Lecture Notes in Computer Science 8567

Commenced Publication in 1973
Founding and Former Series Editors:
Gerhard Goos, Juris Hartmanis, and Jan van Leeuwen

More information about this series at http://www.springer.com/series/7410

Dongdai Lin · Shouhuai Xu
Moti Yung (Eds.)

Information Security and Cryptology

9th International Conference, Inscrypt 2013
Guangzhou, China, November 27–30, 2013
Revised Selected Papers

 Springer

Editors
Dongdai Lin
Chinese Academy of Sciences
Beijing
China

Moti Yung
Columbia University
New York, NY
USA

Shouhuai Xu
University of Texas
San Antonio, TX
USA

ISSN 0302-9743
ISBN 978-3-319-12086-7
DOI 10.1007/978-3-319-12087-4

ISSN 1611-3349 (electronic)
ISBN 978-3-319-12087-4 (eBook)

Library of Congress Control Number: 2014953264

LNCS Sublibrary: SL4 – Security and Cryptology

Springer Cham Heidelberg New York Dordrecht London

Printed on acid-free paper

Springer is part of Springer Science+Business Media (www.springer.com)

Preface

This volume contains the papers presented at Inscrypt 2013: The Ninth China International Conference on Information Security and Cryptology held during November 27–30, 2013 in Guangzhou, China. Inscrypt 2013 was collocated with the 2013 Workshop on RFID and IOT Security (RFIDsec 2013 Asia), which was held on November 27, 2013. Since its inauguration in 2005, Inscrypt has become a well-recognized annual international forum for security researchers and cryptographers to exchange ideas.

The conference received 93 submissions. Each submission was reviewed by at least three, and mostly four Program Committee members. The Program Committee decided to accept 25 papers, including 4 short papers, and 1 full paper that was a merge of two submissions. The overall acceptance rate was, therefore, about 26.8 %. The program also included three invited talks.

Inscrypt 2013 was held in cooperation with the International Association of Cryptologic Research (IACR), and co-organized by the State Key Laboratory of Information Security (SKLOIS) of the Chinese Academy of Sciences (CAS), the Chinese Association for Cryptologic Research (CACR), and Guangzhou University. Inscrypt 2013 was partly supported by the Natural Science Foundation of China (NSFC), the Institute of Information Engineering (IIE) of the Chinese Academy of Sciences, and Guangzhou University. Inscrypt 2013 could not have been a success without the support of these organizations, and we sincerely thank them for their continued assistance and help.

We would also like to thank the authors who submitted their papers to Inscrypt 2013, and the conference attendees for their interest and support that made the conference possible. We thank the Organizing Committee for their time and efforts that allowed us to focus on selecting papers. We thank the Program Committee members and the external reviewers for their hard work in reviewing the submissions; the conference would not have been possible without their expert reviews. Last but not least, we thank the EasyChair system and its operators for making the entire process of the conference convenient.

November 2013

Dongdai Lin
Shouhuai Xu
Moti Yung

Inscrypt 2013

9th China International Conference on Information Security and Cryptology

Guangzhou, China
November 27–30, 2013

Sponsored and organized by

State Key Laboratory of Information Security
(Chinese Academy of Sciences)
Chinese Association for Cryptologic Research
Guangzhou University

in cooperation with
International Association for Cryptologic Research

Conference Chair

Dingyi Pei   Guangzhou University, China

Conference Organizing Committee

Zhijun Qiang   Chinese Association for Cryptologic Research,
                                    China
Chunming Tang   Guangzhou University, China
Chuankun Wu   SKLOIS, Chinese Academy of Sciences, China

Program Co-chairs

Dongdai Lin   SKLOIS, Chinese Academy of Sciences, China
Shouhuai Xu   University of Texas at San Antonio, USA
Moti Yung   Google Inc. and Columbia University, USA

Program Committee

Guoqiang Bai   Tsinghua University, China
Elisa Bertino   Purdue University, USA
Zhenfu Cao   Shanghai Jiao Tong University, China
Bogdan Carbunar   Florida International University, USA
Kefei Chen   Shanghai Jiao Tong University, China

Liqun Chen	Hewlett-Packard Laboratories, UK
Zhong Chen	Peking University, China
Sherman S.M. Chow	Chinese University of Hong Kong, Hong Kong
Ed Dawson	Queensland University of Technology, Australia
Jintai Ding	University of Cincinnati, USA
Cunsheng Ding	Hong Kong University of Science and Technology, Hong Kong
Xuhua Ding	Singapore Management University, Singapore
Shlomi Dolev	Ben-Gurion University of the Negev, Israel
Yingfei Dong	University of Hawaii, USA
Lei Hu	SKLOIS Chinese Academy of Sciences, China
Miroslaw Kutylowski	Wrocław University of Technology, Poland
Xuejia Lai	Shanghai Jiao Tong University, China
Jiangtao Li	Intel Corporation, USA
Hui Li	Xidian University, China
Zhiqiang Lin	University of Texas at Dallas, USA
Donggang Liu	University of Texas at Arlington, USA
Peng Liu	Pennsylvania State University, USA
Di Ma	University of Michigan-Dearborn, USA
Subhamoy Maitra	Indian Statistical Institute, India
Florian Mendel	Graz University of Technology, Austria
Atsuko Miyaji	Japan Advanced Institute of Science and Technology, Japan
Yi Mu	University of Wollongong, Australia
Claudio Orlandi	Aarhus University, Denmark
Xinming Ou	Kansas State University, USA
Ludovic Perret	UPMC/LIP6 Inria/SALSA, France
Giuseppe Persiano	Università di Salerno, Italy
Bertram Poettering	Royal Holloway, University of London, UK
Kouichi Sakurai	Kyushu University, Japan
Nitesh Saxena	University of Alabama at Birmingham, USA
Jae Hong Seo	Myongji University, Republic of Korea
Claudio Soriente	ETH Zurich, Switzerland
Wen-Guey Tzeng	National Chiao Tung University, Taiwan
Yevgeniy Vahlis	AT&T Labs, USA
Xiaofeng Wang	Indiana University, USA
Wenling Wu	Institute of Software, Chinese Academy of Sciences, China
Huaxiong Wang	Nanyang Technological University, Singapore
Guilin Wang	University of Wollongong, Australia
Duncan Wong	City University of Hong Kong, Hong Kong
Maozhi Xu	Peking University, China
Danfeng Yao	Virginia Tech, USA
Chung-Huang Yang	National Kaohsiung Normal University, Taiwan
Yunlei Zhao	Fudan University, China
Fangguo Zhang	Sun Yat-sen University, China

Rui Zhang   Chinese Academy of Sciences, China
Hong-Sheng Zhou   University of Maryland, USA
Yuliang Zheng   UNC Charlotte, USA
Cliff Zou   University of Central Florida, USA
Giovanni Russello   The University of Auckland, New Zealand

External Reviewers

Adhikari, Avishek	Juang, Wen-Shenq
Asghar, Muhammad Rizwan	Kantarcioglu, Murat
Azimpurkivi, Mozhgan	Kubota, Ayumu
Bai, Guoqiang	Kuo, Po-Chun
Bao, Zhenzhen	Lamberger, Mario
Barni, Mauro	Langlois, Adeline
Baum, Carsten	Lee, Hyung Tae
Chen, I-Te	Li, Nan
Chen, Jiageng	Lin, Jiao
Chen, Kai	Liu, Zhen
Cheng, Chen-Mou	Lomne, Victor
Chien, Hung-Yu	Long, Yu
Dalla Preda, Mila	Lv, Xixiang
Ding, Yi	Machado David, Bernardo
Eichlseder, Maria	Mao, Xianping
Fan, Chun-I	Marson, Giorgia Azzurra
Fan, Leo	Ming, Tang
Fiore, Dario	Mohamed, Manar
Fitzpatrick, Robert	Mouha, Nicky
Futa, Yuichi	Mukherjee, Pratyay
Gao, Song	Neupane, Ajaya
Gao, Wei	Nishide, Takashi
George, Wesley	Panwar, Nisha
Gligoroski, Danilo	Paterson, Kenny
Gong, Boru	Pattuk, Erman
Guo, Fuchun	Polychroniadou, Antigoni
Gupta, Aditi	Qin, Baodong
Gupta, Kishan	Rao, Fang-Yu
Habibi, Mohammad	Ren, Chuangang
Han, Jinguang	Renault, Guenael
Hanzlik, Lucjan	Schläffer, Martin
Huang, Jialin	Shebaro, Bilal
Huang, Yun	Shirvanian, Maliheh
Hwang, Ren Junn	Shrestha, Babins
Jhanwar, Mahabir Prasad	Snook, Michael
Jiao, Lin	Song, Fang

Su, Chunhua
Su, Ming
Sun, Xiaoyan
Tang, Fei
Tang, Qiang
Tang, Ying-Kai
Tso, Raylin
Wang, Chih Hung
Wang, Kunpeng
Wang, Liangliang
Wang, Yanfeng
Wei, Puwen
Wu, Shenbao
Xagawa, Keita
Xiao, Gaoyao
Xu, Hong
Xue, Weijia

Yasunaga, Kenji
Yoneyama, Kazuki
Yuen, Tsz Hon
Zeitoun, Rina
Zeng, Xiangyong
Zhang, Cong
Zhang, Haibin
Zhang, Huiling
Zhang, Lei
Zhang, Su
Zhang, Tao
Zhao, Chang-An
Zhao, Fangming
Zhao, Mingyi
Zhao, Yongjun
Zhou, Xuhua

Contents

Computational Number Theory

Public Key Cryptography

Hash Function

Side-Channel and Leakage

Application and System Security

Boolean Function and Block Cipher

A Note on Semi-bent and Hyper-bent Boolean Functions

Chunming Tang[1,2], Yu Lou[2], Yanfeng Qi[2,3]([✉]), Maozhi Xu[2], and Baoan Guo[3]

[1] School of Mathematics and Information, China West Normal University,
Nanchong 637002, Sichuan, China
[2] LMAM, School of Mathematical Sciences,
Peking University, Beijing 100871, China
{tangchunmingmath,qiyanfeng07}@163.com
[3] Aisino Corporation Inc., Beijing 100195, China

Abstract. Semi-bent and hyper-bent funcitons as two classes of Boolean functions with low Walsh transform, are applied in cryptography and commnunications. This paper considers a new class of semi-bent quadratic Boolean function and a generalization of a new class of hyper-bent Boolean functions. The new class of semi-bent quadratic Boolean function of the form $f(x) = \sum_{i=1}^{\lfloor \frac{m-1}{2} \rfloor} Tr_1^n(c_i x^{1+4^i})(c_i \in \mathbb{F}_4, n = 2m)$ is simply characterized and enumerated. Then we present the characterization of a generalization of a new class of hyper-bent Boolean functions of the form $f_{a,b}^{(r)} := Tr_1^n(ax^{r(2^m-1)}) + Tr_1^4(bx^{\frac{2^n-1}{5}})$, where $n = 2m$, $m \equiv 2 \pmod 4$, $a \in \mathbb{F}_{2^m}$ and $b \in \mathbb{F}_{16}$.

Keywords: Boolean function · Quadratic boolean function · Semi-bent function · Bent function · Hyper-bent function

1 Introduction

A Boolean function is a function from $\mathbb{F}_2^n$ to $\mathbb{F}_2$. Since finite fields have many rich structures and properties, we often study Boolean functions as functions from $\mathbb{F}_{2^n}$ to $\mathbb{F}_2$. Boolean functions with low Walsh transform are of great interest because of their wide applications in cryptography and communications. For application in cryptography, these functions can resist linear cryptanalysis on block ciphers [15] and the fast correlation attack on stream ciphers [21]. As for application in communications, they can be used to design m-sequnces with low cross-correlation [9,10].

Two classes of Boolean functions with low Walsh transform are bent functions [6,24] and semi-bent functions [5,17,22,23]. For even n, the spectra of bent functions attains the value $\pm 2^{n/2}$. Later, Youssef and Gong [29] introduced a class of bent functions called hyper-bent functions, which achieve the maximal minimum distance to all the coordinate functions of all bijective monomials. The spectra of semi-bent functions is $\{0, \pm 2^{\lfloor (n+2)/2 \rfloor}\}$.

© Springer International Publishing Switzerland 2014
D. Lin et al. (Eds.): Inscrypt 2013, LNCS 8567, pp. 3–21, 2014.
DOI: 10.1007/978-3-319-12087-4_1

The quadratic Boolean functions of the form

$$f(x) = \sum_{i=1}^{\lfloor \frac{n-1}{2} \rfloor} c_i Tr_1^n(x^{1+2^i}), c_i \in \mathbb{F}_2.$$

is studied in [2,5,7,13,14]. The Boolean function $f(x)$ is semi-bent if and only if

$$gcd(c(x), x^n + 1) = \begin{cases} x+1, & \text{for odd } n; \\ x^2+1, & \text{for even } n. \end{cases}$$

where $c(x) = \sum_{i=1}^{\lfloor \frac{n-1}{2} \rfloor} c_i(x^i + x^{n-i})$.

The bent quadratic Boolean functions of the form

$$f(x) = \sum_{i=1}^{\frac{n-2}{2}} c_i Tr_1^n(x^{1+2^i}) + Tr_1^{n/2}(x^{1+2^{\frac{n}{2}}}), \quad c_i \in \mathbb{F}_2;$$

$$f(x) = \sum_{i=1}^{\frac{m-2}{2}} c_i Tr_1^n(\beta x^{1+2^{ei}}) + Tr_1^{n/2}(\beta x^{1+2^{\frac{n}{2}}}), c_i \in \mathbb{F}_2, n = em, 2|m, \beta \in \mathbb{F}_{2^e};$$

$$f(x) = \sum_{i=1}^{\frac{m}{2}-1} Tr_1^n(c_i x^{1+2^{ei}}) + Tr_1^{n/2}(c_{m/2}x^{1+2^{n/2}}), n = em, 2|m, c_i \in \mathbb{F}_{2^e}$$

are studied in [8,16,27,30].

The hyper-bentness of Boolean functions of the form $f_{a,b}^{(r)} := Tr_1^n(ax^{r(2^m-1)}) + Tr_1^2(bx^{\frac{2^n-1}{3}})$ and $f_{a,b}^{(r)} := Tr_1^n(ax^{(2^m-1)}) + Tr_1^4(bx^{\frac{2^n-1}{5}})$ is characterized in [18–20] and [26] respectively.

In this paper, we first consider quadratic Boolean functions of the form

$$f(x) = \sum_{i=1}^{\lfloor \frac{m-1}{2} \rfloor} Tr_1^n(c_i x^{1+4^i}), \quad c_i \in \mathbb{F}_4$$

where $n = 2m$. Then $f(x)$ is semi-bent if and only if $gcd(c_f(x), x^m + 1) = x + 1$, where $c_f(x) = \sum_{i=1}^{\lfloor \frac{m-1}{2} \rfloor} c_i(x^i + x^{m-i})$. Further, for even m, $f(x)$ is not a semi-bent function. We give the enumeration of semi-bent functions for the case $m = 2^v p^r$, where p is not a Wieferich prime, $p \equiv 3 \mod 4$, $ord_p(2) = p - 1$ or $\frac{p-1}{2}$. The semi-bentness of $f(x)$ is characterized by conditions of coefficients c_i. In particular, any nonzero $f(x)$ is a semi-bent function for the case $m = p$, where p is an odd prime, $p \equiv 3 \mod 4$, $ord_p(2) = p - 1$ or $\frac{p-1}{2}$. Finally, we characterize the hyper-bentness of Boolean functions defined over $\mathbb{F}_{2^n}$ by the form: $f_{a,b}^{(r)} := Tr_1^n(ax^{r(2^m-1)}) + Tr_1^4(bx^{\frac{2^n-1}{5}})$, where $n = 2m$, $m \equiv 2 \pmod 4$, $a \in \mathbb{F}_{2^m}$ and $b \in \mathbb{F}_{16}$.

This paper is organized as follows. Section 2 introduces some notations and basic knowledge. Section 3 presents the characterization and enumeration of a class of semi-bent quadratic Boolean functions and characterizes a class of hyper-bent Boolean functions. Section 4 concludes for this paper.

2 Preliminaries

In this section, some notations are given first. Let $\mathbb{F}_{2^n}$ be the finite field with 2^n elements. Let $\mathbb{F}_{2^n}^*$ be the multiplicative group of $\mathbb{F}_{2^n}$. Let $e|n$, the trace function $Tr_e^n(x)$ from $\mathbb{F}_{2^n}$ to $\mathbb{F}_{2^e}$ is defined by

$$Tr_e^n(x) = x + x^{2^e} + \cdots + x^{2^{e(n/e-1)}}, \quad x \in \mathbb{F}_{2^n}.$$

The trace function satisfies that
(1) $Tr_e^n(x^{2^e}) = Tr_e^n(x)$, where $x \in \mathbb{F}_{2^n}$.
(2) $Tr_e^n(ax + by) = aTr_e^n(x) + bTr_e^n(y)$, where $x, y \in \mathbb{F}_{2^n}$ and $a, b \in \mathbb{F}_{2^e}$.

2.1 Bent Functions and Semi-bent Functions

The Walsh transform of a Boolean function $f(x)$ is defined by

$$\widehat{f}(\lambda) = \sum_{x \in \mathbb{F}_{2^n}} (-1)^{f(x)+Tr_1^n(\lambda x)}, \quad \lambda \in \mathbb{F}_{2^n}.$$

The distribution of values of the Walsh transform can define bent functions and semi-bent functions.

Definition 1. *A Boolean function $f : \mathbb{F}_{2^n} \longrightarrow \mathbb{F}_2$ is called a bent function if $\widehat{f}(\lambda) = \pm 2^{\frac{n}{2}}$ for all $\lambda \in \mathbb{F}_{2^n}$.*

Obviously, bent functions do not exist for odd n.

Definition 2. *A bent function $f : \mathbb{F}_{2^n} \longrightarrow \mathbb{F}_2$ is called a hyper-bent function, if, for any i satisfying $(i, 2^n - 1) = 1$, $f(x^i)$ is also a bent function.*

Definition 3. *A Boolean function $f : \mathbb{F}_{2^n} \longrightarrow \mathbb{F}_2$ is called a semi-bent function if $\widehat{f}(\lambda) \in \{0, \pm 2^{\lfloor \frac{n+2}{2} \rfloor}\}$ for all $\lambda \in \mathbb{F}_{2^n}$.*

2.2 Quadratic Boolean Functions

A quadratic Boolean function can be represented by trace functions. When n is even, a quadratic Boolean function from $\mathbb{F}_{2^n}$ to $\mathbb{F}_2$ can be represented by

$$f(x) = \sum_{i=0}^{\frac{n}{2}-1} Tr_1^n(c_i x^{1+2^i}) + Tr_1^{n/2}(c_{n/2} x^{1+2^{n/2}})$$

where $c_i \in \mathbb{F}_{2^n}$ for $0 \leq i \leq \frac{n}{2}$ and $c_{n/2} \in \mathbb{F}_{2^{\frac{n}{2}}}$. When n is odd, $f(x)$ can be represented by

$$f(x) = \sum_{i=0}^{\frac{n-1}{2}} Tr_1^n(c_i x^{1+2^i}),$$

where $c_i \in \mathbb{F}_{2^n}$.

For a quadratic Boolean function $f(x)$, the distribution of the Walsh transform can be described by the bilinear form

$$Q_f(x,y) = f(x+y) + f(x) + f(y).$$

For the quadratic form Q_f, define

$$K_f = \{x \in \mathbb{F}_{2^n} : Q_f(x,y) = 0, \forall y \in \mathbb{F}_{2^n}\}$$

and $k_f = dim_{\mathbb{F}_2}(K_f)$. Then $2|(n - k_f)$. The distribution of the Walsh transform values of $\hat{f}(\lambda)$ is given in the following theorem [10].

Theorem 1. Let $f(x)$ be a quadratic Boolean function and $k_f = dim_{\mathbb{F}_2}(K_f)$. The distribution of the Walsh transform values of $f(x)$ is given by

$$\hat{f}(\lambda) = \begin{cases} 0, & 2^n - 2^{n-k_f} \; times \\ 2^{\frac{n+k_f}{2}}, & 2^{n-k_f-1} + 2^{\frac{n-k_f}{2}-1} \; times \\ -2^{\frac{n+k_f}{2}}, & 2^{n-k_f-1} - 2^{\frac{n-k_f}{2}-1} \; times. \end{cases}$$

Corollary 1. When n is even, a quadratic function $f(x)$ is a bent function if and only if $k_f = 0$, and $f(x)$ is a semi-bent function if and only if $k_f = 2$; When n is odd, $f(x)$ is a semi-bent function if and only if $k_f = 1$.

The set K_f can also be described by the derivatives of f.

Definition 4. Let $f(x)$ be a Boolean function from $\mathbb{F}_{2^n}$ to $\mathbb{F}_2$. Let $z \in \mathbb{F}_{2^n}$. The derivative of $f(x)$ with respect to z is the function $D_z f(x)$ defined by $D_z f(x) = f(x+z) + f(x)$. z is called a linear structure of $f(x)$ if $D_z f(x)$ is constant. The set of all the linear structures is called the linear space of f.

Precisely, K_f' is exact the linear space of $f(x)$.

2.3 Hyper-bent Functions

Charpin and Gong [4] gave the following property to determine a hyper-bent function.

Proposition 1. Let $n = 2m$, α be a primitive element of $\mathbb{F}_{2^n}$ and f be a Boolean function over $\mathbb{F}_{2^n}$ satisfying $f(\alpha^{2^{m+1}} x) = f(x)$ ($\forall x \in \mathbb{F}_{2^n}$) and $f(0) = 0$. Let ξ be a primitive $2^m + 1$-th root in $\mathbb{F}_{2^n}^*$. Then f is a hyper-bent function if and only if the cardinality of the set $\{i|f(\xi^i) = 1, 0 \leq i \leq 2^m\}$ is 2^{m-1}.

Kloosterman sum is a powerful tool to study the hyper-bentness of some classes of boolean functions.

Kloosterman sums on $\mathbb{F}_{2^m}$ are defined as

$$K_m(a) := \sum_{x \in \mathbb{F}_{2^m}} \chi(\mathrm{Tr}_1^m(ax + \frac{1}{x})), \quad a \in \mathbb{F}_{2^m},$$

where $\chi(f)$ is the *sign* function of f defined as $\chi(f) := (-1)^f$. Some properties of Kloosterman sums are given by the following proposition.

Proposition 2. *([11], Theorem 3.4]) Let $a \in \mathbb{F}_{2^m}$. Then $K_m(a) \in [1 - 2^{(m+2)/2}, 1 + 2^{(m+2)/2}]$ and $4 \mid K_m(a)$.*

Quintic Weil sums on $\mathbb{F}_{2^m}$ are

$$Q_m(a) := \sum_{x \in \mathbb{F}_{2^m}} \chi(\mathrm{Tr}_1^m(a(x^5 + x^3 + x))), \quad a \in \mathbb{F}_{2^m}.$$

And the value of $Q_m(a)$ is related to the factorization of the polynomial $P(x) = x^5 + x + a^{-1}$ [26].

2.4 Self-reciprocal Polynomials

Definition 5. *Let N be a positive integer and a be a positive integer coprime to N. The positive integer k is called the order of a module N if k is the least positive integer such that $N|(a^k - 1)$. And k is denoted by $\mathrm{ord}_N(a)$.*

Lemma 1. *Let p be an odd prime. Then*
(1) Let $\mathrm{ord}_p(4) = s$ and $p \nmid \frac{4^s - 1}{p}$, then $\mathrm{ord}_{p^k}(4) = s_k = p^{k-1}s$.
(2) $\mathrm{ord}_p(4) \neq p - 1$. Further, $\mathrm{ord}_p(4) = \frac{p-1}{2}$ if and only if $\mathrm{ord}_p(2) = p - 1$ or $\mathrm{ord}_p(2) = \frac{p-1}{2}$ ($\frac{p-1}{2}$ is odd).

Proof. The proof follows immediately from [12].

If p is not a Wieferich prime, then p satisfies $p \nmid \frac{4^s - 1}{p}$. The definition of a Wieferich prime is given below.

Definition 6. *Let p be a prime. Then p is called a Wieferich prime if $p | \frac{2^{p-1} - 1}{p}$ [28].*

Wieferich primes are rare. Between 1 and 17×10^{15}, there are only two Wieferich primes 1093 and 3511. Silverman [25] proved that there are infinite Wieferich primes if the abc conjecture holds.

The polynomial $c_f(x)$ for determining semi-bent functions has a close relation with self-reciprocal polynomials.

Definition 7. *The reciprocal polynomial of a polynomial $h(x)$ of degree d is $x^d h(\frac{1}{x})$, denoted by $h^*(x)$. The polynomial $h(x)$ is called a self-reciprocal polynomial if $h^*(x) = h(x)$, that is, $h(x) = \sum_{i=0}^d a_i x^i$ with $a_i = a_{d-i}$.*

Some results on self-reciprocal polynomials are given below.

Lemma 2. *(1) Let $A(x) = \sum_{i=0}^{n_1} a_i x^i$ be a self-reciprocal polynomial of degree n_1. Let $B(x) = \sum_{i=0}^{n_2} b_i x^i$ be a polynomial of degree n_2. Then $A(x)B(x)$ is a self-reciprocal polynomial of degree $n_1 + n_2$ if and only if $B(x)$ is a self-reciprocal polynomial.*
(2) Let $A(x), g(x) \in \mathbb{F}_4[x]$. Let $A(x)$ be self-reciprocal and $g(x)$ be irreducible. Let $g(x)|A(x)$. Then $g^*(x)|A(x)$, where $g^*(x)$ is the reciprocal polynomial of $g(x)$. Further, if $g(x)$ is not self-reciprocal, then $\widetilde{g}(x)|A(x)$, where $\widetilde{g}(x) = g(x)g^*(x)$.

Proof. The proof follows immediately from the definition of self-reciprocal polynomials.

Two important classes of self-reciprocal polynomials are $x^N + 1$ and d-th cyclotomic polynomials $Q_d(x)$ [1,12]. The d-th cyclotomic polynomial $Q_d(x)$, whose roots are primitive d-th roots of unity, is a monic polynomial of degree $\phi(d)$, where $\phi(\cdot)$ is Euler-totient function. The following lemma gives the factorization of cyclotomic polynomials.

Lemma 3. *Let p be an odd prime. Then*

(1) *Let* $\mathrm{ord}_{p^k}(4) = s_k$ *and* $t_k = \frac{p^k - p^{k-1}}{s_k}$. *The p^k-th cyclotomic polynomial $Q_{p^k}(x)$ over $\mathbb{F}_4$ has the following monic irreducible factorization.*

$$Q_{p^k}(x) = h_1(x) \cdots h_{t_k}(x),$$

where $deg(h_i(x)) = s_k$ for $1 \le i \le t_k$. Further, if there exists l such that $p^k | (4^l + 1)$, then $h_i(x) = x^{s_k} h_i(\frac{1}{x})$, that is, $h_i(x)$ is self-reciprocal for any i. Otherwise, the factorization of $Q_{p^k}(x)$ is of the form

$$Q_{p^k}(x) = C h_1(x) h_1^*(x) \cdots h_{\frac{t_k}{2}}(x) h_{\frac{t_k}{2}}^*(x),$$

where $h_i^*(x) = x^{s_k} h_i(\frac{1}{x})$ for $1 \le i \le \frac{t_k}{2}$ and $C \in \mathbb{F}_4^*$.

(2) *Let $\mathrm{ord}_p(4) = s$, $p \nmid \frac{4^s - 1}{p}$ and $t = \frac{p-1}{s}$. Then $Q_p(x)$ over $\mathbb{F}_4$ has the following monic irreducible factorization:*

$$Q_p(x) = h_1(x) \cdots h_t(x),$$

For any $k \ge 2$, $Q_{p^k}(x)$ over $\mathbb{F}_4$ has the irreducible factorization:

$$Q_{p^k}(x) = h_1(x^{p^{k-1}}) \cdots h_t(x^{p^{k-1}}).$$

(3) *Let p be a prime such that $p \equiv 3 \mod 4$, $\mathrm{ord}_p(2) = p - 1$ or $\frac{p-1}{2}$ ($\frac{p-1}{2}$ is odd). Then $Q_p(x)$ over $\mathbb{F}_4$ has the following monic irreducible factorization:*

$$Q_p(x) = C h(x) h^*(x)$$

Suppose that $k \ge 2$. If p is not a Wieferich prime, $Q_{p^k}(x)$ over $\mathbb{F}_4$ has the irreducible factorization

$$Q_{p^k}(x) = C h(x^{p^{k-1}}) h^*(x^{p^{k-1}})$$

where $h^*(x)$ is the self-polynomial of $h(x)$ and $C \in \mathbb{F}_4^*$.

(4) $x^{p^k} + 1 = (x+1) Q_p(x) \cdots Q_{p^k}(x)$.

Proof. The proof follows immediately from [12] and is omitted.

3   Semi-bent Quadratic Boolean Functions and Hyper-bent Boolean Functions

Let $n = 2m$ for this section. And we consider semi-bent quadratic Boolean functions and hyper-bent Boolean functions.

3.1   The Characterization and Enumeration of Semi-bent Quadratic Boolean Functions

In this subsection, we consider quadratic Boolean functions of the form

$$f(x) = \sum_{i=1}^{\lfloor \frac{m-1}{2} \rfloor} Tr_1^n(c_i x^{4^i+1}), \quad c_i \in \mathbb{F}_4. \tag{1}$$

Let $\mathcal{Q}_m$ be the set of all the functions of the form (1). Let $\mathcal{SB}_m$ be the set of all the semi-bent quadratic Boolean functions in $\mathcal{Q}_m$.

The Characterization of Semi-bent Quadratic Boolean Functions. For a quadratic Boolean function defined by (1), the derivative with respect to $z \in \mathbb{F}_{2^n}$ is

$$D_z f(x) = f(x+z) + f(x) = \sum_{i=1}^{\lfloor \frac{m-1}{2} \rfloor} Tr_1^n(c_i(z^{4^i} + z^{4^{m-i}})x) + \sum_{i=1}^{\lfloor \frac{m-1}{2} \rfloor} Tr_1^n(c_i z^{4^i+1}).$$

Then z is a linear structure of $f(x)$ if and only if $\sum_{i=1}^{\lfloor \frac{m-1}{2} \rfloor} c_i(z^{4^i} + z^{4^{m-i}}) = 0$. We call $\sum_{i=1}^{\lfloor \frac{m-1}{2} \rfloor} c_i(x^{4^i} + x^{4^{m-i}})$ the adjoint linear transformation of $f(x)$, which is denoted by $L_f(x)$. Then

$$K_f = \{x \in K_f : L_f(x) = 0\} = Ker(L_f(x)).$$

The following theorem presents the characterization of the semi-bentness of quadratic Boolean functions defined by (1).

Theorem 2. *Let* $n = 2m$. *A Boolean function defined by* (1) *is a semi-bent quadratic Boolean function if and only if* $gcd(c_f(x), x^m + 1) = x + 1$, *where*

$$c_f(x) = \sum_{i=1}^{\lfloor \frac{m-1}{2} \rfloor} c_i(x^i + x^{m-i}). \tag{2}$$

In particular, for even m, *there is no semi-bent quadratic Boolean function of the form* (1), *that is,* $\mathcal{SB}_m = \emptyset$.

Proof. The adjoint linear transformation of $f(x)$ defined by (1) is

$$L_f(x) = \sum_{i=1}^{\lfloor \frac{m-1}{2} \rfloor} c_i(x^{4^i} + x^{4^{m-i}}).$$

Then $L_f(x)$ can be seen as a linear transformation from $\mathbb{F}_{2^n}$ to $\mathbb{F}_{2^n}$ over $\mathbb{F}_4$. Take a regular element α of $\mathbb{F}_{2^n}$ over $\mathbb{F}_4$, that is, $\alpha, \alpha^4, \cdots, \alpha^{4^{m-1}}$ is a basis of $\mathbb{F}_{2^n}$ over $\mathbb{F}_4$. The corresponding matrix of the linear transformation $L_f(x)$ under this basis is

$$M_f = \begin{bmatrix} 0 & c_1 & c_2 & \cdots & c_{m-1} \\ c_{m-1} & 0 & c_1 & \cdots & c_{m-2} \\ c_{m-2} & c_{m-1} & 0 & \cdots & c_{m-3} \\ \vdots & \vdots & \vdots & \cdots & \vdots \\ c_1 & c_2 & c_3 & \cdots & 0 \end{bmatrix}$$

where $c_{m-i} = c_i$ for $(1 \le i \le \lfloor \frac{m-1}{2} \rfloor)$ and $c_{m/2} = 0$ for even m. From Corollary 1 and K_f, $f(x)$ is semi-bent if and only if the dimension of the kernel $Ker(L_f(x))$ over $\mathbb{F}_2$ is $dim_{\mathbb{F}_2}(Ker(L_f(x))) = 2$. Since $L_f(x)$ is also a linear transformation over $\mathbb{F}_4$, $dim_{\mathbb{F}_2}(Ker(L_f(x))) = 2$ if and only if $dim_{\mathbb{F}_4}(Ker(L_f(x))) = 1$ or the rank of M_f is $Rank(M_f) = m - 1$. Note that M_f is the generator matrix of a cyclic code over $\mathbb{F}_4$ with length m and generator polynomial $c_f(x)$. From theories of cyclic codes, $Rank(M_f) = m - deg(gcd(c_f(x), x^m + 1))$. Hence $f(x)$ is semi-bent if and only if $deg(gcd(c_f(x), x^m + 1)) = 1$. Obviously $deg(gcd(c_f(x), x^m + 1)) = 1$ if and only if $gcd(c_f(x), x^m + 1) = x + 1$.

When m is even,

$$c_f(x) = \sum_{i=1}^{\lfloor \frac{m-1}{2} \rfloor} c_i x^i (1 + x^{\frac{m}{2}-i})^2, \quad x^m + 1 = (x^{\frac{m}{2}} + 1)^2,$$

We obtain that $(x+1)^2 | gcd(c_f(x), x^m + 1)$ and $f(x)$ is not semi-bent.

Hence, this theorem follows.

From Theorem 2, we just consider quadratic Boolean functions for odd m.

Corollary 2. *Let $n = 2m$, where m is odd. The quadratic Boolean function*

$$f(x) = Tr_1^n(cx^{4^i+1}), \quad c \in \mathbb{F}_4^*$$

is semi-bent if and only if $gcd(i, m) = 1$.

Proof. Note that $c_f(x) = c(x^i + c^{m-i})$. Then

$$gcd(c(x^i + x^{m-i}), x^m + 1) = gcd(x^{2i} + 1, x^m + 1) = x^{gcd(2i,m)} + 1.$$

Since m is odd, then $gcd(2i, m) = gcd(i, m)$. From Theorem 2, $f(x)$ is semi-bent if and only if $gcd(i, m) = 1$.

For further characterization, let p be not a Wieferich prime, $p \equiv 3 \mod 4$, $ord_p(2) = p-1$ or $\frac{p-1}{2}$. The following theorem presents a simpler characterization of semi-bent quadratic Boolean functions defined by (1).

Theorem 3. *Let $n = 2m$ and $m = p^r$, where $r \ge 2$, p is not a Wieferich prime, $p \equiv 3 \mod 4$, $ord_p(2) = p - 1$ or $\frac{p-1}{2}$. The quadratic Boolean function $f(x)$ defined by (1) is semi-bent if and only if $(x^{p^{k-1}} + 1)c_f(x) \not\equiv 0 \mod x^{p^k} + 1$ for any $1 \le k \le r$.*

Proof. From (4) in Lemma 2,

$$gcd(c_f(x), x^{p^r} + 1) = (x + 1)gcd(c_f(x)/(x+1), \prod_{k=1}^{r} Q_{p^k}(x)).$$

From Lemma 2, $f(x)$ is semi-bent if and only if $gcd(c_f(x)/(x+1), \prod_{k=1}^{r} Q_{p^k}(x)) = 1$. Note that $(x + 1) \nmid \prod_{k=1}^{r} Q_{p^k}(x)$. Then $gcd(c_f(x), \prod_{k=1}^{r} Q_{p^k}(x)) = 1$. Equivalently, for any $1 \le k \le r$, $gcd(c_f(x), Q_{p^k}(x)) = 1$. From (3) in Lemma 3 and (2) in Lemma 2, $gcd(c_f(x), Q_{p^k}(x)) = 1$ if and only if $Q_{p^k}(x) \nmid c_f(x)$. Since $gcd(x^{p^{k-1}} + 1, Q_{p^k(x)}) = 1$ and $(x^{p^{k-1}} + 1) \cdot Q_{p^k(x)} = x^{p^k} + 1$, then $c_f(x) \not\equiv 0$ mod $Q_{p^k}(x)$ is equivalent to $(x^{p^{k-1}} + 1)c_f(x) \not\equiv 0$ mod $x^{p^k} + 1$. Hence, this theorem follows.

Lemma 4. *Let $m = p^r$, where p is an odd prime. Let $c_f(x)$ be defined by (2). Then*

(1) For any $1 \le k \le r$, define $c_i = c_{p^r-i}(\frac{p^r+1}{2} \le i \le p^r - 1)$, $w_{i,k} = \sum_{j=0}^{p^{r-k}-1} c_{i+jp^k}(1 \le i \le p^k - 1)$. Then $w_{i,k} = w_{p^k-i,k}$ for any $1 \le i \le p^k - 1$. Further,

$$c_{f,k}(x) \equiv c_f(x) \equiv \sum_{i=1}^{p^k-1} w_{i,k}x^i \equiv \sum_{i=1}^{(p^k-1)/2} w_{i,k}(x^i + x^{p^k-i}) \mod x^{p^k} + 1.$$

(2) For $i = i_0 + jp^k$ and $0 \le i_0 \le p^k - 1$, define $w_{0,k} = 0$ and $w_{i,k} = w_{i_0,k}$. Then

$$(x^{p^{k-1}} + 1)c_f(x) \equiv (x^{p^{k-1}} + 1)c_{f,k}(x) \equiv \sum_{i=0}^{p^k-1} (w_{i,k} + w_{i-p^{k-1},k})x^i \mod x^{p^k} + 1.$$

(3) Let W_k be the matrix

$$\begin{bmatrix} w_{0,k} & w_{1,k} & \cdots & w_{\frac{p^{k-1}-1}{2},k} & \cdots & w_{p^{k-1}-1,k} \\ w_{p^{k-1},k} & w_{p^{k-1}+1,k} & \cdots & w_{p^{k-1}+\frac{p^{k-1}-1}{2},k} & \cdots & w_{2p^{k-1}-1,k} \\ w_{2p^{k-1},k} & w_{2p^{k-1}+1,k} & \cdots & w_{2p^{k-1}+\frac{p^{k-1}-1}{2},k} & \cdots & w_{3p^{k-1}-1,k} \\ \vdots & \vdots & \vdots & \vdots & \vdots & \vdots \\ w_{(\frac{p-1}{2})p^{k-1},k} & w_{(\frac{p-1}{2})p^{k-1}+1,k} & \cdots & w_{\frac{p^k-1}{2},k} & \cdots & w_{\frac{p^k-1}{2}+\frac{p^{k-1}-1}{2},k} \\ \vdots & \vdots & \vdots & \vdots & \vdots & \vdots \\ w_{(p-1)p^{k-1},k} & w_{(p-1)p^{k-1}+1,k} & \cdots & w_{(p-1)p^{k-1}+\frac{p^{k-1}-1}{2},k} & \cdots & w_{p^k-1,k} \end{bmatrix}$$

Let $A_{i,k} = [A_{i,k}(0), A_{i,k}(1), \cdots, A_{i,k}(p-1)]'$ be the i-th column of W_k, that is, $W_k = [A_{0,k}, A_{1,k}, \cdots, A_{p^{k-1}-1,k}]$. Then

(i) For any $1 \le i \le p^{k-1} - 1$ and $0 \le j \le p-1$, $A_{i,k}(j) = A_{p^{k-1}-i,k}(p-1-j)$;

(ii) For any $1 \le i \le p^{k-1} - 1$, $A_{i,k}$ is constant if and only if $A_{p^{k-1}-i,k}$ is constant.

Proof. The proof follows immediately from the above definitions.

Theorem 4. *Let $n = 2m = 2p^r$, where $r \geq 2$, p is not a Wieferich prime, $p \equiv 3$ mod 4, $ord_p(2) = p - 1$ or $\frac{p-1}{2}$. The quadratic Boolean function $f(x)$ defined by (1) is semi-bent if and only if for any $1 \leq k \leq r$, there exists $0 \leq i \leq \frac{p^{k-1}-1}{2}$ such that $A_{i,k}$ is not constant.*

Proof. From Theorem 3, $f(x)$ is semi-bent if and only if for any $1 \leq k \leq r$,

$$(x^{p^{k-1}} + 1)c_f(x) \not\equiv 0 \mod x^{p^k} + 1.$$

From (2) in Lemma 4, that is equivalent to that there exists $0 \leq i \leq p^k - 1$ such that $w_{i,k} + w_{i-p^{k-1},k} \neq 0$. For $i = i_0 + jp^{k-1}$ and $0 \leq i_0 \leq p^{k-1} - 1$, $w_{i,k} + w_{i-p^{k-1},k} \neq 0$ is equivalent to

$$A_{i_0,k} = [w_{i_0,k}, w_{i_0+p^{k-1},k}, \cdots, w_{i_0+(p-1)p^{k-1},k}]'$$

is not constant. From (3) in Lemma 4, this theorem follows.

The Enumeration for Semi-bent Quadratic Boolean Functions. Before the enumeration of semi-bent quadratic Boolean functions, two sets of self-reciprocal polynomials are defined.

Let m be an odd positive integer and $A(x)$ be a nonzero self-reciprocal polynomial. Let $\mathcal{SM}_m(A(x))$ be the set of polynomials $g(x) \in \mathbb{F}_4[x]$ such that

  (i) $A(x)|g(x)$;
 (ii) $deg(g(x)) = m - 1 - 2t(1 \leq t \leq \frac{m-1}{2})$;
(iii) $g^*(x) = g(x)$.

For convenience, suppose that $0 \in \mathcal{SM}_m(A(x))$.

Let m be odd and $B(x)$ is a nonzero self-reciprocal polynoial. Let $\mathcal{SR}_m(B(x))$ be the set of polynomials $g(x) \in \mathbb{F}_4[x]$ such that

  (i) $gcd(g(x), B(x)) = 1$;
 (ii) $deg(g(x)) = m - 1 - 2t(1 \leq t \leq \frac{m-1}{2})$;
(iii) $g^*(x) = g(x)$.

Let $\mathcal{C}_m$ be the set of $c_f(x)$ satisfying that $gcd(c_f(x), x^m + 1) = x + 1$, where $f(x)$ is defined by (1).

Lemma 5. *Let notations be defined above. Then $\#(\mathcal{C}_m) = \#(\mathcal{SR}_m(\frac{x^m+1}{x+1}))$.*

Proof. To complete the proof, we just consider the bijection between $\mathcal{C}_m$ and $\mathcal{SR}_m(\frac{x^m+1}{x+1})$. Define a map

$$F : \mathcal{C}_m \longrightarrow \mathcal{SR}_m(\frac{x^m+1}{x+1}) \quad c_f(x) \longmapsto \frac{x^{-t}c_f(x)}{x+1} = \tilde{c}_f(x).$$

where t is the least positive integer such that $c_t \neq 0$ for $1 \leq t \leq \frac{m-1}{2}$.

We then verify the definition first. From the definition of $c_f(x)$, the integer t naturally exists. Let $c_i = c_{m-i}$ for $\frac{m+1}{2} \le i \le m - 1$. Then

$$\widetilde{c}_f(x) = \frac{x^{-t}c_f(x)}{x+1} = \frac{1}{x+1}(c_{m-t}x^{m-2t} + c_{m-t-1}x^{m-2t-1} + \cdots + c_{t+1}x + c_t).$$

From Lemma 2, the polynomial $\widetilde{c}_f(x)$ is self-reciprocal of degree $deg(\widetilde{c}_f(x)) = m-1-2t$. Hence, $\widetilde{c}_f(x)$ satisfies (ii) and (iii) in the definition of $\mathcal{SR}_m(\cdot)$. Finally, we just verify that $\widetilde{c}_f(x)$ satisfies (i).

$$gcd(\widetilde{c}_f(x), \frac{x^m+1}{x+1}) = gcd(c_f(x), x^m+1)/(x+1) = 1.$$

Hence, the map F is well defined.

Define another map

$$G :\mathcal{SR}_m(\frac{x^m+1}{x+1}) \longrightarrow \mathcal{C}_m \quad \widetilde{c}(x) \longrightarrow (x+1)x^t\widetilde{c}(x) = c(x),$$

where $deg(\widetilde{c}(x)) = m - 1 - 2t$. The map G is also well defined. Then we have

$$F(G(\widetilde{c}(x))) = \widetilde{c}(x)(\widetilde{c}(x) \in \mathcal{SR}_m(\frac{x^m+1}{x+1})), \quad G(F(c_f(x))) = c_f(x)(c_f(x) \in \mathcal{C}_m).$$

Hence, this lemma follows.

Lemma 6. (1) *Let $A(x)$ be a monic self-reciprocal polynomial of even degree d, where $0 \le d \le p^r - 3$. Then $\#(\mathcal{SM}_{p^r}(A(x))) = 2^{p^r-1-d}$. If $d > p^r - 3$, then $\#(\mathcal{SM}_{p^r}(A(x))) = 1$.*

(2) *Let p be not a Wieferich prime such that $p \equiv 3 \mod 4$, $ord_p(2) = p - 1$ or $\frac{p-1}{2}$. Then*

$$\#(\mathcal{SR}_{p^r}(\frac{x^{p^r}+1}{x+1})) = 2^{p^r-1}\prod_{k=1}^{r}(1 - (\frac{1}{2})^{p^k-p^{k-1}}).$$

Proof. (1) Let $g(x)$ be a nonzero polynomial. From Lemma 2, $g(x) \in \mathcal{SM}_{p^r}(A(x))$ if and only if $h(x) = \frac{g(x)}{A(x)}$ is a self-reciprocal polynomial of degree $deg(h(x)) \in \{0, 2, \cdots, p^r - 5 - d, p^r - 3 - d\}$. The number of self-reciprocal polynomials of $deg(h(x)) \in \{0, 2, \cdots, p^r - 5 - d, p^r - 3 - d\}$ is

$$3 + 3 \cdot 4^{\frac{2}{2}} + \cdots 3 \cdot 4^{\frac{p^r-5-d}{2}} + 3 \cdot 4^{\frac{p^r-3-d}{2}} = 2^{p^r-1-d} - 1.$$

Note that $0 \in \mathcal{SM}_{p^r}(A(x))$, then $\#(\mathcal{SM}_{p^r}(A(x))) = 2^{p^r-1-d}$.

(2) From (3) in Lemma 3 and (2) in Lemma 2, $g(x) \in \mathcal{SR}_{p^r}(\frac{x^{p^r}+1}{x+1})$ if and only if $g(x) \in \mathcal{SM}_{p^r}(1)$ and $g(x) \notin \mathcal{SM}_{p^r}(Q_{p^k}(x))$ for $1 \le k \le r$. Note that if $1 \le k_1 < \cdots < k_i \le r$, then $\bigcap_{1 \le j \le i} \mathcal{SM}_{p^r}(Q_{p^{k_j}}(x)) = \mathcal{SM}_{p^r}(\prod_{j=1}^{r} Q_{p^{k_j}}(x))$.

For convenience, let $d_k = deg(Q_{p^k}(x)) = p^k - p^{k-1}$. Then $deg(\prod_{j=1}^r Q_{p^{k_j}}(x)) = \sum_{j=1}^r d_{k_j}$. From Result (1) and the inclusion-exclusion principle,

$$\#(\mathcal{SR}_{p^r}(\frac{x^{p^r}+1}{x+1})) = 2^{p^r-1-0} + (-1)^1 \sum_{1 \le k_1 \le r} 2^{p^r-1-d_{k_1}} \cdots$$

$$+ (-1)^i \sum_{1 \le k_1 < \cdots < k_i \le r} 2^{p^r-1-d_{k_1}-\cdots-d_{k_i}} + \cdots$$

$$+ (-1)^r 2^{p^r-1-d_1-\cdots-d_r}$$

$$= 2^{p^r-1} \prod_{k=1}^r (1 - (\frac{1}{2})^{p^k-p^{k-1}}).$$

Hence, this lemma follows.

Theorem 5. *Let $n = 2m = 2p^r$, where $r \ge 1$, p is not a Wieferich prime, $p \equiv 3$ mod 4, $ord_p(2) = p - 1$ or $\frac{p-1}{2}$. The number of semi-bent functions of the form (1) is*

$$\#(\mathcal{SB}_{p^r}) = 2^{p^r-1} \prod_{k=1}^r (1 - (\frac{1}{2})^{p^k-p^{k-1}}).$$

Proof. From Theorem 2, $\#(\mathcal{SB}_{p^r}) = \#(\mathcal{C}_{p^r})$. From Lemma 5, $\#(\mathcal{C}_{p^r}) = \#(\mathcal{SR}_{p^r})$. From Lemma 6, $\#(\mathcal{SB}_{p^r}) = 2^{p^r-1} \prod_{k=1}^r (1 - (\frac{1}{2})^{p^k-p^{k-1}})$.

Remark 1. If $r = 1$, it is not necessary that p is not a Wieferich prime in Theorem 5.

Corollary 3. *Let $n = 2m = 2p$, where $p \equiv 3 \mod 4$, $ord_p(2) = p - 1$ or $\frac{p-1}{2}$. The quadratic Boolean function defined by (1) is semi-bent, that is, $\mathcal{SB}_m = \mathcal{Q}_m$.*

Proof. Obviously, $\mathcal{SB}_m \subseteq \mathcal{Q}_m$. From the definition of $\mathcal{Q}_m$, $\#(\mathcal{Q}_m) = 2^{p-1} - 1$. From Theorem 5, $\#(\mathcal{SB}_m) = 2^{p-1} - 1$. Hence, $\#(\mathcal{SB}_m) = \#(\mathcal{Q}_m)$, that is, $\mathcal{SB}_m = \mathcal{Q}_m$.

The reverse of Corollary 3 also holds.

Theorem 6. *Let $\mathcal{SB}_m = \mathcal{Q}_m$ for a positive integer m. Then m is an odd prime p such that $p \equiv 3 \mod 4$, $ord_p(2) = p - 1$ or $\frac{p-1}{2}$.*

Proof. From Theorem 2 and Corollary 2, m is an odd prime p.

We first prove that $ord_p(4) = \frac{p-1}{2}$. Suppose that $ord_p(4) = s < \frac{p-1}{2}$. Then $t = \frac{p-1}{s} > 2$.

(1) When s is even, then $p|(4^{\frac{s}{2}} + 1)$. From (1) in Lemma 3, we have the factorization $Q_p(x) = h_1(x) \cdots h_t(x)$, where $h_i^*(x) = h_i(x)$ and $t = \frac{p-1}{s}$. We take $c(x) = (x+1)x^{\frac{p-1-s}{2}} h_1(x)$.

(2) When s is odd, there does not exist l such that $p|(4^l + 1)$. From (1) in Lemma 3, we have the factorization $Q_p(x) = h_1(x)h_1^*(x) \cdots h_{\frac{t}{2}}(x)h_{\frac{t}{2}}^*(x)$, where $deg(h_1(x)h_1(x)^*) = p-1-2 \cdot \frac{p-1-2s}{2}$. We take $c(x) = (x+1)x^{\frac{p-1-2s}{2}} h_1(x)h_1(x)^*$.

It can be verified that $c(x)$ has the form $c(x) = \sum_{i=1}^{\frac{p-1}{2}} c_i(x^i + x^{m-i})$. The quadratic Boolean function with respect to c_i is

$$f(x) = \sum_{i=1}^{\frac{p-1}{2}} Tr_1^{2p}(c_i x^{4^i+1}).$$

Hence, we have

$$gcd(c_f(x), x^p + 1) = (x+1)gcd(\frac{c(x)}{x+1}, Q_p(x))$$

$$= \begin{array}{ll} (x+1)h_1(x), & s \equiv 0 \mod 2 \\ (x+1)h_1(x)h_1^*(x), & s \equiv 1 \mod 2 \end{array}$$

From Theorem 2, $f(x) \notin \mathcal{SB}_m$, which contradicts that $\mathcal{SB}_m = \mathcal{Q}_m$.

Hence, $ord_p(4) = \frac{p-1}{2}$. Suppose that $p \not\equiv 3 \mod 4$, then $\frac{p-1}{2}$ is even. With the similar discussion, $p \not\equiv 3 \mod 4$ contradicts that $\mathcal{SB}_m = \mathcal{Q}_m$.

Hence, this theorem follows.

3.2   Hyper-bent Boolean Functions

In the this subsection, we consider the Boolean function

$$f_{a,b}^{(r)}(x) := Tr_1^n(ax^{r(2^m-1)}) + Tr_1^4(bx^{\frac{2^n-1}{5}}), \tag{3}$$

where $n = 2m$, $m \equiv 2$ (mod 4), $a \in \mathbb{F}_{2^m}$ and $b \in \mathbb{F}_{16}$. As the cyclotomic coset of 2 module $2^n - 1$ containing $\frac{2^n-1}{5}$ is $\{\frac{2^n-1}{5}, 2 \cdot \frac{2^n-1}{5}, 2^2 \cdot \frac{2^n-1}{5}, 2^3 \cdot \frac{2^n-1}{5}\}$. Its size is 4, or $o(\frac{2^n-1}{5}) = 4$, which means $f_{a,b}^{(r)}$ is neither in the class considered by Charpin and Gong [4] nor in the class studied by Mesanager [18,19].

We introduce some notations on character sums in [26]. Let $\xi = \alpha^{2^m-1}$, $U = <\xi>$, $V = <\xi^5>$. Since $5|(2^m+1)$, V is the subgroup of U and $\#V = \frac{2^m+1}{5}$. Let α be a primitive element of $\mathbb{F}_{2^n}$, and $\beta = \alpha^{\frac{2^n-1}{5}}$.

For any $i \in \mathbb{F}_{2^m}$ and an integer i, we define

$$S_i = \sum_{v \in V} \chi(Tr_1^n(a\xi^{i(2^m-1)}v)) = \sum_{v \in V} \chi(Tr_1^n(a\xi^{3i}v)).$$

From the definition of S_i, $S_i = S_j \pmod 5$.

The Hyper-bentness of Boolean Functions $f_{a,b}^{(5)}(x)$. We consider the hyper-bentness of $f_{a,b}^{(r)}(x)$ with $r = 5$ of the form

$$f_{a,b}^{(5)}(x) := Tr_1^n(ax^{5(2^m-1)}) + Tr_1^4(bx^{\frac{2^n-1}{5}}), \tag{4}$$

where $n = 2m$, $m \equiv 2$ (mod 4), $a \in \mathbb{F}_{2^m}$ and $b \in \mathbb{F}_{16}$.

Since $m \equiv 2$ (mod 4), $5 \mid 2^m + 1$. For any $y \in \mathbb{F}_{2^m}$, $y^{2^m-1} = 1$. Then $f_{a,b}^{(5)}(\alpha^{2^m+1}x) = f_{a,b}^{(5)}(x)$, where α is a primitive element of $\mathbb{F}_{2^n}$. Further, $f_{a,b}^{(5)}(0) = 0$. Then, from Proposition 1 and Similar to the proof of Proposition 9 in [26], we have the following proposition on the hyper-bentness of $f_{a,b}^{(5)}(x)$.

Proposition 3. *Let $f_{a,b}^{(5)}$ be the Boolean function defined by (4), where $a \in \mathbb{F}_{2^m}$ and $b \in \mathbb{F}_{16}$. Define the following character sum $\Lambda_5(a,b) := \sum_{u \in U} \chi(f_{a,b}^{(5)}(u))$. Then $f_{a,b}^{(5)}$ is a hyper-bent function if and only if $\Lambda_5(a,b) = 1$. Further, the hyper-bent function $f_{a,b}^{(5)}$ lies in $\mathcal{PS}_{ap}$ if and only if $\mathrm{Tr}_1^4(b) = 0$.*

Proposition 4. *Let $n = 2m$ and $m \equiv \pm 2, \pm 6 \pmod{20}$, If $b \in \{0\} \bigcup \{\beta^i | i = 0, 1, 2, 3, 4\}$, then the Boolean function $f_{a,b}^{(5)}$ in (4) is not a hyper-bent function. Further, if $b \in \mathbb{F}_{16}^* \backslash \{\beta^i | 0 \leq i \leq 4\}$, $f_{a,b}^{(5)}$ is a hyper-bent function if and only if $\sum_{v \in V} \chi(\mathrm{Tr}_1^n(av)) = 1$.*

Proof. We have

$$\Lambda_5(a,b) = \sum_{u \in U} \chi(f_{a,b}^{(5)}(u)) = \sum_{u \in U} \chi(\mathrm{Tr}_1^n(au^{5(2^m-1)}))\chi(\mathrm{Tr}_1^4(bu^{\frac{2^n-1}{5}})).$$

Note that $U = <\xi>$, $V = <\xi^5>$, we have $U = \xi^0 V \bigcup \xi^1 V \bigcup \xi^2 V \bigcup \xi^3 V \bigcup \xi^4 V$. Then $\Lambda_5(a,b) = \sum_{i=0}^4 \sum_{v \in V} \chi(\mathrm{Tr}_1^4(b(\xi^i v)^{\frac{2^n-1}{5}}))\chi(\mathrm{Tr}_1^n(a(\xi^{5i})^{2^m-1}v^{5(2^m-1)}))$. Since $(\xi^{5i})^{2^m-1} \in V$ and $m \equiv \pm 2, \pm 6 \pmod{20}$, $(5(2^m-1), \#V) = (5, \frac{2^m+1}{5}) = 1$. Then $v \longmapsto (\xi^{5i})^{2^m-1}v^{5(2^m-1)}$ is a permutation of V. Hence,

$$\Lambda_5(a,b) = (\sum_{i=0}^4 \chi(\mathrm{Tr}_1^4(b\xi^{i\frac{2^n-1}{5}})))(\sum_{v \in V} \chi(\mathrm{Tr}_1^n(av))).$$

Since $\xi^{\frac{2^n-1}{5}} = (\alpha^{2^m-1})^{\frac{(2^m-1)(2^m+1)}{5}} = \beta^{2^m-1} = \beta^{2^m+1-2} = \beta^3$, then :

$$\Lambda_5(a,b) = (\sum_{i=0}^4 \chi(\mathrm{Tr}_1^4(b\beta^{3i}))(\sum_{v \in V} \chi(\mathrm{Tr}_1^n(av))) = (\sum_{i=0}^4 \chi(\mathrm{Tr}_1^4(b\beta^i))(\sum_{v \in V} \chi(\mathrm{Tr}_1^n(av))).$$

When $b = 0$, $\Lambda_5(a,0) = 5 \sum_{v \in V} \chi(\mathrm{Tr}_1^n(av))$. Hence, $\Lambda_5(a,0) \neq 1$.

From Proposition 3, $f_{a,0}^{(5)}$ is not a hyper-bent function.

When $b \neq 0$, b can be represented by $b = \omega\beta^j$, where $\omega^3 = 1$ and $0 \leq j \leq 4$. Then $\sum_{i=0}^4 \chi(\mathrm{Tr}_1^4(b\beta^i)) = \sum_{i=0}^4 \chi(\mathrm{Tr}_1^4(\omega\beta^{i+j})) = \sum_{i=0}^4 \chi(\mathrm{Tr}_1^4(\omega\beta^i))$. Since $\omega^3 = 1$ and $\omega^4 = \omega$, we have $\mathrm{Tr}_1^4(\omega\beta^i) = \mathrm{Tr}_1^4(\omega^4\beta^{4i}) = \mathrm{Tr}_1^4(\omega\beta^{4i})$. If $\omega = 1$, $\sum_{i=0}^4 \chi(\mathrm{Tr}_1^4(b\beta^i)) = \sum_{i=0}^4 \chi(\mathrm{Tr}_1^4(\beta^i))$. Since β satisfies $\beta^4 + \beta^3 + \beta^2 + \beta + 1 = 0$, $\mathrm{Tr}_1^4(\beta^i) = 1$. Then $\sum_{i=0}^4 \chi(\mathrm{Tr}_1^4(b\beta^i)) = -3$. Therefore,

$$\Lambda_5(a,b) = -3 \sum_{v \in V} \chi(\mathrm{Tr}_1^n(av)), b = \beta^j, 0 \leq j \leq 4.$$

From Propsition 3, $f_{a,\beta^j}^{(5)}$ is not a hyper-bent function. When $\omega \neq 1$, we have

$$\mathrm{Tr}_1^4(\omega\beta) + \mathrm{Tr}_1^4(\omega\beta^2) = \mathrm{Tr}_1^4(\omega(\beta + \beta^2)) = 1.$$

Then $\chi(\mathrm{Tr}_1^4(\omega\beta)) + \chi(\mathrm{Tr}_1^4(\omega\beta^2)) = 0$. Similarly, $\chi(\mathrm{Tr}_1^4(\omega\beta^3)) + \chi(\mathrm{Tr}_1^4(\omega\beta^4)) = 0$. Therefore,

$$\Lambda_5(a,b) = \sum_{v\in V} \chi(\mathrm{Tr}_1^n(av)), b = \omega\beta^j, 0 \le j \le 4, \omega^3 = 1, \omega \ne 1.$$

From Proposition 3, the second part of this proposition follows.

In Proposition 4, we consider the hyper-bentness of the Boolean function $f_{a,b}^{(5)}$ for $m \equiv \pm 2, \pm 6 \pmod{20}$. The proposition below discusses the hyper-bentness of $f_{a,b}^{(5)}$ for $m \equiv 10 \pmod{20}$.

Proposition 5. *Let* $n = 2m$, $m \equiv 10 \pmod{20}$, $a \in \mathbb{F}_{2^m}$, $b \in \mathbb{F}_{16}$. *then the Boolean function* $f_{a,b}^{(5)}$ *in* (4) *is not a hyper-bent function.*

Proof. Note that $\Lambda_5(a,b) = \sum_{i=0}^4 \sum_{v\in V} \chi(\mathrm{Tr}_1^4(b\xi^{i\frac{2^n-1}{5}}))\chi(\mathrm{Tr}_1^n(a(\xi^{5i})^{2^m-1}v^{5(2^m-1)}))$. Since $m \equiv 10 \pmod{20}$, $25|(2^m + 1)$ and $(5(2^m - 1), \frac{2^m+1}{5}) = 5$. Then $v \longmapsto v^{5(2^m-1)}$ is 5 to 1 from V to $V^5 := \{v^5|v \in V\}$. Therefore,

$$\Lambda_5(a,b) = 5\sum_{i=0}^4 \sum_{v\in V^5} \chi(\mathrm{Tr}_1^4(b\xi^{i\frac{2^n-1}{5}}))\chi(\mathrm{Tr}_1^n(a(\xi^{5i})^{2^m-1}v)).$$

Hence, $5|\Lambda_5(a,b)$ and $\Lambda_5(a,b)$ is not equal to 1, From Proposition 3, $f_{a,b}^{(5)}$ is not a hyper-bent function.

From Proposition 4, $\sum_{v\in V} \chi(\mathrm{Tr}_1^n(av)) = \sum_{v\in V} \chi(\mathrm{Tr}_1^n(av^{2^m-1}))$. Note that $\sum_{v\in V} \chi(\mathrm{Tr}_1^n(av)) = S_0$ in [26]. From Proposition 15 in [26],

$$\sum_{v\in V} \chi(\mathrm{Tr}_1^n(av)) = \frac{1}{5}[1 - K_m(a) + 2Q_m(a)]. \tag{5}$$

Further, from Proposition 16 and 18 in [26], we have the following results.

Theorem 7. *Let* $n = 2m$, $m \equiv \pm 2, \pm 6 \pmod{20}$, $m \ge 6$ *and* $b \in \mathbb{F}_{16}^* \setminus \{\beta^i | 0 \le i \le 4\}$, *then* $f_{a,b}^{(5)}$ *is a hyper-bent function if and only if one of the assertions* (1) *and* (2) *holds.*
  (1) $Q_m(a) = 0$, $K_m(a) = -4$.
  (2) $Q_m(a) = 2^{m_1}$, $K_m(a) = 2 \cdot 2^{m_1} - 4$.

The Hyper-bentness of $f_{a,b}^{(r)}(x)$. Now, we consider the general case of the hyper-bentness of $f_{a,b}^{(r)}(x)$. Define the character sum $\Lambda_r(a,b) := \sum_{u\in U} \chi(f_{a,b}^{(r)}(u))$.
Similarly, $f_{a,b}^{(5)}(x)$ is a hyper-bent function if and only if $\Lambda_r(a,b) = 1$.

Theorem 8. *Let* $n = 2m$, $m \equiv 2 \pmod 4$, $a \in \mathbb{F}_{2^m}$ *and* $b \in \mathbb{F}_{16}$. *If* $(r, \frac{2^m+1}{5}) > 1$, *then* $f_{a,b}^{(r)}$ *is not a hyper-bent function. Further, if* $(r, \frac{2^m+1}{5}) = 1$, *then*

(1) If $r \equiv 0 \pmod 5$, then $f_{a,b}^{(r)}$ and $f_{a,b}^{(5)}$ have the same hyper-bentness.

(2) If $r \equiv \pm 1 \pmod 5$, then $f_{a,b}^{(r)}$ and $f_{a,b}^{(1)}$ have the same hyper-bentness.

(3) If $r \equiv \pm 2 \pmod 5$, then $f_{a,b}^{(r)}$ and $f_{a,b}^{(2)}$ have the same hyper-bentness.

Proof. Note that $\Lambda_r(a,b) = \sum_{i=0}^{4} \sum_{v \in V} \chi(\mathrm{Tr}_1^4(b\xi^{i\frac{2^n-1}{5}}))\chi(\mathrm{Tr}_1^n(a\xi^{ri(2^m-1)}v^{r(2^m-1)}))$. Let $d := (r(2^m-1), \#V) = (r, \frac{2^m+1}{5})$, then

$$\Lambda_r(a,b) = d\sum_{i=0}^{4}\chi(\mathrm{Tr}_1^4(b\xi^{i\frac{2^n-1}{5}})) \sum_{v \in V^d}\chi(\mathrm{Tr}_1^n(a\xi^{ri(2^m-1)}v^{r(2^m-1)})),$$

where $V^d = \{v^d | v \in V\}$. If $d = (r, \frac{2^m+1}{5}) > 1$, $d | \Lambda_r(a,b)$ and $\Lambda_r(a,b) \neq 1$. Hence, $f_{a,b}^{(r)}$ is not a hyper-bent function.

When $d = (r, \frac{2^m+1}{5}) = 1$, $\Lambda_r(a,b) = \sum_{i=0}^4 \chi(\mathrm{Tr}_1^4(b\xi^{i\frac{2^n-1}{5}})) \sum_{v \in V} \chi(\mathrm{Tr}_1^n(a\xi^{ri(2^m-1)}v))$. If $r \equiv 0 \pmod 5$, from $\xi^{\frac{2^n-1}{5}} = \beta^3$, we have

$$\Lambda_r(a,b) = \sum_{i=0}^{4}\chi(\mathrm{Tr}_1^4(b\beta^i)) \sum_{v \in V}\chi(\mathrm{Tr}_1^n(av)).$$

Then $\Lambda_r(a,b) = \Lambda_5(a,b)$. Therefore, $f_{a,b}^{(r)}$ and $f_{a,b}^{(5)}$ have the same hyper-bentness.

If $r \equiv 1 \pmod 5$, then $\Lambda_r(a,b) = \sum_{i=0}^4 \chi(\mathrm{Tr}_1^4(b\xi^{i\frac{2^n-1}{5}})) \sum_{v \in V} \chi(\mathrm{Tr}_1^n(a\xi^{i(2^m-1)}v))$. From Proposition 10 in [26], $\Lambda_r(a,b) = \Lambda_1(a,b)$. Hence, $f_{a,b}^{(r)}$ and $f_{a,b}^{(1)}$ have the same hyper-bentness.

If $r \equiv 2 \pmod 5$, then $\Lambda_r(a,b) = \sum_{i=0}^4 \chi(\mathrm{Tr}_1^4(b\xi^{i\frac{2^n-1}{5}})) \sum_{v \in V} \chi(\mathrm{Tr}_1^n(a\xi^{2i(2^m-1)}v))$ $= \sum_{i=0}^4 \chi(\mathrm{Tr}_1^4(b\beta^{3i}))S_{2i} = \sum_{i=0}^4 \chi(\mathrm{Tr}_1^4(b\beta^{9i}))S_{6i} = \sum_{i=0}^4 \chi(\mathrm{Tr}_1^4(b\beta^{4i}))S_i$. From Lemma 1 in [26], then

$$\Lambda_r(a,b) = \chi(\mathrm{Tr}_1^4(b))S_0 + (\chi(\mathrm{Tr}_1^4(b\beta)) + \chi(\mathrm{Tr}_1^4(b\beta^4)))S_1$$
$$+ (\chi(\mathrm{Tr}_1^4(b\beta^2)) + \chi(\mathrm{Tr}_1^4(b\beta^3)))S_2. \tag{6}$$

Hence, $\Lambda_r(a,b) = \Lambda_2(a,b)$. $f_{a,b}^{(r)}$ and $f_{a,b}^{(2)}$ have the same hyper-bentness.

If $r \equiv 3 \pmod 5$, $\Lambda_r(a,b) = \sum_{i=0}^4 \chi(\mathrm{Tr}_1^4(b\xi^{i\frac{2^n-1}{5}})) \sum_{v \in V} \chi(\mathrm{Tr}_1^n(a\xi^{3i(2^m-1)}v))$ $= \sum_{i=0}^4 \chi(\mathrm{Tr}_1^4(b\beta^{3i}))S_{3i} = \sum_{i=0}^4 \chi(\mathrm{Tr}_1^4(b\beta^i))S_i$. From Lemma 1 in [26],

$$\Lambda_r(a,b) = \chi(\mathrm{Tr}_1^4(b))S_0 + (\chi(\mathrm{Tr}_1^4(b\beta)) + \chi(\mathrm{Tr}_1^4(b\beta^4)))S_1$$
$$+ (\chi(\mathrm{Tr}_1^4(b\beta^2)) + \chi(\mathrm{Tr}_1^4(b\beta^3)))S_2. \tag{7}$$

Hence, $\Lambda_r(a,b) = \Lambda_3(a,b)$. From (6) and (7), we have $\Lambda_2(a,b) = \Lambda_3(a,b)$. Thus, $f_{a,b}^{(r)}$ and $f_{a,b}^{(2)}$ have the same hyper-bentness.

Similarly, if $r \equiv 4 \pmod 5$, then $\Lambda_r(a,b) = \Lambda_4(a,b) = \Lambda_1(a,b)$. Thus, $f_{a,b}^{(r)}$ and $f_{a,b}^{(1)}$ have the same hyper-bentness.

Above all, this theorem follows.

From Theorem 8, to characterize the hyper-bentness of $f_{a,b}^{(r)}$, we just consider the hyper-bentness of $f_{a,b}^{(1)}$, $f_{a,b}^{(2)}$ and $f_{a,b}^{(5)}$. The hyper-bentness of $f_{a,b}^{(1)}$ is considered in [26]. And the hyper-bentness of $f_{a,b}^{(5)}$ is discussed before. Next, we just study the hyper-bentness of $f_{a,b}^{(2)}$.

When $b = 0$, the hyper-bentness of $f_{a,0}^{(2)}$ is given in [3]. Then we just consider the case $b \neq 0$. We first give properties of $\Lambda_2(a,b)$ in the following proposition.

Proposition 6. *Let $a \in \mathbb{F}_{2^m}$ and $b \in \mathbb{F}_{16}^*$, then*
(1) *If $b = 1$, then $\Lambda_2(a,b) = S_0 - 2(S_1 + S_2) = 2S_0 - \Lambda_2(a,0)$.*
(2) *If $b \in \{\beta + \beta^2, \beta + \beta^3, \beta^2 + \beta^4, \beta^3 + \beta^4\}$, that is, b is a primitive element satisfying $\mathrm{Tr}_1^4(b) = 0$, then $\Lambda_2(a,b) = S_0$.*
(3) *If $b = \beta$ or β^4, then $\Lambda_2(a,b) = -S_0 - 2S_2$.*
(4) *If $b = \beta^2$ or β^3, then $\Lambda_2(a,b) = -S_0 - 2S_1$.*
(5) *If $b = 1 + \beta$ or $1 + \beta^4$, then $\Lambda_2(a,b) = -S_0 + 2S_2$.*
(6) *If $b = 1 + \beta^2$ or $1 + \beta^3$, then $\Lambda_2(a,b) = -S_0 + 2S_1$.*
(7) *If $b = \beta + \beta^4$, then $\Lambda_2(a,b) = S_0 + 2S_2 - 2S_1$.*
(8) *If $b = \beta^2 + \beta^3$, then $\Lambda_2(a,b) = S_0 - 2S_2 + 2S_1$.*

Proof. From (6) and the similar proof of Proposition 13 in [26], this proposition follows.

Corollary 4. *Let $a \in \mathbb{F}_{2^m}$ and $b \in \mathbb{F}_{16}^*$, then $f_{a,b}^{(2)}$ and $f_{a,b^2}^{(1)}$ have the same hyper-bentness.*

Proof. From Proposition 13 in [26] and Proposition 6, we have $\Lambda_2(a,b^2) = \Lambda_1(a,b)$. Hence, $f_{a,b}^{(2)}$ and $f_{a,b^2}^{(1)}$ have the same hyper-bentness.

From Corollary 4, the hyper-bentness of $f_{a,b}^{(2)}$ can be characterized by that of $f_{a,b}^{(1)}$.

From the above discussion, we have the following result on $f_{a,b}^{(r)}$.

Theorem 9. *Let $a \in \mathbb{F}_{2^m}$ and $(r, \frac{2^m+1}{5}) = 1$, then*
(1) *If $\frac{1}{5}[1 - K_m(a) + 2Q_m(a)] = 1$, then the following Boolean functions*
    (a) *$f_{a,b}^{(r)}$ $b \in \mathbb{F}_{16}^* \setminus \{\beta^i | i = 0, 1, 2, 3, 4\}$, $r \equiv 0 \pmod 5$.*
    (b) *$f_{a,b}^{(r)}$, $r \not\equiv 0 \pmod 5$, $b^4 + b + 1 = 0$.*
    are hyper-bent functions.
(2) *If $-\frac{1}{5}[3(1 - K_m(a)) - 4Q_m(a)] = 1$, then the Boolean function $f_{a,1}^{(r)}$ $(r \not\equiv 0 \pmod 5)$ is a hyper-bent function.*

Proof. From Proposition 16 in [26] and Theorem 8, Equation (5) and Proposition 4, this theorem follows.

4   Conclusion

This paper presents a new class of semi-bent quadratic Boolean functions and a new class of hyper-bent Boolean functions with even variable n. The semi-bentness and hyper-bentness are characterized. Moreover, for some special cases, the number of semi-bent quadratic Boolean functions is enumerated. The techniques used in this paper can be utilized into the study of generalized bent functions and generalized semi-bent functions.

Acknowledgements. The authors would like to thank anonymous reviewers for their helpful advice and comments. This work was supported by the National Natural Science Foundation of China (Grant Nos. 10990011, 11401480, 61272499), and Science and Technology on Information Assurance Laboratory (Grant No. KJ-11-02). Yanfeng Qi acknowledges support from Aisino Corporation Inc.

References

1. Berlekamp, E.R.: Algebraic Coding Theory. Revised edn. Aegean Park, Laguna Hills, CA (1984)
2. Boztas, S., Kumar, P.V.: Binary sequences with Gold-like correlation but larger linear span. IEEE Trans. Inf. Theory **40**, 532–537 (1994)
3. Canteaut, A., Charpin, P., Kyureghyan, G.: A new class of monomial bent functions. Finite Fields Applicat. **14**(1), 221–241 (2008)
4. Charpin, P., Gong, G.: Hyperbent functions, Kloosterman sums and Dickson polynomials. IEEE Trans. Inf. Theory **9**(54), 4230–4238 (2008)
5. Charpin, P., Pasalic, E., Tavernier, C.: On bent and semi-bent quadratic Boolean functions. IEEE Trans. Inf. Theory **51**(12), 4286–4298 (2005)
6. Dobbertin, H., Leander, G.: A survey of some recent results on bent functions. In: Helleseth, T., Sarwate, D., Song, H.-Y., Yang, K. (eds.) SETA 2004. LNCS, vol. 3486, pp. 1–29. Springer, Heidelberg (2005)
7. Gold, R.: Maximal recursive sequences with 3-valued recursive crosscorrelation functions. IEEE Trans. Inf. Theory **14**(1), 154–156 (1968)
8. Hu, H., Feng, D.: On quadratic bent functions in polynomial forms. IEEE Trans. Inform. Theory **53**, 2610–2615 (2007)
9. Helleseth, T.: Correlation of m-sequences and related topics. In: Ding, C., Helleseth, T., Niederreiter, H. (eds.) Sequences and Their Applications, pp. 49–66. Springer, London (1998)
10. Helleseth, T., Kumar, P.V.: Sequences with low correlation. In: Pless, V.S., Huffman, W.C. (eds.) Handbook of Coding Theory, vol. II, pp. 1765–1853. North-Holland, Amsterdam (1998)
11. Lachaud, G., Wolfmann, J.: The weights of the orthogonal of the extended quadratic binary Goppa codes. IEEE Trans. Inform. Theory **36**, 686–692 (1990)
12. Lidl, R., Niederreiter, H.: Finite fields. In: Encyclopedia of Mathematics and its Applications, vol. 20. Addison-Wesley, Reading (1983)
13. Khoo, K., Gong, G., Stinson, D.R.: A new family of Gold-like sequences. In: Proceedings of IEEE International Symposium on Information Theory, Lausanne, Switzerland, p. 181, June/July 2002

14. Khoo, K., Gong, G., Stinson, D.R.: A new characterization of semi-bent and bent functions on finite fields. Des. Codes. Cryptogr. **38**(2), 279–295 (2006)
15. Matsui, M.: Linear cryptanalysis method for DES cipher. In: Helleseth, T. (ed.) EUROCRYPT 1993. LNCS, vol. 765, pp. 386–397. Springer, Heidelberg (1994)
16. Ma, W., Lee, M., Zhang, F.: A new class of bent functions. IEICE Trans. Fundam. **E88–A**(7), 2039–2040 (2005)
17. MacWilliams, F.J., Sloane, N.J.A.: The Theory of Error-Correcting Codes. North-Holland, Amsterdam (1977)
18. Mesnager, S.: A new class of bent boolean functions in polynomial forms. In: Proceedings of International Workshop on Coding and Cryptography, WCC 2009, pp. 5–18 (2009)
19. Mesnager, S.: A new class of bent and hyper-bent boolean functions in polynomial forms. Des. Codes Crypt. **59**(1–3), 265–279 (2011)
20. Mesnager, S.: A new family of hyper-bent boolean functions in polynomial form. In: Parker, M.G. (ed.) Cryptography and Coding 2009. LNCS, vol. 5921, pp. 402–417. Springer, Heidelberg (2009)
21. Meier, W., Staffelbach, O.: Fast correlation attacks on stream ciphers. In: Günther, C.G. (ed.) EUROCRYPT 1988. LNCS, vol. 330, pp. 301–314. Springer, Heidelberg (1988)
22. Patterson, N., Wiedemann, D.H.: The covering radius of the $(2^{15}, 16)$ Reed-Muller code is at least 16276. IEEE Trans. Inf. Theory **29**, 354–356 (1983)
23. Patterson, N.J., Wiedemann, D.H.: Correction to The covering radius of the $(2^{15}, 16)$ Reed-Muller code is at least 16276. IEEE Trans. Inf. Theory **36**, 443 (1990)
24. Rothaus, O.S.: On bent functions. J. Combin. Theory A **20**, 300–305 (1976)
25. Silverman, J.: Wieferich's criterion and the abc-conjecture. J. Number Theory **30**(2), 226–237 (1988)
26. Tang, C., Qi, Y., Xu, M., Wang, B., Yang, Y.: A new class of hyper-bent Boolean functions in binomial forms. CoRR, abs/1112.0062v2 (2012)
27. Tang, C., Qi, Y., Xu, M.: New quadratic bent functions in polynomial forms with coefficients in extension fields. IACR Crypt. ePrint Archive **2013**, 405 (2013)
28. Wieferich, A.: Zum letzten Fermat'Schen Theorem. J. Reine Angew. Math. **136**, 293–302 (1909)
29. Youssef, A.M., Gong, G.: Hyper-bent Functions. In: Pfitzmann, B. (ed.) EUROCRYPT 2001. LNCS, vol. 2045, pp. 406–419. Springer, Heidelberg (2001)
30. Yu, N.Y., Gong, G.: Constructions of quadratic bent functions in polynomial forms. IEEE Trans. Inf. Theory **52**(7), 3291–3299 (2006)

New Construction of Differentially
4-Uniform Bijections

Claude Carlet[1], Deng Tang[1,2]([✉]), Xiaohu Tang[2], and Qunying Liao[3]

[1] LAGA, Department of Mathematics, University of Paris 8, CNRS, UMR 7539,
2 Rue de la Liberté, 93526 Saint-Denis Cedex 02, France
claude.carlet@univ-paris8.fr
[2] Provincial Key Lab of Information Coding and Transmission,
Institute of Mobile Communications, Southwest Jiaotong University,
Chengdu 610031, China
deng.tang@etud.univ-paris8.fr, xhutang@ieee.org
[3] Institute of Mathematics and Software Science, Sichuan Normal University,
Chengdu 610066, China
qunyingliao@sicnu.edu.cn

Abstract. Block ciphers use Substitution boxes (S-boxes) to create confusion into the cryptosystems. For resisting the known attacks on these cryptosystems, the following criteria for functions are mandatory: low differential uniformity, high nonlinearity and not low algebraic degree. Bijectivity is also necessary if the cipher is a Substitution-Permutation Network, and balancedness makes a Feistel cipher lighter. It is well-known that almost perfect nonlinear (APN) functions have the lowest differential uniformity 2 (the values of differential uniformity being always even) and the existence of APN bijections over $\mathbb{F}_{2^n}$ for even $n \geq 8$ is a big open problem. In real practical applications, differentially 4-uniform bijections can be used as S-boxes when the dimension is even. For example, the AES uses a differentially 4-uniform bijection over $\mathbb{F}_{2^8}$. In this paper, we first propose a method for constructing a large family of differentially 4-uniform bijections in even dimensions. This method can generate at least $\left(2^{n-3} - \lfloor 2^{(n-1)/2-1} \rfloor - 1\right) \cdot 2^{2^{n-1}}$ such bijections having maximum algebraic degree $n - 1$. Furthermore, we exhibit a subclass of functions having high nonlinearity and being CCZ-inequivalent to all known differentially 4-uniform power bijections and to quadratic functions.

Keywords: Block cipher · Substitution box · Differential uniformity · CCZ-equivalence · Nonlinearity

1 Introduction and Preliminaries

In Shannon's terms [12], the generally accepted design principles for conventional ciphers are confusion and diffusion. These two design principles are very general

© Springer International Publishing Switzerland 2014
D. Lin et al. (Eds.): Inscrypt 2013, LNCS 8567, pp. 22–38, 2014.
DOI: 10.1007/978-3-319-12087-4_2

and informal. In practice, every block cipher uses Substitution boxes (S-boxes) to create confusion and uses some well chosen linear transformations (related to codes of large minimum distance) to bring diffusion into the cryptosystem. If the cipher is a Substitution-Permutation Network as in the AES, then we need the S-boxes to be bijections (to ensure invertibility).

Given two integers n and m, any S-box with n input bits and m output bits, which is often called an (n, m)-function or a vectorial Boolean function if the values n and m are omitted, can be viewed as a function G from the vectorial space $\mathbb{F}_2^n$ to the vectorial space $\mathbb{F}_2^m$. Particularly, G is called a Boolean function when $m = 1$. We denote by $\mathcal{B}_n$ the set of Boolean functions of n variables. The basic representation of any Boolean function $f \in \mathcal{B}_n$ is by its truth table, i.e.,

$$f = \big[f(0, 0, \cdots, 0), f(1, 0, \cdots, 0), \cdots, f(0, 1, \cdots, 1), f(1, 1, \cdots, 1) \big].$$

We say that a Boolean function $f \in \mathcal{B}_n$ is balanced if its truth table contains an equal number of ones and zeros, that is, if its Hamming weight equals 2^{n-1}, where the Hamming weight of f, denoted by $\mathrm{wt}(f)$, is the number of nonzero values in its truth table. Given two Boolean functions f and g on n variables, the Hamming distance between f and g is defined as $d_H(f, g) = |\{x \in \mathbb{F}_2^n \mid f(x) \neq g(x)\}|$.

Let G be an (n, m)-function, the Boolean functions $g_1(x), \cdots, g_m(x)$ defined by $G(x) = (g_1(x), \cdots, g_m(x))$ are called the coordinate functions of G. Further, the Boolean functions, which are the linear combinations, with non all-zero coefficients of the coordinate functions of G, are called component functions of G. The component functions of G can be expressed as $a \cdot G$ where $a \in \mathbb{F}_2^{m*}$. If we identify every element of $\mathbb{F}_2^m$ with an element of finite field $\mathbb{F}_{2^m}$, then the component functions of G can be expressed as $tr_1^n(\alpha G)$, where $\alpha \in \mathbb{F}_{2^n}^*$ and $tr_1^n(x) = \sum_{i=0}^{n-1} x^{2^i}$ is the trace function from $\mathbb{F}_{2^n}$ to $\mathbb{F}_2$. To resist the known attacks on each model of block cipher (and hopefully, to resist future attacks), the S-boxes used in ciphers should satisfy various design criteria simultaneously. The design criteria on S-boxes result in necessary properties of the component functions and of the vectorial function itself.

Let $x = (x_1, x_2, \cdots, x_n)$ and $\alpha = (\alpha_1, \alpha_2, \cdots, \alpha_n)$ both belong to $\mathbb{F}_2^n$ and let $x \cdot \alpha$ be any inner product, for instance the usual one, defined as $x \cdot \alpha = x_1\alpha_1 \oplus x_2\alpha_2 \oplus \cdots \oplus x_n\alpha_n$, then the Walsh transform of G at $(a, b) \in \mathbb{F}_2^{m*} \times \mathbb{F}_2^n$ is defined as

$$W_G(a, b) = \sum_{x \in \mathbb{F}_2^n} (-1)^{a \cdot G(x) + b \cdot x}.$$

Usually, we call extended Walsh spectrum of G the multi-set of their absolute values. To resist linear cryptanalysis [10], S-boxes used in cryptosystems should have high nonlinearity. The nonlinearity $nl(G)$ of an (n, m)-function G is the minimum Hamming distance between all the component functions of G and all affine functions on n variables. According to the definition of Walsh transform, we have

$$nl(G) = 2^{n-1} - \frac{1}{2} \max_{(a,b) \in \mathbb{F}_2^{m*} \times \mathbb{F}_2^n} |W_G(a,b)|$$

$$= 2^{n-1} - \frac{1}{2} \max_{(\alpha,\beta) \in \mathbb{F}_{2^m}^* \times \mathbb{F}_{2^n}} |W_G(\alpha,\beta)|.$$

It is well-known that the nonlinearity $nl(G)$ is upper-bounded by $2^{n-1} - 2^{\frac{n-1}{2}}$ when $n = m$ and the best known value of $nl(G)$ is $2^{n-1} - 2^{\frac{n}{2}}$ when $n = m$ is even.

Any (n,m)-function G can be represented in univariate form:

$$G(x) = \sum_{i=0}^{2^n-1} a_i x^i, a_i \in \mathbb{F}_{2^n}.$$

The algebraic degree, denoted by $\deg(G)$, equals the maximal 2-weight of the exponent i such that $a_i \neq 0$, where the 2-weight of a given integer i is the number of ones in its binary expansion. It is known that the maximum algebraic degree of bijective functions in dimension n is $n - 1$. Functions used as S-boxes should have high (or at least not low) algebraic degree to withstand the higher order differential attack [7] which is described by Knudsen when the degree is 2 but a degree 3 seems still insufficient and a degree at least 4 is safer.

The differential attack introduced by Biham and Shamir [1] is a powerful cryptanalytic method for attacking block ciphers. For measuring the ability of a given function to resist the differential attack [1], Nyberg [11] introduced a concept which is called differential δ-uniformity:

Definition 1. *An (n,m)-function G is called differentially δ-uniform if, for every nonzero $a \in \mathbb{F}_2^n$ and every $b \in \mathbb{F}_2^m$, the equation $G(x) + G(x + a) = b$ has at most δ solutions.*

For every $a \in \mathbb{F}_2^{n*}$ and every $b \in \mathbb{F}_2^m$, if we denote by $\delta_G(a,b)$ the size of the set $\{x \in \mathbb{F}_2^n \mid G(x) + G(x + a) = b\}$, then we can see that δ equals the maximum value of $\delta_G(a,b)$. The multi-set $[\delta_G(a,b) \mid a \in \mathbb{F}_2^{n*}, b \in \mathbb{F}_2^m]$ is called the differential spectrum of G. The smaller δ is, the better is the contribution of G to a resistance to differential attack. When $m = n$, the smallest possible value of δ is 2 (since if x is a solution of equation $G(x) + G(x + a) = b$ then $x + a$ is also a solution, hence the values of δ are even); the functions achieving this value are called almost perfect nonlinear (APN) functions. APN functions have the lowest differential uniformity. Up to now, there is only one sporadic example of APN bijection for $n = 6$, found in [3] and it is a big open problem to know whether there exist APN bijections over $\mathbb{F}_{2^n}$ for even $n \geq 8$. So, for resisting differential attacks in even dimension, we need to choose differentially 4-uniform bijections as S-boxes (differential 4-uniformity is not optimal but it can withstand differential attacks in an efficient way; for example, the AES uses a differentially 4-uniform bijection with 8 input bits). For the convenience of the readers, we give in Sect. 2 a brief description of known APN bijections and differentially 4-uniform bijections in even dimensions.

These notions are preserved by extended affine equivalence (in brief, EA equivalence) and Carlet-Charpin-Zinoviev equivalence (CCZ-equivalence): two (n, n)-functions G and H are called affine equivalent if one is equal to the other, composed on the left and on the right by affine permutations; they are called EA-equivalent if one is affine equivalent to the other, added with an affine function; they are called CCZ-equivalent if their graphs $\{(x, y) \in \mathbb{F}_2^n \times \mathbb{F}_2^n \,|\, y = G(x)\}$ and $\{(x, y) \in \mathbb{F}_2^n \times \mathbb{F}_2^n \,|\, y = H(x)\}$ are affine equivalent, that is, if there exists an affine automorphism $L = (L_1, L_2)$ of $\mathbb{F}_2^n \times \mathbb{F}_2^n$ such that $y = G(x) \Leftrightarrow L_2(x, y) = H(L_1(x, y))$ (where L_1 and L_2 are two affine functions from $\mathbb{F}_2^n \times \mathbb{F}_2^n$ to $\mathbb{F}_2^n$). It is well-known that EA equivalence implies CCZ-equivalence, but the converse is false. Both EA and CCZ-equivalence preserve the differential spectrum and extended Walsh spectrum. But CCZ-equivalence does not respect the algebraic degree, while EA equivalence does.

Ideally, the dimension n of bijections used in cryptosystems should be a power of 2 for an efficient implementation in both hardware and software since it allows decomposing optimally the computation of the output in $\mathbb{F}_{2^n}$ into computations in subfields. This is also more convenient for the design of the whole cipher, for instance the number of input bits of the AES is 8. In practice, S-boxes used in cryptosystems should satisfy a tradeoff between security and efficient implementation simultaneously. Therefore, it is very interesting to construct bijections with good cryptographic properties in even dimensions. In the present paper, we construct a family of differentially 4-uniform bijections of even dimensions $n \geq 6$ by concatenating two $(n - 1, n)$-functions. For every even $n \geq 6$, this family includes at least $\left(2^{n-3} - \lfloor 2^{(n-1)/2 - 1} \rfloor - 1\right) \cdot 2^{2^{n-1}}$ bijections, all of algebraic degree $n - 1$. We also mathematically prove that, for any even $n \geq 8$, bijections in this family are CCZ-inequivalent to the Gold functions, the Kasami functions, the functions discussed in [2] and to quadratic functions. Further, we show a subclass of the family which has nonlinearity at least $2^{n-1} - 2\lfloor 2^{(n+1)/2} \rfloor - 4$ and is CCZ-inequivalent to all known differentially 4-uniform power bijections and to quadratic functions.

The paper is organized in the following way: Sect. 2 summarizes the known differentially 4-uniform bijections in even dimensions. A family of differentially 4-uniform bijections is presented in Sect. 3, and its algebraic degree, Walsh spectrum and CCZ-equivalence with known functions is studied. In Sect. 4, we give a subclass of differentially 4-uniform bijections with good cryptographic properties. Finally, Sect. 5 concludes the paper.

2 The Known Bijections with Low Differential Uniformity in Even Dimensions

Up to now, only a few classes of bijections with very low differential uniformity in even dimensions have been found, some of them are listed in [4,14]. We summarize them here for the convenience of the reader. It is clear that the functions

x^d and $x^{2^i d}$ are affine equivalent for every i, so we only list one value of d for each cyclotomic coset of 2 mod $2^n - 1$. Besides, we also omit d^{-1} when d is co-prime with $2^n - 1$ since arbitrary bijection is CCZ-equivalent to its compositional inverse.

- There is only one example of APN bijection on 6 variables, which is found by J. Dillon in [3], and the problem whether there exist APN bijections over $\mathbb{F}_{2^n}$ for even $n \geq 8$ is still open. This example is CCZ-equivalent to a quadratic function (which may represent a risk with respect to the higher order differential attack) and its expression is complex (this leads to inefficient implementation in both hardware and software).
- The inverse function x^{2^n-2} is differentially 4-uniform when n is even (and is APN when n is odd) [11]; it is used as the S-box of the AES with $n = 8$. It has best known nonlinearity $2^{n-1} - 2^{n/2}$ and maximum algebraic degree $n - 1$. But the inverse function satisfies the bilinear relation $x^2 y = x$ where $y = x^{2^n-2}$, which is the core of the algebraic attacks and so may represent a thread.
- The Gold functions x^{2^i+1} such that $\gcd(i, n) = 2$ are differentially 4-uniform. Functions in this class are bijective when $\gcd(2^i + 1, 2^n - 1) = 1$, but they are quadratic and can not be used as S-boxes.
- The Kasami functions $x^{2^{2i}-2^i+1}$ such that n is divisible by 2 but not by 4 and $\gcd(i, n) = 2$ are differentially 4-uniform. Functions in this class have best known nonlinearity $2^{n-1} - 2^{n/2}$ (in fact, they have same Walsh spectrum as the Gold functions and we do not know whether this can represent a weakness) and are bijective when $\gcd(2^{2i} - 2^i + 1, 2^n - 1) = 1$. This class of functions never reaches the maximum algebraic degree $n - 1$. Note that $2^{2i} - 2^i + 1 = \frac{2^{3i}+1}{2^i+1}$ and $2^i + 1$ is co-prime with $2^n - 1$ when n is divisible by 2 but not by 4 and $\gcd(i, n) = 2$. This means that the Kasami functions have the form $F(x) = Q_1(Q_2^{-1}(x))$ where Q_1 and Q_2 are quadratic permutations, which has some similarity with a function CCZ-equivalent to a quadratic function. Maybe this could be used in an extended higher order differential attack.
- The function $x^{2^{n/2+n/4+1}}$ is differentially 4-uniform [2] and has best known nonlinearity $2^{n-1} - 2^{n/2}$ as well. This class of functions is bijective if n is divisible by 4 but not by 8. It has algebraic degree 3 which is too low.
- In [8], the authors modified the method introduced in [4], initially designed for constructing differentially 4-uniform bijections in odd dimensions, to construct differentially 4-uniform bijections in even dimensions. They obtained three classes of differentially 4-uniform bijections with best known nonlinearity $2^{n-1} - 2^{n/2}$ and algebraic degree $(n+2)/2$. Those functions are interesting but the authors did not discuss whether they are CCZ-equivalent to power functions and quadratic functions.
- Recently, a construction has been introduced in [14] to build differentially 4-uniform bijections in even dimensions by adding some special Boolean functions to the inverse function. Based on it, the authors have discovered two infinite classes of differentially 4-uniform bijections. The first class of functions is of the form $x^{2^n-2} + tr_1^n(x^2(x + 1)^{2^n-2})$, which has optimal algebraic

degree $n-1$ and the nonlinearity is no less than $2^{n-1} - 2^{n/2+1} - 2$. The second one is of the form $x^{2^n-2} + tr_1^n\left(x^{(2^n-2)d} + (x^{2^n-2}+1)^d\right)$, where $d = 3(2^t+1)$, $2 \leq t \leq n/2 - 1$. The latter has algebraic degree $n-1$ as well and the nonlinearity is at least $2^{n-2} - 2^{n/2-1} - 1$. The authors didn't mathematically prove whether their functions are CCZ-inequivalent to the inverse function (but we can easily check, with the help of computer, that those two classes of functions are CCZ-inequivalent to the inverse function for even $n = 6, 8, 10, 12$). These two classes of functions are interesting and they are worthy of a further investigation.

We can see from above that except for the inverse function (which has however a potential weakness), the Kasami functions (whose algebraic degree is enough to resist the higher order differential attack but which is not maximum, whose Walsh spectrum is the same as that of the Gold function and which seems related with quadratic functions - in a way which could not be used yet to design attacks, though), the functions proposed in [8] (which have not been proven CCZ-inequivalent to power functions) and the functions constructed in [14] (which have not been proven CCZ-inequivalent to the inverse function), there is no known bijection with low differential uniformity, which can be used as S-box. Hence, finding more bijections with all the desired features is very interesting from theoretical and practical viewpoints.

3 A Family of Differentially 4-Uniform Bijections

For any finite field $\mathbb{F}_{2^n}$ we define $0^{-1} = 0$ by convention (we shall always use this convention in the sequel). Any finite field $\mathbb{F}_{2^n}$ can be viewed as an n-dimensional vector space over $\mathbb{F}_2$; each of its elements can be identified with a binary vector of length n, the element $0 \in \mathbb{F}_{2^n}$ is identified with the all-zero vector. From now on, any given element $x = (x_1, \cdots, x_{n-1}, x_n) \in \mathbb{F}_2^n$ can be identified with $(x', x_n) \in \mathbb{F}_{2^{n-1}} \times \mathbb{F}_2$, where $x' \in \mathbb{F}_{2^{n-1}}$ is identified with the vector $(x_1, \cdots, x_{n-1}) \in \mathbb{F}_2^{n-1}$.

Construction 1. *Let $n \geq 6$ be an even number. For any element $c \in \mathbb{F}_{2^{n-1}} \setminus \{0, 1\}$ such that $tr_1^{n-1}(c) = tr_1^{n-1}(1/c) = 1$, we define an (n,n)-function F as follows:*

$$F(x_1, \cdots, x_{n-1}, x_n) = \begin{cases} (1/x', f(x')), & \text{if } x_n = 0 \\ (c/x', f(x'/c) + 1), & \text{if } x_n = 1 \end{cases}.$$

where $x' \in \mathbb{F}_{2^{n-1}}$ is identified with $(x_1, \cdots, x_{n-1}) \in \mathbb{F}_2^{n-1}$ and f is an arbitrary Boolean function defined on $\mathbb{F}_{2^{n-1}}$.

3.1 Bijectivity

Theorem 1. *The function F defined in Construction 1 is bijective.*

Proof. We first prove that F is an injection. For any two elements $x, y \in \mathbb{F}_2^n$, if $x_n = y_n$ and $x \neq y$, then we can easily see that $F(x) \neq F(y)$ since $1/x', c/y'$ are two bijections on $\mathbb{F}_{2^{n-1}}$. If $x_n = y_n+1$, then without loss of generality, we assume that $x_n = 0$ and $y_n = 1$. We can see that $F(x) = F(y)$ leads to $1/x' = c/y'$ which is equivalent to $y' = cx'$. Note that the last bit of $F(x)$ is $f(x')$ and the last bit of $F(y)$ equals $f(y'/c) + 1 = f(cx'/c) + 1 = f(x') + 1$, which does not equal $f(x')$. So F is an injection. Therefore, F is bijective.   □

3.2   Differential 4-Uniformity

In this subsection, we will prove that F is differentially 4-uniform. For doing this, we first need a few preliminary results. The following lemma is well known.

Lemma 1. [9]. *Let n be a positive integer. For any $(a, b) \in \mathbb{F}_{2^n}^* \times \mathbb{F}_{2^n}$ let us define the polynomial $\mu(x) = ax^2 + bx + c \in \mathbb{F}_{2^n}[x]$, then the equation $\mu(x) = 0$ has 2 solutions if and only if $tr_1^n(b^{-2}ac) = 0$.*

The proof of the differential 4-uniformity of our functions will be based on the following lemma.

Lemma 2. *Let n be an even integer and $c \in \mathbb{F}_{2^{n-1}} \setminus \{0, 1\}$ such that $tr_1^{n-1}(c) = tr_1^{n-1}(1/c) = 1$, let us consider the following four equations defined on $\mathbb{F}_{2^{n-1}}$:*

$$1/x' + 1/(x' + a') = b' \tag{1}$$
$$c/x' + c/(x' + a') = b' \tag{2}$$

where $(a', b') \in \mathbb{F}_{2^{n-1}}^* \times \mathbb{F}_{2^{n-1}}$, and

$$1/x' + c/(x' + a') = b' \tag{3}$$
$$c/x' + 1/(x' + a') = b' \tag{4}$$

where $(a', b') \in \mathbb{F}_{2^{n-1}} \times \mathbb{F}_{2^{n-1}}$. Then the following statements hold:

(1) For $a'b' \neq 1$, (1) has two solutions on $\mathbb{F}_{2^{n-1}}$ if $b' \neq 0$ and $tr_1^{n-1}(1/(a'b')) = 0$ and has no solution otherwise. For $a'b' = 1$, (1) has two distinct solutions $0, a'$.

(2) For $a'b' \neq c$, (2) has two solutions on $\mathbb{F}_{2^{n-1}}$ if $b' \neq 0$ and $tr_1^{n-1}(c/(a'b')) = 0$ and has no solution otherwise. For $a'b' = c$, (2) has two distinct solutions $0, a'$.

(3) For any $x_0' \in \mathbb{F}_{2^{n-1}}$, x_0' is a solution of (3) if and only if $x_0' + a'$ is a solution of (4). Furthermore:
  - *for $a'b' \neq 0, 1, c$, both of (3) and (4) have two solutions if $tr_1^{n-1}(a'b'/(a'b' + c + 1)) = 0$ and have no solution otherwise;*
  - *for $a'b' = 1$, (3) has unique solution a' and (4) has unique solution 0;*
  - *for $a'b' = c$, (3) has unique solution 0 and (4) has unique solution a';*
  - *for $a'b' = 0$, both (3) and (4) have unique solution.*

Proof. Our proof mainly relies on Lemma 1.

(1) If $a'b' \neq 1$, which is equivalent to saying that both 0 and a' are not solutions of (1), then (1) is equivalent to $b'x'^2 + a'b'x' + a' = 0$. By Lemma 1, this new equation has two solutions if $b' \neq 0$ and $tr_1^{n-1}(1/(a'b')) = 0$. Note that (1) has no solution if $b' = 0$ since $a' \neq 0$. Therefore, for $a'b' \neq 1$, (1) has two solutions if $b' \neq 0$ and $tr_1^{n-1}(1/(a'b')) = 0$ and has no solution otherwise. If $a'b' = 1$ then $tr_1^{n-1}(1/(a'b')) = tr_1^{n-1}(1) = 1$ and therefore $b'x'^2 + a'b'x' + a' = 0$ has no solution. This implies that (1) has only two solutions $0, a'$ when $a'b' = 1$.

(2) If $a'b' \neq c$, which is equivalent to saying that both 0 and a' are not solutions of (2), then (2) is equivalent to $b'x'^2 + a'b'x' + ca' = 0$, which, by Lemma 1, has two solutions if $b' \neq 0$ and $tr_1^{n-1}(c/(a'b')) = 0$ and has no solution otherwise since (2) has no solution for $b' = 0$. If $a'b' = c$ then $tr_1^{n-1}(c/(a'b')) = tr_1^{n-1}(1) = 1$, which implies that $b'x'^2 + a'b'x' + ca' = 0$ has no solution. Thus, (2) has only two solutions $0, a'$ for $a'b' = c$.

(3) We can directly check that, for any $x_0' \in \mathbb{F}_{2^{n-1}}$, if x_0' is a solution of (3) then $x_0' + a'$ is a solution of (4) and the converse is true.

If $a'b' \neq 1, c$ in (3), which is equivalent to saying that both 0 and a' are not solutions of (3), then (3) is equivalent to $b'x'^2 + (a'b' + c + 1)x' + a' = 0$. Note that $a'b' \neq 0$ gives $b' \neq 0$. Hence, for $a'b' \neq 0, 1, c$, $b'x'^2 + (a'b' + c + 1)x' + a' = 0$ has two solutions if $tr_1^{n-1}(a'b'/(a'b' + c + 1)^2) = 0$ and has no solution if $tr_1^{n-1}(a'b'/(a'b' + c + 1)^2) = 1$ by Lemma 1. Note that $a'b' = 1$ implies that $tr_1^{n-1}(a'b'/(a'b'+c+1)^2) = tr_1^{n-1}(1/c) = 1$ and $a'b' = c$ leads to $tr_1^{n-1}(a'b'/(a'b'+c+1)^2) = tr_1^{n-1}(c) = 1$. Hence, (3) has unique solution a' if $a'b' = 1$ and has unique solution 0 if $a'b' = c$. If $a'b' = 0$, we can easily check that (3) has unique solution for $b' \neq a' = 0$, $a' \neq b' = 0$ and $a' = b' = 0$, respectively. Then the statement for (4) is direct.

$\square$

Now we are ready to prove our main theorem.

Theorem 2. *For any even $n \geq 6$, the bijection F defined in Construction 1 is differentially 4-uniform.*

Proof. Let us check that

$$F(x) + F(x + a) = b \tag{5}$$

has at most 4 solutions for every fixed $(a, b) \in \mathbb{F}_2^{n*} \times \mathbb{F}_2^n$. Let us write $x = (x', x_n)$, $a = (a', a_n)$ and $b = (b', b_n)$. Then Eq. (5) is equivalent to

$$F(x', x_n) + F(x' + a', x_n + a_n) = (b', b_n), \tag{6}$$

s If $a_n = 0$ and $a' \neq 0$ then the solutions of Eq. (6) are constituted by $(x', 0)$ such that

$$1/x' + 1/(x' + a') = b', f(x') + f(x' + a') = b_n \tag{7}$$

and by $(x', 1)$ such that

$$c/x' + c/(x' + a') = b', f(x'/c) + f((x' + a')/c) = b_n. \tag{8}$$

If $a_n = 1$ then the solutions of Eq. (6) are constituted by $(x', 0)$ such that

$$1/x' + c/(x' + a') = b', f(x') + f((x' + a')/c) = b_n + 1 \tag{9}$$

and by $(x', 1)$ such that

$$c/x' + 1/(x' + a') = b', f(x'/c) + f((x' + a')) = b_n + 1. \tag{10}$$

For $a_n = 0$ and $a' \neq 0$, by (1) and (2) of Lemma 2, we can see that the sum of the numbers of solutions of Eqs. (7) and (8) is at most 4. Similarly, for $a_n = 1$, it follows from (3) of Lemma 2 that the sum of the numbers of solutions of Eqs. (9) and (10) is at most 4. This completes the proof. □

Remark 1. Given an integer n, let us define $T(n)$ as the number of $c \in \mathbb{F}_{2^n}$ such that $tr_1^n(c) = tr_1^n(1/c) = 1$. Then there are $T(n) - 1$ elements $c \in \mathbb{F}_{2^n} \setminus \{0, 1\}$ such that $tr_1^n(c) = tr_1^n(1/c) = 1$ when n is odd, since $tr_1^n(0) = 0$ and $tr_1^n(1) = 1$. Let $K_n(a) = \sum_{x \in \mathbb{F}_{2^n}} (-1)^{tr_1^n(1/x + ax)}$, where $a \in \mathbb{F}_{2^n}^*$, be the so-called Kloosterman sums on $\mathbb{F}_{2^n}$. Note that $K_n(1) = \sum_{x \in \mathbb{F}_{2^n}} (-1)^{tr_1^n(x + 1/x)} = 2^n - 2\text{wt}(tr_1^n(x) + tr_1^n(1/x)) = 2^n - 2\text{wt}(tr_1^n(x)) - 2\text{wt}(tr_1^n(1/x)) + 4T(n) = -2^n + 4T(n)$. We have $T(n) = 2^{n-2} + K_n(1)/4$, which is at least $2^{n-2} - \lfloor 2^{n/2-1} \rfloor$ according to Lemma 3 (see below). Hence, for any even $n \geq 6$, Construction 1 can generate $(T(n-1) - 1) \cdot 2^{2^{n-1}} \geq (2^{n-3} - \lfloor 2^{(n-1)/2-1} \rfloor - 1) \cdot 2^{2^{n-1}}$ differentially 4-uniform bijections.

In fact, our method for constructing differentially 4-uniform bijections on n variables can be viewed as concatenating the value-tables of two almost bent bijections on $n - 1$ variables and completing each value by concatenating it with the value of a Boolean function. Some work to find new infinite classes of APN or differentially 4-uniform functions (not bijective) has been done by concatenation method [5,6], but the concatenation was on two functions in n variables whose outputs have length $n/2$.

3.3 Algebraic Degree

We shall now show the algebraic degree of F.

Theorem 3. *For every even $n \geq 6$, F with any Boolean function $f \in \mathcal{B}_{n-1}$ has algebraic degree $n - 1$.*

Proof. It is obvious that F has algebraic degree at most $n - 1$ since F is bijective. So we only need to prove that F has algebraic degree at least $n - 1$. Let $a_0 \in \mathbb{F}_{2^n}$ be an element which is identified with $(a', 0)$ such that $a' \neq 0$. Then the component function $a_0 \cdot F$ is identified with $tr_1^{n-1}(a'F(x', x_n))$. This implies that $a_0 \cdot F(x', x_n) = (1 + x_n)tr_1^{n-1}(a'/x') + x_n tr_1^{n-1}(a'c/x') = x_n tr_1^{n-1}((a' + a'c)/x') + tr_1^{n-1}(a'/x')$. Note that $a' + a'c \neq 0$ since $a' \neq 0$ and $c \neq 1$. So we have the component function $a_0 \cdot F$ has algebraic degree $n - 1$ thanks to $tr_1^{n-1}((a' + a'c)/x')$ has degree $n - 2$. Therefore, F has algebraic degree $n - 1$. □

3.4 Walsh Transform

Theorem 4. *Let $n \geq 6$ be an integer and $f \in \mathcal{B}_{n-1}$ be the function defined in Construction 1. For any $(a,b) \in \mathbb{F}_2^{n*} \times \mathbb{F}_2^n$, we have*

$$W_F(a,b) =$$
$$\begin{cases}
\displaystyle\sum_{x' \in \mathbb{F}_{2^{n-1}}} (-1)^{tr_1^{n-1}(a'/x'+b'x')} + \sum_{x' \in \mathbb{F}_{2^{n-1}}} (-1)^{tr_1^{n-1}(a'c/x'+b'x')}, \text{ if } a_n = 0, b_n = 0 \\[2ex]
\displaystyle\sum_{x' \in \mathbb{F}_{2^{n-1}}} (-1)^{tr_1^{n-1}(a'/x'+b'x')} - \sum_{x' \in \mathbb{F}_{2^{n-1}}} (-1)^{tr_1^{n-1}(a'c/x'+b'x')}, \text{ if } a_n = 0, b_n = 1 \\[2ex]
\displaystyle\sum_{x' \in \mathbb{F}_{2^{n-1}}} (-1)^{tr_1^{n-1}(a'/x'+b'x')+f(x')} - \sum_{x' \in \mathbb{F}_{2^{n-1}}} (-1)^{tr_1^{n-1}(a'c/x'+b'x')+f(x'/c)}, \\[1ex]
\hfill \text{if } a_n = 1, b_n = 0 \\[2ex]
\displaystyle\sum_{x' \in \mathbb{F}_{2^{n-1}}} (-1)^{tr_1^{n-1}(a'/x'+b'x')+f(x')} + \sum_{x' \in \mathbb{F}_{2^{n-1}}} (-1)^{tr_1^{n-1}(a'c/x'+b'x')+f(x'/c)}, \\[1ex]
\hfill \text{if } a_n = 1, b_n = 1
\end{cases}$$

where a is identified with (a', a_n) and b is identified with (b', b_n), where $a', b' \in \mathbb{F}_{2^{n-1}}$.

Proof. Note that the linear function $(b_1, \cdots, b_{n-1}, b_n) \cdot (x_1, \cdots, x_{n-1}, x_n)$ can be identified with $tr_1^{n-1}(b'x') + b_n x_n$ and the component function $a \cdot F$, denoted by $g_a(x_1, \cdots, x_{n-1}, x_n)$, can be identified with $g_a(x', x_n)$, where $g_a(x', x_n)$ is defined as $g_a(x', x_n) = tr_1^{n-1}(a'/x') + a_n f(x')$ if $x_n = 0$ and $g_a(x', x_n) = tr_1^{n-1}(a'c/x') + a_n(f(x'/c) + 1)$ if $x_n = 1$. Therefore, we have

$$W_F(a,b) = \sum_{x \in \mathbb{F}_2^n} (-1)^{a \cdot F + bx}$$

$$= \sum_{(x', x_n) \in \mathbb{F}_{2^{n-1}} \times \{0\}} (-1)^{tr_1^{n-1}(a'/x')+a_n f(x')+tr_1^{n-1}(b'x')+b_n x_n}$$

$$+ \sum_{(x', x_n) \in \mathbb{F}_{2^{n-1}} \times \{1\}} (-1)^{tr_1^{n-1}(a'c/x')+a_n(f(x'/c)+1)+tr_1^{n-1}(b'x')+b_n x_n}$$

$$= \sum_{x' \in \mathbb{F}_{2^{n-1}}} (-1)^{tr_1^{n-1}(a'/x'+b'x')+a_n f(x')}$$

$$+ \sum_{x' \in \mathbb{F}_{2^{n-1}}} (-1)^{tr_1^{n-1}(a'c/x'+b'x')+a_n f(x'/c)+b_n+a_n}.$$

Then our assertion follows from above equality.   □

Remark 2. By Theorem 4, we can see that the nonlinearity of F can take value 0 if the Boolean function f used in Construction 1 is an affine function.

3.5 CCZ-inequivalence

In this subsection, we will prove that, for any even $n \geq 8$, F is CCZ-inequivalent to the Gold functions, the Kasami functions, the functions discussed in [2] and to quadratic functions. With the help of computer, we checked that for even n ranging from 8 to 16, F is CCZ-inequivalent to the inverse function.

Here and subsequently, I denotes the inverse function. We need the nonlinearities of component functions of I.

Lemma 3 [13]. *For any positive integer n and arbitrary $a \in \mathbb{F}_{2^n}^*$, the Walsh spectrum of $tr_1^n(ax^{-1})$ defined on $\mathbb{F}_{2^n}$ can take any value divisible by 4 in the range $[-2^{n/2+1}+1, 2^{n/2+1}+1]$.*

We now study the CCZ-inequivalence of F.

Theorem 5. *For every even $n \geq 8$, F is CCZ-inequivalent to the Gold functions, the Kasami functions, the functions discussed in [2] and quadratic functions.*

Proof. Note that the extended Walsh spectrum is a CCZ-invariant parameter. It is well known that, for even n, the elements of the extended Walsh spectra of the Gold functions, the Kasami functions and the functions discussed in [2] belong to the set $\{0, \pm 2^{n/2}, \pm 2^{n/2+1}\}$ and that the elements of the extended Walsh spectrum of quadratic functions can be divisible by $2^{n/2}$ (indeed, the component functions of any quadratic function have algebraic degree at most 2. We know that the nonlinearity of any affine function is equal to 0 and the Walsh spectrum of any quadratic Boolean function is $\pm 2^{n/2}$ or $0, \pm 2^{n/2+l}$, where $l \geq 1$). Hence, for proving F is CCZ-inequivalent to those functions, we only need to prove that F has different extended Walsh spectrum compared to theirs. Let us take $a' = 1$ in Theorem 4. Then there must be an element $b_0' \in \mathbb{F}_{2^{n-1}}$ such that $\sum_{x' \in \mathbb{F}_{2^{n-1}}} (-1)^{tr_1^{n-1}(1/x'+b_0'x')} = 4$, according to Lemma 3. Define $\lambda = \sum_{x' \in \mathbb{F}_{2^{n-1}}} (-1)^{tr_1^{n-1}(c/x'+b_0'x')}$. It follows from Theorem 4 that $4 + \gamma$ and $4 - \gamma$ belong to the extended Walsh spectra of F. We can see that, for even $n \geq 8$, $4 + \gamma$ and $4 - \gamma$ can not be divisible by $2^{n/2}$ simultaneously. This is the desired conclusion. □

Theorem 6. *Let $n \geq 8$ be an even integer. Define $f_3 \in \mathcal{B}_n$ on variables $x_1, \cdots, x_n$ as $f_3 = (1+x_n)f_1 + x_n f_2$, where $f_1, f_2 \in \mathcal{B}_{n-1}$ are defined as $f_1 = tr_1^{n-1}(1/x)$ and $f_2 = tr_1^{n-1}(c/x)$ where $c \in \mathbb{F}_{2^{n-1}} \setminus \{0, 1\}$ is such that $tr_1^{n-1}(c) = tr_1^{n-1}(1/c) = 1$. If $nl(f_3) < 2^{n-1} - 2^{n/2}$, then F with any $f \in \mathcal{B}_{n-1}$ is CCZ-inequivalent to the inverse function and therefore F is CCZ-inequivalent to all known differentially 4-uniform power functions and to quadratic functions.*

Proof. Let us take $a' = 1 \in \mathbb{F}_{2^{n-1}}$ and $a_n = 0$ in the function $g_a(x_1, \cdots, x_{n-1}, x_n)$ which is defined in the proof of Theorem 4. Then we can see that $g_a(x_1, \cdots, x_{n-1}, x_n)$ is equal to f_3 and so f_3 is a component function of F. If $nl(f_3) < 2^{n-1} - 2^{n/2}$, then we have $nl(F) < 2^{n-1} - 2^{n/2}$ and therefore F is CCZ-inequivalent to the inverse function since the nonlinearity is a CCZ-invariant parameter and $nl(I) = 2^{n-1} - 2^{n/2}$. The rest of proof follows from Theorem 5. □

Remark 3. By computer investigation, we checked that $nl(f_3) < 2^{n-1} - 2^{n/2}$ (but the nonlinearity of f_3 is very close to $2^{n-1} - 2^{n/2}$ and we will show below a class of highly nonlinear bijections by choosing a special Boolean function f in Construction 1) for even n ranging from 8 to 16, where f_3 is defined in Theorem 6. This implies that F is CCZ-inequivalent to all known differentially 4-uniform power functions and to quadratic functions when $8 \leq n \leq 16$.

4   A Class of Differentially 4-Uniform Bijections with Good Cryptographic Properties

Hereinafter, for any even integer $n \geq 6$, we define F_1 as the function F with $f(x') = tr_1^{n-1}(1/(x'+1))$. By Theorems 1 and 2, we can see that F_1 is a differentially 4-uniform bijection. It follows from Theorem 3 that F_1 has maximum algebraic degree $n - 1$. In what follows, we will prove that the function F_1 has high nonlinearity and is CCZ-inequivalent to known differentially 4-uniform power functions and to quadratic functions.

We first give a lower bound on the nonlinearity of F_1. For doing this, we need the following lemma.

Lemma 4 [14]. *Let n be a positive integer such that $n \geq 4$, then we have* $\sum_{x\in\mathbb{F}_{2^n}} (-1)^{tr_1^n(ax+bx^{-1}+x^2(x+1)^{-1})}| \leq 2\lfloor 2^{n/2+1} \rfloor + 4$ *for any* $(a,b) \in \mathbb{F}_{2^n} \times \mathbb{F}_{2^n}$.

Note that $x^2(x+1)^{-1} = x+1+(x+1)^{-1}$. Then Lemma 4 is equivalent to:

Corollary 1. *For any $n \geq 4$, we have* $|\sum_{x\in\mathbb{F}_{2^n}} (-1)^{tr_1^n(ax+bx^{-1}+(x+1)^{-1})}| \leq 2\lfloor 2^{n/2+1} \rfloor + 4$ *for any* $(a,b) \in \mathbb{F}_{2^n} \times \mathbb{F}_{2^n}$.

We are now ready to give a lower bound on the nonlinearity of F_1.

Theorem 7. *For any even $n \geq 6$, we have $nl(F_1) \geq 2^{n-1} - 2\lfloor 2^{(n+1)/2} \rfloor - 4$.*

Proof. For any $(a,b) \in \mathbb{F}_2^{n*} \times \mathbb{F}_2^n$, we identify a with (a',a_n) and b with (b',b_n). By Lemma 4, we have

$$W_F(a,b) =$$

$$\begin{cases} \sum_{x'\in\mathbb{F}_{2^{n-1}}} (-1)^{tr_1^{n-1}(a'/x'+b'x')} + \sum_{x'\in\mathbb{F}_{2^{n-1}}} (-1)^{tr_1^{n-1}(a'c/x'+b'x')}, & \text{if } a_n = 0, b_n = 0 \\[2mm] \sum_{x'\in\mathbb{F}_{2^{n-1}}} (-1)^{tr_1^{n-1}(a'/x'+b'x')} - \sum_{x'\in\mathbb{F}_{2^{n-1}}} (-1)^{tr_1^{n-1}(a'c/x'+b'x')}, & \text{if } a_n = 0, b_n = 1 \\[2mm] \sum_{x'\in\mathbb{F}_{2^{n-1}}} (-1)^{tr_1^{n-1}\left(a'/x'+1/(x'+1)+b'x'\right)} \\[1mm] \quad - \sum_{x'\in\mathbb{F}_{2^{n-1}}} (-1)^{tr_1^{n-1}\left(a'/x'+1/(x'+1)+b'cx'\right)}, & \text{if } a_n = 1, b_n = 0 \\[2mm] \sum_{x'\in\mathbb{F}_{2^{n-1}}} (-1)^{tr_1^{n-1}\left(a'c/x'+1/(x'+1)+b'x'\right)} \\[1mm] \quad + \sum_{x'\in\mathbb{F}_{2^{n-1}}} (-1)^{tr_1^{n-1}\left(a'/x'+1/(x'+1)+b'cx'\right)}, & \text{if } a_n = 1, b_n = 1 \end{cases}$$

Table 1. The exact values of $nl(F_1)$ on small number of variables

n	6	8	10	12
$2^{n-1} - 2^{n/2}$	24	112	480	1984
$nl(F_1)$	20	94	436,438,440,442	1888,1892,1894,1896,1898,1900,1902
Our lower bound	6	80	418	1864

By Lemma 3 and Corollary 1, we have

$$|W_F(a,b)| \leq \begin{cases} 2\lfloor 2^{(n+1)/2} \rfloor, & \text{if } a_n = 0, b_n \in \mathbb{F}_2 \\ 4\lfloor 2^{(n+1)/2} \rfloor + 8, & \text{if } a_n = 1, b_n \in \mathbb{F}_2 \end{cases}.$$

This implies that $nl(F_1) \geq 2^{n-1} - 2\lfloor 2^{(n+1)/2} \rfloor - 4$. $\square$

With the help of computer, we get the exact values of $nl(F_1)$ for even numbers of variables ranging from 6 to 12, which are given in the following table.

4.1   CCZ-inequivalence

We shall now show that F_1 is CCZ-inequivalent to known differentially 4-uniform power functions and to quadratic functions.

To prove our main result, we need the following lemma.

Lemma 5. *Let $n \geq 7$ be an integer. For any $\gamma \in \mathbb{F}_{2^n}^*$ and $\beta_i, \alpha_i \in \mathbb{F}_{2^n}$ where $1 \leq i \leq 3$, we have*

$$\Big| \sum_{x \in \mathbb{F}_{2^n}} (-1)^{tr_1^n\left(\frac{\alpha_1}{x+\beta_1} + \frac{\alpha_2}{x+\beta_2} + \frac{\alpha_3}{x+\beta_3} + \gamma x\right)} \Big| \leq 3\lfloor 2^{\frac{n}{2}+1} \rfloor + 6.$$

Proof. Define $S = \{(x,y) \in \mathbb{F}_{2^n} \times \mathbb{F}_{2^n} \,|\, y^2 + y = \frac{\alpha_1}{x+\beta_1} + \frac{\alpha_2}{x+\beta_2} + \frac{\alpha_3}{x+\beta_3} + \gamma x\}$. Then we have

$$\sum_{x \in \mathbb{F}_{2^n}} (-1)^{tr_1^n\left(\frac{\alpha_1}{x+\beta_1} + \frac{\alpha_2}{x+\beta_2} + \frac{\alpha_3}{x+\beta_3} + \gamma x\right)} = |S| - 2^n, \tag{11}$$

since $tr_1^n(z) = 0$ if and only if there exists an element $y \in \mathbb{F}_{2^n}$ such that $z = y^2 + y$, and $y \mapsto y^2 + y$ is a 2-to-1 mapping. Let us consider the function field $K = \mathbb{F}_{2^n}(x,y)$ with defining equation

$$y^2 + y = \frac{\alpha_1}{x + \beta_1} + \frac{\alpha_2}{x + \beta_2} + \frac{\alpha_3}{x + \beta_3} + \gamma x. \tag{12}$$

Then we can deduce that the genus g of K is equal to

$$g = \begin{cases} 1, & \text{if } \beta_1 = \beta_2 = \beta_3 \\ 2, & \text{if } \beta_1 = \beta_2 \neq \beta_3 \text{ or } \beta_1 \neq \beta_2 = \beta_3 \text{ or } \beta_1 = \beta_3 \neq \beta_2 \\ 3, & \text{if } \beta_1 \neq \beta_2 \neq \beta_3 \neq \beta_1 \end{cases}. \tag{13}$$

Denote by N the number of the places with degree one of K/F_{2^n}. Then by Serre bound, we have

$$|N - (2^n + 1)| \leq g\lfloor 2^{n/2+1} \rfloor. \tag{14}$$

In what follows, we compute the points at infinity of (12). We first consider the case that $\alpha_1, \alpha_2, \alpha_3$ are pairwise distinct. The homogeneous equation of Equation (12) is equal to

$$(\frac{Y}{Z})^2 + \frac{Y}{Z} = \frac{\alpha_1 Z}{X + \beta_1 Z} + \frac{\alpha_2 Z}{X + \beta_2 Z} + \frac{\alpha_3 Z}{X + \beta_3 Z} + \gamma \frac{X}{Z}. \tag{15}$$

If we multiply both sides of Eq. (15) by Z^2, we get

$$Y^2 + YZ = [\frac{\alpha_1 Z}{X + \beta_1 Z} + \frac{\alpha_2 Z}{X + \beta_2 Z} + \frac{\alpha_3 Z}{X + \beta_3 Z}]Z^2 + \gamma XZ. \tag{16}$$

Multiply both sides of Eq. (16) by $(X + \beta_1 Z)(X + \beta_2 Z)(X + \beta_3 Z)$ and then let $Z = 0$, we have $X^3 Y^2 = 0$. Hence, there are two points at infinity satisfying the Eq. (15), which are $(0 : 1 : 0)$ and $(1 : 0 : 0)$. We now compute the multiplicity of roots of $(0 : 1 : 0)$ and $(1 : 0 : 0)$, respectively. Let us first consider $(0 : 1 : 0)$, i.e., $Y = 1$. We can use

$$(\frac{1}{z})^2 + \frac{1}{z} = \frac{\alpha_1 z}{x + \beta_1 z} + \frac{\alpha_2 z}{x + \beta_2 z} + \frac{\alpha_3 z}{x + \beta_3 z} + \gamma \frac{x}{z} \tag{17}$$

to calculate the multiplicity of root. It should be note that $(0 : 1 : 0)$ is corresponding to $(0,0)$. Multiply Eq. (17) by z^2, we get

$$1 + [\frac{\alpha_1}{x + \beta_1 z} + \frac{\alpha_2}{x + \beta_2 z} + \frac{\alpha_3}{x + \beta_3 z}]z^3 = z + \gamma xz.$$

Multiply this new equation by $(x + \beta_1 z)(x + \beta_2 z)(x + \beta_3 z)$, we have

$$(x + \beta_1 z)(x + \beta_2 z)(x + \beta_3 z) + R(x, z) = 0,$$

where $R(x, z)$ is a polynomial such that its every monomial has algebraic degree at least 3. This gives $(0 : 1 : 0)$ is a root of multiplicity 3. For the point $(1 : 0 : 0)$, i.e. $X = 1$, we can use

$$(\frac{y}{z})^2 + \frac{y}{z} = \frac{\alpha_1 z}{1 + \beta_1 z} + \frac{\alpha_2 z}{1 + \beta_2 z} + \frac{\alpha_3 z}{1 + \beta_3 z} + \gamma \frac{1}{z} \tag{18}$$

to calculate the multiplicity of root. Similar with Eq. (17), Eq. (18) can be deduced as

$$\gamma z + (Y^2 + yz) + [\frac{\alpha_1}{1 + \beta_1 z} + \frac{\alpha_2}{1 + \beta_2 z} + \frac{\alpha_3}{1 + \beta_3 z}]z^3 = 0.$$

Multiply this new equation by $(1 + \beta_1 z)(1 + \beta_2 z)(1 + \beta_3 z)$. Two cases can then occur, according to the values of γ.

- For $\gamma \neq 0$, we have $\gamma z + R_1(y, z) = 0$, where $R_1(y, z)$ is such that its every monomial has algebraic degree at least 1. This implies that $(1 : 0 : 0)$ is a root of multiplicity 1.
- For $\gamma = 0$, we can deduce that $(y^2 + yz) + R_2(y, z) = 0$ where $R_2(y, z)$ is such that its every monomial has algebraic degree at least 2, which implies $(1 : 0 : 0)$ is a root of multiplicity 2.

Therefore, Eq. (12) has at most five points at infinity in the case that $\alpha_1, \alpha_2, \alpha_3$ are pairwise distinct. Then

$$N \geq S - 5. \tag{19}$$

Similarly, we can deduce that Eq. (12) has at most four points at infinity if $\alpha_1, \alpha_2, \alpha_3$ are not pairwise distinct. So we have

$$N \geq S - 4. \tag{20}$$

Equations (11), (14), (19) and (20) combined give our statement.   □

We are ready now to state and prove the main result of this subsection.

Theorem 8. *For any even $n \geq 8$, F_1 is CCZ-inequivalent to all known differentially 4-uniform power functions and to quadratic functions.*

Proof. By Theorem 5, we can see that F_1 is CCZ-inequivalent to the Gold functions, the Kasami functions, the functions discussed in [2] and to quadratic functions. So, for proving our statement, we only need to prove that F_1 is CCZ-inequivalent to the inverse function. It is well-known that the number of pairs $(a, b) \in \mathbb{F}_2^{n*} \times \mathbb{F}_2^n$ such that $I(x) + I(x + a) = b$ has 4 solutions is $2^n - 1$. Recall that the differential spectrum is a CCZ-invariant parameter. So we only need to prove that the number of pairs $(a, b) \in \mathbb{F}_2^{n*} \times \mathbb{F}_2^n$ such that $F_1(x) + F_1(x + a) = b$ has 4 solutions is at least 2^n.

We identify a with (a', a_n) and b with (b', b_n). Let us first give a sufficient condition for the sum of the numbers of distinct solutions (9) and (10) to equal 4. For every $a' \in \mathbb{F}_{2^{n-1}}$ and for every fixed $x_0 \in \mathbb{F}_{2^{n-1}} \setminus \{0, a', a'/(c+1)\}$, if we assume that x_0 is a solution of $1/x' + c/(x' + a') = b'$ which is equivalent to

$$b'x'^2 + (a'b' + c + 1)x' + a' = 0 \tag{21}$$

thanks to $x_0 \neq 0, a$, then we have $b'x_0^2 + (a'b' + c + 1)x_0 + a' = 0$ and hence $b' = (a' + (c+1)x_0)/(x_0^2 + a'x_0)$ which is nonzero since $x_0 \neq a'/(c+1), 0, a'$. Further, we can deduce that the other solution of (21) is $x_1 = x_0 + a' + (c+1)/b' = ca'^2/((c+1)(cx_0 + x_0 + a')) + a'/(c+1)$. For ensuring $x_0 \neq x_1$, $a' + (c+1)/b'$ should not be equal to 0, which is equivalent to saying that x_0 should not be a solution of equation $(a' + (c+1)x')/(x'^2 + a'x') = (c+1)/a'$. This implies that $x_0 \neq a'(c+1)^{2^{n-2}}$. Hence, for every $a' \in \mathbb{F}_{2^{n-1}}^*$, then for every fixed $x_0 \in \mathbb{F}_{2^{n-1}} \setminus \{0, a', a'(c+1)^{2^{n-2}}, a'/(c+1)\}$, equation $1/x' + c/(x' + a') = b'$ with $b' = (a' + (c+1)x_0)/(x_0^2 + a'x_0)$ has two distinct solutions x_0, x_1. Further, by (3) of Lemma 2, $x_0 + a', x_1 + a'$ are two distinct solutions of $c/x' + 1/(x' + a') = b'$. We can see that $x_1 + a' \neq x_0$ since $(c+1)/b' \neq 0$. This gives that $x_0, x_1, x_0 + a', x_1 + a'$ are four distinct elements. Therefore, for every $a' \in \mathbb{F}_{2^{n-1}}^*$ and for every fixed $x_0 \in \mathbb{F}_{2^{n-1}} \setminus \{0, a', a'(c+1)^{2^{n-2}}, a'/(c+1)\}$, (9) and (10) have four pairwise distinct solutions if $f(x') + f((x' + a')/c) = f(x'/c) + f((x' + a'))$, in which $b' = (a' + (c+1)x_0)/(x_0^2 + a'x_0)$ and $b_n = f(x') + f((x' + a')/c)$, and therefore (6) has four distinct solutions. For every $a' \in \mathbb{F}_{2^{n-1}}^*$, let us define $T_{a'} = \{x \in \mathbb{F}_{2^{n-1}} \setminus \{0, a', a'(c+1)^{2^{n-2}}, a'/(c+1)\} | f(x') + f((x' + a')/c) + f(x'/c) + f((x' + a')) = 0\}$. Note that (21) has at most two solutions when a', b' are fixed. Thus, for every $a' \in \mathbb{F}_{2^{n-1}}^*$, there are at least $T_{a'}/2$ distinct pairs $(a, b) = \big((a', 1), (b', b_n)\big)$ such that (6) has four distinct solutions.

We now show that the number of pairs $(a, b) \in \mathbb{F}_2^{n*} \times \mathbb{F}_2^n$ such that $F_1(x) + F_1(x + a) = b$ has 4 solutions is not less than 2^n. We replace $f(x')$ in $T_{a'}$ by $tr_1^{n-1}(1/(x'+1))$, then $T_{a'}$ becomes $T_{a'} = \{x_0 \in \mathbb{F}_{2^{n-1}} \setminus \{0, a', a'(c+1)^{2^{n-2}}, a'/(c+1)\} | tr_1^n(1/(x_0 + 1) + 1/((x_0 + a')/c + 1) + 1/(x_1 + 1) + 1/((x_1 + a')/c + 1)) = 0\}$. Recall that $x_1 = x_0 + a' + (c+1)/b' = ca'^2/((c+1)(cx_0 + x_0 + a')) + a'/(c+1)$. Then for every $a' \in \mathbb{F}_{2^n} \setminus \{0, 1 + c, (c+1)^{2^{n-2}}\}$, we have

$$T_{a'} = \Big\{x_0 \in \mathbb{F}_{2^{n-1}} \setminus \{0, a', a'(c+1)^{2^{n-2}}, a'/(c+1)\} | tr_1^{n-1}\Big(\frac{\frac{c}{(a'+c+1)^2}}{x_0 + \frac{1}{a'+c+1}} + \frac{\frac{ca'^2}{(a'^2+c+1)^2}}{x_0 + \frac{a'+c+1}{a'^2+c+1}}$$

$$+ \frac{\frac{a'^2}{(c+1)^2}}{x_0 + \frac{a'+c+1}{c+1}} + x_0 + \frac{c}{a'+c+1} + \frac{ca'^2}{(a'+c+1)(a'^2+c+1)} + \frac{a'^2}{(a'+c+1)(c+1)}\Big) = 0\Big\}.$$

Therefore, the number of pairs $(a, b) \in \mathbb{F}_2^{n*} \times \mathbb{F}_2^n$ such that $F_1(x) + F_1(x + a) = b$ has 4 solutions is greater than $(2^{n-1} - 3)T_{a'}/2$, which is not less than $2^n - 1$ since $T_{a'} \geq 2^{n-2} - \frac{3}{2}\lfloor 2^{\frac{n-1}{2}+1}\rfloor - 7$ for every $a' \in \mathbb{F}_{2^n} \setminus \{0, 1 + c, (c+1)^{2^{n-2}}\}$ according to Lemma 5. This completes the proof. $\square$

Remark 4. By computer investigation, we checked that the extended Walsh spectrum of F_1 for even numbers of variables ranging from 6 to 12 are different from those of all the known differentially 4-uniform bijections listed in Sect. 2. This implies that functions F_1 are CCZ-inequivalent to all known differentially 4-uniform bijections in the dimensions ranging over even integers from 6 to 12.

5 Conclusion

In this paper, we first presented a construction of differentially 4-uniform bijections on $\mathbb{F}_{2^n}$, where $n \geq 6$ is even. For any even $n \geq 6$, this construction can generate at least $(2^{n-3} - \lfloor 2^{(n-1)/2-1}\rfloor - 1) \cdot 2^{2^{n-1}}$ bijections having algebraic degree $n - 1$. In addition, we exhibited a subclass of these bijections which have high nonlinearity and are CCZ-inequivalent to all known differentially 4-uniform power bijections and to quadratic functions. The research of finding more subclasses with high nonlinearity from our construction is very interesting and is worthy of a further investigation.

Acknowledgement. The authors wish to thank Sihem Mesnager for helpful informa-tion. The work of D. Tang was supported by the program of China Scholarships Council (No. 201207000049). The work of X.H. Tang was supported by the Youngth Innova-tive Research Team of Sichuan Province under Grant 2011JTD0007. The work of Q.Y. Liao was supported by the National Science Foundation of China (No. A10990011), the Ph.D. Programs Foundation of Ministry of Education of China(No. 20095134120001) and Sichuan Provincial Advance Research Program for Excellent Youth Leaders of Disciplines in Science of China (No. 2011JQ0037).

References

1. Biham, E., Shamir, A.: Differential cryptanalysis of DES-like cryptosystems. J. Cryptol. **4**(1), 3–72 (1991)
2. Bracken, C., Leander, G.: A highly nonlinear differentially 4 uniform power map-ping that permutes fields of even degree. Finite Fields Appl. **16**(4), 231–242 (2010)
3. Browning, K.A., Dillon, J.F., McQuistan, M.T., Wolfe, A.J.: An APN permuta-tion in dimension six. In: Postproceedings of the 9th International Conference on Finite Fields and their Applications Fq'9. Contemporary Mathematics Journal of American Mathematical Society, vol. 518, pp. 33–42 (2010)
4. Carlet, C.: On known and new differentially uniform functions. In: Parampalli, U., Hawkes, P. (eds.) ACISP 2011. LNCS, vol. 6812, pp. 1–15. Springer, Heidelberg (2011)
5. Carlet, C.: Relating three nonlinearity parameters of vectorial functions and build-ing APN functions from bent functions. Des. Codes Cryptogr. **59**(1–3), 89–109 (2011)
6. Carlet, C.: More constructions of APN and differentially 4-uniform functions by concatenation. Sci. China Math. **56**(7), 1373–1384 (2013)
7. Knudsen, L.: Truncated and higher order differentials. In: Preneel, B. (ed.) FSE 1994. LNCS, vol. 1008, pp. 196–211. Springer, Heidelberg (1995)
8. Li, Y., Wang, M.: Constructing differentially 4-uniform permutations over $GF(2^{2m+1})$ from quadratic APN permutations over $GF(2^{2m})$. To appear in Des. Codes Cryptogr. (2012). doi:10.1007/s10623-012-9760-9
9. MacWilliams, F.J., Sloane, N.J.: The Theory of Error-Correcting Codes. North Holland, Amsterdam (1977)
10. Matsui, M.: Linear cryptanalysis method for DES cipher. In: Helleseth, T. (ed.) EUROCRYPT 1993. LNCS, vol. 765, pp. 386–397. Springer, Heidelberg (1994)
11. Nyberg, K.: Differentially uniform mappings for cryptography. In: Helleseth, T. (ed.) EUROCRYPT 1993. LNCS, vol. 765, pp. 55–64. Springer, Heidelberg (1994)
12. Shannon, C.E.: Communication theory of secrecy systems. Bell Syst. Tech. J. **28**, 656–715 (1949)
13. Lachaud, G., Wolfmann, J.: The weights of the orthogonals of the extended quadratic binary Goppa codes. IEEE Trans. Inf. Theory **36**(3), 686–692 (1990)
14. Qu, L., Tan, Y., Tan, C., Li, C.: Constructing Differentially 4-Uniform Permuta-tions over $\mathbb{F}_2^{2k}$ via the Switching Method. IEEE Trans. Inf. Theory **59**(7), 4675–4686 (2013)

Automatic Security Evaluation of Block Ciphers with S-bP Structures Against Related-Key Differential Attacks

Siwei Sun[✉], Lei Hu, Ling Song, Yonghong Xie, and Peng Wang

State Key Laboratory of Information Security, Institute of Information Engineering,
Chinese Academy of Sciences, Beijing 100093, China
{swsun,hu}@is.ac.cn

Abstract. Counting the number of active S-boxes is a common way to evaluate the security of symmetric key cryptographic schemes against differential attack. Based on Mixed Integer Linear Programming (MILP), Mouha et al. proposed a method to accomplish this task automatically for word-oriented symmetric-key ciphers with SPN structures. However, this method can not be applied directly to block ciphers of SPN structures with bitwise permutation diffusion layers (S-bP structures), due to its ignorance of the diffusion effect derived collaboratively by nonlinear substitution layers and bitwise permutation layers. In this paper we extend Mouha et al.'s method for S-bP structures by introducing new representations for exclusive-or (XOR) differences to describe bit/word level differences simultaneously and by taking the collaborative diffusion effect of S-boxes and bitwise permutations into account. Our method is applied to the block cipher PRESENT-80, an international standard for lightweight symmetric key cryptography, to automatically evaluate its security against differential attacks. We obtain lower bounds on the numbers of active S-boxes in the single-key model for full 31-round PRESENT-80 and in related-key model for round-reduced PRESENT-80 up to 12 rounds, and therefore automatically prove that the full-round PRESENT-80 is secure against single-key differential attack, and the cost of related-key differential attack on the full-round PRESENT-80 is close to that of an exhaustive search: the best related-key differential characteristic for full PRESENT-80 is upper bounded by 2^{-72}.

Keywords: Block cipher · SPN structure · Differential attack · Active S-box · Mixed-integer linear programming

1 Introduction

Differential cryptanalysis [6] and linear cryptanalysis [20] are two of the most important attacks on symmetric-key cryptographic schemes, based on which a whole bunch of techniques for analysing block ciphers are devised, such as related-key differential attack [4], impossible differential attack [5] and zero correlation attack [8]. Resistance against differential and linear attacks is a basic requirement for today's design of block ciphers.

© Springer International Publishing Switzerland 2014
D. Lin et al. (Eds.): Inscrypt 2013, LNCS 8567, pp. 39–51, 2014.
DOI: 10.1007/978-3-319-12087-4_3

After the introduction of the wide trail strategy [13] by the designers of AES, provable security against differential cryptanalysis comes from a similar argument for almost all newly designed block ciphers. That is, the designers provide a very small upper bound for the probability of the best differential characteristic of the cipher by showing a lower bound on the number of active S-boxes for any consecutive r rounds of the cipher. Therefore, how to find the minimum number of active S-boxes is of great interest.

Actually, lots of works have been done in this direction for both classes of block ciphers with substitution-permutation network (SPN) and Feistel structures. These methods can be classified into two categories.

In the first category, the lower bound is proved mathematically. In [14], the wide trail design strategy ensures that there are at least 25 active S-boxes for any 5-round AES, and the designers of PRESENT [7] proved that any 5-round differential characteristic of PRESENT-80 had a minimum of 10 active S-boxes. Results concerning block ciphers with Feistel or generalized Feistel structure can be found in [17,24,27,29]. This kind of methods is tricky, and sometimes many possible cases of the differential propagation must be considered.

In the second category, algorithms are designed to count the number of active S-boxes automatically. In [3], Aoki et al. used a variant of Matsui's algorithm [21] to compute a lower bound on the minimal number of active S-boxes for the block cipher Camellia, and therefore proved its security against differential attack. The minimum number of active S-boxes for generalized Feistel structure was obtained in [24] by an algorithm which searches word-based truncated differentials. Sareh Emami et al. proved that no related-key differential characteristic exists with probability higher than 2^{-64} for the full-round PRESENT-80 by a new method called extended split approach [23]. Highly automatic methods employing Mixed Integer Liner Programming (MILP) were presented in [22,26] to determine the minimum number of active S-boxes for SPN structures and Feistel structures with SPN round functions.

In this paper, we are mostly interested in the methods based on MILP since they are the most automatic methods and require less programming effort compared with other methods. Using this method, what an analyst need to do is just to write a program to generate the MILP instance with suitable objective function and constraints imposed by the differential propagation of the cipher. The remaining work for determining the bounds can be done by a highly optimized open-source or commercially available software such as CPLEX [12], SCIP [1] and Gurobi [15].

Contribution of this Paper. In this paper, we focus on how to determine the minimum number of active S-boxes in the single-key or related-key model for block ciphers of SPN structures with bitwise permutation diffusion layers (S-bP structures). We point out that Mouha et al.'s method is not applicable to block ciphers with bitwise permutations or non-MDS, even almost MDS diffusion layers. By extending Mouha et al.'s method, we propose an MILP based approach to prove the security of block ciphers of S-bP structures against single-key or related-key differential attacks automatically. Compared with other proving methods like that presented in [7], it is highly automatic.

We have implemented our method on a personal computer: a Python module was developed to generate the MILP instances, and the Gurobi optimizer [15] was employed as the underlying MILP solver. Experimental results showed that we can automatically prove that the block cipher PRESENT-80 is secure against single-key differential attack within only 222 s. We have also found that there are at least 15 active S-boxes in any related-key differential characteristic for 12-round PRESENT-80, and the probability of the best related-key differential characteristic for the full 31-round PRESENT-80 is at most 2^{-72}, which leads to the conclusion that the workload of related-key differential attack on the full-round PRESENT-80 is close to that of an exhaustive search.

The paper is organized as follows. In Sect. 2 we recall the Mixed Integer Linear Programming and its applications to analysing word-oriented block ciphers. In Sect. 3 we extend Mouha et al.'s method to block ciphers of S-bP structures with bitwise permutation diffusion layers. We apply our method to the block cipher PRESENT-80 in Sect. 4. Section 5 is the discussion and conclusion.

2   MILP and Mouha et al.'s Method

Mixed integer linear programming is an optimization method that tries to minimize or maximize a linear objective function of several variables subjected to certain linear constraints on the variables. An MILP problem can be formally stated as follows.

MILP: Given $A \in \mathbb{R}^{m \times n}$, $b \in \mathbb{R}^m$ and $c_1, \cdots, c_n \in \mathbb{R}^n$, find an $x \in \mathbb{Z}^k \times \mathbb{R}^{n-k} \subseteq \mathbb{R}^n$ with $Ax \leq b$, such that the linear function $c_1 x_1 + c_2 x_2 + \cdots + c_n x_n$ is minimized (or maximized) with respect to the linear constraint $Ax \leq b$.

This kind of problems arises in many areas and the study of linear programming can be traced back, at least, to World War II [18]. However, it is only in recent years that MILP was applied in cryptographic research.

In [10], Borghoff et al. devised a general method to transform the problem of solving a system of quadratic equations over $\mathbb{F}_2$ into a mixed-integer linear programming problem. With this method, the authors of [10] were able to recover the internal state of the stream cipher Bivium A within 4.5 h. The same method was also employed in [2] to analyze polynomial systems with noises arising in the context of cold boot key recovery attacks [16]. In [11], Bulygin and Walter investigated the invariant coset attack on PrintCipher [19] by finding invariant projected subsets with techniques of mixed integer linear programming. A technique of MILP was also employed in optimizing the guessing strategies for algebraic attack on EPCBC [25].

Mouha et al. [22] and Wu et al. [26] applied MILP to automatically determine lower bounds of the numbers of active S-boxes for some word-oriented symmetric-key ciphers. In the following we give a description of Mouha et al.'s method introduced in [22].

Mouha et al.'s method uses 0–1 variables to describe the word-level differentials propagating through r rounds of the cipher. These variables are subjected to constraints imposed by the specific operations and structures of the cipher under consideration. Assume a block cipher consists of the following three operations:

1. S-box, $\mathcal{S} : \mathbb{F}_2^\omega \to \mathbb{F}_2^\omega$;
2. XOR, $\oplus : \mathbb{F}_2^\omega \times \mathbb{F}_2^\omega \to \mathbb{F}_2^\omega$; and
3. Linear transformation $L : \mathbb{F}_{2^\omega}^m \to \mathbb{F}_{2^\omega}^m$. The branch number of L is defined as

$$\mathcal{B}_L = \min_{a \neq 0}\{wt(a\|L(a)) : a \in \mathbb{F}_{2^\omega}^m\}$$

where $wt(a\|L(a))$ is the number of non-zero entries of the $2m$-dimensional vector $a\|L(a) \in \mathbb{F}_{2^\omega}^{2m}$.

Representation of active S-boxes and objective function. For an input difference $\Delta_i \in \mathbb{F}_{2^\omega}$ of each S-box appearing in the schematic diagram of the cipher, Mouha et al. introduced a new 0–1 variable A_i to describe the corresponding S-box is active or not, i.e., $A_i = 1$ or $A_i = 0$ depending on $\Delta_i \neq 0$ or $\Delta_i = 0$. Then, the total number of active S-boxes, $\sum_i A_i$, is chosen as the objective function to be minimized subjecting to constraints imposed by the operations of the cipher.

Constraints imposed by XOR operations. Assume that a, $b \in \mathbb{F}_2^\omega$ are the input differences of the XOR operation, and $c \in \mathbb{F}_2^\omega$ is the output difference. Then we have

$$\begin{cases} a + b + c \geq 2d_\oplus \\ d_\oplus \geq a \\ d_\oplus \geq b \\ d_\oplus \geq c \end{cases} \tag{1}$$

where $d_\oplus$ is a dummy variable taking values from $\{0,1\}$.

Constraints imposed by linear transformation. Suppose $\{i_0, \cdots, i_{m-1}\}$ and $\{j_0, \cdots, j_{m-1}\}$ are permutations of $\{0, \cdots, m-1\}$. Let x_{i_k} and y_{j_k}, $k \in \{0,1,\ldots,m-1\}$, be 0–1 variables to denote the word-level input and output differences respectively for a linear transformation. Then these variables are subjected to the following constraints

$$\begin{cases} \sum_{k=0}^{m-1}(x_{i_k} + y_{j_k}) \geq \mathcal{B}_L d_L \\ d_L \geq x_{i_0} \\ \cdots \\ d_L \geq x_{i_{m-1}} \\ d_L \geq y_{j_0} \\ \cdots \\ d_L \geq y_{j_{m-1}} \end{cases} \tag{2}$$

where d_L is a dummy variable taking values in $\{0,1\}$ and $\mathcal{B}_L$ is the branch number of the linear transformation L.

With the objective function and constraints presented as above, the problem of calculating a lower bound of the number of active S-boxes is modelled as an MILP instance which can be solved by the CPLEX [12] optimizer. The minimum numbers of active S-boxes were obtained in [22] for r-round Enocoro-128V2 ($r \leq 96$) and full-round AES. We refer the reader to [22] for more information.

These results are impressive especially for that Mouha et al.'s method is able to show the resistance of AES against related-key differential attacks automatically. However, Mouha et al.'s method is not applicable to SPN ciphers with bitwise permutation diffusion layers since it does not consider the collaborative diffusion effect of the S-box layer and bitwise permutation linear diffusion layer. In the next section, we will extend Mouha et al.'s method by introducing new representations linking bit-level and word-level differentials and adding new constraints concerning the diffusion effect of S-boxes to make it suitable to SPN ciphers with bitwise permutation diffusion layers.

3   Calculating the Minimum Number of Active S-boxes for S-bP Structures

In this section, we consider an r-round SP block cipher with n-bit block size, $\omega \times \omega$ S-box, and a bitwise permutation diffusion layer. We call this is a block cipher of S-bP(n, ω, r) structure. Under this notation, PRESENT-80 is an S-bP$(64, 4, 31)$ structure, PRINTCIPHER is an S-bP$(32, 3, 48)$ structure, and EPCBC$(48,96)$ is an S-bP$(96, 4, 32)$ structure.

Each round of an S-bP(n, ω, r) structure consists of a key addition (XOR) layer, a substitution layer where the n input bits are divided into n/ω words which will be substituted by new ones according to the underlying S-boxes, and a bitwise permutation layer that permutes the position of the output bits of the substitution layer (Fig. 1).

3.1   Representation of the Differentials

Bit-level representation. For every bit-level difference in S-bP structure, we introduce a new 0–1 variable to denote it if necessary. For differences that can be represented by variables already introduced (e.g., the r-th round input difference is the bitwise permutation of the $(r-1)$-th round output difference in single-key differential analysis), we do not introduce new variables. The reason is that we should make the number of variables as small as possible in the resulting MILP instance.

Word-level representation. For every S-box in the schematic diagram (including the encryption process and the key schedule algorithm) of the block cipher, we introduce a new 0–1 variable A_j.

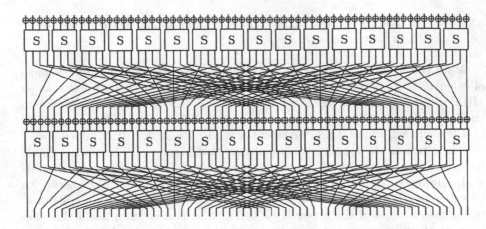

Fig. 1. Two consecutive rounds of the PRESENT-80 encryption algorithm

3.2   Constructing the MILP Instance for S-bP Structure

If we follow the way of variable usage introduced in Subsect. 3.1 and obey the rules of variable assignment as follows:

$$x_i = \begin{cases} 0, & \text{there is no bit level difference at this position,} \\ 1, & \text{otherwise,} \end{cases}$$

$$A_i = \begin{cases} 0, & \text{the Sbox marked by } A_i \text{ is not active,} \\ 1, & \text{otherwise,} \end{cases}$$

then it is natural to choose the objective function f as $\sum A_j$, which will be minimized to determine the lower bound of the number of active S-boxes for S-bP(n, ω, r) structure. The tricky part is to pinpoint the constraints under which the objective function f should be minimized.

Constraints Imposed by XOR Operations. For every XOR operation that may receive more than one nonzero input difference, we add the constraints (1) presented in Sect. 2, here the corresponding input and output variable should be changed to bit-level representation.

Constraints Describing the S-box Operation. Assume $(x_{i_0}, \cdots, x_{i_{\omega-1}})$ and $(y_{j_0}, \ldots, y_{j_{\omega-1}})$ are the input and output bits of an S-box marked by A_t respectively. Firstly, to ensure $A_t = 1$ when any one of $x_{i_0}, \ldots, x_{i_{\omega-1}}$ is 1, we require

$$\begin{cases} x_{i_0} - A_t \leq 0 \\ x_{i_1} - A_t \leq 0 \\ \cdots \\ x_{i_{\omega-1}} - A_t \leq 0 \end{cases} \tag{3}$$

Secondly, when $A_t = 1$, one of $x_{i_0}, \ldots, x_{i_{\omega-1}}$ must be 1:

$$x_{i_0} + x_{i_1} + \cdots + x_{i_{\omega-1}} - A_t \geq 0 \tag{4}$$

Thirdly, input difference must result in output difference and vice versa:

$$\begin{cases} \omega y_{j_0} + \omega y_{j_1} + \cdots + \omega y_{j_{\omega-1}} - (x_{i_0} + x_{i_1} + \cdots + x_{i_{\omega-1}}) \geq 0 \\ \omega x_{i_0} + \omega x_{i_1} + \cdots + \omega x_{i_{\omega-1}} - (y_{j_0} + y_{j_1} + \cdots + y_{j_{\omega-1}}) \geq 0 \end{cases} \tag{5}$$

Here we stress that similar constraints must be added for invertible linear transformation $L : \mathbb{F}_{2^\omega}^m \to \mathbb{F}_{2^\omega}^m$ with branch number $\mathcal{B}_L < \omega + 1$. For example, the block cipher PRINCE in [9] applies an almost-MDS linear diffusion layer L with $\mathcal{B}_L = \omega$.

In Mouha et al.'s method, the variables representing input and output differences of a linear diffusion transformation are subjected to (2). It is easy to check that the following assignment

$$\begin{cases} d_L = 1 \\ x_{i_0} = 1 \\ \vdots \\ x_{i_{m-1}} = 1 \\ y_{j_0} = 0 \\ \vdots \\ y_{j_{m-1}} = 0 \end{cases}$$

does not violate (2) if $\mathcal{B}_L < \omega + 1$. However, this contradicts the invertibility of L since a nonzero input difference must result in a nonzero output difference. This defect can be remedied by adding (5) as additional constraints.

Finally, since a single active S-box may lead to more than one active S-box in the next round in S-bP structure, the collaborative diffusion effect of the S-boxes and bitwise permutations can not be ignored.

Definition 1. *The branch number $\mathcal{B}_S$ of an $\omega \times \omega$ S-box $S : \mathbb{F}_2^\omega \to \mathbb{F}_2^\omega$ is defined as follows*

$$\mathcal{B}_S = \min_{a \neq b} \{ wt((a \oplus b) \| (\mathcal{S}(a) \oplus \mathcal{S}(b)) : a, b \in \mathbb{F}_2^\omega \}$$

where $wt(\cdot)$ is the Hamming weight of a 2ω-bit word.

Similarly to the constraints describing the diffusion effect of linear transformations in Mouha et al.'s method, we have

$$\begin{cases} \sum_{k=0}^{\omega-1} (x_{i_k} + x_{j_k}) \geq \mathcal{B}_S d_t \\ d_t \geq x_{i_0} \\ \cdots \\ d_t \geq x_{i_{\omega-1}} \\ d_t \geq y_{j_0} \\ \cdots \\ d_t \geq y_{j_{\omega-1}} \end{cases} \tag{6}$$

Additional Constraints. Add an extra constraint to ensure nonzero input difference to rule out the trivial result where zero input difference results in 0 active S-box. Let $(x_1, \cdots, x_n)$ be the input difference, we require a constraint that $x_1 + \cdots + x_n \geq 1$.

0–1 Variables Vs Mixed-Integer Linear Programming. If we restrict all variables appearing in the objective function and constraints to be 0–1, the resulting instance is a pure integer programming problem. In practice, as suggested in [10], we only require all variables representing differences of plaintexts and all dummy variables to be 0–1 whilst other variables are only required to be real numbers, this may lead to a faster solving process.

4   Applications to the Block Cipher PRESENT-80

The increasing popularity of small computing devices with restrictive cost, power and size makes it a crucial task to design lightweight block ciphers. However, designing a secure lightweight block cipher suitable for extremely constrained devices is still a challenging goal.

Some designers employ the well understood SPN structure to meet the lightweight requirement with smaller S-boxes and bitwise permutation diffusion layers, both of which can be implemented in hardware with very low cost. For example, PRESENT [7] and EPCBC [28] use 4×4 S-boxes, and PrintCipher [19] uses 3×3 S-boxes. All these schemes have bitwise permutation diffusion layers. It is remarkable that the PRESENT cipher has become an international standard for lightweight cryptography. Hence, it is of great importance to evaluate the security of S-bP structures.

In [23], Sareh Emami et al. examined the security of the 64-bit lightweight block cipher PRESENT-80 against related-key differential attacks. With a computer search they proved that no related-key differential characteristic exists with probability higher than 2^{-64} for the full-round PRESENT-80. In the following subsection, we analyze the security of PRESENT-80 with regard to differential attack using the MILP approach.

4.1   Experimental Results for PRESENT-80

The numbers of differentially active S-boxes in the single-key and related-key model are summarized in Tables 1 and 2 respectively. The MILP instances were generated by a Python script and solved by the Gurobi5.5 optimizer running on a PC with Intel(R) Core(TM) Quad CPU (2.83 GHz, 3.25 GB RAM), and to make full use of the CPU, all computations were performed parallelly with four threads.

From Table reftab1 we know that the MILP instance corresponding to the full-round PRESENT-80 in the single-key model consists of 1056 0–1 variables, 1984 continuous variables, and 7937 constraints. This instance can be solved

Table 1. Results for the single-key differential analysis

Rounds	#Variables	#Constraints	#Active S-boxes	Timing (in seconds)
1	96 + 64	257	1	1
2	128 + 128	513	2	1
3	160 + 192	769	4	1
4	192 + 256	1025	6	1
5	224 + 320	1281	10	1
6	256 + 384	1537	12	1
7	288 + 448	1739	14	2
8	320 + 512	2049	16	5
9	352 + 576	2305	18	3
10	384 + 640	2561	20	6
11	416 + 704	2817	22	14
12	448 + 768	3073	24	13
13	480 + 832	3329	26	14
14	512 + 896	3585	28	17
15	544 + 960	3841	30	22
16	576 + 1024	4097	32	27
17	608 + 1088	4353	34	35
18	640 + 1152	4609	36	33
19	672 + 1216	4865	38	46
20	704 + 1280	5121	40	39
21	736 + 1344	5377	42	43
22	768 + 1408	5633	44	82
23	800 + 1472	5889	46	69
24	832 + 1536	6145	48	88
25	864 + 1600	6401	50	107
26	896 + 1664	6657	52	105
27	928 + 1728	6913	54	116
28	960 + 1792	7169	56	140
29	992 + 1856	7425	58	165
30	1024 + 1920	7681	60	262
31	1056 + 1984	7937	62	222

Table 2. Results for related-key differential analysis

Rounds	#Variables	#Constraints	#Active S-boxes	Timing (in seconds)
1	97 + 277	530	0	1
2	130 + 474	1058	0	1
3	163 + 671	1586	1	1
4	196 + 868	2114	2	1
5	229 + 1065	2642	3	3
6	262 + 1262	3170	4	10
7	295 + 1459	3698	6	26
8	328 + 1656	4226	8	111
9	361 + 1853	4754	9	171
10	394 + 2050	5282	12	1540
11	427 + 2247	5810	13	8136
12	460 + 2444	6338	15	18102
13	493 + 2641	8192	–	> 5 days

within 222 s and the number of active S-boxes is 62. Since the S-box of PRESENT-80 achieves a maximum probability of differentials 2^{-2}, the maximum probability for differentials of the PRESENT-80 cipher is roughly $(2^{-2})^{62} = 2^{-124}$, which is less than 2^{-80}, the probability of success for an exhaustive search, thus, we have proved that PRESENT-80 is secure against single-key differential attack.

For PRESENT-80 in the related-key differential attack, we are only able to obtain the results for its round-reduced version up to 12 rounds within a reasonable timing, and the results are listed in Table 2. For example, the probability of the best related-key differential characteristics for 7-round and 12-round PRESENT-80 are upper bounded by $(2^{-2})^6$, and $(2^{-2})^{15}$ respectively. From these results, the probability of the best related-key differential characteristic for full 31-round PRESENT-80 is upper bounded by $(2^{-2})^{15+15+6} = 2^{-72}$. Although this is slightly larger than the probability of success for an exhaustive search, we conjecture that the actual minimum number of active S-boxes is greater than 40. How to reduce the gap and completely prove the security of the full-round PRESENT-80 against related-key differential attack is still an open question.

5   Conclusion and Discussion

In this paper, we extended Mouha et al.'s method and propose an approach for automatically computing a lower bound on the number of active S-boxes for block ciphers with S-bP structures based on mixed-integer linear programming (MILP). We applied this method to the PRESENT-80 block cipher and successfully obtained the minimal numbers of active S-boxes in any single-key differential characteristic for the full-round PRESENT-80, and any related-key differential characteristic for its round reduced versions. We proved that PRESENT-80 is secure against the single-key differential attack, and that the cost of related-key differential attack against the full-round PRESENT-80 is close to the cost of an exhaustive search.

Finally, we would like to mention some related topics that deserve further investigation: 1. Completely prove the security of the full-round PRESENT-80 with respect to the related-key differential attack. A direct approach is to solve the MILP instance generated from the 31-round PRESENT-80 in the related-key model. However, according to our experiment, we are not even able to solve the MILP instance corresponding to 13-round PRESENT-80 within 5 days. 2. The MILP instances generated from cryptographic problems are in general very hard to solve compared to usual MILP instances coming from other fields. To practically solve the MILP instances derived from the full-round PRESENT-80 against related-key differential attack, it is an interesting research topic to develop methods to utilize specific structures in the MILP instances generated from cryptography and speed up the solving process.

Acknowledgements. The authors would like to thank the anonymous reviewers for their helpful comments and suggestions. The work of this paper was supported by the National Key Basic Research Program of China (2013CB834203), the National Natural Science Foundation of China (Grants 61070172, 10990011, and 61272477), and the Strategic Priority Research Program of Chinese Academy of Sciences under Grant XDA06010702.

References

1. Achterberg, T.: SCIP-a framework to integrate constraint and mixed integer programming. Report 04–19, Zuse Institute, Berlin (2004)
2. Albrecht, M., Cid, C.: Cold boot key recovery by solving polynomial systems with noise. In: Lopez, J., Tsudik, G. (eds.) ACNS 2011. LNCS, vol. 6715, pp. 57–72. Springer, Heidelberg (2011)
3. Aoki, K., Ichikawa, T., Kanda, M., Matsui, M., Moriai, S., Nakajima, J., Tokita, T.: *Camellia*: A 128-bit block cipher suitable for multiple platforms - design and analysis. In: Stinson, D.R., Tavares, S. (eds.) SAC 2000. LNCS, vol. 2012, pp. 39–56. Springer, Heidelberg (2001)
4. Biham, E.: New types of cryptanalytic attacks using related keys. J. Crypt. **7**(4), 229–246 (1994)
5. Biham, E., Biryukov, A., Shamir, A.: Cryptanalysis of skipjack reduced to 31 rounds using impossible differentials. In: Stern, J. (ed.) EUROCRYPT 1999. LNCS, vol. 1592, pp. 12–23. Springer, Heidelberg (1999)
6. Biham, E., Shamir, A.: Differential cryptanalysis of DES-like cryptosystems. J. Crypt. **4**(1), 3–72 (1991)
7. Bogdanov, A.A., Knudsen, L.R., Leander, G., Paar, C., Poschmann, A., Robshaw, M., Seurin, Y., Vikkelsoe, C.: PRESENT: An ultra-lightweight block cipher. In: Paillier, P., Verbauwhede, I. (eds.) CHES 2007. LNCS, vol. 4727, pp. 450–466. Springer, Heidelberg (2007)

8. Bogdanov, A., Rijmen, V.: Zero correlation linear cryptanalysis of block ciphers. IACR Eprint Archive report 123 (2011)
9. Borghoff, J., Canteaut, A., Güneysu, T., Kavun, E.B., Knezevic, M., Knudsen, L.R., Leander, G., Nikov, V., Paar, C., Rechberger, C., Rombouts, P., Thomsen, S.S., Yalçın, T.: PRINCE – a low-latency block cipher for pervasive computing Applications. In: Wang, X., Sako, K. (eds.) ASIACRYPT 2012. LNCS, vol. 7658, pp. 208–225. Springer, Heidelberg (2012)
10. Borghoff, J., Knudsen, L.R., Stolpe, M.: Bivium as a mixed-integer linear programming problem. In: Parker, M.G. (ed.) Cryptography and Coding 2009. LNCS, vol. 5921, pp. 133–152. Springer, Heidelberg (2009)
11. Bulygin, S., Walter, M.: Study of the invariant coset attack on printcipher: more weak keys with practical key recovery. Technical report, Cryptology eprint Archive, Report 2012/85 (2012)
12. CPLEX, I.I.: IBM software group. User-Manual CPLEX 12 (2011)
13. Daemen, J., Rijmen, V.: The wide trail strategy. In: Honary, B. (ed.) The Design of Rijndael. Information Security and Cryptography, pp. 123–147. Springer, Heidelberg (2002)
14. Daemen, J., Rijmen, V.: AES Proposal: Rijndael. In: Proceedings from the First Advanced Encryption Standard Candidate Conference, National Institute of Standards and Technology (NIST) (1998)
15. Gurobi: Gurobi optimizer reference manual (2012). http://www.gurobi.com
16. Halderman, J.A., Schoen, S.D., Heninger, N., Clarkson, W., Paul, W., Calandrino, J.A., Feldman, A.J., Appelbaum, J., Felten, E.W.: Lest we remember: cold-boot attacks on encryption keys. Commun. ACM **52**(5), 91–98 (2009)
17. Kanda, M.: Practical security evaluation against differential and linear cryptanalyses for feistel ciphers with SPN round function. In: Stinson, D.R., Tavares, S. (eds.) SAC 2000. LNCS, vol. 2012, pp. 324–338. Springer, Heidelberg (2001)
18. Kantorovich, L.V.: A new method of solving some classes of extremal problems. Dokl. Akad. Sci. USSR. **28**, 211–214 (1940)
19. Knudsen, L., Leander, G., Poschmann, A., Robshaw, M.J.B.: PRINTCIPHER: a block cipher for IC-printing. In: Mangard, S., Standaert, F.-X. (eds.) CHES 2010. LNCS, vol. 6225, pp. 16–32. Springer, Heidelberg (2010)
20. Matsui, M.: Linear cryptanalysis method for DES cipher. In: Helleseth, T. (ed.) EUROCRYPT 1993. LNCS, vol. 765, pp. 386–397. Springer, Heidelberg (1994)
21. Matsui, M.: Differential path search of the block cipher E2. Technical report, ISEC99-19, pp. 57–64 (1999)
22. Mouha, N., Wang, Q., Gu, D., Preneel, B.: Differential and linear cryptanalysis using mixed-integer linear programming. In: Wu, C.-K., Yung, M., Lin, D. (eds.) Inscrypt 2011. LNCS, vol. 7537, pp. 57–76. Springer, Heidelberg (2012)
23. Emami, S., Ling, S., Nikolić, I., Pieprzyk, J., Wang, H.: The resistance of present-80 against related-key differential attacks. Cryptology ePrint Archive, Report 2013/522 (2013). http://eprint.iacr.org/
24. Shibutani, K.: On the diffusion of generalized feistel structures regarding differential and linear cryptanalysis. In: Biryukov, A., Gong, G., Stinson, D.R. (eds.) SAC 2010. LNCS, vol. 6544, pp. 211–228. Springer, Heidelberg (2011)
25. Walter, M., Bulygin, S., Buchmann, J.: Optimizing guessing strategies for algebraic cryptanalysis with applications to EPCBC. In: Kutyłowski, M., Yung, M. (eds.) Inscrypt 2012. LNCS, vol. 7763, pp. 175–197. Springer, Heidelberg (2013)
26. Wu, S., Wang, M.: Security evaluation against differential cryptanalysis for block cipher structures. Technical report, Cryptology ePrint Archive, Report 2011/551 (2011)

27. Wu, W., Zhang, W., Lin, D.: On the security of generalized feistel scheme with SP round function. Int. J. Netw. Secur. **3**(3), 215–224 (2006)
28. Yap, H., Khoo, K., Poschmann, A., Henricksen, M.: EPCBC - a block cipher suitable for electronic product code encryption. In: Lin, D., Tsudik, G., Wang, X. (eds.) CANS 2011. LNCS, vol. 7092, pp. 76–97. Springer, Heidelberg (2011)
29. Zhang, M., Liu, J., Wang, X.: The upper bounds on differential characteristics in block cipher sms4. Cryptology ePrint Archive, Report 2010/155 (2010)

Sequence and Stream Cipher

On the Key-Stream Periods
Probability of Edon80

Yunqing Xu[✉]

Mathematics Department, Ningbo University, Ningbo 315211, China
xuyunqing@nbu.edu.cn

Abstract. Edon80 is a hardware binary additive synchronous stream cipher submitted to the third and last phase of the eSTREAM project. It's properties are: (1) The internal structure is highly pipelined; (2) It is highly parallelizable, making it scalable from the speed of processing point of view; (3) Its design principles offer possibilities to achieve significant speed asymmetry — it belongs to a family of stream ciphers that in hardware can have a constant speed of one bit per clock cycle, but in software implementation on popular modern CPUs can be made as slow as needed. Since its first description in 2005, it has been analyzed by several cryptographers, have been implemented in a more compact way and a MAC functionality have been added. The key stream generator of Edon80 employed four quasigroups of order 4. The quasigroups are chosen by experiments and the period probabilities of the key stream are also discussed by experiments. In this paper, we research the period probabilities of Edon80 with mathematical theory, and also we discuss quasigroups with larger periods factors.

Keywords: Stream cipher · Edon80 · Key-stream period · Quasigroup · Latin square

1 Introduction

A quasigroup is an ordered pair $(Q, *)$, where Q is a set and $*$ is a binary operation on Q such that the equations $a * x = b$ and $y * a = b$ are uniquely solvable for every pair of elements a, b in Q. A Latin square on a set Q is an $|Q| \times |Q|$ array such that every symbol occurs in every row once, and also in every column once. It is fairly well known that (e.g., see [1]) the multiplication table of a quasigroup defines a Latin square; that is, a Latin square can be viewed as the multiplication table of a quasigroup with the headline and the sideline removed. Therefore the notions of a quasigroup and a Latin square will be freely interchanged in this paper.

Consider an alphabet (i.e. a finite set) Q, and denote by Q^+ the set of all nonempty words (i.e. finite strings) formed by the elements of Q. The elements of Q^+ will be denoted by $x_1 x_2 \cdots x_m$, where $x_i \in Q$ ($i = 1, 2, \cdots, m$). Let $*$ be a

© Springer International Publishing Switzerland 2014
D. Lin et al. (Eds.): Inscrypt 2013, LNCS 8567, pp. 55–69, 2014.
DOI: 10.1007/978-3-319-12087-4_4

quasigroup operation on set Q, i.e. consider a quasigroup $(Q, *)$. For each $a \in Q$, we define a function $E_{a,*} \colon Q^+ \to Q^+$ as follows. $\forall\, X = x_1 x_2 \cdots x_m \in Q^+$,

$$E_{a,*}(x_1 x_2 \cdots x_m) = y_1 y_2 \cdots, y_m,$$

where

$$\begin{cases} y_1 = a * x_1, \\ y_{i+1} = y_i * x_{i+1},\ i = 1, 2, \cdots, m-1 \end{cases}$$

The function $E_{a,*}$ is called an *e-transformation* of Q^+ based on the operation $*$ with leader a. And the graphical representation of $E_{a,*}$ is shown in Fig. 1.

Fig. 1. Graphical representation of the transformation $E_{a,*}$

Edon80 was submitted to the eSTREAM project as a hardware stream cipher under the Profile 2. It was designed by Gligoroski, Markovski, Kocarev, and Gusev and its original description is given in [2]. It has a unique design among known stream cipher designs: it concatenates 80 basic building blocks derived from four small quasigroups of order 4 in Fig. 2.

$\bullet_0$	0	1	2	3
0	0	2	1	3
1	2	1	3	0
2	1	3	0	2
3	3	0	2	1

$\bullet_1$	0	1	2	3
0	1	3	0	2
1	0	1	2	3
2	2	0	3	1
3	3	2	1	0

$\bullet_2$	0	1	2	3
0	2	1	0	3
1	1	2	3	0
2	3	0	2	1
3	0	3	1	2

$\bullet_3$	0	1	2	3
0	3	2	1	0
1	1	0	3	2
2	0	3	2	1
3	2	1	0	3

Fig. 2. Quasigroups used for the design of Edon80

Edon80 process e-transformations to the initial string consisting of letters "0 1 2 3 0 1 2 3 0 ..." in 80 steps and output every second letter that forms the keystream of the stream cipher (see Fig. 3). The processing in every step is done by a quasigroup $*_i$ operation in $\{\bullet_1, \bullet_2, \bullet_3, \bullet_4\}$ and a leader $a_i \in \{0, 1, 2, 3\}$, $i = 0, 1, \cdots 79$ chosen in the IVSetup process that have the property to map the initial 80-bit key (40 2-bit letters) and initial 64-bit IV (32 2-bit letters) equiprobable in the space $\{0, 1, 2, 3\}^{80}$.

For the four quasigroup operations in Fig. 2, it is indicated in [2] that:

1. $\bullet_0$ in average increases the period of an input string by factor of 2.66.
2. $\bullet_1$ in average increases the period of an input string by factor of 2.48.
3. $\bullet_2$ in average increases the period of an input string by factor of 2.43.
4. $\bullet_3$ in average increases the period of an input string by factor of 2.37.

$*_i$		0	1	2	3	0	1	2	3	0	$\cdots$
$*_0$	a_0	$a_{0,0}$	$a_{0,1}$	$a_{0,2}$	$a_{0,3}$	$a_{0,4}$	$a_{0,5}$	$a_{0,6}$	$a_{0,7}$	$a_{0,8}$	$\cdots$
$*_1$	a_1	$a_{1,0}$	$a_{1,1}$	$a_{1,2}$	$a_{1,3}$	$a_{1,4}$	$a_{1,5}$	$a_{1,6}$	$a_{1,7}$	$a_{1,8}$	$\cdots$
$\vdots$	$\vdots$	$\vdots$	$\vdots$	$\vdots$	$\vdots$	$\vdots$	$\vdots$	$\vdots$	$\vdots$	$\vdots$	
$*_{79}$	a_{79}	$a_{79,0}$	$\mathbf{a_{79,1}}$	$a_{79,2}$	$\mathbf{a_{79,3}}$	$a_{79,4}$	$\mathbf{a_{79,5}}$	$a_{79,6}$	$\mathbf{a_{79,7}}$	$a_{79,8}$	$\cdots$

Fig. 3. Representation of quasigroups e-transformation of Edon80 during the Keystream mode

Thus, in average, each e-transformation increases the period of an input string by factor of 2.48. The projected period of the keystream in Edon80 after applying 80 e-transformation is $\frac{1}{2}2.48^{80} \approx 2^{103}$.

The attack on Edon80 presented in [3] is based on analyzing $(key, state)$ pairs (concrete assignment of working quasigroups $*_i$ and initial values for a_i) that give small periods. The small period probabilities summary of his findings are given in Table 1.

Table 1. Summary periods probabilities in [3]

Periods less then	Probability	Period less then	Probability
2^{63}	2^{-60}	2^{55}	2^{-71}
2^{62}	2^{-66}	2^{54}	2^{-78}
2^{61}	2^{-75}	2^{53}	2^{-88}

Gligoroski et al. [4] gives more small periods probabilities as shown in Table 2.

Table 2. Summary periods probabilities in [4]

Periods less then	Probability	Period less then	Probability
2^{80}	$2^{-4.48}$	2^{48}	$2^{-35.02}$
2^{76}	$2^{-6.57}$	2^{44}	$2^{-41.24}$
2^{72}	$2^{-9.13}$	2^{40}	$2^{-48.03}$
2^{68}	$2^{-12.16}$	2^{36}	$2^{-55.46}$
2^{64}	$2^{-15.67}$	2^{32}	$2^{-63.59}$
2^{60}	$2^{-19.70}$	2^{28}	$2^{-72.46}$
2^{56}	$2^{-24.25}$	2^{24}	$2^{-82.14}$
2^{52}	$2^{-29.35}$	2^{20}	$2^{-92.86}$

All the above probabilities are obtained by experiments of performing e-transformations. It can be seen that the probabilities in Table 1 and in 2 are not coherent.

A precise mathematical description of the periods of the keystreams of Edon80 was attempt to get in [5], but the distributions of the random variables were still obtained by numerous numerical experiments of performing e-transformations. In this paper, we discuss the period probabilities of the keystream of Edon80 based on mathematical theory, especially the theory of permutation groups.

The structure of this paper is as follows. Section 2 give the concept and the probability distributions of the period factors of a quasigroup in general. The period factors probability distributions of the four quasigroups employed in Edon80 are discussed in Sect. 3. The period probabilities of Edon80 are given in Sect. 4. In Sect. 5, more suitable quasigroups for the key-stream generator are discussed from the point of view of periods of the key stream. Finally, conclusions are given in Sect. 6.

2   The Period Factors of Quasigroups

Let $X = x_1 x_2 \cdots x_m \in Q^+$. If there exist positive integers k and p such that $x_{i+p} = x_i$ when $i \geq k$, then we say that X is *eventually periodic*. If $k = 0$, then we say that X is *periodic*. If p is the least number of such integers, then p is called the *period* of X.

Definition 1. *Let Q be a n-set and σ be a permutation on Q. $\forall\, x \in Q$, the period of sequence $x\ \sigma(x)\ \sigma^2(x)\ \cdots \sigma^i(x) \cdots$ is called the period factor of σ at x and denoted by $f_\sigma(x)$.*

For example, if $Q = \{1, 2, 3, 4\}$ and $\sigma = (1)(2\ 3\ 4)$, then $f_\sigma(1) = 1$, $f_\sigma(2) = f_\sigma(3) = f_\sigma(4) = 3$. It is easy to see that if $x \in Q$ is in a cycle of σ of length k, then $f_\sigma(x) = k$.

It is obvious that $f_\sigma(x)$ is an integer and $1 \leq f_\sigma(x) \leq n$. The function $f_\sigma = f_\sigma(x)$ with domain Q is a random variable with sample space $N = \{1, 2, \cdots, n\}$. The following is a restatement of Theorem 3 in [6].

Theorem 1. *Let Q be an n-set and $Y^{(0)} = y_1^{(0)} y_2^{(0)} \cdots y_m^{(0)} \in Q^+$, $*_1, *_2, \cdots, *_p$ be p quasigroup operations on Q, and $a_1, a_2, \cdots, a_p$ be p letters in Q. Let*

$$\begin{cases} y_1^{(k)} = a_k *_k y_1^{(k-1)}, \\ y_{i+1}^{(k)} = y_i^{(k)} *_k y_{i+1}^{(k-1)}, \, i = 1, 2, \cdots, m-1 \end{cases}$$

for $k = 1, 2, \cdots, p$ recursively and denote $Y^{(p)} = y_1^{(p)} y_2^{(p)} \cdots y_m^{(p)}$. Let l be an integer with $1 \leq l \leq p$(we suppose that $l, p \ll m$). Then the distribution of substrings of length l in $Y^{(p)}$ is uniform.

Let $Y = y_1 y_2 y_3 \cdots \in Q^+$ be a sequence get by an e-transformation defined in Sect. 1. From Theorem 1 we know that the appearance probability of each letter $x \in Q$ at any place of Y is $1/|Q|$.

Theorem 2. *Suppose Q is an n-set and σ is a permutation on Q. If the type of σ is $1^{\lambda_1} 2^{\lambda_2} \cdots n^{\lambda_n}$, i.e., σ has λ_i cycles of length i $(i = 1, 2, \cdots, n)$, and the probability distribution of the letters in Q is uniform: $\{P(x) = \frac{1}{n} : x \in Q\}$, then the probability distribution of f_σ*

$$\begin{pmatrix} 1 & 2 & \cdots & n \\ P(f_\sigma = 1) & P(f_\sigma = 2) & \cdots & P(f_\sigma = n) \end{pmatrix} = \begin{pmatrix} 1 & 2 & \cdots & n \\ \frac{\lambda_1}{n} & \frac{2\lambda_2}{n} & \cdots & \frac{n\lambda_n}{n} \end{pmatrix}.$$

Proof. Let $Q_i = |\{x \in Q \mid f_\sigma(x) = i\}|$, then $Q = \cup_{i=1}^n Q_i$ and $P(f_\sigma = i) = \frac{|Q_i|}{|Q|} = \frac{1}{n} \cdot i \cdot \lambda_i$ for $i = 1, 2, \cdots, n$. □

Definition 2. *Let $Q = \{1, 2, \cdots, n\}$ and $(Q, *)$ be a quasigroup, $L = (l_{ij})_{n \times n}$ be the Latin square of the multiplication table of $(Q, *)$. $\forall\, i \in Q$, the permutation*

$$\sigma_i = \begin{pmatrix} 1 & 2 & \cdots & n \\ l_{1i} & l_{2i} & \cdots & l_{ni} \end{pmatrix} = \begin{pmatrix} 1 & 2 & \cdots & n \\ 1 * i & 2 * i & \cdots & n * i \end{pmatrix}$$

is called the ith column permutation of L (or $(Q, *)$).

Theorem 3. *Let $Q = \{1, 2, \cdots, n\}$, $(Q, *)$ be a quasigroup and $\sigma_1, \sigma_2, \cdots, \sigma_n$ be the column permutations of $(Q, *)$. Suppose $X = x_1 x_2 \cdots x_m \cdots \in Q^+$ is periodic with period p. $E_{a_0, *}$ is the e-transformation function of Q^+ based on the operation $*$ with leader $a_0 \in Q$ and*

$$Y = y_1 y_2 \cdots y_m \cdots = E_{a_0, *}(x_1 x_2 \cdots x_m \cdots).$$

If a_0 is in a cycle of length k of the permutation $\sigma = \sigma_{x_p} \sigma_{x_{p-1}} \cdots \sigma_{x_1}$, then Y is periodic and the period of Y is $k \cdot p$.

Proof. Suppose $(a_0\, a_1\, a_2\, \cdots a_{k-1})$ is a cycle of $\sigma = \sigma_{x_p} \sigma_{x_{p-1}} \cdots \sigma_{x_1}$. From the definition of e-transformation we know

$$\begin{cases} y_1 = a_0 * x_1 = \sigma_{x_1}(a_0), \\ y_2 = y_1 * x_2 = \sigma_{x_2} \sigma_{x_1}(a_0), \\ \quad\vdots \\ y_p = y_{p-1} * x_p = \sigma_{x_p} \sigma_{x_{p-1}} \cdots \sigma_{x_1}(a_0) = \sigma(a_0) = a_1, \end{cases}$$

and

$$\begin{cases} y_{2p} = \sigma_{x_{2p}} \sigma_{x_{2p-1}} \cdots \sigma_{x_{p+1}}(a_1) = \sigma(a_1) = a_2, \\ y_{3p} = \sigma_{x_{3p}} \sigma_{x_{3p-1}} \cdots \sigma_{x_{2p+1}}(a_2) = \sigma(a_2) = a_3, \\ \quad\vdots \\ y_{kp} = \sigma_{x_{kp}} \sigma_{x_{kp-1}} \cdots \sigma_{x_{(k-1)p+1}}(a_{k-1}) = \sigma(a_{k-1}) = a_0, \end{cases} \tag{2.1}$$

Let i be a positive integer and denote $i = sp + r$, where s and r are non-negative integers with $r < p$, then

$$y_i = \sigma_{x_r}\sigma_{x_{r-1}}\cdots\sigma_{x_1}(\sigma^s(a)) = \sigma_{x_r}\sigma_{x_{r-1}}\cdots\sigma_{x_1}(a_{s \ (\text{mod } k)}),$$

$$\begin{aligned}
y_{i+kp} &= \sigma_{x_r}\sigma_{x_{r-1}}\cdots\sigma_{x_1}(a_{s+k \ (\text{mod } k)}) \\
&= \sigma_{x_r}\sigma_{x_{r-1}}\cdots\sigma_{x_1}(a_{s \ (\text{mod } k)}) \\
&= y_i.
\end{aligned}$$

Suppose the period of Y is t, t must be a divisor of kp and we denote $kp = \ell t$. Then we have

$$y_t = y_{2t} = \cdots = y_{\ell t} = y_{kp} = a_0 \overset{\triangle}{=} y_0. \tag{2.2}$$

Since

$$y_{i-1} * x_{t+i} = y_{t+i-1} * x_{t+i} = y_{t+i} = y_i = y_{i-1} * x_i$$

and $*$ is a quasigroup operation, we have

$$x_{t+i} = x_i.$$

So, t must be a multiple of p, the period of X. Suppose $t = sp$, by Formulas (2.2) and (2.1) we have

$$a_0 = y_t = y_{sp} = a_{s \ (\text{mod } k)}.$$

From the minimality of t we $s = k$ and the period of Y is $t = kp$. □

Definition 3. *Suppose Q is an n-set, $(Q, *)$ is a quasigroup and L is the Latin square of the multiplication table of $(Q, *)$, $\sigma_1, \sigma_2, \cdots, \sigma_n$ are the column permutations of L and $S_* = \{\sigma_1, \sigma_2, \cdots, \sigma_n\}$. For any positive integer p, let $S_*^p = \{\sigma_{i_p}\sigma_{i_{p-1}}\cdots\sigma_{i_1} : 1 \leq i_1, i_2, \cdots, i_p \leq n\}$ be a multi-set. $\forall (\sigma, x) \in S_*^p \times Q$, the period of sequence $x \ \sigma(x) \ \sigma^2(x) \ \cdots\sigma^p(x)\cdots$ is the period factor of σ at x. The function $f_*^{(p)}(\sigma, x) = f_\sigma(x)$ with domain $S_*^p \times Q$ is a random variable with sample space $N = \{1, 2, \cdots, n\}$. $f_*^{(p)}(\sigma, x)$ is called the period factor of degree p of L (or $(Q, *)$) and denoted by $f_*^{(p)}$.*

Theorem 4. *Suppose Q is an n-set and $(Q, *)$ is a quasigroup, and $S_* = \{\sigma_1, \sigma_2, \cdots, \sigma_n\}$ is from Definition 3. Let $\{\tau_1, \tau_2, \cdots, \tau_v\} = \langle S_* \rangle$ be the permutation group generated by S_* and suppose the type of τ_i is $1^{\lambda_{i1}} 2^{\lambda_{i2}} \cdots n^{\lambda_{in}}$ $(i = 1, 2, \cdots, v)$. Suppose the probability distribution of the letters in Q is uniform: $\{P(x) = \frac{1}{n} : x \in Q\}$. For any positive integer p, if the multi-set $S_*^p = \{\sigma_{i_p}\sigma_{i_{p-1}}\cdots\sigma_{i_1} : 1 \leq i_1, i_2, \cdots, i_p \leq n\} = \{n_1^{(p)} \cdot \tau_1, \ n_2^{(p)} \cdot \tau_2, \ \cdots, \ n_v^{(p)} \cdot \tau_v\}$, then the probability distribution of $f_*^{(p)}$ is*

$$\begin{pmatrix} 1 & 2 & \cdots & n \\ \frac{1}{n^{p+1}}\sum\limits_{i=1}^{v} n_i^{(p)}\lambda_{i1} & \frac{2}{n^{p+1}}\sum\limits_{i=1}^{v} n_i^{(p)}\lambda_{i2} & \cdots & \frac{n}{n^{p+1}}\sum\limits_{i=1}^{v} n_i^{(p)}\lambda_{in} \end{pmatrix}.$$

Proof. Let $P_k = \{(\sigma, x) \in S_*^p \times Q \mid f_*^{(p)}(\sigma, x) = k\}$ be a multi-set, then

$$P_k = \{(\sigma, x) \in S_*^p \times Q \mid f_\sigma(x) = k\}$$

$$= \bigcup_{i=1}^{v} n_i^{(p)} \{x \in Q \mid f_{\sigma_i}(x) = k\}.$$

Apply Theorem 2 we get

$$P(f_*^{(p)} = k) = \frac{|P_k|}{|S_*^p \times Q|}$$

$$= \frac{1}{n^{p+1}} \sum_{i=1}^{v} n_i^{(p)} k \lambda_{ik}.$$

This completes the proof. □

Definition 4. *Let L be a Latin square based on set $Q = \{1, 2, \cdots, n\}$ with column permutations $\sigma_1, \sigma_2, \cdots, \sigma_n$, and denote $L = L(\sigma_1, \sigma_2, \cdots, \sigma_n)$. Suppose $i_1, i_2, \cdots, i_n$ is a permutation of $1, 2, \cdots, n$, then $L(\sigma_{i_1}, \sigma_{i_2}, \cdots, \sigma_{i_n})$ is also a Latin square. We call the set*

$$\mathcal{A}(L) = \{L(\sigma_{i_1}, \sigma_{i_2}, \cdots, \sigma_{i_n}) \mid i_1, i_2, \cdots, i_n \text{ is a permutation of } 1, 2, \cdots, n\}$$

the column isomorphism class *of L.*

It is easy to see that if L is a Latin square of order n, then $|\mathcal{A}(L)| = n!$.

Let $L_1 = L(\sigma_1, \sigma_2, \cdots, \sigma_n)$ and τ is a permutation on Q. Then $L_2 = L(\tau\sigma_1\tau^{-1}, \tau\sigma_2\tau^{-1}, \cdots, \tau\sigma_n\tau^{-1}))$ is also a Latin square. L_2 is said to be a *column conjugate* of L_1 and denote $L_2 = \tau L_1 \tau^{-1}$.

Suppose $\mathcal{A}_1$ and $\mathcal{A}_2$ are two column isomorphism classes of Latin squares on set Q. If there exist $L_1 \in \mathcal{A}_1$, $L_2 \in \mathcal{A}_2$ and a permutation τ on Q such that $L_2 = \tau L_1 \tau^{-1}$, then we say the $\mathcal{A}_2$ is a *conjugate* of $\mathcal{A}_1$ and denoted by $\mathcal{A}_2 \wr \mathcal{A}_1$. It is easy to see that the map $\psi : L \mapsto \tau L \tau^{-1}$ is a bijection from $\mathcal{A}_1$ to $\mathcal{A}_2$ and each column isomorphism classes is a conjugate of itself.

Definition 5. *Let L be a Latin square, the set of all conjugates of $\mathcal{A}(L)$*

$$\mathcal{C}(L) = \bigcup_{\mathcal{A} \wr \mathcal{A}(L)} \mathcal{A}$$

is called the column conjugate class *of L.*

Let $S = \{\sigma_1, \sigma_2, \cdots, \sigma_n\}$ and $T = \tau S \tau^{-1} = \{\tau\sigma_1\tau^{-1}, \tau\sigma_2\tau^{-1}, \cdots, \tau\sigma_n\tau^{-1}\}$, then $T^p = \tau S^p \tau^{-1}$. The following is a restatement of Theorem 2.9 in [7].

Theorem 5. *Permutations ξ and ξ' on Q have the same cycle structure, i.e., have the same type, if and only if there exists a permutation τ on Q such that $\xi' = \tau\xi\tau^{-1}$.*

Combine Theorems 4 and 5, we have the following theorem.

Theorem 6. *L_1 and L_2 are two Latin squares on Q, if L_2 is in the column conjugate class of L_1, then L_1 and L_2 have the same period factors of degree p for every positive integer p.*

3   The Period Factors Probability Distribution of the Four Quasigroups Used in Edon80

In this section, we discuss the period factor distribution of the four quasigroups used in Edon80. Let $Q = \{0, 1, 2, 3\}$ be a set and Ω_Q be the symmetric group on Q. We denote the elements of Ω_Q as shown in Table 3.

Table 3. Elements of symmetric group Ω_Q

$\tau_1 = 1$	$\tau_5 = (12)$	$\tau_9 = (021)$	$\tau_{13} = (032)$	$\tau_{17} = (02)(13)$	$\tau_{21} = (0213)$
$\tau_2 = (01)$	$\tau_6 = (13)$	$\tau_{10} = (013)$	$\tau_{14} = (123)$	$\tau_{18} = (03)(12)$	$\tau_{22} = (0231)$
$\tau_3 = (02)$	$\tau_7 = (23)$	$\tau_{11} = (031)$	$\tau_{15} = (132)$	$\tau_{19} = (0123)$	$\tau_{23} = (0312)$
$\tau_4 = (03)$	$\tau_8 = (012)$	$\tau_{12} = (023)$	$\tau_{16} = (01)(23)$	$\tau_{20} = (0132)$	$\tau_{24} = (0321)$

Denote the Latin square of order 4 with the lexicographic number m by $L_{\#m}$, then the multiplication table of $(Q, \bullet_0)$ shown in Fig. 2 is $L_{\#61}$. Let $M_0 = \{15, 35, 61, 85, 105, 129, 167, 187, 215, 239, 257, 281, 298, 322, 352, 376, 394, 422, 436, 460, 488, 512, 530, 558\}$. Then the column isomorphism class

$$\mathcal{A}_0 = \mathcal{A}(L_{\#61}) = \{L_{\#m} \mid m \in M_0\}.$$

The multiplication table of $(Q, \bullet_1)$ is $L_{\#241}$. Let $M_1 = \{10, 34, 64, 88, 108, 136, 149, 173, 199, 219, 241, 265, 312, 336, 358, 378, 404, 428, 441, 469, 489, 513, 543, 567\}$. Then
$$\mathcal{A}_1 = \mathcal{A}(L_{\#241}) = \{L_{\#m} \mid m \in M_1\}.$$

The multiplication table of $(Q, \bullet_2)$ is $L_{\#350}$. Let $M_2 = \{23, 45, 72, 94, 115, 140, 158, 180, 204, 227, 251, 273, 304, 326, 350, 373, 397, 419, 437, 462, 483, 505, 532, 554\}$. Then
$$\mathcal{A}_2 = \mathcal{A}(L_{\#350}) = \{L_{\#m} \mid m \in M_2\}.$$

The multiplication table of $(Q, \bullet_3)$ is $L_{\#564}$. Let $M_3 = \{12, 38, 58, 81, 109, 131, 165, 191, 214, 236, 261, 286, 294, 317, 344, 366, 387, 413, 443, 465, 493, 518, 538, 564\}$. Then
$$\mathcal{A}_3 = \mathcal{A}(L_{\#564}) = \{L_{\#m} \mid m \in M_3\}.$$

It can be easily check that

$$L_{\#61} = \tau_3 L_{\#265} \tau_3^{-1} = \tau_{12} L_{\#94} \tau_{12}^{-1} = \tau_4 L_{\#131} \tau_4^{-1}.$$

So, $\mathcal{A}_i \wr \mathcal{A}_0$ for $i = 1, 2, 3$. From Theorem 6 we know that $(Q, \bullet_0)$, $(Q, \bullet_1)$, $(Q, \bullet_2)$, $(Q, \bullet_3)$ have the same period factor of degree p for every positive integer p, and we need only to calculate the period factors probability distribution of $(Q, \bullet_0)$.

The column permutations of $(Q, \bullet_0)$ are $\sigma_0 = \tau_5$, $\sigma_1 = \tau_{12}$, $\sigma_2 = \tau_{20}$, $\sigma_3 = \tau_{11}$. The permutation multiplications $\sigma_i \tau_j$ ($0 \leq i \leq 3$, $1 \leq j \leq 24$) are shown in Table 4. Let $S = \{\sigma_0, \sigma_1, \sigma_2, \sigma_3\}$, and denote $S^p = \{\sigma_{i_p}\sigma_{i_{p-1}} \cdots \sigma_{i_1} : 1 \le i_1, i_2, \cdots, i_p \le 4\}$ be a **multi-set**, then it is easy to get

$$
\begin{cases}
S^2 = \{\tau_1, \tau_2, \tau_3, \tau_6, \tau_7, \tau_9, \tau_{10}, \tau_{13}, \tau_{14}, \tau_{16}, \tau_{17}, \tau_{18}, \tau_{19}, \tau_{21}, \tau_{23}, \tau_{24}\}, \\
S^3 = 2 \cdot S^2 \cup 4 \cdot \{\tau_4, \tau_5, \tau_8, \tau_{11}, \tau_{12}, \tau_{15}, \tau_{20}, \tau_{22}\}.
\end{cases}
\tag{3.1}
$$

For any positive integer p, denote

$$
S^p = \{n_i^{(p)} \cdot \tau_i \mid i = 1, 2, \cdots, 24\}.
$$

From Table 4 we have the recursion Eq. (3.2).

Table 4. Permutation multiplication table

·	τ_1	τ_2	τ_3	τ_4	τ_5	τ_6	τ_7	τ_8	τ_9	τ_{10}	τ_{11}	τ_{12}
σ_0	τ_5	τ_8	τ_9	τ_{18}	τ_1	τ_{14}	τ_{15}	τ_2	τ_3	τ_{19}	τ_{23}	τ_{21}
σ_1	τ_{12}	τ_{22}	τ_7	τ_3	τ_{19}	τ_{21}	τ_4	τ_{14}	τ_{16}	τ_{17}	τ_9	τ_{13}
σ_2	τ_{20}	τ_{15}	τ_{10}	τ_{16}	τ_{17}	τ_{13}	τ_8	τ_{21}	τ_6	τ_{24}	τ_7	τ_2
σ_3	τ_{11}	τ_4	τ_{23}	τ_6	τ_{24}	τ_2	τ_{22}	τ_{13}	τ_{18}	τ_1	τ_{10}	τ_{14}
·	τ_{13}	τ_{14}	τ_{15}	τ_{16}	τ_{17}	τ_{18}	τ_{19}	τ_{20}	τ_{21}	τ_{22}	τ_{23}	τ_{24}
σ_0	τ_{24}	τ_6	τ_7	τ_{20}	τ_{22}	τ_4	τ_{10}	τ_{16}	τ_{12}	τ_{17}	τ_{11}	τ_{13}
σ_1	τ_1	τ_{18}	τ_{10}	τ_{11}	τ_{15}	τ_8	τ_{23}	τ_6	τ_{20}	τ_{24}	τ_5	τ_2
σ_2	τ_{19}	τ_3	τ_{23}	τ_5	τ_4	τ_{22}	τ_9	τ_{18}	τ_{11}	τ_1	τ_{12}	τ_{14}
σ_3	τ_{17}	τ_{16}	τ_9	τ_{12}	τ_8	τ_{15}	τ_7	τ_3	τ_5	τ_{19}	τ_{20}	τ_{21}

$$
\begin{cases}
n_1^{(p+1)} = n_5^{(p)} + n_{13}^{(p)} + n_{22}^{(p)} + n_{10}^{(p)}, & n_{13}^{(p+1)} = n_{24}^{(p)} + n_{12}^{(p)} + n_6^{(p)} + n_8^{(p)}, \\
n_2^{(p+1)} = n_8^{(p)} + n_{24}^{(p)} + n_{12}^{(p)} + n_6^{(p)}, & n_{14}^{(p+1)} = n_6^{(p)} + n_8^{(p)} + n_{24}^{(p)} + n_{12}^{(p)}, \\
n_3^{(p+1)} = n_9^{(p)} + n_4^{(p)} + n_{14}^{(p)} + n_{20}^{(p)}, & n_{15}^{(p+1)} = n_7^{(p)} + n_{17}^{(p)} + n_2^{(p)} + n_{18}^{(p)}, \\
n_4^{(p+1)} = n_{18}^{(p)} + n_7^{(p)} + n_{17}^{(p)} + n_2^{(p)}, & n_{16}^{(p+1)} = n_{20}^{(p)} + n_9^{(p)} + n_4^{(p)} + n_{14}^{(p)}, \\
n_5^{(p+1)} = n_1^{(p)} + n_{23}^{(p)} + n_{16}^{(p)} + n_{21}^{(p)}, & n_{17}^{(p+1)} = n_{22}^{(p)} + n_{10}^{(p)} + n_5^{(p)} + n_{13}^{(p)}, \\
n_6^{(p+1)} = n_{14}^{(p)} + n_{20}^{(p)} + n_9^{(p)} + n_4^{(p)}, & n_{18}^{(p+1)} = n_4^{(p)} + n_{14}^{(p)} + n_{20}^{(p)} + n_9^{(p)}, \\
n_7^{(p+1)} = n_{15}^{(p)} + n_3^{(p)} + n_{11}^{(p)} + n_{19}^{(p)}, & n_{19}^{(p+1)} = n_{10}^{(p)} + n_5^{(p)} + n_{13}^{(p)} + n_{22}^{(p)}, \\
n_8^{(p+1)} = n_2^{(p)} + n_{18}^{(p)} + n_7^{(p)} + n_{17}^{(p)}, & n_{20}^{(p+1)} = n_{16}^{(p)} + n_{21}^{(p)} + n_1^{(p)} + n_{23}^{(p)}, \\
n_9^{(p+1)} = n_3^{(p)} + n_{11}^{(p)} + n_{15}^{(p)} + n_{15}^{(p)}, & n_{21}^{(p+1)} = n_{12}^{(p)} + n_6^{(p)} + n_8^{(p)} + n_{24}^{(p)}, \\
n_{10}^{(p+1)} = n_{19}^{(p)} + n_{15}^{(p)} + n_3^{(p)} + n_{11}^{(p)}, & n_{22}^{(p+1)} = n_{17}^{(p)} + n_2^{(p)} + n_{18}^{(p)} + n_7^{(p)}, \\
n_{11}^{(p+1)} = n_{23}^{(p)} + n_{16}^{(p)} + n_{21}^{(p)} + n_1^{(p)}, & n_{23}^{(p+1)} = n_{11}^{(p)} + n_{19}^{(p)} + n_{15}^{(p)} + n_3^{(p)}, \\
n_{12}^{(p+1)} = n_{21}^{(p)} + n_1^{(p)} + n_{23}^{(p)} + n_{16}^{(p)}, & n_{24}^{(p+1)} = n_{13}^{(p)} + n_{22}^{(p)} + n_{10}^{(p)} + n_5^{(p)}.
\end{cases}
\tag{3.2}
$$

From Eq. (3.1) we have

$$
n_i^{(2)} = \begin{cases}
1, & i \in \{1, 2, 3, 6, 7, 9, 10, 13, 14, 16, 17, 18, 19, 21, 23, 24\}, \\
0, & i \in \{4, 5, 8, 11, 12, 15, 20, 22\}.
\end{cases}
$$

$$n_i^{(3)} = \begin{cases} 2, i \in \{1,2,3,6,7,9,10,13,14,16,17,18,19,21,23,24\}, \\ 4, i \in \{4,5,8,11,12,15,20,22\}. \end{cases}$$

Let

$$N_1 = \{1,2,3,6,7,9,10,13,14,16,17,18,19,21,23,24\},$$
$$N_2 = \{4,5,8,11,12,15,20,22\}.$$

If

$$n_i^{(p)} = \begin{cases} a(p), i \in N_1, \\ b(p), i \in N_2, \end{cases}$$

then from Eq. (3.2) we obtain

$$n_i^{(p+1)} = \begin{cases} 2a(p) + 2b(p), i \in N_1, \\ 4a(p), \quad\quad\quad i \in N_2. \end{cases}$$

So, we have

$$\begin{cases} a(p+1) = 2a(p) + 2b(p), \\ b(p+1) = 4a(p), \\ a(3) = 2, \\ b(3) = 4. \end{cases} \tag{3.3}$$

The solution of Eq. (3.3) is

$$a(p) = \begin{cases} 2^{p-2}\left(1 + \sum\limits_{i=0}^{(p-4)/2} 2^{2i+1}\right), & \text{if } p \geq 4 \text{ is even}, \\ 2^{p-2}\sum\limits_{i=0}^{(p-3)/2} 2^{2i}, & \text{if } p \geq 5 \text{ is odd}, \end{cases} \tag{3.4}$$

$$b(p) = \begin{cases} 2^{p-1}\sum\limits_{i=0}^{(p-4)/2} 2^{2i}, & \text{if } p \geq 4 \text{ is even}, \\ 2^{p-1}\left(1 + \sum\limits_{i=0}^{(p-5)/2} 2^{2i+1}\right), & \text{if } p \geq 5 \text{ is odd}, \end{cases} \tag{3.5}$$

Suppose the type of τ_i is $1^{\lambda_{i1}}2^{\lambda_{i2}}3^{\lambda_{i3}}4^{\lambda_{i4}}$ ($i = 1,2,\cdots,24$). Applying Theorem 4, when $p \geq 4$ is even we have

$$P(f_{\bullet_0}^{(p)} = 1) = \frac{1}{4^{p+1}} \sum_{i=1}^{24} n_i^{(p)} \lambda_{i1}$$
$$= \frac{1}{4^{p+1}}\left(16a(p) + 8b(p)\right)$$
$$= \frac{1}{4}$$

$$P(f_{\bullet_0}^{(p)} = 2) = \frac{2}{4^{p+1}} \sum_{i=1}^{24} n_i^{(p)} \lambda_{i2}$$
$$= \frac{2}{4^{p+1}}\left(10a(p) + 2b(p)\right)$$
$$= \frac{1}{4} + \frac{1}{2^{p+2}}$$

$$P(f_{\bullet_0}^{(p)} = 3) = \frac{3}{4^{p+1}} \sum_{i=1}^{24} n_i^{(p)} \lambda_{i3}$$

$$= \frac{3}{4^{p+1}} \Big(4a(p) + 4b(p) \Big)$$

$$= \frac{1}{4} - \frac{1}{2^{p+2}}$$

$$P(f_{\bullet_0}^{(p)} = 4) = \frac{4}{4^{p+1}} \sum_{i=1}^{24} n_i^{(p)} \lambda_{i4}$$

$$= \frac{4}{4^{p+1}} \Big(4a(p) + 2b(p) \Big)$$

$$= \frac{1}{4}$$

So, the probability distribution of $f_{\bullet_0}^{(p)}$ is

$$\begin{pmatrix} 1 & 2 & 3 & 4 \\ \frac{1}{4} & \frac{1}{4} + \frac{1}{2^{p+2}} & \frac{1}{4} - \frac{1}{2^{p+2}} & \frac{1}{4} \end{pmatrix}$$

when $p \geq 4$ is even (it is also true when $p = 2$).

Similarly, we can get the probability distribution of $f_{\bullet_0}^{(p)}$ is

$$\begin{pmatrix} 1 & 2 & 3 & 4 \\ \frac{1}{4} & \frac{1}{4} - \frac{1}{2^{p+2}} & \frac{1}{4} + \frac{1}{2^{p+2}} & \frac{1}{4} \end{pmatrix}$$

when $p \geq 1$ is odd. So, the probability distribution of $f_{\bullet_0} = \lim_{p \to \infty} f_{\bullet_0}^{(p)}$ is

$$\begin{pmatrix} 1 & 2 & 3 & 4 \\ \frac{1}{4} & \frac{1}{4} & \frac{1}{4} & \frac{1}{4} \end{pmatrix}$$

4   The Period Probabilities of Edon80

Every application of an e-transformation in Edon80 can be viewed as a random variable ξ that receives values from the set $\{1, 2, 3, 4\}$. Since Edon80 has 80 e-transformations, we have 80 random variables $\xi_1, \xi_2, \cdots, \xi_{80}$ and every ξ_i ($1 \leq i \leq 80$) has the same probability distribution as $f_{\bullet_0}^{(p)}$ with $p \geq 4$ and approximately the distribution of $f_{\bullet_0}$:

$$\begin{pmatrix} 1 & 2 & 3 & 4 \\ \frac{1}{4} & \frac{1}{4} & \frac{1}{4} & \frac{1}{4} \end{pmatrix}$$

Denote Y_{80} the period of the sequence get by 80 e-transformations to the initial sequence, then $Y_{80} = \frac{1}{2} \cdot 4\xi_1\xi_2 \cdots \xi_{80}$.

In a process of 80 e-transformations in Edon80, let $r_k = |\{\xi_i \mid \xi_i = k, 1 \leq i \leq 80\}|$ for $k = 1, 2, 3, 4$ and suppose that $Y_{80} \leq 2^r$, then $2 \cdot 1^{r_1} 2^{r_2} 3^{r_3} 4^{r_4} \leq 2^r$, i.e.,

$$r_2 + \log_2 3 r_3 + 2r_4 \leq r - 1 \tag{4.1}$$

Each ξ_i has four possibilities, so, the probability of the event $Y_{80} \leq 2^r$

$$P(Y_{80} \leq 2^r) = \frac{1}{4^{80}} \sum_{(r_1, r_2, r_3) \in R} \binom{80}{r_2} \binom{80 - r_2}{r_3} \binom{80 - r_2 - r_3}{r_4} \tag{4.2}$$

Where R is the solution set of inequation (4.1). Apply Eq. (4.2) we get the period probabilities of Y_{80} shown in Table 5, it ia quite different with the probabilities shown in Table 1. Compared with Table 2, the probabilities in Table 5 are smaller when the upper bounds of the period are large, and are larger when the upper bounds are small.

Table 5. Periods probabilities of Edon80

Periods less then	Probability	Period less then	Probability
2^{161}	1	2^{52}	$2^{-29.164}$
2^{100}	0.8611	2^{48}	$2^{-34.514}$
2^{80}	$2^{-5.019}$	2^{44}	$2^{-40.391}$
2^{76}	$2^{-7.118}$	2^{40}	$2^{-46.829}$
2^{72}	$2^{-9.649}$	2^{36}	$2^{-53.863}$
2^{68}	$2^{-12.625}$	2^{32}	$2^{-61.530}$
2^{64}	$2^{-16.055}$	2^{28}	$2^{-69.895}$
2^{60}	$2^{-19.949}$	2^{24}	$2^{-79.076}$
2^{56}	$2^{-24.316}$	2^{20}	$2^{-89.237}$

5   Order 4 Quasigroups Suitable for E-Transformations

5.1   The Column Conjugate Class of $L_{\#61}$

Let $M_4 = \{6, 30, 56, 76, 98, 122, 153, 177, 207, 231, 249, 277, 310, 330, 360, 384, 402, 426, 434, 458, 482, 510, 536, 560\}$,

$M_5 = \{8, 32, 50, 74, 104, 124, 162, 186, 210, 238, 264, 288, 289, 313, 339, 367, 391, 415, 453, 473, 503, 527, 545, 569\}$;

$M_6 = \{13, 39, 59, 84, 112, 134, 164, 190, 211, 233, 260, 283, 291, 316, 341, 363, 386, 412, 446, 468, 496, 519, 539, 565\}$;

$M_7 = \{16, 36, 62, 86, 106, 130, 168, 188, 216, 240, 258, 282, 297, 321, 351, 375, 393, 421, 435, 459, 487, 511, 529, 557\}$;

$M_8 = \{17, 41, 67, 95, 119, 143, 151, 175, 193, 217, 247, 267, 300, 328, 346, 370, 400, 424, 455, 479, 501, 521, 547, 571\}$;

$M_9 = \{19, 47, 65, 89, 117, 141, 155, 183, 201, 225, 255, 279, 296, 320, 338,$
$362, 390, 410, 448, 472, 492, 516, 542, 562\}$;

$M_{10} = \{20, 48, 66, 90, 118, 142, 156, 184, 202, 226, 256, 280, 295, 319, 337,$
$361, 389, 409, 447, 471, 491, 515, 541, 561\}$;

$M_{11} = \{22, 44, 69, 91, 114, 137, 159, 181, 205, 230, 254, 276, 301, 323, 347,$
$372, 396, 418, 440, 463, 486, 508, 533, 555\}$.

Then $\mathcal{A}_i = \{L_{\#m} \mid m \in M_i\}$ $(4 \le i \le 11)$ are eight different column isomorphism classes. It can be easily check that

$$L_{\#61} = \tau_{10} L_{\#6} \tau_{10}^{-1} = \tau_6 L_{\#74} \tau_6^{-1} = \tau_{20} L_{\#565} \tau_{20}^{-1} = \tau_2 L_{\#321} \tau_2^{-1}$$
$$= \tau_9 L_{\#175} \tau_9^{-1} = \tau_{16} L_{\#472} \tau_{16}^{-1} = \tau_7 L_{\#118} \tau_7^{-1} = \tau_8 L_{\#418} \tau_8^{-1},$$

where $\tau_{10}, \tau_6, \tau_{20}, \tau_2, \tau_9, \tau_{16}, \tau_7, \tau_8$ are from Table 3. So, $\mathcal{A}_i \wr \mathcal{A}_0$ for $1 \le i \le 11$, where $\mathcal{A}_i$ $(i = 0, 1, 2, 3)$ are the column isomorphism classes in Sect. 3. This implies that $\bigcup_{i=0}^{11} \mathcal{A}_i \subseteq \mathcal{C}(L_{\#61})$, the column conjugate class of $L_{\#61}$.

The proof of $\bigcup_{i=0}^{11} \mathcal{A}_i \supseteq \mathcal{C}(L_{\#61})$ is tedious, but, by a computer program, it can be easily check that except the Latin squares in $\bigcup_{i=0}^{11} \mathcal{A}_i$, there is no other Latin square has the same period factor of degree p as that of $L_{\#61}$ has for every positive integer p. This conclude that $\bigcup_{i=0}^{11} \mathcal{A}_i = \mathcal{C}(L_{\#61})$ and there are just 288 Latin squares have the same period factor of degree p shown in Sect. 3.

There are 576 quasigroups of order 4. By the experiments of Gligoroski et al. [8], most suitable for Edon80 are the following 64 (given by their lexicographic numbers): 12, 19, 23, 30, 32, 58, 59, 61, 74, 76, 85, 90, 115, 117, 134, 136, 143, 149, 155, 158, 162, 167, 173, 177, 188, 190, 204, 205, 226, 231, 241, 255, 265, 286, 319, 320, 339, 350, 358, 362, 366, 384, 386, 391, 394, 404, 413, 419, 424, 428, 446, 459, 487, 493, 496, 503, 512, 513, 519, 530, 541, 558, 562, 564. These Latin squares are all in $\mathcal{C}(L_{\#61})$. By the above discussion, all the Latin square in the column conjugate class $\mathcal{C}(L_{\#61})$ have the same "period property".

5.2 Quasigroups of Order 4 with Better Period Factors

Figure 4 is the quasigroup $(Q, *)$ with multiplication table $L_{\#309}$. The column permutations are $\sigma_0 = (02)(13)$, $\sigma_1 = 1$, $\sigma_2 = (0123)$, $\sigma_3 = (0321)$. Since $\langle \sigma_0, \sigma_1, \sigma_2, \sigma_3 \rangle = \{\sigma_0, \sigma_1, \sigma_2, \sigma_3\}$, we have

$$\{\sigma_0, \sigma_1, \sigma_2, \sigma_3\}^p = 4^{p-1}\{\sigma_0, \sigma_1, \sigma_2, \sigma_3\},$$

$$P(f_*^{(p)} = 1) = \frac{1}{4^p+1} 4^{p-1} \cdot 4 = \frac{1}{4},$$

$$P(f_*^{(p)} = 2) = \frac{2}{4^p+1} 4^{p-1} \cdot 2 = \frac{1}{4},$$

$$P(f_*^{(p)} = 3) = \frac{3}{4^p+1} 4^{p-1} \cdot 0 = 0,$$

$$P(f_*^{(p)} = 4) = \frac{4}{4^p+1} 4^{p-1} \cdot 2 = \frac{1}{2},$$

and the probability distribution of $f_*^{(p)}$ is

$$\begin{pmatrix} 1 & 2 & 4 \\ \frac{1}{4} & \frac{1}{4} & \frac{1}{2} \end{pmatrix}$$

for all positive integer p. The expected value $E(f_*^{(p)}) = 2.75$ is quite larger than that of $f_{\bullet 0}^{(p)}$:

$$E(f_{\bullet 0}^{(p)}) = \begin{cases} 2.5 - \frac{1}{2^{p+2}}, & \text{if } p \text{ is even,} \\ 2.5 + \frac{1}{2^{p+2}}, & \text{if } p \text{ is odd.} \end{cases}$$

Let $N_1 =\{5, 29, 55, 75, 97, 121, 154, 178, 208, 232, 250, 278, 309, 329, 359,$ $383, 401, 425, 433, 457, 481, 509, 535, 559\}$,

$N_2 =\{2, 25, 52, 78, 99, 125, 148, 171, 198, 224, 245, 271, 307, 333, 356, 382,$ $407, 432, 449, 475, 498, 524, 549, 574\}$,

$N_3 =\{7, 49, 31, 73, 103, 123, 161, 185, 209, 237, 263, 287, 290, 314, 340, 368,$ $392, 416, 454, 474, 504, 528, 546, 570\}$,

Then $\mathcal{B}_i = \{L_{\#m} \mid m \in N_i\}$ $(1 \le i \le 3)$ are eight different column isomorphism classes. It can be easily check that

$$L_{\#309} = \tau_4 L_{\#171} \tau_4^{-1} = \tau_7 L_{\#454} \tau_7^{-1}.$$

So, $\mathcal{B}_1 \wr \mathcal{B}_2 \wr \mathcal{B}_3$. It can be proved that $\mathcal{C}(L_{\#309}) = \mathcal{B}_1 \cup \mathcal{B}_2 \cup \mathcal{B}_3$, and so there are just 72 Latin squares of order 4 have period factors the same as $L_{\#309}$.

*	0	1	2	3
0	2	0	1	3
1	3	1	2	0
2	0	2	3	1
3	1	3	0	2

Fig. 4. Quasigroup of $L_{\#309}$

6   Conclusion

Based on the theory of permutation groups, we can give a precise mathematical description of the periods of the keystreams of Edon80.

There are 576 quasigroups of order 4. By the experiments of Gligoroski et al. [8], 384 of them are suitable, and 64 of them are very suitable. By our investigations, all the four quasigroup use in Edon80 are in the same column conjugate class $\mathcal{C}(L_{\#61})$ which contains 288 quasigroups, all the 288 quasigroups have the same period probability distributions and the same period expected value approximately equal to 2.5.

There are 72 quasigroups in column conjugate class $\mathcal{C}(L_{\#309})$ and they have the same period expected value 2.75. From the point of view of periods, the quasigroups in $\mathcal{C}(L_{\#309})$ are more suitable for key stream generators.

Acknowledgement. The author would like to acknowledge the support of the National Natural Science Foundation of China under Grant No. 61373007 and Zhejiang Provincial Natural Science Foundation of China under Grant No. LY13F020039.

References

1. Dénes, J., Keedwell, A.D.: Latin Squares and Their Applications. Academic Press, New York (1974)
2. Gligoroski, D., Markovski, S., Kocarev, L., Gusev, M.: Edon80, eSTREAM, Report 2005/007 (2005)
3. Hong, J.: Remarks on the Period of Edon80, ECRYPT database, June 2005
4. Gligoroski, D., Markovski, S., Kocarev, L., Gusev, M.: Understanding Periods in Edon80, ECRYPT database, July 2005
5. Gligoroski, D., Markovski, S., Knapskog, S.J.: On periods of Edon-(2m, 2k) family of stream ciphers. In: The State of the Art of Stream Ciphers, Workshop Record, SASC 2006, Leuven, Belgium (2006)
6. Markovski, S., Gligoroski, D., Bakeva, V.: Quasigroup string processing: Part 1. Proc. of Maced. Acad. of Sci. Arts for Math. and Tech. Sci **XX 1–2**, 13–28 (1999)
7. Rotman, J.J.: Advanced Modern Algebra. Prentice Hall, Upper Saddle River (2002)
8. Gligoroski, D., Markovski, S., Knapskog, S.J.: The stream cipher Edon80. In: Robshaw, M., Billet, O. (eds.) New Stream Cipher Designs. LNCS, vol. 4986, pp. 152–169. Springer, Heidelberg (2008)

Cube Theory and Stable k-Error Linear Complexity for Periodic Sequences

Jianqin Zhou[1,3][✉], Wanquan Liu[1], and Guanglu Zhou[2]

[1] Department of Computing, Curtin University, Perth 6102, Australia
zhou9@yahoo.com, w.liu@curtin.edu.au
[2] Department of Mathematics and Statistics,
Curtin University, Perth 6102, Australia
g.zhou@curtin.edu.au
[3] School of Computer Science, Anhui University of Technology,
Ma'anshan 243032, China

Abstract. The linear complexity of a sequence has been used as an important measure of keystream strength, hence designing a sequence with high linear complexity and k-error linear complexity is a popular research topic in cryptography. In this paper, the concept of stable k-error linear complexity is proposed to study sequences with stable and large k-error linear complexity. In order to study linear complexity of binary sequences with period 2^n, a new tool called cube theory is developed. By using the cube theory, one can easily construct sequences with the maximum stable k-error linear complexity. For such purpose, we first prove that a binary sequence with period 2^n can be decomposed into some disjoint cubes. Second, it is proved that the maximum k-error linear complexity is $2^n - (2^l - 1)$ over all 2^n-periodic binary sequences, where $2^{l-1} \leq k < 2^l$. Finally, continuing the work of Kurosawa et al., a characterization is presented about the minimum number k for which the second decrease occurs in the k-error linear complexity of a 2^n-periodic binary sequence s.

Keywords: Periodic sequence · Linear complexity · k-error linear complexity · Stable k-error linear complexity · Cube theory

1 Introduction

It is well known that stream ciphers have broad applications in network security. The linear complexity of a sequence s, denoted as $L(s)$, is defined as the length of the shortest linear feedback shift register (LFSR) that can generate s. The concept of linear complexity is very useful in the study of the security for stream ciphers. A necessary condition for the security of a key stream generator is that it produces a sequence with large linear complexity. However, high linear complexity can not necessarily guarantee the sequence is secure. The linear complexity of some sequences is unstable. If a small number of changes to a sequence greatly

© Springer International Publishing Switzerland 2014
D. Lin et al. (Eds.): Inscrypt 2013, LNCS 8567, pp. 70–85, 2014.
DOI: 10.1007/978-3-319-12087-4_5

reduce its linear complexity, then the resulting key stream would be cryptographically weak. Ding, Xiao and Shan in their book [1] noticed this problem first, and presented the weight complexity and sphere complexity. Stamp and Martin [10] introduced k-error linear complexity, which is similar to the sphere complexity, and proposed the concept of k-error linear complexity profile. Suppose that s is a sequence over $GF(q)$ with period N. For $k(0 \leq k \leq N)$, the k-error linear complexity of s, denoted as $L_k(s)$, is defined as the smallest linear complexity that can be obtained when any k or fewer of the terms of the sequence are changed within one period. It is worthy to mention that $L_k(s) = \min\{SC_k(s), L(s)\}$, where $SC_k(s)$ is the sphere complexity and $L(s)$ is the linear complexity. Hence the k-error linear complexity is the minimum of the two complexities proposed earlier.

For small k, Niederreiter [9] presented some sequences over $GF(q)$ which possess high linear complexity and the k-error linear complexity. By using the generalized discrete Fourier transform, Hu and Feng [5] constructed some periodic sequences over $GF(q)$ which possess very large 1-error linear complexity.

One important result, proved by Kurosawa et al. in [6] is that the minimum number k for which the k-error linear complexity of a 2^n-periodic binary sequence s is strictly less than the linear complexity $L(s)$ is determined by $k_{\min} = 2^{W_H(2^n - L(s))}$, where $W_H(a)$ denotes the Hamming weight of the binary representation of an integer a. In [7], for the period length p^n, where p is an odd prime and 2 is a primitive root modulo p^2, the relationship is showed between the linear complexity and the minimum value k for which the k-error linear complexity is strictly less than the linear complexity. In [11], for sequences over $GF(q)$ with period $2p^n$, where p and q are odd primes, and q is a primitive root modulo p^2, the minimum value k is presented for which the k-error linear complexity is strictly less than the linear complexity. For $k = 1, 2$, Meidl [8] characterized the complete counting functions on the k-error linear complexity of 2^n-periodic binary sequences with the maximal possible linear complexity 2^n. Fu et al. [4] studied the linear complexity and the 1-error linear complexity of 2^n-periodic binary sequences, and then characterized such sequences with the 1-error linear complexity. For $k = 2, 3$, Zhu and Qi [13] further derived the complete counting functions on the k-error linear complexity of 2^n-periodic binary sequences with linear complexity $2^n - 1$. The complete counting functions for the number of 2^n-periodic binary sequences with the 3-error linear complexity are given by Zhou and Liu recently in [12].

The motivation of studying the stability of linear complexity is that changing a small number of elements in a sequence may lead to a sharp decline of its linear complexity. Therefore we really need to study such stable sequences in which even a small number of changes do not reduce their linear complexity. The stable k-error linear complexity is introduced in this paper to deal with this problem. Suppose that s is a sequence over $GF(q)$ with period N. For $k(0 \leq k \leq N)$, the k-error linear complexity of s is defined as stable when any k or fewer of the terms of the sequence are changed within one period, the linear complexity does not decline.

Algebra [4,7,8,13] and discrete Fourier transform [5] are two important tools to study the k-error linear complexity for periodic sequences. Etzion et al. [2] studied the sequences with only two k-error linear complexity values exactly, namely its k-error linear complexity is only $L(s)$ or 0. To further investigate this concept, we present a new tool called cube theory to study the stable k-error linear complexity of binary sequences with period 2^n. By using the cube theory, we are capable of investigating the k-error linear complexity for periodic sequences from a new perspective. One significant benefit is that one can construct sequences with the maximum stable k-error linear complexity. Some examples are also given to illustrate the approach. As a by product, it is proved that a binary sequence with period 2^n can be decomposed into some disjoint cubes. With such decomposition, it is proved that the maximum k-error linear complexity is $2^n - (2^l - 1)$ over all 2^n-periodic binary sequences, where $2^{l-1} \leq k < 2^l$. Continuing the work of Kurosawa et al. in [6] with different approaches, a characterization is presented about the minimum number k for which the second decrease occurs in the k-error linear complexity.

The rest of this paper is organized as follows. In Sect. 2, some preliminary results are presented. In Sect. 3, the definition of cube theory and our main results are presented. Our conclusion is presented in Sect. 4.

2   Preliminaries

We will consider sequences over $GF(q)$, which is the finite field of order q. Let $x = (x_1, x_2, \cdots, x_n)$ and $y = (y_1, y_2, \cdots, y_n)$ be vectors over $GF(q)$. Then we define

$$x + y = (x_1 + y_1, x_2 + y_2, \cdots, x_n + y_n).$$

The Hamming weight of an N-periodic sequence s is defined as the number of nonzero elements in per period of s, denoted by $W_H(s)$. Let s^N be one period of s. If $N = 2^n$, s^N is also denoted as $s^{(n)}$. The distance of two elements is defined as the difference of their indexes. Specifically, for an N-periodic sequence $s = \{s_0, s_1, s_2, s_3, \cdots, \}$, the distance of s_i, s_j is $j - i$, where $0 \leq i \leq j \leq N$.

The generating function of a sequence $s = \{s_0, s_1, s_2, s_3, \cdots, \}$ is defined by

$$s(x) = s_0 + s_1 x + s_2 x^2 + s_3 x^3 + \cdots = \sum_{i=0}^{\infty} s_i x^i$$

The generating function of a finite sequence $s^N = \{s_0, s_1, s_2, \cdots, s_{N-1}, \}$ is defined by $s^N(x) = s_0 + s_1 x + s_2 x^2 + \cdots + s_{N-1} x^{N-1}$. If s is a periodic sequence with the first period s^N, then,

$$s(x) = s^N(x)(1 + x^N + x^{2N} + \cdots) = \frac{s^N(x)}{1 - x^N}$$

$$= \frac{s^N(x)/\gcd(s^N(x), 1 - x^N)}{(1 - x^N)/\gcd(s^N(x), 1 - x^N)}$$

$$= \frac{g(x)}{f_s(x)}$$

where $f_s(x) = (1 - x^N)/\gcd(s^N(x), 1 - x^N), g(x) = s^N(x)/\gcd(s^N(x), 1 - x^N)$.

Obviously, $\gcd(g(x), f_s(x)) = 1, \deg(g(x)) < \deg(f_s(x))$. $f_s(x)$ is called the minimal polynomial of s, and the degree of $f_s(x)$ is called the linear complexity of s, that is $\deg(f_s(x)) = L(s)$.

Suppose that $N = 2^n$, then $1 - x^N = 1 - x^{2^n} = (1 - x)^{2^n} = (1 - x)^N$. Thus for binary sequences with period 2^n, to find its linear complexity is equivalent to computing the degree of factor $(1 - x)$ in $s^N(x)$.

For $k(0 \leq k \leq N)$, the k-error linear complexity of s is defined as stable when any k or fewer of the terms of the sequence are changed within one period, the linear complexity does not decline. Therefore, the k-error linear complexity of s is its linear complexity in this case.

The following three lemmas are well known results on 2^n-periodic binary sequences. Please refer to [4,8,12,13] for details.

Lemma 2.1. Suppose that s is a binary sequence with period $N = 2^n$, then $L(s) = N$ if and only if the Hamming weight of a period of the sequence is odd.

If an element one is removed from a sequence whose Hamming weight is odd, the Hamming weight of the sequence will be changed to even, so the main concern hereinafter is about sequences whose Hamming weights are even.

Lemma 2.2. Let s_1 and s_2 be binary sequences with period $N = 2^n$. If $L(s_1) \neq L(s_2)$, then $L(s_1 + s_2) = \max\{L(s_1), L(s_2)\}$; otherwise if $L(s_1) = L(s_2)$, then $L(s_1 + s_2) < L(s_1)$.

Suppose that the linear complexity of s can decrease when at least k elements of s are changed. By Lemma 2.2, the linear complexity of the binary sequence, in which elements at exactly those k positions are all nonzero, must be $L(s)$. Therefore, for the computation of the k-error linear complexity, we only need to find the binary sequence whose Hamming weight is minimum and its linear complexity is $L(s)$.

Lemma 2.3. Suppose that E_i is a 2^n-periodic binary sequence with one nonzero element at position i and 0 elsewhere in each period, $0 \leq i \leq N$. If $j - i = 2^r(1 + 2a), a \geq 0, 0 \leq i < j < N, r \geq 0$, then $L(E_i + E_j) = 2^n - 2^r$.

Denote E_{ij} by a binary sequence with period 2^n, and it has only 2 nonzero elements in a period. If there are only 2 adjacent positions with nonzero elements in E_{ij}, then its linear complexity is $2^n - 1$, namely E_{ij} is a sequence with even Hamming weight and the largest linear complexity. According to Lemma 2.2, if sequence s can be decomposed into the superposition of several E_{ij}s, in which each has linear complexity $2^n - 1$, and the number of E_{ij}s is odd, then $L(s) = 2^n - 1$. After a symbol of s is changed, its Hamming weight will be odd, so its linear complexity will be 2^n, namely the 1-error linear complexity of sequence s is $2^n - 1$.

Proposition 2.1. If s is a binary sequence with period 2^n, then its maximum 1-error linear complexity is $2^n - 1$.

In order to discuss the maximal 2-error linear complexity of a binary sequence with period 2^n, we now consider a binary sequence which has only 4 positions with nonzero elements. Please refer to [12] for the proof of Lemma 2.4.

Lemma 2.4. If s is a binary sequence with period $N = 2^n$ and there are only four non-zero elements, thus s can be decomposed into the superposition of E_{ij} and E_{kl}. Suppose that non-zero positions of E_{ij} are i and j with $j-i = 2^d(1+2u)$, and non-zero positions of E_{kl} are k and l with $l - k = 2^e(1 + 2v), i < k, k - i = 2c + 1$. If $d = e$, the linear complexity is $2^n - (2^d + 1)$, otherwise the linear complexity is $2^n - 2^{\min(d,e)}$.

More specifically, we have the following result.

Lemma 2.5. If s is a binary sequence with period 2^n and there are only 4 non-zero elements, and s can be decomposed into the superposition of E_{ij} and E_{kl}, in which each has linear complexity $2^n - 1$, then the linear complexity of s is $2^n - (2^d + 1)$ or $2^n - 2^d, d > 0$.

Proof. Suppose that the non-zero positions of E_{ij} are i and j, whose linear complexity is $2^n - 1, j - i = 2a + 1$, and non-zero positions of E_{kl} are k and l, whose linear complexity is also $2^n - 1$, $i < k, l - k = 2b + 1$.

Next we will investigate the problem with the following 6 cases:

(1) $i < k < l < j$, and $k - i = 2c$.
As $j - i = 2a + 1, l - k = 2b + 1$, so

$$j - l = 2a + 1 - (2b + 1 + 2c) = 2(a - b - c)$$

If $j - l = 2^d + 2u2^d, k - i = 2^e + 2v2^e$, without loss of generality, assume $d < e$, by Lemma 2.2, $L(s) = 2^n - 2^d, d > 0$.
If $d = e$, by Lemma 2.4, since $l - i = 2(b + c) + 1$, so $L(s) = 2^n - (2^d + 1)$.

(2) $i < k < l < j$, and $k - i = 2c + 1$.
As $j - i = 2a + 1, l - k = 2b + 1$, so $l - i = 2b + 1 + 2c + 1 = 2(b + c + 1), j - k = 2a + 1 - (2c + 1) = 2(a - c)$
If $j - k = 2^d + 2u2^d, l - i = 2^e + 2v2^e$, without loss of generality, assume $d < e$, by Lemma 2.2, $L(s) = 2^n - 2^d, d > 0$.
Since $k - i = 2c + 1$, by Lemma 2.4, if $d = e$, then $L(s) = 2^n - (2^d + 1)$.

(3) $i < k < j < l$, and $k - i = 2c$.
As $j - i = 2a + 1, l - k = 2b + 1$, so $j - k = 2a + 1 - 2c = 2(a - c) + 1, l - j = 2b + 1 - [2(a - c) + 1] = 2(b + c - a)$
If $l - j = 2^d + 2u2^d, k - i = 2^e + 2v2^e$, without loss of generality, assume $d < e$, by Lemma 2.2, $L(s) = 2^n - 2^d, d > 0$.
Since $j - i = 2a + 1$, by Lemma 2.4, if $d = e$, then $L(s) = 2^n - (2^d + 1)$.

(4) $i < k < j < l$, and $k - i = 2c + 1$.
As $j - i = 2a + 1, l - k = 2b + 1$, so $j - k = 2a + 1 - (2c + 1) = 2(a - c), l - i = 2b + 1 + 2c + 1 = 2(b + c + 1)$.
If $l - i = 2^d + 2u2^d, j - k = 2^e + 2v2^e$, without loss of generality, assume $d < e$, by Lemma 2.2, $L(s) = 2^n - 2^d, d > 0$.
Since $k - i = 2c + 1$, by Lemma 2.4, if $d = e$, then $L(s) = 2^n - (2^d + 1)$.

(5) $i < j < k < l$, and $k - i = 2c$.
As $j - i = 2a + 1, l - k = 2b + 1$, so $k - j = 2c - (2a + 1) = 2(c - a) - 1, l - j = 2b + 1 + [2(c - a) - 1] = 2(b + c - a)$

If $l - j = 2^d + 2u2^d, k - i = 2^e + 2v2^e$, without loss of generality, assume $d < e$, by Lemma 2.2, $L(s) = 2^n - 2^d, d > 0$.

Note that $j - i = 2a + 1$, by Lemma 2.4, if $d = e$, then $L(s) = 2^n - (2^d + 1)$.

(6) $i < j < k < l$, and $k - i = 2c + 1$.

As $j - i = 2a + 1, l - k = 2b + 1$, so $k - j = 2c + 1 - (2a + 1) = 2(c - a), l - i = 2b + 1 + 2c + 1 = 2(b + c + 1)$

If $l - i = 2^d + 2u2^d, k - j = 2^e + 2v2^e$, without loss of generality, assume $d < e$, by Lemma 2.2, $L(s) = 2^n - 2^d, d > 0$.

Note that $k - i = 2c + 1$, by Lemma 2.4, if $d = e$, then $L(s) = 2^n - (2^d + 1)$.

Based on above 6 cases, we conclude that the lemma can be established. $\square$

Corollary 2.1. Suppose that s is a binary sequence with period 2^n and there are only 4 non-zero elements, and s can be decomposed into the superposition of E_{ij} and E_{kl}. If non-zero positions of E_{ij} are i and $j, j - i$ is an odd number, and non-zero positions of E_{kl} are k and $l, l - k$ is also an odd number, and $i < k, k - i = 4c + 2, |l - j| = 4d + 2$, or $|k - j| = 4c + 2, |l - i| = 4d + 2$, then the linear complexity of s is $2^n - 3$.

Proof. According to case (1), (3) and (5) of Lemma 2.5, if $k - i = 4c + 2, |l - j| = 4d + 2$, then $|l - j| = 2 + 4d, k - i = 2 + 4c$. By Lemma 2.4, noting that $j - i = 2a + 1$, so $L(s) = 2^n - (2 + 1)$.

According to case (2), (4) and (6) of Lemma 2.5, if $|k - j| = 4c + 2, |l - i| = 4d + 2$, then it is easy to know that $k - i$ is odd, thus $|k - j| = 2 + 4c, |l - i| = 2 + 4d$. By Lemma 2.4, $L(s) = 2^n - (2 + 1)$. $\square$

Corollary 2.2. If s is a binary sequence with period 2^n and there are only 4 non-zero elements, and s can be decomposed into the sum of two E_{ij}, in which each has linear complexity $2^n - 2$, then the linear complexity of s is $2^n - (2 + 1)$ or $2^n - (2^d + 1)2, d > 0$ or $2^n - 2^d, d > 1$.

Proof. Suppose that non-zero positions of the first E_{ij} are i and $j, j - i = 4a + 2$, and non-zero positions of the second E_{ij} are k and $l, l - k = 4b + 2$, where $i < k$.

If $k - i = 2c + 1$, according to Lemma 2.4, then $L(s) = 2^n - (2 + 1)$.

If $k - i = 2c$, the corresponding polynomial of $E_i + E_j + E_k + E_l$ is given by

$x^i + x^j + x^k + x^l = x^i(1 + x^{j-i} + x^{k-i} + x^{l-k+k-i})$

Therefore, we only need to consider

$1 + x^{j-i} + x^{k-i} + x^{l-k+k-i} = 1 + (x^2)^{2a+1} + (x^2)^c + (x^2)^{2b+1+c} = 1 + y^{2a+1} + y^c + y^{2b+1+c}$

According to Lemma 2.5, $L(s) = 2^n - (2^d + 1)2, d > 0$ or $2^n - 2^d, d > 1$. $\square$

Now we can obtain the following conclusions according to Lemma 2.5 and Corollary 2.2.

Proposition 2.2. Suppose that s is a binary sequence with period 2^n and there are four non-zero elements, then the necessary and sufficient conditions for the linear complexity of s being $2^n - 3$ are given by: s can be decomposed into the superposition of E_{ik} and E_{jl}, in which each has linear complexity $2^n - 2$.

Further, if non-zero positions of E_{ik} are i and k, with $k - i = 4c + 2$, and non-zero positions of the second E_{jl} are j and l, with $l - j = 4d + 2$, where $i < j$, then $j - i = 2a + 1$(or $|l - k| = 2b + 1$ or $|l - i| = 2e + 1$ or $|k - j| = 2f + 1$).

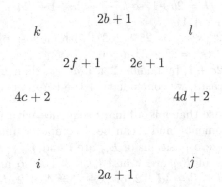

Fig. 1. A graphic illustration of Proposition 2.2

We can also illustrate this with a graph in Fig. 1. The only 4 non-zero positions of sequence s are i, j, k and l. As $k - i = 4c + 2$, $l - j = 4d + 2$, and $j - i = 2a + 1$, so $l - k = l - j + j - i - (k - i) = 4d + 2 + 2a + 1 - (4c + 2)$ is odd. Next we give a result on the stable sequence.

Proposition 2.3. Suppose that s is a binary sequence with period 2^n and its Hamming weight is even, then the maximum stable 2-error linear complexity of s is $2^n - 3$.

Proof. Assume that $L(s) = 2^n - 1$, then s can be decomposed into the sum of several E_{ij}s and the number of E_{ij}s with linear complexity $2^n - 1$ is odd. According to Lemma 2.2, if an E_{ij} with linear complexity $2^n - 1$ is removed, then the linear complexity of s will be less than $2^n - 1$, namely the 2-error linear complexity of s is less than $2^n - 1$.

Assume that $L(s) = 2^n - 2$, then s can be decomposed into the sum of several E_{ij}s and the number of E_{ij}s with linear complexity $2^n - 2$ is odd. If an E_{ij} with linear complexity $2^n - 2$ is removed, then the linear complexity of s will be less than $2^n - 2$, namely the 2-error linear complexity of s is less than $2^n - 2$.

Assume that $L(s) = 2^n - 3$, without loss of generality, here we only discuss the case that s has 4 non-zero elements: e_i, e_j, e_k and e_l, and $L(E_i + E_j + E_k + E_l) = 2^n - 3$. If any two of them are removed, by Proposition 2.2, the linear complexity of remaining elements of the sequence is $2^n - 1$ or $2^n - 2$. From Fig. 1, after e_i and e_l are changed to zero, we can see that the linear complexity of the sequence composed by e_j and e_k is $2^n - 1$.

If the position of one element from e_i, e_j, e_k and e_l is changed, then there exist two elements, of which the position difference remains unchanged as odd, thus $L(s) \geq 2^n - 3$.

If two nonzero elements are added to the position outside e_i, e_j, e_k and e_l, namely an E_{ij} with linear complexity $2^n - 2^d$ is added to sequence s, according to Lemma 2.2, the linear complexity will be $2^n - 1$, $2^n - 2$ or $2^n - 3$.

Summarizing all above discussions, the proof is completed.   □

The following is an example to illustrate Proposition 2.3.

The linear complexity of $11110 \cdots 0$ is $2^n - 3$

The linear complexity of $01010 \cdots 0$ or $10100 \cdots 0$ is $2^n - 2$

The linear complexity of $01100 \cdots 0$ or $10010 \cdots 0$ is $2^n - 1$

If two additional nonzero elements are added to $11110 \cdots 0$, namely an E_{ij} whose linear complexity is $2^n - 2^d$ is added to it, according to Lemma 2.2, the linear complexity will become $2^n - 1$, $2^n - 2$ or $2^n - 3$.

For instance, suppose that $1110 \cdots 010 \cdots 0$ is the addition of $11110 \cdots 0$ and $0001 \cdots 010 \cdots 0$. We here only consider the case that the position difference of the last two nonzero elements is $2c + 1$. According to case (5) of Lemma 2.5, $j - i = 1, l - k = 2c + 1$, so $k - j = 1, l - j = 2(c + 1)$.

Noticed that $k - i = 2$, if $l - j = 2^d(2u + 1)$, according to Lemma 2.2, $L(s) = 2^n - 2$ when $d > 1$.

If $d = 1$, since $j - i = 1$, according to Lemma 2.4, $L(s) = 2^n - 3$.

3   Cube Theory and Main Results

Before presenting main results, we first give a special case.

Lemma 3.1. Suppose that s is a binary sequence with period 2^n and there are 8 non-zero elements, thus s can be decomposed into the superposition of E_{ij}, E_{kl}, E_{mn} and E_{pq}. Suppose that non-zero positions of E_{ij} are i and $j, j - i = 2a + 1$, and non-zero positions of E_{kl} are k and $l, l - k = 2b + 1$, and $k - i = 4c + 2, l - j = 4d + 2$, and non-zero positions of E_{mn} are m and n, non-zero positions of E_{pq} are p and q, and $m - i = 4 + 8u, n - j = 4 + 8v, p - k = 4 + 8w, q - l = 4 + 8y$, where a, b, c, d, u, v, w and y are all non-negative integers, then the linear complexity of s is $2^n - 7$.

Proof. According to Corollary 2.1, $L(E_i + E_j + E_k + E_l) = 2^n - 3$.

As $m - n = m - i - (n - j) - (j - i)$, $p - q = p - k - (q - l) - (l - k)$, thus both $m - n$ and $p - q$ are odd numbers.

As $p - m = p - k - (m - i) + (k - i)$, $q - n = q - l - (n - j) + (l - j)$, thus both $p - m$ and $q - n$ are multiples of 2, but not multiples of 4. According to Corollary 2.1, $L(E_m + E_n + E_p + E_q) = 2^n - 3$.

Similar to the proof of Lemma 2.4 [12], the corresponding polynomial of $E_i + E_k + E_m + E_p$ is given by

$$x^i + x^k + x^m + x^p$$
$$= x^i(1 - x^4)[(1 + x^4 + x^{2 \cdot 4} + \cdots + x^{2u \cdot 4})$$
$$\qquad + x^{k-i}(1 + x^4 + x^{2 \cdot 4} + \cdots + x^{2w \cdot 4})]$$
$$= x^i(1 - x^4)[1 + x^{k-i} + (x^4 + x^{2 \cdot 4} + \cdots + x^{2u \cdot 4})$$
$$\qquad + x^{k-i}(x^4 + x^{2 \cdot 4} + \cdots + x^{2w \cdot 4})]$$

$$= x^i(1-x^4)[1 + x^{4c+2} + (x^4 + x^{2\cdot4} + \cdots + x^{2u\cdot4})$$
$$+x^{k-i}(x^4 + x^{2\cdot4} + \cdots + x^{2w\cdot4})]$$
$$= x^i(1-x)^6[(1 + x^2 + x^4 + \cdots + x^{4c})$$
$$+(x^4 + x^{3\cdot4} + \cdots + x^{(2u-1)\cdot4})(1+x)^2$$
$$+x^{k-i}(x^4 + x^{3\cdot4} + \cdots + x^{(2w-1)\cdot4})(1+x)^2]$$

The corresponding polynomial of $E_j + E_l + E_n + E_q$ is given by

$$x^j + x^l + x^n + x^q$$
$$= x^j(1-x^4)[(1 + x^4 + x^{2\cdot4} + \cdots + x^{2v\cdot4})$$
$$+x^{l-j}(1 + x^4 + x^{2\cdot4} + \cdots + x^{2y\cdot4})]$$
$$= x^j(1-x)^6[(1 + x^2 + x^4 + \cdots + x^{4d})$$
$$+(x^4 + x^{3\cdot4} + \cdots + x^{(2v-1)\cdot4})(1+x)^2$$
$$+x^{l-j}(x^4 + x^{3\cdot4} + \cdots + x^{(2y-1)\cdot4})(1+x)^2]$$

The corresponding polynomial of $E_i + E_j + E_k + E_l + E_m + E_n + E_p + E_q$ is given by

$$x^i + x^j + x^k + x^l + x^m + x^n + x^p + x^q$$
$$= x^i(1-x)^6\{(1 + x^2 + x^4 + \cdots + x^{4c})$$
$$+(x^4 + x^{3\cdot4} + \cdots + x^{(2u-1)\cdot4})(1+x)^2$$
$$+x^{k-i}(x^4 + x^{3\cdot4} + \cdots + x^{(2w-1)\cdot4})(1+x)^2$$
$$+x^{j-i}[(1 + x^2 + x^4 + \cdots + x^{4d})$$
$$+(x^4 + x^{3\cdot4} + \cdots + x^{(2v-1)\cdot4})(1+x)^2$$
$$+x^{l-j}(x^4 + x^{3\cdot4} + \cdots + x^{(2y-1)\cdot4})(1+x)^2]\}$$
$$= x^i(1-x)^6\{1 + x^{j-i} + (x^2 + x^4 + \cdots + x^{4c})$$
$$+(x^4 + x^{3\cdot4} + \cdots + x^{(2u-1)\cdot4})(1+x)^2$$
$$+x^{k-i}(x^4 + x^{3\cdot4} + \cdots + x^{(2w-1)\cdot4})(1+x)^2$$
$$+x^{j-i}[(x^2 + x^4 + \cdots + x^{4d})$$
$$+(x^4 + x^{3\cdot4} + \cdots + x^{(2v-1)\cdot4})(1+x)^2$$
$$+x^{l-j}(x^4 + x^{3\cdot4} + \cdots + x^{(2y-1)\cdot4})(1+x)^2]\}$$
$$= x^i(1-x)^7\{1 + x + x^2 + \cdots + x^{2a}$$
$$+x^2(1+x)(1 + x^4 + \cdots + x^{4(c-1)})$$
$$+(x^4 + x^{3\cdot4} + \cdots + x^{(2u-1)\cdot4})(1+x)$$
$$+x^{k-i}(x^4 + x^{3\cdot4} + \cdots + x^{(2w-1)\cdot4})(1+x)$$
$$+x^{j-i}[x^2(1+x)(1 + x^4 + \cdots + x^{4(d-1)})$$
$$+(x^4 + x^{3\cdot4} + \cdots + x^{(2v-1)\cdot4})(1+x)$$
$$+x^{l-j}(x^4 + x^{3\cdot4} + \cdots + x^{(2y-1)\cdot4})(1+x)]\}$$

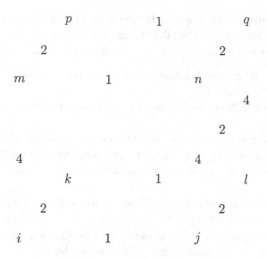

Fig. 2. A graphic illustration of Lemma 3.1

The number of items in $(1 + x + x^2 + \cdots + x^{2a})$ is odd, thus there is no factor $(1 + x)$ in $(1 + x + x^2 + \cdots + x^{2a})$.

$$\gcd((1 - x)^{2^n}, x^i + x^j + x^k + x^l + x^m + x^n + x^p + x^q) = (1 - x)^7$$

It is followed by $L(s) = 2^n - 7$. $\qquad\qquad\square$

For the convenience of presentation, we introduce some definitions.

Definition 3.1. Suppose that the difference of positions of two non-zero elements of sequence s is $(2x + 1)2^y$, both x and y are non-negative integers, then the distance between the two elements is defined as 2^y.

Definition 3.2. Suppose that s is a binary sequence with period 2^n, and there are 2^m non-zero elements in s, and $0 \leq i_1 < i_2 < \cdots < i_m < n$. If $m = 1$, then there are 2 non-zero elements in s and the distance between the two elements is 2^{i_1}, so it is called as a 1-cube. If $m = 2$, then s has 4 non-zero elements which form a rectangle, the lengths of 4 sides are 2^{i_1} and 2^{i_2} respectively, so it is called as a 2-cube. In general, s has 2^{m-1} pairs of non-zero elements, in which there are 2^{m-1} non-zero elements which form a $(m - 1)$-cube, the other 2^{m-1} non-zero elements also form a $(m - 1)$-cube, and the distance between each pair of elements are all 2^{i_m}, then the sequence s is called as an m-cube, and the linear complexity of s is called as the linear complexity of the cube as well.

Definition 3.3. A non-zero element of sequence s is called a vertex. Two vertexes can form an edge. If the distance between the two elements (vertices) is 2^y, then the length of the edge is defined as 2^y.

Now we consider the linear complexity of a cube.

Theorem 3.1. Suppose that s is a binary sequence with period 2^n, and non-zero elements of s form a m-cube, if lengths of edges are $i_1, i_2, \cdots, i_m$ ($0 \le i_1 < i_2 < \cdots < i_m < n$) respectively, then $L(s) = 2^n - (2^{i_1} + 2^{i_2} + \cdots + 2^{i_m})$.

Proof. Similar to the proof of Lemma 3.1, it is easy to prove Theorem 3.1 with mathematical induction.

Based on Games-Chan algorithm [3], we give another proof from different perspective.

In the kth step, $1 \le k \le n$, if and only if one period of the sequence can not be divided into two equal parts, then the linear complexity should be increased by half period. In the kth step, the linear complexity can be increased by maximum 2^{n-k}.

Suppose that non-zero elements of sequence s form a m-cube, lengths of edges are $i_1, i_2, \cdots, i_m$ ($0 \le i_1 < i_2 < \cdots < i_m < n$) respectively. Then in the $(n - i_m)$th step, one period of the sequence can be divided into two equal parts, then the linear complexity should not be increased by 2^{i_m}.

......

In the $(n - i_2)$th step, one period of the sequence can be divided into two equal parts, then the linear complexity should not be increased by 2^{i_2}.

In the $(n - i_1)$th step, one period of the sequence can be divided into two equal parts, then the linear complexity should not be increased by 2^{i_1}.

Therefore, $L(s) = 1 + 1 + 2 + 2^2 + \cdots + 2^{n-1} - (2^{i_1} + 2^{i_2} + \cdots + 2^{i_m}) = 2^n - (2^{i_1} + 2^{i_2} + \cdots + 2^{i_m})$.

The proof is complete now.   □

There is a 3-cube in Fig. 2. $L(s) = 2^n - (1 + 2 + 4)$, and lengths of edges are $1, 2$ and 4 respectively. Next we give a decomposition result.

Theorem 3.2. Suppose that s is a binary sequence with period 2^n, and $L(s) = 2^n - (2^{i_1} + 2^{i_2} + \cdots + 2^{i_m})$, where $0 \le i_1 < i_2 < \cdots < i_m < n$, then the sequence s can be decomposed into several disjoint cubes, and only one cube has the linear complexity $2^n - (2^{i_1} + 2^{i_2} + \cdots + 2^{i_m})$, other cubes possess distinct linear complexity which are all less than $2^n - (2^{i_1} + 2^{i_2} + \cdots + 2^{i_m})$. If the sequence s consists of only one cube, then the Hamming weight of s is 2^m.

Proof. The mathematical induction will be applied to the degree d of $s^N(x)$. For $d < 3$, by Lemma 2.3, the theorem is obvious.

We first consider a simple case.

(A) Suppose that $L(s) = 2^n - (2^{i_1} + 2^{i_2} + \cdots + 2^{i_m} + 2^{i_{m+1}})$, and the Hamming weight of s is the minimum, namely $L(s) \ne 2^n - (2^{i_1} + 2^{i_2} + \cdots + 2^{i_m} + 2^{i_{m+1}})$ when we remove 2 or more non-zero elements. Next we prove that s consists of one $(m + 1)$-cube exactly. Let

$$s^N(x) = (1 - x^{2^{i_1}})(1 - x^{2^{i_2}}) \cdots (1 - x^{2^{i_m}})(1 - x^{2^{i_{m+1}}})$$
$$[1 + f(x)(1 - x)]$$

Then $t^N(x) = (1 - x^{2^{i_1}})(1 - x^{2^{i_2}}) \cdots (1 - x^{2^{i_m}})[1 + f(x)(1 - x)]$ corresponds to a sequence t whose linear complexity is $L(t) = 2^n - (2^{i_1} + 2^{i_2} + \cdots + 2^{i_m})$.

The degree of $t^N(x)$ is less than the degree of $s^N(x)$, so the mathematical induction can be applied.

In the following, we consider two cases. We will prove that the second case is equivalent to the first case.

(1) The Hamming weight of sequence t is 2^m. By mathematical induction, t is an m-cube. Since $s^N(x) = t^N(x)(1 - x^{2^{i_{m+1}}}) = t^N(x) + x^{2^{i_{m+1}}}t^N(x)$, and $0 \le i_1 < i_2 < \cdots < i_m < i_{m+1} < n$, so s is a $(m+1)$-cube and its Hamming weight is 2^{m+1}.

(2) The Hamming weight of sequence t is $2^m + 2y$. By mathematical induction, the sequence t can be decomposed into several disjoint cubes, and only one cube has the linear complexity $2^n - (2^{i_1} + 2^{i_2} + \cdots + 2^{i_m})$. Thus

$$t^N(x) = (1 - x^{2^{i_1}})(1 - x^{2^{i_2}}) \cdots (1 - x^{2^{i_m}})[1 + g(x)(1 - x) + h(x)(1 - x)], \text{ and}$$

$u^N(x) = (1 - x^{2^{i_1}})(1 - x^{2^{i_2}}) \cdots (1 - x^{2^{i_m}})[1 + g(x)(1 - x)]$, corresponds to an m-cube, its non-zero elements form a set denoted by A.

$v^N(x) = (1 - x^{2^{i_1}})(1 - x^{2^{i_2}}) \cdots (1 - x^{2^{i_m}})h(x)(1 - x)$ corresponds to several cubes, whose $2y$ non-zero elements form a set denoted by B.

Assume that $b \in B, bx^{2^{i_{m+1}}} \in A$, we swap b and $bx^{2^{i_{m+1}}}$, namely let $b \in A, bx^{2^{i_{m+1}}} \in B$. It is easy to show that the linear complexity of the sequence to which $u^N(x)$ corresponds remains unchanged. The new $u^N(x)$ is still an m-cube.

$$s^N(x) = t^N(x)(1 - x^{2^{i_{m+1}}}) = u^N(x) + v^N(x) - u^N(x)x^{2^{i_{m+1}}} - v^N(x)x^{2^{i_{m+1}}},$$

$u^N(x)x^{2^{i_{m+1}}}$ corresponds to 2^m non-zero elements which form a set denoted by C. $v^N(x)x^{2^{i_{m+1}}}$ corresponds to $2y$ non-zero elements which form a set denoted by D.

By definition, set A and set C disjoint, set B and set D disjoint.

Suppose that set A and set D intersects. Thus there exists $b \in B$, such that $bx^{2^{i_{m+1}}} \in A$, which contradicts the assumption that $b \in A, bx^{2^{i_{m+1}}} \in B$. So set A and set D disjoint.

As set A and set B disjoint, we know that set C and set D disjoint.

We now prove that Set C and B disjoint by contradiction approach.

Suppose that $b \in B, b = ax^{2^{i_{m+1}}} \in C, a \in A$, then $ax^{2(2^{i_{m+1}})}$ must be in D, so sequence s has non-zero elements a and $ax^{2(2^{i_{m+1}})}$. The linear complexity of the sequence with only non-zero elements a and $ax^{2(2^{i_{m+1}})}$ is

$$2^n - 2 \cdot 2^{i_{m+1}} < 2^n - (2^{i_1} + 2^{i_2} + \cdots + 2^{i_m} + 2^{i_{m+1}}).$$

By Lemma 2.2, if the two non-zero elements are changed to zero, the linear complexity of s remains unchanged. This contradicts to the assumption that the Hamming weight is the minimum, so A and C form a $(m+1)$-cube exactly, and its linear complexity is $2^n - (2^{i_1} + 2^{i_2} + \cdots + 2^{i_m} + 2^{i_{m+1}})$.

By the assumption of Case (A), s has minimum Hamming weight, so s consists of a $(m+1)$-cube exactly.

(B) Let $s^N(x) = u^N(x) + v^N(x)$, where the Hamming weight of $u^N(x)$ is the minimum, and

$$L(u) = 2^n - (2^{i_1} + 2^{i_2} + \cdots + 2^{i_m} + 2^{i_{m+1}}).$$

From Case (A), $u^N(x)$ consists of a $(m+1)$-cube exactly.

Let $v^N(x) = y^N(x) + z^N(x)$, where the Hamming weight of $y^N(x)$ is minimum, and $L(y) = L(v)$. By Case (A), $y^N(x)$ consists of only one cube exactly. By analogy, we can prove that s consists of several cubes, and only one cube has the linear complexity of $2^n - (2^{i_1} + 2^{i_2} + \cdots + 2^{i_m} + 2^{i_{m+1}})$, other cubes possess distinct linear complexity which are all less than $2^n - (2^{i_1} + 2^{i_2} + \cdots + 2^{i_m} + 2^{i_{m+1}})$.

This completes proof.   □

The following examples can help us understand the proof of Theorem 3.2.

$(1+x)(1+x^2)[1+x^5(1+x^2)] = 1+x+x^2+x^3+x^5+x^6+x^9+x^{10}$ corresponds to a sequence in which there are 8 non-zero elements. It consists of two 2-cubes: $(1+x)(1+x^2)$ and $(1+x)(1+x^4)x^5$.

$(1+x)(1+x^2)[1+x^5(1+x^2)](1+x^4) = 1+x+x^2+x^3+x^4+x^7+x^{13}+x^{14}$ corresponds a sequence in which there are also 8 non-zero elements, but only one 3-cube. The linear complexity is $2^n - (1+2+4)$, and the lengths of edges are 1, 2 and 4 respectively.

Suppose that the linear complexity of s can reduce when at least k elements of s are changed. By Lemma 2.2, the linear complexity of the binary sequence, in which elements at exactly those k positions are all nonzero, must be $L(s)$. According to Theorems 3.1 and 3.2, it is easy to achieve the following conclusion.

Corollary 3.1. Suppose that s is a binary sequence with period 2^n, and $L(s) = 2^n - (2^{i_1} + 2^{i_2} + \cdots + 2^{i_m})$, where $0 \le i_1 < i_2 < \cdots < i_m < n$. If $k_{\min}$ is the minimum, such that $k_{\min}$-error linear complexity is less than $L(s)$, then $k_{\min} = 2^m$.

Corollary 3.1 was first proved by Kurosawa et al. [6], and later it was proved by Etzion et al. [2] with different approaches.

Obviously, previous Propositions 2.2 and 2.3 are also corollaries of Theorems 3.1 and 3.2.

Consider a k-cube, if lengths of edges are $1, 2, 2^2, \cdots$, and 2^{k-1} respectively, and the linear complexity is $2^n - (2^k - 1)$. By Theorems 3.1 and 3.2, we can obtain the following results on stability.

Corollary 3.2. Suppose that s is a binary sequence with period 2^n and its Hamming weight is even, then the maximum stable $2^{k-1}, \cdots, (2^k - 2)$ or $(2^k - 1)$-error linear complexity of s are all $2^n - (2^k - 1)(k > 0)$.

The following is an example to illustrate Corollary 3.2.

Let s be the binary sequence $\overbrace{11\cdots11}^{2^k}0\cdots0$. Its period is 2^n, and there are only 2^k continuous nonzero elements at the beginning of the sequence. Then it is a k-cube, and the $2^{k-1}, \cdots, (2^k - 2)$ or $(2^k - 1)$-error linear complexity of s are all $2^n - (2^k - 1)$.

After at most $e(0 \le e \le 2^k - 1)$ elements of a period in the above sequence are changed, the linear complexity of all new sequences are not decreased, so the original sequence possesses stable e-error linear complexity.

According to Lemma 2.2, if a sequence whose linear complexity is less than $2^n - (2^k - 1)$ is added to the sequence with linear complexity $2^n - (2^k - 1)$, then the linear complexity of the new sequence is still $2^n - (2^k - 1)$, and the $2^{k-1}, \cdots, (2^k - 2)$ or $(2^k - 1)$-error linear complexity of the new sequence are all $2^n - (2^k - 1)$.

By combining Corollaries 3.1 and 3.2, we can achieve the following theorem.

Theorem 3.3. For $2^{l-1} \leq k < 2^l$, there exists a 2^n-periodic binary sequence s with stable k-linear complexity $2^n - (2^l - 1)$, such that

$$L_k(s) = \max_t L_k(t)$$

where t is any 2^n-periodic binary sequence.

It is reminded that CELCS (critical error linear complexity spectrum) is studied by Etzion et al. [2]. The CELCS of the sequence s consists of the ordered set of points $(k, L_k(s))$ satisfying $L_k(s) > L_{k'}(s)$, for $k' > k$; these are the points where a decrease occurs in the k-error linear complexity, and thus are called critical points.

Let s be a binary sequence with period 2^n and it has only one m-cube. Then s has only two critical points: $(0, l(s)), (2^m, 0)$.

In the following, we will study binary sequences with several cubes. By Theorem 3.2, if s is a 2^n-periodic binary sequence, then it can be decomposed into several disjoint cubes. The following examples show that the cube decomposition of a sequence is not unique.

For example, $1 + x + x^3 + x^4 + x^7 + x^8$ can be decomposed into a 1-cube $1 + x$, whose linear complexity is $2^n - 1$, and a 2-cube $x^3 + x^4 + x^7 + x^8$, whose linear complexity is $2^n - (1 + 4)$.

It can also be decomposed into a 1-cube $x^3 + x^4$, whose linear complexity is $2^n - 1$, a 1-cube $x + x^7$, whose linear complexity is $2^n - 2$, and another 1-cube $1 + x^8$, whose linear complexity is $2^n - 8$.

It can also be decomposed into a 1-cube $x^7 + x^8$, whose linear complexity is $2^n - 1$, a 1-cube $x + x^3$, whose linear complexity is $2^n - 2$, and another 1-cube $1 + x^4$, whose linear complexity is $2^n - 4$.

It can also be decomposed into a 1-cube $1 + x^3$, whose linear complexity is $2^n - 1$, a 1-cube $x + x^7$, whose linear complexity $2^n - 2$, and another 1-cube $x^4 + x^8$, whose linear complexity is $2^n - 4$.
......

In fact, we do not know how many possible ways for such decomposition. However, in order to achieve the maximal decrease of the linear complexity of the new sequence by superposing another sequence over the original one, a direct method is, if possible, that the linear complexity of the first cube is changed to the same as the linear complexity of the second cube.

As an illustrative example, noting that the linear complexity of $x^3 + x^4 + x^7 + x^8$ is $2^n - 5$, thus in order to achieve the maximum decrease of linear complexity, we superpose $x^{12} + x^{13}$ over $1 + x + x^3 + x^4 + x^7 + x^8$, so that the linear complexity of $1 + x + x^{12} + x^{13}$ is also $2^n - 5$. As a result, the linear complexity of $1 + x + x^3 + x^4 + x^7 + x^8 + x^{12} + x^{13}$ is reduced to $2^n - 6$, which can be decomposed into a 2-cube $x + x^3 + x^7 + x^{13}$, whose linear complexity is $2^n - 6$, and another 2-cube $1 + x^4 + x^8 + x^{12}$, whose linear complexity is $2^n - 12$.

To construct the sequence possessing high stable k-error linear complexity, both the first cube and the second cube should possess higher linear complexity. Specifically, it is easy to verify the following.

Theorem 3.4. Suppose that s is a binary sequence with period 2^n, the linear complexity of the largest cube of s is $L(s) = 2^n - (2^{i_1} + 2^{i_2} + \cdots + 2^{i_m})$, where $0 \leq i_1 < i_2 < \cdots < i_m < n$, and the linear complexity of the second largest cube of s is $2^n - (2^{j_1} + 2^{j_2} + \cdots + 2^{j_l})$, where $0 \leq j_1 < j_2 < \cdots < j_l < n$. If the largest cube of s is unique, then $2^m + 2^l$ is the minimum number k for which the second decrease occurs in the k-error linear complexity of s. Namely,

$$L(s) > L_{2^m}(s) > L_{2^m + 2^l}(s).$$

For example, $1 + x + x^3 + x^4 + x^7 + x^8$ has a 1-cube $1 + x$, whose linear complexity is $2^n - 1$. It also has 1-cube $x^3 + x^4$ and $x^7 + x^8$, all with linear complexity $2^n - 1$. So Theorem 3.4 can not be applied to this sequence. In fact, $L(s) > L_2(s) > L_4(s) > 0$.

4   Conclusion

A small number of element changes may lead to a sharp decline of linear complexity, so the concept of stable k-error linear complexity has been introduced in this paper. By studying the linear complexity of binary sequences with period 2^n, especially the linear complexity may decline when the superposition of two sequences with the same linear complexity is operated. In this paper, a new approach to construct the sequence with stable k-error linear complexity based on cube theory has been derived. It has been proved that a binary sequence whose period is 2^n can be decomposed into several disjoint cubes, so a new approach to study k-error linear complexity has been given.

In future, by using methods similar to that of the binary sequence, we may study a sequence with period p^n over F_p, where p is a prime number. The polynomial $1 - x^{p^n} = (1 - x)^{p^n}$ over F_p. Thus for a sequence with period p^n over F_p, its linear complexity is equal to the degree of factor $(1 - x)$ in $s^N(x)$.

The following are some similar conclusions, whose proofs are omitted here.

Lemma 1. *Suppose that s is a sequence with period p^n over F_p. Necessary and sufficient conditions for $L(s) < p^n$ are: the element sum of one period of the sequence s is divisible by p.*

Lemma 2. *Both s_1 and s_2 are sequences with period p^n over F_p. If $L(s_1) \neq L(s_2)$, then $L(s_1 + s_2) = \max\{L(s_1), L(s_2)\}$. If $L(s_1) = L(s_2)$, then $L(s_1 + s_2) \leq L(s_1)$.*

Lemma 3. *Suppose that s is a sequence with period p^n over F_p, and $s^N(x) = ax^k(1 - x^l), a \neq 0 \pmod p$, $l = bp^m, b \neq 0 \pmod p$, then both the linear complexity and 1-error linear complexity of sequence s are $p^n - p^m$.*

References

1. Ding, C., Xiao, G., Shan, W., et al. (eds.): The Stability Theory of Stream Ciphers. LNCS, vol. 561, pp. 85–88. Springer, Heidelberg (1991)
2. Etzion, T., Kalouptsidis, N., Kolokotronis, N., Limniotis, K., Paterson, K.G.: Properties of the error linear complexity spectrum. IEEE Trans. Inf. Theory **55**(10), 4681–4686 (2009)
3. Games, R.A., Chan, A.H.: A fast algorithm for determining the complexity of a binary sequence with period 2^n. IEEE Trans. Inf. Theory **29**(1), 144–146 (1983)
4. Fu, F.-W., Niederreiter, H., Su, M.: The characterization of 2^n-periodic binary sequences with fixed 1-error linear complexity. In: Gong, G., Helleseth, T., Song, H.-Y., Yang, K. (eds.) SETA 2006. LNCS, vol. 4086, pp. 88–103. Springer, Heidelberg (2006)
5. Hu, H., Feng, D.: Periodic sequences with very large 1-error linear complexity over Fq. J. Softw. **16**(5), 940–945 (2005)
6. Kurosawa, K., Sato, F., Sakata, T., Kishimoto, W.: A relationship between linear complexity and k-error linear complexity. IEEE Trans. Inf. Theory **46**(2), 694–698 (2000)
7. Meidl, W.: How many bits have to be changed to decrease the linear complexity? Des. Codes Cryptogr. **33**, 109–122 (2004)
8. Meidl, W.: On the stability of 2^n-periodic binary sequences. IEEE Trans. Inf. Theory **51**(3), 1151–1155 (2005)
9. Niederreiter, H.: Periodic sequences with large k-error linear complexity. IEEE Trans. Inf. Theory **49**, 501–505 (2003)
10. Stamp, M., Martin, C.F.: An algorithm for the k-error linear complexity of binary sequences with period 2^n. IEEE Trans. Inf. Theory **39**, 1398–1401 (1993)
11. Zhou, J.Q.: On the k-error linear complexity of sequences with period $2p^n$ over GF(q). Des. Codes Cryptogr. **58**(3), 279–296 (2011)
12. Zhou, J.Q., Liu, W.Q.: The k-error linear complexity distribution for 2^n-periodic binary sequences. Des. Codes Cryptogr. (2013). http://link.springer.com/article/10.1007/s10623-013-9805-8
13. Zhu, F.X., Qi, W.F.: The 2-error linear complexity of 2^n-periodic binary sequences with linear complexity $2^n - 1$. J. Electron. (China) **24**(3), 390–395 (2007). http://www.springerlink.com/content/3200vt810p232769/

Autocorrelation Values of New Generalized Cyclotomic Sequences of Order Six Over Z_{pq}

Xinxin Gong[1]([✉]), Bin Zhang[2], Dengguo Feng[3], and Tongjiang Yan[4]

[1] Trusted Computing and Information Assurance Laboratory, Institute of Software, Chinese Academy of Sciences, Beijing 100190, People's Republic of China
gongxinxin@is.iscas.ac.cn
[2] Institute of Information Engineering, Chinese Academy of Sciences, Beijing 100093, People's Republic of China
zhangbin@is.iscas.ac.cn
[3] Institute of Software, Chinese Academy of Sciences, Beijing 100190, People's Republic of China
[4] China College of Sciences, China University of Petroleum, Beijing, China

Abstract. Let p, q $(p < q)$ be two odd primes with $gcd(p-1, q-1) = 6$. In this paper, based on the Whiteman generalized cyclotomy, new generalized cyclotomic sequences with order six and length pq are constructed. We first calculate the autocorrelation values of these sequences and get conditions of p and q such that they are four-valued. Besides, we find some specific examples such that the autocorrelation function takes on only a few values.

Keywords: Whiteman generalized cyclotomy · Generalized cyclotomic sequences · Pseudo-random sequences · Stream cipher

1 Introduction

Pseudo-random sequences are used extensively for their high speed and security level and less errors. As a branch, the cyclotomic sequences and the generalized ones are studied widely because of their simple mathematical structures and excellent pseudo-random properties [1,2,6]. The autocorrelation function of Pseudo-random sequence is used to measure the similarity between a sequence and its shift sequence, which is an important indicator of randomness. Sequences with low autocorrelation values and uniform distribution have wide applications in stream cipher, software testing and radar navigation and other fields [2], the construction and analysis are important parts in the sequence construction theory.

In this paper, we always assume p, q $(p < q)$ are two odd primes with $gcd(p-1, q-1) = 6$. Based on the Whiteman generalized cyclotomy [3,7], new generalized cyclotomic sequences with order six and length pq are constructed. let $D_0, D_1, D_2, D_3, D_4, D_5$ be generalized cyclotomic classes with $Z_{pq}^* = \overset{5}{\underset{i=0}{\cup}} D_i$.

© Springer International Publishing Switzerland 2014
D. Lin et al. (Eds.): Inscrypt 2013, LNCS 8567, pp. 86–98, 2014.
DOI: 10.1007/978-3-319-12087-4_6

let $R = \{0\}$, $P = \{p, 2p, ..., (q-1)p\}$, $Q = \{q, 2q, ..., (p-1)q\}$, we compute the periodic autocorrelation function $AC_s(w)$ of binary sequences $\{s_i\}$ from $D = P \cup D_0 \cup D_1 \cup D_3$, and give conditions of p and q such that $AC_s(w)$ are four-valued. Besides, we find specific examples from another perspective such that the autocorrelation function takes on only a few values.

2 Preliminaries

Let p, q $(p < q)$ be two odd primes with $gcd(p-1, q-1) = d$ and let $N = pq$, $e = (p-1)(q-1)/d$, by the Chinese Remainder Theorem, there exists a common primitive root g of both p and q. In fact, suppose that m is a primitive root modulo p, and n a primitive root modulo q, then g should satisfy the simultaneous congruences

$$g \equiv m(\text{mod } p), g \equiv n(\text{mod } q)$$

we get the common primitive root

$$g \equiv qi_q m + pi_p n(\text{mod } pq)$$

where $qi_q \equiv 1(\text{mod } p)$ and $pi_p \equiv 1(\text{mod } q)$. Let $\bar{x}$ be an integer satisfying the simultaneous congruences

$$\bar{x} \equiv g(\text{mod } p) , \bar{x} \equiv 1(\text{mod } q).$$

The existence and uniqueness of $\bar{x}$ modulo pq are guaranteed by the Chinese Remainder Theorem.

Since g is a primitive root of both p and q, by the Chinese Remainder Theorem once more

$$ord_N(g) = lcm(ord_p(g), ord_q(g)) = lcm(p-1, q-1) = e$$

where $ord_m(g)$ denotes the multiplicative order of g modulo m, and $lcm(a, b)$ denotes the lowest common multiple of a and b.

In $Z_N = \{0, 1, ..., N-1\}$, the residue class ring modulo N, the Whiteman's generalized cyclotomic classes of order d are defined by

$$D_i = \{g^s \bar{x}^i : s = 0, 1, ..., e-1\}, i = 0, 1, ..., d-1$$

It is easy to see that

$$Z_N^* = \bigcup_{i=0}^{d-1} D_i, \ D_i \cap D_j = \emptyset, i \neq j$$

where $\emptyset$ denotes the empty set and Z_N^* the multiplicative group of the ring Z_N.

The corresponding generalized cyclotomic numbers of order d are defined by

$$(i, j) = |(D_i + 1) \cap D_j|, i, j = 0, 1, ..., d-1;$$

Here and hereafter we define $A + a = \{x + a : x \in A\}$ and $aA = \{ax : x \in A\}$ for any subset A of Z_N and $a \in Z_N$.

When $d = 6$, $\gcd(p - 1, q - 1) = 6$, i.e., $p \equiv 1 \bmod 6$, $q \equiv 1 \bmod 6$, matrices $\bar{A}$, $\bar{B}$ are of size 6×6, and

$$\bar{A} = \begin{bmatrix} A\,B\,C\,D\,E\,F \\ G\,H\,I\,E\,C\,I \\ H\,J\,G\,F\,I\,B \\ A\,G\,H\,A\,G\,H \\ G\,F\,I\,B\,H\,J \\ H\,I\,E\,C\,I\,G \end{bmatrix} \quad \bar{B} = \begin{bmatrix} A\,B\,C\,D\,E\,F \\ B\,F\,G\,H\,I\,G \\ C\,G\,E\,I\,J\,H \\ D\,H\,I\,D\,H\,I \\ E\,I\,J\,H\,C\,G \\ F\,G\,H\,I\,G\,B \end{bmatrix}$$

where the ith row and jth column represents the generalized cyclotomic number $(i - 1, j - 1), i, j \in \{1, 2, 3, 4, 5, 6\}$. We have the following lemmas about the generalized cyclotomic numbers of order six [9].

Lemma 1. *When $(p - 1)(q - 1)/36$ is even, the generalized cyclotomic numbers of order six are determined by matrix $\bar{A}$, together with the relations*
$72A = 12\dot{M} + 20 - 8x - 2a + 2c$
$72B = 12\dot{M} - 4 - 3a - c - 9b + 9d$
$72C = 12\dot{M} - 4 - 8x + a - c + 24y - 3b - 9d$
$72D = 12\dot{M} - 4 + 24x + 6a + 2c$
$72E = 12\dot{M} - 4 - 8x + a - c - 24y + 3b + 9d$
$72F = 12\dot{M} - 4 - 3a - c + 9b - 9d$
$72G = 12\dot{M} + 8 + 4x + a - c + 12y + 3b + 9d$
$72H = 12\dot{M} + 8 + 4x + a - c - 12y - 3b - 9d$
$72I = 12\dot{M} - 4 + 4x - 2a + 2c$
$72J = 12\dot{M} - 4 - 12x + 6a + 2c$
where $pq = x^2 + 3y^2$, $6\dot{M} = (p - 2)(q - 2) - 1$ and $4pq = a^2 + 3b^2 = c^2 + 27d^2$.

Lemma 2. *When $(p - 1)(q - 1)/36$ is odd, the generalized cyclotomic numbers of order six are determined by matrix $\bar{B}$, together with the relations*
$72A = 12\dot{M} + 32 + 6a - 24x + 2c$
$72B = 12\dot{M} + 8 + a + 3b + 8x + 24y - c + 9d$
$72C = 12\dot{M} + 8 - 3a + 9b - c - 9d$
$72D = 12\dot{M} + 8 - 2a + 8x + 2c$
$72E = 12\dot{M} + 8 - 3a - 9b - c + 9d$
$72F = 12\dot{M} + 8 + a - 3b + 8x - 24y - c - 9d$
$72G = 12\dot{M} - 4 - 2a - 4x + 2c$
$72H = 12\dot{M} - 4 + a + 3b - 4x - 12y - c + 9d$
$72I = 12\dot{M} - 4 + a - 3b - 4x + 12y - c - 9d$
$72J = 12\dot{M} - 4 + 6a + 12x + 2c$
where $pq = x^2 + 3y^2$, $6\dot{M} = (p - 2)(q - 2) - 1$ and $4pq = a^2 + 3b^2 = c^2 + 27d^2$.

Proof. Matrix $\bar{B}$ can be obtained by Lemma 3(b)(c) of p. 86 in [9], and by Lemma 3(d), we have the four linear relations

$$\begin{cases} A + B + C + D + E + F = \dot{M} + 1 \\ B + F + 2G + H + I = \dot{M} \\ C + E + G + H + I + J = \dot{M} \\ 2D + 2H + 2I = \dot{M} \end{cases}$$

Further, a reduced set of $R(m,n)$ for $d = 6$ is $R(1,1), R(1,2), R(2,2)$. By Lemma 11(b) of p. 99 in [9], setting

$$2R(1,1) = 2\sum_{k=0}^{5} \gamma^k \sum_{h=0}^{5} \gamma^{-2h}(k,h) = a + i\sqrt{3}b.$$

$$R(1,2) = \sum_{k=0}^{5} \gamma^{2k} \sum_{h=0}^{5} \gamma^{-3h}(k,h) = -x + i\sqrt{3}y$$

$$2R(2,2) = 2\sum_{k=0}^{5} \gamma^{2k} \sum_{h=0}^{5} \gamma^{-4h}(k,h) = c + 3i\sqrt{3}d$$

We obtain the additional six equations

$$\begin{cases} 2A + B - 3C - 2D - 3E + F - 4G + 2H + 2I + 4J = a \\ B + 3C - 3E - F + 2H - 2I = b \\ A - B - D - F + G + H + I - J = -x \\ B - F - H + I = y \\ 2A - 3B - 3C + 6D - 3E - 3F + 12G - 6H - 6I + 4J = c \\ B - C + E - F + 2H - 2I = d \end{cases}$$

The simultaneous solution of the above ten equations in ten unknowns is given in the statement of the lemma.

With notations as above, given two odd primes p, q $(p < q)$ with $\gcd(p - 1, q - 1) = 6$, suppose that $pq = x^2 + 3y^2 = x'^2 + 3y'^2$, $4pq = a^2 + 3b^2 = a'^2 + 3b'^2$ and $4pq = c^2 + 27d^2 = c'^2 + 27d'^2$, then a change in the choice of g may lead to the replacement of x, y, a, b, c, d by x', y', a', b', c', d' respectively in Lemmas 1 and 2. If g is fixed, we cannot determine how to choose x, y, a, b, c, d. In the following part, we will first calculate the exact autocorrelation values of corresponding sequences theoretically without considering the choice of g, i.e., we take the autocorrelation values only as the function of x, y, a, b, c, d. Next, consider only the choice of g, we find some examples of $(p, q, m, n, g, \bar{x})$, such that the autocorrelation function is four-valued, five-valued, or six-valued by a computer calculation.

3   Autocorrelation Values

In this section, we discuss autocorrelation values of a new Whiteman's generalized cyclotomic sequence of order six. Let $\gcd(p-1, q-1) = 6$, we define

$$C_0 = R \cup Q \cup D_2 \cup D_4 \cup D_5, C_1 = P \cup D_0 \cup D_1 \cup D_3$$

The new generalized cyclotomic sequences s^∞ of order six with respect to the primes p and q (denoted by $NGCS_6$) is defined by

$$s_i = \begin{cases} 1, & if \ (i \bmod N) \in C_1, \\ 0, & if \ (i \bmod N) \in C_0. \end{cases}$$

The periodic autocorrelation function of the binary sequence s^∞ is defined by

$$AC_s(w) = \sum_{i \in Z_N} (-1)^{s_{i+w} - s_i}, w \in Z_N.$$

The main results of this correspondence are summarized in the following two theorems. The proofs will be given later.

Theorem 1. *With notations as Lemma 1.*
  Let $(p-1)(q-1)/36$ be even, then $(q-p)/6$ is odd, and the autocorrelation function of $NGCS_6$ is

$$AC_s(w) = \begin{cases} q - p - 3, & w \in P \\ p - q + 1, & w \in Q \\ -3 + (4x - 12y + a - 3b + 3c + 27d)/18, & w \in D_0 \cup D_3 \\ -1 - (4x + a + 3c)/9, & w \in D_1 \cup D_4 \\ 1 + (4x + 12y + a + 3b + 3c - 27d)/18, & w \in D_2 \cup D_5 \end{cases} \quad (1)$$

Theorem 2. *With notations as Lemma 2.*
  Let $(p-1)(q-1)/36$ be odd, then $(q-p)/6$ is even, and the autocorrelation function of $NGCS_6$ is

$$AC_s(w) = \begin{cases} q - p - 3, & w \in P \\ p - q + 1, & w \in Q \\ -3 + (16x + 5a + 9b + 3c + 27d)/18, & w \in D_0 \\ -3 - (8x + 48y - 2a - 12b + 6c)/18, & w \in D_1 \\ 1 - (8x - 24y + 7a - 3b - 3c + 27d)/18, & w \in D_2 \\ -3 - (8x + 24y + 7a + 3b - 3c - 27d)/18, & w \in D_3 \\ 1 - (8x - 48y - 2a + 12b + 6c)/18, & w \in D_4 \\ 1 + (16x + 5a - 9b + 3c - 27d)/18, & w \in D_5 \end{cases} \quad (2)$$

By Theorem 1, we have the following conclusion.

Corollary 1. *Define $M := 4x + a + 3c$, $N := 12y + 3b - 27d$, $h := q - p - 2$. If $(p-1)(q-1)/36$ is even, then $AC_s(w)$ is at most four-valued if and only if one of the following systems of equations holds:*

$M = -9h$, and $N = -27h - 36$

$M = 18h$, and $N = -36$

$M = -9h$, and $N = 27h - 36$

$M = 9h$, and $N = 27h - 36$

$M = -18h$, and $N = -36$

$M = 9h$, and $N = -27h - 36$

$M = 0$, and $N = -36$

$M = 9h$, and $N = -9h - 36$

$M = 0$, and $N = -18h - 36$

$M = 9h/2$, and $N = -27h/2 - 36$

$M = -9h$, and $N = 9h - 36$

$M = -9h$, and $N = -9h - 36$

$M = -9h$, and $N = -36$

$M = 0$, and $N = 18h - 36$

$M = 9h$, and $N = 9h - 36$

$M = 9h/2$, and $N = 27h/2 - 36$

$M = -9h/2$, and $N = 27h/2 - 36$

$M = 9h$, and $N = -36$

$M = -9h/2$, and $N = -27h/2 - 36$

Especially, when $M = 0$ and $N = -36$, $AC_s(w) = -1$ for each $w \in Z_{pq}^*$.

Proof. Let $(p-1)(q-1)/36$ be even, by Theorem 1, we will find conditions such that several values of $AC_s(w)$ can be equal. For convenience, we give labels for the values of $AC_s(w)$ as follows:

$U := q - p - 3$, $V := p - q + 1$, $W := -3 + (M - N)/18$

$X := -1 - M/9$, $Y := 1 + (M + N)/18$

Now we will find conditions such that $AC_s(w)$ is at most four-valued.

If $U = W = X$, or $U = W = Y$, or $U = X = Y$, or $V = W = X$, or $V = W = Y$, or $V = X = Y$, or $W = X = Y$, then $AC_s(w)$ is at most four-valued, from which we can get the first seven systems of equations.

If both $U = W$ and $V = X$, or both $U = W$ and $V = Y$, or both $U = W$ and $X = Y$, or both $U = X$ and $V = W$, or both $U = X$ and $V = Y$, or both $U = X$ and $W = Y$, or both $U = Y$ and $V = W$, or both $U = Y$ and $V = X$, or both $U = Y$ and $W = X$, or both $V = W$ and $X = Y$, or both $V = X$ and $W = Y$, or both $V = Y$ and $W = X$, then $AC_s(w)$ is also at most four-valued, from which we can get the last twelve systems of equations.

The converse is true as well.

Example 1: With notations as Lemma 1. Let $(p-1)(q-1)/36$ be even, by the last part of Lemma 3, we find some examples of (p, q) such that $M = 0$ and $N = -36$, i.e., $AC_s(w) = -1$ for each $w \in Z_{pq}^*$(See Table 1 in Appendix)[1].

To prove Theorems 1 and 2, we need the following lemmas. Define

$$d_s(i, j; w) = |C_i \cap (C_j + w)|, w \in Z_N, i, j = 0, 1.$$

---

[1] We only list part of the results, many others can be found by a computer calculation.

Lemma 3. *With notations as before. In the residue class ring Z_N, we have*
(1) *If $a \in P$, then $aP = P$, $aQ = \{0\}$.*
(2) *If $a \in Q$, then $aP = \{0\}$, $aQ = Q$.*
(3) *If $a \in D_j$, then $aP = P$, $aQ = Q$, $aD_i = D_{i+j(\text{modd})}, i, j = 0, 1, ..., d-1$.*

Lemma 4. *For each $w \neq 0(\text{mod } N)$, $AC_s(w) = N - 4d_s(1, 0, w)$.*

Proof. See Lemma 1 of [4].

For $NGCS_6$, note that

$$
\begin{aligned}
d_s(1, 0; w) &= |C_1 \cap (C_0 + w)| \\
&= |P \cap (R \cup Q + w)| + |P \cap (D_2 + w)| + |P \cap (D_4 + w)| \\
&\quad + |P \cap (D_5 + w)| + |D_0 \cap (R \cup Q + w)| + |D_1 \cap (R \cup Q + w)| \\
&\quad + |D_3 \cap (R \cup Q + w)| + |D_0 \cap (D_2 + w)| + |D_0 \cap (D_4 + w)| \\
&\quad + |D_0 \cap (D_5 + w)| + |D_1 \cap (D_2 + w)| + |D_1 \cap (D_4 + w)| \\
&\quad + |D_1 \cap (D_5 + w)| + |D_3 \cap (D_2 + w)| + |D_3 \cap (D_4 + w)| \\
&\quad + |D_3 \cap (D_5 + w)|.
\end{aligned}
$$

Hence we only need to determine values of $|P \cap (R \cup Q + w)|$, $|P \cap (D_i + w)|$, $|D_j \cap (R \cup Q + w)|$ and $|D_j \cap (D_i + w)|$, where $i = 2, 4, 5$, $j = 0, 1, 3$.
A proof of the following lemma can be found in [4].

Lemma 5

$$
|P \cap (R \cup Q + w)| = \begin{cases} 1, & w \in P \\ 0, & w \in Q \\ 1, & w \in Z_N^* \end{cases}
$$

To determine $|P \cap (D_i + w)|, i = 2, 4, 5$, we need the following Generalized Chinese Remainder Theorem [8].

Lemma 6. *Let $m_1, m_2, ..., m_t$ be positive integers. For a set of integers $a_1, a_2, ..., a_t$, the system of congruences*

$$
x \equiv a_i(\text{mod } m_i), i = 1, 2, ..., t
$$

has solutions if and only if

$$
a_i \equiv a_j(\text{mod } \gcd(m_i, m_j)), i \neq j, 1 \leq i, j \leq t \tag{3}
$$

If (3) is satisfied, the solution is unique modulo $lcm(m_1, m_2, ..., m_t)$.

Lemma 7. *If $(q-p)/6$ is even, $-1 \in D_0$; If $(q-p)/6$ is odd, $-1 \in D_3$.*

Proof. $-1 \in D_i$ if and only if there is an integer s with $0 \leq s \leq e-1$ such that

$$
g^s \bar{x}^i \equiv -1(\text{mod } pq) \tag{4}
$$

Which is by the Chinese Remainder Theorem equivalent to

$$g^s \bar{x}^i \equiv -1(\text{mod } p), g^s \bar{x}^i \equiv -1(\text{mod } q)$$

That is $g^{s+i} \equiv -1(\text{mod } p), g^s \equiv -1(\text{mod } q)$. Since g is a common primitive root of p and q, we have

$$g^{(p-1)/2} \equiv -1(\text{mod } p), \ g^{(q-1)/2} \equiv -1(\text{mod } q)$$

Thus (4) is further equivalent to

$$g^{s+i-(p-1)/2} \equiv 1(\text{mod } p), g^{s-(q-1)/2} \equiv 1(\text{mod } q)$$

Which is equivalent to

$$\begin{cases} s + i - (p-1)/2 \equiv 0(\text{mod } p-1) \\ s - (q-1)/2 \equiv 0(\text{mod } q-1) \end{cases}$$

By Lemma 6, (4) has a solution if and only if $(q-p)/2 = -i(\text{mod } 6)$, then we get the conclusion.

Since $|P \cap (D_i + w)| = |(P \cup R) \cap (D_i + w)| - |R \cap (D_i + w)|, i = 2, 4, 5$, then we will compute $|(P \cup R) \cap (D_i + w)|$ and $|R \cap (D_i + w)|$ respectively.

Lemma 8

$$|(P \cup R) \cap (D_i + w)| = \begin{cases} 0, & w \in P \cup R \\ (q-1)/6, & otherwise \end{cases}$$

Proof. The first part is clear. We now prove the second part.

If $w \notin P \cup R$, then an element $z = g^s \bar{x}^i + w \in P \cup R$ if and only if

$$g^s \bar{x}^i + w \equiv 0(\text{mod } p) \tag{5}$$

Note that $\bar{x} \equiv g(\text{mod } p)$. Let v be the inverse of $w(\text{mod } p)$. Since g is a primitive root of p, there must be an integer t with $0 \le t \le p-1$ such that $v \equiv g^t(\text{mod } p)$. Thus (5) is equivalent to

$$g^{s+t+i} \equiv -1(\text{mod } p)$$

Note that $g^{(p-1)/2} \equiv -1(\text{mod } p)$, then (5) is also equivalent to

$$g^{s+t+i-(p-1)/2} \equiv 1(\text{mod } p)$$

Which is further equivalent to

$$s + i + t - (p-1)/2 \equiv 0(\text{mod } p-1)$$

It follows that the number of solution s of (5) with $0 \le s \le e-1$ is $e/(p-1) = (q-1)/6$.

Lemma 9

$$|R \cap (D_i + w)| = \begin{cases} 0, & w \in Q \\ 1, & w \in D_i, \; and (q-p)/6 \; is \; even \\ 1, & w \in D_{i+3}, and \; (q-p)/6 \; is \; odd \\ 0, & otherwise \end{cases}$$

Proof. The first part and last part are clear.

If $(q-p)/6$ is even, by Lemma 7, $-1 \in D_0$. Further more, if $w \in D_i$, by Lemma 3, $-w \in D_i$. Thus $|R \cap (D_i + w)| = 1$.

Similarly, we know that $|R \cap (D_i + w)| = 1$ if $(q-p)/6$ is odd and $w \in D_{i+3}$.

By Lemmas 8 and 9, we get the following Lemma.

Lemma 10

$$|P \cap (D_i + w)| = \begin{cases} 0, & w \in P \\ (q-7)/6, & w \in D_i, \; and \; (q-p)/6 \; is \; even \\ (q-7)/6, & w \in D_{i+3}, \; and \; (q-p)/6 \; is \; odd \\ (q-1)/6, & otherwise \end{cases}$$

Similar to the proof of Lemma 8, we can get the following result.

Lemma 11

$$|D_j \cap (R \cup Q + w)| = \begin{cases} 0, & w \in Q \cup R \\ (p-1)/6, & otherwise \end{cases}$$

Lemma 12. *Suppose that $w \in D_i$, then $w^{-1} \in D_{i+j}$ if and only if $2i + j \equiv 0(\mod 6)$.*

Proof. Since $w \in D_i$, there is an integer s with $0 \leq s \leq e - 1$ such that $w \equiv g^s \bar{x}^i (\mod pq)$, which is by the Chinese Remainder Theorem equivalent to

$$w \equiv g^s \bar{x}^i (\mod p), w \equiv g^s \bar{x}^i (\mod q)$$

that is $w \equiv g^{s+i} (\mod p)$ and $w \equiv g^s (\mod q)$.

Similarly, $w^{-1} \in D_{i+j}$ if and only if there is an integer k with $0 \leq k \leq e - 1$ such that

$$w^{-1} \equiv g^{k+i+j} (\mod p), w^{-1} \equiv g^k (\mod q) \tag{6}$$

Thus (6) is equivalent to

$$1 \equiv w \cdot w^{-1} \equiv g^{k+s+2i+j} (\mod p)$$
$$1 \equiv w \cdot w^{-1} \equiv g^{k+s} (\mod q)$$

Which is further equivalent to

$$\begin{cases} k + s + 2i + j = 0(\mod \; p-1) \\ k + s = 0(\mod \; q-1) \end{cases}$$

By Lemma 6, (6) has a solution if and only if $2i + j = 0(\mod 6)$, then we get the conclusion.

Lemma 13

$$|D_j \cap (D_i + w)| = \begin{cases} (p-1)(q-1)/36, & w \in P \cup Q \\ (i,j), & w \in D_0 \\ (i+5, j+5), & w \in D_1 \\ (i+4, j+4), & w \in D_2 \\ (i+3, j+3), & w \in D_3 \\ (i+2, j+2), & w \in D_4 \\ (i+1, j+1), & w \in D_5 \end{cases}$$

Proof. The first part is clear.

For the second part, note that if $w \notin P \cup Q$, then $|D_j \cap (D_i + w)| = |(w^{-1} \cdot D_i + 1) \cap w^{-1} \cdot D_j|$. We get the conclusion by Lemma 3 and Lemma 12.

We are now ready to prove Theorems 1 and 2.

Proof of Theorem 1: Define $m_1, m_2, m_3, m_4, m_5, m_6$ as follows.

$$m_1 = \sum_{\substack{i \in \{2,4,5\} \\ j \in \{0,1,3\}}} (i,j), \quad m_2 = \sum_{\substack{i \in \{1,3,4\} \\ j \in \{5,0,2\}}} (i,j)$$

$$m_3 = \sum_{\substack{i \in \{0,2,3\} \\ j \in \{4,5,1\}}} (i,j), \quad m_4 = \sum_{\substack{i \in \{5,1,2\} \\ j \in \{3,4,0\}}} (i,j)$$

$$m_5 = \sum_{\substack{i \in \{4,0,1\} \\ j \in \{2,3,5\}}} (i,j), \quad m_6 = \sum_{\substack{i \in \{3,5,0\} \\ j \in \{1,2,4\}}} (i,j)$$

By Lemmas 5, 10, 11, 13, if $(p-1)(q-1)/36$ is even, then

$$d_s(1,0;w) = \begin{cases} (pq+p-q+3)/4, & w \in P \\ (pq-p+q-1)/4, & w \in Q \\ (p+q)/2 + m_1, & w \in D_0 \\ (p+q-2)/2 + m_2, & w \in D_1 \\ (p+q-2)/2 + m_3, & w \in D_2 \\ (p+q)/2 + m_4, & w \in D_3 \\ (p+q)/2 + m_5, & w \in D_4 \\ (p+q-2)/2 + m_6, & w \in D_5 \end{cases}$$

By Lemma 1, we have

$$72m_1 = 108\dot{M} - 4x + 12y - a + 3b - 3c - 27d$$
$$72m_2 = 108\dot{M} + 36 + 8x + 2a + 6c$$
$$72m_3 = 108\dot{M} - 4x - 12y - a - 3b - 3c + 27d$$
$$72m_4 = 108\dot{M} - 4x + 12y - a + 3b - 3c - 27d$$
$$72m_5 = 108\dot{M} - 36 + 8x + 2a + 6c$$
$$72m_6 = 108\dot{M} - 4x - 12y - a - 3b - 3c + 27d$$

Formula (1) then follows from

$$AC_s(w) = N - 4d_s(1,0;w), \quad w \neq 0 (\text{mod} N).$$

Similarly, we can prove Theorem 2.

4   Experimental Results

In this section, consider only the choice of g, we present some specific experimental results, such that the autocorrelation function takes on only a few values.

Let the symbols be the same as above, given fixed $(p, q, m, n, g, \bar{x})$, the Whiteman's generalized cyclotomic classes of order six defined by $D_i = \{g^s x^i : s = 0, 1, ..., e-1\}, i = 0, 1, ..., 5$ is fixed, then the corresponding $NGCS_6$ is also determined. Actually, for a given g, m and n are both determined by $m \equiv g(\bmod p)$ and $n \equiv g(\bmod q)$, $\bar{x}$ is also determined by both $\bar{x} \equiv g(\bmod p)$ and $\bar{x} \equiv 1(\bmod q)$.

Example 2:   Let p, q $(p < q)$ be two odd primes with $gcd(p - 1, q - 1) = d$. By a computer calculation, we find some specific results of $(p, q, m, n, g, \bar{x})$ such that $AC_s(w)$ is four-valued, five-valued or six-valued. We list in the last column whether $AC_s(w) = -1$ for each $w \in Z_{pq}^*$ (see Table 2 in Appendix) (see Footnote 1).

5   Conclusion

In this paper, we constructed the new generalized cyclotomic sequences with order six and length pq, and determined the autocorrelation values of the corresponding sequences. Besides, we found examples involving p, q such that the autocorrelation function takes on only a few values.

Theorem 1 shows that the sequences have six-valued autocorrelations when $(p - 1)(q - 1)/36$ is even, while Theorem 2 shows that the sequences have nine-valued autocorrelations when $(p - 1)(q - 1)/36$ is odd. In the former case, we got conditions of p, q such that the autocorrelation function $AC_s(w)$ is four-valued. Besides, consider only the choice of g, primitive root of both p and q, we present some specific experimental results such that the autocorrelation function takes on only a few values. The construction contributes to the understanding of the periodic autocorrelation structure of cyclotomically-constructed binary sequences.

Acknowledgment. The authors would like to thank the anonymous reviewers for their helpful comments. This work is supported by the National Grand Fundamental Research 973 Program of China(Grant No. 2013CB338002, 2013CB338003), the Strategic Priority Research Program of the Chinese Academy of Sciences (Grant No. XDA06010701), IIE's Research Project on Cryptography (Grant No. Y3Z0016102), and the programs of the National Natural Science Foundation of China (Grant No. 60833008, 60603018, 61173134, 91118006, 61272476).

6   Appendix

We list in Table 1 part of the results in *Example* 1, and Table 2 part of the results in *Example* 2.

Table 1. Some result that $AC_s(w) = -1$ for each $w \in Z^*_{pq}$

Period $N = p * q$	x, y, a, b, c, d in Lemma 1	Property
$91 = 7 * 13$	$4, 5, 16, -6, -11, 3$	four-valued
$91 = 7 * 13$	$4, 5, 17, -5, -11, 3$	four-valued
$91 = 7 * 13$	$-8, 3, -11, -9, 16, 2$	four-valued
$91 = 7 * 13$	$-8, 3, -16, -6, 16, 2$	four-valued
$427 = 7 * 61$	$-20, 3, -40, -6, 40, 2$	four-valued
$427 = 7 * 61$	$-20, -3, -40, 6, 41, 1$	four-valued
$511 = 7 * 73$	$22, 3, 44, -6, -44, 2$	four-valued
$511 = 7 * 73$	$22, -3, 37, 15, -44, 2$	four-valued
$247 = 13 * 19$	$10, 7, -25, 11, -4, 6$	four-valued
$403 = 13 * 31$	$16, 7, -17, 21, -17, 7$	four-valued
$403 = 13 * 31$	$-20, -1, -32, 14, 37, 3$	four-valued
$559 = 13 * 43$	$-14, 11, 28, 22, 7, 9$	four-valued
$559 = 13 * 43$	$22, -5, 47, -3, -47, -1$	four-valued
$1339 = 13 * 103$	$16, 19, -41, 35, -8, 14$	four-valued
$1147 = 31 * 37$	$-8, 19, 49, 27, -5, 13$	four-valued
$1591 = 37 * 43$	$-2, 23, 59, 31, -17, 15$	four-valued
$9991 = 97 * 103$	$58, 47, 17, 115, -83, 35$	four-valued
$13483 = 97 * 139$	$-116, 3, -232, -6, 232, 2$	four-valued
$21823 = 139 * 157$	$34, 83, 185, 133, -107, 53$	four-valued
$31243 = 157 * 199$	$-116, 77, -115, 193, 193, 57$	four-valued
$107143 = 307 * 349$	$214, 143, 275, 343, -377, 103$	four-valued

Table 2. some results that $AC_s(w)$ is four, five or six-valued

Primes p, q	Choice of g	$m, n, \bar{x}$	Property	$AC_s(w) = -1$ for each $w \in Z^*_{pq}$
$7, 13$	80	$3, 2, 66$	four-valued	no
$7, 13$	54	$5, 2, 40$	four-valued	no
$13, 19$	162	$6, 10, 58$	four-valued	no
$61, 67$	2	$2, 2, 3418$	four-valued	no
$67, 97$	1950	$7, 10, 2620$	four-valued	no
$73, 103$	2787	$13, 6, 1546$	four-valued	no
$79, 97$	6800	$6, 10, 3008$	four-valued	no
$7, 13$	45	$3, 6, 66$	four-valued	yes
$7, 61$	124	$5, 2, 306$	four-valued	yes

Table 2. (*Continued*)

Primes p, q	Choice of g	$m, n, \bar{x}$	Property	$AC_s(w) = -1$ for each $w \in Z_{pq}^*$
7, 73	159	5, 13, 439	four-valued	yes
13, 151	1371	6, 12, 1813	four-valued	yes
13, 379	2	2, 2, 2654	four-valued	yes
19, 409	21	2, 21, 819	four-valued	yes
43, 157	2841	3, 15, 6281	four-valued	yes
67, 181	4362	7, 18, 10861	four-valued	yes
67, 373	2	2, 2, 11191	four-valued	yes
67, 373	1066	61, 320, 21635	four-valued	yes
67, 373	14533	61, 359, 21635	four-valued	yes
73, 211	5488	13, 2, 7386	four-valued	yes
97, 139	975	5, 2, 10287	four-valued	yes
7, 19	40	5, 2, 96	five-valued	no
31, 43	476	11, 3, 259	five-valued	no
7, 19	59	3, 2, 115	six-valued	no
7, 31	166	5, 11, 187	six-valued	no

References

1. Ding, C.: Binary cyclotomic generators. In: Preneel, B. (ed.) FSE 1994. LNCS, vol. 1008, pp. 29–60. Springer, Heidelberg (1995)
2. Helleseth, T., Kumar, P.V.: Sequences with low correlation. In: Pless, V., Huffman, W.C. (eds.) Handbook of Coding Theory, vol. II, pp. 1765–1854. Elsevier, The Nether-lands (1998)
3. Whiteman, A.L.: A family of difference sets. Ill. J. Math. **6**, 107–121 (1962)
4. Ding, C.: Autocorrelation values of generalized cyclotomic sequences of order two. IEEE Trans. Inf. Theory **44**(4), 1699–1702 (1998)
5. Ding, C.: Linear complexity of the generalized cyclotomic sequence of order 2. Finite Fields Appl. **3**(2), 159–174 (1997)
6. Bai, E., Liu, X.: Generalized cyclotomic sequences of order four over Z_{pq} and their autocorrelation values. Gongcheng Shuxue Xuebao **25**(5), 894–900 (2008)
7. Hu, L., Yue, Q.: Autocorrelation value of Whiteman generalized cyclotomic sequence. J. Math. Res. Appl. **32**(4), 415–422 (2012)
8. Ding, C., Pei, D., Salomaa, A.: Chinese Remainder Theorem: Applications in Computing, Coding, Cryptography, Chap. 2. World Scientific, Singapore (1996)
9. Storer, T.: Cyclotomy and Difference Sets. Markham, Chicago (1967)

Applications: Systems and Theory

Automatic Detection and Analysis
of Encrypted Messages in Malware

Ruoxu Zhao$^{(\boxtimes)}$, Dawu Gu, Juanru Li, and Yuanyuan Zhang

Department of Computer Science and Engineering,
Shanghai Jiao Tong University, Shanghai, China
zhaoruoxu@gmail.com, dwgu@sjtu.edu.cn

Abstract. Encryption is increasingly used in network communications, especially by malicious software (malware) to hide its malicious activities and protect itself from being detected or analyzed. Understanding malware's encryption schemes helps researchers better analyze its network protocol, and then derive the internal structure of the malware. However, current techniques of encrypted protocol analysis have a lot of limitations. For example, they usually require the encryption part being separated from message processing which is hardly satisfied in today's malware, and they cannot provide detailed information about the encryption parameter such as the algorithm used and its secret key. Therefore, these techniques cannot fulfill the needs of today's malware analysis.

In this paper, we propose a novel and enhanced approach to automatically detect and analyze encryption and encoding functions within network applications. Utilizing dynamic taint analysis and data pattern analysis, we are able to detect encryption, encoding and checksum routines within the normal processing of protocol messages without prior knowledge of the protocol, and provide detailed information about its encryption scheme, including the algorithms used, secret keys, ciphertext and plaintext. We can also detect private or custom encryption routines made by malware authors, which can be used as signature of the malware. We evaluate our method with several malware samples to demonstrate its effectiveness.

Keywords: Network protocols · Encryption detection · Data analysis · Reverse engineering

1 Introduction

Today protocol reverse engineering is widely used in many security applications, especially in malware detection and analysis. To fully understand the intention and behavior of malware, security analysts usually have to obtain detailed network protocol information. However, current circumstance of the wider use of

Supported by the National Science and Technology Major Projects (Grant No.: 2012ZX03002011-002), the National Key Technology R&D Program (2012BAH426B02) and NSFC under Grant No. 61103040.

D. Lin et al. (Eds.): Inscrypt 2013, LNCS 8567, pp. 101–117, 2014.
DOI: 10.1007/978-3-319-12087-4_7

sophisticated encryption schemes in malware's network communication renders it very difficult to analyze the protocol directly. Several techniques were proposed to solve this problem [3,15,19], however these techniques have several critical weaknesses which make them inadequate in the analysis of current malware. First, these techniques usually require encryption or decryption to be in a separated phase from normal processing of protocol messages. This condition is hardly satisfied in today's malware, which usually uses several layers of different encryption or encoding schemes. Second, they usually detect encryption routines by the ratio of bitwise or arithmetic instructions. This condition also cannot be met when malware uses weaker but simpler encoding scheme instead of encryption, or with the existence of obfuscation. And third, these techniques only detect the existence of encryption routines but not the parameters such as the secret key. The lack of this information makes it very difficult to give a comprehensive view of the malware's internal structure.

We propose an in-depth approach to detect and analyze the encryption, encoding and checksum routines within a program using dynamic taint analysis [16] and dynamic data pattern analysis [23], and then uncover the complete structure of malware's protocol messages. First we construct the hierarchical structure of a protocol message using its procedure-level execution context. Then, we perform dynamic taint analysis on the possible procedures to discover encryption and encoding routines. After that, dynamic data pattern analysis is used to reveal the parameters of encryption or decryption, and to produce possible submessages. At last, we reconstruct sub-messages to the original protocol message to provide comprehensive analysis result of encrypted protocol content.

Some of our contributions are listed below.

- We use dynamic taint analysis as the primary tool to locate encryption or encoding within the message processing, eliminating the former requirement of the separation of encryption and message processing. We also propose methods to distinguish different layers of encryption, revealing the internal structure of encrypted message.
- Dynamic data pattern analysis is used to extract the high-value parameters of encryption, including the algorithm used, secret keys, ciphertext, plaintext, etc. This information is valuable to security analysts, and can be used as signature to malware detection and classification.
- We provide methods to detect non-public or custom made encryption or encoding routines used in malware's protocols automatically, with no prior knowledge of the malware. Some of the parameters used in custom algorithms can be extracted at the same time.
- We use entropy metrics and data characteristics as powerful supplements to distinguish encryption routines (focusing on confusion and diffusion) and encoding routines (focusing on transformation). The entropy metrics provide a convenient way to discover the underlying nature of detected algorithm.
- We evaluate our method with custom programs as well as several real world malware samples to show the effectiveness of our approach, including ZeuS P2P botnet, Mega-D botnet, Storm botnet, etc.

2   Background and Related Work

Protocol reverse engineering has gained significant attention in recent years. Polyglot [4] took the first step to automatically reverse engineer the message format using dynamic program analysis techniques. Utilizing dynamic taint analysis, it can discover different kinds of message fields such as direction fields and keywords. AutoFormat [14] took a step further to detect the structural information about protocol messages. The work by Wondracek et al. [20] combined multiple messages together to deduce the internal structure of messages. All these approaches worked on plain unencrypted messages. There are other systems [6,7] proposed to automatically infer the protocol state machine using program analysis techniques. The first effort to reverse engineer encrypted protocol content automatically was made by the system ReFormat [19], and then Dispatcher [3]. They took similar approaches with the assumption of the separation of decryption and message processing, and used instruction characteristics to detect the decryption function. The lack of flexibility and detailed information about cryptographic parameters limited their usages. There are other approaches [8,17,18] that used network traces to analyze protocols. These approaches arc mostly probabilistic and require prior knowledge about the protocol, which are less accurate than the program analysis based approaches.

Automatic detection and analysis of cryptographic algorithms is also a hot topic of security research in recent years. Gröbert's work [11] took the first step to detect cryptographic primitives in software using dynamic data analysis techniques. Zhao et al. [22,23] extended this work using dynamic data pattern analysis, which is more effective and accurate. The system Aligot [5] focused on detecting cryptographic algorithms in obfuscated software using loop detection techniques. CipherXRay [13] used the avalanche effect of cryptographic algorithms and dynamic taint analysis to detect the input-output dependency of cryptographic algorithms.

In this paper, we combine protocol reverse engineering techniques with cryptographic algorithm detection techniques to provide in-depth and comprehensive detection and analysis of encrypted protocol messages. We also extend the cryptographic algorithm detection to encoding functions and propose information entropy based metrics to distinguish encryption and encoding functions. Our approach requires no prior knowledge of the protocol or the algorithms, and tries to detect generic patterns and reveal complete structures of encrypted messages.

3   System Description

3.1   System Overview

Our system is designed to automatically extract the detailed internal structure and data protection schemes of an encrypted protocol message. Given a sample of a program, our system runs it within the execution monitor, and outputs the complete structure of encrypted network messages, with detailed information about its encryption, hashing and checksums used in different layers of the processing of the message. To achieve this goal, our system takes the following steps: (a) Run the program in the execution monitor (emulator) and obtain runtime traces containing low-level context data. (b) Upon receiving a message, our system analyzes the procedure call hierarchy and the message structure. (c) Analyze possible encryption (or decryption), encoding (or decoding) and checksum routines with the message processing. The decrypted (or decoded) data is extracted as sub-messages. (d) We continue step (b) on all sub-messages and subsequent messages until the analysis is complete, and output all analysis result. An overview of the architecture of our system is shown in Fig. 1.

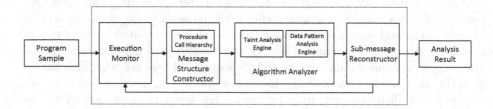

Fig. 1. System architecture

Dynamic Execution Monitoring. In order to obtain program runtime data, the program to be analyzed is run in a formerly available program emulation system [22]. Fine-grained information, including CPU instructions, register values, memory accesses and parameters of system API calls, can be visited conveniently. All networking APIs are hooked to notify our system when a network message is received, including the message data and context information. All subsequent processing of the message is monitored by our system to analyze possibly encrypted message content. The analysis and program execution are done simultaneously for better performance.

3.2   Message Structure Inference

The first step during analysis is to construct the internal hierarchical structure of a message into a tree structure. The message tree is later used to reconstruct the meaningful hierarchy of an encrypted message and its sub-messages. To achieve this, our system is based on the simple observation: Most functionality units of a program are implemented as procedures, especially encryption routines, hashing routines and checksums. This fact accords with the software engineering principle of modularized design, and is common in today's software even in malware.

During program execution, our message structure analyzer maintains a virtual call stack to track current procedure call hierarchy. Whenever message data is accessed (to byte granularity), we record its call stack context, and append it

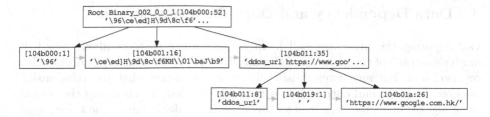

Fig. 2. A sample message tree

to the message tree properly. All message data with the same context are merged in the final tree. A sample of constructed message tree is shown in Fig. 2.

The sole purpose of message structure reconstruction is for the reconstruction of decrypted or decoded sub-messages. We can also analyze message field format in this step, which has been extensively studied [3,4,9,14,20]. So here we omit the analysis of message field format and focus on encrypted data.

3.3 Data-Oriented Analysis and Algorithm Detection

After the inference of message structure, we conduct data-oriented analysis on each of the possible procedures. The data analysis mainly includes dynamic data taint analysis for the detection of data dependency, and dynamic data pattern analysis for the detection of specific algorithms. We'll discuss this in detail in Sect. 4.

3.4 Sub-message Generation

A sub-message is an encrypted or encoded partial message which is embedded within its parent message. A sub-message often indicates a new layer of the original message, which usually has different semantic meanings and is processed in different routines. After each successful detection of an algorithm in the previous step, we spot the beginning of a sub-message starting at the completion point of the algorithm. We then analyze the sub-message recursively until all sub-messages are detected and analyzed.

3.5 Message Reconstruction

Upon the completion of analysis of each sub-message, we discard the original analysis of the sub-message in its parent message and append the newly generated sub-message. The final result is a tree-like structure where all layers of the processing of the original message and the conversions of message data are clear to analysts. Examples of our final result are shown in Sect. 5.

4 Data Dependency and Data Pattern Analysis

On acquiring the procedure call hierarchy, we are able to conduct data flow analysis on each of the procedure call that possibly contains encryption, encoding or checksum. For any deterministic algorithm, we argue that the relationship between its input and output data is uniquely decided, which means the output of an algorithm is predetermined for any fixed input data. This is the key concept in the whole analysis phase.

For each trace of procedure call, we conduct dynamic taint analysis first to test if the input-output data dependency satisfies the characteristics of a certain algorithm. We use every byte of the received message as the taint source, and track the flow of the message in each procedure. For those whose output data is tainted, we perform further analysis on it to test if a specific algorithm exists. This approach has the limitation that not all input parameters of an algorithm can be tainted in the same procedure. This limitation can be resolved using dynamic data pattern analysis.

To certify the existence of an algorithm, we conduct dynamic data pattern analysis on selected procedures. For each procedure, all possible combinations of input and output data are iterated to see if the data pattern is satisfied. In the meantime, the parameters of an algorithm can be extracted as side products. We further discuss the analysis details using these techniques for different kinds of algorithms.

4.1 Detecting Block Ciphers

For block ciphers, we use the avalanche effect as theoretical basis for our analysis. The avalanche effect says that flipping a single bit in input results in about half of the output bits being flipped in a well-designed block cipher. In fact, if we consider the situation for each byte, the possibility of an output byte not being affected by any one of the input byte is so low that it cannot happen in one experiment, even for a short 64-bit block [13]. Hence, we argue that every byte in the output data of a block cipher is dependent on every byte of its input data. Dynamic taint analysis is just the right tool to detect this dependency. Whenever we found a block of output data being completely tainted by a block of input data, we further analyze this block using data pattern analysis to verify. A demonstration of the data dependency of block ciphers is shown in Fig. 3.

Key Scheduling. Before actual encryption of a block cipher, a program must perform key scheduling first to generate the sub-keys. In most of the malware, the secret key is embedded in its binary, thus won't be tainted in procedure input. We use the strategy of retainting the input using some special taint tags, and test if every byte of the possible sub-key is tainted by a subset of input key. Then data pattern analysis is performed to verify its belonging to an algorithm.

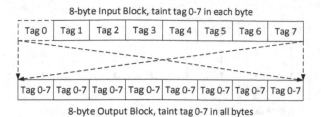

8-byte Input Block, taint tag 0-7 in each byte

| Tag 0 | Tag 1 | Tag 2 | Tag 3 | Tag 4 | Tag 5 | Tag 6 | Tag 7 |

| Tag 0-7 | Tag 0-7 | Tag 0-7 | Tag 0-7 | Tag 0-7 | Tag 0-7 | Tag 0-7 | Tag 0-7 |

8-byte Output Block, taint tag 0-7 in all bytes

Fig. 3. Block cipher data dependency

Modes of Operation. With the power of taint analysis and data pattern analysis, detecting modes of operation of block ciphers is fairly straightforward. We demonstrate how some of modes of operation is detected.

Electronic Codebook (ECB). There's no initialization vector (IV) in ECB mode, so it can be detected using taint analysis only.

Cipher-Block Chaining (CBC). In CBC mode, the IV is first XORed with plaintext, and then encrypted to produce the ciphertext. We first detect the block encryption and get the actual input, which is the XORed result. We then perform XOR with the tainted message input, and get the IV used in encryption.

Cipher Feedback (CFB) and Output Feedback (OFB). In CFB and OFB mode, the IV is encrypted and then XORed with the plaintext to produce the ciphertext. For most of the malware implementations, the IV is embedded in the malware's binary, just like the secret key. So we detect the IV first using data pattern analysis in the first block, and detect subsequent encryptions using taint analysis.

Counter (CTR). In CTR mode, each block input can be untainted in our analysis, so we detect all blocks using data pattern analysis.

4.2 Detecting Stream Ciphers

Most stream ciphers don't have a strong data dependency like the block ciphers. The plaintext of stream ciphers is usually XORed with some value to produce the ciphertext. Hence, each byte of the ciphertext of stream ciphers must be tainted by at least the corresponding byte in plaintext. We then use data pattern analysis to verify the data dependency.

Key Scheduling. Stream ciphers like RC4 may also have a key scheduling process. This process is actually quite similar to the key scheduling of block ciphers where each byte of the scheduled key is tainted by a part of the secret key. As most of the secret keys are untainted in our analysis, we also detect them using data pattern analysis (Fig. 4).

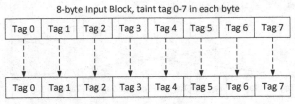

Fig. 4. Stream cipher data dependency

4.3 Detecting Hash Functions

Like block ciphers, well designed hash functions also have the property of the avalanche effect. Unlike block ciphers, they produce the same length of output regardless of the length of their input. The strong data dependency is a notable signature of hash functions. We take similar approaches as before to detect hash functions.

4.4 Detecting Encoding Functions

The encoding functions we refer to are used to transform data into another format for network transmission, such as the widely used Base64. They don't have cryptographic characteristics and their encoded message can be decoded easily. However, they still remain some weak data dependency which is similar to stream ciphers, and can be used as a signature to detect these functions. Some of the encoding functions produce different length of output to the input, so we modify the method used in stream ciphers to handle variable length of output data.

Some of the malware authors don't care much about the security of their encryption functions, and just use a simpler encoding scheme instead. However, this approach is usually good enough to bypass most of the intrusion detection systems or black-box analysis [10]. We further describe this situation in Sect. 4.6.

4.5 Detecting Checksums

Malware usually uses checksums to detect errors or modifications of network data. Unlike hash functions, checksums usually have a small length and can be easily forged. Most of the checksums don't exceed 32-bit, and can fit into a register of x86 CPUs. Therefore, we detect checksum routines using register values as well as memory data, to see if a small-size datum is dependent on the whole input block. Data pattern analysis includes common checksum algorithms like CRC-32, Alder-32, bitwise XOR and arithmetic sum.

4.6   Inferring Private Algorithms

Apart from using standard algorithms, many malware authors choose to use custom or modified algorithms to avoid detection. Doing so further increases the difficult to reverse engineer the malware samples or to analyze network traffic. It's of great importance to detect these kinds of algorithms, since they provide valuable information to security analysts. Here we discuss the techniques we use to detect custom or private encryption and encoding algorithms.

Although the details of private algorithms remain unknown prior to our analysis, they do exhibit many of the features of standard algorithms mentioned earlier. We still use data analysis techniques as weapons to uncover the nature of these algorithms. Since many of the details are unavailable to our analysis, we have to introduce extra techniques to extract them. We introduce information entropy based metrics for algorithm classification, and discuss in detail about the detection of each kind of algorithms.

Entropy Metrics.   In information theory, entropy is used to quantify the expected value of the information contained in a message. We use Shannon entropy here for the measurement of the randomness of data. Given a block of binary data d(length $n > 0$), and $c_i(0 \le i < 256)$ denoting the total occurrences of byte i in d, we defined the normalized entropy $H(d)$ as:

$$H(d) = -\frac{\sum_{i=0}^{255} \frac{c_i}{n} \log_2 \frac{c_i}{n}}{\log_2 n} (0 < H(d) \le 1)$$

Unencrypted messages or texts usually have a low $H(d)$ value, yet encrypted binary data tends to have a high (nearly 1) $H(d)$ value. In this way, we further define the quotient of the entropy of the output data d_o and the input data d_i for a procedure trace p as:

$$Q(p) = \frac{H(d_o)}{H(d_i)}$$

For short messages, the $H(d)$ or $Q(p)$ value may not be meaningful, as information entropy is a statistical concept. However, our experiments suggest that for medium length (tens or hundreds of bytes) messages, the $H(d)$ and $Q(p)$ value can be used to measure the randomness indeed. We'll discuss the usages of entropy metrics below, and show our experiment results in Sect. 5.

Block Ciphers.   For the detection of private block ciphers, we use taint analysis to discover the data dependency. The key scheduling and modes of operation (other than ECB), however, cannot be easily detected because of the unavailability of data pattern analysis. For most of block cipher decryptions, the Q value is usually below 0.8, which is the lowest among all kinds of algorithms.

Stream Ciphers and Encoding Functions. Private stream ciphers and encoding functions exhibit almost the same features in our analysis, as they all show byte-to-byte mapping in our data dependency analysis. The first difference is that encoding (or decoding) functions may have input and output data with different lengths, yet in stream ciphers the length is always the same. Another difference is that the Q value of stream ciphers is generally lower than encoding functions. We use an empirical Q value of 0.9 as the boundary, where procedures of Q below 0.9 as stream ciphers and above as encoding functions.

Many malware authors use XOR-based encryption schemes. There are mainly two kinds of XOR-based encryptions: one is chained-XOR, where each byte is XORed with previous value to get the encrypted byte; the other one is keyed-XOR, where each byte is XORed with a short custom-scheduled key (similar to RC4). In our analysis, we treat the chained-XOR as encoding, whereas the keyed-XOR as encryption, which is supported by the experiment results of entropy metrics.

Hash Functions and Checksums. Hash functions have very distinguishable data characteristics. They have a strong data dependency, and their Q value is usually above 1.1. Checksum routines share the data characteristics of hash functions, except that their output is too short for entropy metrics.

5   Implementation and Evaluation

We implemented our system as a plugin module of the LochsEmu emulator [21, 22], which can be used to analyze 32-bit Windows programs. This infrastructure enables us to conduct efficient and convenient data-oriented analysis. Other available frontend options include QEMU [2] and PIN [1], but they usually require tracing the intermediate result into hard disk first, which introduces considerable performance deduction. We implemented the taint analysis engine, the data pattern analysis engine and algorithm analyzers as loosely coupled submodules with about 10k lines of C++ code.

We chose some custom made programs for test purposes, and some variants or self-compiled versions of real-world malware (botnet) for validation and evaluation, including ZeuS P2P botnet, Mega-D, Storm, ZeroAccess, Festi and Mariposa. Most of the test samples are botnet clients which have extensive network communication. Our target algorithms include block cipher DES (ECB, CBC and CFB modes), stream cipher RC4 and chained XOR, hash function MD5, encoding function Base64 and checksum functions CRC32 and Alder32. We also detect private or custom algorithms which we call generic symmetric ciphers, generic stream ciphers and generic encoding/decoding algorithms. An overview of our evaluation result is in Table 1.

Table 1. Evaluation result overview

Sample	Result
Mega-D	DES key schedule; DES-ECB decryption
ZeuS P2P	Chained XOR; MD5; RC4 key schedule; RC4 decryption
Storm	Generic decoding; Checksum (XOR 8-bit); Checksum (ADD 8-bit)
ZeroAccess	Generic stream decryption; Checksum (CRC32)
Festi	Generic stream decryption
Mariposa	Generic stream decryption
Test Sample 1	DES key schedule; DES-CBC decryption; DES-CFB decryption
Test Sample 2	Base64 decoding

5.1 Entropy Metrics

We use entropy metrics for the distinguishing of encryption and encoding. The Q values of the samples above are shown in Fig. 5.

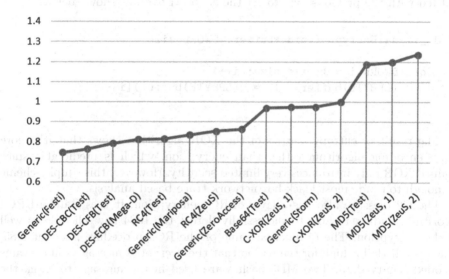

Fig. 5. Values of Q function

There's a huge gap between MD5 hash function and other algorithms because MD5 acts like encryption which makes entropy higher, while others are decryption or decoding which reduces entropy. Generally, we treat procedures with $Q > 1.1$ as encryption functions or hash functions. We set the Q range $0.9 < Q \leq 1.1$ for encoding and decoding. All detected decoding routines fell into this range with Q values near 1.0. All decryption routines met the condition that $Q \leq 0.9$, generally within the range from 0.75 to 0.85. These decryption routines include both symmetric ciphers and stream ciphers.

5.2   Case Study

ZeuS P2P Botnet.   The C2 message (type 0xCC) is the most complicated encrypted message we analyzed. It contains three layers of encryption or encoding, and two MD5 hash data blocks used as checksums. The layout of a ZeuS C2 message is shown in Fig. 6, and the complete structure of a ZeuS message is in Appendix A.

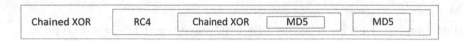

Fig. 6. ZeuS message layout

The chained XOR algorithm is a fundamental algorithm used in ZeuS botnet, and the outmost layer of every ZeuS message is encoded using chained XOR. This algorithm uses a single fixed byte as initialization byte, and each byte is XORed with the previous byte to get the encoded byte, as shown below.

```
void _visualEncrypt (void *buffer, DWORD size)
{
    for (DWORD i = 1; i < size; i++)
        ((LPBYTE)buffer)[i] ^= ((LPBYTE)buffer)[i - 1];
}
```

The result of entropy metrics of the XOR algorithm shows that it's more of an encoding algorithm rather than encryption, which is predictable since chained XOR only introduces very limited security. However, this simple scheme is enough to evade most black-box network trace based analysis.

The C2 message also has a layer of RC4 encryption. It uses standard RC4 algorithm, and we're able to successfully detect the RC4 key schedule as well as the encryption. The Q function value of the RC4 procedure is about 0.85, which is a little bit high for the reason that the decrypted message still contains encoded binary data. Two MD5 hashes are used in the message to check the message's integrity. They're both successfully detected and their occurrences are linked with MD5's output, shown in Appendix A.

With the information above, security analysts can easily grasp the high-level structure of a large complicated message, and focus on an interesting point to do further manual analysis. This information can also be used to study the evolvement of a particular malware.

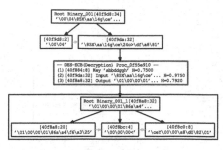

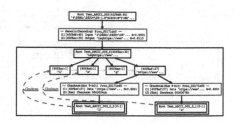

Fig. 7. The Mega-D message   **Fig. 8.** The storm message

Mega-D Botnet. The Mega-D botnet uses DES-ECB encryption to protect its network communication. A sample analysis result of Mega-D message is shown in Fig. 7.

The Mega-D messages begin with a two-byte field specifying the number of DES blocks. The example above shows that there're 4 blocks in this message. The decryption is detected including its secret key, ciphertext and plaintext. The decrypted plaintext is further divided into several parts, and in this example they indicate some ID fields.

One thing worth mentioning is that Mega-D encrypts its message with embedded secret key 'abcdefgh', however the detected secret key is 'abbddggh'. That's because 'abbddggh' is the parity-fixed value of 'abcdefgh', and obviously they produce the same S-box for DES decryption after fixing parity.

Storm Botnet. The Storm botnet uses a encoding algorithm which is similar to Base64 [12]. The plaintext is first padded and separated into 6-bit units and then each unit is added with 0x21 to get the encoded byte. The decoded data contains two bytes for checksum, one is 8-bit sum modulo 256 and the other is 8-bit bitwise XOR, as shown in Fig. 8.

ZeroAccess, Festi and Mariposa. The encryption schemes for these three botnet samples are all custom XOR-based stream ciphers. ZeroAccess uses a custom scheduled 256-byte S-box, which is similar to RC4. It also uses a CRC32 checksum within the decrypted message to validate integrity, shown in Fig. 9.

Festi uses a 4-byte embedded key, and performs bitwise XOR of the plaintext and the key every 4 bytes to get the ciphertext. Mariposa uses a 2-byte key derived from the plaintext. It's easy to see that these encryption algorithms are not cryptographically secure, but very easy to implement and use. There's really no point in using the encryption algorithms that are proven to be secure under the circumstance that the software binary can be obtained and analyzed, so this kind of simple encryption schemes is widely used by malware authors.

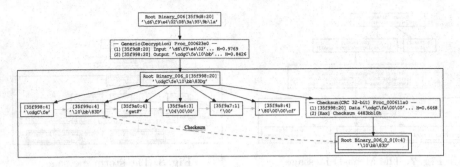

Fig. 9. The ZeroAccess message

6   Conclusion

In this paper, we present a novel encrypted protocol analysis technique that can be used to reveal the complicated encrypted message structure of today's malware. We first infer the message structure using runtime context, and reconstruct the message into a tree hierarchy. We then use data-oriented analysis techniques including taint analysis and data pattern analysis to detect encryption, encoding and checksum routines and extract possible sub-messages. At last, we analyze recursively on all sub-messages to uncover the complete structure of an encrypted message.

With the power of dynamic taint analysis and dynamic data pattern analysis, we're able to detect public encryption and encoding algorithms such as DES, RC4 and Base64. We can also locate possible custom or private algorithms, which are widely used by malware. The use of entropy metrics makes it possible to find out the data characteristics and distinguish encryption and encoding functions. We evaluate our technique using 6 malware samples as well as some custom made test programs. The evaluation result shows that our technique is reliable and accurate to detect both public and private algorithms, and to extract the complete structure of messages with complicated encryption and encoding schemes.

A   ZeuS Botnet Message Format

See Fig. 10.

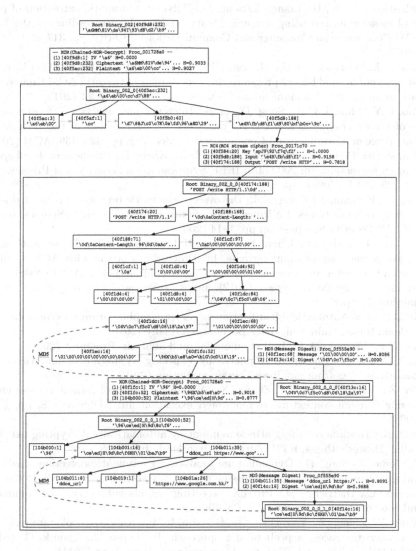

Fig. 10. ZeuS message format

References

1. PIN - a dynamic binary instrumentation tool. http://software.intel.com/en-us/articles/pin-a-dynamic-binary-instrumentation-tool
2. QEMU open source processor emulator. http://wiki.qemu.org/Main_Page

3. Caballero, J., Poosankam, P., Kreibich, C., Song, D.: Dispatcher: enabling active botnet infiltration using automatic protocol reverse-engineering. In: Proceedings of the 16th ACM Conference on Computer and Communications Security, pp. 621–634. ACM (2009)

4. Caballero, J., Yin, H., Liang, Z., Song, D.: Polyglot: automatic extraction of protocol message format using dynamic binary analysis. In: Proceedings of the 14th ACM Conference on Computer and Communications Security, pp. 317–329. ACM (2007)

5. Calvet, J., Fernandez, J.M., Marion, J.Y.: Aligot: cryptographic function identification in obfuscated binary programs. In: Proceedings of the 2012 ACM Conference on Computer and Communications Security, pp. 169–182. ACM (2012)

6. Cho, C.Y., Shin, E.C.R., Song, D., et al.: Inference and analysis of formal models of botnet command and control protocols. In: Proceedings of the 17th ACM Conference on Computer and Communications Security, pp. 426–439. ACM (2010)

7. Comparetti, P.M., Wondracek, G., Kruegel, C., Kirda, E.: Prospex: protocol specification extraction. In: 2009 30th IEEE Symposium on Security and Privacy, pp. 110–125. IEEE (2009)

8. Cui, W., Kannan, J., Wang, H.J.: Discoverer: automatic protocol reverse engineering from network traces. In: Proceedings of 16th USENIX Security Symposium on USENIX Security Symposium, pp. 1–14 (2007)

9. Cui, W., Peinado, M., Chen, K., Wang, H.J., Irun-Briz, L.: Tupni: automatic reverse engineering of input formats. In: Proceedings of the 15th ACM Conference on Computer and Communications Security, pp. 391–402. ACM (2008)

10. Elisan, C.: The XOR bypass (2012). https://blog.damballa.com/archives/tag/malware-dropper

11. Gröbert, F.: Automatic identification of cryptographic primitives in software. Diploma thesis, Ruhr-University Bochum, Germany (2010)

12. Lee, C.P.: Framework for botnet emulation and analysis. ProQuest (2009)

13. Li, X., Wang, X., Chang, W.: CipherXRay: exposing cryptographic operations and transient secrets from monitored binary execution (2012)

14. Lin, Z., Jiang, X., Xu, D., Zhang, X.: Automatic protocol format reverse engineering through context-aware monitored execution. In: NDSS, vol. 8, pp. 1–15 (2008)

15. Lutz, N.: Towards revealing attackers intent by automatically decrypting network traffic. Master's thesis, ETH, Zürich, Switzerland, July 2008

16. Newsome, J., Song, D.: Dynamic taint analysis for automatic detection, analysis, and signature generation of exploits on commodity software. In: NDSS (2005)

17. Rossow, C., Dietrich, C.J.: ProVeX: detecting botnets with encrypted command and control channels. In: DIMVA (2013)

18. Wang, Y., Zhang, Z., Yao, D.D., Qu, B., Guo, L.: Inferring protocol state machine from network traces: a probabilistic approach. In: Lopez, J., Tsudik, G. (eds.) ACNS 2011. LNCS, vol. 6715, pp. 1–18. Springer, Heidelberg (2011)

19. Wang, Z., Jiang, X., Cui, W., Wang, X., Grace, M.: ReFormat: automatic reverse engineering of encrypted messages. In: Backes, M., Ning, P. (eds.) ESORICS 2009. LNCS, vol. 5789, pp. 200–215. Springer, Heidelberg (2009)

20. Wondracek, G., Comparetti, P.M., Kruegel, C., Kirda, E., Anna, S.S.S.: Automatic network protocol analysis. In: NDSS, vol. 8, pp. 1–14 (2008)

21. Zhao, R.: Lochsemu process emulator for windows x86. https://github.com/zhaoruoxu/lochsemu

22. Zhao, R., Gu, D., Li, J., Liu, H.: Detecting encryption functions via process emulation and IL-based program analysis. In: Chim, T.W., Yuen, T.H. (eds.) ICICS 2012. LNCS, vol. 7618, pp. 252–263. Springer, Heidelberg (2012)
23. Zhao, R., Gu, D., Li, J., Yu, R.: Detection and analysis of cryptographic data inside software. In: Lai, X., Zhou, J., Li, H. (eds.) ISC 2011. LNCS, vol. 7001, pp. 182–196. Springer, Heidelberg (2011)

EAdroid: Providing Environment Adaptive Security for Android System

Hongliang Liang[1(✉)], Yu Dong[1], Bin Wang[2], and Shuchang Liu[1]

[1] Beijing University of Posts and Telecommunications, Beijing, China
hliang@bupt.edu.cn
[2] Beijing Institute of Technology, Beijing, China

Abstract. With the rapid popularization of Android system around the world, of the increase in Android malwares post serious threats to the security of users' Android device and the privacy stored in it. At the same time, many trusted third party institutions (such as military, government institutions) need to customize the security policy of their Android devices according to their regulations, but most of them do not have this capability. This paper proposed an environment adaptive security mechanism for Android platform called EAdroid, which providing a simple way for trusted third party institutions to customize the security policy of their Android devices. EAdroid reforms the framework layer of Android system and synthetically applies Smack security module of Linux. At the same time, the security rules of framework layer and kernel layer in EAdroid can adapt to the current environment context. Series of tests show that EAdroid can efficiently protect the security of user's devices and privacy with negligible overhead of performance.

Keywords: Environment adaptive · Security · Android system · Access control

1 Introduction

In recent years, the Android devices have become increasingly popular [1]. At the same time, due to the shortage of Android's default security mechanism, the number of the Android malwares is in fast growth too, and they have posted serious threats to the security of users' Android device and the privacy stored in it.

The Android system is developed based on Linux kernel. In addition to the fine process isolation mechanism, discretionary access control (DAC) and other security mechanisms inherited from Linux system, Android also provides a Permission Mechanism to classify the behaviors of applications and control them by different permissions. Developers have to specify the corresponding permissions in the installation package based on the functionality of their applications. Users will get the permissions information of the applications and decide if the applications will be installed or not.

Although Android used a variety of security mechanisms to protect mobile devices, the imperfection of these security mechanisms leads to the rapidly spread of malwares. First, most users do not have the ability to judge the security of the

© Springer International Publishing Switzerland 2014
D. Lin et al. (Eds.): Inscrypt 2013, LNCS 8567, pp. 118–131, 2014.
DOI: 10.1007/978-3-319-12087-4_8

applications they are going to install based on the permission information; Even assuming that the users have the ability above, the way of granting permission (for example, install or not) in Android system is still coarse-grained. Users will likely choose to use of applications and ignore the security. More importantly, Android's security mechanisms were based on the DAC mechanism of Linux kernel, which consigns the security management capabilities of the files and other objects to their owner user. The process started by the user has the same permissions as the user. If the programs that run as root contains vulnerabilities, malwares may gain the root privilege through them [2, 3].

Beyond that, only some mobile phone manufacture and mobile telecom carrier have the abilities to develop and customize Android system. Some trusted third party (TTP), such as government agencies, military, scientific research departments, commercial organizations, need to allot Android device for their staffs. Nevertheless, they don't have the capacities to customize Android system according to their security regulations, which means the behavior of the APPs in their Android devices cannot be controlled by their regulations.

Motivated by these problems, this paper proposes a mobile-device oriented, fine-grained and environment adaptive security mechanism called EAdroid, which bring users or TTP institutions a simple way to customize the security policy of their devices. Our main contributions are that:

- We present an environment adaptive security mechanism called EAdroid, which can protect users against malwares according to the environment context. It means EAdroid can bring TTP or normal users with a more flexible and fine-grained way to control their Android devices.
- We build a prototype system of EAdroid to control the behavior of Android applications on both framework layer and kernel layer. Moreover, we have unified the control in the both layers seamlessly.
- Experiments show the effectiveness of EAdroid in protecting against a variety of attacks including privacy leakage, money stealing and root exploit with negligible performance overhead.

The paper is organized as follows: Sect. 2 shows the detailed design of EAdroid in policy forms and architecture. In Sect. 3 we present some obstacles when implementing EAdroid and our methods to solve them. Section 4 describes the evaluation of EAdroid. Related works are discussed in Sects. 5 and 6 concludes.

2 Environment Adaptive Security Mechanism for Android

EAdroid aims to provide an environment adaptive security mechanism for Android system. With this mechanism, users or TTP can specify their security regulations as EAdroid rules on their Android devices. In addition, the rules can control the behaviors of the applications according to the environment. For example, users can make the applications labeled with "untrusted" unable to send SMS during 8:00 am to 8:00 pm. The policy forms and the architecture of EAdroid are described below.

2.1 Policy Forms

To make the policy rules for EAdroid, the users first need to know the forms of the rule. EAdroid defines the forms of the rule as follow:

Definition 1. $R = (\langle L \rangle, \langle P \rangle, \langle E \rangle, \langle C \rangle)$ is the set of all the possible rules. And the single rule belongs to R is represented as $r = (l, p, e, c)$. "**L**" is the set of all applications' labels "**l**", where $L ::= system|trusted|untrusted$. "**P**" is the set of all the permissions "**p**" controlled by EAdroid (such as *android.permission.INTERNET*). "**E**" is the set of all environment types "**e**" that can be detected by EAdroid, where $E ::= time|location$. "**C**" is the set of all possible environments context "**c**", and the content of "**c**" is decided by the value of "**e**".

The three values of "**L**" represent three categories of applications, which are system applications (system), trusted applications (trusted) and untrusted applications (untrusted). The "system" label corresponds to the applications that are installed by default in the system and are necessary to the completeness of the device functions, such as telephone, message, browser, etc. Label "trusted" corresponds to the applications that preset by TTP for their terminal and are used to complete specific tasks. "Untrusted" label corresponds to the applications download and installed by the actual users of device. The three labels is a general division of the APPs in security levels. The value of "E" is not fixed. The values of "L" will be extended in future work.

The set "P" includes permissions that may affect users' privacy together with the security of device, such as sending text messages, making phone calls, collecting contact information, setting system options etc. Users can choose permissions from P to control when they are setting each rule.

If the user selects "time" as the "e" of rule "r", then he need to set the beginning and ending time that the rule takes effect at the "c". For the same reason, if the user selects "location" as "e", then he need to set the range of the location (latitude and longitude) that the rule takes effect at the "c". The two environment types are the most common ones in the regulations of the TTP. Therefore, it can apply to most of the scenarios. Rule-makers only need to set "c" to zero in order to make the rule take effect permanently.

2.2 EAdroid Architecture

Android has hierarchical structure. In order to improve the security of the system and defense against various attacks, EAdroid adds some modules to both framework layer and kernel layer of Android. EAdroid uses user-generated security rules to guide the acts of these modules, and brings unity control on multi-layers of Android. The architecture of EAdroid is shown in Fig. 1.

The bold frames in Fig. 1 are the primary modules of EAdroid. When a new application is installed, the application initialization module will allot label for the application and label the process of it. The permission control module will intercept the behavior of the application and enquire the policy management module about whether to block the behavior. Except for responding to the permission control module, the policy management module keeps detecting the environment and updates the current policy in framework layer and kernel layer. We use and modify Smack module in kernel layer. Smack is a mandatory access control module inside Linux kernel [4]. On one hand, the Smack security module using the default smack rules to protect the root, and on the other hand, Smack control the behavior of applications in kernel layer according to the rules provided by policy management module.

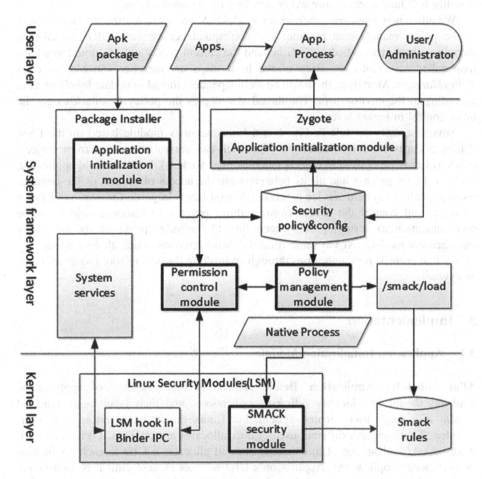

Fig. 1. The architecture of EAdroid

During installing an application, the Android system will make a series of operations on apk packages, some of the operations are implemented in the class *com.android.server.pm.Setting*. The application initialization module judges the type of the application to be installed according to user's configuration, and allot corresponding label to the application, and all the above logic are implemented inside the installation related methods of class Setting. When the application is launched into a process, the application initialization module will label the processes for Smack security module to distinguish. In addition, the label procedure is implemented inside Zygote daemon (a background process in Android that is in charge of forking a process for an App and loading the byte code of the App into the process).

The class *com.android.server.pm.PackageManagerService* of Android includes some methods involving permission checking. We insert the interception functionality of permission control module into these methods. Therefore, the interception functionality will take effect before every behavior of the applications.

We add a new class *com.android.server.PolicyManager* to realize the functionality of the policy management module. The correspondence between UID and label is stored in a hash map called *uidToLabel* and the current policy will be stored in a hash map called *labelToAccess*. Both of the hash maps are member variables of class *PolicyManager*. Moreover, there will be an independent thread to update *labelToAccess* according to the environment. The thread also copies the policy to smack to get the unity control in kernel layer.

Smack security module in Fig. 1 is a Linux security module based on the LSM (Linux Security Module) framework [4], which can control the access from subjects (such as Linux processes) to objects (such as files, sockets). Each Android application run as a Linux process and all its behaviors are the access of objects or the communication with the system service process. EAdroid labels important resource objects in advance, and control the access from Android process to resource objects or the communication to system process according to the rules provided by the policy management module. At the same time, EAdroid provides a default Smack security policy that protects root authorities through controlling the acts of root processes (such as *zygote*).

3   Implementation

3.1   Application Initialization Module

Allot Label for Application. Before controlling the behaviors of applications, EAdroid should first identify different applications, and then label them. Android system is a single-user-oriented system, but Linux that it based on is multi-user-oriented. To distinguish different users, Linux allocates a user ID (UID) to each user. Android takes advantage of this mechanism and allocates a UID to each application or to minority applications. Application's UID will not change until it is uninstalled. Android system also use the user-isolation mechanism of Linux to isolate applications.

EAdroid use UID to identify applications, and allocate corresponding labels to them. Two tables are used to record the correspondence between UID and label. One of them is the hash map *uidToLabel* mentioned above, which is stored in main memory as primary search target while another one is a table in a database as a permanent storage.

By modifying class *Setting*, we can initialize and update *uidToLabel* together with the database, Method *AddUserIdLPw* of class Setting is used to load UID information of applications during system's boot time. In this method, EAdroid adds codes to copy the content of database to the hash map *uidToLabel*, which complete the initialization of the hash map. Method *NewUserIdLPw* of class *Setting* is used to load UID information in the process of newly installed applications. In this method, EAdroid uses the UID to search the database for the corresponding label. If there is any related record, EAdroid will update the hash table. If there is not any record in database, EAdroid will use UID and "untrusted" as a key-value pair and write it to the hash map and database.

Label the Application Process. To make the unity control in both framework layer and kernel layer, the label of an application must be the same to the different modules in the different layers. Smack provide a way for a native process to inherit the label stored in the extended attributes of its binary program file. Nevertheless, the mechanism is only applicable to the native programs like *vold* (volume daemon), *rild* (radio interface layer daemon), and so on, and it doesn't fit for the ordinary Android applications installed with apk file. Which means, even giving a label to the *dex* file of an application, the process forked from it will not have the same label.

The reason is that the startup procedures between the native executable file and the Android application are different. The Android application executes *fork()* system call to create a subprogram through the *zygote* process, and loads *dex* file of the application to make it a different process. The *exec()* system call was not called, so the extended attributes of the executable file was not read. Therefore, if EAdroid cannot label Android application process, it can't use Smack security module to control the behavior of the Android applications.

To solve the problem, we modify the codes of *zygote* to add a function that can give label to the application process. Firstly, the function read the database mentioned above, then get the label of the application and write it into the */proc/self/attr/current* interface, which means writing the label into the security field of the *task_struct* kernel object corresponding to the process.

3.2 Permission Control Module

In the framework layer of Android system, method *checkPermission* and method *checkUidPermission* included in class *PackageManagerService* are responsible for checking the permissions of application's behavior. The way to implement permission control module is to call the method *checkPermission* of class *PolicyManager* in these methods, provide it with the parameters needed, and judge that if the application has the permission to implement the act according to the return value.

3.3 Policy Management Module

Responding the Permission Control Module. In order to control an application's behavior, EAdroid searches corresponding UID in *uidToLabel* to get the label, and then use the label to inquire in *labelToAccess* hash map to find whether it has the permission. If there is not any related rule in the hash map, the access is granted, otherwise corresponding results will be returned according to specific rules.

Environment Adaptive. The content in *labelToAccess* is the specific expression of user's rules under current environment context. To be environment adaptive, the content of *labelToAccess* has to change according to the change of the environment context. There is an inner class in class *PolicyManager* called *ContextDetector*, which launch an independent thread to detect environment context periodically and update *labelToAccess* according to the user rules. There is an example to show it: If the user wants to make a rule like "applications labeled with untrusted are not allowed accessing the permission *android.permission.SEND_SMS* between 8:00 and 18:00", the standard form of the rule r is as follows:

$$r = (untrusted, android.permission.SEND\_SMS, time, 8:00:18:00)$$

When the current time changes from 7:59 to 8:00, the thread that the instance of *ContextDetector* class launched will add a rule to *labelToAccess* table. The rule shows that the accesses from "untrusted" labeled applications to *android.permission. SEND_SMS* are all denied. If an application labeled "untrusted" want to send SMS at 9:00, then the rule added in *labelToAccess* table will be inquired and rejection decision will be returned. When current time changes from 18:00 to 18:01, the thread will delete the rule. After that, all SMS sending behavior by untrusted labeled application will be allowed. It is worth noting that the thread updates the *labelToAccess* periodically, and the modification of the user rules will take effect at the next thread updating.

The Unity of Security Rules. In order to prevent the malwares from bypassing the permissions mechanism in the Android framework layer, EAdroid unities the rules of Smack module in the kernel layer with the security rules of framework layer. So even if the malware has bypassed the permissions mechanism in framework layer, its malicious behavior can still be blocked by Smack security module.

Inner class *ContextDetector* of class *PolicyManager* mentioned above provides an independent thread, which updates *labelToAccess* hash map in class *PolicyManager* according to the rules set by the user and the current environment context. In fact, this thread also copy the content of *labelToAccess* hash table into the */Smack/load* interface with the Smack-module-accepted format, which achieves the unity of the security rules between the kernel and framework layers.

3.4 Smack Security Module

Adding New Hook into Binder IPC. Binder IPC mechanism is a communication mechanism of Android system [21]. It provides applications with remote process call to the methods or functions in system service processes. In fact, the Android system applications call the service system mainly through Binder IPC. Therefore, EAdroid modified the LSM framework, added a new hook function specific to Binder IPC mechanism. In addition, the Binder IPC mechanism was modified to cooperate with the new LSM hook.

Binder IPC mechanism relies on a kernel driver named Binder drive. In binder driver, the system services are represented in the form of *binder_node* structure. Applications' access to system services can be regarded as the access to the corresponding *binder_node*. There are some LSM hooks existing in Binder driver to control a process's access to the service-providing process. However, a service process can provide a variety of services in Android system (such as the media service process), and these services can't be respectively controlled by the existing hook functions. The new LSM hook we added can control the process's access to the binder_node.

We assign ID for all services related to security and privacy, and extend the definition of *binder_node* structure by adding a service ID of integer. When the server process registers each service, it shall provide the name corresponding to the service, and the service ID is written into its binder_node. In this way, the corresponding relationship between the *binder_node* and the name of its representative service is maintained. When an access from a process to a *binder_node* is captured, the service ID number in the *binder_node* is mapped to the corresponding service name as the label of the object. Moreover, the label of the process is used as the label of subject. The labels of object and subject are provided to the newly added hook as parameters for access decision. We modify Smack module to implement the decision logic of the newly added hook function, and modify the *security_operations* structure of the module, to link this function with the hook function.

Default Mandatory Access Control Rules. One of the dangerous security threats in Android is the abuse of root privilege. Malwares can obtain root by exploiting the vulnerabilities in the system process that run as root. The behavior of the system process running as root is relatively fixed, so we use Smack module and formulate a set of default mandatory access control rules that limit the behavior of the system process. Notably, this default policy does not change with environmental context.

When labeling the system process and key resources, the challenge is that the labels adding to the extended attributes of the files under "/" and "/system" will be lost when the device reboots. In order to solve this problem, we first record the path of the programs and key resources and their corresponding labels in a file. Then we added a local program *smackinit* to label the key system program file and resources according to this file during system's startup. To ensure that the rules can be loaded in the early stage of the boot process, we adopt a local program *smackload* to write the rules of the file to the */smack/load* interface.

In order to make *smackinit* and *smackload* programs launched before other system programs, we modified the *init.rc* file to make them start instantly after the file systems were mounted. Through the above changes, the default mandatory access control rules could be loaded and the root in the device can be protected when the device boots.

4 Evaluation

4.1 Security

To test the protect capability of EAdroid, we created two scenarios where Android device could be compromised. Under the first scenario, a malware from real world collects private information stored in the device and performs money stealing through SMS. Under the second scenario, another malware tries to gain root access. This section describes the results of analysis and testing performed to assess the effectiveness of EAdroid in defending these threats.

Privacy Leakage and Money Stealing. As [11] shown, the main motivations of android malwares is money-stealing and privacy collection. To check the capability of EAdroid against these threats, we choose a malware called HippoSMS that can't be detected by some leading mobile AV [12]. The malware collects information about the device and incurs additional phone charges by sending SMS messages to a hard-coded premium-rated number, and it also blocks/removes short messages from legitimate mobile phone service providers (whose number start with 10) to prevent users from knowing about the additional charges [13]. In attracting users to download it, the malware pretends itself as a popular video client called Ku6 and provides user with a user interface that is similar to the real one. When HippoSMS is installed, it requests for permissions listed in Table 1.

Table 1. The permissions requested by HippoSMS and related behaviors.

Permissions	Related behaviors
android.permission.SEND_SMS	Send SMS messages
android.permission.RECEIVE_BOOT_COMPLETED	Automatically start at boot
android.permission.WRITE_SMS	Edit SMS or MMS
android.permission.ACCESS_NETWORK_STATE	View network status
android.permission.RECEIVE_SMS	Receive SMS
android.permission.INTERNET	Full Internet access
android.permission. MOUNT_UNMOUNT_FILESYSTEMS	Mount/unmount file systems
android.permission.WRITE_EXTERNAL_STORAGE	Modify/delete SD card contents
android.permission.READ_SMS	Read SMS or MMS

In order to defense against the malware, rules as below were added to EAdroid.
untrusted, android.permission.SEND_SMS, time, 8:00:18:00
untrusted, android.permission.READ_SMS, time, 8:00:18:00
untrusted, android.permission.WRITE_SMS, time, 8:00:18:00
untrusted, android.permission.RECEIVE_SMS, time, 8:00:18:00
With all these rules, we intended to restrict all SMS related behaviors of all applications labeled with "untrusted" between 8:00 and 18:00. When the time of the device is between 8:00 and 18:00, we tried to launch HippoSMS and we found that there was not any access from HippoSMS to isms in binder driver. We sent SMS to the device again, and we found that all SMS could be found in SMS box no matter what number it was sent from, which revealed that EAdroid blocked the behaviors of HippoSMS.

When the time was 18:05, we did all tests above again. We found that all the SMS sent from "10XXXXX" were gone. Moreover, the access from HippoSMS to isms in binder driver showed again. Further, we changed the environment condition from time to location and tested it again. All the malicious behaviors of HippoSMS were gone when the location of device moved into the boundary set in rules.

The test showed that EAdroid could protect the Android device against the malicious behaviors like privacy leakage and money stealing.

Root Exploits. EAdroid was developed based on Android 4.2.2 for which no documented vulnerabilities or root exploits are released. Therefore, we developed a native daemon with a vulnerability similar to GingerBreak and a malware exploiting the vulnerability. CVE-2011-1823 describes the GingerBreak vulnerability in *vold*'s handling of the net link messages [14]. The GingerBreak exploit code is able to dynamically survey the device in order to find all of the information it needs to launch a successful attack on vold. It first obtains the PID of the vold process from the proc file system, and it also changes the binary code of vold to change its GOT table and replace the address of strcmp() and atoi() with the address of system() to create root shell.

According to the above steps, the malware we developed does three things, which will read proc file system, write /system/bin/vold, create net link socket and send its UID in its message to vold. To simplify the exploit process, the native daemon we developed did two things, which were listening to the net link socket and creating a setuid-root shell to the UID written in the payload received.

EAdroid labels dir "/proc" with label "procdir", and labels files "/dev/socket/vold" and "/system/bin/vold" with "vold", and labels file "/system/bin/sh" with "shell" during the boot process. To defend the above attack, we add three Smack rules in EAdroid: The malware's proc directory reading is blocked by the smack rule "*untrusted procdir -*", and the /system/bin/vold writing and payload sending are blocked by the rule "*untrusted vold -*", and the setuid-root shell creating was blocked by "*vold shell -*". In summary, EAdroid can block the exploit and made it impossible for the malware to gain root privilege.

4.2 Overhead

This section describes the performance overheads introduced by EAdroid compared with AOSP version. The AOSP images were built from the android 4.2.2 for the emulator with 1 GB RAM and a 1 GB SD card. The EAdroid images were built for the same emulator and from the same source code branch with our all modifications. The results for SEAndroid images are compared against the AOSP results to determine the overhead introduced by EAdroid.

We ran for 100 times the AnTuTu benchmark applications [19] on both AOSP and EAdroid, and the results are shown in Table 2. It is necessary to note that only the tests involving system call could be affected by EAdroid, the tests of *memory, integer, float, 3d* and *2d* would not be affected by EAdroid. The tests of *sdwrite* and *sdread* perform writes and reads of the SD card storage, measuring the data transfer rate. The test of database I/O exercises the functionality of Android SQLite database. We expect some small overhead from EAdroid due to the need of Smack security module to create and fetch the extended attributes for file security labeling and due to the additional permission checking performed by EAdroid. For most of the tests, the EAdroid shows negligible overhead and the result of EAdroid is within one standard deviation of the AOSP result.

We finished 100 runs of the Benchmark by Softweg benchmark [20] on both AOSP and EAdroid, and the results are shown in Table 3. The memory, CPU and the graphics scores would not be affected by EAndroid either. The write and read tests of filesystem

Table 2. AnTuTu benchmarking comparison

Test	AOSP		EAdroid	
	Mean	SD	Mean	SD
Total score	1189.8	103.25	1191.91	114.2
Memory	330.7	32.77	330.92	27.59
Integer	321.4	30.05	321.55	24.48
Float	70.36	8.73	70.71	10.25
2D	54.14	7.25	54.2	5.31
3D	34.6	1.28	34.22	1.19
SDread	52	2.95	51.62	4.16
SDwrite	197.3	9.33	196.81	11
Database	133	13.56	131.88	11.74

Table 3. Softweg benchmarking comparison

Test	AOSP		EAdroid	
	Mean	SD	Mean	SD
Total memory	162.42	33.58	161.83	30.8
Copy memory	140.13	29.71	141.78	32.15
Total CPU	706.31	72.07	696.22	68.244
MFLOPS DP	5.99	0.536	5.88	0.72
MFLOPS SP	13.19	0.12	12.51	0.283
MWIPS DP	43.23	1.003	41.9	1.15
MWIPS SP	48.33	1.24	47.84	1.23
VAX MIPS DP	42.67	2.05	42.53	2.16
VAX MIPS SP	42.93	1.986	42.42	1.877
Graphics scores				
Total score	131.39	4.28	130.92	4.57
Opacity	43.48	3.55	42.75	4.57
Transparent	39.96	4.87	40.26	4.92
Filesystem scores				
Total score	112.438	16.5	111.33	19.24
Create files	3.186	0.13	3.57	0.34
Delete files	1.313	0.52	1.392	0.37
Read file	222.22	18.99	216.96	16.73
Write file	3.99	0.21	3.876	0.34

measured the speed (M/sec) of writing and reading 1 M. The files create and delete tests in Table 3 were a measure of the time (seconds) it took to create and delete 1000 empty files. These create and delete tests can be viewed as the worst case overhead for EAdroid since the overhead of creating and removing extended attribute is not amortized over any real usage of the file. For most of the tests, the EAdroid result shows negligible overhead and is within one standard deviation of the AOSP result.

Table 4. Overhead ratio comparison

Test	SEAndroid	EAdroid
AnTuTu		
SD read	0.052 %	0.73 %
SD write	0.26 %	0.248 %
Database	3.81 %	0.84 %
Softweg		
Create files	15.79 %	12.05 %
Delete files	8.7 %	6.01 %
Read file	1.9 %	2.36 %
Write file	3.31 %	2.85 %

Table 4 shows the result of overhead ratio comparison between EAdroid and SE Android. We compare SE Android with EAdroid because they both use LSM security module in their kernel level. To stress the key point, we only listed the tests that were affected by EAdroid and SEAndroid. As we can see from the table, EAdroid, even with additional security mechanism in framework layer, shows its advantages over SE Android in overhead. In some tests like "SD read" and "Read file" the overhead ratio of EAdroid is even higher. However, it is hard to provide a completely fair comparison, since the tests of EAdroid and SEAndroid are executed on different devices and different Android versions (in fact, SEAndroid was tested with a higher configuration machine and a lower Android version), Therefore, we only use overhead ratio as comparison index which can eliminate the differences above to some extent. The overhead tests and comparison above show that the overhead introduced by EAdroid is negligible and acceptable.

We will carry out power consumption test in future. For now, the Sensor-Hub chip in devices like Samsung S4 and Apple iPhone 5s can effectively reduce the power consumption of the sensors. The technology is believed to become widespread soon.

5   Related Work

The majority of research related to securing Android focused on security policy extension and enforcement for Android. AppGuard [22] and XPrivacy [23] implemented their policy enforcement on application layer and brought more flexibility in permission mechanism. TaintDroid [5] tainted private data to detect leakage of users' private information. TaintDroid modified both Binder and the Dalvik VM, but extended only partially to native code. Quire [6] used provenance to track permissions across application boundaries through the IPC call chain to prevent permission escalation of privilege attacks. CREePE [7] allowed access to system services only in a certain context at runtime. Similarly, Apex [8] used user-defined runtime rules to regulate applications' access to system services. AppFence [9] blocked imperious applications' behaviors that demand information unnecessary to perform their advertised functionality, and covertly substitute shadow data in place. These researches together with the ones like Kirin [15], SAINT [16], Porscha [17] and IPC Inspection [18] paid close attention to one layer of Android system, but didn't take the ability of the security mechanism into multi-layers, especially the kernel level, to protect the root, which made them possible to be bypassed.

SEAndroid (Security-Enhanced Android) ported the mandatory access control module SELinux from Linux to Android [10]. It can strengthen the Android operating system's access control of the App and establish the isolation similar to sandbox, which ensure the independence between each App. Therefore, it can prevent the malicious App's attack to the system or other applications. SEAndroid is similar to the EAdroid that both protect the Android system through the framework layer and the kernel layer. However, compared with EAdroid, the TE model used by SEAndroid is too complex. If users want to set the security rules for device with SEAndroid, they need to spend a lot of energy to learn the specific configuration method and define protection rules.

6   Conclusion and Future Work

This paper proposed an environment adaptive security mechanism for Android platform called EAdroid, which providing a simple way for users to customize their security policies. EAdroid improves the framework layer of Android system and integrated uses Smack security module of Linux. At the same time, the security rules of the framework layer and kernel layer in Android system can adapt to the current environment context. Series of tests show that EAdroid can efficiently protect the security of user's devices and privacy against malwares with small overhead of performance.

In future, we will focus on providing a complete mechanism for the TTP to define, update, and distribute the security rules. Under this mechanism, the security policy will be defined by specific security administrator of the TTP, and sent through Internet or text message to every device. We will also test the power consumption and extend the set of application labels of EAdroid.

References

1. Gartner. Market Share Analysis: Mobile Phones, Worldwide (2013)
2. Davi, L., Dmitrienko, A., Sadeghi, A.-R., Winandy, M.: Privilege escalation attacks on android. In: Burmester, M., Tsudik, G., Magliveras, S., Ilić, I. (eds.) ISC 2010. LNCS, vol. 6531, pp. 346–360. Springer, Heidelberg (2011)
3. Bugiel, S., Davi, L., Dmitrienko, A., Fischer, T., Sadeghi, A.R.: Xmandroid: a new android evolution to mitigate privilege escalation attacks. Technical report, Technische Univercity at Darmstadt (2011)
4. Schaufler, C.: The Smack project home page. http://schaufler-ca.com/
5. Enck, W., Gilbert, P., Chun, B.G., Cox, L.P., Jung, J., Mcdaniel, P., Andsheth, A.N.: TaintDroid: an information-flow tracking system for realtime privacy monitoring on smartphones. In: 9th USENIX Conference on Operating Systems Design and Implementation, pp. 1–6. USENIX Association (2010)

6. Dietz, M., Shekhar, S., Pisetsky, Y., Shu, A., Wallach, D.S.: Quire: lightweight provenance for smart phone operating systems. In: 20th USENIX Conference on Security, pp. 23–23. USENIX Association (2011)

7. Conti, M., Nguyen, V.T.N., Crispo, B.: CRePE: context-related policy enforcement for android. In: Burmester, M., Tsudik, G., Magliveras, S., Ilić, I. (eds.) ISC 2010. LNCS, vol. 6531, pp. 331–345. Springer, Heidelberg (2011)

8. Nauman, M., Khan, S., Zhang, X.: Apex: extending Android permission model and enforcement with user-defined runtime constraints. In: 5th ACM Symposium on Information, Computer and Communications Security, pp. 328–332. ACM, New York (2010)

9. Hornyack, P., Han, S., Jung, J., Schechter, S., Wetherall, D.: These aren't the droids you're looking for: retrofitting Android to protect data from imperious applications. In: 18th ACM Conference on Computer and Communications Security, pp. 639–652. ACM, New York (2011)

10. Smally, S., Craig, R.: Security Enhanced (SE) Android: bringing flexible MAC to Android. In: NDSS. The Internet Society (2013)

11. Chien, E.: Motivations of Recent Android Malware. Symantec Corporation. http://www.symantec.com/content/en/us/enterprise/media/security_response/whitepapers/motivations_of_recent_android_malware.pdf

12. Virustotal. Virus report of HippoSMS. https://www.virustotal.com/

13. Jiang, X.: Security Alert: New Android Malware-HippoSMS-Found in Alternative Android Markets. http://www.cs.ncsu.edu/faculty/jiang/HippoSMS/

14. CVE-2011-1823. http://cve.mitre.org/cgi-bin/cvename.cgi?name=CVE-2011-1823

15. Enck, W., Ongtang, M., McDaniel, P.: On lightweight mobile phone application certification. In: 16th ACM Conference on Computer and Communications Security, pp. 235–245. ACM, New York (2009)

16. Ongtang, M., McLaughlin, S., Enck, W., McDaniel, P.: Semantically rich application-centric security in android. In: 25th Annual Computer Security Applications Conference, pp. 340–349. IEEE Computer Society Washington (2009)

17. Ongtang, M., Butler, K., McDaniel, P.: Porscha: policy oriented secure content handling in Android. In: 26th Annual Computer Security Applications Conference, pp. 221–230. ACM New York (2010)

18. Felt, A.P., Wang, H.J., Moshchuk, A., Hanna, S., Chin, E.: Permission re-delegation: attacks and defenses. In: 20th USENIX Security Symposium, p. 22. USENIX Association Berkeley (2011)

19. AnTuTu Benchmark. http://www.antutu.net/index.shtml

20. Softweg Benchmark. https://play.google.com/store/apps/details?id=softweg.hw.performance

21. Pandiyan, D., Paranjape, S.: Android Architecture and Binder. http://rts.lab.asu.edu/web_438/project_final/Talk%208%20AndroidArc_Binder.pdf

22. Backes, M., Gerling, S., Hammer, C., Maffei, M., von Styp-Rekowsky, P.: AppGuard – enforcing user requirements on android apps. In: Piterman, N., Smolka, S. (eds.) TACAS 2013 (ETAPS 2013). LNCS, vol. 7795, pp. 543–548. Springer, Heidelberg (2013)

23. XPrivacy home page. https://github.com/M66B/XPrivacy

24. Elish, K.O., Yao, D., Ryder, B.G.: User-centric dependence analysis for identifying malicious mobile apps. In: Workshop on Mobile Security Technologies (2012)

Supervised Usage of Signature Creation Devices

Przemysław Kubiak and Mirosław Kutyłowski[⊠]

Faculty of Fundamental Problems of Technology,
Wrocław University of Technology, Wrocław, Poland
{przemyslaw.kubiak,miroslaw.kutylowski}@pwr.wroc.pl

Abstract. We propose an effective scheme for controlling usage of secure
signature creation devices (SSCD). With cryptographic means we assure
that an inspector can check whether an (ordered) list of signatures at
hand is the complete list of signatures created by the device. Our scheme
is devoted to some applications like automatic creation of invoices or con-
tract signing by a legal representative of a company.

The inspection procedure is probabilistic with no false-negatives and
low probability of false-positives. It requires extra private keys known
only by the inspector. So it cannot be executed by the holder of an
SSCD – this has to prevent testing integrity of the list after list manipulations searching for a false-positive result.

Our solution works for a wide class of signatures based on Discrete
Logarithm Problem without any changes of the signature format.

We provide formal security proofs as well as discuss implementation
issues.

Keywords: Secure signature creation device (sscd) · Smart card · Qual-
ified signature · Controlled usage · Discrete Logarithm Problem · Diffie-
Hellman Problem · ElGamal signature · Schnorr signature · DSA ·
ECDSA

1 Introduction

The security concept of digital signatures (or *advanced electronic signatures* as
named by European Directive [8]) is based on three factors:

1. strength of an asymmetric cryptographic signature scheme,
2. security of the private key stored in a dedicated hardware unit, which is called
   secure signature creation device (SSCD for short) in [8],
3. guarding physical access to the SSCD.

From the three factors the strongest one are cryptographic algorithms. There is
a lot of research devoted to these issues, despite that the cryptographic part does
not contribute the most significant risks for using digital signatures in practice.

During the work on this paper the second author has been supported by Foundation
for Polish Science, MISTRZ Programme, and by the IBM Faculty Award.

© Springer International Publishing Switzerland 2014
D. Lin et al. (Eds.): Inscrypt 2013, LNCS 8567, pp. 132–149, 2014.
DOI: 10.1007/978-3-319-12087-4_9

In turn, the security of SSCD is mainly in focus of R&D work of the hardware manufacturers. Their approach is quite different: many technical details for securing the chips are kept secret and we have to do with a kind of race between the hardware manufacturers and the attackers. In order to be able to recognize which device is suited (secure enough) for a particular application, *Common Criteria* framework [6] has been introduced. However, a Common Criteria evaluation does not provide security guarantees but only testifies conformance with certain development procedures that should support creating a secure product. Nevertheless, in many cases the manufacturers provide just a declaration of conformance of their products with the rules imposed e.g. by [8], and are liable for any design faults.

The third factor - protection of an SSCD against illegitimate use – is the most critical issue. There is a tradeoff between the ease of use and the unit price on one hand and security on the other hand. The dominant solution is to use a secret PIN number to activate the device. However, the effectiveness of this solution is limited:

- As SSCD devices with an integrated input channel are rare, typically the PIN number is entered through a keyboard of a PC. So the PIN can be leaked.
- A third person may learn a PIN number by observing the owner of an SSCD during activation of the SSCD. This is a major problem since a large number of smart card users do not follow even fundamental rules of the PIN protection.
- Occasionally, some people provide own signature cards together with the PIN to other people for doing some work on behalf of them.

Once a PIN is not secret anymore, the only defense is keeping control over the device. However, this is not always possible. A typical case is a *lunch time attack*: a secretary uses the SSCD left in the office of his or her boss to sign some documents.

One approach to deal with these problems is to provide own input channel for the SSCD. For example, smart cards with two buttons have been developed and studied in the context of the German personal identity card (finally, this solution has not been deployed). However this solves only the first problem. Another approach is biometric identification. In this case the major problems are costs, usability and high false acceptance/rejection rates.

Problem Statement. In this paper we do not attempt to provide new techniques that could replace PIN protection. Instead we provide means of monitoring usage of the SSCD devices. Our goal is to provide an effective procedure that would protect against illegitimate use of an SSCD.

Note that our goal is much broader than preventing problems arising from insufficient protection via the PIN. In many application scenarios the adversary is the SSCD owner himself. This may sound strange (as *it makes no sense to steal own money*), however in many cases the SSCD is restricted for use in specific situations and all signed documents must be available to some parties.

One example of this kind is using an SSCD by a representative of a legal person for signing legally binding obligations. There are many legal rules that prohibit hiding documents of this kind. However, the real life is full of violations of the law, just as in the case of ENRON, where the frauds would be prevented if one could easily detect that some documents are missing in the official book-keeping.

Another application case are all kinds of registries that provide reference data, but where the entries are created and signed by a certain official. In this case an SSCD of the official should be used exclusively in a strictly defined scope and we have to make sure that all documents are indeed included in the registry.

Similar requirements apply for many procedures in the court and law enforcement practice, where all steps of the procedure are strictly regulated and the complete documentation has to be maintained.

Note that the traditional digital signatures framework does not guarantee that:

- the holder of the SSCD enters all signed documents to the system,
- the signatures are created in the sequence indicated by the signing time entered on the document.

In particular, the holder of the SSCD may replace an old document with a new one.

Our solution is an inspection procedure that takes a list of signatures created by a device within some time – allegedly a complete one – and checks whether some signatures created by the device have been omitted.

1.1 Simple Solutions and Related Work

Counters. The first possible solution is to add an internal counter to an SSCD and append the counter value to the text before signing. This approach has obvious advantages but also critical disadvantages. The first one is leaking how many messages have been signed by the device to every recipient of a signature. This is unacceptable in most business cases. The second problem is that introducing such a field might be incompatible with the current legal framework. Namely, [8] states that:

> Secure signature-creation devices must not alter the data to be signed or prevent such data from being presented to the signatory prior to the signature process.

The third problem is that the smart card gets no document to be signed but its hash value. So the counter value should be appended to the hash value of the document. Then we would have to hash again before applying algebraic signing operations as, in general, these operations should not be applied to plaintexts.

Another approach is to add an encrypted value of the counter. In this case the information is hidden from unauthorized viewers. However, again there are legal concerns. Moreover, in this case the problem is even more acute as the SSCD adds an information field that cannot be inspected by the signatory.

On the other hand, there is an easy implementation in case of RSA-PSS signatures created according to PKCS#1 standard [17]. Recall that the hash value of the document to be signed is augmented by a bit string (*salt*) that might be set arbitrarily – e.g. it may contain the encrypted value of the counter. What is more, this bit string is recoverable during the signature verification process. Note that this approach does not require any change of the standard and of the verification software. However, the solution is limited to the RSA-PSS signatures.

Mediated Signatures. Mediated signatures [4] have been proposed for eliminating a single point of trust failure in the system of electronic signatures. Creating a mediated signature requires cooperation of at least two holders of corresponding secret keys. A single key does not even suffice to create a digital proof that this key has been used: the public key of the signatory is useless for this purpose. Elegant constructions for mediated signatures exist for RSA [4] and Schnorr signatures [15].

The main advantage of the mediated signatures is that they provide effective control means over SSCD usage, allowing for instance immediate blocking the SSCD when the owner looses control over it or monitoring detects suspicious activities. Their disadvantage is that some infrastructure is required and no simple solution for signatures such as ECDSA is known.

Stamp and Extend. According to [14] the signatures are created and stored in a form of a list with a hidden tree structure. If n signatures are created, then simultaneously there are n commitments for the next n signatures to be created by the device. The scheme enables to check whether a given list of n signatures is the list of all first n signatures created by the device. If an attacker replaces one of the signatures of the list with another signature that can be verified positively, then the private signing key gets revealed. So the protection mechanism in [14] is quite aggressive. While it is well suited for time-stamping (*nobody would ruin own business*), in case of regular users instant invalidation of all signatures in case of a forgery is not always welcome.

1.2   Design Objectives

The CTRL-Sign scheme designed in this paper has to provide the following features:

- If the owner of an SSCD presents an incomplete list of signatures created with it, then the entitled verifier can detect that some signatures have been omitted.
- The entitled verifier should be able to recognize positions of missing signatures, if there are any.

In order to get a solution easy to apply in practice, we impose the following requirements:

- the signatures created with the scheme should be standard ones, so that no adjustment of the verification process would be necessary,

- the signed values may not contain additional fields such as serial numbers, additional signatures, ciphertexts and so on,
- unless some secret keys are used, it should be infeasible to distinguish between the SSCD devices with supervision mechanism from the regular SSCDs.

1.3 Some Applications

Let us describe a few application areas where the proposed inspection procedures of CTRL-Sign might be of significant importance.

Electronic seals: the primary application field of electronic signatures is authenticating documents created automatically in IT systems. (In this case the term *electronic seal* is used (see [7]), but exactly the same technology can be used as for electronic signatures.) For instance, an overwhelming majority of invoices is created in the electronic form. Electronic seals may be used to authenticate and protect their integrity. One of important problems is that sometimes the invoices are deleted in order to hide some transactions from the tax authorities. The SSCD devices implementing the mechanism proposed provide an effective inspection mechanism for the tax authorities against certain tax frauds.

Financial records: Progress in hardware design makes it possible to use asymmetric cryptography for securing the financial transactions. In particular, issuing signatures for transactions would be a great help against frauds. However, the instrument holder could claim that the secret key installed by a financial organization in the electronic authentication device has a copy retained by the organization and that certain signatures have been created with this key. The CTRL-Sign mechanism prevents undetected insertion of new signatures in the list.

Controlling staff activity: if a corporation provides SSCD devices to own staff members, then it might be necessary to check whether all signed documents are stored in the data system of the corporation and no documents are created without awareness of the corporation.

2 Description of the CTRL-Sign Scheme

2.1 Setup

Algebraic Setup. Let $\mathcal{G}$ be an abelian group of prime order q, in which the Discrete Logarithm Problem is hard. Let us fix an arbitrary generator g of $\mathcal{G}$. We use multiplicative notation for group $\mathcal{G}$. Unless otherwise specified the operations are executed in the group $\mathcal{G}$. If we are performing algebraic operations on exponents of elements of $\mathcal{G}$ we assume silently that the operations are performed modulo q.

We use independent hash functions $Hash_1$, $Hash_2$, $Hash_3$, $Hash_4$ and $Hash_5$ with appropriate range following from the context. We assume that the hash functions are strong in the cryptographic sense.

System Actors and their Keys. There are the following actors in the system: the Card Issuer, the signatories holding SSCDs, the Certification Authority (CA), and the Inspection Authority (IA).

The following keys are associated with each of the actors:

Inspection Authority: the IA has a long period secret key k_{master}, the secret inspection key ins, and the public inspection key Ins. For a user U, the IA determines the control key $c_U := Hash_1(U, k_{master})$.

Card Issuer: for a user U, the Card Issuer obtains the keys c_U and Ins from the IA and installs them in the SSCD issued for U.

Signatories: the SSCD of a user U holds the preinstalled keys c_U and Ins as well as the private signature key x_U created at random by the SSCD, and the public key $X_U = g^{x_U}$. (Note that the SSCD does not hold the private inspection key ins).

Certification Authority: the CA has standard keys for issuing certificates for the public keys of the users, just as in PKI built according to the X.509 framework.

The SSCD of a user U and the IA share the secret c_U. It serves as a seed for a PRNG, thereby SSCD of the user U and the IA share a string $\text{RAND}_U = \text{PRNG}(c_U)$. The string RAND_U is divided into d-bit substrings, where d is a small integer (e.g. $d = 4$), say $\text{RAND}_U = \rho_U^1 \rho_U^2 \ldots$. The substring ρ_U^i is a control sequence for the ith signature created by the SSCD of the user U.

2.2   Creating a Signature

In our construction we may use any signature scheme based on the Discrete Logarithm Problem, where one if the components included in the final signature is g^k for k chosen at random – as for ElGamal signatures. Alternatively, we may apply a signature scheme where $r = g^k$ is not included in the final message but can be derived from it. This is the case for DSA, ECDSA [1,11,13,16], Guillou-Quisquater signatures [10]) and Schnorr signatures [18].

In order to fix our attention let recall the process of creating a Schnorr signature for a message M:

1. choose $k \in [1, q - 1]$ uniformly at random,
2. $r := g^k$,
3. $e := \text{Hash}(M, r)$,
4. $s := (k - x \cdot e) \bmod q$.
5. output signature (e, s).

Recall that $g^s y^e = g^k g^{-xe} g^{xe} = g^k = r$, where $y = g^x$ is the public key corresponding to x. Hence, as claimed, r can be easily recovered from the signature.

The general approach of CTRL-Sign is as follows:

1. generate k at random,
2. check the *hidden footprint* of k; if it is incorrect return to step 1,
3. proceed signing steps of the basic procedure Sign for the parameter k chosen.

First we present the construction of the hidden footprints borrowed from [20]:

Generating $f_U(k)$ - a hidden footprint for k and user U.

    input: Ins, k
    $f := Hash_3(Ins^k)$;
    output d least significant bits of f

For the inspection procedure carried out by Inspection Authority there is an alternative way for computing $f_U(k)$ (this is essential, since k is an ephemeral value existing only on the SSCD):

Alternative generation of $f_U(k)$.

    input: $ins, r = g^k$
    $f := Hash_3(r^{ins})$;
    output d least significant bits of f

Note that the both methods of computing the footprint are equivalent, as

$$r^{ins} = g^{k \cdot ins} = (g^{ins})^k = Ins^k .$$

Abusing notation we also write $f_U(r)$ instead of $f_U(k)$. Also, given a signature $S = (r, s)$, with $r = g^k$, we write $f_U(S)$ instead of $f_U(k)$.

Creating the ith signature by SSCD of user U for message M.

    input: a message M, signing key x_U, $RAND_U$
    "choose k at random so that $f_U(k) = \rho_U^i$"
    proceed with the signing algorithm Sign with
        the first signature component $r = g^k$

Let us explain what does it mean "choose k at random so that $f_U(k) = \rho_U^i$". We apply the following procedure:

Choosing k at random so that $f_U(k) = \rho_U^i$.

    input: i, c_U, d
    compute ρ_U^i as the ith d-bit block of $PRNG(c_U)$;
    choose k at random;
    $R := Ins^k$;
    while $Hash_3(R) \neq \rho_U^i$ do
        $k =: k + 1$;
        $R := R \cdot Ins$

Signature verification.

    We apply the standard verification procedure of Sign.

2.3   Inspection Procedure of CTRL-Sign

Below we describe an inspection of a signature list created by a user.

1. User U presents a list $S_1, S_2, \ldots, S_t$ of allegedly all signatures created with his SSCD, according to the order in which they have been created.

2. Apart from the regular verification of each signature S_i, the Inspection Authority checks all footprints. Namely, for each signature $S_j = (r_j, s_j)$, $j \leq t$, the IA computes the footprint $\omega_j := f_U(r_j)$.
3. If $(\omega_1, \omega_2, \ldots, \omega_t) = (\rho_U^1, \rho_U^2, \ldots, \rho_U^t)$, then inspection result is positive.

For the extended inspection procedure, the user has to create some number of additional signatures for void messages and append them to the list $S_1, S_2, \ldots,$ S_t before the IA starts the inspection.

2.4   Inspection Result in Case of Manipulations

Below we consider diverse cases of manipulations of the list of signatures. We assume that the SSCD is secure so we do not discuss here what happens if the adversary can manipulate or clone the SSCD.

The general observation is the following: if the original list is $S_1, \ldots, S_t$ while the signatory presents for inspection a list $S_1', \ldots, S_w'$ of valid signatures, then the fraud remains undetected with probability approximately 2^{-dN}, where N is the number of indexes $j \leq w$ such that $S_j \neq S_j'$. This follows from the fact that it is infeasible to guess the footprint with probability non-negligibly higher than 2^{-d} (see Sect. 4), while on the other hand the probability that an SSCD ever creates two signatures with the same component $r = g^k$ is negligible and therefore we may assume that the signatory never gets two signatures that he *knows* that they have the same fingerprint.

Below we discuss some chosen manipulation scenarios.

Omitting a Signature: *a user U takes the list of signatures $S_1, S_2, \ldots, S_t$ created by his SSCD and removes at least one of signatures before the inspection.*

Assume that the omitted signatures are $S_{j_1}, \ldots, S_{j_b}$, where $j_1 < j_2 < \cdots < j_b < t$. Assume that the inspection procedure yields the positive result for the reduced list of signatures. Hence in particular $f_U(S_{j_1+i}) = \rho_U^{j_1+i-1}$ for $j_1+i < j_2$. On the other hand, $f_U(S_{j_1+i}) = \rho_U^{j_1+i}$ due to the construction. So $\rho_U^{j_1} = \rho_U^{j_1+1} = \cdots = \rho_U^{j_2-1}$.

Analogously, we get

$$\rho_U^{j_2-1} = \rho_U^{j_2+1} = \rho_U^{j_2+3} = \ldots = \rho_U^{j_2+1+2a_2}$$

where a_2 is the biggest $j_2 + 1 + 2a_2 < j_3$, and

$$\rho_U^{j_2} = \rho_U^{j_2+2} = \rho_U^{j_2+4} = \ldots = \rho_U^{j_2+2a_2'}$$

where a_2' is the biggest index such that $j_2 + 2a_2' < j_3$. Proceeding in this way, for each ρ_U^j, $j > j_1$, $j \neq j_2, j_3, \ldots, j_b$ we may assign one equality with some $\rho_U^{j'}$, where $j' < j$. So in total there are $t - j_1 - b + 1$ equations to be satisfied.

We see that an attack of this kind requires a very careful choice of the signatures removed. However, the user does not see the footprints, so it is hard to make decisions which signatures can be removed.

As we see, the only safe choice for the signatory is to truncate the list of signatures. Then of course no irregularities will be detected. However, then the extended inspection procedure helps a lot and we are back in the previous scenario where omissions occur not at the end of the list. If m extra signatures are added, then we have at least m equations on d-bit values to be satisfied. Probability of an undetected fraud is then 2^{-dm}. So for $d = 4$ and $m = 15$ we get probability 2^{-60}, which is much better than we need.

Changing the Order of the Signatures: Assume that an adversary permutes the signatures using a permutation π. As π is a superposition of disjoint cycles, the attack succeeds if in each cycle the values of the footprints are fixed. So if the attacker fails to guess a footprint in at least one position, then the attack becomes detected.

Adding Forged Signatures: adding signatures without removing the old ones causes the same problems for the adversary as removing signatures and requires fulfilling quite many equations between the footprints. The analysis is similar as in the first case.

3   Security of CTRL-Sign Scheme

The proposed scheme CTRL-Sign changes substantially the signature creation process, since the choice of the parameter k is not fully random, since the footprint created with k has to satisfy certain conditions. Potentially, this may convert a secure signature scheme into an insecure one. We show that this is not the case. For the proof we apply the security games framework from [19].

3.1   Key Privacy

We consider the following attack models for deriving the private signing key x_U of the user U. The attacker has access to the following data:

Model 1: a list of signatures $S_1, \ldots, S_t$, the inspection key ins and $RAND_U$,
Model 2: a list of signatures $S_1, \ldots, S_t$, the inspection key ins and c_U.

Note that in real life the adversaries have typically less data, e.g. only the list $S_1, \ldots, S_t$. Note also that there is a subtle difference between the Model 1 and the Model 2: in the second case the signatures are created in some particular way and having a list of signatures created in a regular way we usually cannot find a matching c_U.

Model 1. First we define a game describing an attack for breaking the signing key:

Game 0
    choose x_U, ins at random
    choose c_U at random

$\text{RAND}_U := \text{PRNG}(c_U)$

create $S_1, \ldots, S_t$ with x_U, ins, RAND_U

$b := F(x_U)$

$\bar{b} := \mathcal{A}(S_1, \ldots, S_t, \text{RAND}_U, ins)$

The adversary wins, if $\bar{b} = b$, i.e. if the property F of x_U has been correctly derived. If $\Pr(F(x_U) = 1) = p$, then in case of a random answer $\bar{b}$ the probability to win is $2p(1 - p)$. Hence the advantage of the adversary may be defined as $|\Pr(\bar{b} = b) - 2p(1 - p)|$.

Let us transform the game to the following form:

Game 1

choose x_U, ins at random

~~choose c_U at random~~

choose RAND_U at random ~~$\text{RAND}_U := \text{PRNG}(c_U)$~~

create $S_1, \ldots, S_t$ with x_U, ins, RAND_U

$b := F(x_U)$

$\bar{b} := \mathcal{A}(S_1, \ldots, S_t, \text{RAND}_U, ins)$

If there is any no-negligible difference between advantages for the Game 0 and the Game 1, then we can easily build a distinguisher that for a candidate string C decides with a fairly high probability whether C has been created at random, or it has been computed as $C := \text{PRNG}(c)$ for some c chosen at random.

Game 2

choose x_U, ins at random

~~choose RAND_U at random~~

create $S_1, \ldots, S_t$ with x_U, ~~ins, RAND_U~~

reconstruct RAND_U from the signatures $S_1, \ldots, S_t$ and ins according to
   the inspection procedure

$b := F(x_U)$

$\bar{b} := \mathcal{A}(S_1, \ldots, S_t, \text{RAND}_U, ins)$

Note that the Game 2 creates RAND_U with exactly the same probability distribution as the Game 1. Therefore the advantage of the adversary does not change.

Since in the Game 2 the random key ins does not influence the signature creation and is used to compute RAND_U, we may remove it from the game and ask the adversary to create them during the procedure $\mathcal{A}$. Thereby we get the following game with exactly the same advantage:

Game 3

choose x_U at random, ~~choose ins at random~~

create $S_1, \ldots, S_t$ with x_U

~~reconstruct RAND_U from the signatures $S_1, \ldots, S_t$ and ins according to~~
   ~~the inspection procedure~~

$b := F(x_U)$

$\bar{b} := \mathcal{A}(S_1, \ldots, S_t , \text{~~RAND}_U, ins~~})$

Note that the Game 3 describes the security of the signing key in the regular model.

Theorem 1. *If the adversary has a non-negligible chance to break the signing key in the Model 1 for CTRL-Sign, then the same applies for the underlying signature scheme, provided that the PRNG creates strings indistinguishable from the random strings.*

Model 2. We show that given a set of signatures $S_1, \ldots, S_t$ we can create a case for the Model 2. However, during the reduction the number of signatures decreases. Let us describe the reduction:

> choose ins at random
> choose c_U at random
> $\text{RAND}_U := \text{PRNG}(c_U)$, put $\text{RAND}_U = (\rho_U^1, \rho_U^2, \ldots)$,
> choose a sequence $v_1 < v_2 < \ldots < v_m \leq t$ such that ρ_U^j equals the last
> d bits of $Hash_3(r_{v_j}^{ins})$ for $j \leq m$, where $S_{v_j} = (r_{v_j}, s_{v_j})$

For finding $v_1, v_2, \ldots, v_m$ we apply the greedy procedure. After finding v_{j-1} we look for the smallest $l > v_{j-1}$ such that the last d bits of $Hash_3(r_l^{ins})$ are equal to ρ_U^j.

The number m is a random variable. It is easy to see that the greedy procedure leads to the biggest possible m. The value of m can be estimated as follows: Consider $j < m$. Let χ_j denote $v_j - v_{j-1}$. We may assume that the process of generating RAND_U is a *lazy* random process, that is, after finding v_{j-1} we generate ρ_U^j at random. Then we generate the next signatures $S = (r, \ldots)$ with r generated at random. The process of finding a match behaves in the same way for each value of ρ_U^j, so we may assume without loss of generality that each ρ_U^j is an all-zero string. Thereby, the probability distribution of m is the same as for the number of zeroes in a string of length t, where the entries are chosen at random from the set $0, 1, \ldots, 2^d - 1$. The expected number of zeroes in such a string equals $t/2^d$, and according to the Chernoff Bounds

$$\Pr[m < \frac{t}{2^d}(1 - \delta)] < e^{-\frac{\delta^2 t}{2^{d+1}}} .$$

Theorem 2. *The advantage of an adversary attacking the basic signature scheme for a list of signatures of length t is not lower then the advantage of an adversary attacking in Model 2 for a list of signatures of length m where m is a random variable denoting the number of zeroes in a random string of length t consisting of elements chosen uniformly at random from the set $\{0, 1, \ldots, 2^d - 1\}$.*

3.2 Forging a Signature

As the process of signature creation is based on the regular signature creation (with some signatures dropped) forging a signature is not easier than in the regular case.

4   Secrecy of Footprints – an Enhanced CTRL-Sign Scheme

The aim of the construction is to make a SSCD implementing CTRL-Sign indistinguishable from a regular SSCD under the assumption that the SSCD is a black box device. This implies in particular that no guess about footprint values can be obtained.

Intuitively, a signature $S = (r, s)$, where $r = g^k$, reveals no information about Ins^k. Computing any information about Ins^k is closely related to the Decisional Diffie-Hellman Problem: one could take an instance (g, g^a, g^b, z) of the Decisional Diffie-Hellman Problem, assign $r = g^a$, $Ins = g^b$, derive some information about $Ins^k = g^{ab}$, and compare it with the same information related to z. However, this argument is not formally correct, since the adversary is also given the second component s of the signature S, which depends on the private signing key x_U and the exponent k. So in the reduction argument it would be necessary to construct the signature component s. However, the reduction cannot use a signing key x_U chosen by the reduction algorithm, as it would enable to compute k from s. On the other hand, if x_U is unknown for the reduction algorithm, then such a construction would create electronic signatures without the secret key x_U, which is infeasible.

The problem that we are faced with is whether it is possible to derive any information about y^k, given $r = g^k$ and a signature, say $s = k + H(M, r) \cdot x$ (the Schnorr signature), and the public key g^x. The parameter y is here random and independent from g^x – the public verification key for the signatures. It seems that a Schnorr signature does not enable to derive any information about y^k. However, in order to be on the safe side we present below a slight modification of CTRL-Sign scheme for which there is a formal indistinguishability argument.

Note that a somewhat related problem arises in [2], where $Y_A = g^{y_A}$ from the Diffie-Hellman key exchange is reused for creating a Schnorr signature authenticating the smart card executing the protocol. The workaround used in [2] for security of the session key is that it is derived as a hash of the key obtained via the Diffie-Hellman algorithm. Thereby, one can apply Random Oracle Model arguments and hide the problem via application of this model.

Main Idea. The main concern is the second component of the signature. To make the hidden footprint completely independent from the second component of the signature we use a decomposition trick. Namely, for the ith signature we use $k = k_1 + k_2^{(i)}$, where $k_2^{(i)}$ is derived from a key shared by the SSCD and the IA; the key k_1 is chosen at random. On the other hand, for the footprint the exponent k_1 is used. Note that Inspection Authority will be able to derive g^{k_1}, since $g^{k_1} = r/g^{k_2^{(i)}}$.

Enhanced CTRL-Sign Scheme. There is another key b_U shared by the Inspection Authority and a SSCD of user U. For instance, we may set $b_U = Hash_4(U, k_{master})$.

Creation of the ith signature by user U with Enhanced CTRL-Sign

input: i, message M, secret keys b_U, c_U, x_U, public key Ins

recompute $\mathrm{RAND}_U := \mathrm{PRNG}(c_U)$ and extract ρ_U^i from RAND_U

$k_2^{(i)} := Hash_5(b_U, i)$

choose k_1 at random

$z := Ins^{k_1}$

while the last d bits of ρ_U^i and $Hash_3(z)$ are not the same do

$\qquad k_1 =: k_1 + 1,$

$\qquad z := z \cdot Ins$

$k := k_1 + k_2^{(i)}$

$r := g^k$

generate a signature $S = (r, s)$ for the message M using k and r

For the ith signature $S = (r, s)$ of user U the inspection procedure computes the footprint value as d last bits of

$$Hash_3(r^{ins}/Ins^{Hash_5(b_U, i)}) \ .$$

Sketch of the Indistinguishability Proof. Again we consider a sequence of games, where the starting game describes the enhanced CTRL-Sign scheme. The adversary is given Ins and the whole string RAND_U – as it can facilitate the attack trying to recover the footprints.

Game 0 this is the same as the original procedure for creating the ith signature by Enhanced CTRL-Sign, appended with the extra step representing information extraction by the adversary:

$\qquad out := \mathcal{A}(M, S, i, X_U, ins, \mathrm{RAND}_U)$

Only the key b_U is not given to the adversary.

Now we use the fact that $k_2^{(i)}$ is created by a kind of pseudorandom number generator. Therefore the output of the Game 0 must be indistinguishable from the output of the following game:

Game 1

input: i, message M, secret keys b_U, c_U, x_U, public key Ins

recompute $\mathrm{RAND}_U := \mathrm{PRNG}(c_U)$ and extract ρ_U^i from RAND_U

choose $k_2^{(i)}$ at random $\xcancel{k_2^{(i)} := Hash_5(b_U, i)}$

choose k_1 at random

$z := Ins^{k_1}$

while the last d bits of ρ_U^i and $Hash_3(z)$ are not the same do

$\qquad k_1 =: k_1 + 1,$

$\qquad z := z \cdot Ins$

$k := k_1 + k_2^{(i)}$

$r := g^k$

generate a signature $S = (r, s)$ for the message M using k and r

$out := \mathcal{A}(M, S, i, X_U, ins, \mathrm{RAND}_U)$

Now let us consider the probability distribution of the exponents k generated by the Game 1. First observe that the probability distribution of k_1 is non-uniform and depends very much on ρ_U^i. However, $k_2^{(i)}$ has the uniform distribution and therefore $k = k_1 + k_2^{(i)}$ has the uniform probability distribution as well. So we conclude that from the point of view of the adversary we may replace the complicated method of generating k by the following simple algorithm:

Game 2
input: i, message M, secret keys b_U, c_U, x_U, public key Ins
~~recompute $\text{RAND}_U := \text{PRNG}(c_U)$ and extract ρ_U^i from RAND_U~~
~~choose $k_2^{(i)}$ at random~~
~~choose k_1 at random~~
~~$z := Ins^{k_1}$~~
~~while the last d bits of ρ_U^i and $Hash_3(z)$ are not the same do~~
~~ $k_1 := k_1 + 1$,~~
~~ $z := z \cdot Ins$~~
choose k at random ~~$k := k_1 + k_2^{(i)}$~~
$r := g^k$
generate a signature $S = (r, s)$ for the message M using k and r
$out := \mathcal{A}(M, S, i, X_U, ins, \text{RAND}_U)$

Now observe that the Game 2 describes the adversary holding an SSCD that implements electronic signatures in a regular way, without the inspection features and adjusting the exponents k. So we may conclude that the output out is indistinguishable between the cases of a regular SSCD and the case of an enhanced CTRL-Sign SSCD.

The above proof can be easily extended to the case that the adversary is given multiple signatures and may ask a device to sign messages of his choice. Thereby we get the following theorem:

Theorem 3. *Assume that $Hash_4(b, i)$ is a PRNG with seed b which produces outputs indistinguishable from the random numbers in the range of the order of group $\mathcal{G}$ used for creating electronic signatures. Then it is infeasible to distinguish an SSCD implementing the enhanced CTRL-Sign scheme from the regular SSCD implementing the same signature scheme, given all public values (the signatures and the public key X_U) as well as the secret inspection parameter ins.*

Corollary 1. *Assume that the assumptions of Theorem 3 hold. Then given a list of signatures created by the enhanced CTRL-Sign SSCD, it is infeasible to derive any non-negligible amount of information about the footprints for the signatures.*

Proof. Assume conversely that there is an algorithm $\mathcal{A}$ that can derive such information. Then we use $\mathcal{A}$ to construct an adversary $\mathcal{A}'$ that contradicts the claim of Theorem 3. Indeed, given RAND_U and a sequence of signatures, we can present the signatures to $\mathcal{A}$, get the output from $\mathcal{A}$ and compare the data obtained for compliance with RAND_U. If the data do not fit to each other, then $\mathcal{A}'$ says that the SSCD is a regular device. Otherwise $\mathcal{A}'$ claims that

SSCD implements enhanced CTRL-Sign scheme. Obviously, if the information obtained by $\mathcal{A}$ is non-negligible, then $\mathcal{A}'$ is a distinguisher with a non-negligible advantage.   □

5   Chosen Implementation Issues

Since in quite many cases signatures are created by cryptographic smart cards, we have to consider additional computational effort due to CTRL-Sign implementation on these weak devices. Note that the computational complexity is not a problem for the inspection procedure, as presumably it will be executed by a server. For generating a signature the extra effort is:

- generating the current footprint ρ_U^i,
- computing $R := Ins^k$ for the exponent k chosen at random,
- some number of iterations of the following loop:
        while $Hash_3(R) \neq \rho_U^i$ do
          $k =: k + 1;$
          $R := R \cdot Ins$

Note that it is not necessary to compute g^k at each iteration of the while loop. We either compute it once the final value of k has been found, or compute $r := g^k$ and $R := Ins^k$ together before starting the while loop (we take advantage of the fact that one can save time when computing these two powers at once), and then updating $r := r \cdot g$ at each iteration of the loop.

An important question is how many executions of the *while* loop are necessary in order to find a k yielding the correct value. If we treat $Hash_3$ according to the Random Oracle Model, then the probability that in $N = 2^d \cdot h$ executions of the loop we do not get an appropriate k equals

$$(1 - \frac{1}{2^d})^N \approx \frac{1}{e^h} \ .$$

For $d = 4$ and 160 loop executions the probability of not finding the proper k is about 0.00003. The question is how long it takes to execute this number of loops.

The best way to check the efficiency of CTRL-Sign would be to implement it directly on a smart card using an open architecture such as Java Card with the efficient elliptic curve arithmetic. However, the problem is that the cryptographic functions are implemented in a secure way and there is no access to modify their code or get access to intermediate values such as the exponent k of $r = g^k$. Moreover, there is no direct way of adding two points of the elliptic curve. Implementing such operations on application layer is usually too slow and a good solution is to find a workaround – an implementation using hardware supported operations (see e.g. [3]). However, an implementation of CTRL-Sign has to use point addition in the protected section of the card for the sheer reason that k must not leave this section (otherwise the signing key might be exposed). So a reasonable implementation must use the native code in the protected section.

As there is no public data on the execution time of all low level primitives we may derive some data indirectly. We have tested Gemalto Java Cards equipped with Infineon and NXP processors. Example results are presented in Table 1.

Table 1. Some experimental results on Gemalto Java cards and 256-bit elliptic curve

Operation	MultiApp ID Dual Citizen 144 K CC v2.0 (Infineon)	MultiApp ID 144 KECC v2.1 (NXP)
Scalar multiplication	186 ms	104 ms
ECDSA signature with SHA1	191 ms	111 ms
ECDSA signature with SHA256	194 ms	112 ms
Verification of ECDSA with SHA1	140 ms	112 ms
Verification of ECDSA with SHA256	141 ms	115 ms
SHA-1 computation	4 ms	4 ms
SHA-256 computation	8.6 ms	6.4 ms

One can see that computing the hash functions in the `while` loop is not very costly concerning the execution time. The question is how long it take to add points of an elliptic curve.

The longer computation times for a signature creation than for a signature verification may follow from countermeasures against side channel time analysis. This indicates that for the signature creation the Montgomery ladder algorithm might have been used. In this case the computation consists of *add* operations and *double* operations, and the number of these operations is logarithmic in the scalar. This in turn would suggest that the addition of elliptic curve points takes a few milliseconds on the cards inspected. Thereby, the whole execution would take about half a second at average, and less than 1.5 s with probability 0.99997. Of course, due to time analysis attacks, a fixed number of iterations of the loop should be executed. If no appropriate k is found in this time, then the card should restart with a fresh k.

6   Conclusions and Future Work

CTRL-Sign has to be implemented in the protected areas of a smart card. Today, the smart card manufacturers give no access to these areas for the third parties, so an implementation attempt would be technically difficult and would violate intellectual property rights.

Particularly interesting would be choosing the best implementation of CTRL-Sign against time analysis. However this depends very much on the card specific data.

Finally, let us note that similar constructions are possible for some other schemes, like for instance Feige-Fiat-Shamir [9] and Nyberg-Rueppel [12] schemes.

Thereby, we see that with an exception for RSA all algorithms recommended by German authorities for practical use (see the list [5]) admit control mechanisms proposed in this paper.

References

1. ANSI: X9.62:2005 public key cryptography for the financial services industry: The elliptic curve Digital Signature Algorithm (ECDSA) (2005)
2. Bender, J., Dagdelen, Ö., Fischlin, M., Kügler, D.: The PACE|AA protocol for machine readable travel documents, and its security. In: Keromytis, A.D. (ed.) FC 2012. LNCS, vol. 7397, pp. 344–358. Springer, Heidelberg (2012)
3. Bichsel, P., Camenisch, J., Groß, T., Shoup, V.: Anonymous credentials on a standard Java card. In: Al-Shaer, E., Jha, S., Keromytis, A.D. (eds.) ACM Conference on Computer and Communications Security, pp. 600–610. ACM (2009)
4. Boneh, D., Ding, X., Tsudik, G., Wong, C.M.: Instantenous revocation of security capabilities. In: USENIX Security Symposium (2001)
5. Bundesnetzagentur für Elektrizität, Gas, Telekommunikation, Post und Eisenbahnen: Bekanntmachung zur elektronischen Signatur nach dem Signaturgesetz und der Signaturverordnung (Übersicht über geeignete Algorithmen). Draft, 10 October 2013
6. Common Criteria. http://www.commoncriteriaportal.org
7. European Commision: Proposal for a regulation of the European Parliament and of the Council on electronic identification and trust services for electronic transactions in the internal market, 4 June 2012
8. European Parliament and of the European Council: Directive 1999/93/EC of the European Parliament and of the Council of 13 December 1999 on a Community framework for electronic signatures. Official Journal of the European Communities L(13), 19 Jan 2000
9. Feige, U., Fiat, A., Shamir, A.: Zero-knowledge proofs of identity. J. Cryptol. 1(2), 77–94 (1988)
10. Guillou, L.C., Quisquater, J.-J.: A practical zero-knowledge protocol fitted to security microprocessor minimizing both transmission and memory. In: Günther, C.G. (ed.) EUROCRYPT 1988. LNCS, vol. 330, pp. 123–128. Springer, Heidelberg (1988)
11. IEEE: IEEE P1363: Standard specification for public key cryptography (2000)
12. ISO: ISO/IEC 9796–3:2006 Information technology - Security techniques - Digital signature schemes giving message recovery - Part 3: Discrete logarithm based mechanisms (2006)
13. ISO/IEC: 14888–3:2006 Information technology - Security techniques - Digital signatures with appendix - Part 3: Discrete logarithm based mechanisms (2006)
14. Krzywiecki, Ł., Kubiak, P., Kutyłowski, M.: Stamp and extend – instant but undeniable timestamping based on lazy trees. In: Mitchell, C.J., Tomlinson, A. (eds.) INTRUST 2012. LNCS, vol. 7711, pp. 5–24. Springer, Heidelberg (2012)
15. Nicolosi, A., Krohn, M.N., Dodis, Y., Mazières, D.: Proactive two-party signatures for user authentication. In: NDSS, The Internet Society (2003)
16. NIST: FIPS publication 186–4: Digital Signature Standard (DSS) (2013)
17. RSA Laboratories: PKCS#1 v2.1 – RSA Cryptography Standard + Errata (2005)
18. Schnorr, C.-P.: Efficient identification and signatures for smart cards. In: Brassard, G. (ed.) CRYPTO 1989. LNCS, vol. 435, pp. 239–252. Springer, Heidelberg (1990)

19. Shoup, V.: Sequences of games: a tool for taming complexity in security proofs. IACR Cryptology ePrint Archive 332 (2004)
20. Young, A., Yung, M.: Kleptography: using cryptography against cryptography. In: Fumy, W. (ed.) EUROCRYPT 1997. LNCS, vol. 1233, pp. 62–74. Springer, Heidelberg (1997)

A Practical Attack on *Patched* MIFARE Classic

Yi-Hao Chiu[1], Wei-Chih Hong[2], Li-Ping Chou[3], Jintai Ding[4,5],
Bo-Yin Yang[2]([⊠]), and Chen-Mou Cheng[1]

[1] National Taiwan University, Taipei, Taiwan
[2] Academia Sinica, Taipei, Taiwan
by@crypto.tw
[3] Chinese Culture University, Taipei, Taiwan
[4] University of Cincinnati, Cincinnati, USA
[5] Chongqing University, Chongqing, China

Abstract. MIFARE Classic is the world's most widely deployed RFID
(radio-frequency identification) technology. It was claimed to be cryptographically protected by the proprietary Crypto-1 stream cipher. However,
it proved inadequate after weaknesses in the design and implementation of
Crypto-1 and MIFARE Classic started surfacing since late 2007
[7,8,12–17]. Some operators of MIFARE Classic-based systems reacted by
upgrading to more secure alternatives such as MIFARE DESFire. However, many (especially in Asia) opted to "patch" MIFARE Classic instead.
Their risk analysis might have gone as follows: *"The most serious threat
comes from efficient card-only attacks, where the attacker only needs an
off-the-shelf reader and a PC to tamper a target tag. All efficient card-only
attacks depend on certain implementation flaws. Ergo, if we just fix these
flaws, we can stop the most serious attacks without an expensive infrastructure upgrade."* One such prominent case is "EasyCard 2.0," today accepted
in Taiwan as a means of electronic payment not only in public transporta-
tion but also in convenient stores, drug stores, eateries, cafes, supermarkets, book stores, movie theaters, etc. Obviously, the whole "patching"
approach is questionable because Crypto-1 is fundamentally a weak cipher.
In support of the proposition, we present a new card-only attack based on
state-of-the-art algebraic differential cryptanalytic techniques [1,2]. Still
using the same cheap reader as previous attacks, it takes 2–15 min of computation on a PC to recover a secret key of EasyCard 2.0 after 10–20 h of
data collection. We hope the new attack makes our point sufficiently clear,
and we urge that all MIFARE-Classic operators with important transactions such as electronic payment upgrade their systems to the more secure
alternatives soon.

Keywords: RFID security · MIFARE Classic · Card-only attack · Algebraic cryptanalysis

1 Introduction

MIFARE Classic, a brand owned by the NXP Semiconductors, is the most
widely used RFID technology in the world today, with billions of chips sold

© Springer International Publishing Switzerland 2014
D. Lin et al. (Eds.): Inscrypt 2013, LNCS 8567, pp. 150–164, 2014.
DOI: 10.1007/978-3-319-12087-4_10

worldwide. It is used in many public-transportation ticketing systems in, e.g., Beijing, Chongqing, Guangzhou, Boston, the Netherlands, London, Seoul, Taipei, etc. In recent years, it has even found its way into electronic payment systems in several Asian countries including China and Taiwan.

The proprietary Crypto-1 stream cipher is designed to provide cryptographic protection to MIFARE Classic. NXP Semiconductors has never made public the detailed algorithm of Crypto-1. Nevertheless, starting from late 2007 in a series of papers, the specifications and several weaknesses of the cipher have been found via reverse engineering and cryptanalysis [7,8,12,13,15–17]. As Courtois *et al.* concluded: "The security of this cipher is therefore close to zero" [8]. Users of MIFARE Classic around the world responded differently to this incident. Some kept silent, while others promptly announced plans of replacing MIFARE Classic—unfortunately not always with more secure technologies.

In this paper, we shall investigate in detail one such replacement being deployed in Taipei, an early adopter and aggressive user of MIFARE Classic. Branded under the name "EasyCard," more than 35 million cards have been issued in Taipei since the official release in 2002, with more than 4.6 million transactions per day in 2012. Starting from 2010, the card is also accepted as a means of electronic payment by almost all convenient store chains, as well as drug stores, eateries, cafes, supermarkets, book stores, movie theaters, etc. Similar use of MIFARE Classic is reported in several cities in China including Beijing, Chongqing, and Guangzhou.

In a nutshell, not only does Crypto-1 use way too short a key (48 bits) by today's standards, its cipher structure also allows very easy recovery of its internal state (and hence the secret key) if the attacker learns a small number of contiguous keystream bits [12]. This allows a sniffer to recover the secret key if it is placed in proximity when a pair of legitimate reader and tag are in a transaction.

In addition, there are two serious implementation flaws which also cause weaknesses: (i) *parity bits are computed over plaintext and then encrypted*; (ii) *the 32-bit tag nonces used in the authentication satisfy a degree-16 linear recurrence relation and can be controlled by appropriately timing the authentication attempts.* Furthermore, there is a convenient way for the attacker to extract information on keystream bits from (i), as a tag would respond *differently* depending on whether the parity bits are correct or not. Together, they allow extremely efficient attacks even when the attacker only has access to the tag [13].

Compared with sniffer-based attacks, these efficient card-only attacks are arguably *much more serious* because of the low entry barriers. All the attacker needs is a PC and a cheap, off-the-shelf reader, so any ordinary person can launch such an attack in private by downloading the appropriate software from the Internet.

In late 2012, the EasyCard Corporation rolled out "EasyCard 2.0," a dual-interface smart card that is compatible with existing EasyCard readers, yet with all implementation flaws *fixed*. The tag nonces seem random, both unpredictable and uncontrollable, and the tag responses are indistinguishable whether the parities sent by the reader are correct or not. This renders all existing efficient card-only attacks [7,8,12,13,15] *ineffective*, as we have verified through experiments. This does not stop, of course, brute-force attacks, which are arguably less threatening because it takes years of computation on an ordinary PC. The attacker would need to have access to expensive supercomputers, e.g., GPU or FPGA clusters, in order to recover the keys within a reasonably short amount of time [5]. As a result, the EasyCard Corporation seems confident that Easy-Card 2.0 can be "reasonably secure," as the computational power required by brute-force attacks is way beyond the reach of an ordinary person.

In this paper, we will show that such a sense of security is *false*. Namely, we will present a new card-only attack based on state-of-the-art algebraic differential cryptanalytic techniques [1]. The attack is highly practical: it uses the same cheap reader as previous attacks [7,8,12,13,15] and takes 2–15 min on a PC to recover the secret key of EasyCard 2.0 or other similar implementations of MIFARE Classic. The extra price the attacker needs to pay for the new attack is a slightly longer time for data collection, typically 10–20 h. We note that this is not atypically long for differential attacks and still makes the new attack a serious threat because the data collection can be done by the attacker in private without needing access to a legitimate reader. Overall, this is a significant improvement over the brute-force attacks, which would take about 4 years on the same PC.

The rest of this paper is organized as follows. In Sect. 2, we will first give some background information on the cipher itself and the cryptanalytic techniques we have used to attack it. We will then present our new attack in Sect. 3 and experiment results in Sect. 4. Finally, we will discuss the implications and conclude this paper in Sect. 5.

2   Background and Related Work

2.1   Crypto-1 and the MIFARE Classic Authentication Protocol

Crypto-1 is a stream cipher used to provide cryptographic protection to MIFARE Classic tags and contactless smart cards. For more than a decade, its design was kept secret by NXP, along with the rest of MIFARE Classic. After the details of MIFARE Classic was reverse-engineered in 2007 [12,16,17], many weaknesses have been discovered, and with them many attacks. These attacks vary greatly in efficacy. The first few key-recovery attacks exploit the weaknesses of the cipher and gather the required information either by direct communication with a legitimate reader or by eavesdropping a communication session. Although some system vendors argue even today that these attacks are impractical, the cipher itself was by then considered cryptographically broken.

A few months later, better, card-only attacks were published [13]. These exploit several properties in the authentication protocol of MIFARE Classic as well as flaws in generating tag nonces.

For the sake of completeness, we include here a brief description of Crypto-1 and its use in the authentication protocol of MIFARE Classic. Crypto-1 uses a 48-bit linear feedback shift register (LFSR) with nonlinear output filter [12]. The feedback function of the LFSR is $F(s_0, s_1, \ldots, s_{47}) := s_0 \oplus s_5 \oplus s_9 \oplus s_{10} \oplus s_{12} \oplus$

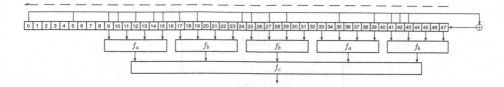

Fig. 1. The structure of the Crypto-1 stream cipher

$s_{14} \oplus s_{15} \oplus s_{17} \oplus s_{19} \oplus s_{24} \oplus s_{25} \oplus s_{27} \oplus s_{29} \oplus s_{35} \oplus s_{39} \oplus s_{41} \oplus s_{42} \oplus s_{43}$. With every tick of the clock, 20 bits from the LFSR are fed into the function f to generate one new bit of the keystream. Then the LFSR shifts one bit to the left, and the new rightmost bit is filled by the output of F—or, if the operational phase calls for inputs, F XORed with an input bit. F is *primitive*: the LFSR has a period of $2^{48} - 1$, the maximum possible.

The function f or *output filter* consists of two layers of nonlinear functions. The first layer is a mixed combination of two 4-input nonlinear functions f_a and f_b, and the second layer is a 5-input function f_c. Here, $f_a = \texttt{0x2c79}$, $f_b = \texttt{0x6617}$, $f_c = \texttt{0x7907287b}$ in "table form" (collating the output bits as the input goes lexicographically over its range), and f can then be expressed as

$$f(s_0, \ldots, s_{47}) := f_c(f_a(s_9, s_{11}, s_{13}, s_{15}),$$
$$f_b(s_{17}, s_{19}, s_{21}, s_{23}), f_b(s_{25}, s_{27}, s_{29}, s_{31}),$$
$$f_a(s_{33}, s_{35}, s_{37}, s_{39}), f_b(s_{41}, s_{43}, s_{45}, s_{47})). \tag{1}$$

Note that each has an equal number of 0 and 1 bits and hence outputs 0 or 1 each with probability $1/2$ if input bits are independently and uniformly distributed over $\mathbb{F}_2$ [13].

On being powered up by the reader's electromagnetic field, the tag sends its unique identifier uid to the reader to start the anti-collision phase. The reader may then request to authenticate a specific block. On receiving the request, the tag loads the secret key for the block as the initial state of the cipher and sends a randomly chosen challenge nonce n_T to the reader. Meanwhile, $n_T \oplus$ uid is shifted into the LFSR. All subsequent communication is encrypted with the keystream, and we will use the notation $\{X\}$ to represent the ciphertext of X, i.e., $X \oplus$ keystream. Next, the reader picks its challenge n_R, which will also be shifted into the LFSR, and sends $\{n_R\}$ followed by the answer $\{a_R\}$ to the tag's challenge. Finally, the tag replies with its answer $\{a_T\}$ to conclude the authentication procedure (see Fig. 2). If the tag and the reader used the same secret key for the initial state of their ciphers, this authentication procedure should bring the ciphers on either side to the same internal state, and the two keystreams generated by both ends will be henceforth in synchronization.

2.2 Existing Card-Only Attacks Against MIFARE Classic

The best known attacks have been summarized by Garcia *et al.* [13], which we will recapitulate here for the sake of completeness. The card-only attacks mainly exploited the following weaknesses.

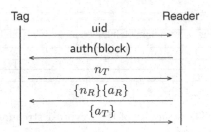

Fig. 2. The authentication protocol in MIFARE Classic

1. The communication of MIFARE Classic follows the ISO 14443-A standard, which requires that a parity bit be sent after every 8 bits of transmission. However, in MIFARE Classic, these parity bits are computed over the plaintext, and the keystream bit used to encrypt the parity bits is reused to encrypt the next bit of plaintext. Furthermore, during authentication, the tag would not reply anything if the received messages have incorrect parity, i.e., the tag checks the authenticity of the reader's answer only if the parity bits are correct.

2. If all parity bits are correct but the encrypted answer $\{a_R\}$ to the tag's nonce cannot be correctly verified, the tag responds with an encrypted 4-bit NACK code. Since the NACK code is fixed, this leaks 4 keystream bits.

3. The 32-bit tag nonce is actually generated by a 16-bit LFSR that runs in a deterministic cycle after it powers up, i.e., timing is used as the source of randomness to the internal random number generator (RNG). Therefore, controlling or measuring when the reader sends every authentication request basically gives us control or a very good guess to the next tag nonce.

4. When a reader is already communicating with a tag (i.e., having authenticated to certain sector), the protocol of a subsequent authentication for a new sector differs slightly from the initial one in that the tag nonce will be encrypted by the new sector key before transmitted to the reader. Since the first tag nonce was sent in plaintext, and the timing between two authentication attempts is known, the attacker can guess the second tag nonce and recover 32 bits of keystream with high accuracy.

Taking advantage of the weakness in the parity bits, the attacker can ask to authenticate for a sector of the tag at hand and answer the tag's challenge with random $\{n_R\}$ and $\{a_R\}$ (totally 8 bytes) accompanied with 8 random parity bits. On average, one out of 256 trials will the attacker receive the encrypted NACK code from the tag. Each such trace reveals 12 bits of information (8 from parity bits and 4 from NACK code) on the secret key. In practice, six traces are enough for the offline brute-force check of the secret key. It takes $6 \cdot 256 = 1536$ trials on average to gather these traces and can be accomplished within a minute. The offline part of this attack is to check which key out of the 2^{48} possible keys generates all "correct" parity and NACK code bits in these traces, and the computing time depends on the implementation realized by the attacker. Pessimistically, the run-time of checking on a powerful FPGA cluster like COPACOBANA is around half an hour.

Two other attacks try to trade online communication for the offline computing time using the weakness that tag nonces n_T can be controlled precisely by timing the authentication requests. The attacker may substantially reduce offline search space by fixing either tag or reader nonce while varying the other, and look for specific properties.

In the second card-only attack [13], the tag nonce n_T is fixed. The attacker searches for a reader nonce n_R such that flipping the last bit in each byte of n_R also flips the following encrypted parity bit, which averages around 28500 authentication attempts or 15 min. Such an n_R let us cut approximately 15 bits from the offline search space, enabling a standard desktop to finish the computation in around 1 min.

For the third attack [13], the attacker fixes response of the reader to $\{n_R\} = 0 = \{a_R\} = 0$, and searches for an n_T such that the tag responds with the desired encrypted NACK code. For example, it might be desired that the keystream bits are all zero, which means that the ciphertext would be identical to the plaintext. Such search takes 4096 attempts on average since we need 12 bits (8 parity plus 4 keystream bits) to be exactly zero. The direct offline search in a huge precomputed table (with around 2^{36} entries) of the cipher states that could lead to such pattern may take about one day. However, with some further attempts to find the parity bits that correspond to the same n_T but different n_R and a_R (e.g., $\{n_R\} = \{a_R\} = \texttt{0xffffffff}$), one can split the table into 4096 parts. This not only makes it easier to store and read the table but also speeds up the offline search significantly.

A fourth attack [13] tries to derive from a known sector key 32 keystream bits generated by another unknown sector key. Because Crypto-1 is structured such that the internal state can be separated into odd- and even-numbered bits, this allows us to further reduce the search space in exploiting the parity-bit weakness. As a result, the attacker can determine the second sector key in less than a second of computation time after about three nested authentication attempts.

Impact and current countermeasures. The last attack is particularly critical as it takes very little time to recover additional keys once a first key is known, making it feasible to "pickpocket" a card wirelessly if a deployed system leaves unused sectors with default keys or does not diversify keys. In response to the attacks outlined above, several countermeasures have been implemented in newer versions of MIFARE Classic cards, such as EasyCard 2.0, that are still compatible with legacy systems.

First and most importantly, the generator of the tag nonce is replaced by a better RNG such that we can no longer control or predict n_T. From our experiments, it seems a true 32-bit RNG instead of having a period of 2^{16}. This improvement breaks almost all efficient card-only attacks depicted above except the brute-force attack, as all the techniques to reduce search space make use of the flaw in tag nonce generation. Furthermore, these new cards now always reply with encrypted NACK code if the authentication fails, whether the parity bits are correct or not. This closes the last loophole of the brute-force attack described above, as it is no longer possible to gather the required information to attack the parity-bit weakness.

2.3 Algebraic Differential Cryptanalysis

Algebraic cryptanalysis brings the concept of applying algebraic techniques to attack various cryptographic primitives, e.g., block ciphers, stream ciphers, and public key systems. It is usually done in two major steps. First, a set of multivariate polynomial equations over a finite field is constructed to describe the cryptographic scheme. This system of equations is formulated in a way that its solutions correspond to certain secret information of the cryptographic scheme. The second step is then to solve the system using techniques such as SAT solvers or Gröbner-basis algorithms. As a result, the efficiency of this category of attacks is strongly related to the quality of the constructed equations as well as the performance of the system-solving technique in use.

The idea of algebraic cryptanalysis is not new. Back in 1949, Shannon already noted the relationship between breaking a good cipher and solving a complex system of equations [18]. Shannon was probably thinking about how to build a good cipher, but this concept gives us a hint of checking possible weaknesses of cryptosystems using algebraic techniques. However, it was not until the huge progress in the efficiency of system solving, especially the solving of multivariate polynomial systems, that people started to consider system-solving as legitimate attacks. The invention of F_4 [10], XL [6], F_5 [11], and their variants greatly boosted the speed of solving multivariate polynomial systems. Also, the substantial advances in the performance of SAT solvers [9,19] provides us with an alternative, namely to transform problems into boolean formulas and search for solutions.

Differential cryptanalysis exploits information leaked by special pairs of input and output differences, called *differentials*, in a block cipher to distinguish its output from random or to recover (some of) its key bits [3]. Such an attack is statistical in nature and usually requires a large number of plaintext-ciphertext pairs, especially in the context of known-plaintext or ciphertext-only attacks, for which the attacker cannot freely choose the plaintexts. Even before its publication, differential cryptanalysis has played a very important role in cipher design. It is so successful that today's standard procedures for designing a new cipher include checking differential immunity.

In the recent seminal work [1], Albrecht and Cid tried to incorporate the information obtained from differential characteristics into algebraic attacks. They proposed three methods, labeled simply as Attack A, B, and C, of obtaining and using such information. Even though Attack B was not very effective against the PRESENT cipher [20], it did inspire our attack, which we will describe in more detail in Sect. 3.

3   Construction of Attacks

In this section, we illustrate the proposed attack against the patched MIFARE Classic cards based on modern cryptanalysis techniques. The critical step of a successful algebraic attack is to construct as many informative multivariate equations as possible. Three types of algebraic equations are collected in our attack, namely NACK equations, differential equations, and filter equations.

3.1   NACK Equations

As mentioned in Sect. 2.2, the patched MIFARE Classic cards, e.g., EasyCard 2.0, blocks all existing efficient card-only attacks by incorporating better RNG and replying every authentication error with encrypted NACK while maintaining compatibility with legacy readers. Since the plaintext of the 4-bit NACK code is fixed (0x0 for EasyCard 2.0), replying encrypted NACK codes leaks four keystream bits per authentication failure. The data collected in each failed authentication attempt is called a *trace* and can be used to construct a set of four algebraic equations as the following.

Let $\mathbf{x} = (x_0, \dots, x_{47})$ denote the initial state of the LFSR, i.e., the secret key. The new state of the LFSR after an input of n-bit sequence $\mathbf{i}$ can be written in a form like:

$$\mathbf{A_i}(\mathbf{x}) = \mathbf{L}^n \mathbf{x} + \mathbf{v_i}, \tag{2}$$

where $\mathbf{L}$ is a linear transformation that depends only on the LFSR's feedback function F, and $\mathbf{v_i}$ is a 48-bit vector that depends on the input $\mathbf{i}$ (and, of course, the LFSR's feedback function F). Here the important thing to note is that $\mathbf{v_i}$ *does not* depend on the secret key and hence can be computed based on the information available in a trace. Then the keystream bit generated by the nonlinear filter right after the input $\mathbf{i}$ can be obtained by

$$a_{\mathbf{i}} = f(\mathbf{A_i}(\mathbf{x})). \tag{3}$$

Both uid and n_T are transmitted in plaintext. It is then easy to express the LFSR state after the input of uid $\oplus\, n_T$ in terms of the unknowns $x_0, \dots, x_{47}$ using Eq. (2). Although only the encrypted reader nonce is available (in fact, it is generated by the attacker in card-only attacks), it is still possible to *decrypt* $\{n_R\}$ using the keystream bits obtained by Eq. (3) and derive subsequent LFSR states and keystream bits in the form of polynomials of $x_0, \dots, x_{47}$. By equating the 4 keystream bits to their corresponding polynomials, we get 4 *NACK equations* per trace of failed authentication session. It is then possible, at least in theory, to collect sufficiently many equations (≥ 12) and solve the resulted system using Gröbner-basis or SAT solvers.

In practice, however, the main difficulty of the algebraic attack described above lies in the last step, namely, solving the resulted polynomial system. In fact, the degree of such systems saturates due to the nonlinearity introduced by the recurrent decryption of $\{n_R\}$. In order to speed up the solving procedure, we need to extract more information from the traces using algebraic differential cryptanalytic techniques.

3.2 Differential Equations

From Eq. (2), we can see that the difference of two LFSR states that descend from a common initial state would be $A_i(x) \oplus A_j(x) = v_i \oplus v_j$ if i and j are two input bit streams of the same length. It means that we can *know* the LFSR state difference after two different tag nonces even though we *cannot control* them. This is easy to circumvent, however, as one can keep authenticating with a card at hand, hoping that the desired differences will eventually show up. For example, we are interested in those pairs that have only one bit difference in the LFSR state after an input of $\text{uid} \oplus n_T$, especially when the different bit lies at the leftmost possible position. As will be clear later, the reason why we are interested in such pairs is because such pairs of difference are easy to "cancel," which gives more information in recovery of the secret key. More specifically, let y_{n_T}, $y_{n_T'}$ denote the LFSR states after inputting two different tag nonces n_T and n_T', then our targets would be the pairs such that $\Delta y = y_{n_T} \oplus y_{n_T'} = \text{0x000080000000}$. Since n_T has only 32 bits, one bit difference at position 16 (cf. Fig. 1) is the furthest we can get. Thanks to the birthday paradox, it does not take too long to gather sufficiently many such pairs.

Once such a pair is observed, we then try to "cancel" the state difference by properly manipulating the reader's nonce in the second trace. This could be done by carefully selecting and guessing $\{n_R'\}$ in the second trace according to $\{n_R\}$ in the first trace because the reader's nonces are transmitted in ciphertext and we, as the attacker, do not have the secret key to produce the correct keystream bits. More specifically, our goal in this stage is to keep pushing bits with zero difference into the LFSR. Since there is only one bit of difference at position 16 of the LFSR state at the beginning of this stage, we only need to keep our eyes on it. When it is shifted to a position that is not part of input to the nonlinear filter function f, the output keystream bits of these two traces should be the same. In this case, we can obtain the exact difference in the corresponding bits of $\{n_R\}$ by simply inspecting the feedback function of LFSR and then cancel it by altering the input accordingly. However, for positions 15, 13, 11, and 9 (cf. Fig. 1), we need to guess the output keystream bits of the nonlinear function f. If all four guesses are correct, we will arrive at a target pair of traces with identical LFSR states.

Figure 3 demonstrates how the first three bits of $\{n_R'\}$ are decided or guessed by showing the differential view of the LFSR states of target pairs. Let z_k, z_k' be the LFSR states of the pair after shifting in k bits (including n_T). For any target pair of traces, we have

$$\Delta z_{32} = z_{32} \oplus z_{32}' = v_{n_T} \oplus v_{n_T'} = \text{0x000080000000}. \tag{4}$$

In this state, both the outputs of the feedback function and the filter function are identical for these two traces, so the first bit of $\{n_R'\}$ should be the same as $\{n_R\}$ (cf. the zero values in Fig. 3a). When the bit difference is pushed to position 15, we can only choose the second bit of $\{n_R'\}$ by guessing since the difference of $f(z_{33})$ and $f(z_{33}')$ cannot be obtained purely from this differential

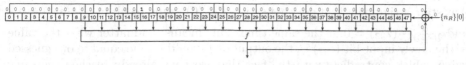

(a) Before inputting the first bit of the reader's nonce ($\Delta \mathbf{z}_{32}$).

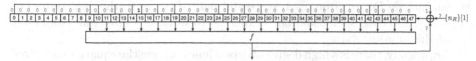

(b) Before inputting the second bit of the reader's nonce ($\Delta \mathbf{z}_{33}$).

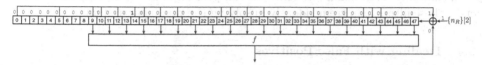

(c) Before inputting the third bit of the reader's nonce ($\Delta \mathbf{z}_{34}$).

Fig. 3. Differential view of Crypto-1's LFSR states

view (cf. Fig. 3b). For the third bit, the difference of $\{n_R\}$ and $\{n'_R\}$ should be 1 because of the feedback function (cf. Fig. 3c).

Following similar procedure, we push the bit difference out of the LFSR and hope to cancel the differences in the input bits. Such cancellation of input difference could be examined by checking whether the tag responds with an identical encrypted NACK code. In other words, the four keystream bits obtained after each authentication failure are used as an oracle for confirming whether our guesses in $\{n'_R\}$ successfully produce the desired differential or not. There are, of course, false positives from this oracle due to collision in practice, and we leave the discussion about this issue to Sect. 3.4.

If the guessed bits successfully cancel the differences, the following 4 *differential equations*, corresponding to the four guessed bits, should hold.

$$f(\mathbf{z}'_k) \oplus f(\mathbf{z}_k) = f(\mathbf{z}_k \oplus \mathbf{e}_{48-k}) \oplus f(\mathbf{z}_k) = \frac{\partial f}{\partial z_{48-k}}(\mathbf{z}_k) = \delta_k, \qquad (5)$$

where $\mathbf{e}_k$ is the 48-bit vector with 1 in the k-th position and 0 elsewhere, and δ_k is the guessed difference, for $k = 33, 35, 37, 39$.

3.3   Filter Equations

In addition to Eq. (5), by taking a closer look at state $\mathbf{z}_{33}$, we devise the following formula as the *filter equation* to further reduce the search space of our attack.

$$\left(\frac{\partial f}{\partial z_{15}}(\mathbf{z}_{33}) \oplus \delta_{33} \right) \left(\frac{\partial^2 f}{\partial z_{15} \partial z_{47}}(\mathbf{z}_{33}) \oplus 1 \right) = 0. \qquad (6)$$

Any state assignment that does not satisfy Eq. (6) would result in $\frac{\partial f}{\partial z_{15}}(\mathbf{z}_{33}) \neq \delta_{33}$ and $\frac{\partial^2 f}{\partial z_{15} \partial z_{47}}(\mathbf{z}_{33}) = 0$ at the same time. This means, no matter what the value of the newly input bit (z_{47}) is, the output of f would not be equal to our guessed value, which contradicts with the fact that we have already reached the same LFSR state in both traces at the end of the authentication session. As a result, we can include Eq. (6) from each successful pair of traces to the final system of equations, and each such equation is expected to work as a filter that eliminates $1/4$ of the solution space.

Empirically, there is a high degree of dependency among the equations acquired from different traces, but it does not take too long to collect sufficiently many pairs such that only a few candidate solutions can pass all filters. Based on our experience, these filters help tremendously in solving the nonlinear system.

3.4   Dealing with False Positives

Up until this point, we have assumed that our oracle can 100 % accurate in telling whether two internal states are the same or not. This does not hold in practice: as we can only observe four keystream bits, it is possible for two traces to have the same keystream bits yet different internal states. In our experiments, around 26 % of the cases where the four keystream bits agree are actually false positives. As a result, not all the collected differential relations, i.e., Eqs. (5) and (6), can be incorporated in the final system to solve. In this section, we will describe how we deal with this problem by more aggressive filtering.

We note that only 18 bits ($z_9, z_{11}, z_{13}, z_{17}, z_{19}, \ldots, z_{45}$) might have an effect on the evaluation of Eq. (6). Random assignments to these 18 bits should be in the solution space of the filter equation with probability $q = 3/4$, given that the filter function f is unbiased. Additionally, the correct assignment should be a solution to those filter equations collected from the true positive results. If we collect sufficiently many pairs and rank all 2^{18} possible assignments by their number of correct evaluations to the collected filter equations, the correct assignment should be very close to the top of the list with high probability. Therefore, the list serves as a good guide for guessing the 18 bits in the resultant system of equations. We can substitute the 18 variables with the bit assignments according to the list and try solving the system using SAT solvers. Note that we should eliminate the equations derived from the traces where Eq. (6) evaluates to `false` while trying each 18-bit assignment. According to our empirical results, it takes around 2 to 15 min for CryptoMiniSat to solve the system if the 18 bits are assigned with correct values.

The next question is how many pairs are sufficient to put the correct assignment at the top of the list with high probability. Assume that in total N such differential pairs are collected, among which $\tilde{N}$ are true positives. The number of filter equations that the correct assignment would evaluate to true, denoted by N_1, should have the following probability mass function.

$$Pr[N_1 = n] = \binom{N - \tilde{N}}{n - \tilde{N}} q^{n - \tilde{N}} (1 - q)^{N - n}, n = \tilde{N}, \ldots, N. \tag{7}$$

Furthermore, if we denote the rank of the correct assignment in the list by ρ, then we have

$$Pr[\rho = k | N_1 = n] = \binom{M-1}{k-1} a(n)^{M-k} [1 - a(n)]^{k-1}, \qquad (8)$$

where $M = 2^{18}$ and $a(n) = \sum_{i=0}^{n-1} \binom{N}{i} q^i (1-q)^{N-i}$ is the probability that an incorrect assignment evaluates less than n filter equations to true. Using Eqs. (7) and (8), it is straightforward to compute the probability function of the rank of the correct assignment by

$$Pr[\rho = k] = \sum_{n=\tilde{N}}^{N} Pr[\rho = k | N_1 = n] Pr[N_1 = n]. \qquad (9)$$

We compute the percentiles of the rank of the correct bit assignments for various numbers of filter equations and summarize the most useful results in Table 1. This gives us an estimate of how many pairs would be sufficient to substantially reduce the expected number of trials we have to perform before finally solving the system. For example, given 150 filter equations collected, we are able to solve the system in less than 7 trials with a probability of 99 %. This is a very good result because in most cases, we just need to repeat the computation a few times before we can recover the key.

3.5   The Complete Attack

We summarize our attack procedure as follows.

1. Initiate (failing) authentication sessions with the target tag and record in a database each n_T received, $\mathbf{v}_{n_T}$, and four keystream bits $\mathbf{s}$ used to encrypt the returned NACK code.
2. For each $(n_T, \mathbf{v}_{n_T}, \mathbf{s})$ received, check whether $\mathbf{v}_{n_T} \oplus$ 0x000080000000, matches any $\mathbf{v}_{n_T'}$ already recorded. If so go to Step 3, having found a pair of n_T's that produce the state difference $\Delta \mathbf{y} =$ 0x000080000000. Otherwise, repeat Step 1.
3. Guess four δ_k's and manipulate $\{n_R\}$ accordingly. Check whether we see the same four keystream bits. If so, record the four differential relations (cf. Eq. (5)) thus found.

Table 1. The percentiles of ρ ($\tilde{N}/N = 74\%$)

Number of filter equations (N)	Percentile	Rank(ρ)
90	75	11
110	90	8
130	95	4
150	99	6

4. Repeat Steps 1–3 until we have collected enough differential relations (about 600–1000, or 150 to 250 successful attempts), then we use the method from Sect. 3.4 to remove the false positives.
5. Feed the differential equations, along with (i) some NACK equations, to a Gröbner-basis or SAT solver, and (ii) the 18-bit solution to the filter equations (cf. Sect. 3.4) as hint bits, to the solver and solve for the key. Empirically, we need about 1 NACK equation for every 4–5 differential equations.

4   Empirical Results and Discussion

We have tried several different solvers including the built-in Gröbner-basis solver in Maple, as well as PolyBoRi [4]. Empirically, CryptoMiniSat outperforms the other solvers by a large margin. Hence we only report the timings obtained using CryptoMiniSat for the rest of the paper. The results also show that the hint bits are extremely helpful to CryptoMiniSat, usually resulting in a tremendous speed-up.

We also note that the differential relations, as a system of equations, tend to be highly redundant and have multiple solutions. It is to avoid ending up with such a wrong solution, that in step 5 we must add a few equations on keystream bits in order to obtain a unique solution with high probability.

A submarine patch. We had bought a fair number of EasyCards on the streets of Taipei between 2009 and 2012 trying to track there were different editions of EasyCards. Surprisingly, we discovered that EasyCard 2.0 was actually not the first "patch" attempted by the EasyCard Corporation. There is actually another different kind of EasyCard, that we shall refer to as EasyCard 1.5, which has been surreptitiously in circulation since late 2010 or early 2011.

Although to all outward appearances EasyCard 1.5 is identical to EasyCard 1.0, it has a better RNG which makes n_T neither predictable nor controllable based on timing. This already defeats some (but not all) existing card-only attacks, even though EasyCard 1.5 performs otherwise identically to the original. For example, since the parities attack relies on the capability of controlling n_T, such an improved RNG already makes the attack time much longer if still possible at all. We represent this fact using a question mark in Table 3, in which we summarize the time required to carry out various attacks. It is perhaps surprising that the EasyCard Corporation managed to resist the temptation of announcing a security upgrade and kept this modification under wraps for so long. The differences among the three types of EasyCards are summarized in Table 2.

From Table 3, it is clear that our attack is the most practical one among the effective attacks against EasyCard 2.0 in the sense that our attack can be carried out by an ordinary person in private with an off-the-shelf reader and a PC.

In Table 3, the GPU result is taken from Chih *et al.* [5], while all other experiments are all carried out on a PC with 2.3 GHz AMD CPU. The data collection, on the other hand, is performed on a laptop PC with 2.0 GHz Intel

Table 2. Types of EasyCards attacked in our experiments

Card type	Parities checked	n_T generation
EasyCard 1.0	Yes	Predictable
EasyCard 1.5	Yes	Somewhat random
EasyCard 2.0	No (always 0x0)	Random

Table 3. Timing comparison of all known attacks

Attack type	Online time	Compute time	1.0	1.5	2.0
Sniffing attack	2 s	< 2 s	√	√	√
GPU brute-force [5]	5 s	14 h	√	√	√
CPU brute-force	5 s	4 years	√	√	√
Parities attack	> 3 min	< 30 s	√	?	
Nested authentications	15–75 s	25–125 s	√	√	
Our attack	10–20 h	2–15 min			√

CPU. For CPU brute-force attack, we obviously have not run it to completion but extrapolate based on the timing result of a partial run instead. We use open-source software whenever possible, but we have also implemented and optimized some of the attacks.

5   Concluding Remarks

In this paper, we have demonstrated a highly practical attack against the Easy-Card 2.0, which is marketed as having patched the vulnerabilities of previous implementations of MIFARE Classic. By applying algebraic differential crypt-analysis techniques, our card-only attack can recover the secret key of EasyCard 2.0 within one day. This includes the time for online data collection and offline computation, both of which can be carried by a working platform that costs no more than a few hundreds of US dollars and is affordable even to the least wealthy attacker. This again shows the weakness of the Crypto-1 cipher, and highlights the unfortunate the fact that "security" protocols based on unsound ciphers, such as MIFARE Classic, is not suitable for important transactions such as electronic payment.

References

1. Albrecht, M., Cid, C.: Algebraic techniques in differential cryptanalysis. In: Dunkelman, O. (ed.) FSE 2009. LNCS, vol. 5665, pp. 193–208. Springer, Heidelberg (2009)

2. Albrecht, M., Cid, C., Dullien, T., Faugère, J.-C., Perret, L.: Algebraic precomputations in differential and integral cryptanalysis. In: Lai, X., Yung, M., Lin, D. (eds.) Inscrypt 2010. LNCS, vol. 6584, pp. 387–403. Springer, Heidelberg (2011)
3. Biham, E., Shamir, A.: Differential cryptanalysis of DES-like cryptosystems. In: Menezes, A., Vanstone, S.A. (eds.) CRYPTO 1990. LNCS, vol. 537, pp. 2–21. Springer, Heidelberg (1991)
4. Brickenstein, M., Dreyer, A.: PolyBoRi: a framework for Gröbner-basis computations with boolean polynomials. J. Symb. Comput. **44**(9), 1326–1345 (2009)
5. Chih, M.-Y., Shih, J.-R., Yang, B.-Y., Ding, J., Cheng, C.-M.: MIFARE Classic: Practical attacks and defenses. In: 19th Cryptology and Information Security Conference (CISC 2010), Hsinchu, Taiwan May 2010
6. Courtois, N., Klimov, A., Patarin, J., Shamir, A.: Efficient algorithms for solving overdefined systems of multivariate polynomial equations. In: Preneel, B. (ed.) EUROCRYPT 2000. LNCS, vol. 1807, pp. 392–407. Springer, Heidelberg (2000)
7. Courtois, N.T.: The dark side of security by obscurity and cloning MiFare Classic rail and building passes anywhere, anytime. Cryptology ePrint Archive, Report 2009/137 (2009). http://eprint.iacr.org/
8. Courtois, N.T., Nohl, K., O'Neil, S.: Algebraic attacks on the Crypto-1 stream cipher in MiFare Classic and Oyster cards. Cryptology ePrint Archive, Report 2008/166 (2008). http://eprint.iacr.org/
9. Davis, M., Logemann, G., Loveland, D.: A machine program for theorem-proving. Commun. ACM **5**(7), 394–397 (1962)
10. Faugère, J.C.: A new efficient algorithm for computing Gröbner bases (F_4). J. Pure Appl. Algebra **139**(1), 61–88 (1999)
11. Faugère, J.C.: A new efficient algorithm for computing Gröbner bases without reduction to zero (F_5). In: Proceedings of the 2002 International Symposium on Symbolic and Algebraic Computation, ISSAC '02, pp. 75–83. ACM, New York (2002)
12. Garcia, F.D., de Koning Gans, G., Muijrers, R., van Rossum, P., Verdult, R., Schreur, R.W., Jacobs, B.: Dismantling MIFARE Classic. In: Jajodia, S., Lopez, J. (eds.) ESORICS 2008. LNCS, vol. 5283, pp. 97–114. Springer, Heidelberg (2008)
13. Garcia, F.D., van Rossum, P., Verdult, R., Schreur, R.W.: Wirelessly pickpocketing a Mifare Classic card. In Proceedings of the 2009 30th IEEE Symposium on Security and Privacy, S&P '09, pp. 3–15. IEEE Computer Society, Washington, DC (2009)
14. Golić, J.D.: Cryptanalytic attacks on MIFARE Classic protocol. In: Dawson, E. (ed.) CT-RSA 2013. LNCS, vol. 7779, pp. 239–258. Springer, Heidelberg (2013)
15. de Koning Gans, G., Hoepman, J.-H., Garcia, F.D.: A practical attack on the MIFARE Classic. In: Grimaud, G., Standaert, F.-X. (eds.) CARDIS 2008. LNCS, vol. 5189, pp. 267–282. Springer, Heidelberg (2008)
16. Nohl, K., Evans, D., Starbug, S., Plötz, H.: Reverse-engineering a cryptographic RFID tag. In: Proceedings of the 17th Conference on Security Symposium, Security '08, pp. 185–193. USENIX Association, Berkeley (2008)
17. Nohl, K., Plötz, H.: Mifare: Little security, despite obscurity. In: 24th Chaos Communication Congress, 24C3, Berlin, Germany, Dec 2007
18. Shannon, C.E.: Communication theory of secrecy systems. Bell Syst. Tech. J. **28**(4), 656–715 (1949)
19. Soos, M.: CryptoMiniSat. https://github.com/msoos/cryptominisat
20. Wang, M., Sun, Y., Mouha, N., Preneel, B.: Algebraic techniques in differential cryptanalysis revisited. In: Parampalli, U., Hawkes, P. (eds.) ACISP 2011. LNCS, vol. 6812, pp. 120–141. Springer, Heidelberg (2011)

Computational Number Theory

Omega Pairing on Hyperelliptic Curves

Shan Chen[1,2]($\boxtimes$), Kunpeng Wang[1], Dongdai Lin[1], and Tao Wang[3]

[1] State Key Laboratory of Information Security, Institute of Information Engineering,
Chinese Academy of Sciences, Beijing 100093, People's Republic of China
{chenshan,ddlin}@iie.ac.cn, kunpengwang@263.net
[2] University of Chinese Academy of Sciences,
Beijing 100049, People's Republic of China
[3] China Electric Power Research Institute,
Beijing 100192, People's Republic of China
13911556154@139.com

Abstract. The omega pairing is proposed as a variant of Weil pairing on special elliptic curves using automorphisms. In this paper, we generalize the omega pairing to general hyperelliptic curves and use the pairing lattice to construct the optimal omega pairing which has short Miller loop length and simple final exponentiation. On some special hyperelliptic curves, the optimal omega pairing could be super-optimal.

Keywords: Pairing-based cryptography · Hyperelliptic curves · Automorphism · Omega pairing · Super-optimal pairing

1 Introduction

In recent years, the pairing-based cryptography is regarded as an attractive area in public key cryptography. Since the implementation of pairing-based cryptosystems involves pairing evaluation, the development of efficient pairing calculations becomes a significant topic of research.

The most common pairings used in applications are the Tate and Weil pairings on elliptic curves over finite fields. They are calculated by an iterative algorithm called Miller's algorithm [1]. The Miller iteration loop of the Tate and Weil pairings is roughly $\log_2 r$, where r is the order of the bilinear cyclic group. Motivated by shortening Miller loop length, various variants of Tate pairing are proposed, such as eta pairing [3], Ate pairing [4], Ate$_i$ pairing [5] and R-ate pairing [6]. Zhao $et\ al.$ [7] used the automorphisms to propose a super-optimal pairing called omega pairing based on Weil pairing on two families of ordinary elliptic curves. Vercauteren [2] introduced the concept of an optimal pairing and gave an algorithm to construct optimal ate pairings. Generally, if the Miller iteration loop is roughly $\log_2 r/\varphi(k)$, where k is the embedding degree of elliptic curves and φ is the Euler function, the pairing is called optimal. And if the number of the Miller iteration loop is less than $\log_2 r/\varphi(k)$, the corresponding pairing is called super-optimal. Meanwhile, Vercauteren gave the Optimality

D. Lin et al. (Eds.): Inscrypt 2013, LNCS 8567, pp. 167–184, 2014.
DOI: 10.1007/978-3-319-12087-4_11

Conjecture: any non-degenerate pairing on an elliptic curve without efficiently computable endomorphisms different from powers of Frobenius requires at least $\mathcal{O}(\log_2 r/\varphi(k))$ basic Miller iterations. Hess [8] provided a mathematical framework that encompasses almost all known pairing functions and proved the Optimality Conjecture. So far, the theory of pairings on elliptic curves has become mature.

As an alternative to that on elliptic curves, pairings on hyperelliptic curves have been also investigated. Granger et al. [9] generalized Ate pairing on ordinary elliptic curves to non-supersingular hyperelliptic curves. Zhang [10] proposed Ate_i pairing and twisted Ate pairing on hyperelliptic curves. Fan et al. [11] implemented pairing computation on genus 2 hyperelliptic curves with efficiently computable automorphisms. Tang et al. [13] improved some results of [11]. Balakrishnan et al. [14] generalized the work of Hess [8] and Vercauteren [2] to Tate pairing for hyperelliptic curves and constructed HV pairings. At the same time, they proposed some open problems on hyperelliptic pairings, asking whether there are other non-degenerate, bilinear hyperelliptic pairings which are not part of the HV framework and exploring more improvements in loop length by using the automorphisms.

In fact, our work gives part solutions about above open problems. In this paper, we generalize the omega pairing originally defined on elliptic curves to hyperelliptic curves. The strategy of construction for hyperelliptic omega pairing is similar to [7], but from points to divisors, many technical problems must be solved. On the other hand, we utilize the idea of pairing lattice to construct many new pairings and even give optimal omega pairings in some curves. As the variants based on Weil pairing, all these pairings are different from HV pairings, which are variants based on Tate pairing. On the other hand, our new pairings are obtained by using automorphisms and the HV pairings are obtained by using the powers of Frobenius endomorphism. The Miller iteration loop of the optimal pairing in HV pairings is roughly $\log_2 r/\varphi(k)$. And the Miller iteration loop of the optimal omega pairing is roughly $\log_2 r/\varphi(n)$, where n is the order of the automorphism. If $\varphi(n) > \varphi(k)$, the optimal omega pairing will be super-optimal. For most ordinary elliptic curves, $\varphi(n) \leq \varphi(k)$, so the optimal omega pairing does not generally give an improved loop length. However, hyperelliptic curves have a larger automorphism group Aut(C) and the case $\varphi(n) > \varphi(k)$ is easy to satisfied, so it would be worth-while to study the omega pairing. Not only the short Miller loop length, the optimal omega pairing also has simple final exponentiation. Therefore, if the final exponentiation of the variants based on Tate pairing is complex enough, the optimal omega pairing will be faster than all of them. The example in Sect. 5 shows that, the omega pairing is more efficient than most hyperelliptic pairings.

This paper is organized as follows: Sect. 2 provides some fundamental definitions; Sect. 3 presents the main results; Sect. 4 shows how the omega pairing can be constructed on some genus 2 hyperelliptic curves over large prime fields; Sect. 5 analyze an example curve; Sect. 6 concludes the paper and the appendix provides detailed proofs of all lemmas in Sect. 3.

2   Preliminaries

In this section, we recall the arithmetic on hyperelliptic curves, the definitions of the Tate-Lichtenbaum, Weil pairings, and the omega pairing on elliptic curves.

2.1   Hyperelliptic Curves and Their Jacobians

Let C be a nonsingular curve of genus g defined over a finite field $\mathbb{F}_q$ with $q = p^n$ elements. In this paper, we assume that C has a unique point P_∞ at infinity and the affine part is in the form

$$y^2 + h(x)y = f(x)$$

where $h, f \in \mathbb{F}_q[x], \deg(h) \le g$, f monic and $\deg(f) = 2g + 1$. For any algebraic extension $\mathbb{F}_{q^k}$ of $\mathbb{F}_q$, the set

$$C(\mathbb{F}_{q^k}) := \{(x, y) \in \mathbb{F}_{q^k} \times \mathbb{F}_{q^k} \mid y^2 + h(x)y = f(x)\} \cup \{P_\infty\}$$

is called the set of $\mathbb{F}_{q^k}$-rational points on C. The hyperelliptic involution on the set $C(\mathbb{F}_{q^k})$ is defined by $\iota(x, y) = (x, -y - h(x))$ and the Frobenius morphism $\pi_q : C \longrightarrow C$ is given by $\pi_q(x, y) = (x^q, y^q)$. Since the set $C(\mathbb{F}_{q^k})$ for $g \ge 2$ does not form a group, we embed C into an abelian variety of dimension g called the Jacobian of C and denoted by $\mathcal{J}_C$.

A divisor D on C is a formal sum of points over the algebraic closure $\overline{\mathbb{F}}_q$, denoted by

$$D = \sum_{P \in C(\overline{\mathbb{F}}_q)} n_P(P),$$

with only finitely many non-zero coefficients $n_P \in \mathbb{Z}$. The degree of the divisor D is defined as $\deg(D) = \sum_{P \in C(\overline{\mathbb{F}}_q)} n_P$. The definition of the divisor class group of degree zero divisors $Div_C^0 / Princ_C$ can be found in [9]. Here we introduce an important relation that $\mathcal{J}_C = Div_C^0 / Princ_C$ and $\mathcal{J}_C(\mathbb{F}_{q^k}) = Div_C^0(\mathbb{F}_{q^k}) / Princ_C(\mathbb{F}_{q^k})$.

In fact, each divisor class of degree zero $\overline{D}$ in $\mathcal{J}_C$ can be uniquely represented by a so called reduced divisor, i.e. a divisor in the form

$$\sum_{i=1}^{m} (P_i) - m(P_\infty), m \le g$$

where $P_i = (x_i, y_i) \in C(\overline{\mathbb{F}}_q), P_i \ne P_\infty$ and $P_i \ne \iota(P_j)$ for $i \ne j$. Then we can introduce two maps on $\mathcal{J}_C$: given a divisor class $\overline{D}$, we define $\rho(\overline{D})$ the unique reduced divisor in $\overline{D}$ and $\varepsilon(\overline{D})$ the effective part of $\rho(\overline{D})$, i.e. $\rho(\overline{D}) = \varepsilon(\overline{D}) - \deg(\varepsilon(\overline{D}))(P_\infty)$. Given a $\mathbb{F}_{q^k}$-rational divisor D and an integer n, a *Miller function* $f_{n,D} \in \mathbb{F}_{q^k}(C)$ is any function for which $div(f_{n,D}) = nD - [n]D$, where $[n]D := \rho(nD)$.

In practice, the Mumford representation [16] is often used. Any reduced $\mathbb{F}_{q^k}$-rational divisor admits a Mumford representation $[u(x), v(x)]$, i.e. a pair of polynomials $u, v \in \mathbb{F}_{q^k}[x]$, with $u = \prod_{i=1}^{m}(x - x_i), \deg(v) \le \deg(u) \le g$ and $u \mid v^2 + vh - f$. Cantors algorithm [15] can be used to compute the Mumford representation of the sum of two reduced divisors.

2.2   Pairings on Hyperelliptic Curves

Let r be a prime with $r \mid \sharp \mathcal{J}_C(\mathbb{F}_q)$ and $\gcd(r,q) = 1$. Let k be the smallest integer such that $r \mid (q^k - 1)$, then k is called the embedding degree with respect to r. This implies that the r-th roots of unity are contained in $\mathbb{F}_{q^k}$ and in no strictly smaller extension of $\mathbb{F}_q$. The r-torsion points on $\mathcal{J}_C$ defined over $\mathbb{F}_{q^k}$ is denoted by $\mathcal{J}_C(\mathbb{F}_{q^k})[r]$. Let $h(x) = \sum_{i=0}^{d} h_i x^i \in \mathbb{Z}[x]$ with $h(n) \equiv 0 \pmod{r}$. Define a *generalized Miller function* $f_{n,h,D} \in \mathbb{F}_{q^k}(C)$ is any function with divisor $\sum_{i=0}^{d} h_i \rho(n^i D)$. For the properties of function $f_{n,h,D}$, please refer to [14]. In the remainder of the paper, we will assume that all Miller functions are normalised.

Let $\overline{D}_1 \in \mathcal{J}_C(\mathbb{F}_{q^k})[r]$ be represented by a divisor D_1, then the function $f_{r,D_1} \in \mathbb{F}_{q^k}(C)^*$ has divisor $div(f_{r,D_1}) = rD_1 - [r]D_1 = rD_1$. Let $\overline{D}_2 \in \mathcal{J}_C(\mathbb{F}_{q^k})[r]$ be represented by a divisor D_2, and $supp(D_1) \cap supp(D_2) = \emptyset$. The Tate-Lichtenbaum pairing of the divisor classes $\overline{D}_1$ and $\overline{D}_2$ is then defined by

$$(\cdot,\cdot) : \mathcal{J}_C(\mathbb{F}_{q^k})[r] \times \mathcal{J}_C(\mathbb{F}_{q^k})/r\mathcal{J}_C(\mathbb{F}_{q^k}) \to \mathbb{F}_{q^k}^*/\mathbb{F}_{q^k}^{*r},$$
$$(\overline{D}_1, \overline{D}_2) \mapsto f_{r,D_1}(D_2).$$

This pairing is bilinear, non-degenerate and the result is independent of the choice of representatives of the divisor classes. If the function f_{r,D_1} is normalised, the Tate pairing can simply be computed as $f_{r,D_1}(\varepsilon(\overline{D}_2))$ [21]. For cryptographic applications, one often requires a unique pairing value in the group of r-th roots of unity μ_r. So one can define the reduced Tate-Lichtenbaum pairing as

$$e(\overline{D}_1, \overline{D}_2) = f_{r,D_1}(\varepsilon(\overline{D}_2))^{\frac{q^k-1}{r}}.$$

The Weil pairing is another non-degenerate and bilinear pairing, which is defined as [17]

$$e_r(\cdot,\cdot) : \mathcal{J}_C(\mathbb{F}_{q^k})[r] \times \mathcal{J}_C(\mathbb{F}_{q^k})[r] \to \mu_r,$$
$$(\overline{D}_1, \overline{D}_2) \mapsto (-1)^{rm_1 m_2} \frac{f_{r,D_2}(D_1)}{f_{r,D_1}(D_2)},$$

where $m_1 = \deg(\varepsilon(\overline{D}_1))$ and $m_2 = \deg(\varepsilon(\overline{D}_2))$. Lemma 2.1 in [7] stated that if f_{r,D_1} and f_{r,D_2} are normalized functions and the supports of $\varepsilon(\overline{D}_1)$ and $\varepsilon(\overline{D}_2)$ are disjoint, then

$$e_r(\overline{D}_1, \overline{D}_2) = (-1)^{rm_1 m_2} \frac{f_{r,D_2}(\varepsilon(D_1))}{f_{r,D_1}(\varepsilon(D_2))}.$$

Let $\overline{\mathbb{F}}_q$ be the algebraic closure of the field $\mathbb{F}_q$. Let π_q denote the endomorphism on the divisor class group $\mathcal{J}_C(\overline{\mathbb{F}}_q)$ induced by the Frobenius morphism π_q on C. Since $\mathcal{J}_C(\overline{\mathbb{F}}_q)[r]$ is a vector space with dimension $2g$ over $\mathbb{F}_r$, so the endomorphism π_q can be viewed as linear transformations on $\mathcal{J}_C(\overline{\mathbb{F}}_q)[r]$. Let $\mathbb{G}_1 = \mathcal{J}_C(\overline{\mathbb{F}}_q)[r] \cap Ker(\pi_q - [1])$, $\mathbb{G}_q = \mathcal{J}_C(\overline{\mathbb{F}}_q)[r] \cap Ker(\pi_q - [q])$ denote the 1-eigenspace and q-eigenspace of π_q on $\mathcal{J}_C(\overline{\mathbb{F}}_q)[r]$. In order to improve the efficiency, many pairings are defined on $\mathbb{G}_1$ and $\mathbb{G}_q$, such as Ate pairing [21], twisted Ate pairing [10], HV pairings [14].

2.3   Omega Pairing on Elliptic Curves

In [7], Zhao *et al.* constructed an efficient pairing based on the Weil pairing, which they called the omega pairing. The omega pairing is constructed for two special classes of ordinary elliptic curves. Here we only introduce the pairing for one class.

Suppose p is a prime such that $p \equiv 1 (\mathrm{mod}\ 3)$, and E_1 is an ordinary elliptic curve over $\mathbb{F}_p$. It's equation is $E_1 : y^2 = x^3 + B$. Let r be a large prime satisfying $r \mid \sharp E_1(\mathbb{F}_p)$ and $r^2 \nmid \sharp E_1(\mathbb{F}_p)$. And assume that E_1 has the embedding degree $k = 2$ with respect to r. Let β be an element of order three in $\mathbb{F}_p$. Then there are two automorphisms ϕ and $\widehat{\phi}$ of E_1 given by $\phi : E_1 \longrightarrow E_1, (x, y) \longrightarrow (\beta x, y)$ and $\widehat{\phi} : E_1 \longrightarrow E_1, (x, y) \longrightarrow (\beta^2 x, y)$, respectively. Assume that λ is a root of the equation $x^2 + x + 1 = 0 (\mathrm{mod}\ r)$ such that $\phi(P) = \lambda, \widehat{\phi}(Q) = \lambda Q$. Let a be the integer such that $ar = \lambda^2 + \lambda + 1$. Then we have the following results: the function

$$\omega(P, Q) = \left(\frac{f_{\lambda, P}(Q)}{f_{\lambda, Q}(P)} \right)^{p-1}$$

defines a bilinear pairing.

3   Omega Pairing on Hyperelliptic Curves

In this section, we construct the hyperelliptic omega pairing and give a general algorithm of the pairing.

3.1   Construction of the Omega Pairing

In this subsection, we give our main results. By using the automorphisms on hyperelliptic curves, we propose an efficient variant of Weil pairing. Since the new pairing on hyperelliptic curves can be regarded as a generation of the omega pairing on elliptic curves, we call it hyperelliptic omega pairing. Furthermore, we use the idea of pairing lattice to give more new pairings and even the optimal omega pairing.

Balakrishnan *et al.* [14] discussed hyperelliptic HV pairings and the twisted Ate pairing. All of them are variants of the Tate pairing restricted on the eigenspaces of the Frobenius endomorphism. In a different way, the hyperelliptic omega pairing is the improvement of the Weil pairing restricted on two special eigenspaces of the automorphism on $\mathcal{J}_C[r]$ whose corresponding eigenvalues are reciprocal. The main result is concluded in the following theorem.

Theorem 1. *Let C be a hyperelliptic curve over $\mathbb{F}_q$ and $r \mid \#\mathcal{J}_C(\mathbb{F}_q)$ be a large prime number with $(r, q - 1) = 1$. Let ϕ be a $\mathbb{F}_q$-rational automorphism of order n on $\mathcal{J}_C(\overline{\mathbb{F}}_q)$ and have two eigenvalues λ and λ^{-1} on $\mathcal{J}_C[r]$. The corresponding eigenspaces are denoted by $\mathbb{G}_\lambda = \langle \overline{D}_1 \rangle$ and $\mathbb{G}_{\lambda^{-1}} = \langle \overline{D}_2 \rangle$, where $\overline{D}_1 \in \mathcal{J}_C(\mathbb{F}_q)[r]$ and $\overline{D}_2 \in \mathcal{J}_C(\overline{\mathbb{F}}_q)[r]$. Suppose $m \in \mathbb{Z}$ satisfies $mr = \lambda^n - 1$ and $supp(\varepsilon(D_1)) \cap supp(\varepsilon(D_2)) = \emptyset$, then*

$$\omega : \mathbb{G}_\lambda \times \mathbb{G}_{\lambda^{-1}} \to \mu_r, (\overline{D}_1, \overline{D}_2) \mapsto \left(\frac{f_{\lambda, D_1}(\varepsilon(D_2))}{f_{\lambda, D_2}(\varepsilon(D_1))} \right)^{q-1}$$

with $D_1 = \rho(\overline{D}_1)$ and $D_2 = \rho(\overline{D}_2)$, defines a bilinear pairing called the hyperelliptic omega pairing. Furthermore, the pairing will be non-degenerate if the Weil pairing restricted on $\mathbb{G}_\lambda \times \mathbb{G}_\lambda^{-1}$ is non-degenerate and $r \nmid m$.

In order to prove the theorem, we need the following three lemmas. Due to space constraints, the proofs of all lemmas are given in the appendix.

Lemma 1. *Suppose D_1 is a $\mathbb{F}_q$-rational reduced divisor and D_2 is a reduced divisor, then for $i, j \in \mathbb{Z}$, we have*

$$\left(\frac{f_{i,D_1}(\varepsilon([j]D_2))}{f_{j,D_2}(\varepsilon([i]D_1))} \right)^{q-1} = \left(\frac{f_{i,D_1}^j(\varepsilon(D_2))}{f_{j,D_2}^i(\varepsilon(D_1))} \right)^{q-1}.$$

Lemma 2. *With notation as above, for $i \in \mathbb{Z}$, we have*

$$\left(\frac{f_{\lambda, D_1}(\varepsilon([\lambda^i]D_2))}{f_{\lambda, D_2}(\varepsilon([\lambda^i]D_1))} \right)^{q-1} = \left(\frac{f_{\lambda, D_1}(\varepsilon(D_2))}{f_{\lambda, D_2}(\varepsilon(D_1))} \right)^{\lambda^i(q-1)}.$$

Lemma 3. *With notation as above, we have* $\left(\frac{f_{\lambda, D_1}(\varepsilon(D_2))}{f_{\lambda, D_2}(\varepsilon(D_1))} \right)^{q-1} \in \mu_r.$

Now we can prove the statement of Theorem 1.

Proof of Theorem 1: For D_1 is reduced, then $div(f_{\lambda^n-1,D_1}) = (\lambda^n - 1)D_1 - [\lambda^n - 1]D_1 = \lambda^n D_1 - D_1 - [\lambda^n]D_1 + D_1 = \lambda^n D_1 - [\lambda^n]D_1 = div(f_{\lambda^n,D_1})$. So we can take $f_{\lambda^n-1,D_1} = f_{\lambda^n,D_1}$. According to Lemma 2 in [11], it's easy to obtain that

$$f_{\lambda^n,D_1} = \prod_{i=0}^{n-1} f_{\lambda,[\lambda^{n-i-1}]D_1}^{\lambda^i}.$$

Since $f_{\lambda,[\lambda]D_1} = \alpha f_{\lambda, D_1} \circ \widehat{\phi}$ and $\alpha \in \mathbb{F}_q$, we can calculate that

$$
\begin{aligned}
(f_{r,D_1}^m(\varepsilon(D_2)))^{q-1} &= f_{mr,D_1}(\varepsilon(D_2))^{q-1} \\
&= f_{\lambda^n-1,D_1}(\varepsilon(D_2))^{q-1} \\
&= f_{\lambda^n,D_1}(\varepsilon(D_2))^{q-1} \\
&= \prod_{i=0}^{n-1} f_{\lambda,[\lambda^{n-i-1}]D_1}^{\lambda^i}(\varepsilon(D_2))^{q-1} \\
&= \prod_{i=0}^{n-1} f_{\lambda,D_1}^{\lambda^i}(\varepsilon(\widehat{\phi}^{n-i-1}(D_2)))^{q-1} \\
&= \prod_{i=0}^{n-1} f_{\lambda,D_1}^{\lambda^i}(\varepsilon([\lambda^{n-i-1}]D_2))^{q-1}.
\end{aligned}
\tag{1}
$$

By using the same reasoning, we obtain

$$(f_{r,D_2}^m(\varepsilon(D_1)))^{q-1} = \prod_{i=0}^{n-1} f_{\lambda, D_2}^{\lambda^i}(\varepsilon([\lambda^{n-i-1}]D_1))^{q-1}.$$

From Lemma 2.1 in [7], we know that the Weil pairing

$$e_r(\overline{D}_1, \overline{D}_2) = e_r(D_1, D_2) = (-1)^{rm_1 m_2} \frac{f_{r,D_2}(\varepsilon(D_1))}{f_{r,D_1}(\varepsilon(D_2))}.$$

Then Lemma 2 shows that

$$
\begin{aligned}
((-1)^{rm_1 m_2} e_r^{-1}(D_1, D_2))^{m(q-1)} &= \left(\frac{f_{r,D_1}^m(\varepsilon(D_2))}{f_{r,D_2}^m(\varepsilon(D_1))} \right)^{q-1} \\
&= \frac{\prod_{i=0}^{n-1} f_{\lambda, D_1}^{\lambda^i}(\varepsilon([\lambda^{n-i-1}]D_2))^{q-1}}{\prod_{i=0}^{n-1} f_{\lambda, D_2}^{\lambda^i}(\varepsilon([\lambda^{n-i-1}]D_1))^{q-1}} \\
&= \prod_{i=0}^{n-1} \left(\frac{f_{\lambda, D_1}(\varepsilon([\lambda^{n-i-1}]D_2))}{f_{\lambda, D_2}(\varepsilon([\lambda^{n-i-1}]D_1))} \right)^{\lambda^i(q-1)} \\
&= \left(\frac{f_{\lambda, D_1}(\varepsilon(D_2))}{f_{\lambda, D_2}(\varepsilon(D_1))} \right)^{n\lambda^{n-1}(q-1)}
\end{aligned}
$$

So we obtain

$$((-1)^{rm_1 m_2} e_r^{-1}(D_1, D_2))^{m(q-1)} = \left(\frac{f_{\lambda, D_1}(\varepsilon(D_2))}{f_{\lambda, D_2}(\varepsilon(D_1))} \right)^{n\lambda^{n-1}(q-1)}.$$

Suppose $M = (n\lambda^{n-1})^{-1} \pmod{r}$ and consider Lemma 3, then it follows that

$$\omega(D_1, D_2) = \left(\frac{f_{\lambda, D_1}(\varepsilon(D_2))}{f_{\lambda, D_2}(\varepsilon(D_1))} \right)^{q-1} = ((-1)^{rm_1 m_2} e_r^{-1}(D_1, D_2))^{m(q-1)M}.$$

All bilinear pairings forms a group [24], so $\omega(D_1, D_2)$ defines a bilinear pairing and its non-degeneracy depends on Weil pairing. $\square$

Remark 1. When C is an elliptic curve, $E[r]$ is a vector space with dimension 2 over $\mathbb{F}_r$. And the endomorphisms π_q and ϕ have the same two eigenspaces. We can assum $\mathbb{G}_\lambda = \mathbb{G}_1$ and $\mathbb{G}_{\lambda^{-1}} = \mathbb{G}_q$. Obviously the Weil pairing defined on $\mathbb{G}_1 \times \mathbb{G}_q$ is non-degenerate.

For ordinary elliptic curves, Hess [8] proposed pairing lattices as a convenient mathematical framework to use existing pairing to construct new pairings. The pairing lattice may contain efficient pairings whose Miller loop length are short or even optimal. For the details, please refer to [8]. Following the idea of pairing lattice, we can use the omega pairing ω to construct new pairings $\omega_{\lambda, h}$. When the Miller iteration loop is roughly $\log_2 r / \varphi(n)$, the corresponding pairing $\omega_{\lambda, h}$ is called *optimal omega pairing*. In order to give our result, we recall the following Theorem.

Theorem 2. [8] *Assume that r is a prime number, that n is co-prime to r and that s is a primitive n-th root of unity modulo r^2. Let*

$$a_s : I^{(1)} \longrightarrow W_n, h \longmapsto a_{s,h}$$

be a map with the following properties:

1. $a_{s,g+h} = a_g a_h$ for all $g, h \in I^{(1)}$,
2. $a_{s,hx} = a_{s,h}^s$ for all $h \in I^{(1)}$ with $a_{s,h} \in W_n^{bilin}$,
3. $a_{s,r} \in W_n^{bilin} \setminus \{1\}$ and $a_{s,t-s} = 1$.

Then $im(a_s) = W_n^{bilin}$ and $ker(a_s) = I^{(2)}$. More precisely,

$$a_{s,h} = a_{s,r}^{h(s)/r}$$

for all $h \in I^{(1)}$. There exists an efficiently computable $h \in I^{(1),\varphi(n)}$ with $\|h\|_1 = O(r^{1/\varphi(n)})$ and $a_{s,h} \neq 1$. The O-constant depends on n. Any $h \in I^{(1)}$ with $a_{s,h} \neq 1$ satisfies $\|h\|_1 \geq r^{1/\varphi(n)}$.

Theorem 3. We use the notations of Theorems 1 and 2. Let λ be a primitive n-th root of unity modulor r^2. Let $h(x) = \sum_{i=0}^n h_i x^i$ with $h(\lambda) \equiv 0 (mod\, r)$. Then

$$\omega_{\lambda,h} : \mathbb{G}_\lambda \times \mathbb{G}_{\lambda^{-1}} \to \mu_r, (\overline{D}_1, \overline{D}_2) \mapsto \left(\frac{f_{\lambda,h,D_1}(\varepsilon(D_2))}{f_{\lambda,h,D_2}(\varepsilon(D_1))} \right)^{q-1}$$

defines a bilinear pairing. Furthermore, the pairing will be non-degenerate if and only if $\gcd(h(\lambda)/r, r) = 1$. There exists an efficiently computable $h \in \mathbb{Z}[x]$ with $h(\lambda) \equiv 0 (mod\, r), \deg(h) \leq \varphi(n) - 1$ and $\|h\|_1 = O(r^{1/\varphi(n)})$ such that the above pairings are non-degenerate. Any h such that $\omega_{\lambda,h}(\cdot, \cdot)$ are non-degenerate satisfies $\|h\|_1 \geq r^{1/\varphi(n)}$.

Proof. The proof of this theorem is similar with the proof of Theorem 3 in [8]. Here we have the function

$$\omega_\lambda : I^{(1)} \to W_1, h \mapsto \omega_{\lambda,h}.$$

It is sufficient to show that the function ω_λ satisfies the three properties of Theorem 2. Propertys 1 and 2 are clear for ω_λ, since the function $f_{\lambda,h,R}$ satisfies $f_{\lambda,h+g,R} = f_{\lambda,h,R} f_{\lambda,g,R}$ and $f_{\lambda,hx,R} = f_{\lambda,h,\lambda R}$ for any $h, g \in I^{(1)}$ with $\omega_{\lambda,h} \in W_1^{bilin}$ and $R \in E(\mathbb{F}_{q^k})[r]$.

Since the divisors D_1 and D_2 reduced, $(f_{\lambda,r,D_1}) = r\rho(D_1) = rD_1 = f_{r,D_1}$ and $(f_{\lambda,r,D_2}) = r\rho(D_2) = rD_2 = f_{r,D_2}$. Furthermore,

$$\omega_{\lambda,r}(D_1, D_2) = \left(\frac{f_{\lambda,r,D_1}(\varepsilon(D_2))}{f_{\lambda,r,D_2}(\varepsilon(D_1))} \right)^{q-1} = e_r(D_1, D_2)^{-(q-1)}.$$

So that we have $\omega_{\lambda,r} = e_r^{-(q-1)} \in W_1 \setminus \{1\}$. In fact, the pairing ω in Theorem 1 is equal to the function $\omega_{\lambda,x-\lambda}$. Because $\lambda^n \equiv 1 (mod\, r^2)$, so $\omega_{\lambda,x-\lambda} = \omega = 1$. So Property 3 is also satisfied. This concludes the proof of Theorem 3. $\square$

Theorem 2 shows that, the pairing lattice based on the omega pairing contains pairings with Miller iterations not less than $\log_2 r/\varphi(n)$. If there exists the optiaml pairing with Miller iteration $\log_2 r/\varphi(n)$ and $\varphi(n) > \varphi(k)$, then the optimal omega pairing is super-optimal.

3.2   Algorithm of the Omega Pairing

In this subsection, we give the general algorithm of computing the omega pairing. For the explicit cases, the algorithm could be simplified because some special optimization techniques can be used.

Assume $\mathbb{G}_\lambda \subseteq \mathcal{J}_C(\mathbb{F}_q)$, $\mathbb{G}_{\lambda-1} \subseteq \mathcal{J}_C(\mathbb{F}_{q^{k'}})$ with k' even. There is an easy fact that: if $x \in \mathbb{F}_{q^{k'}}$, we can replace inversions with conjugations, $i.e.$

$$\left(\frac{1}{x}\right)^{q^{\frac{k'}{2}}-1} = \left(\frac{1}{a+bi}\right)^{q^{\frac{k'}{2}}-1} = (a-bi)^{q^{\frac{k'}{2}}-1} = \overline{x}^{q^{\frac{k'}{2}}-1},$$

where $x = a+bi \in \mathbb{F}_{q^{k'}}$ and $a, b \in \mathbb{F}_{q^{\frac{k'}{2}}}$. This fact can be used to avoid computing the denominator. If $(r, q^{\frac{k'}{2}} - 1) = 1$, we can raise the final exponentiation of omega pairing from $q - 1$ to $q^{\frac{k'}{2}} - 1$. Then the final exponentiation of $f^{q^{\frac{k'}{2}}-1}$ can be finished by an inversion and an multiplication, $i.e. f^{q^{\frac{k'}{2}}-1} = \overline{f} \cdot \frac{1}{f}$.

Since the final exponentiation of hyperelliptic omega pairing is very simple, so computing the pairing is mainly an evaluation of $\frac{f_{\lambda,D_1}(\varepsilon(D_2))}{f_{\lambda,D_2}(\varepsilon(D_1))}$. The explicit algorithm is given below.

Algorithm 1. Miller's Algorithm for $\frac{f_{\lambda,D_1}(\varepsilon(D_2))}{f_{\lambda,D_2}(\varepsilon(D_1))}$ with even k'

Input: $D_1 \in \mathbb{G}_\lambda, D_2 \in \mathbb{G}_{\lambda-1}, \lambda = [e_l, e_{l-1}, ..., e_0]_2$, where $e_l \neq 0$
Output: $\frac{f_{\lambda,D_1}(\varepsilon(D_2))}{f_{\lambda,D_2}(\varepsilon(D_1))}$
1: $T \leftarrow D_1, R \leftarrow D_2, f \leftarrow 1, g \leftarrow 1$
2: for i from $l-1$ down to 0 do
2.1: compute T' and $G_{T,T}(x,y) = \frac{c_{T,T}}{d_{T,T}}$ where $T' = 2T - div(G_{T,T})$
    compute R' and $G_{R,R}(x,y) = \frac{c_{R,R}}{d_{R,R}}$ where $R' = 2R - div(G_{R,R})$
2.2: $T \leftarrow 2T, R \leftarrow 2R$
2.3: $f \leftarrow f^2 \cdot G_{T,T}(\varepsilon(D_2)) \cdot \overline{G_{R,R}(\varepsilon(D_1))}, g \leftarrow g \cdot lc_\infty(G_{R,R}(x,y))$
2.4: if $e_i = 1$ then
2.4.1: compute T' and $G_{T,D_1} = \frac{c_{T,D_1}}{d_{T,D_1}}$ where $T' = T + D_1 - div(G_{T,D_1})$
    compute R' and $G_{R,D_2} = \frac{c_{R,D_2}}{d_{R,D_2}}$ where $R' = R + D_2 - div(G_{R,D_2})$
2.4.2: $T = T \oplus D_1, R = R \oplus D_2$
2.4.3: $f \leftarrow f \cdot G_{T,D_1}(\varepsilon(D_2)) \cdot \overline{G_{R,D_2}(\varepsilon(D_1))}, g \leftarrow g \cdot lc_\infty(G_{R,D_2}(x,y))$
3: $f \leftarrow f \cdot g^{m_1}$
4: return f

To estimate the theoretical complexity of Algorithm 1, we need some notations. Let

- T_{D_i} : time for doubling divisor D_i
- T_{A_i} : time for adding divisor D_i
- T_{G_i} : time for evaluation of G defined by D_i at effective part
- $T_{mk'}, T_{sk'}$: time for squaring and multiplication in $\mathbb{F}_{p^{k'}}$
- T_3 : time for Step 3

Assume the hamming weight of λ is $\frac{l}{2}$, *i.e.* $\frac{1}{2} \log_2(\lambda)$. Then the total cost of Algorithm 1 is given by

$$\log_2(\lambda)(T_{D_1} + T_{D_2} + T_{G_1} + T_{G_2} + 3T_{mk'} + T_{sk'})$$

$$+ \frac{1}{2} \log_2(\lambda)(T_{A_1} + T_{A_2} + T_{G_1} + T_{G_2} + 3T_{mk'}) + T_3,$$

where $T_3 = T_{mk'} + T_{sk'}$ when D_1 is general and $T_3 = T_{mk'}$ when D_1 is degenerate.

4   Genus 2 Hyperelliptic Curves over Large Prime Fields

In this section, we recall two families of non-supersingular genus 2 curves over large prime field $\mathbb{F}_p$, which have been studied by Fan *et al.* [11]. We show that the omega pairing can be constructed on them by using automorphisms.

4.1   Family I

We first discuss a family of hyperelliptic curves defined by the equation

$$C : y^2 = x^5 + ax, a \in \mathbb{F}_p^*, p \equiv 1 (\text{mod } 8),$$

where the embedding degree is 4. However our results can be generalised easily to other curves in this form with the embedding degree k is divisible by 4. Curves of this form have automorphisms $\phi : (x, y) \mapsto (\zeta_8^2 x, \zeta_8 y)$ and $\widehat{\phi} : (x, y) \mapsto (\zeta_8^{-2} x, \zeta_8^{-1} y)$, where ζ_8 is a primitive 8-th root of unity in $\mathbb{F}_p$. A rational automorphism on C induces an automorphism on the divisor class group $\mathcal{J}_C(\mathbb{F}_p)$. ϕ induces a non-trivial automorphism of order 8, which is also denoted by ϕ.

$$\phi : \mathcal{J}_C(\overline{\mathbb{F}}_p) \longrightarrow \mathcal{J}_C(\overline{\mathbb{F}}_p),$$
$$[x^2 + u_1 x + u_0, v_1 x + v_0] \longmapsto [x^2 + \zeta_8^2 u_1 x - u_0, \zeta_8^{-1} v_1 x + \zeta_8 v_0],$$
$$[x + u_0, v_0] \longmapsto [x + \zeta_8^2 u_0, \zeta_8 v_0],$$
$$0 \longmapsto 0.$$

Similarly, $\widehat{\phi}$ also induces an automorphism on $\mathcal{J}_C(\overline{\mathbb{F}}_p)$.

$$\widehat{\phi} : \mathcal{J}_C(\overline{\mathbb{F}}_p) \longrightarrow \mathcal{J}_C(\overline{\mathbb{F}}_p),$$
$$[x^2 + u_1 x + u_0, v_1 x + v_0] \longmapsto [x^2 + \zeta_8^{-2} u_1 x - u_0, \zeta_8 v_1 x + \zeta_8^{-1} v_0],$$
$$[x + u_0, v_0] \longmapsto [x + \zeta_8^{-2} u_0, \zeta_8^{-1} v_0],$$
$$0 \longmapsto 0.$$

It's easy to check that $\phi \circ \widehat{\phi} = \widehat{\phi} \circ \phi = [1]$. Tang *et al.* [13] studied this family of curves carefully, here we cite some useful facts. π_p, ϕ and $\widehat{\phi}$ have the same eigenspaces on $\mathcal{J}_C(\overline{\mathbb{F}}_p)[r]$ and two eigenvalues of ϕ and $\widehat{\phi}$ on the same eigenspace are reciprocal. Since ϕ and $\widehat{\phi}$ have the same characteristic polynomial $P(t) = t^4 + 1$, so all eigenvalues of ϕ and $\widehat{\phi}$ are primitive 8-th root of unity in $\mathbb{F}_r$.

Let $\mathbb{G}_1$ and $\mathbb{G}_p$ denote the 1-eigenspace and p-eigenspace of π_p acting on $\mathcal{J}_C(\overline{\mathbb{F}}_p)[r]$, where $\mathbb{G}_1 = \langle \overline{D}_1 \rangle$ and $\mathbb{G}_p = \langle \overline{D}_2 \rangle$. Let $D_1 = \rho(\overline{D}_1)$ and $D_2 = \rho(\overline{D}_2)$. The proof of Theorem 3.2 in Tang *et al.* [13] suggested that, if $\phi(D_1) = [\lambda]D_1$, $\widehat{\phi}^2(D_2) = [p]D_2 = [\lambda^2](D_2)$. It follows that $\widehat{\phi}(D_2) = [\lambda](D_2)$ or $\widehat{\phi}(D_2) = [-\lambda](D_2)$. Here we can prove the former is correct.

Lemma 4. *With notation as above, we have* $\widehat{\phi}(D_2) = [\lambda](D_2)$.

Proof. Since the eigenvalue of $\widehat{\phi}^2$ on $\mathbb{G}_p$ is λ^2, so the eigenvalue of ϕ^2 on $\mathbb{G}_p$ is $(\lambda^2)^{-1}$. On the other hand, the eigenvalue of ϕ^2 on $\mathbb{G}_1$ is λ^2 because $\phi^2(D_1) = [\lambda^2]D_1$. Therefore, for the automorphism ϕ^2, the eigenspace $\mathbb{G}_{\lambda^2} = \mathbb{G}_1$ and the eigenspace $\mathbb{G}_{\lambda^{-2}} = \mathbb{G}_p$. Then we can use Theorem 1 in Sect. 3 to obtain that

$$((-1)^{rm_1 m_2} e_r^{-1}(D_1, D_2))^{m(p-1)} = \left(\frac{f_{\lambda^2, D_1}(\varepsilon(D_2))}{f_{\lambda^2, D_2}(\varepsilon(D_1))} \right)^{4\lambda^6(p-1)}.$$

If $\widehat{\phi}(D_2) = [-\lambda]$, then $f_{-\lambda, [-\lambda]D_2} = f_{-\lambda, D_2} \circ \phi$ up to a scalar multiply in $\mathbb{F}_p$. Following Lemma 1 we have

$$\left(\frac{f_{\lambda^2, D_1}(\varepsilon(D_2))}{f_{\lambda^2, D_2}(\varepsilon(D_1))} \right)^{p-1} = \left(\frac{f_{\lambda^2, D_1}(\varepsilon(D_2))}{f_{(-\lambda)^2, D_2}(\varepsilon(D_1))} \right)^{p-1}$$

$$= \left(\frac{f_{\lambda, D_1}^\lambda(\varepsilon(D_2))}{f_{-\lambda, D_2}^{-\lambda}(\varepsilon(D_1))} \frac{f_{\lambda, [\lambda]D_1}(\varepsilon(D_2))}{f_{-\lambda, [-\lambda]D_2}(\varepsilon(D_1))} \right)^{p-1}$$

$$= \left(\frac{f_{\lambda, D_1}^\lambda(\varepsilon(D_2))}{f_{-\lambda, D_2}^{-\lambda}(\varepsilon(D_1))} \frac{f_{\lambda, D_1}(\varepsilon([-\lambda]D_2))}{f_{-\lambda, D_2}(\varepsilon([\lambda]D_1))} \right)^{p-1}$$

$$= \left(\frac{f_{\lambda, D_1}^\lambda(\varepsilon(D_2))}{f_{-\lambda, D_2}^{-\lambda}(\varepsilon(D_1))} \frac{f_{\lambda, D_1}^{-\lambda}(\varepsilon(D_2))}{f_{-\lambda, D_2}^\lambda(\varepsilon(D_1))} \right)^{p-1}$$

$$= 1$$

Then $((-1)^{rm_1 m_2} e_r^{-1}(D_1, D_2))^{m(p-1)} = \left(\frac{f_{\lambda^2, D_1}(\varepsilon(D_2))}{f_{\lambda^2, D_2}(\varepsilon(D_1))} \right)^{4\lambda^6(p-1)} = 1$. It follows that the Weil pairing restricted on $\mathbb{G}_1 \times \mathbb{G}_p$ is degenerate. That's incorrect. So $\widehat{\phi}(D_2) = [\lambda]D_2$. □

Therefore, on this family of curves, we can get $\mathbb{G}_\lambda = \mathbb{G}_1$ and $\mathbb{G}_{\lambda^{-1}} = \mathbb{G}_p$ and use automorphism ϕ to define the omega pairing. Therefore, the new pairing is non-degenerate since the Weil pairing on $\mathbb{G}_1 \times \mathbb{G}_p$ is non-degenerate.

4.2 Family II

In this subsection, we study another family of non-supersingular hyperelliptic curves defined by the equation [11]

$$C : y^2 = x^5 + a, a \in \mathbb{F}_p^*, p \equiv 1 (\mathrm{mod}\ 5),$$

where the embedding degree is 5. In this case, our results also can be generalised easily to other curves in this form with the embedding degree k is divisible by

5. Curves of this form have automorphisms $\phi : (x, y) \mapsto (\zeta_5 x, y)$ and $\widehat{\phi} : (x, y) \mapsto (\zeta_5^{-1} x, y)$, where ζ_5 is a primitive 5-th root of unity in $\mathbb{F}_p$. Then ϕ induces a non-trivial automorphism of order 5, which is also denoted by ϕ.

$$\phi : \mathcal{J}_C(\overline{\mathbb{F}}_p) \longrightarrow \mathcal{J}_C(\overline{\mathbb{F}}_p),$$
$$[x^2 + u_1 x + u_0, v_1 x + v_0] \longmapsto [x^2 + \zeta_5 u_1 x + \zeta_5^2 u_0, \zeta_5^{-1} v_1 x + v_0],$$
$$[x + u_0, v_0] \longmapsto [x + \zeta_5 u_0, v_0],$$
$$0 \longmapsto 0.$$

Similarly, $\widehat{\phi}$ also induces an automorphism on $\mathcal{J}_C(\overline{\mathbb{F}}_p)$.

$$\widehat{\phi} : \mathcal{J}_C(\overline{\mathbb{F}}_p) \longrightarrow \mathcal{J}_C(\overline{\mathbb{F}}_p),$$
$$[x^2 + u_1 x + u_0, v_1 x + v_0] \longmapsto [x^2 + \zeta_5^{-1} u_1 x + \zeta_5^{-2} u_0, \zeta_5 v_1 x + v_0],$$
$$[x + u_0, v_0] \longmapsto [x + \zeta_5^{-1} u_0, v_0],$$
$$0 \longmapsto 0.$$

It's easy to check that $\phi \circ \widehat{\phi} = \widehat{\phi} \circ \phi = [1]$. With the similar reasons as the first family of curves, π_p, ϕ and $\widehat{\phi}$ have the same eigenspaces on $\mathcal{J}_C(\overline{\mathbb{F}}_p)[r]$ and two eigenvalues of ϕ and $\widehat{\phi}$ on the same eigenspace are reciprocal. Since ϕ and $\widehat{\phi}$ have the same characteristic polynomial $P(t) = t^4 + t^3 + t^2 + t + 1$, so all eigenvalues of ϕ and $\widehat{\phi}$ are primitive 5-th root of unity in $\mathbb{F}_r$.

Let $\mathbb{G}_1$ and $\mathbb{G}_p$ denote the 1-eigenspace and p-eigenspace of π_p, where $\mathbb{G}_1 = \langle \overline{D}_1 \rangle$ and $\mathbb{G}_p = \langle \overline{D}_2 \rangle$. Let $D_1 = \rho(\overline{D}_1)$, $D_2 = \rho(\overline{D}_2)$ and $\phi(D_1) = [\lambda] D_1$. Then we can prove $\widehat{\phi}(D_2) = [\lambda](D_2)$.

Lemma 5. *With notation as above, we have $\widehat{\phi}(D_2) = [\lambda](D_2)$.*

Proof. Suppose the eigenvalues of $\widehat{\phi}$ on $\mathbb{G}_p$ is ν such that $\widehat{\phi}(D_2) = [\nu](D_2)$. Since the embedding degree is 5, $p^5 \equiv 1 \pmod{r}$. Therefore, p, ν and λ are primitive 5-th roots of unity in $\mathbb{F}_r$. Let $\nu = p^j \pmod{r}$ with $j \in \mathbb{Z}$, then $\widehat{\phi}(D_2) = [\nu](D_2) = [p^j] D_2 = \pi_p^j(D_2)$. Let $mr = \lambda^5 - 1$ with $m \in \mathbb{Z}$. Following Eq. (1), we know the power of the Tate pairing

$$e_t(\overline{D}_1, \overline{D}_2)^m = f_{r, D_1}^m(\varepsilon(D_2))^{\frac{p^5 - 1}{r}}$$
$$= \prod_{i=0}^4 f_{\lambda, D_1}^{\lambda^i}(\varepsilon(\widehat{\phi}^{4-i}(D_2)))^{\frac{p^5 - 1}{r}}$$
$$= \prod_{i=0}^4 f_{\lambda, D_1}^{\lambda^i}(\varepsilon(\pi_p^{j(4-i)}(D_2)))^{\frac{p^5 - 1}{r}}$$
$$= f_{\lambda, D_1}(\varepsilon(D_2))^{\sum_{i=0}^4 \lambda^i p^{j(4-i)} \frac{p^5 - 1}{r}}.$$

It's easy to check that, $\sum_{i=0}^4 \lambda^i p^{j(4-i)} \neq 0 \pmod{r}$ if and only if $\lambda = p^j \pmod{r}$. Since the Tate pairing is non-degenerate, so $\lambda = p^j$. Thus $\widehat{\phi}(D_2) = [\nu](D_2) = [p^j] D_2 = [\lambda](D_2)$. □

The result above shows that, on this family of curves, we can also use automorphism ϕ to define the omega pairing over $\mathbb{G}_1 \times \mathbb{G}_p$.

5   Efficiency Analysis

Generally, the Tate pairing can be computed more efficiently than the Weil pairing because the latter involves two Miller iteration loops. However, the Weil pairing computation does not need the final exponentiation. So when the Miller iterations is less costly than the final exponentiation, the Weil pairing could be faster than the original Tate pairing. As a variant based on the Weil pairing, the omega pairing has advantages that its Miller loop length is very short and the final exponentiation is simple.

In the following, we analysis an example curve in Family I proposed by Fan et al. [11] which is given by the equation

$$C : y^2 = x^5 + 9x,$$

and the hexadecimal representation of parameters are as follows

$p =$ 0000016b 953ca333 acf202b3 0476f30f ff085473 6d0a0be4
     c542fa48 66e5$a fba$ 7bc6cd6d 21ca9fad $ee f$796f1 (329 bits),
$r =$ 00000006 a37991af 81$ddfa$3a ead6ec83 1ca0fc44 75d5add9 (163 bits),
$\lambda = 2^{43} + 2^{10}$.

For this curve we have $\mathbb{G}_\lambda = \mathbb{G}_p \subseteq \mathcal{J}_C(\mathbb{F}_{p^4})$. According to Algorithm 1 in Sect. 3.2, the total cost of computing this omega pairing is given as

$$43 \cdot (T_{D_1} + T_{D_2} + T_{G_1} + T_{G_2} + 3T_{m4} + T_{s4})$$

$$+2(T_{A_1} + T_{A_2} + T_{G_1} + T_{G_2} + 3T_{m4}) + 2T_{m4} + T_{s4} + I_4,$$

where I_4 denotes the inversion in $\mathbb{F}_{p^4}$.

Choie and Lee [19] showed that the Miller rational function is $G(x, y) = \frac{y - l(x)}{u_3(x)}$. Suppose that the above divisors $D_1 = [u_1(x), v_1(x)], D_2 = [u_2(x), v_2(x)]$ are general. since $\pi_p^2(D_2) = [p^2](D_2) = [-1](D_2)$, then $u_2(x) \in \mathbb{F}_{p^2}[x]$. Denote $[n]D_i = [u_{in}(x), v_{in}(x)]$ with $n \in \mathbb{Z}$, we can similarly obtain $u_{1n}(x) \in \mathbb{F}_p[x]$, $u_{2n}(x) \in \mathbb{F}_{p^2}[x]$. Then denominator elimination can be applied to avoid the computation of $u_3(x)$ when we evaluate $G(x, y)$ for both D_1 and D_2.

In [19], Choie and Lee gave costs of doubling and adding general divisors for the most common case in affine coordinates. Although Fan et al. [12] has improved the results in project coordinates, the corresponding Miller rational function $G(x, y)$ is only efficient for the Tate-like pairings. Here we need to compare Tate-like and Ate-like pairings, so we utilize the costs from [19] for our rough estimation. Let M_s, S_s, I_s denote multiplication, squaring and inversion in the finite field $\mathbb{F}_{q^s}$. If we use the pairing-friendly fields with $s = 2^i 3^j$, then we estimate $M_s = 3^i 5^j M_1, S_s = 3^i 5^j S_1$ [4]. Follwing above relations, the corresponding costs in Algorithm 2 are given as follow

- $T_{D_1} = I + 4S + 22M, T_{D_2} = I + 38S + 164M$
- $T_{A_1} = I + 3S + 23M, T_{A_2} = I + 23S + 149M$
- $T_{G_1} = 21M,$ $T_{G_2} = 33M,$

where M, S, I denote multiplication, squaring and inversion in the finite field $\mathbb{F}_p$.

Generally, the final exponentiation of the Tate pairing $f^{\frac{p^4-1}{r}}$ can be divided into two parts. The easy part is to compute f^{p^2-1}, which costs $I_4 + M_4$. The hard part $f^{\frac{p^2+1}{r}}$ can be obtained by Lucas Exponentiation. The specific details of the analysis can be found in [20, 22].

In order to show the efficiency of the omega pairing, we estimate the costs of the original Tate pairing, the improved Tate pairing, the optimal Ate pairing, Weil pairing and the omega pairing in Table 1. In [13], the authors improved the original Tate pairing and computed costs for degenerate divisors in project coordinates. Here we use the same pairing and computed costs for general divisors. The hyperelliptic Ate pairing has no final exponentiation, but its Miller loop is $\log_2 p = 329$. Therefore, the whole costs is obviously more expensive than that of other pairings. So we omit the hyperelliptic Ate pairing and consider the optimal Ate pairing. Since the specific form of the optimal Ate pairing is unknown, we estimate the costs roughly by supposing the Miller loop is $\frac{r}{\varphi(k)} \approx 82$ and the hamming weight of Mliier loop is 41.

Table 1. Costs of Computing Pairings for General Divisors.

Pairing	Doubling	Adding	Miller Loop	Final Expo.	Total
original Tate	$I + 13S + 52M$	$I + 3S + 53M$	163	$I + 1493S + 1502M$	$253I + 3879S + 14695M$
Tate [13]	$I + 22S + 82M$	$I + 3S + 83M$	43	$I + 1493S + 1502M$	$46I + 2445S + 5470M$
optimal Ate	$I + 47S + 215M$	$I + 23S + 200M$	82	$I + 1493S + 1502M$	$124I + 6299S + 27341M$
Weil	$2I + 51S + 267M$	$2I + 26S + 253M$	163	no cost	$504I + 10636S + 66047M$
Omega	$2I + 51S + 267M$	$2I + 26S + 253M$	43	$I + 8S + 17M$	$91I + 2262S + 12013M$

Table 1 shows that, as a super-optimal pairing, the omega pairing is more efficient than other pairings except the improved Tate pairing. This result is mainly benefits from its short Miller loop. Since the embedding degree in the example is small and the final exponentiation is not expensive, the simple exponentiation of the omega pairing hasn't made great contribution. Therefore, when the Miller loop of the improved Tate pairing becomes as short as its Miller loop, the omega pairing loses competitiveness. So when the embedding degree is large and the final exponentiation of the Tate pairing is very expensive, the omega pairing may be more competitive.

6   Conclusion and Future Work

In this paper, we generalize the omega pairing on elliptic curves to hyperelliptic curves. As the variant of the Weil pairing, the omega pairing has advantages that its Miller loop length is very short and the final exponentiation is simple. So it can be faster than most pairings in some hyperelliptic curves.

Generally speaking, the Tate-like pairings are always more efficient than the Ate-like pairings on hyperelliptic curves. Because the costs of doubling and adding general divisors in extension field are many times more expensive than in the base field. Though the optimal omega pairing has short Miller loop length and simple final exponentiation, it is slower than the improved Tate pairing. So the research on how to use high degree twists for faster computations of hyperelliptic pairings is one of our future work.

On the other hand, this is the first time to construct the variant of weil pairing using authorphisms on hyperelliptic curve. Since the authorphisms group on hyperelliptic curves are large and complex, it would be worth to study how to speed up pairing computation using automorphisms. That's also a direction of our future work.

Acknowledgments. We would like to thank the anonymous reviewers for their helpful comments. This work is supported by the National 973 Program of China (No. 2011CB302400), the Strategic Priority Research Program of Chinese Academy of Sciences (No. XDA06010701, No. XDA06010702), the National Natural Science Foundation of China (No. 61303257) and Institute of Information Engineering's Research Project on Cryptography (No. Y3Z0023103, No. Y3Z0011102).

A   Explicit Proofs

Proof of Lemma 1: We denote $D_l = \varepsilon(D_l) - m_l(P_\infty)$ for $l = 1, 2$ and $[k]D_l = \varepsilon([k]D_l) - m_{lk}(P_\infty)$ for $k = i, j$. Let u_∞ be a $\mathbb{F}_q$-rational uniformizer for P_∞ and assume $supp(div(u_\infty)) \cap supp(\varepsilon(D_1)) = \emptyset$. Thus

$$supp(div(f_{i,D_1})) \cap supp((jm_2 - m_{2j})(P_\infty) + div(\frac{1}{u_\infty^{(jm_2-m_{2j})}})) = \emptyset.$$

Since f_{i,D_1} is a $\mathbb{F}_q$-rational function, so

$$\left(f_{i,D_1}((jm_2 - m_{2j})(P_\infty) + div(\frac{1}{u_\infty^{(jm_2-m_{2j})}})) \right)^{q-1} = 1$$

by Fermat's Little Theorem. According to Weil reciprocity [23] , we have

$$\left(f_{i,D_1}(\varepsilon([j]D_2))f_{i,D_1}^{-j}(\varepsilon(D_2)) \right)^{q-1}$$
$$= \left(f_{i,D_1}(\varepsilon([j]D_2) - j\varepsilon(D_2) + (jm_2 - m_{2j})(P_\infty) + div(\frac{1}{u_\infty^{(jm_2-m_{2j})}})) \right)^{q-1}$$
$$= \left(f_{i,D_1}([j]D_2 - jD_2 + div(\frac{1}{u_\infty^{(jm_2-m_{2j})}})) \right)^{q-1}$$
$$= \left(f_{i,D_1}(div((f_{j,D_2}u_\infty^{(jm_2-m_{2j})})^{-1})) \right)^{q-1}$$
$$= \left((f_{j,D_2}u_\infty^{(jm_2-m_{2j})})^{-1}(div(f_{i,D_1})) \right)^{q-1}$$
$$= \left(f_{j,D_2}u_\infty^{(jm_2-m_{2j})}([i]D_1 - iD_1) \right)^{q-1}$$
$$= (f_{j,D_2}(\varepsilon([i]D_1) - i\varepsilon(D_1)))^{q-1} \left(u_\infty^{(jm_2-m_{2j})}(\varepsilon([i]D_1) - i\varepsilon(D_1)) \right)^{q-1}$$
$$\cdot (f_{j,D_2}u_\infty^{(jm_2-m_{2j})}((im_1 - m_{1i})(P_\infty)))^{q-1}$$
$$= \left(f_{j,D_2}(\varepsilon([i]D_1))f_{j,D_2}^{-i}(\varepsilon(D_1)) \right)^{q-1}.$$

In fact, u_∞ and reduced divisor D_1 are $\mathbb{F}_q$-rational, so

$$\left(u_\infty^{(jm_2-m_{2j})}(\varepsilon([i]D_1) - i\varepsilon(D_1)) \right)^{q-1} = 1.$$

On the other hand, $ord_{P_\infty}(f_{j,D_2}u_\infty{}^{(jm_2-m_{2j})}) = 0$ shows that this function is defined on P_∞. Then $f_{j,D_2}u_\infty{}^{(jm_2-m_{2j})}$ is normalised implies that

$$f_{j,D_2}u_\infty{}^{(jm_2-m_{2j})}(P_\infty) = lc_\infty(f_{j,D_2}u_\infty{}^{(jm_2-m_{2j})}) = 1. \qquad (2)$$

So the last indentity holds and it is followed by the equation

$$\left(\frac{f_{i,D_1}(\varepsilon([j]D_2))}{f_{j,D_2}(\varepsilon([i]D_1))}\right)^{q-1} = \left(\frac{f^j_{i,D_1}(\varepsilon(D_2))}{f^i_{j,D_2}(\varepsilon(D_1))}\right)^{q-1}.$$

$\square$

Proof of Lemma 2: Let ϕ be the $\mathbb{F}_q$-rational automorphism defined in Theorem 1, then $[\lambda]D_1 = \phi(D_1)$. Since the automorphism is also an isogeny, so we can denote its daul isogeny as $\widehat{\phi}$, where $\phi \circ \widehat{\phi} = [1]$ and $\widehat{\phi}$ is also $\mathbb{F}_q$-rational. Thus $[\lambda]D_2 = \widehat{\phi}(D_1)$. According to Lemma 3 in [11], we have $f_{\lambda,[\lambda]D_1} = \alpha f_{\lambda,D_1} \circ \widehat{\phi}$ with $\alpha \in \mathbb{F}_q$. By mathematical induction, the identity can be obtained. Following Lemma 1, let $i = j = \lambda$, we have

$$\left(\frac{f_{\lambda,D_1}(\varepsilon([\lambda]D_2))}{f_{\lambda,D_2}(\varepsilon([\lambda]D_1))}\right)^{q-1} = \left(\frac{f_{\lambda,D_1}(\varepsilon(D_2))}{f_{\lambda,D_2}(\varepsilon(D_1))}\right)^{\lambda(q-1)}.$$

Suppose the identity in Lemma 2 holds for i, we can prove it also holds for $i+1$. In fact,

$$\left(\frac{f_{\lambda,D_1}(\varepsilon([\lambda^{i+1}]D_2))}{f_{\lambda,D_2}(\varepsilon([\lambda^{i+1}]D_1))}\right)^{q-1} = \left(\frac{f_{\lambda,D_1}(\varepsilon(\widehat{\phi}^i([\lambda]D_2)))}{f_{\lambda,D_2}(\varepsilon([\lambda][\lambda^i]D_1))}\right)^{q-1}$$

$$= \left(\frac{f_{\lambda,D_1}(\widehat{\phi}^i(\varepsilon([\lambda]D_2)))}{f_{\lambda,D_2}(\varepsilon([\lambda][\lambda^i]D_1))}\right)^{q-1}$$

$$= \left(\frac{f_{\lambda,[\lambda^i]D_1}(\varepsilon([\lambda]D_2))}{f_{\lambda,D_2}(\varepsilon([\lambda][\lambda^i]D_1))}\right)^{q-1}$$

$$= \left(\frac{f_{\lambda,[\lambda^i]D_1}(\varepsilon(D_2))}{f_{\lambda,D_2}(\varepsilon([\lambda^i]D_1))}\right)^{\lambda(q-1)}$$

$$= \left(\frac{f_{\lambda,D_1}(\varepsilon([\lambda^i]D_2))}{f_{\lambda,D_2}(\varepsilon([\lambda^i]D_1))}\right)^{\lambda(q-1)}$$

$$= \left(\frac{f_{\lambda,D_1}(\varepsilon(D_2))}{f_{\lambda,D_2}(\varepsilon(D_1))}\right)^{\lambda^{i+1}(q-1)}.$$

The mathematical induction gives the result of this lemma. $\square$

Proof of Lemma 3: To prove the result, it suffices to show that $\left(\left(\frac{f_{\lambda,D_1}(\varepsilon(D_2))}{f_{\lambda,D_2}(\varepsilon(D_1))}\right)^{q-1}\right)^r = 1$. As is stated in Lemma 1, u_∞ is a $\mathbb{F}_q$-rational uniformizer for P_∞. For the similar reasons with Equation (2),

$$f_{\lambda,D_2}u_\infty{}^{((\lambda-1)m_2)}(P_\infty) = f_{r,D_2}u_\infty{}^{rm_2}(P_\infty) = 1.$$

Assume $div(u_\infty) = P_\infty + D_\infty$ and $supp(D_\infty) \cap supp(div(f_{r,D_1})) = \emptyset$. According to Weil reciprocity [23] and Fermat's Little Theorem, we have

$$\left(\frac{f_{\lambda,D_1}(\varepsilon(D_2))}{f_{\lambda,D_2}(\varepsilon(D_1))} \right)^{(q-1)r}$$

$$= \left(\frac{f_{\lambda,D_1}(\varepsilon(D_2) - m_2(P_\infty) + div(u_\infty^{m_2}))}{f_{\lambda,D_2}u_\infty^{(\lambda-1)m_2}(\varepsilon(D_1) - m_1(P_\infty))} \right)^{(q-1)r}$$

$$= \left(\frac{f_{\lambda,D_1}(rD_2 + div(u_\infty^{rm_2}))}{f_{\lambda,D_2}u_\infty^{(\lambda-1)m_2}(rD_1)} \right)^{(q-1)r}$$

$$= \left(\frac{f_{r,D_2}u_\infty^{rm_2}(\lambda D_1 - [\lambda]D_1)}{f_{r,D_1}(\lambda D_2 - [\lambda]D_2 + div(u_\infty^{(\lambda-1)m_2}))} \right)^{q-1}$$

$$= \left(\frac{f_{r,D_2}(\lambda\varepsilon(D_1) - \varepsilon([\lambda]D_1))u_\infty^{rm_2}(\lambda\varepsilon(D_1) - \varepsilon([\lambda]D_1))f_{r,D_2}u_\infty^{rm_2}(-(\lambda-1)m_1(P_\infty))}{f_{r,D_1}(\lambda\varepsilon(D_1) - \varepsilon([\lambda]D_1))f_{r,D_1}(D_\infty)} \right)^{q-1}$$

$$= \left(\frac{f_{r,D_2}(\lambda\varepsilon(D_1))}{f_{r,D_1}(\lambda\varepsilon(D_2))} \frac{f_{r,D_1}(\varepsilon([\lambda]D_2))}{f_{r,D_2}(\varepsilon([\lambda]D_1))} \right)^{q-1}$$

$$= \left(\frac{f_{r,D_2}(\varepsilon(D_1))}{f_{r,D_1}(\varepsilon(D_2))} \right)^\lambda \left(\frac{f_{r,[\lambda]D_1}(\varepsilon(D_2))}{f_{r,D_2}(\varepsilon([\lambda]D_1))} \right)^{q-1}$$

$$= \left((-1)^{rm_1m_2}e_r(D_1, D_2)^\lambda(-1)^{rm_1m_2}e_r(D_2, [\lambda]D_1) \right)^{q-1}$$

$$= \left(e_r(D_1, D_2)^\lambda e_r(D_2, D_1)^\lambda \right)^{q-1}$$

$$= 1$$

This complete the proof of Lemma 3.

$\square$

References

1. Miller, V.S.: The Weil Pairing and its efficient calculation. J. Cryptol. **17**(4), 235–261 (2004)
2. Vercauteren, F.: Optimal pairings. IEEE Trans. Inf. Theory **56**(1), 455–461 (2010)
3. Barreto, P.S.L.M., Galbraith, S., OhEigeartaigh, C., Scott, M.: Efficient pairing computation on supersingular abelian varieties. Des. Codes Crypt. **42**(3), 239–271 (2007)
4. Hess, F., Smart, N.P., Vercauteren, F.: The eta pairing revisited. IEEE Trans. Inf. Theory **52**(10), 4595–4602 (2006)
5. Zhao, C.A., Zhang, F., Huang, J.: A note on the Ate pairing. Int. J. Inf. Secur. Arch. **7**(6), 379–382 (2008)
6. Lee, E., Lee, H., Park, C.: Efficient and generalized pairing computation on Abelien varieties. IEEE Trans. Inf. Theory **55**(4), 1793–1803 (2009)
7. Zhao, C.A., Xie, D., Zhang, F., Zhang, J., Chen, B.L.: Computing bilinear pairings on elliptic curves with automorphisms. Des. Codes Crypt. **58**(1), 35–44 (2011)
8. Hess, F.: Pairing lattices. In: Galbraith, S.D., Paterson, K.G. (eds.) Pairing 2008. LNCS, vol. 5209, pp. 18–38. Springer, Heidelberg (2008)
9. Granger, R., Hess, F., Oyono, R., Thériault, N., Vercauteren, F.: Ate pairing on hyperelliptic curves. In: Naor, M. (ed.) EUROCRYPT 2007. LNCS, vol. 4515, pp. 430–447. Springer, Heidelberg (2007)
10. Zhang, F.: Twisted Ate pairing on hyperelliptic curves and applications Sciece China. Inf. Sci. **53**(8), 1528–1538 (2010)

11. Fan, X., Gong, G., Jao, D.: Speeding up pairing computations on genus 2 hyper-elliptic curves with efficiently computable automorphisms. In: Galbraith, S.D., Paterson, K.G. (eds.) Pairing 2008. LNCS, vol. 5209, pp. 243–264. Springer, Heidelberg (2008)

12. Fan, X., Gong, G., Jao, D.: Efficient pairing computation on genus 2 curves in projective coordinates. In: Avanzi, R.M., Keliher, L., Sica, F. (eds.) SAC 2008. LNCS, vol. 5381, pp. 18–34. Springer, Heidelberg (2009)

13. Tang, C., Xu, M., Qi, Y.: Faster pairing computation on genus 2 hyperelliptic curves. Inf. Process. Lett. **111**, 494–499 (2011)

14. Balakrishnan, J., Belding, J., Chisholm, S., Eisenträger, K., Stange, K., Teske, E.: Pairings on hyperelliptic curves (2009). http://www.math.uwaterloo.ca/~eteske/teske/pairings.pdf

15. Cantor, D.G.: Computing in the Jacobian of a hyperelliptic curve. Math. Comp **48**(177), 95–101 (1987)

16. Mumford, D.: Tata Lectures on Theta I, II. Birkhäuser, Boston (1983/84)

17. Howe, E.W.: The Weil pairing and the Hilbert symbol. Math. Ann. **305**, 387–392 (1996)

18. Joux, A.: A one round protocol for tripartite Diffie-Hellman. J. Cryptol. **17**, 263–276 (2004)

19. Choie, Y., Lee, E.: Implementation of Tate pairing on hyperelliptic curves of genus 2. In: Lim, J.-I., Lee, D.-H. (eds.) ICISC 2003. LNCS, vol. 2971, pp. 97–111. Springer, Heidelberg (2004)

20. Scott, M., Barreto, P.S.L.M.: Compressed pairings. In: Franklin, M. (ed.) CRYPTO 2004. LNCS, vol. 3152, pp. 140–156. Springer, Heidelberg (2004)

21. Granger, R., Hess, F., Oyono, R., Thériault, N., Vercauteren, F.: Ate pairing on hyperelliptic curves. In: Naor, M. (ed.) EUROCRYPT 2007. LNCS, vol. 4515, pp. 430–447. Springer, Heidelberg (2007)

22. Granger, R., Page, D.L., Smart, N.P.: High security pairing-based cryptography revisited. In: Hess, F., Pauli, S., Pohst, M. (eds.) ANTS 2006. LNCS, vol. 4076, pp. 480–494. Springer, Heidelberg (2006)

23. Silverman, H.: The Arithmetic of Elliptic Curves. GTM, vol. 106, 2nd edn. Springer, New York (2009)

24. Zhao, C.A., Zhang, F., Huang, J.: All pairings are in a group. IEICE Trans. Fundam. **E91−A**(10), 3084–3087 (2008)

Pairing Computation on Edwards Curves with High-Degree Twists

Liangze Li[1,3], Hongfeng Wu[2](✉), and Fan Zhang[1]

[1] LMAM, School of Mathematical Sciences, Peking University, Beijing 100871, China
viczf@pku.edu.cn
[2] College of Sciences, North China University of Technology, Beijing 100144, China
whfmath@gmail.com
[3] Beijing International Center for Mathematical Research, Beijing 100871, China
liliangze2005@163.com

Abstract. Elliptic curve can be seen as the intersection of two quadratic surfaces in space. In this paper, we used the geometry approach to explain the group law for general elliptic curves given by intersection of two quadratic surfaces, then we construct the Miller function over the intersection of quadratic surfaces. As an example, we obtain the Miller function of Tate pairing computation on twisted Edwards curves. Then we present the explicit formulae for pairing computation on Edwards curves. Our formulae for the doubling step are a littler faster than that proposed by Arène et al.. Moreover, when $j = 1728$ and $j = 0$ we consider quartic and sextic twists to improve the efficiency respectively. Finally, we present the formulae of refinements technique on Edwards curves to obtain gain up when the embedding degree is odd.

Keywords: Edwards curves · Tate pairing · Miller functions · Cryptography

1 Introduction

To compute pairings efficiently is always a bottleneck for implementing pairing-based cryptography. The basic method of computing pairings is Miller's algorithm [20]. Consequently, various improvements were presented in [1,13,14,17,21]. One way to improve the efficiency is to find other models of elliptic curves which can provide more efficient algorithms for pairing computation. Edwards curves were one of the popular models. Edwards curve was discovered by Edwards [9] and was applied in cryptography by Bernstein and Lange [2]. Then twisted Edwards curves which are the generalization of Edwards curves were introduced by Bernstein et al. in [3]. Bernstein and Lange also pointed out several advantages of applying the Edwards curves to cryptography. Edwards curves are far superior in elliptic curve cryptography because of fast addition formulae. Pairing computation over Edwards curves was first considered in [8,16]. In 2009, Arène et al. [1]

© Springer International Publishing Switzerland 2014
D. Lin et al. (Eds.): Inscrypt 2013, LNCS 8567, pp. 185–200, 2014.
DOI: 10.1007/978-3-319-12087-4_12

gave the geometric interpretation of the group law and presented explicit formulae for computing the Tate pairing on twisted Edwards curves. Their formulae are faster than all previously proposed formulas for pairings computation on twisted Edwards curves. Their formulae are even competitive with all published formulae for pairing computation on Weierstrass curves.

Any elliptic curve defined over a field K with characteristic different from 2 is birationally equivalent to an Edwards curve over some extension of K, i.e. a curve given by $x^2 + y^2 = 1 + dx^2y^2$ with $d \notin \{0, 1\}$. In fact, the twisted Edwards can be seen as the intersection of two quadratic surfaces in space. That is to say the twisted Edwards curves can be given by $S_{a,d} : aX^2 + Y^2 = Z^2 + dW^2$, $XY = ZW$. For general elliptic curves given by intersection of two quadratic surfaces, the geometric interpretation of group law had been discussed by Merriman et al. in [19]. In some situations it is more effectively to write an elliptic curve as the intersection of two quadratic surfaces in space. Jacobi quartic curve is another example of the importance [7, 18]. In [22], we use a straightforward way give the elaborate geometric interpretation of the group law on twisted Edwards curves which are seen as the intersection of two quadric surfaces in space. In this paper, we used the geometry approach of [19] to explain the group law for general elliptic curves given by intersection of two quadratic surfaces, then we construct the Miller function over the intersection of quadratic surfaces. As an example, we obtain the Miller function of Tate pairing computation on twisted Edwards curves. Of course, you can use a similar approach to compute Tate pairing on any elliptic curves given by intersection of two quadratic surfaces. However, for the sake of integrity, we recalculate the explicit formulae for pairing computation on twisted Edwards curves. The high-twists had been sufficiently studied by Costello, Lange and Naehrig [6] on Weierstrass curves. As the result given by [11], one elliptic curve and its quartic/sextic twist can't both be written in a rational twisted Edwards form, so we turn to Weierstrass curves for the high-degree twists of twisted Edwards curves. These twists enable us to reduce the cost of substituting to a half and a third respectively in $j = 1728$ case and $j = 0$ case. For Edwards curves, it is an interesting problem to find an efficient way to compute ate pairing on twisted Edwards curves.

When the embedding degree is even, the traditional denominator elimination technique is used. While the denominator elimination can not be used if the embedding degree is odd, so we consider the refinement technique to improve the efficiency. In [5], Blake et al. presented three refinements to Miller's algorithm over Weierstrass curves by reducing the total number of vertical lines in Miller's algorithm. This method can be used for both Weil and Tate Pairing over Weierstrass curves with any embedding degree. In [23], L. Xu and D. Lin study the refinements formulas for Edwards curves. If we see the Edwards curves as the intersection of two quadratic surfaces in space, our refinements over Edwards curves cost less than the refinements of L. Xu and D. Lin [23], because in our method we use one plane to replace two lines of the Miller function in [23].

In this paper, we use $\mathbf{m}$ and $\mathbf{s}$ denote the costs of multiplication and squaring in the base field $\mathbb{F}_q$ while $\mathbf{M}$ and $\mathbf{S}$ denote the costs of multiplication and squaring in the extension $\mathbb{F}_{q^k}$.

2   Tate Pairing

Let $p > 3$ be a prime and $\mathbb{F}_q$ be a finite field with $q = p^n$. E is an elliptic curve defined over $\mathbb{F}_q$ with neutral element denoted by O. r is a prime such that $r | \#E(\mathbb{F}_q)$. Let $k > 1$ denote the embedding degree with respect to r, i.e. k is the smallest positive integer such that $r | q^k - 1$. For any point $P \in E(\mathbb{F}_q)[r]$, there exists a rational function f_P defined over $\mathbb{F}_q$ such that $\text{div}(f_P) = r(P) - r(O)$, which is unique up to a non-zero scalar multiple. The group of r-th roots of unity in $\mathbb{F}_{q^k}$ is denoted by μ_r. The reduced Tate pairing is then defined as follows:

$$T_r : E(\mathbb{F}_q)[r] \times E(\mathbb{F}_{q^k}) \to \mu_r : (P, Q) \mapsto f_P(Q)^{(q^k - 1)/r}.$$

The rational function f_P can be computed in polynomial time by using Miller's algorithm [20]. The main ideal of Miller's algorithm is to inductively build up such a function f_P by constructing the function $f_{n,P}$. The function $f_{n,P}$ is defined by $(f_{n,P}) = n(P) - ([n]P) - (n-1)(O)$, n is an integer smaller than r.

Let $g_{P,T} \in \mathbb{F}_q(E)$ be the rational function satisfying $\text{div}(g_{P,T}) = (P) + (T) - (O) - (P+T)$, where $P+T$ denotes the sum of P and T on E, and additions of the form $(P) + (T)$ denote formal additions in the divisor group.

If $P \in E$, define $f_{0,P} = f_{1,P} = 1$. Inductively, for $n > 0$, define $f_{n+1,P} := f_{n,P} g_{P,nP}$, then we have

$$f_{m+n,P} = f_{m,P} \cdot f_{n,P} \cdot g_{mP,nP}.$$

3   Edwards Curves

In this section, we review the preliminaries of Edwards curves. Let $\mathbb{F}_q$ be a finite field with characteristic greater than 3. A twisted Edwards curve is a quartic curve over $\mathbb{F}_q$, defined by

$$E_{a,d} : \ ax^2 + y^2 = 1 + dx^2 y^2,$$

where a, d are distinct nonzero elements of $\mathbb{F}_q$. In [3], Bernstein et al. proved that an elliptic curve over a field K with the group $4 | \sharp E(K)$ if and only if E is birationally equivalent over K to a twisted Edwards curve. The sum of two points (x_1, y_1) and (x_2, y_2) on the twisted Edwards curve $E_{a,d}$ is

$$(x_1, y_1) + (x_2, y_2) = \left(\frac{x_1 y_2 + x_2 y_1}{1 + dx_1 x_2 y_1 y_2}, \frac{y_1 y_2 - a x_1 x_2}{1 - dx_1 x_2 y_1 y_2} \right).$$

The point $(0, 1)$ is the unit of the addition law. The inverse of a point (x, y) on $E_{a,d}$ is $(-x, y)$.

In fact, the twisted Edwards curve can be seen as the intersection of two quadric surfaces in space. That is, the twisted Edwards curve can be written as:

$$S_{a,d} : \ aX^2 + Y^2 = Z^2 + dW^2, \quad XY = ZW. \tag{1}$$

Set $O = (0 : 1 : 0 : 1)$ as the neutral element, the group law on (1) is given by

$$-(X : Y : W : Z) = (-X : Y : -W : Z)$$

and

$$(X_1 : Y_1 : W_1 : Z_1) + (X_2 : Y_2 : W_2 : Z_2) = (X_3 : Y_3 : W_3 : Z_3)$$

where

$$
\begin{aligned}
X_3 &= (X_1 Y_2 + Y_1 X_2)(Z_1 Z_2 - dW_1 W_2), \\
Y_3 &= (Y_1 Y_2 - aX_1 X_2)(Z_1 Z_2 + dW_1 W_2), \\
W_3 &= (Y_1 Y_2 - aX_1 X_2)(X_1 Y_2 + X_2 Y_1), \\
Z_3 &= (Z_1 Z_2 - dW_1 W_2)(Z_1 Z_2 + dW_1 W_2)
\end{aligned}
\tag{2}
$$

The point $O' = (0 : -1 : 0 : 1)$ has order 2. Note that the above formula is unified, that is it can be applied to both adding two distinct points and doubling a point. The fast arithmetic on twisted Edwards given by $S_{a,d}$ can be found in [4,15].

4 Group Law Over the Intersection of Quadratic Surfaces

Let E denote the intersection of quadratic surfaces. The group law of this kind of curve is different from that of cubic curves. We consider projective planes which are given by homogeneous projective equations $\Pi = 0$. In this paper, we still use the symbol Π to denote projective planes. In fact, any plane Π intersects E at exactly four points. Although these planes are not functions on E, their divisors can be well defined as:

$$(\Pi) = \sum_{P \in \Pi \cap E} n_P (P) \tag{3}$$

where n_P is the intersection multiplicity of Π and E at P. Then the quotient of two projective planes is a well defined function which gives principal divisor. Let $O \in E(\mathbb{F}_q)$ be the neutral element, there must be a plane intersects E with multiply three at O, and its fourth intersecting points with E is O'. It is also obvious that P_1, P_2, P_3 and P_4 are coplaner if and only if $P_1 + P_2 + P_3 + P_4 = O'$.

4.1 Miller Function Over the Intersection of Quadratic Surfaces

In this section we construct the Miller function over the intersection of quadratic surfaces.

Let E be the intersection of two quadratic surfaces, O is the neutral element; P_1 and P_2 be two different points on E, $\Pi_{P_1,P_2,O'}$ denote the projective plane passing through P_1, P_2 and O'. The group law given above shows that $-P_1 - P_2$ is the third intersection, by (3) we can get:

$$(\Pi_{P_1,P_2,O'}) = (P_1) + (P_2) + (-P_1 - P_2) + (O')$$

Similarly, $\Pi_{T+P,O,O'}$ intersects with E at $P_1 + P_2$, O', O and $-P_1 - P_2$. Then:

$$(\Pi_{P_1+P_2,O,O'}) = (P_1 + P_2) + (O) + (O') + (-P_1 - P_2)$$

Thus,

$$(\frac{\Pi_{P_1,P_2,O'}}{\Pi_{P_1+P_2,O,O'}}) = (P_1) + (P_2) - (P_1 + P_2) - (O)$$

The geometry interpolation derives the formula of Miller's function directly. The Miller's function with divisor $(P_1) + (P_2) - (P_1 + P_2) - (O)$ can be given

$$g_{P_1,P_2} = \frac{\Pi_{P_1,P_2,O'}}{\Pi_{P_1+P_2,O,O'}} \qquad (4)$$

In Miller's algorithm, P is always a fixed point, T is always nP for some integer n. For the addition steps, Miller function $g_{T,P}$ over E can be given by setting $P_1 = T, P_2 = P$. For the doubling steps, Miller function $g_{T,T}$ over E is given by setting $P_1 = P_2 = T$.

Note that the planes appear in the formula always pass through O'. Particularly, if P_1, P_2 and O' are pairwise distinct points on $S_{a,d}$. We use the equation $C_X X + C_Y Y + C_Z Z + C_W W = 0$ to denote a projective plane. By solving linear equations, we get the coefficients of the plane $\Pi_{P_1,P_2,O'}$ in Miller function of twisted Edwards curves as follows:

$$\begin{aligned}
C_X &= W_2(Z_1 + Y_1) - W_1(Z_2 + Y_2), \\
C_Y &= X_2 W_1 - X_1 W_2, \\
C_W &= X_1(Y_2 + Z_2) - X_2(Z_1 + Y_1)
\end{aligned} \qquad (5)$$

In the case that $P_1 = P_2$, we have

$$C_X = Y_1 Z_1 - a X_1^2, \ C_Y = X_1 Z_1 - X_1 Y_1, \ C_W = d X_1 W_1 - Z_1^2. \qquad (6)$$

5 Pairing Computation on $S_{a,d}$ with Even Embedding Degrees

In this section, we analysis computation steps in Miller's algorithm explicitly. The results in this section are mainly from [22]. For an addition step or doubling step, each addition or doubling steps consist of three parts: computing the point $T + P$ or $2T$ and the function $g_{T,P}$ or $g_{T,T}$, evaluating $g_{T,P}$ or $g_{T,P}$ at Q, then updating the variable f by $f \leftarrow f \cdot g_{T,P}(Q)$ or by $f \leftarrow f^2 \cdot g_{T,T}(Q)$. The updating part, as operation in $\mathbb{F}_{q^k}$, costs 1M for addition step and 1M + 1S for doubling step. For the evaluating part, some standard methods such as denominator elimination and subfield simplification can be used, as we introduce below.

As usual, we choose $P \in S_{a,d}(\mathbb{F}_q)[r]$ and $Q \in S_{a,d}(\mathbb{F}_{q^k})$, where $k > 1$ is the embedding degree. In fact as stated in [13], Q can be chosen from a subgroup which is given by a twist of $S_{a,d}$. More precisely, for $d = \#\mathrm{Aut}(S_{a,d})$, there is degree-$d$ twist of $S_{a,d}$ over $\mathbb{F}_{q^{k/d}}$ denoted as E' such that $Q \in \psi(E'(\mathbb{F}_{q^{k/d}}))$ with $\psi : E' \to S_{a,d}$ an isomorphism over $\mathbb{F}_{q^{k/d}}$. It is noticeable that E' is not necessary to have a twisted Edwards model.

In this part, we assume that embedding degree k is even. Let δ be a generator of $\mathbb{F}_{q^k}$ over $\mathbb{F}_{q^{k/2}}$ with $\delta^2 \in \mathbb{F}_{q^{k/2}}$. Suppose $Q' = (X_0 : Y_0 : W_0 : Z_0) \in$

$S_{a\delta-2,d\delta-2}(\mathbb{F}_{q^{k/2}})$, we can see that $Q = (X_0 : \delta Y_0 : W_0 : \delta Z_0) \in S_{a,d}(\mathbb{F}_{q^k})$. If $P_3 = P_1 + P_2 \neq O, O'$, for evaluation of $g_{P_1,P_2}(Q)$, we have

$$g_{P_1,P_2}(Q) = \frac{\Pi_{P_1,P_2,O'}(Q)}{\Pi_{P_3,O,O'}(Q)} = \frac{C_X X_0 + C_Y \delta(Y_0 + Z_0) + C_W W_0}{W_3 X_0 - X_3 W_0}$$

$$= \frac{C_X \frac{X_0}{Y_0+Z_0} + C_Y \delta + C_W \frac{W_0}{Y_0+Z_0}}{(W_3 X_0 - X_3 W_0)/(Y_0 + Z_0)} \in (C_X \theta + C_Y \delta + C_W \eta)\mathbb{F}_{q^{k/2}}^*,$$

where $\theta = \frac{X_0}{Y_0+Z_0}$ and $\eta = \frac{W_0}{Y_0+Z_0}$. It is clearly that $(W_3 X_0 - X_3 W_0)/(Y_0 + Z_0)$ in $\mathbb{F}_{q^{k/2}}^*$, then it can be discarded in pairing computation thanks to the final exponentiation, This fact is usually called the denominator elimination technique.

In generally, Let $\mathbb{F}_q$ be an ordinary elliptic curve with neutral elements $O \in E(\mathbb{F}_q)$, then Miller function $g_{P_1,P_2} = \frac{\Pi_{P_1,P_2,O'}}{\Pi_{P_1+P_2,O,O'}} = \frac{\Pi_{P_1,P_2,O'}/\Pi_{O,O,O'}}{\Pi_{P_1+P_2,O,O'}/\Pi_{O,O,O'}}$. let $E'/\mathbb{F}_q$ is a degree-d twist of $E/\mathbb{F}_q$ with d even, thus the isomorphism $\phi : E' \to E$ is defined over $\mathbb{F}_{q^d}$. Then for any $Q' \in E'(\mathbb{F}_q)$ and $P \neq O \in E(\mathbb{F}_q)$, the value of function $\Pi_{P,O,O'}/\Pi_{O,O,O'} \in \mathbb{F}_q(E)$ at $Q = \phi(Q') \in \mathbb{F}_{q^{d/2}}^*$ if $Q \neq \pm P$. Thus it is eliminated by the final exponential.

Note that $\theta, \eta \in \mathbb{F}_{q^{k/2}}$ are fixed during pairing computation, so they can be precomputed. The coefficients C_X, C_Y and C_W are in $\mathbb{F}_q$, thus the evaluation at Q given the coefficients of the plane can be computed in $k\mathbf{m}$ (multiplications by θ and η need $\frac{k}{2}\mathbf{m}$ each).

Addition Steps. Let $P_1 = T$ and $P_2 = P$ be distinct points with $Z_1 Z_2 \neq 0$. By variant of formula (2) and (5), the explicit formulas for computing $P_3 = T + P$ and C_X, C_Y, C_W are given as follows:

$$A = X_1 \cdot X_2, B = Y_1 \cdot Y_2, C = Z_1 \cdot W_2, D = Z_2 \cdot W_1, E = W_1 \cdot W_2,$$
$$F = (X_1 - Y_1) \cdot (X_2 + Y_2) - A + B, G = B + aA, H = D - C,$$
$$I = D + C, X_3 = I \cdot F, Y_3 = G \cdot H, Z_3 = F \cdot G, W_3 = I \cdot H,$$
$$C_X = (W_1 - Y_1) \cdot (W_2 + Y_2) - E + B + H, C_W = X_2 \cdot Z_1 - X_1 \cdot Z_2 - F,$$
$$C_Y = (X_1 - W_1) \cdot (X_2 + W_2) - A + E.$$

With these formulas $T + P$ and C_X, C_Y, C_W can be computed in $14\mathbf{m} + 1\mathbf{m_c}$, where $1\mathbf{m_c}$ is constant multiplication by a. For a mixed addition step, in which the base point P is chosen to have $Z_2 = 1$, the costs reduce to $12\mathbf{m} + 1\mathbf{m_c}$. Therefore, the total costs of an addition step are $1\mathbf{M} + k\mathbf{m} + 14\mathbf{m} + 1\mathbf{m_c}$, while a mixed addition step costs $1\mathbf{M} + k\mathbf{m} + 12\mathbf{m} + 1\mathbf{m_c}$.

Doubling Steps. For $P_1 = P_2 = T$, $P_3 = 2T$. By the formulae of (2) and (6), our explicit formulas for computing $P_3 = 2T$ and C_X, C_Y, C_W are given as follows:

$$A = X_1{}^2, B = Y_1{}^2, C = Z_1{}^2, D = aA, E = B + D, F = 2C - E,$$
$$G = (X_1 + Y_1)^2 - A - B, H = (Y_1 + Z_1)^2 - B - C,$$
$$X_3 = G \cdot F, Y_3 = E \cdot (B - D), Z_3 = E \cdot F, W_3 = G \cdot (B - D),$$
$$2C_X = H - 2D, 2C_Y = (X_1 + Z_1)^2 - A - C - G,$$
$$2C_W = d((X_1 + W_1)^2 - A) - C - E.$$

By the above formulae, $2T$ and C_X, C_Y, C_W can be computed in $4\mathbf{m} + 7\mathbf{s} + 2\mathbf{m_c}$, where $2\mathbf{m_c}$ are constant multiplications by a and d. So total costs of our formulae for a doubling step are $1\mathbf{M} + 1\mathbf{S} + k\mathbf{m} + 4\mathbf{m} + 7\mathbf{s} + 2\mathbf{m_c}$. While the total costs of the formulae for the doubling step proposed in [1] are $1\mathbf{M} + 1\mathbf{S} + k\mathbf{m} + 6\mathbf{m} + 5\mathbf{s} + 2\mathbf{m_c}$, where $2\mathbf{m_c}$ are both constant multiplication by a.

The following table shows the concrete comparison for doubling step(DBL), mixed addition step (mADD) and addition step (ADD).

	DBL	mADD	ADD
Arène et.al. [1]	$1\mathbf{M} + 1\mathbf{S} + k\mathbf{m}$	$1\mathbf{M} + k\mathbf{m}$	$1\mathbf{M} + k\mathbf{m}$
	$+6\mathbf{m} + 5\mathbf{s} + 2\mathbf{m_c}$	$+12\mathbf{m} + 1\mathbf{m_c}$	$+14\mathbf{m} + 1\mathbf{m_c}$
This paper	$1\mathbf{M} + 1\mathbf{S} + k\mathbf{m}$	$1\mathbf{M} + k\mathbf{m}$	$1\mathbf{M} + k\mathbf{m}$
	$+4\mathbf{m} + 7\mathbf{s} + 2\mathbf{m_c}$	$+12\mathbf{m} + 1\mathbf{m_c}$	$+14\mathbf{m} + 1\mathbf{m_c}$

5.1 Pairing Computation on $S_{a,d}$ with Twists of Degree 4 or 6

Let $d|k$, an elliptic curve E' over $\mathbb{F}_{q^{k/d}}$ is called a twist of degree d of $E/\mathbb{F}_{q^{k/d}}$ if there is an isomorphism $\psi : E' \to E$ defined over $\mathbb{F}_{q^k}$, and this is the smallest extension of $\mathbb{F}_{q^{k/d}}$ over which ψ is defined. Depending on the j-invariant $j(E)$ of E, there exist twists of degree at most 6, since $\text{char}(\mathbb{F}_q) > 3$. Pairing friendly curves with twists of degree higher than 2 arise from constructions with j-invariants $j(E) = 0$ and $j(E) = 1728$.

The twisted Edwards curve $ax^2 + y^2 = 1 + dx^2y^2$ has j-invariant $j_{a,d} = 16(a^2 + 14ad + d^2)^3/ad(a - d)^4$, hence, the j-invariant of $E_{a,-a} : ax^2 + y^2 = 1 - ax^2y^2$ equal to 1728, thus, there exist twists of degree 4. The case $a = 1$ is the "classical" Edwards curve $x^2 + y^2 = 1 - x^2y^2$ with complex multiplication $D = -4$ [12]. Furthermore, $j_{a,d} = 0$ if and only if $a = (-7 \pm 4\sqrt{3})d$. Note that 3 is a square in finite field $\mathbb{F}_q$ if and only if $q \equiv \pm 1 \pmod{12}$. Now we assume that $q \equiv \pm 1 \pmod{12}$ and a, d satisfy the relation $a = (-7 \pm 4\sqrt{3})d$. Then Edwards curve $E_{a,d} : ax^2 + y^2 = 1 + dx^2y^2$ has j-invariant equal to 0, hence, there exist twists of degree 6. The case $a = 1$ is the Edwards curve $x^2 + y^2 = 1 - (7 + 4\sqrt{3})x^2y^2$ with complex multiplication $D = -3$ [12]. But Galbraith showed one elliptic curve and its quartic/sextic twist can't both be written in a rational twisted Edwards form [11], so we turn to Weierstrass curves for the high-degree twists of twisted Edwards curves.

Twists of Degree 4

Lemma 1 ([22], Lemma 2). *Assume that $4|k$, δ is a generator of $\mathbb{F}_{q^k}$ over $\mathbb{F}_{q^{k/4}}$ and $\delta^4 \in \mathbb{F}_{q^{k/4}}$, which implies $\delta^2 \in \mathbb{F}_{q^{k/2}}$. Then the Weierstrass curve $W_a : \frac{2}{a}v^2 = u^3 + \frac{1}{\delta^4}u$ is a twist of degree 4 over $\mathbb{F}_{q^{k/4}}$ of $E_{a,-a}$. The isomorphism can be given as*

$$\psi : W_a \longrightarrow E_{a,-a}, \quad (u,v) \longmapsto (x,y) = \left(u/\delta v, (\delta^2 u - 1)/(\delta^2 u + 1)\right).$$

The inverse transformation is $(x,y) \mapsto ((1+y)/(\delta^2(1-y)), (1+y)/(\delta^3 x(1-y)))$. For $Q' \in W_a(\mathbb{F}_{q^{k/4}})$, we have $(x_Q, y_Q) = \psi(Q') \in E_{a,-a}(\mathbb{F}_{q^k})$. Then its corresponding point $Q \in S_{a,-a}(\mathbb{F}_{q^k})$ can be given as $(X_Q : Y_Q : W_Q : Z_Q) = (x_Q : y_Q : x_Q y_Q : 1)$. One can check by substitution that:

$$\frac{X_Q + W_Q}{Y_Q + Z_Q} = x_Q = \frac{u}{\delta v}, \quad \frac{X_Q - W_Q}{Y_Q + Z_Q} = x_Q \cdot \frac{1 - y_Q}{1 + y_Q} = \frac{1}{\delta^3 v}.$$

For $\theta = \frac{u}{2v}$ and $\eta = \frac{1}{2v}$, we have $\frac{X_Q}{Y_Q + Z_Q} = \theta\delta^{-1} + \eta\delta^{-3}$ and $\frac{W_Q}{Y_Q + Z_Q} = \theta\delta^{-1} - \eta\delta^{-3}$ with $\theta, \eta \in \mathbb{F}_{q^{k/4}}$. Then for the evaluation of $g_{P_1,P_2}(Q)$ with $P_3 = P_1 + P_2 \neq O, O'$, we get

$$
\begin{aligned}
g_{P_1,P_2}(Q) &= \frac{\Pi_{P_1,P_2,O'}(Q)}{\Pi_{P_3,O,O'}(Q)} = \frac{C_X \frac{X_Q}{Y_Q+Z_Q} + C_Y + C_W \frac{W_Q}{Y_Q+Z_Q}}{W_3 \frac{X_Q}{Y_Q+Z_Q} - X_3 \frac{W_Q}{Y_Q+Z_Q}} \\
&= \frac{C_X(\theta\delta^{-1} + \eta\delta^{-3}) + C_Y + C_W(\theta\delta^{-1} - \eta\delta^{-3})}{W_3(\theta\delta^{-1} + \eta\delta^{-3}) - X_3(\theta\delta^{-1} - \eta\delta^{-3})} \\
&= \frac{(C_X - C_W)\eta + (C_X + C_W)\theta\delta^2 + C_Y\delta^3}{(W_3 + X_3)\eta + (W_3 - X_3)\theta\delta^2} \\
&\in ((C_X - C_W)\eta + (C_X + C_W)\theta\delta^2 + C_Y\delta^3)\mathbb{F}_{q^{k/2}}^*.
\end{aligned}
$$

So we can reduce $g_{P_1,P_2}(Q)$ to $(C_X - C_W)\eta + (C_X + C_W)\theta\delta^2 + C_Y\delta^3$. Moreover we may precompute θ and η since they are fixed during the whole computation. When $C_X, C_Y, C_W \in \mathbb{F}_q$ and $\theta, \eta \in \mathbb{F}_{q^{k/4}}$ are given, the evaluation at Q can be computed in $\frac{k}{2}\mathbf{m}$, with $\frac{k}{4}\mathbf{m}$ each for multiplications by θ and η.

Consider $\mathbb{F}_{q^k}$ as an $\mathbb{F}_{q^{k/4}}$-vector space with basis $1, \delta, \delta^2, \delta^3$. Then an arbitrary element $\alpha \in \mathbb{F}_{q^k}$ can be denoted as $a_0 + a_1\delta + a_2\delta^2 + a_3\delta^3$ with $a_i \in \mathbb{F}_{q^{k/4}}, i = 0, 1, 2, 3$. And the reduced value of $g(Q)$ we've gotten above can be denoted as $\beta = b_0 + b_2\delta^2 + b_3\delta^3$, where $b_3 \in \mathbb{F}_q$ and $b_0, b_2 \in \mathbb{F}_{q^{k/4}}$. This special representation may lead to some optimization of the main multiplication in $\mathbb{F}_{q^k}$, but when using the field towering the cost will remain approximately $1\mathbf{M}$.

Therefore, the addition step costs $1\mathbf{M} + (\frac{k}{2} + 14)\mathbf{m} + 1\mathbf{m_c}$, where $1\mathbf{m_c}$ is constant multiplication by a. For a mixed addition step, the costs reduce to $1\mathbf{M} + (\frac{k}{2} + 12)\mathbf{m} + 1\mathbf{m_c}$. The doubling step costs $1\mathbf{M} + 1\mathbf{S} + (\frac{k}{2} + 4)\mathbf{m} + 7\mathbf{s} + 2\mathbf{m_c}$, where $2\mathbf{m_c}$ are constant multiplications by a and d.

When using the Schoolbook method, multiplying α by β costs $4 \cdot \frac{k}{4}\mathbf{m}$ for computing $a_i \cdot b_3, i = 0, 1, 2, 3$ and costs $8(\frac{k}{4})^2\mathbf{m}$ for $a_i \cdot b_0$ and $a_i \cdot b_2$. The total cost $(\frac{k^2}{2} + k)\mathbf{m}$ equals to $(\frac{1}{2} + \frac{1}{k})\mathbf{M}$, considering that a general multiplication in $\mathbb{F}_{q^k}$ costs $\mathbf{M} = k^2\mathbf{m}$. Namely the quartic twist may reduce the cost of the main multiplication in Miller's algorithm to $(\frac{1}{2} + \frac{1}{k})\mathbf{M}$. Therefore, the addition step costs $(\frac{1}{2} + \frac{1}{k})\mathbf{M} + (\frac{k}{2} + 14)\mathbf{m} + 1\mathbf{m_c}$, where $1\mathbf{m_c}$ is constant multiplication by a. For a mixed addition step, the costs reduce to $(\frac{1}{2} + \frac{1}{k})\mathbf{M} + (\frac{k}{2} + 12)\mathbf{m} + 1\mathbf{m_c}$. The doubling step costs $(\frac{1}{2} + \frac{1}{k})\mathbf{M} + 1\mathbf{S} + (\frac{k}{2} + 4)\mathbf{m} + 7\mathbf{s} + 2\mathbf{m_c}$, where $2\mathbf{m_c}$ are constant multiplications by a and d.

By the way, according to the definition of Ate pairing, the point addition and doubling are performed in $\mathbb{F}_{q^k}$. Thanks to the Lemma 1, we can choose $Q' \in W_a$ such that $Q = \psi(Q') \in S_{a,-a}$. So, is there a efficient way to compute ate pairing on twisted Edwards curves?

Twists of Degree 6. We denote $M = \frac{2(a+d)}{a-d}$ and $N = \frac{4}{a-d}$ when given a, d.

Lemma 2 ([22], Lemma 3). *Assume that $6|k$, δ is a generator of $\mathbb{F}_{q^k}$ over $\mathbb{F}_{q^{k/6}}$ with $\delta^6 \in \mathbb{F}_{q^{k/6}}$, which implies $\delta^2 \in \mathbb{F}_{q^{k/2}}$ and $\delta^3 \in \mathbb{F}_{q^{k/3}}$. Then the Weierstrass elliptic curve $W_{M,N} : v^2 = u^3 - \frac{M^3 N^3}{27}\delta^6$ is a twist of degree 6 over $\mathbb{F}_{q^{k/6}}$ of $E_{a,d}$. The isomorphism can be given as*

$$\psi : W_a \longrightarrow E_{a,d}, \quad (u,v) \longmapsto (x,y) = \left(\frac{N\delta(3u - MN\delta^2)}{3v}, \frac{3u - MN\delta^2 - 3N\delta^2}{3u - MN\delta^2 + 3N\delta^2} \right).$$

The inverse transformation is $(x,y) \mapsto ((y(MN\delta^2 - 3N\delta^2) - (MN\delta^2 + 3N\delta^2))/3$ $(y-1), -N^2\delta^3(1+y)/x)$.

Similarly with the twists of degree 4 case, for the evaluation of $g_{P_1,P_2}(Q)$ with $P_3 = P_1 + P_2 \neq O, O'$, we get

$$
\begin{aligned}
g_{P_1,P_2}(Q) &= \frac{\Pi_{P_1,P_2,O'}(Q)}{\Pi_{P_3,O,O'}(Q)} = \frac{C_X \frac{X_Q}{Y_Q+Z_Q} + C_Y + C_W \frac{W_Q}{Y_Q+Z_Q}}{W_3 \frac{X_Q}{Y_Q+Z_Q} - X_3 \frac{W_Q}{Y_Q+Z_Q}} \\
&= \frac{C_X(\theta\delta^{-5} + (3 - M)\eta\delta^{-3}) + C_Y + C_W(\theta\delta^{-5} - (3 + M)\eta\delta^{-3})}{W_3(\theta\delta^{-5} + (3 - M)\eta\delta^{-3}) - X_3(\theta\delta^{-5} - (3 + M)\eta\delta^{-3})} \\
&= \frac{(C_X + C_W)\theta + (3(C_X - C_W) - M(C_X + C_W))\eta\delta^2 + C_Y\delta^5}{(W_3 - X_3)\theta + (3(W_3 + X_3) - M(W_3 - X_3))\eta\delta^2} \\
&\in ((C_X + C_W)\theta + (3(C_X - C_W) - M(C_X + C_W))\eta\delta^2 + C_Y\delta^5)\mathbb{F}_{q^{k/2}}^*.
\end{aligned}
$$

So we can reduce $g_{P_1,P_2}(Q)$ to the representative in the last line. Moreover we may precompute θ and η since they are fixed during the whole computation. When $C_X, C_Y, C_W \in \mathbb{F}_q$ and $\theta, \eta \in \mathbb{F}_{q^{k/6}}$ are given, the evaluation at Q can be computed in $\frac{k}{3}\mathbf{m} + \mathbf{m_c}$, with $\frac{k}{6}\mathbf{m}$ each for multiplications by θ and η and a constant multiplication by $M = \frac{2(a+d)}{a-d}$.

Furthermore, the reduced $g(Q)$ can be denoted as $\beta = b_0 + b_2\delta^2 + b_5\delta^5$, where $b_5 \in \mathbb{F}_q$ and $b_0, b_2 \in \mathbb{F}_{q^{k/6}}$. The cost of main multiplication is still $1\mathbf{M}$ with some possibilities of further optimization. Therefore, the addition step costs

$1M + (\frac{k}{3} + 14)m + 2m_c$. For a mixed addition step, the costs reduce to $1M + (\frac{k}{3} + 12)m + 2m_c$. The doubling step costs $1M + 1S + (\frac{k}{3} + 4)m + 7s + 3m_c$.

Likewise, when using the Schoolbook method, multiplying α by β costs $6 \cdot \frac{k}{6}m$ for computing $a_i \cdot b_5, i = 0, 1, 2, 3$ and costs $12(\frac{k}{6})^2 m$ for $a_i \cdot b_0$ and $a_i \cdot b_2$. The total cost $(\frac{k^2}{3} + k)m$ equals to $(\frac{1}{3} + \frac{1}{k})M$, considering that a general multiplication in $\mathbb{F}_{q^k}$ costs $M = k^2 m$. Namely the sextic twist may reduce the cost of the main multiplication in Miller's algorithm to $(\frac{1}{3} + \frac{1}{k})M$. Therefore, the addition step costs $(\frac{1}{3} + \frac{1}{k})M + (\frac{k}{3} + 14)m + 2m_c$, where $2m_c$ are multiplications by a and $\frac{2(a+d)}{a-d}$. For a mixed addition step, the costs reduce to $(\frac{1}{3} + \frac{1}{k})M + (\frac{k}{3} + 12)m + 2m_c$. The doubling step costs $(\frac{1}{3} + \frac{1}{k})M + 1S + (\frac{k}{3} + 4)m + 7s + 3m_c$, where $3m_c$ are multiplications by a, d and $\frac{2(a+d)}{a-d}$.

The following table shows the total cost of Tate pairing computation on twisted Edwards curves with $j = 1728$ or $j = 0$.

	DBL	mADD	ADD
This paper	$1M + 1S + \frac{k}{2}m$	$1M + \frac{k}{2}m$	$1M + \frac{k}{2}m$
$j = 1728$	$+4m + 7s + 2m_c$	$+12m + 1m_c$	$+14m + 1m_c$
This paper	$1M + 1S + \frac{k}{3}m$	$1M + \frac{k}{3}m$	$1M + \frac{k}{3}m$
$j = 0$	$+4m + 7s + 3m_c$	$+12m + 2m_c$	$+14m + 2m_c$

6   Refinements Over Twisted Edwards Curves

When the embedding degree is odd, to improve the efficiency we may use the refinements technique to reduce the cost of the multiplication and squaring in the extension field $\mathbb{F}_{q^k}$. The refinements technique is first prosed by [5]. In [23], L. Xu and D. Lin study the refinements formulas for Edwards curves. From formula (4), the iterative formula over the intersection of quadratic surfaces can be rewritten as:

$$f_{n,P} \cdot f_{m,P} \cdot g_{nP,mP} = f_{n,P} \cdot f_{m,P} \cdot \frac{\Pi_{nP,mP,O'}}{\Pi_{(n+m)P,O',O}}$$

In fact, we can study the refinements over Edwards curves based on the following observations.

Theorem 1.

$$\frac{\Pi_{T,T,O'}}{\Pi_{2T,O',O}} \cdot \frac{\Pi_{2T,P,O'}}{\Pi_{2T+P,O',O}} = \frac{\Pi_{T,T,O'}}{\Pi_{-2T,-P,O'}} \cdot \frac{\Pi_{P,O',O}}{\Pi_{O',O,O}}$$

Proof. By the group law described in Sect. 4, we can get

$$(\frac{\Pi_{T,T,O'}}{\Pi_{2T,O',O}} \cdot \frac{\Pi_{2T,P,O'}}{\Pi_{2T+P,O',O}}) = 2(T) + (P) - (2T + P) - 2(O)$$

we reconstruct the divisor $2(T) + (P) - (2T + P) - 2(O)$ as:

$$\frac{(T) + (T) + (O') + (-2T) + (P) + (O') + (O) + (-P)}{(-2T) + (-P) + (O') + (2T + P) + (O) + 3(O')}$$

while, from the formula (3) the above divisor is exactly

$$\left(\frac{\Pi_{T,T,O'}}{\Pi_{-2T,-P,O'}} \cdot \frac{\Pi_{P,O',O}}{\Pi_{O',O,O}}\right)$$

Since, in the Miller's algorithm we choose all the rational functions to be normalized. Thus,

$$\frac{\Pi_{T,T,O'}}{\Pi_{2T,O',O}} \cdot \frac{\Pi_{2T,P,O'}}{\Pi_{2T+P,O',O}} = \frac{\Pi_{T,T,O'}}{\Pi_{-2T,-P,O'}} \cdot \frac{\Pi_{P,O',O}}{\Pi_{O',O,O}}$$

$\square$

Theorem 2.

$$\frac{\Pi_{4T,r_iP,O'}}{\Pi_{4T+r_iP,O',O}} \cdot \frac{\Pi_{2T,2T,O'}}{\Pi_{4T,O',O}} \cdot \frac{\Pi^2_{T,T,O'}}{\Pi^2_{2T,O',O}} = \frac{\Pi^2_{T,T,O'}}{\Pi_{-2T,-2T,O'} \cdot \Pi_{4T+r_iP,O',O}} \cdot \frac{\Pi_{4T,r_iP,O'}}{\Pi_{O',O,O}}$$

Proof. By the group law described in Sect. 4, we can get

$$\left(\frac{\Pi_{4T,r_iP,O'}}{\Pi_{4T+r_iP,O',O}} \cdot \frac{\Pi_{2T,2T,O'}}{\Pi_{4T,O',O}} \cdot \frac{\Pi^2_{T,T,O'}}{\Pi^2_{2T,O',O}}\right) = 4(T) + (r_iP) - (4T + r_iP) - 4(O)$$

we reconstruct the divisor $4(T) + (r_iP) - (4T + r_iP) - 4(O)$ as:

$$\frac{2(T) + 2(T) + 2(O') + 2(-2T) + (4T) + (r_iP) + (O') + (-4T - r_iP)}{2(-2T) + (O') + (4T) + (4T + r_iP) + (O') + (O) + (-4T - r_iP) + (O') + 3(O)}$$

while, by the formula (3) we can get the above divisor is exactly

$$\left(\frac{\Pi^2_{T,T,O'}}{\Pi_{-2T,-2T,O'} \cdot \Pi_{4T+r_iP,O',O}} \cdot \frac{\Pi_{4T,r_iP,O'}}{\Pi_{O',O,O}}\right)$$

since, in the Miller's algorithm we choose all the rational functions to be normalized. So we have:

$$\frac{\Pi_{4T,r_iP,O'}}{\Pi_{4T+r_iP,O',O}} \cdot \frac{\Pi_{2T,2T,O'}}{\Pi_{4T,O',O}} \cdot \frac{\Pi^2_{T,T,O'}}{\Pi^2_{2T,O',O}} = \frac{\Pi^2_{T,T,O'}}{\Pi_{-2T,-2T,O'} \cdot \Pi_{4T+r_iP,O',O}} \cdot \frac{\Pi_{4T,r_iP,O'}}{\Pi_{O',O,O}}$$

$\square$

$2T+P$-form Refinement. In the *ith* basic Miller iteration of Algorithm 1, we can displace the explicit formula of f as follows:

$$f \leftarrow f^2 \cdot \frac{\Pi_{T,T,O'}(Q)}{\Pi_{2T,O',O}(Q)} \cdot \frac{\Pi_{2T,P,O'}(Q)}{\Pi_{2T+P,O',O}(Q)}$$

Our $2T + P$-form refinement is based on Theorem 1, the formula of f in the ith basic Miller iteration in our algorithm is:

$$f \leftarrow f^2 \cdot \frac{\Pi_{T,T,O'}(Q)}{\Pi_{-2T,-P,O'}(Q)} \cdot \frac{\Pi_{P,O',O}(Q)}{\Pi_{O',O,O}(Q)}$$

$4T + r_i P$–form Refinements. When $r_i = 0, 1, 2, 3$, in the ith basic Miller iteration of Algorithm 4.1 in [5], we can display an explicit formula of f in the ith basic Miller iteration as follows:

$$f \leftarrow f^4 \cdot f_{r_i,P} \cdot \frac{\Pi_{4T,r_iP,O'}(Q)}{\Pi_{4T+r_iP,O',O}(Q)} \cdot \frac{\Pi_{2T,2T,O'}(Q)}{\Pi_{4T,O',O}(Q)} \cdot \frac{\Pi^2_{T,T,O'}(Q)}{\Pi^2_{2T,O',O}(Q)}$$

where $f_{2,P} = \frac{\Pi_{P,P,O'}}{\Pi_{2P,O',O}}$, $f_{3,P} = \frac{\Pi_{2P,P,O'}}{\Pi_{3P,O',O}} \cdot \frac{\Pi_{P,P,O'}}{\Pi_{2P,O',O}}$, $2P$ and $3P$ can be precalculated. When $r_i = 0$, the above formula turns to:

$$f \leftarrow f^4 \cdot \frac{\Pi_{2T,2T,O'}(Q)}{\Pi_{4T,O',O}(Q)} \cdot \frac{\Pi^2_{T,T,O'}(Q)}{\Pi^2_{2T,O',O}(Q)}$$

Our $4T + r_i P$-form refinement is based on Theorem 2. The original formula of updating f in the ith basic Miller's iteration can be replaced as:

$$f \leftarrow f^4 \cdot f_{r_i,P} \cdot \frac{\Pi^2_{T,T,O'}(Q)}{\Pi_{-2T,-2T,O'}(Q) \cdot \Pi_{4T+r_iP,O',O}(Q)} \cdot \frac{\Pi_{4T,r_iP,O'}(Q)}{\Pi_{O',O,O}(Q)}$$

When $r_i = 0$ the above formula turns to:

$$f \leftarrow f^4 \cdot \frac{\Pi^2_{T,T,O'}(Q)}{\Pi_{-2T,-2T,O'}(Q) \cdot \Pi_{O',O,O}(Q)}$$

6.1   Pairing Computation on $S_{a,d}$ with Odd Embedding Degrees

For a projective line Π, we define $\Pi(Q)$ to be the value of $\frac{\Pi}{Z}(Q)$, which is actually the value of Π when substituting the coordinates of Q with $Z_Q = 1$. If we precalculate the coordinates of Q such that $\Pi_{O',O,O}(Q) = 1$ (this can easily be done in practice), then the plane $\Pi_{O',O,O}$ can be eliminated in our formulae. In this case, we can save one multiplication. In most cases (see $3T + r_iP$ and $4T + r_i P$-form refinements), the total number of the planes which present in each new formula is smaller than that in original formula. This also can save some multiplications of the extension field $\mathbb{F}_q^k$.

In fact, the plane $\Pi_{T,O',O}$ is the equation $W_T X - X_T W = 0$. For any point Q, if we precalculate its coordinates with $W_Q = 1$, then:

$$\Pi_{T,P,O'}(Q) = C_X X_Q + C_Y (Y_Q + Z_Q) + C_W, \ \Pi_{T,O',O}(Q) = W_T X_Q - X_T.$$

so, it takes **2km** to evaluate $\Pi_{T,P,O}$ at Q, and **km** to evaluate $\Pi_{T,O',O}$ at Q.

If we calculate the coordinates of Q such that $X_Q - W_Q = 1$, that is $\Pi_{O',O,O}(Q) = 1$, then:

$$\Pi_{T,P,O'}(Q) = C_X + C_Y(Y_Q + Z_Q) + (C_W + C_X)W_Q, \quad \Pi_{T,O',O}(Q) = (W_T - X_T)X_Q + X_T.$$

so, it takes **2km** to evaluate $\Pi_{T,P,O}$ at Q, and **km** to evaluate $\Pi_{T,O',O}$ at Q.

The cost of updating points in our formulae is the same with the original ones, so we ignore this cost in the base field in the following table.

Iteration forms	$2T + P$	$3T$	$4T$
Original algorithm	$2S + 4M + 6km$	$2S + 4M + 6km$	$4S + 4M + 6km$
Our algorithm	$2S + 3M + 4km$	$2S + 3M + 5km$	$4S + 2M + 4km$
Iteration forms	$4T + P$	$4T + 2P$	$4T + 3P$
Original algorithm	$4S + 6M + 9km$	$4S + 8M + 9km$	$4S + 8M + 9km$
Our algorithm	$4S + 4M + 7km$	$4S + 6M + 7km$	$4S + 6M + 7km$

The refinements over Edwards curves in [23] are corresponding to our $4T + r_iP$-refinements. Our $4T$ and $4T + P$-refinement cost less than the "00" and "01" cases in [23]. By combining their two lines into one plane we can reduce one **M**. Comparing to their "10" and "11" cases, our $4T + 2P$ and $4T + 3P$-refinement use precalculation to get more improvements. See the comparison in the following table.

	$4T$(case "00")	$4T + P$(case "01")	$4T + 2P$(case "10")	$4T + 3P$(case "11")
Result 1 [23]	$5S + 3M$	$4S + 7M$	$4S + 7M$	$4S + 11M$
Result 2 [23]	$5S + 3M$	$4S + 8M$	$4S + 8M$	$4S + 10M$
Result this paper	$4S + 2M$	$4S + 4M$	$4S + 6M$	$4S + 6M$

Acknowledgment. This work was supported by National Natural Science Foundation of China (No. 11101002, No. 11271129 and No. 61370187) and Beijing Natural Science Foundation (No. 1132009).

A   Examples of Pairing-Friendly Edwards Curves

We list some pairing friendly Edwards curves with various k=6,12,24. We use construction 6.6 in [10] to present it. $h = \#S_{1,d}(\mathbb{F}_p)/r$, $\rho = \log_2(p)/\log_2(r)$.

$k = 6, \rho = 1.99, \lceil \log_2(p) \rceil = 511, \lceil \log_2(r) \rceil = 257, \lceil \log_2(p^k) \rceil = 3063,$

$p = 4469269309980865699858008332735282459011729442283504212242920046$
$\quad 5254107669101255894363776709837049695943172869161549919107677836$
$\quad 2077660002788747108519621 7,$

$r =$ 11579208923731619542357098500868791324912747693096177917818873403461721558841,

$h =2^6 \cdot 3 \cdot 11^4 \cdot 31^2 \cdot 15659837533^2 \cdot 2413758894233920819865272^2,$

$d =$ 366425155244101230756453936536666913965662096471642988800396217503855065157940074941206695810480629869345608774421066373731513792257475802242152436128857163612885716.

$k =12, \rho = 1.48, \lceil \log_2(p) \rceil = 239, \lceil \log_2(r) \rceil = 161, \lceil \log_2(p^k) \rceil = 2861,$

$p =$ 58894903106944413307390115487123818149518495524631244315292117307863211778632117,

$r =$ 14615016530104764195638243240757034706068926150011,

$h =2^4 \cdot 3 \cdot 13^2 \cdot 19^2 \cdot 331^2 \cdot 1120711^2,$

$d =$ 30396860491943229775788480386744182493625811817306896009185905395643295656432956.

$k =12, \rho = 1.49, \lceil \log_2(p) \rceil = 383, \lceil \log_2(r) \rceil = 257, \lceil \log_2(p^k) \rceil = 4589,$

$p =$ 13134002065464890777046310593953455923303708146914070616694187178169845236078372714249135715340284274851981554471437816984523607837271424913571534028427485198155447143781437,

$r =$ 1157920892373165737821551871767212460418194942614239462794724036612657092114016126570921140161265709211401,

$h =2^4 \cdot 3^5 \cdot 3245503^2 \cdot 52627646891^2,$

$d =$ 20867503875200968960704186101877766814698529594417025750443951739878029727037407150289955081384025519663622179242689878029727037407150289955081384025519663622179242689878029727037407150289955081384025519663622179242689878029727037407150289955081384025519663622179242689878029727037407150289955081384025519663622179242689878029727037407150289955081384025519663622179242682089878029727037407150289955081384025519663622179242689878029727037407150289955081384025519663622179242689878029727037407150289955081384025519663622179242689878029727037407150289955081384025519663622179242682089878029727037407150289955081384025519663622179242682089878029727037407150289955081384025519663622179242682089878029727037407150289955081384025519663622179242682089878029727037407150289955081384025519663622179242682089878029727037407150289955081384025519663622179242682089878029727037407150289955081384025519663622179242682089878029727037407150289955081384025519663622179242682089878029727037407150289955081384025519663622179242682089878029727037407150289955081384025519663622179242682089878029727037407150289955081384025519663622179242682089878029727037407150289955081384025519663622179242682089878029727037407150289955081384025519663622179242682089878029727037407150289955081384025519663622179242682689.

$k =24, \rho = 1.24, \lceil \log_2(p) \rceil = 319, \lceil \log_2(r) \rceil = 257, \lceil \log_2(p^k) \rceil = 7642,$

$p =$ 71200032829467886887678328250478929631220397703435069480903502414914344046446418005717712764010149143440464464180057177127640101,

$r =$ 11579269421990228310489685747211428643336304196941369448237502161601500010040116015000100401,

$h =2^4 \cdot 3^3 \cdot 5^4 \cdot 17^2 \cdot 280717^2,$

$d =$ 6563654562067688285838956119740898916476600058476145431602456870265159610161444513017361855027326515961016144451301736185502726515961016144513017361855027326515961016144513017361855027326515961016144451301736185502732651596101614445130173618550273.

References

1. Arene, C., Lange, T., Naehrig, M., Ritzenthaler, C.: Faster computation of the tate pairing. J. Number Theory **131**, 842–857 (2011)
2. Bernstein, D.J., Lange, T.: Faster addition and doubling on elliptic curves. In: Kurosawa, K. (ed.) ASIACRYPT 2007. LNCS, vol. 4833, pp. 29–50. Springer, Heidelberg (2007)
3. Bernstein, D.J., Birkner, P., Joye, M., Lange, T., Peters, C.: Twisted Edwards curves. In: Vaudenay, S. (ed.) AFRICACRYPT 2008. LNCS, vol. 5023, pp. 389–405. Springer, Heidelberg (2008)
4. Bernstein, D.J., Lange, T.: A complete set of addition laws for incomplete Edwards curves. J. Number Theory **131**, 858–872 (2011)
5. Blake, I.F., Murty, V.K., Xu, G.: Refinements of Miller's algorithm for computing the Weil/Tate pairing. J. Algorithm **58**, 134–149 (2006)
6. Costello, C., Lange, T., Naehrig, M.: Faster pairing computations on curves with high-degree twists. In: Nguyen, P.Q., Pointcheval, D. (eds.) PKC 2010. LNCS, vol. 6056, pp. 224–242. Springer, Heidelberg (2010)
7. Duquesne, S., Fouotsa, E.: Tate pairing computation on Jacobi's elliptic curves. In: Abdalla, M., Lange, T. (eds.) Pairing 2012. LNCS, vol. 7708, pp. 254–269. Springer, Heidelberg (2013)
8. Das, M.P.L., Sarkar, P.: Pairing computation on twisted Edwards form elliptic curves. In: Galbraith, S.D., Paterson, K.G. (eds.) Pairing 2008. LNCS, vol. 5209, pp. 192–210. Springer, Heidelberg (2008)
9. Edwards, H.M.: A normal form for elliptic curves. Bull. Am. Math. Soc. **44**, 393–422 (2007)
10. Freeman, D., Scott, M., Teske, E.: A taxonomy of pairing-friendly elliptic curves. J. Cryptol. **23**(2), 224–280 (2010)
11. Galbraith, S.D.: Mathematics of Public Key Cryptography. Cambridge University Press, Cambridge (2012)
12. Galbraith, S.D., Lin, X., Scott, M.: Endomorphisms for faster elliptic curve cryptography on a large class of curves. J. Cryptogr. **24**(3), 446–469 (2011)
13. Hess, F., Smart, N.P., Vercauteren, F.: The eta pairing revisited. IEEE Trans. Inf. Theory **52**, 4595–4602 (2006)
14. Hess, F.: Pairing lattices. In: Galbraith, S.D., Paterson, K.G. (eds.) Pairing 2008. LNCS, vol. 5209, pp. 18–38. Springer, Heidelberg (2008)
15. Hisil, H., Wong, K.K.-H., Carter, G., Dawson, E.: Twisted Edwards curves revisited. In: Pieprzyk, J. (ed.) ASIACRYPT 2008. LNCS, vol. 5350, pp. 326–343. Springer, Heidelberg (2008)
16. Ionica, S., Joux, A.: Another approach to pairing computation in Edwards coordinates. In: Chowdhury, D.R., Rijmen, V., Das, A. (eds.) INDOCRYPT 2008. LNCS, vol. 5365, pp. 400–413. Springer, Heidelberg (2008)
17. Koblitz, N., Menezes, A.: Pairing-based cryptography at high security levels. In: Smart, N.P. (ed.) Cryptography and Coding 2005. LNCS, vol. 3796, pp. 13–36. Springer, Heidelberg (2005)
18. Li, L., Wu, H., Zhang, F.: Faster pairing computation on Jacobi quartic curves with high-degree twists. http://eprint.iacr.org/2012/551.pdf
19. Merriman, J.R., Siksek, S., Smart, N.P.: Explicit 4-descents on an elliptic curve. Acta Arithmetica **77**(4), 385–404 (1996)
20. Miller, V.S.: The weil pairing and its efficient calculation. J. Cryptol. **17**(44), 235–261 (2004)

21. Vercauteren, F.: Optimal pairings. IEEE Trans. Inf. Theory **56**, 455–461 (2010)
22. Wu, H., Li, L., Zhang, F.: The pairing computation on Edwards curves. Math. Prob. Eng. **2013**, Article ID 136767, 8 pp. (2013). doi:10.1155/2013/136767
23. Xu, L., Lin, D.: Refinement of Miller's algorithm over Edwards curves. In: Pieprzyk, J. (ed.) CT-RSA 2010. LNCS, vol. 5985, pp. 106–118. Springer, Heidelberg (2010)

The Gallant-Lambert-Vanstone Decomposition Revisited

Zhi Hu[1,2](✉) and Maozhi Xu[3]

[1] Beijing International Center for Mathematical Research, Peking University,
Beijing 100871, People's Republic of China
[2] School of Mathematics and Statistics, Central South University,
Changsha 410083, Hunan, People's Republic of China
huzhi@math.pku.edu.cn
[3] LMAM, School of Mathematical Sciences, Peking University,
Beijing 100871, People's Republic of China
mzxu@math.pku.edu.cn

Abstract. The Gallant-Lambert-Vanstone method accelerates the computation of scalar multiplication $[k]P$ of a point (or a divisor) P of prime order r on some algebraic curve (or its Jacobian) by using an efficient endomorphism ϕ on such curve. Suppose ϕ has minimal polynomial $h(x) = \sum_{i=0}^{d} a_i x^i \in \mathbb{Z}[x]$, the question how to efficiently decompose the scalar k as $[k]P = \sum_{i=0}^{d-1} [k_i] \phi^i(P)$ with $\max_i \log |k_i| \approx \frac{1}{d} \log r$ has drawn a lot of attention. In this paper we show the link between the lattice based decomposition and the division in $\mathbb{Z}[\phi]$ decomposition, and propose a hybrid method to decompose k with $\max_i |k_i| \leq 2^{(d-5)/4} d(dN(h))^{(d-1)/2} r^{1/d}$, where $N(h) = \sum_{i=0}^{d-1} a_i^2$. In particular, we give explicit and efficient GLV decompositions for some genus 1 and 2 curves with efficient endomorphisms through decomposing the Frobenius map in $\mathbb{Z}[\phi]$, which also indicate that the complex multiplication usually implies good properties for GLV decomposition. Our results well support the GLV method for faster implementations of scalar multiplications on desired curves.

Keywords: GLV method · Scalar multiplication · Complex multiplication

1 Introduction

Elliptic and hyperelliptic curve cryptography has become a popular and standardized approach to instantiate public-key cryptography [1]. There are subexponential attacks on the discrete logarithm problem for large genus curves [10,12] but still not known on those for genus 1 (elliptic) and 2 (hyperelliptic) curves. The Gallant-Lambert-Vanstone (a.k.a GLV) method [14] is an important approach for speeding up scalar multiplication on algebraic curve $\mathcal{C}$ (or its Jacobian) with genus 1 or 2 defined over fields of large prime characteristic p. To compute $[k]P$ for $P \in \mathcal{C}/\mathbb{F}_q$ (or its Jacobian) of order r and k selected uniformly at

© Springer International Publishing Switzerland 2014
D. Lin et al. (Eds.): Inscrypt 2013, LNCS 8567, pp. 201–216, 2014.
DOI: 10.1007/978-3-319-12087-4_13

random from the interval $[0, r-1]$, the basic idea is stated as follows. Suppose the curve $\mathcal{C}/\mathbb{F}_q$ has an efficiently computable endomorphism ϕ of degree d such that $\phi(P) = [\lambda]P$ for some $\lambda \in \mathbb{Z}/r\mathbb{Z}$. If we can efficiently decompose $k \equiv \sum_{i=0}^{d-1} k_i \lambda^i \bmod r$, then $[k]P = \sum_{i=0}^{d-1} [k_i]\phi^i(P)$. This multi-scalar multiplication with dimension d can be computed by employing the Straus-Shamir trick. If the decomposed coefficients satisfy $\max_i \log_2 |k_i| \approx 1/d \log_2 |k|$, then the number of doublings would be approximately reduced at most to $1/d$.

The original idea of Gallant et al. [14] works on some elliptic curves with special complex multiplication, and their decomposition is based on a short lattice basis. Several work have been done to decompose the scalar and give a theoretic upper bound for the decomposed coefficients [14,20,24]. Park, Jeong and Lim [25] extended Gallant et al.'s work to hyperelliptic curves with efficient endomorphism, and described another method to decompose k by using a division in the ring $\mathbb{Z}[\phi]$ generated by the endomorphism ϕ. Sica, Ciet and Quisquater [28] first gave a theoretic upper bound for the decomposed coefficients from this method. Since hyperelliptic curves usually have larger automorphism group than those of elliptic curves, it can be expected that higher GLV method can be applied in this scenario. Bos, Costello, Hisil and Lauter [3,4] realized fast genus 2 curves based cryptography.

Galbraith, Lin, and Scott (GLS) [15] showed that over $\mathbb{F}_{p^2}$ one can expect to find some curves with efficient endomorphisms derived from Frobenius map and twist map. They also analyzed the using of such endomorphisms in GLV method. It is expected that higher dimensional GLV method could be achieved on genus 1 or 2 GLS curves over extension fields. Hu et al. [18] and Longa et al. [23] considered 4 dimensional GLV method for some GLS elliptic curves over $\mathbb{F}_{p^2}$ with special complex multiplication, they gave proper decompositions for these curves and implemented high-performance scalar multiplications on such curves by using the GLV method. Bos et al. [4] implemented high-performance scalar multiplication on GLS genus 2 curves using 8 dimensional GLV decomposition.

Fast implementations of scalar multiplications on genus 1 or 2 curves mentioned above by using GLV method rely on the efficient decomposition of the scalar. In this paper we show that the division in $\mathbb{Z}[\phi]$ method can also be viewed as some lattice based decomposition, and propose a hybrid GLV decomposition method. If ϕ has minimal polynomial $h(x) = a_0 + a_1 x + \cdots + a_{d-1} x^{d-1} + x^d$, then our method decomposes k as $[k]P = \sum_{i=0}^{d-1} [k_i]\phi^i(P)$, with $\max_i |k_i| \leq 2^{(d-5)/4} d(dN(h))^{(d-1)/2} r^{1/d}$, where $N(h) = \sum_{i=0}^{d-1} a_i^2$. In particular, we propose explicit and natural GLV decompositions for some genus 1 and 2 curves with efficient endomorphisms through decomposing Frobenius map in $\mathbb{Z}[\phi]$, and give the "almost ideal" theoretic upper bound for decomposed coefficients. While the previous methods usually need d Round operations and $d^2 + d$ multiplications for d dimensional GLV decomposition, our approach can save at most $d^2/2$ multiplications. Our results indicate that the complex multiplication (CM) implies good properties for GLV decomposition, and the experiments also show that these decompositions well support the GLV method for faster implementations of scalar multiplications on desired curves.

The remaining of this paper is organized as follows. In Sect. 2 we recall the necessary background for point counting and endomorphisms on algebraic curves with CM. Section 3 outlines the two existent approaches for the GLV decompositions, and proposes our hybrid method. Section 4 gives the explicit decompositions for some genus 1 and 2 curves with special CM. Section 5 presents our examples and experimental results. At last in Sect. 6 we conclude this work.

2 Preliminaries

We present the preliminaries in a somewhat general setting. Let $\mathcal{C} : y^2 = f(x)$ be an algebraic curve of genus g over finite field $\mathbb{F}_q$, where f is a monic polynomial with $\deg(f) = 2g+1$ and $q = p^n$ for some prime $p > 3$ and integer $n \geq 1$. Denote $\mathcal{J}_{\mathcal{C}}$ as the jacobian variety of $\mathcal{C}$, and $\mathcal{J}_{\mathcal{C}}(\mathbb{F}_q)$ as the group of $\mathbb{F}_q$-rational elements of $\mathcal{J}_{\mathcal{C}}$ together with the identity element $\mathcal{O}_\infty$. For simplicity, we also use $\mathcal{J}_{\mathcal{C}}(\mathbb{F}_q)$ here to denote the group of $\mathbb{F}_q$-rational points instead of the jacobian elements in the case of elliptic curves. Assume that $\mathcal{J}_{\mathcal{C}}(\mathbb{F}_q)$ is ordinary and simple. Let π_q be the q-th power Frobenius map on $\mathcal{C}$ and $\chi_q(T)$ be the characteristic polynomial of π_q, then the group order of $\mathcal{J}_{\mathcal{C}}(\mathbb{F}_q)$ can be given by $\#\mathcal{J}_{\mathcal{C}}(\mathbb{F}_q) = \chi_q(1)$. Let ζ_k be a k-th primitive root of unity.

2.1 Counting Points on Curves with CM

Let $End(\mathcal{J}_{\mathcal{C}})$ be the endomorphism ring of $\mathcal{J}_{\mathcal{C}}$, and $K = End(\mathcal{J}_{\mathcal{C}}) \otimes \mathbb{Q}$. Suppose $(K, \{\sigma_1, \cdots, \sigma_g : \sigma_i \in Gal(K/\mathbb{Q})\})$ is a CM type, i.e., it satisfies the following two conditions [27, Chap. II, Thm. 1]:

1. There exists a subfield $K_0 \subset K$ such that K_0 is totally real and K is a totally imaginary quadratic extension of K_0 (which also implies $[K : Q] = 2g$);
2. There are no two isomorphisms among the σ_is which are complex conjugate of each other.

The objective of point counting for $\mathcal{C}/\mathbb{F}_q$ is to compute $\chi_q(1)$. If the prime p splits in K as $p = \pi\bar{\pi}$, then

$$\#\mathcal{J}_{\mathcal{C}}(\mathbb{F}_{p^n}) = \prod_{k=1}^{g} (1 - \sigma_k(\pi^n))(1 - \sigma_k(\bar{\pi}^n)). \tag{1}$$

Let m be a positive integer such that the m-th primitive root of unity $\zeta_m \in End(\mathcal{J}_{\mathcal{C}}) \subset K$. For elliptic curves $m \in \{1, 2, 3, 4, 6\}$ [29], while for genus 2 hyperelliptic curves $m \in \{1, 2, 3, 4, 5, 6, 8, 10\}$ [30]. Then the twist curve $\mathcal{C}'_{m,j}$ of $\mathcal{C}$ with degree m has order

$$\#\mathcal{J}_{\mathcal{C}'_{m,j}}(\mathbb{F}_{p^n}) = \prod_{k=1}^{g} (1 - \sigma_k(\zeta_m^j \pi^n))(1 - \sigma_k(\bar{\zeta}_m^j \bar{\pi}^n)). \tag{2}$$

2.2 Curves with Efficient Endomorphisms

An endomorphism $\phi \in End(\mathcal{J}_C)$ is said to be efficiently computable if it can be evaluated in constant time. Gallant et al. illustrated some very efficient endomorphisms on genus 1 curves [14], while Park et al. presented some efficient endomorphisms on genus 2 curves [25]. Both scenarios are with special CM.

Galbraith, Lin and Scott [15] proposed a method to obtain a large class of algebraic curves over extension field with efficient endomorphisms. Let $\mathcal{C}'$ over $\mathbb{F}_{p^n}$ be the m-th twist of $\mathcal{C}/\mathbb{F}_{p^n}$. Let ψ_m be the m-th twist map and π be the p-th Frobenius map, then we can obtain an efficient endomorphism on $\mathcal{C}'/\mathbb{F}_{p^n}$ as

$$\phi : \mathcal{C}'/\mathbb{F}_{p^n} \overset{\psi_m^{-1}}{\to} \mathcal{C}/\mathbb{F}_{p^{mn}} \overset{\pi}{\to} \mathcal{C}/\mathbb{F}_{p^{mn}} \overset{\psi_m}{\to} \mathcal{C}'/\mathbb{F}_{p^n}, \tag{3}$$

and ϕ has characteristic polynomial $h(x) = \Psi_{mn}(x)$, where Ψ_{mn} is the mn-th cyclotomic polynomial. Thus ϕ induces a $\varphi(mn)$ dimensional GLV method, where φ is the Euler function.

Longa and Sica [23] generalized the work of Galbraith et al. [15] and Zhou et al. [31]. They considered the quadratic twisted genus 1 curves over $\mathbb{F}_{p^{2n}}$ with special CM, and obtained two efficient endomorphisms ϕ_1 and ϕ_2 on the same curve, where ϕ_i has the minimal polynomial as $h_1(x) = x^2 + bx + c$ or $h_2(x) = \Psi_{2n}(x)$ respectively. Suppose $\mathbb{Q}(\phi_1) \cap \mathbb{Q}(\phi_2) = \mathbb{Q}$ (This is not contradict with the fact that $End(\mathcal{J}_{\mathcal{C}'})$ is an order in a quadratic imaginary extension of $\mathbb{Q}$, since $\phi, \psi \in End(\mathcal{J}_{\mathcal{C}'}(\mathbb{F}_{p^{2n}}))$ and usually $End(\mathcal{J}_{\mathcal{C}'}(\mathbb{F}_{p^{2n}})) \neq End(\mathcal{J}_{\mathcal{C}'}))$. Let ϕ be a primitive element in $\mathbb{Q}(\phi_1, \phi_2)$ (usually we can choose ϕ as $\phi_1\phi_2$ or $\phi_1 + \phi_2$), then ϕ induces a $2\varphi(2n)$ dimensional GLV method.

3 GLV Decomposition

Let ϕ be an endomorphism of $\mathcal{C}/\mathbb{F}_p$ with degree d, i.e., ϕ satisfies monic irreducible polynomial

$$h(x) = a_0 + a_1 x + a_2 x^2 + \cdots + a_{d-1} x^{d-1} + x^d, \quad a_i \in \mathbb{Z}. \tag{4}$$

Define the field $K = \mathbb{Q}(\phi)$, $[K : \mathbb{Q}] = d$.

Let ϕ act on $\mathcal{C}/\mathbb{F}_p$ as $\phi(P) = [\lambda]P$ for any $P \in \mathcal{C}/\mathbb{F}_p$ of prime order r and some $\lambda \in \mathbb{Z}$. Thus $h(\lambda) = a_0 + a_1\lambda + \cdots + a_{d-1}\lambda^{d-1} + \lambda^d \equiv 0 \bmod r$. Define two useful functions as follows:

$$g : \mathbb{Z}[\phi] \to \mathbb{Z}^d, \quad \sum_{i=0}^{d-1} k_i \phi^i \mapsto (k_0, k_1, \cdots, k_{d-1}). \tag{5}$$

$$f : \mathbb{Z}^d \to \mathbb{Z}/r\mathbb{Z}, \quad (k_0, k_1, \cdots, k_{d-1}) \mapsto \sum_{i=0}^{d-1} k_i \lambda^i \bmod r. \tag{6}$$

Since f is homomorphic and surjective onto $\mathbb{Z}/r\mathbb{Z}$, then $\ker f$ is a sublattice of $\mathbb{Z}^d$ of index r.

For k selected uniformly at random from the interval $[0, r-1]$, the d dimensional GLV method replaces the computation of $[k]P$ by $[k]P = \sum_{i=0}^{d-1} [k_i]\lambda^i(P) = \sum_{i=0}^{d-1} [k_i]\phi^i(P)$.

3.1   Lattice Based Decomposition

Suppose $\{\mathbf{v_0}, \cdots, \mathbf{v_{d-1}}\}$ is a lattice basis of $\ker f$, then by the Babai rounding method [2] $\{\mathbf{v_i}\}$ induce a decomposition as $(k_0, k_1, ..., k_{d-1}) = (k, 0, ..., 0) - (\sum_{i=0}^{d-1} \lfloor b_i \rceil \mathbf{v_i})$, where $b_i \in \mathbb{Q}$ and $(k, 0, ..., 0) = \sum_{i=0}^{d-1} b_i \mathbf{v_i}$. Naturally, the decomposed coefficients satisfies $\max_i |k_i| \leq \frac{1}{2} \sum_{i=0}^{d-1} \|\mathbf{v_i}\| \leq \frac{d}{2} \max_i \|\mathbf{v_i}\|$, where $\| \cdot \|$ is the Euclidean norm on $\mathbb{Q}^d$.

The original 2 dimensional decomposition [14] is based on two short vectors in $\ker f$ derived from the extended Euclidean algorithm.

3.2   Division in Ring $\mathbb{Z}[\phi]$

Park, Jeong and Lim [25] described an algebraic method to decompose k by using a division in the ring $\mathbb{Z}[\phi]$ generated by the endomorphism ϕ. Their basic idea states as follows:

1. Find a short vector $\mathbf{v} = (v_0, ..., v_{d-1}) \in \ker f$, and set $\alpha = g^{-1}(\mathbf{v}) = \sum_{i=0}^{d-1} v_i \phi^i$;
2. Let $s(x)$ be the minimal polynomial of α, and write $s(x) = xm(x) + R$ for some $m(x) \in \mathbb{Z}[x]$, then $R = -\alpha m(\alpha)$, denote $-m(\alpha) = \sum_{i=0}^{d-1} m_i \phi^i$;
3. Represent k as $k = \beta\alpha + \rho$, where $\beta, \rho \in \mathbb{Z}[\phi]$. Since $f \circ g(\alpha) = 0$, then $[\alpha]P = \mathcal{O}_\infty$, and thus $[k]P = [\beta\alpha]P + [\rho]P = [\rho]P$. Moreover, ρ can be given as $\rho = k - \sum_{i=0}^{d-1} \sum_{j=0}^{d-1} v_i \lfloor \frac{k \cdot m_j}{R} \rceil \phi^{i+j} = \sum_{i=0}^{d-1} k_i \phi^i$.

Sica, Ciet and Quisquater [28] first gave a theoretic upper bound for $\max |k_i|$ as $\max |k_i| < B^{d-1} 2^{d(d-1)/4} r^{1/d}$, where B is some constant concerned with the norm function $N_{K/\mathbb{Q}}(\cdot)$ from K to $\mathbb{Q}$.

3.3   Hybrid Decomposition Method

In this section we propose our hybrid decomposition method derived from the above two methods. Let the denotation be the same as above. In addition, we make two assumptions as follows: (1) $|a_i| \ll r$ and $a_0 \neq 0$ as the warning given by Gallant et al. [14]. (2) $h(x)$ splits completely over $\mathbb{F}_r$ as $h(x) \equiv \prod_{i=0}^{d-1}(x - \lambda_i) \bmod r$, where λ_is are distinct. This is reasonable since $h(x)$s concerned in Sect. 2.2 always satisfy this condition.

Let $M(d)$ be the set of all $d \times d$ matrixes over $\mathbb{Z}$. Define $A \in M(d)$ as

$$A = \begin{bmatrix} 0 & 1 & \cdots & 0 & 0 \\ 0 & 0 & \cdots & 0 & 0 \\ \vdots & \vdots & \ddots & \vdots & \vdots \\ 0 & 0 & \cdots & 0 & 1 \\ -a_0 & -a_1 & \cdots & -a_{d-2} & -a_{d-1} \end{bmatrix} \tag{7}$$

thus $h(A) = a_0 I + a_1 A + \cdots + a_{d-1} A^{d-1} + A^d = 0$. Let $\mathbf{0} \neq \mathbf{v} = (v_0, ..., v_{d-1}) \in \mathbb{Z}^d$, $\alpha = g^{-1}(\mathbf{v}) = \sum_{i=0}^{d-1} v_i \phi^i$, $\mathbf{u_\lambda} = (1, \lambda, \cdots, \lambda^{d-1})$, $\mathbf{\Phi} = (1, \phi, \cdots, \phi^{d-1})$, and define $\Lambda_v \in M(d)$ as

$$\Lambda_v = [\mathbf{v}^T, A^T \mathbf{v}^T, \cdots, A^{d-1^T} \mathbf{v}^T]. \tag{8}$$

Proposition 1. *If* $\mathbf{v} \in \ker f$, *then* $L = \sum_{i=0}^{d-1} \mathbf{v} A^i \mathbb{Z}$ *is a sublattice of* $\ker f$ *and* $r \mid \det \Lambda_v$.

Proof. Since $\mathbf{u}_\lambda A^{i^T} \mathbf{v}^T \equiv \lambda^i \sum_{j=0}^{d-1} v_j \lambda^j = 0 \bmod r$, then $\mathbf{v} A^i \in \ker f$, and thus $L \subset \ker f$. Note that $\mathbf{u}_\lambda$ is a non-zero solution for linear equation system $\mathbf{x} \Lambda_v \equiv (0, \cdots, 0) \bmod r$, it follows that $\det \Lambda_v \equiv 0 \bmod r$. $\qquad\square$

Proposition 2. *If* $r \mid \det \Lambda_v$, *then there exists some* λ_j *such that* $\mathbf{v} \in \ker f$ *when choosing* $\lambda = \lambda_j$.

Proof. Let $\lambda_0, \lambda_1, \cdots, \lambda_{d-1}$ are d distinct roots of $h(x) \equiv 0 \bmod r$. Define $\mathbf{u}_{\lambda_j} = (1, \lambda_j, \cdots, \lambda_j^{d-1})$ and $s_j = \sum_{i=0}^{d-1} v_i \lambda_j^i$, then $\Lambda_v \mathbf{u}_{\lambda_j}^T \equiv s_j \mathbf{u}_{\lambda_j}^T \bmod r$. Note that $\mathbf{u}_{\lambda_j}$s are linear independent over $\mathbb{F}_r$ since $[\mathbf{u}_{\lambda_0}^T, \mathbf{u}_{\lambda_1}^T, \cdots, \mathbf{u}_{\lambda_{d-1}}^T]$ is a Vandermonde matrix and has rank d, it follows that $s_j / \mathbf{u}_{\lambda_j}^T$ are the exact d eigenvalues/eigenvectors for Λ_v. If $r \mid \det \Lambda_v$, then there exists some j such that $s_j \equiv 0 \bmod r$, and thus $\mathbf{v} \in \ker f$ if we choose $\lambda = \lambda_j$. $\qquad\square$

Theorem 1. *Let the notation be as above. If* $K = \mathbb{Q}(\alpha)$, *then* $\{\mathbf{v}, \mathbf{v}A, ..., \mathbf{v}A^{d-1}\}$ *induces a lattice based decomposition which is identical to the division decomposition by* $\mathbf{v}$ *in* $\mathbb{Z}[\phi]$.

Proof. Define the map $\varphi_\alpha : K \to K, x \mapsto \alpha x$, then φ_α is a $\mathbb{Q}$ linear transformation over K, while Λ_v is the matrix corresponding to φ_α, and thus $\det \Lambda_v = N_{K/\mathbb{Q}}(\alpha) = R$. Note that in Sect. 3.1, $\{\mathbf{v}, \mathbf{v}A, ..., \mathbf{v}A^{d-1}\}$ induces a lattice based decomposition with

$$\Lambda_v (b_0 \det \Lambda_v, b_1 \det \Lambda_v, \cdots, b_{d-1} \det \Lambda_v)^T = (\det \Lambda_v, 0, \cdots, 0)^T.$$

And in Sect. 3.2, $R = \sum_{i=0}^{d-1} \sum_{j=0}^{d-1} v_i m_j \phi^{i+j} = (m_0, m_1, \cdots, m_{d-1}) \Lambda_v^T \mathbf{\Phi}^T$, then $\Lambda_v (m_0, m_1, \cdots, m_{d-1})^T = (R, 0, \cdots, 0)^T$. Thus $b_i \det \Lambda_v = m_i$ for $i = 0, \cdots, d-1$, which indicates that both decomposition methods give the same decomposed coefficients. $\qquad\square$

Lemma 1. *[17, Sect. 5.6] Let* $\|B\|_d = \max_{\|x\|=1, x \in \mathbb{Q}^d} \|Bx\|$ *for any* $B \in M(d)$. *Then for any* $B, C \in M(d)$ *and* $x \in \mathbb{Q}^d$, $\|B \cdot C\|_d \le \|B\|_d \|C\|_d$ *and* $\|Bx\| \le \|B\|_d \cdot \|x\|$.

Theorem 2. *Define* $N(h) = \sum_{i=0}^{d-1} a_i^2$, *then* $\{\mathbf{v}, \mathbf{v}A, ..., \mathbf{v}A^{d-1}\}$ *induces a decomposition as* $\max_i |k_i| \le \frac{d}{2} (dN(h))^{(d-1)/2} \cdot \|\mathbf{v}\|$.

Proof. Denote A^T as the column vectors form $A^T = [\alpha_0, \cdots, \alpha_{d-1}]$. Since

$$\|A^T\|_d = \max_{\|x\|=1, x \in \mathbb{Q}^d} \|A^T x\| \le \max_{\|x\|=1, x \in \mathbb{Q}^d} \sum_{i=0}^{d-1} |x_i| \cdot \|\alpha_i\|$$

$$\le \max_j \|\alpha_j\| \sum_{i=0}^{d-1} |x_i| \le d^{1/2} \max_j \|\alpha_j\| = (dN(h))^{1/2}.$$

By the lattice based decomposition and Lemma 1, we obtain that

$$\max_i |k_i| \le \frac{d}{2} \max_i ||A^{i^T} \mathbf{v}^T|| \le \frac{d}{2} \cdot (||A^T||_d)^{d-1} \cdot ||\mathbf{v}||$$

$$\le \frac{d}{2}(dN(h))^{(d-1)/2} \cdot ||\mathbf{v}||. \qquad \Box$$

From the above theorem, we deduce that the GLV decomposition problem can be solved from the Shortest Vector Problem (a.k.a. SVP). While the SVP is NP-hard, the *LLL* algorithm [21] can provide a relative short vector in ker f. Let $\mathbf{v}_0 = (r, 0, \cdots, 0)$, $\mathbf{v}_1 = (-\lambda, 1, \cdots, 0)$, ..., $\mathbf{v}_{d-1} = (-\lambda^{d-1}, 0, \cdots, 0, 1)$. Obviously, $\{\mathbf{v}_i\}$ is a basis of ker f and $\det[\mathbf{v}_0, \mathbf{v}_1, \cdots, \mathbf{v}_{d-1}] = r$. Then by [21, Prop. 1.9], a reduced basis $\mathbf{b}_0, \mathbf{b}_1, \cdots, \mathbf{b}_{d-1}$ can be obtained with $||\mathbf{b}_0|| \le 2^{(d-1)/4} r^{1/d}$. The following result is a little more explicit than that in [28].

Corollary 1. *Let the denotation be as above. If set* $\mathbf{v} = \mathbf{b}_0$, *then the above method induces a decomposition as* $\max_i |k_i| \le 2^{(d-5)/4} d(dN(h))^{(d-1)/2} r^{1/d}$.

We conclude the above procedure as Algorithm 1.

Algorithm 1. Hybrid d Dimensional Decomposition

Input: k, r, λ, A.
Output: Coefficients k_i satisfy $k \equiv \sum_{i=0}^{d-1} k_i \lambda^i \mod r$.
Pre-compute Step:
1. Find a short vector $\mathbf{v} \in$ ker f (by *LLL* algorithm or other methods);
2. Construct $d \times d$ matrix Λ_v and compute $\mathbf{m} = (m_0, m_1, \cdots, m_{d-1})$ satisfying $\Lambda_v \mathbf{m}^T = (\det \Lambda_v, 0, \cdots, 0)^T$;
Decompose Step:
3. Compute $(k_0, k_1, \cdots, k_{d-1}) = (k, 0, \cdots, 0) - \sum_{i=0}^{d-1} \lfloor \frac{m_i \cdot k}{\det \Lambda_v} \rceil \mathbf{v} A^i$.

---

4 Explicit Decompositions for Curves with CM

We show in this section that there exist explicit decompositions for genus 1 and 2 curves with special CM. Let $\#\mathcal{J}_{\mathcal{C}}(\mathbb{F}_{p^n}) = hr$, where r is prime and the cofactor h is very small. Usually we require $\log r \approx \log \#\mathcal{J}_{\mathcal{C}}(\mathbb{F}_{p^n}) \approx gn \log p$.

Let ϕ be the efficient endomorphism on $\mathcal{C}$. For any $P \in \mathcal{J}_{\mathcal{C}}(\mathbb{F}_{p^n})$ of order r, assume $[1 - \pi]P = \mathcal{O}_\infty$ by Eq. 1 or assume $[1 - \zeta_{mn}\pi]P = \mathcal{O}_\infty$ by Eq. 2. (In a general setting, if $[1 - \zeta_m^j \pi^n]P = [\prod_{i=1}^n (1 - \zeta_{mn}^{j-mi}\pi)]P = \mathcal{O}_\infty$, we can assume $[1 - \zeta_{mn}^{j-mi}\pi]P = \mathcal{O}_\infty$ for some $i \in \mathbb{Z}$, while this case can be dealt with in an analogous way.) Our basic idea is that, treat π, ζ_{mn}, ϕ as algebraic numbers and decompose $1 - \pi$ (or $1 - \zeta_{mn}\pi$) in $\mathbb{Z}[\phi]$ (or in $\mathbb{Z}[\phi, \zeta_{mn}]$). For example, if $\pi \in \mathbb{Z}[\phi]$, then decompose $1 - \pi = \sum_{k=0}^{d-1} v_k \phi^k$, and thus we obtain a short vector $\mathbf{v} = (v_0, v_1, \cdots, v_{d-1}) \in \mathbb{Z}^d$ for GLV decomposition in Sect. 3, while the CM usually implies that $||\mathbf{v}|| = O(\sqrt{p})$. In the following, we can choose proper ϕ (or replace ϕ by its conjugate root) to meet the desired setting.

4.1   Genus 1 Curves

Gallant et al. illustrated several examples to support 2 dimensional GLV method, and they used the extended Euclidean algorithm to find the short vectors in ker f. Indeed, previous decompositions [20,24,28] are usually derived from the splitting of r in $\mathbb{Z}[\phi]$ which can be done by solving a quadratic form through the Cornacchias algorithm [6, Alg. 1.5.3]. Here we give the explicit $\mathbf{v}$ to get 2 dimensional decomposition.

Proposition 3. *Suppose elliptic curve $\mathcal{C}$ has CM with discriminant $D < 0$, where $D \equiv 0, 1 \bmod 4$. Let $4p = t^2 - Ds^2$, $\pi = (t + s\sqrt{D})/2$, $\#\mathcal{J}_{\mathcal{C}}(\mathbb{F}_p) = p + 1 - t$, the endomorphism ring $End(\mathcal{J}_{\mathcal{C}}) = \mathbb{Z}[(D + \sqrt{D})/2]$, and $\phi \in End(\mathcal{J}_{\mathcal{C}})$ be the efficient endomorphism. Define $\mathbf{\Phi} = (1, \phi)$.*

1. *If $D \equiv 1 \bmod 4$, set $\phi = (1 + \sqrt{D})/2$, and $\mathbf{v} = (1 - \frac{t-s}{2}, \; -s)$. (In this case $t \equiv s \bmod 2$.)*
2. *If $D \equiv 0 \bmod 4$, set $\phi = \sqrt{D}/2$, and $\mathbf{v} = (1 - \frac{t}{2}, \; -s)$. (In this case $t \equiv 0 \bmod 2$.)*

Then $N_{\mathbb{Q}(\phi)/\mathbb{Q}}(\mathbf{v} \cdot \mathbf{\Phi}^T) = hr$ and $||\mathbf{v}|| \leq \sqrt{2p}$.

Proof. Since $\pi = s\phi + (t-s)/2$ if $D \equiv 1 \bmod 4$, and $\pi = s\phi + t/2$ if $D \equiv 0 \bmod 4$, then $N_{\mathbb{Q}(\phi)/\mathbb{Q}}(\mathbf{v} \cdot \mathbf{\Phi}^T) = N_{\mathbb{Q}(\phi)/\mathbb{Q}}(1 - \pi) = hr$. A rough estimate induces that $||\mathbf{v}|| \leq \sqrt{(t^2 + 3s^2)/2} \leq \sqrt{2p}$. $\qquad\square$

Remark 1. We choose ϕ as the above form mainly for efficient evaluation of ϕ. Since by [7, Thm. 10.14] we have $\phi(x, y) = (\phi^{-2}\frac{f(x)}{g(x)}, \; y\phi^{-3}\left(\frac{f(x)}{g(x)}\right)')$, where f, g are polynomial functions over $\mathbb{Q}$ with $\deg f = N_{K/\mathbb{Q}}(\phi)$, $\deg g = N_{K/\mathbb{Q}}(\phi) - 1$, and such $\phi \in End(\mathcal{J}_{\mathcal{C}})\backslash\mathbb{Z}$ has the minimal norm.

Proposition 4. *Let $\mathcal{C}'/\mathbb{F}_{p^n}$ be the quadratic twisted GLS elliptic curve with CM discriminant $D < -4$, $D \equiv 0, 1 \bmod 4$. Let p, π and ϕ be defined in Proposition 3, and ϕ' (acts as ζ_{2n}) be defined in Eq. 3 with $m = 2$. Assume that $\phi \notin \mathbb{Q}(\zeta_{2n})$, and $[1 - \zeta_{2n}\pi]P = \mathcal{O}_\infty$ for any $P \in \mathcal{J}_{\mathcal{C}'}(\mathbb{F}_{p^n})$ of order r. Consider the GLV method based on $\mathbf{\Phi} = (1, \zeta_{2n}, \cdots, \zeta_{2n}^{\varphi(2n)-1}, \phi, \phi\zeta_{2n}, \cdots, \phi\zeta_{2n}^{\varphi(2n)-1})$, and choose $\mathbf{v} \in \mathbb{Z}^{2\varphi(2n)}$ such that $1 - \zeta_{2n}\pi = \mathbf{v} \cdot \mathbf{\Phi}^T$.*

1. *If $D \equiv 1 \bmod 4$, choose $\mathbf{v} = (1, \frac{s-t}{2}, \overbrace{0, \cdots, 0}^{\varphi(2n)-1}, \; -s, \overbrace{0, \cdots, 0}^{\varphi(2n)-2})$.*
2. *If $D \equiv 0 \bmod 4$, choose $\mathbf{v} = (1, \frac{-t}{2}, \overbrace{0, \cdots, 0}^{\varphi(2n)-1}, \; -s, \overbrace{0, \cdots, 0}^{\varphi(2n)-2})$.*

Let $A_{i,j} \in M(2\varphi(2n))$ be the matrix satisfying $\phi^i\zeta_{2n}^j\mathbf{\Phi}^T = A_{i,j}\mathbf{\Phi}^T$, and define $\mathbf{v}_{i,j} = \mathbf{v}A_{i,j}$, $i = 0, 1, j = 0, \cdots, \varphi(2n) - 1$. Then $\{\mathbf{v}_{i,j}\}$ induces a $2\varphi(2n)$ dimensional lattice based decomposition with decomposed coefficients $\max|k_i| \leq \frac{1}{2}(\varphi(2n) + N(\Psi_{2n})^{1/2} - 1)(1 + \sqrt{(5 - D)/8})\sqrt{2p}$.

Proof. By Proposition 3, we have $\mathbf{v}_{i,j} \cdot \mathbf{\Phi}^T = \phi^i \zeta_{2n}^j \mathbf{v} \cdot \mathbf{\Phi}^T = \phi^i \zeta_{2n}^j (1 - \zeta_{2n}\pi)$. Note that for $j = 0, \cdots, \varphi(2n) - 2$, $\|\mathbf{v}_{0,j}\| = \|\mathbf{v}\| \leq \sqrt{2p}$, and $\|\mathbf{v}_{1,j}\| \leq \sqrt{(5-D)/8}\sqrt{2p}$; for $j = \varphi(2n) - 1$, $\|\mathbf{v}_{0,j}\| \leq N(\Psi_{2n})^{1/2}\|\mathbf{v}\| \leq N(\Psi_{2n})^{1/2}\sqrt{2p}$, and $\|\mathbf{v}_{1,j}\| \leq N(\Psi_{2n})^{1/2}\sqrt{(5-D)/8}\sqrt{2p}$. Then the decomposition based on $\{\mathbf{v}_{i,j}\}$ gives the coefficients satisfying

$$\max |k_i| \leq \frac{1}{2} \sum_{i,j} \|\mathbf{v}_{i,j}\| \leq \frac{1}{2}(\varphi(2n) - 1 + N(\Psi_{2n})^{1/2})(1 + \sqrt{(5-D)/8})\sqrt{2p}.$$

$\square$

Remark 2. Proposition 4 can be viewed as a generalization of Longa-Sica 4 dimensional decomposition for the GLS curves with CM [23]. Note that in the case $n = 2$ (4 dimensional GLV), each $\mathbf{v}_{u,v}$ has one entry being 1 and one entry being 0, so our method will save 8 multiplications compared with Longa-Sica method.

The approach of Galbraith et al. [15] also provides the endomorphisms by using higher order twist maps. We have the following explicit result.

Proposition 5. *Let $C'/\mathbb{F}_{p^n}$ be the m-th twisted GLS elliptic curve, where $n \geq 2$ satisfies $\varphi(mn) > n + 1$ for $m \geq 4$. The endomorphism ϕ defined by Eq. 3 acts as ζ_{mn}. Assume $[1 - \zeta_{mn}\pi]P = \mathcal{O}_\infty$ for any $P \in \mathcal{J}_{C'}(\mathbb{F}_{p^n})$ of order r. Consider the GLV method based on $\mathbf{\Phi} = (1, \phi, \cdots, \phi^{\varphi(mn)-1})$.*

1. *$m = 2$ (General case): Since $\Psi_{2n}(\phi) = \sum_{i=0}^{\varphi(2n)} a_i\phi^i = 0$, define $\mathbf{v}$ as $\mathbf{v} = (a_0, a_1, \cdots, a_{\varphi(2n)-3}, a_{\varphi(2n)-2} - p, a_{\varphi(2n)-1} + t)$.*
2. *$m = 4, 6$ (Higher degree twist): Let $\pi = a + b\zeta_m$ such that $p = \pi\bar{\pi}$. Define $\mathbf{v}$ as $\mathbf{v} = (1, \overbrace{-a, \underbrace{0, \cdots, 0}_{n-1}, -b, \underbrace{0, \cdots, 0}_{\varphi(mn)-n-2}})$.*

Then $1 - \zeta_{mn}\pi = \mathbf{v} \cdot \mathbf{\Phi}^T$ and it induces a $\varphi(mn)$ dimensional decomposition with decomposed coefficients $\max |k_i| \leq \frac{\varphi(mn)}{2}(\varphi(mn)N(\Psi_{mn}))^{(\varphi(mn)-1)/2}\|\mathbf{v}\|$, where $\|\mathbf{v}\| < p + 3 + |a_{\varphi(2n)-2}|$ for $m = 2$ and $\|\mathbf{v}\| < \sqrt{2p}$ for $m = 4, 6$.

Proof. For $m = 2$, since ϕ and π satisfy the same characteristic polynomial $x^2 - tx + p$, then $\phi^{\varphi(2n)} = \phi^{\varphi(2n)-2}(t\phi - p)$, and thus $1 - \zeta_{mn}\pi = \mathbf{v} \cdot \mathbf{\Phi}^T$. Note that $\|\mathbf{v}\| = (p^2 + t^2 - 2a_{\varphi(2n)-2}p - 2a_{\varphi(2n)-1}t + \sum_{i=0}^{\varphi(2n)-1} a_i^2)^{1/2} < p + 3 + |a_{\varphi(2n)-2}|$. For $m = 4, 6$, $1 - \zeta_{mn}\pi = 1 - \zeta_{mn}(a + b\zeta_{mn}^n) = \mathbf{v} \cdot \mathbf{\Phi}^T$, and $\|\mathbf{v}\| = (1 + a^2 + b^2)^{1/2} < \sqrt{2p}$. By Theorem 2 we obtain the above result. $\square$

Remark 3. Proposition 5 is a generalization of Galbraith et al.'s work for $m = 2$ [15] and Hu et al.'s work for $m = 4, 6$ [18].

4.2 Genus 2 Curves

There also exist explicit decompositions on some genus 2 curves with efficient endomorphisms, such as the FKT curves [11] and BK curves [5].

Proposition 6. *Let $C/\mathbb{F}_p : y^2 = x^5 + ax$ be the FKT curve, where $p \equiv 1$ mod 8 is prime, $p = c^2 + 2d^2$ for some $c, d \in \mathbb{Z}$, $c \equiv 1$ mod 4 and the Legendre symbol $(\frac{a}{p}) = -1$. Let $\pi = d + c\zeta_8 - d\zeta_8^2$, then $p = \pi\bar{\pi}$. The endomorphism ϕ defined in [25, Exp. 3] acts as ζ_8 on C. We have*

1. *$\#\mathcal{J}_C(\mathbb{F}_p) = p^2 + 1 - s_1(p + 1) + s_2$, where $s_1 = \pm 4d$, $s_2 = 8d^2$.*
2. *Assume $d = s_1/4$ and $[1-\pi]P = \mathcal{O}_\infty$ for any $P \in \mathcal{J}_C(\mathbb{F}_p)$ of order r. Consider the GLV method based on $\boldsymbol{\Phi} = (1, \phi, \phi^2, \phi^3)$. Define $\mathbf{v} = (d - 1, c, -d, 0)$, then $1 - \pi = \mathbf{v} \cdot \boldsymbol{\Phi}^T$, and $\mathbf{v}$ induces a 4 dimensional decomposition with $\max |k_i| < 2(\sqrt{p} + 1)$.*

Proof. (1). Define $\alpha \equiv a^{(p-1)/8}$ mod p. Since $\alpha^4 \equiv -1$ mod p and $p = c^2 + 2d^2$, by [11, Thm. 3] we can deduce that $s_1^2 \equiv 4c^2(\alpha^3 + \alpha)^2 \equiv -8c^2 \equiv 16d^2$ mod p, thus $s_1 \equiv \pm 4d$ mod p. Note that $|s_1| \leq 4\sqrt{p}$, it follows $s_1 = \pm 4d$. Moreover, since $s_2 \equiv 4c^2(-1) \equiv 8d^2$ mod $2p$ according to [11, Thm. 3], then by [26, Thm.1] and $2\sqrt{p}|s_1| = 2\sqrt{p}|4d| > 8d^2 > 4d^2 = |s_1|^2/4$, it turns out that $s_2 = 8d^2$.

(2). Let A be the matrix corresponding to ϕ as defined in Eq. 7. Then we have $\mathbf{v}A^i \cdot \boldsymbol{\Phi}^T = \phi^i \mathbf{v} \cdot \boldsymbol{\Phi}^T = \phi^i(1 - \pi)$, and $\|\mathbf{v}A^i\| = ((d-1)^2 + c^2 + d^2)^{1/2} < \sqrt{p} + 1$ for $i = 0, 1, 2, 3$. □

Remark 4. As mentioned in [11], FKT curves only in the case with $p \equiv 1$ mod 8 and $(\frac{a}{p}) = -1$ are suitable for cryptographic application. Our result also simplifies [11, Alg. 1] and gives the explicit point counting on such curves.

Before giving the decomposition for BK curves, we recall some background of the point counting for this class of curves. Let $C/\mathbb{F}_p : y^2 = x^5 + a$ be the BK curve, where $p \equiv 1$ mod 10 is prime. There exist uniquely $x, u, v, w \in \mathbb{Z}$ satisfying the Dickson's diophantine system [9]

$$16p = x^2 + 50u^2 + 50v^2 + 125w^2, \quad xw = v^2 - 4uv - u^2,$$

$$x \equiv 1 \bmod 5, u \equiv 0 \bmod 2, x + u - v \equiv 0 \bmod 4.$$

Define $\pi = c_1\zeta_5 + c_2\zeta_5^2 + c_3\zeta_5^3 + c_4\zeta_5^4 \in \mathbb{Z}[\zeta_5]$, where

$$c_1 = (-x + 2u + 4v + 5w)/4, \quad c_2 = (-x + 4u - 2v - 5w)/4,$$

$$c_3 = (-x - 4u + 2v - 5w)/4, \quad c_4 = (-x - 2u - 4v + 5w)/4.$$

We have $p = \pi\bar{\pi}$, and $(\sum_{k=1}^{4} c_i^2)^{1/2} < 2\sqrt{p}$. As pointed out by Buhler and Koblitz in [5], (c_1, c_2, c_3, c_4) can also be computed through *LLL* algorithm [21]. Since $\zeta_{10} \in End(\mathcal{J}_C)$, then there exists some $j \in \mathbb{Z}$ such that $\#\mathcal{J}_C(\mathbb{F}_p) = \prod_{k=1}^{2}(1 - \sigma_k(\zeta_{10}^j\pi))(1 - \sigma_k(\bar{\zeta}_{10}^j\bar{\pi}))$. In the following we assume that $j = 0$, while the other cases can be analyzed in an analogous way.

Proposition 7. *Let the denotation be as above, the endomorphism ϕ be defined in [25, Exp. 4] which acts as ζ_5 on BK curve C. Assume $[1-\pi]P = \mathcal{O}_\infty$ for any $P \in \mathcal{J}_C(\mathbb{F}_p)$ of order r. Consider the GLV method based on $\boldsymbol{\Phi} = (1, \phi, \phi^2, \phi^3)$. Define $\mathbf{v}$ as $\mathbf{v} = (1 + c_4, c_4 - c_1, c_4 - c_2, c_4 - c_3)$, then $1 - \pi = \mathbf{v} \cdot \boldsymbol{\Phi}^T$, and $\mathbf{v}$ induces a 4 dimensional lattice based decomposition with coefficients $\max_i |k_i| < \frac{17}{2}\sqrt{p}$.*

Proof. Let A be the matrix corresponding to ϕ as defined in Eq. 7. Define $\mathbf{v}_i = \mathbf{v}A^i$ for $i = 0, \cdots, 3$, then $\mathbf{v}A^i \cdot \mathbf{\Phi}^T = \phi^i \mathbf{v} \cdot \mathbf{\Phi}^T = \phi^i(1 - \pi)$. Suppose $|c_{i1}| \le |c_{i2}| \le |c_{i3}| \le |c_{i4}|$, then by $(\sum_{k=1}^{4} c_k^2)^{1/2} < 2\sqrt{p}$, we have

$$\|\mathbf{v}_{4-i1}\| < (5c_{i1}^2 + 2\sum c_k^2)^{1/2} < \sqrt{5p + 8p},$$

$$\|\mathbf{v}_{4-i2}\| < (5c_{i2}^2 + 2\sum c_k^2)^{1/2} < \sqrt{20p/3 + 8p},$$

$$\|\mathbf{v}_{4-i3}\| < (5c_{i3}^2 + 2\sum c_k^2)^{1/2} < \sqrt{10p + 8p},$$

$$\|\mathbf{v}_{4-i4}\| < (5c_{i4}^2 + 2\sum c_k^2)^{1/2} < \sqrt{20p + 8p}.$$

Thus $\{\mathbf{v}_i\}$ induces a 4 dimensional GLV decomposition with coefficients

$$\max_i |k_i| \le \frac{1}{2}\sum_{i=0}^{3} \|\mathbf{v}_i\| < \frac{1}{2}(\sqrt{13} + \sqrt{44/3} + \sqrt{18} + \sqrt{28})\sqrt{p} < \frac{17}{2}\sqrt{p}.$$

$\square$

Proposition 8. *Let $C'/\mathbb{F}_{p^n}$ be the m-th twisted genus 2 GLS curve, where $n \ge 2$ satisfies $\varphi(mn) > (m-4)n/2 + 1$. The endomorphism ϕ defined by Eq. 3 acts as ζ_{mn}. Assume $[1 - \zeta_{mn}\pi]P = \mathcal{O}_\infty$ for any $P \in \mathcal{J}_{C'}(\mathbb{F}_{p^n})$ of order r. Consider the GLV method based on $\mathbf{\Phi} = (1, \phi, \cdots, \phi^{\varphi(mn)})$.*

1. *$m = 8$ (FKT curves): Define $\mathbf{v} = (1,\ \ -d,\ \ \overbrace{0,\cdots,0}^{n-1},\ \ -c, \overbrace{0,\cdots,0}^{n-1},$*

   $d,\ \overbrace{0,\cdots,0}^{\varphi(8n)-2n-2})$.

2. *$m = 10$ (BK curves): Define $\mathbf{v} = (1,\ c_2, \overbrace{0,\cdots,0}^{n-1}, c_3 - c_2, \overbrace{0,\cdots,0}^{n-1}, c_2 -$*

   $c_1, \overbrace{0,\cdots,0}^{n-1}, c_4 - c_2,\ \overbrace{0,\cdots,0}^{\varphi(10n)-3n-2})$.

Then $1 - \zeta_{mn}\pi = \mathbf{v}\cdot\mathbf{\Phi}^T$, and $\mathbf{v}$ induces a $\varphi(mn)$ dimensional GLV decomposition with decomposed coefficients $\max_i |k_i| < \frac{\varphi(mn)}{2}(\varphi(mn)N(\Psi_{mn}))^{(\varphi(mn)-1)/2}\|\mathbf{v}\|$, where $\|\mathbf{v}\| = \sqrt{p+1}$ for FKT curves, and $\|\mathbf{v}\| < \sqrt{28p}$ for BK curves.

Proof. This is a generalization of Propositions 6 and 7, and the proof is similar to those for the above two propositions. $\square$

Remark 5. In Propositions 5 and 8, the cases that $[1 - \zeta_{mn}^j\pi]P = \mathcal{O}_\infty$ for any $P \in \mathcal{J}_{C'}(\mathbb{F}_{p^n})$ of order r can be analyzed in the same way, which have the same upper bound for the decomposed coefficients. If extensively studying $n = 2$ in Proposition 8 (8 dimensional GLV), we would get a more tight upper bound for decomposed coefficients as $\max_i |k_i| < 4\sqrt{p+1}$ for FKT curves, or $\max_i |k_i| < 16.1\sqrt{p}$ for BK curves.

5 Numerical Experiments

We illustrate several examples using our decomposition method. For generating curves and giving the explicit parameters, we use Magma and Maple for simplicity. Our examples concentrate on 4 or 8 dimensional GLV cases, since the 2 dimensional cases have been extensively studied, while the higher dimensional GLV method might not be very efficient and has not been exploited. Also, the curve defined over $\mathbb{F}_{p^n}$ with $n \geq 4$ might be vulnerable to index calculus attacks [13,19]. In our examples we assume the use of pseudo-Mersenne primes of the form $p = 2^m - c$ with small c and $m \equiv 0, -1 \bmod 64$.

5.1 4 Dimensional GLV Decomposition

GLS Curve-4. Let $p = 2^{127} - 5997 = a^2 + 2b^2$, $a = 6105930783472132209$, $b = 8150423078832062245$ and $\mathbb{F}_{p^2} = \mathbb{F}_p[i]/(1 + i^2)$. Let $u = 1 + i$, the curve $\mathcal{C}'/\mathbb{F}_{p^2} : y^2 = x^3 - \frac{15}{2}u^2x - 7u^3$ has order $\#\mathcal{J}_{\mathcal{C}'}(\mathbb{F}_{p^2}) = 8r$, where r is a 251-bit prime [23]. Let ϕ' (acts as ζ_4) and ϕ (acts as $\sqrt{-2}$) be defined on $\mathcal{C}'/\mathbb{F}_{p^2}$ as Proposition 4, and $[1 + a\zeta_4 + b\phi\zeta_4]P = \mathcal{O}_\infty$ for any $P \in \mathcal{J}_{\mathcal{C}'}(\mathbb{F}_{p^2})$ of order r. Then the 4 dimensional GLV method based on $\Phi = (1, \zeta_4, \phi, \phi\zeta_4)$ can be done by the decomposition from

$$\mathbf{v}_0 = (1, a, 0, b), \quad \mathbf{v}_1 = (a, -1, b, 0), \quad \mathbf{v}_2 = (0, 2b, -1, -a), \quad \mathbf{v}_3 = (2b, 0, -a, 1).$$

Note that $\det[\mathbf{v}_0^T, \mathbf{v}_1^T, \mathbf{v}_2^T, \mathbf{v}_3^T] = 8r$. For comparison, we also use Longa-Sica method [23] to find a basis $\{\mathbf{u}_i\}$, and $\det[\mathbf{u}_0^T, \mathbf{u}_1^T, \mathbf{u}_2^T, \mathbf{u}_3^T] = r$.

FKT Curve-4. Let $p = 2^{128} - 24935 = c^2 + 2d^2$, where $c = -14885537990011998807$ and $d = 7703996549481574306$. The Jacobian of the curve $\mathcal{C}/\mathbb{F}_p : y^2 = x^5 + 3^7x$ has order $\#\mathcal{J}_{\mathcal{C}}(\mathbb{F}_p) = 2 \cdot r$, where r is a 255-bit prime [3]. Let ϕ (acts as ζ_8) be defined on $\mathcal{C}/\mathbb{F}_p$ as Proposition 6, and $[1 - d - c\phi + d\phi^2]P = \mathcal{O}_\infty$ for any $P \in \mathcal{J}_{\mathcal{C}}(\mathbb{F}_p)$ of order r. Then the 4 dimensional GLV method based on $\Phi = (1, \phi, \phi^2, \phi^3)$ can be done by the decomposition from

$$\mathbf{v} = (1 - d, -c, d, 0), \quad \mathbf{v}' = (d - 1 + \frac{c+1}{2}, d - \frac{c+1}{2}, -\frac{c+1}{2}, -\frac{c+1}{2}),$$

where $N_{\mathbb{Q}(\phi)/\mathbb{Q}}(\mathbf{v} \cdot \Phi^T) = 2r$ and $N_{\mathbb{Q}(\phi)/\mathbb{Q}}(\mathbf{v}' \cdot \Phi^T) = r$.

BK Curve-4. Let $p = 2^{127} - 2437$. By Buhler and Koblitz's approach in [5], we can obtain (c_1, c_2, c_3, c_4) as

$$c_1 = -11808507213253603698, c_2 = -8564770837980062142,$$
$$c_3 = 2272889852863029969, c_4 = -4791530919155826320,$$

and $\pi = c_1\zeta_5 + c_2\zeta_5^2 + c_3\zeta_5^3 + c_4\zeta_5^4$. The Jacobian of the curve $\mathcal{C}/\mathbb{F}_p : y^2 = x^5 + 8$ has order $\#\mathcal{J}_{\mathcal{C}}(\mathbb{F}_p) = r$, where r is a 254-bit prime. Let ϕ (acts as ζ_5) be defined on $\mathcal{C}/\mathbb{F}_p$ as Proposition 7, and $[1 - (c_1\phi + c_2\phi^2 + c_3\phi^3 + c_4\phi^4)]P = \mathcal{O}_\infty$ for any $P \in \mathcal{J}_{\mathcal{C}}(\mathbb{F}_p)$ of order r. Then the 4 dimensional GLV method based on $\Phi = (1, \phi, \phi^2, \phi^3)$ can be done by the decomposition from $\mathbf{v} = (1 + c_4, c_4 - c_1, c_4 - c_2, c_4 - c_3)$.

5.2 8 Dimensional GLV Decomposition

BK Curve-8. Let $p = 2^{63} - 28317$. As same as above, we obtain (c_1, c_2, c_3, c_4) as

$$c_1 = 2096758342, c_2 = 1220703958, c_3 = 3728614569, c_4 = 1719430940.$$

Then we can set $\pi = c_1\zeta_5 + c_2\zeta_5^2 + c_3\zeta_5^3 + c_4\zeta_5^4$. Let $\mathbb{F}_{p^2} = \mathbb{F}_p[i]/(1 + i^2)$ and $a = 5805994751994593008 \cdot i + 9196861641891075683$. The Jacobian of the curve $C'/\mathbb{F}_{p^2} : y^2 = x^5 + a$ has order $\#\mathcal{J}_{C'}(\mathbb{F}_{p^2}) = 41 \cdot r$, where r is a 247-bit prime. Let ϕ (acts as ζ_{20}) be defined on $C'/\mathbb{F}_{p^2}$ as Proposition 8, and $[1 - \phi(c_1\phi^4 + c_2\phi^8 + c_3\phi^{12} + c_4\phi^{16})]P = \mathcal{O}_\infty$ for any $P \in \mathcal{J}_{C'}(\mathbb{F}_{p^2})$ of order r. Then the 8 dimensional GLV method based on $\mathbf{\Phi} = (1, \phi, \cdots, \phi^7)$ can be done by the decomposition from $\mathbf{v} = (1, c_2, 0, c_3 - c_2, 0, c_2 - c_1, 0, c_4 - c_2)$. Also, the shortest vector from the LLL algorithm is given as

$$\mathbf{v}' = (212346264, \ -753542338, \ -339753942, \ -564116807,$$
$$-929427609, \ 977905202, \ -727985478, \ -802019931).$$

5.3 Experimental Results

The following tables illustrate the statistics for 10,000,000 scalar decompositions in each of the GLV scenarios. The columns show the percentage frequency corresponding to decompositions with a maximum "mini-scalar" bit-length. Our results show that we can get "GLV friendly property" from the CM method.

In the case of 4 dimensional GLV decompositions for GLS curve-4, Table 1 shows that our method gives the decomposed coefficients with $\max_i |k_i|$ being at most one bit longer than that given by Longa et al. [23]. We note that if the interleaving with width-w ($w \geq 4$ in [23]) non-adjacent form (NAF) [16, Chap. 3.3.1] and the LM scheme [22] for precomputing points are applied, then both decompositions induce the same NAF length (This also holds if the cofactor $h \leq 2^d$), and the extra bit does not affect the cost of scalar multiplication. Our method (the using of $\{\mathbf{v}_i\}$) saves 8 multiplications in the decomposition procedure since each $\mathbf{v}_i$ has one entry being 1 and one entry being 0.

Table 1. GLS curve - 4 dimensional decompositions

Curve-d-vectors	r	$\max\{|k_i|\}$ bits/freq.(%)		
GLS Curve-4-$\{\mathbf{v}_i\}$	251	64/7.73074	63/69.19551	62/21.50849
		61/1.46759	60/0.09121	$\leq$ 59/0.00646
GLS Curve-4-$\{\mathbf{u}_i\}$	251	63/16.53818	62/70.96524	61/11.71210
		60/0.73510	59/0.04643	$\leq$ 58/0.00295

Note that in the 4 dimensional GLV decomposition for FKT curves, the using of $\mathbf{v}$ will save 4 multiplications. Moreover, the second row of Table 2 is approximate the same as those given by Bos et al. in [3], which also implies that our method based on $\mathbf{v}'$ is identical to the division method in $\mathbb{Z}[\phi]$ as proved in Theorem 1.

Table 2. FKT curve - 4 dimensional decompositions

Curve-d-vector	r	max$\{|k_i|\}$ bits/freq.(%)		
FKT Curve-4- $\mathbf{v}$	255	64/30.94233	63/62.81456	62/5.85503
		61/0.36386	60/0.02278	$\leq 59/0.00144$
FKT Curve-4- $\mathbf{v}'$	255	64/23.37061	63/64.27652	62/11.57446
		61/0.72987	60/0.04557	$\leq 59/0.00015$

Table 3 illustrates the 4 or 8 dimensional decompositions for the BK curves. Since for BK curve-4 the group order r is prime, our explicit method is identical to those based on the straight splitting of r. The 8 dimensional decomposition induced by $\mathbf{v}$ saves 32 multiplications compared with that induced by $\mathbf{v}'$, since there are 4 entries of $\mathbf{v}$ belonging to $\{0,1\}$.

Table 3. BK curve - $4, 8$ dimensional decompositions

Curve-d-vector	r	max$\{|k_i|\}$ bits/freq.(%)		
BK Curve-4- $\mathbf{v}$	254	64/15.96638	63/62.99890	62/19.47502
		61/1.46243	60/0.09147	$\leq 59/0.00580$
BK Curve-8- $\mathbf{v}$	247	32/29.44647	31/66.13605	30/4.39273
		29/0.02462	28/0.00013	$\leq 27/0.00000$
BK Curve-8- $\mathbf{v}'$	247	32/ 1.87365	31/66.70874	30/30.57115
		29/0.84271	28/ 0.00374	$\leq 27/0.00001$

6 Conclusion

In this work we give a general algorithm for decomposing scalar in GLV method, which indicates the link between the lattice based decomposition and the division in $\mathbb{Z}[\phi]$ decomposition. We also propose an explicit way to get short lattice bases for GLV decomposition, and such ready-made lattice bases (derived from special CM) usually bring more benefits in scalar multiplications on elliptic curves or genus 2 Jacobians than other new short ones from Lattice basis reduction algorithm (e.g. Euclidean algorithm or *LLL* algorithm) or algebraic division. Note that in our experiments the decomposed coefficients are not uniformly distributed, it might bring some potential security problem (for instance, vulnerable to side channel attack) in realizing faster scalar multiplication through

GLV method. This could be avoided through using differential addition chains. Recently, Costello, Hisil and Smith [8] described an secure implementation of fast elliptic curve scalar multiplication by directly choosing the multi-scalar k_i or using 2 dimensional differential addition chains for 2 dimensional GLV method. We leave it as an open problem for exploring 2 or higher dimensional differential addition chains in above scenarios.

Acknowledgments. The authors would like to thank the anonymous reviewers for their helpful comments and suggestions. This work was supported by the Natural Science Foundation of China (Grants No. 61272499 and No. 10990011) and the Science and Technology on Information Assurance Laboratory (Grant No. KJ-11-02).

References

1. Avanzi, R., Cohen, H., Doche, C., Frey, G., Lange, T., Nguyen, K., Vercauteren, F.: Handbook of Elliptic and Hyperelliptic Cryptography. Chapman and Hall/CRC, Boca Raton (2006)
2. Babai, L.: On lovasz lattice reduction and the nearest lattice point problem. Combinatorica **6**, 1–13 (1986)
3. Bos, J.W., Costello, C., Hisil, H., Lauter, K.: Fast cryptography in genus 2. In: Johansson, T., Nguyen, P.Q. (eds.) EUROCRYPT 2013. LNCS, vol. 7881, pp. 194–210. Springer, Heidelberg (2013)
4. Bos, J.W., Costello, C., Hisil, H., Lauter, K.: High-performance scalar multiplication using 8-dimensional GLV/GLS decomposition. In: Bertoni, G., Coron, J.-S. (eds.) CHES 2013. LNCS, vol. 8086, pp. 331–348. Springer, Heidelberg (2013)
5. Buhler, J., Koblitz, N.: Lattice basis reduction, jacobi sums and hyperelliptic cryptosystems. Bull. Aust. Math. Soc. **58**(1), 147–154 (1998)
6. Cohen, H.: A Course in Computational Algebraic Number Theory. Springer, Berlin (1996)
7. Cox, D.: Primes of the Form $x^2 + ny^2$. Wiley, New York (1989)
8. Costello, C., Hisil, H., Smith, B.: Faster Compact Diffie-Hellman: Endomorphisms on the x-line. Cryptology ePrint Archive Report 2013/692 (2013)
9. Dickson, L.E.: Cyclotomy, higher congruences, and waring's problem. Amer. J. Math. **57**, 391–424 (1935)
10. Enge, A.: Computing discrete logarithms in high-genus hyperelliptic jacobians in provably subexponential time. Math. Comput. **71**, 729–742 (2002)
11. Furukawa, E., Kawazoe, M., Takahashi, T.: Counting points for hyperelliptic curves of type $y^2 = x^5 + ax$ over finite prime fields. In: Matsui, M., Zuccherato, R.J. (eds.) SAC 2003. LNCS, vol. 3006, pp. 26–41. Springer, Heidelberg (2003)
12. Gaudry, P.: An algorithm for solving the discrete log problem on hyperelliptic curves. In: Preneel, B. (ed.) EUROCRYPT 2000. LNCS, vol. 1807, pp. 19–34. Springer, Heidelberg (2000)
13. Gaudry, P.: Index calculus for abelian varieties of small dimension and the elliptic curve discrete logarithm problem. J. Symb. Comput. **44**(12), 1690–1702 (2008)
14. Gallant, R.P., Lambert, R.J., Vanstone, S.A.: Faster point multiplication on elliptic curves with efficient endomorphisms. In: Kilian, J. (ed.) CRYPTO 2001. LNCS, vol. 2139, pp. 190–200. Springer, Heidelberg (2001)

15. Galbraith, S.D., Lin, X., Scott, M.: Endomorphisms for faster elliptic curve cryptography on a large class of curves. In: Joux, A. (ed.) EUROCRYPT 2009. LNCS, vol. 5479, pp. 518–535. Springer, Heidelberg (2009)
16. Hankerson, D., Menezes, A.J., Vanstone, S.: Guide to Elliptic Curve Cryptography. Springer, Heidelberg (2004)
17. Horn, R.A., Johnson, C.R.: Matrix Analysis. Cambridge University Press, New York (1985)
18. Hu, Z., Longa, P., Xu, M.: Implementing the 4-dimensional GLV method on GLS elliptic curves with j-invariant 0. Des. Codes Cryptogr. **63**(3), 331–343 (2012)
19. Joux, A., Vitse, V.: Cover and decomposition index calculus on elliptic curves made practical. In: Pointcheval, D., Johansson, T. (eds.) EUROCRYPT 2012. LNCS, vol. 7237, pp. 9–26. Springer, Heidelberg (2012)
20. Kim, D., Lim, S.: Integer decomposition for fast scalar multiplication on elliptic curves. In: Nyberg, K., Heys, H.M. (eds.) SAC 2002. LNCS, vol. 2595, pp. 13–20. Springer, Heidelberg (2003)
21. Lenstra, A.K., Lenstra, H.W., Lovász, L.: Factoring polynomials with rational coefficients. Math. Ann. **261**(4), 515–534 (1982)
22. Longa, P., Miri, A.: New composite operations and precomputation scheme for elliptic curve cryptosystems over prime fields. In: Cramer, R. (ed.) PKC 2008. LNCS, vol. 4939, pp. 229–247. Springer, Heidelberg (2008)
23. Longa, P., Sica, F.: Four-dimensional gallant-lambert-vanstone scalar multiplication. In: Wang, X., Sako, K. (eds.) ASIACRYPT 2012. LNCS, vol. 7658, pp. 718–739. Springer, Heidelberg (2012)
24. Park, Y.-H., Jeong, S., Kim, C.H., Lim, J.: An alternate decomposition of an integer for faster point multiplication on certain elliptic curves. In: Naccache, D., Paillier, P. (eds.) PKC 2002. LNCS, vol. 2274, pp. 323–334. Springer, Heidelberg (2002)
25. Park, Y.-H., Jeong, S., Lim, J.: Speeding up point multiplication on hyperelliptic curves with efficiently-computable endomorphisms. In: Knudsen, L.R. (ed.) EUROCRYPT 2002. LNCS, vol. 2332, pp. 197–208. Springer, Heidelberg (2002)
26. Rück, H.G.: Abelian surfaces and Jacobian varieties over finite fields. Compos. Math. **76**, 351–366 (1990)
27. Shimura, G.: Abelian Varieties with Complex Multiplication and Modular Functions. Princeton University Press, Princeton (1998)
28. Sica F., Ciet M., Quisquater J.J.: Analysis of Gallant-Lambert-Vanstone Method Based on Efficient Endomophisms: Elliptic and Hyperelliptic Curves. In: Nyberg K., Heys H.M. (eds.) SAC 2002. LNCS, vol. 2595, pp. 21–36. Springer, Heidelberg (2003)
29. Silverman, J.: The Arithmetic of Elliptic Curves. Springer, New York (1986)
30. Zhang, F.G.: Twisted ate pairing on hyperelliptic curves and applications. China Sci. Inf. Sci. **53**(8), 1528–1538 (2010)
31. Zhou, Z., Hu, Z., Xu, M.Z., Song, W.G.: Efficient 3-Dimensional GLV Method for Faster Point Multiplication on Some GLS Elliptic Curves. Inf. Process. Lett. **110**, 1003–1006 (2010)

Low-Weight Primes for Lightweight Elliptic Curve Cryptography on 8-bit AVR Processors

Zhe Liu[1]($\boxtimes$), Johann Großschädl[1], and Duncan S. Wong[2]

[1] Laboratory of Algorithmics, Cryptology and Security,
University of Luxembourg, Luxembourg, Luxembourg
{zhe.liu,johann.groszschaedl}@uni.lu
[2] Department of Computer Science, City University of Hong Kong,
Kowloon Tong, Hong Kong SAR, China
duncan@cityu.edu.hk

Abstract. Small 8-bit RISC processors and micro-controllers based on the AVR instruction set architecture are widely used in the embedded domain with applications ranging from smartcards over control systems to wireless sensor nodes. Many of these applications require asymmetric encryption or authentication, which has spurred a body of research into implementation aspects of Elliptic Curve Cryptography (ECC) on the AVR platform. In this paper, we study the suitability of a special class of finite fields, the so-called *Optimal Prime Fields (OPFs)*, for a "lightweight" implementation of ECC with a view towards high performance and security. An OPF is a finite field $\mathbb{F}_p$ defined by a prime of the form $p = u \cdot 2^k + v$, whereby both u and v are "small" (in relation to 2^k) so that they fit into one or two registers of an AVR processor. OPFs have a low Hamming weight, which allows for a very efficient implementation of the modular reduction since only the non-zero words of p need to be processed. We describe a special variant of Montgomery multiplication for OPFs that does not execute any input-dependent conditional statements (e.g. branch instructions) and is, hence, resistant against certain side-channel attacks. When executed on an Atmel ATmega processor, a multiplication in a 160-bit OPF takes just 3237 cycles, which compares favorably with other implementations of 160-bit modular multiplication on an 8-bit processor. We also describe a performance-optimized and a security-optimized implementation of elliptic curve scalar multiplication over OPFs. The former uses a GLV curve and executes in 4.19 M cycles (over a 160-bit OPF), while the latter is based on a Montgomery curve and has an execution time of approximately 5.93 M cycles. Both results improve the state-of-the-art in lightweight ECC on 8-bit processors.

1 Introduction

The 8-bit AVR architecture [2] has grown increasingly popular in recent years thanks to its rich instruction set that allows for efficient code generation from high-level programming languages. A typical AVR microcontroller, such as the Atmel ATmega128 [3], features 32 general-purpose registers, separate memories

© Springer International Publishing Switzerland 2014
D. Lin et al. (Eds.): Inscrypt 2013, LNCS 8567, pp. 217–235, 2014.
DOI: 10.1007/978-3-319-12087-4_14

and buses for program and data, and some 130 instructions, most of which are executed in a single clock cycle. The AVR platform occupies a significant share of the worldwide smartcard market and other security-critical segments of the embedded systems industry, e.g. wireless sensor nodes. This has made AVR an attractive evaluation platform for research projects in the area of efficient implementation of cryptographic primitives for embedded devices. The literature contains papers dealing with block ciphers [10], hash functions [17], as well as public-key schemes based on Elliptic Curve Cryptography (ECC) [23]. Despite some recent progress [1,5,18], the implementation of ECC on 8-bit smartcards and sensor nodes is still a big challenge due to the resource constraints of these devices. A typical low-cost smartcard contains an 8-bit microcontroller clocked at a frequency of 5 MHz, 256 B RAM, and 16 kB ROM. On the other hand, a typical wireless sensor node, such as the MICAz mote [8], is equipped with an ATmega128 processor clocked at 7.3728 MHz and provides 4 kB RAM and 128 kB programmable flash memory.

1.1   Past Work on Lightweight ECC for 8-bit Processors

One of the first ECC software implementations for an 8-bit processor was presented by Woodbury et al. in 2000 [41]. Their work utilizes a so-called Optimal Extension Field (OEF), which is a finite field consisting of p^m elements where p is a *pseudo-Mersenne prime* [7] (i.e. a prime of the form $p = 2^k - c$) and m is chosen such that an irreducible binomial $x(t) = t^m - \omega$ exists over $GF(p)$. The specific OEF used in [41] is $GF((2^8 - 17)^{17})$ as this field allows the arithmetic operations, especially multiplication and inversion, to be executed efficiently on an 8-bit platform. Woodbury et al. implemented the point arithmetic in affine coordinates and achieved an execution time of $23.4 \cdot 10^6$ clock cycles for a full 134-bit scalar multiplication on an 8051-compatible microcontroller that is significantly slower than the ATmega128. The first really efficient ECC software for an 8-bitter was introduced by Gura et al. at CHES 2004 [15]. They reported an execution time of only $6.48 \cdot 10^6$ clock cycles for a full scalar multiplication over a 160-bit SECG-compliant prime field on the ATmega128. This impressive performance is mainly the result of a smart optimization of the multi-precision multiplication, the nowadays widely used *hybrid method*. In short, the core idea of hybrid multiplication is to exploit the large register file of the ATmega128 to process several bytes (e.g. four bytes) of the operands in each iteration of the inner loop(s), which significantly reduces the number of load/store instructions compared to a conventional byte-wise multiplication.

In the ten years since the publication of Gura et al.'s seminal paper, a large body of research has been devoted to further reduce the execution time of ECC on the ATmega128. The majority of research focussed on advancing the hybrid multiplication technique or devising more efficient variants of it. An example is the work of Uhsadel et al. [37], who improved the handling of carry bits in the hybrid method and managed to achieve an execution time of 2881 cycles for a (160×160)-bit multiplication (without modular reduction), which is about 7.3 % faster than Gura et al.'s original implementation (3106 cycles). Zhang et al. [43]

re-arranged the sequence in which the byte-by-byte multiplications are carried out and measured an execution time of 2846 clock cycles. A further reduction of the cycle count to 2651 was reported by Scott et al. [30], who fully unrolled the loops and used so-called "carry catcher" registers to limit the propagation of carries. This unrolled hybrid multiplication was adopted by Szczechowiak et al. [35] to implement scalar multiplication over a 160-bit generalized-Mersenne prime field $\mathbb{F}_p$. An interesting result of their work is that the reduction modulo $p = 2^{160} - 2^{112} + 2^{64} + 1$ requires 1228 cycles, which means a full modular multiplication (including reduction) executes in 3882 clock cycles altogether. Also Lederer et al. [22] came up with an optimized variant of the hybrid method and performed ECDH key exchange using the 192-bit generalized-Mersenne prime $p = 2^{192} - 2^{64} - 1$ as recommended by the NIST. A scalar multiplication needs $12.33 \cdot 10^6$ cycles for an arbitrary base point, and $5.2 \cdot 10^6$ cycles when the base point is fixed. The currently fastest means of multiplying two large integers on the ATmega128 is the so-called *operand-caching method* [19,31], which follows a similar idea as the hybrid multiplication method, namely to exploit the large number of general-purpose registers to store (parts of) the operands.

Most lightweight ECC implementations for 8-bit AVR processors mentioned above suffer from two notable shortcomings, namely (1) they are vulnerable to side-channel attacks, e.g. *Simple Power Analysis (SPA)* [28], and (2) they make aggressive use of loop unrolling to reduce the execution time of the prime-field arithmetic, which comes at the expense of a massive increase in code size and poor scalability since the operand length is "fixed." SPA attacks exploit conditional statements and other irregularities in the execution of a cryptographic algorithm (e.g. double-and-add method for scalar multiplication [6]), which can leak key-related information through the power-consumption profile of a device executing the algorithm. However, not only the scalar multiplication, but also the underlying field arithmetic can be vulnerable to SPA attacks, e.g. due to conditional subtractions in the modular addition [34], modular multiplication [38], or modular reduction for generalized-Mersenne primes [29]. It was shown in various papers that SPA attacks on unprotected (or insufficiently protected) implementations of ECC pose a real-world threat to the security of embedded devices such as smart cards [25] or wireless sensor nodes [9].

Loop unrolling is a frequently employed optimization technique to increase the performance of the field arithmetic operations, in particular multiplication [1]. The basic idea is to replicate the loop body n times (and adjust the overall number of iterations accordingly) so that the condition for loop termination as well as the branch back to the top of the loop need to be performed only once per n executions. Full loop unrolling may allow some extra optimizations since the first and the last iteration of a loop often differ from the "middle" ones and can, therefore, be specifically tuned. However, full loop unrolling, when applied to operations of quadratic complexity (e.g. multiplication), bloats the code size (i.e. the size of the binary executable) significantly. Moreover, a fully unrolled implementation can only process operands up to a length corresponding to the number of loop iterations, which means it is not scalable anymore.

1.2 Contributions of This Paper

We present an efficient prime-field arithmetic library for the 8-bit AVR architecture that we developed under consideration of the resource constraints and security requirements of smart cards, wireless sensor nodes, and similar kinds of embedded devices. Our goal was to overcome the drawbacks of most existing implementations mentioned in the previous subsection, and therefore we aimed for a good compromise between performance, code size, and resistance against SPA attacks. Instead of using a Mersenne-like prime field, our library supports so-called *Optimal Prime Fields (OPFs)* [12] since this family of fields has some attractive properties that allow for efficient arithmetic on a wide range of platforms. An OPF is a finite field defined by a "low-weight" prime p of the form $p = u \cdot 2^k + v$, where u and v are small (in relation to 2^k) to that they fit into one or two registers of an 8-bit processor. The reduction modulo such a prime can be performed efficiently using Montgomery's algorithm [26] since only the non-zero bytes of p need to be processed. Our implementation is based on the OPF library from [43], but we significantly improved the execution time of all arithmetic operations (especially multiplication) and made it resistant against SPA attacks. We present a new variant of Montgomery modular multiplication for OPFs that does not perform any data-dependent indexing or branching in the final subtraction. A multiplication (including modular reduction) in a 160-bit OPF takes 3237 clock cycles on the ATmega128, which compares very well with previous work on modular multiplication for 8-bit processors.

Our OPF library uses an optimized variant of Gura et al.'s hybrid technique [15] for the multiplication, whereby we process four bytes of the two operands per iteration of the inner loop(s). However, in contrast to the bulk of previous implementations, we do not fully unroll the loops in order to keep the code size small. All arithmetic functions provided by our OPF library are implemented in a parameterized fashion and with "rolled" loops, which means that the length of the operands is not fixed or hard-coded, but is passed as parameter to the function along with other parameters such as the start address of the arrays in which the operands are stored. Consequently, our OPF library can support operands of varying length, ranging from 64 to 2048 bits (in 32-bit steps). This feature makes our OPF library highly scalable since one and the same function can be used for operands of different length without re-compilation.

We provide benchmarking results for operand lengths of 160, 192, 224, and 256 bits on the 8-bit ATmega128 processor, which we obtained with help of the cycle-accurate simulator of AVR Studio. For the purpose of benchmarking, we also implemented and simulated scalar multiplication for two different families of elliptic curves, namely Montgomery curves [27] and GLV curves [11]. In the former case, an SPA-protected scalar multiplication over a 160-bit OPF takes only $5.93 \cdot 10^6$ cycles, which is faster than most unprotected implementations reported in the literature. On the other hand, we use the GLV curve to explore the "lower bound" of the execution time for a scalar multiplication when resistance against SPA is not needed. Such a speed-optimized implementation has an execution time of only $4.19 \cdot 10^6$ clock cycles for a 160-bit scalar.

2   Preliminaries

In this section we recap some basic properties of special families of prime fields and elliptic curves, and discuss how to exploit their distinctive features to speed up the arithmetic operations needed in ECC.

2.1   Prime Fields

Even though elliptic curves can be defined over various algebraic structures, we only consider prime fields in this paper [6]. Formally, a prime field $\mathbb{F}_p$ consists of p elements (namely the integers between 0 and $p-1$) and the arithmetic operations are addition and multiplication modulo p. It is common practice in ECC to use "special" primes to speed up the modular reduction; a well-known example for primes with good arithmetic properties are the so-called Mersenne primes, which are primes of the form $p = 2^k - 1$. Multiplying two k-bit integers $a, b \in \mathbb{F}_p$ yields a $2k$-bit product r that can be written $r = r_H \cdot 2^k + r_L$, where r_H and r_L represent the upper half and the lower half of r, respectively. Since $2^k \equiv 1 \bmod p$, we can simply reduce r via a conventional addition of the form $t = (r_H + r_L) \bmod p$ to obtain a result that is at most $k+1$ bits long. A final subtraction of p may be necessary to get a fully reduced result. In summary, a reduction modulo a Mersenne prime requires just a conventional k-bit addition and, in the worst case, a subtraction of p. Unfortunately, Mersenne primes are rare, and there exist no Mersenne primes between 2^{160} and 2^{512}, which is the interval from which one normally chooses primes for ECC.

A wealth of research has been devoted to find other families of prime fields that allow for similarly efficient arithmetic and many proposals appeared in the literature, e.g. fields based on "Mersenne-like" primes such as pseudo-Mersenne primes [7] and generalized Mersenne primes [33]. A *pseudo-Mersenne prime* is a prime of the form

$$p = 2^k - c \tag{1}$$

where $\log_2(c) \leq \frac{1}{2}k$, i.e. the constant c is small compared to 2^k. However, c is bigger than 1, and hence the reduction operation modulo such a prime is more costly than that for a "real" Mersenne prime. On the other hand, allowing c to be bigger than 1 provides a larger choice of primes for a given bit-length.

The so-called *generalized Mersenne primes* were first described by Solinas in 1999 [33] and shortly thereafter, the NIST recommended a set of five of these special primes for use in ECC cryptosystems. The common form of the primes presented by Solinas is

$$p = 2^k - c_1 2^{k-1} - \cdots - c_i 2^{k-i} - \cdots - c_k \tag{2}$$

where all c_i are integers with a small absolute value, e.g. $c_i \in \{-1, 0, 1\}$. A concrete example is $p = 2^{192} - 2^{64} - 1$, which is one of the primes recommended by the NIST. The reduction operation modulo generalized Mersenne primes is similar to that of real Mersenne primes, namely to exploit congruence relations that stem from the special form of the prime to "shorten" the residue.

2.2   Elliptic Curves

Any elliptic curve over a prime field $\mathbb{F}_p$ can be expressed through a Weierstrass equation of the form $y^2 = x^3 + ax + b$ [16]. When using mixed Jacobian-affine coordinates, a point addition on a Weierstrass curve costs eight multiplications (i.e. 8 M) and three squarings (i.e. 3 S) in the underlying field, whereas a point doubling requires 4 M and 4 S [16]. Similar to prime fields, there exist numerous "special" families of elliptic curves, each having a unique curve equation and a unique addition law. In the past 20 years, a massive research effort was devoted to finding special curves that allow for a more efficient implementation of the scalar multiplication than ordinary Weierstrass curves.

Peter Montgomery introduced in 1997 a family of curves to speed up algorithms for the factorization of big integers [27]. These curves are referred to as Montgomery curves and have the unique property that a scalar multiplication can be carried out using the x coordinate only, which is much faster than when both the x and y coordinate are calculated in each step [6]. In formal terms, a Montgomery curve over $\mathbb{F}_p$ is defined by the equation

$$By^2 = x^3 + Ax^2 + x \tag{3}$$

with $A, B \in \mathbb{F}_p$, $(A^2 - 4)B \neq 0$ and allows for a very fast computation of the x-coordinate of the sum $P + Q$ of two points P, Q whose difference $P - Q$ is known. A point addition performed via the equation from [27, p. 261] requires 4 M and 2 S, whereas a point doubling costs 3 M and 2 S. However, one of the three field multiplications in the point doubling uses the constant $(A + 2)/4$ as operand, which is small if the parameter A is chosen accordingly. Our results show that multiplying a field element by a small constant (up to 16 bits) costs only between 0.2 M and 0.25 M (cf. Sect. 4). Furthermore, the point addition formula given in [27, p. 261] can be optimized when using the so-called Montgomery ladder (Algorithm 13.35 in [6]) for scalar multiplication and representing the base point in projective coordinates with $Z = 1$ (see also Remark 13.36 (ii) in [6]). Even though the number of field multiplications and squarings is low, one has to take into account that the Montgomery ladder always executes both a point addition and a point doubling for each bit of the scalar k. Therefore, the computational cost of a scalar multiplication amounts to $5.25n$ multiplications and $4n$ squarings in $\mathbb{F}_p$, i.e. 5.25 M + 4 S per bit.

The so-called Gallant-Lambert-Vanstone curves, or simply GLV curves, are elliptic curves over $\mathbb{F}_p$ which possess an efficiently computable endomorphism ϕ whose characteristic polynomial has small coefficients [11]. The specific curve we use in this paper belongs to the family of GLV curves that can be described by a Weierstrass equation of the form

$$y^2 = x^3 + b \quad \text{(i.e. } a = 0 \text{ and } b \neq 0) \tag{4}$$

over a prime field $\mathbb{F}_p$ with $p \equiv 1 \bmod 3$ (see Example 4 from [11]). When using mixed Jacobian-affine coordinates, the point addition on such a curve requires 8 M + 3 S, i.e. adding points is exactly as costly as on an ordinary

Weierstrass curve. On the other hand, the double of a point given in Jacobian coordinates can be computed with only $3\,\mathrm{M} + 4\,\mathrm{S}$ since the parameter a of our GLV curve is 0. However, what makes GLV curves really attractive is that the cost for the computation of a scalar multiplication can be significantly reduced thanks to an efficiently-computable endomorphism as described in [11]. This endomorphism allows one to accomplish an n-bit scalar multiplication $k \cdot P$ by a computation of the form $k_1 \cdot P + k_2 \cdot Q$, whereby k_1, k_2 have only half the length of k. The two half-length scalar multiplications can be carried out simultaneously (via "Shamir's trick"), which takes $n/2$ point doublings and roughly $n/4$ additions when k_1, k_2 are represented in Joint Sparse Form (JSF) [16]. Thus, the overall cost of computing $k \cdot P$ amounts to $3.5n$ multiplications and $2.75n$ squarings in $\mathbb{F}_p$, i.e. $3.5\,\mathrm{M} + 2.75\,\mathrm{S}$ per bit.

3   Optimal Prime Fields

The lightweight ECC software we introduce in this paper is based on a special family of prime fields, the so-called *Optimal Prime Fields (OPFs)*, which were first described in the literature in an extended abstract from 2006 [12]. OPFs are defined by "low-weight" primes that can be written as

$$p = u \cdot 2^k + v \tag{5}$$

where u and v are small compared to 2^k, e.g. have a length of 8 or 16 bits so that they fit into one two registers of an 8-bit processor. A concrete example is $p = 65356 \cdot 2^{144} + 1$ (i.e. $u = 65356$, $k = 144$, and $v = 1$), which happens to be a 160-bit prime that looks as follows when written as a hex-string:

$$p = 0\mathrm{xFF4C0000000000000000000000000000000000001}$$

The main characteristic of these primes is their low Hamming weight, which is due to the fact that only a few bits near to the Most Significant Bit (MSB) and the Least Significant Bit (LSB) are non-zero; all the "middle" bits in between are 0. This property distinguishes them from other families of primes used in ECC, in particular Mersenne-like primes (cf. Sect. 2.1), which generally have a high Hamming weight. Using primes with a low Hamming weight allows for a simplification of the modular multiplication and other operations since all the zero-bits (resp. zero-bytes) do not need to be processed in a reduction modulo p. Most modular reduction algorithms, including Barrett and Montgomery reduction [26], can be optimized for OPFs, as will be shown in more detail in the remainder of this section. Another advantage of OPFs is that there exist a large number of primes of the form $p = u \cdot 2^k + v$ for any bitlength, which is not the case for generalized Mersenne primes.

The implementation of most of the arithmetic operations we describe in the following subsections is based on Zhang et al.'s OPF library for AVR processors [43]. However, Zhang's library, in its original form, is not resistant against side-channel attacks because it contains operand-dependent conditional statements such as if-then-else constructs. Therefore, we modified the arithmetic functions in a way so that they exhibit a highly regular execution pattern (and constant execution time) regardless of the actual values of the operands. In addition, we optimized a number of performance-critical code sections in the field arithmetic operations, which improved their execution time by up to 10 % versus Zhang's OPF library. As stated in Sect. 1.2, we strive for a scalable implementation able to process operands of varying length. To achieve this, we implemented all arithmetic functions to support the passing of a length parameter, which is then used by the function to calculate the number of loop iterations. Our library is dimensioned for operands between 64 and 2048 bits in steps of 32 bits, i.e. the operand length has to be a multiple of 32.

3.1   Selection of Primes

The original definition of OPFs in [12] specifies the coefficients u and v of the prime $p = u \cdot 2^k + v$ to "fit into a single register of the target processor," i.e. in our case, u and v would be (at most) 8 bits long. However, the OPF library we describe in this paper expects u to be a 16-bit integer, while v is fixed to 1. In the following, we explain the rationale behind this choice and elaborate on the supported bitlengths of p.

It is common practice in ECC to use primes with a bitlength that is a multiple of 32, e.g. 160, 192, 224 and 256 bits for applications with low to medium security requirements, and 384 and 512 bits for high-security applications. All standardization bodies (e.g. NIST, IEEE, SECG) recommend primes of these lengths and also we follow this approach. However, for efficiency reasons, it can be advantageous to use finite fields of a length slightly smaller than a multiple of 32, e.g. 255 bits instead of 256 [4]. Such slightly reduced field sizes facilitate certain optimization techniques like the so-called "lazy reduction," which means that the result of an addition or any other operation is only reduced when it is necessary so as to prevent overflow. We conducted some experiments with the 159-bit OPF given by $p = 126 \cdot 2^{152} + 1$, but found the performance gain one can achieve through lazy reduction to be less than 5 %. Therefore, we decided to stick with the well-established field lengths of 160, 192, 224 and 256 bits.

Our OPF software uses Montgomery's algorithm [26] for multiplication and squaring modulo p. A standard implementation of Montgomery multiplication based on e.g. the so-called Finely Integrated Product Scanning (FIPS) method [21] has to execute $2s^2 + s$ word-level multiplications (i.e. $(w \times w)$-bit `mul` instructions) for operands consisting of s words [14]. However, when we optimize the FIPS method for primes of the form $p = u \cdot 2^k + v$ with $0 < u, v < 2^w$, then only $s^2 + 3s$ `mul` instructions are required since all the "middle" words of p do not need to be processed because they are 0. A further reduction is achievable if $v = 1$ since this case simplifies the quotient determination in Montgomery's algorithm so that only $s^2 + s$ `mul` instructions need to be executed, as we will show in Sect. 3.3. The situation is similar for $v = 2^w - 1$ (which corresponds to $v = -1$ in two's complement representation) as also this special case allows for a reduction of the number of `mul` instructions. Having $v = 2^w - 1$ implies that the least significant word of p is an "all-one" word, which, in turn, means $p \equiv 3 \bmod 4$ and square roots modulo p can be computed efficiently [6].

The bitlength of a prime of the form $p = u \cdot 2^k + 1$ is not only determined by the exponent k, but also the coefficient u. To maximize performance, it was recommended in [12] to select u so that its length matches the word-size of the underlying processor; in our case, u should be an 8-bit integer in order to fit in a single register of an ATmega128 processor. When doing so, an optimized FIPS Montgomery multiplication ignoring all the zero-bytes of p requires to execute only $s^2 + s$ mul instructions. However, high performance is only one of several design goals; as stated in Sect. 1.2, we also aim for scalability, which means the ability to support fields of different lengths without the need to re-compile the arithmetic library. Besides the common field lengths of 160, 192, 224, and 256 bits, we want our library also to be able to perform arithmetic in 384 and 512-bit OPFs. Unfortunately, neither a 384-bit nor a 512-bit prime of the form $p = u \cdot 2^k + 1$ with $2^7 <= u < 2^8$ exists. It should be noted that the situation is very similar for pseudo-Mersenne primes; none of the 256 integers of the form $2^k - c$ with $k = 384$ and $c < 2^8$ is prime, and the same holds for $k = 512$. As a consequence, we decided to "weaken" the original criterium for the selection of u, namely to fit into a single register on the target processor, and allow u to have a length of 16 bits. While this relaxed condition for the selection of u entails a slight performance degradation, it significantly increases scalability and allows our OPF library to support high-security applications requiring 384 and 512-bit fields. All arithmetic functions of our library assume that u is a 16-bit integer and can be kept in two registers of an 8-bit ATmega128 processor. The second coefficient v of our low-weight primes is fixed to 1.

Notation. In what follows, $\mathbb{F}_p$ denotes an OPF defined by a prime of the form $p = u \cdot 2^k + 1$, whereby u is in the range $[2^{15}, 2^{16} - 1]$, i.e. u has a length of 16 bits. As mentioned above, the bitlength n of the primes we use in this paper is always a multiple of 32, e.g. $n = 160, 192, 224,$ or 256 bits. Field elements are referred to by lowercase italic letters, e.g. $a \in \mathbb{F}_p$. When implementing ECC in software, it is common practice to represent field elements by arrays of single-precision (i.e. w-bit) words so that the arithmetic operations can be executed efficiently on the processor's fast integer unit [16]. Normally, one chooses w to match the word-size of the underlying processor, which would mean $w = 8$ in the case of an 8-bit processor. However, as shown by Gura et al. in [15], it can be more efficient to process several (e.g. four) bytes of the operands at a time (instead of just a single byte), which, in fact, means to work with 32-bit words even though the processor has just an 8-bit datapath. We follow this approach and represent the elements of $\mathbb{F}_p$ via arrays of $s = \lceil n/w \rceil$ words, each having a length of $w = 32$ bits. For example, an element of a 160-bit prime field consists of five 32-bit words since $s = 160/32 = 5$. We use uppercase letters to denote these arrays and indexed uppercase letters to refer to individual words within an array, e.g. $A = (A_{s-1}, ..., A_1, A_0)$ where A_0 is the least significant word and A_{s-1} the most significant word of A, respectively.

3.2 Modular Addition and Subtraction

The typical way to perform a modular addition $z = a + b \bmod p$ is to first add the two n-bit operands $a, b \in \mathbb{F}_p$ to get a temporary sum $t = a + b$ (which can have a length of up to $n + 1$ bits), followed by a comparison between t and p to check whether $t \geq p$. Based on the result of this comparison, it may be necessary to subtract p from t to get a sum in the range of $[0, p - 1]$. However, this approach exhibits an operand-dependent (and, therefore, irregular) execution pattern that leaks information through small variations of both the execution time and power consumption profile, the latter of which may be exploited in an SPA attack as described in e.g. [34]. In fact, this side-channel leakage has two origins, one is the comparison between t and p, and the other is the conditional subtraction of p. Most performance-optimized ECC implementations adopt an "early-abort" strategy to compare two integers, which means the comparison is done word by word, starting at the most significant word-pair, and the result is immediately returned when the first unequal word-pair is found. Therefore, the difference between the operands determines the execution time; it is maximal when the operands are equal. The second origin of side-channel leakage, i.e. the subtraction of p, is more obvious since this subtraction is only performed when the temporary sum t is not smaller than p.

In order to eliminate or, at least, reduce side-channel leakage, we adopt the idea of incomplete modular arithmetic as described by Yanık et al. [42]. Instead of reducing the result t of the addition to the least non-negative residue in the range of $[0, p - 1]$, incomplete modular arithmetic allows (i.e. tolerates) results that are not fully reduced as long as they do not exceed a certain bitlength. In our case, this means that all results of modular operations are (at most) n bits long, but do not necessarily need to be smaller than p. All our modular arithmetic functions also accept incompletely reduced operands as inputs, provided that their length does not exceed n, the bitlength of p. The advantage of this "relaxed" residue representation is the possibility to perform modular addition without an exact comparison between the sum t and the prime p. Instead, we just check whether the length of t exceeds n bits (i.e. whether $t \geq 2^n$), which is only the case when the addition $t = a + b$ produced a "carry bit."

Thanks to the carry bit (which is either 0 or 1), the conditional subtraction of p can be done in an "unconditional" way by applying a mask to each byte of p before it is subtracted. The value of this mask is either an "all-zero" byte or an "all-one" byte and can be easily obtained from the carry bit through negation. For example, when the carry bit $c = 0$, the value of the mask becomes $m = -c = 0$. Applying this mask m to a byte p_i of p (i.e. performing a logical **and** between m and p_i) yields a zero-byte, which means 0 is subtracted from the sum t. Conversely, when $c = 1$, we have $m = -c = -1 = 2^8 - 1 = 0\text{xff}$, and applying this m to the bytes p_i does not change their value, which means p is subtracted from t. Note, however, that a second subtraction may be required to obtain an n-bit result since both operands can be incompletely reduced. To get "branch-less" code, we always perform two masked subtractions of p and update the carry bit c after the first one. More precisely, the first subtraction produces a "borrow bit," which is either 0 or 1 and has to be subtracted from the carry bit to obtain the correct carry bit for the second subtraction.

A modular subtraction $z = a - b \bmod p$ can be implemented on basis of the same principles as the modular addition described above. Our implementation performs an ordinary subtraction $t = a - b$ followed by two masked additions of p, whereby the mask is derived from the borrow bit of the subtraction.

3.3   Modular Multiplication and Squaring

As detailed earlier in this section, our OPF library supports low-weight primes of the form $p = u \cdot 2^k + 1$ where u is 16 bits long. Following the notation from Sect. 3.1, we can represent p via an array $P = (P_{s-1}, \ldots, P_1, P_0)$ consisting of s words, each having a length of w bits, i.e. $w/4$ bytes. The least significant word P_0 is 1, while the most significant word P_{s-1} contains u; all other words are 0. In this subsection, we assume that the two operands a, b to be multiplied have the same length as p, namely n bits, but they do not necessarily need to be smaller than p, i.e. a and b are in the range of $[0, 2^n - 1]$.

We show in the following that Montgomery modular multiplication [26] can be optimized for primes of the form $p = u \cdot 2^k + 1$ by simply ignoring all words P_i with $1 \leq i \leq s - 2$ (i.e. all "zero" words) in the reduction operation. When doing so, the overall number of word-level (i.e. $(w \times w)$-bit) multiplications to compute a Montgomery product amounts to $s^2 + s$, of which s^2 contribute to the multiplication of the s-word operand a by b, and the rest to the reduction modulo p. In other words, the "overhead" of modular reduction is only s word-level multiplications, i.e. reduction has linear complexity. For comparison, the reduction of a $2s$-word product modulo a pseudo-Mersenne prime of the form $p = 2^k - c$ (with c fitting into a single word) also requires exactly s word-level multiplications [6]. However, when performing a modular multiplication with a pseudo-Mersenne prime, the reduction is typically done *after* the multiplication (see e.g. [18]), which is inefficient since the $2s$-word product is first written to memory (during the multiplication), and then it has to be loaded again from memory to accomplish the reduction. To avoid this, our implementation adopts a variant of the so-called Finely Integrated Product Scanning (FIPS) method [21] for Montgomery multiplication, which interleaves multiplication steps and reduction steps instead of executing them one after the other, thereby saving a number of load/store instructions and reducing the RAM footprint.

The standard FIPS technique for arbitrary primes, as described in [14,21], has a nested-loop structure with two outer and two simple inner loops. In each iteration of the inner loops, two Multiply-Accumulate (MAC) operations are carried out; one with the words of the operands a and b, which contributes to the computation of $a \cdot b$. The second MAC operation involves words of the prime p and, hence, contributes to the reduction operation. Algorithm 1 shows a special variant of the FIPS method optimized for "low-weight" primes of the form $p = u \cdot 2^k + 1$. This variant differs from the generic FIPS method for arbitrary primes in three main aspects. First, we eliminated all multiplications and MAC operations performed on zero words of p since they do not contribute to

---

Algorithm 1. FIPS Montgomery modular multiplication for OPFs

Input: An n-bit prime $p = u \cdot 2^k + 1$ given as s-word array $P = (P_{s-1}, \ldots, P_1, P_0)$, two
integers $a, b \in [0, 2^n - 1]$ given as $A = (A_{s-1}, \ldots, A_1, A_0)$, $B = (B_{s-1}, \ldots, B_1, B_0)$.
Output: An $(s+1)$-word array $Z = (Z_s, \ldots, Z_1, Z_0)$ with $Z_s \in \{0, 1\}$ representing a
possibly incompletely reduced Montgomery product $z = a \cdot b \cdot 2^{-n} \bmod p$.

1: $T \leftarrow A_0 \times B_0$
2: **for** i from 1 by 1 to $s - 1$ **do**
3:    $Z_{i-1} \leftarrow -(T \bmod 2^w)$
4:    $T \leftarrow T + Z_{i-1}$
5:    $T \leftarrow T / 2^w$
6:    **for** j from 0 by 1 to i **do**
7:       $T \leftarrow T + A_j \times B_{i-j}$
8:    **end for**
9: **end for**
10: $T \leftarrow T + Z_0 \times P_{s-1}$
11: $Z_{s-1} \leftarrow -(T \bmod 2^w)$
12: $T \leftarrow T + Z_{s-1}$
13: **for** i from s by 1 to $2s - 2$ **do**
14:    $T \leftarrow T / 2^w$
15:    **for** j from $i - s + 1$ by 1 to $s - 1$ **do**
16:       $T \leftarrow T + A_j \times B_{i-j}$
17:    **end for**
18:    $T \leftarrow T + Z_{i-s+1} \times P_{s-1}$
19:    $Z_{i-s} \leftarrow T \bmod 2^w$
20: **end for**
21: $T \leftarrow T / 2^w$
22: $Z_{s-1} \leftarrow T \bmod 2^w$
23: $Z_s \leftarrow T / 2^w$ { Z_s is either 0 or 1 }
24: $Z \leftarrow (Z_s, \ldots, Z_1, Z_0)$
25: **return** Z

---

the final result. Consequently, the inner loops of Algorithm 1 perform only one
MAC operation, similar to the product-scanning method for multiple-precision
multiplication [16]. In fact, the inner loops in lines 6–8 and 15–17 are the same
as in product-scanning multiplication, which makes Algorithm 1 fairly easy to
implement. Another difference between our FIPS variant and the generic FIPS
method for arbitrary primes is that the former is optimized for $P_0 = 1$ and, as
a consequence, the Montgomery reduction requires only s MAC operations; one
is performed in line 10 and the remaining $s - 1$ in the second outer loop (line
18). When $P_0 = 1$, we have $-P_0^{-1} \bmod 2^w = -1 \bmod 2^w = 2^w - 1$, which simplifies the quotient-determination part of the reduction operation compared to
the original FIPS method (see [43, Sect. 4.3] for a detailed explanation). Due
to this optimization, the total number of word-level multiplications and MAC
operations of the FIPS method for $p = u \cdot 2^k + 1$ amounts to only $s^2 + s$. The
third difference between our FIPS variant and the classic one is that we peeled
off the computation of $A_0 \times B_0$ from the first nested loop and re-arranged the

loop structure accordingly. Because of this modification, all loops of Algorithm 1 iterate at least one time if $s \geq 2$, which simplifies their implementation.

Our AVR Assembly implementation of the FIPS Montgomery multiplication is based on the pseudo-code from Algorithm 1. However, in order to maximize performance, we adopt a variant of Gura et al.'s hybrid multiplication method [15], which means all word-level multiplications and MAC operations are performed on four bytes (i.e. 32 bits) of the operands instead of just a single byte (i.e. our word-size w is 32). In each iteration of the two inner loops, four bytes of operand a (i.e. the word A_j) and operand b (i.e. the word B_{i-j}) are loaded from memory and multiplied together to a 64-bit product. This product is then added to a cumulative sum T held in nine 8-bit registers. Our implementation of the inner loops follows [24, Sect. 3.1] and is, therefore, slightly faster than Zhang et al.'s inner-loop operation from [43]. Each iteration of the inner loops consists of eight ld (i.e. load), 16 mul, 49 add (or adc), and four movw instructions (excluding loop overhead). When taking the updating of the loop-control variable and branch instruction into account, the overall execution time of one full iteration of the inner loop amounts to exactly 104 clock cycles.

Besides excellent performance, the inner-loop implementation from [24] has the further advantage that it occupiers only 30 out of the 32 working registers of an AVR processor. We use the two free registers to accommodate the 16-bit coefficient u of the prime $p = u \cdot 2^k + 1$. Hence, we have to maintain only three pointers, namely the pointers to the arrays A, B, and Z, which we hold in the three pointer registers X, Y, and Z during the execution of a multiplication. In each iteration of the inner loop, the pointer to A gets incremented by 4, while the pointer to B is decremented. Therefore, the pointers need to be initialized with the correct start addresses, and this initialization has to performed in the outer loop, immediately before the start of the inner loop. Zhang et al. [43] did this pointer initialization with help of the "original" start address of the arrays A and B (i.e. the address of A_0 and B_0), which they pushed on the stack at the very beginning of the multiplication and then popped whenever needed. Unfortunately, this approach is quite expensive since push and pop instructions take two cycles each. We found it more efficient to re-calculate the original address of these pointers using the end-value of the loop counter.

Algorithm 1 does not include the so-called "final subtraction" of p, which is generally required in Montgomery multiplication to guarantee that the result is smaller than p or, in our case, smaller than 2^n. Therefore, the array Z consists of $s + 1$ words, whereby its most significant word Z_s is either 0 or 1. Note that (at most) one subtraction of p is required to get an s-word result in the range of $[0, 2^n - 1]$, even when both inputs are not completely reduced. To minimize SPA leakage, we perform this subtraction of p in the same way as described in Sect. 3.2, but use Z_s to derive an "all-zero" or "all-one" mask.

We implemented modular squaring for our low-weight primes similar to the multiplication, using the same optimizations in the reduction. Furthermore, the squaring adopts the well-known "trick" that allows one to cut the total number of word-level multiplications by almost one half (from s^2 to $\frac{s^2+s}{2}$) [6].

4   Performance Evaluation and Comparison

In the following, we present execution times of both field and group arithmetic operations, including scalar multiplication, for OPFs (and appropriate elliptic curves) ranging from 160 to 256 bits. As mentioned before, we implemented all OPF arithmetic operations in Assembly language to achieve peak performance on 8-bit AVR processors. The group operations (i.e. the point arithmetic) and the algorithms for scalar multiplication were written in ANSI C and compiled using WinAVR. We determined the execution time of all arithmetic operations with help of the cycle-accurate instruction-set simulator of AVR Studio 4.

Table 1. Execution time (in clock cycles) of arithmetic operations in OPFs

Operation	160 bit	192 bit	224 bit	256 bit
Addition	530	631	732	833
Subtraction	530	631	732	833
Multiplication	3237	4500	5971	7650
Squaring	2901	3909	5058	6347
Mul. by 16-bit integer	873	1039	1295	1461
Inversion	223374	311828	416758	531901

Table 1 summarizes the execution times we obtained using the ATmega128 processor as target platform, whereby all timings include the full function-call overhead. A multiplication in a 160-bit OPF takes 3237 clock cycles, which is almost 10 % faster than the average multiplication time of 3542 cycles reported by Zhang et al. [43]. For comparison, Szczechowiak et al.'s NanoECC [35] needs a total of 3882 clock cycles for a 160-bit modular multiplication (2654 cycles to do the multiplication, 1228 cycles for a reduction modulo a 160-bit generalized Mersenne prime), even though they fully unrolled the loops. The overhead due to the reduction operation accounts for about 31.6 % of the total multiplication time. On the other hand, the reduction overhead of multiplication in a 160-bit OPF is 459 clock cycles (or 14.2 %) since, according to [24], a conventional 160-bit multiplication (without modular reduction) requires 2778 cycles.

As analyzed in Sect. 3.3, our FIPS Montgomery multiplication for OPFs has to perform $s^2 + s$ word-level multiplications or MAC operations, which are essentially (32×32)-bit multiplications in our case. On an 8-bit processor, this translates into $16s^2 + 8s$ mul instructions since the two least significant bytes of P_{s-1} are 0, i.e. the s MAC operations in line 10 and 18 of Algorithm 1 need only eight mul instructions instead of 16. On the other hand, an OPF squaring including reduction involves $(s^2 + 3s)/2$ word-level multiplications (resp. MAC operations), which means $8s^2 + 12s$ mul instructions on the ATmega128. As a consequence, one would expect OPF squaring to be (almost) 50 % faster than OPF multiplication. However, an optimized squaring function has to carry out some auxiliary operations, e.g. left-shifts of word-level (i.e. 64-bit) products in order to double them, which significantly impacts the total execution time, the more so the shorter the operands are. The results given in Table 1 show that, in a 160-bit OPF, squaring is just some 10.4 % faster than multiplication, but the gain increases to roughly 17 % in a 256-bit OPF. We implemented the inversion based on the binary version of the well-known Extended Euclidean Algorithm (EEA) [16], whereby we exploited the special form of our primes to accelerate certain low-level operations, e.g. additions and subtractions of p. Note that the inversion has an irregular execution profile, which means the execution time is not constant but depends on the input. Table 1 specifies the average execution time of 100 inversions performed on random field elements.

Table 2. Execution time (in cycles) of point arithmetic and scalar multiplication

Operation	160 bit	192 bit	224 bit	256 bit
GLV point addition	40305	54417	70418	88550
GLV point doubling	26684	36539	45369	56296
GLV scalar mul.	4191073	6918518	10064582	14178625
Montgomery point add.	19479	25890	33207	41428
Montgomery point dbl.	15950	21072	26884	33390
Montgomery scalar mul.	5928088	9445554	14109549	20158840

Table 2 lists the simulated execution times of point addition/doubling and full scalar multiplication for both GLV and Montgomery curves. As explained in Sect. 2.2, the addition and doubling of points on a Montgomery curve is less costly (in terms of arithmetic operations in the underlying prime field) than the point addition/doubling on a GLV curve, and the simulation results from Table 2 clearly confirm this. However, the situation becomes different when we compare the execution times of a full scalar multiplication since the GLV curve outperforms its Montgomery counterpart by a factor of 1.41 in the 160-bit case (i.e. $4.19 \cdot 10^6$ versus $5.93 \cdot 10^6$ cycles on an ATmega128). We implemented the scalar multiplication on the Montgomery curve in a straightforward way based on a "Montgomery ladder" [6], while the scalar multiplication on the GLV curve exploits an efficiently computable endomorphism as described in [11,16]. Since the Montgomery curves we used have a positive trace and a co-factor of 4, we evaluated the execution time using scalars that are two bits shorter than the underlying OPF. On the other hand, our GLV curves have a co-factor of 1 and we used scalars k that satisfy the following conditions: (1) the two sub-scalars k_1, k_2 of the decomposition of k are both positive and $n/2$ bit long (n is the bitlength of the underlying OPF), and (2) their JSF contains $n/4$ zero bits.

Table 3 compares the scalar multiplication time of our two implementations with previous results reported in the literature. Our GLV variant outperforms all previous implementations, with two exceptions, namely the implementation

Table 3. Comparison of execution time of scalar multiplication over fields of an order of roughly 160 bits (evaluation platform is an ATmega128 clocked at 7.3728 MHz)

Implementation	Field order	Fixed P.	Rand. P.	SPA resistant
Seo et al. [32]	GF(2^m), 163 bit	1.14 s	1.14 s	No
Kargl et al. [20]	GF(2^m), 167 bit	0.76 s	0.76 s	No
Aranha et al. [1]	GF(2^m), 163 bit	0.29 s	0.32 s	No
Liu et al. [23]	GF(p), 160 bit	2.05 s	2.30 s	No
Szczechowiak et al. [35]	GF(p), 160 bit	1.27 s	1.27 s	No
Wang et al. [39]	GF(p), 160 bit	1.24 s	1.35 s	No
Gura et al. [15]	GF(p), 160 bit	0.88 s	0.88 s	No
Chu et al. [5]	GF(p), 160 bit	0.79 s	0.79 s	No
Großschädl et al. [13]	GF(p), 160 bit	0.74 s	0.74 s	No
Ugus et al. [36]	GF(p), 160 bit	0.57 s	1.03 s	No
Wenger et al. [40] (Mon.)	GF(p), 160 bit	0.75 s	0.75 s	Yes
Wenger et al. [40] (GLV)	GF(p), 160 bit	0.53 s	0.53 s	No
Our work (Montg. curve)	GF(p), 160 bit	0.80 s	0.80 s	Yes
Our work (GLV curve)	GF(p), 160 bit	0.57 s	0.57 s	No

of Aranha et al. [1] and Wenger et al. [40]. However, both applied extensive loop unrolling in the field arithmetic operations, which in general entails large code size and poor scalability. Furthermore, the implementation of Aranha et al. can only be made SPA resistant at the expense of a massive performance hit.

5   Conclusions

The aim of this paper was to provide new insights into certain implementation aspects of OPFs on 8-bit AVR processors. First, we argued that OPFs defined by primes of the form $p = u \cdot 2^k + 1$, where u is a 16-bit integer, represent an optimal trade-off between performance and scalability. Then, we described in detail how to implement arithmetic operations for OPFs, taking the properties (e.g. low Hamming weight) of these primes into account. In particular, we proposed a new variant of Montgomery multiplication for low-weight primes based on the FIPS method. Our Montgomery variant has the same loop structure as the ordinary product-scanning method for multiplication and can, therefore, be well optimized for ATmega processors. We implemented the multiplication and all other arithmetic operations needed for ECC in a parameterized fashion with rolled loops so as to achieve high scalability and small code size. Furthermore, we wrote the Assembly code of all arithmetic functions (bar inversion) in such a way that always the same instruction sequence is executed, irrespective of the actual value of the operands, which helps to foil SPA attacks. Simulation results obtained with AVR Studio 4 indicate an execution time of 3237 cycles for a multiplication in a 160-bit OPF, while squaring takes 2901 cycles. These results compare very favorably with previous work and outperform even some implementations with unrolled loops. We also evaluated the execution time of a full scalar multiplication on Montgomery as well as GLV curves over OPFs. In the former case, the scalar multiplication is "intrinsically" SPA resistant and executes in 5.93 million cycles over a 160-bit OPF, while, in the latter case, we have an execution time of 4.19 million cycles. Both results confirm that OPFs are an excellent implementation option for ECC on 8-bit AVR processors.

References

1. Aranha, D.F., Dahab, R., López, J.C., Oliveira, L.B.: Efficient implementation of elliptic curve cryptography in wireless sensors. Adv. Math. Commun. 4(2), 169–187 (2010)
2. Atmel Corporation. 8-bit ARV® Instruction Set. User Guide, July 2008. http://www.atmel.com/dyn/resources/prod_documents/doc0856.pdf
3. Atmel Corporation. 8-bit ARV® Microcontroller with 128K Bytes In-System Programmable Flash: ATmega128, ATmega128L. Datasheet, June 2008. http://www.atmel.com/dyn/resources/prod_documents/doc2467.pdf
4. Bernstein, D.J.: Curve25519: New Diffie-Hellman Speed Records. In: Yung, M., Dodis, Y., Kiayias, A., Malkin, T. (eds.) PKC 2006. LNCS, vol. 3958, pp. 207–228. Springer, Heidelberg (2006)
5. Chu, D., Großschädl, J., Liu, Z., Müller, V., Zhang, Y.: Twisted Edwards-form elliptic curve cryptography for 8-bit AVR-based sensor nodes. In: Xu, S., Zhao, Y. (eds.) Proceedings of the 1st ACM Workshop on Asia Public-Key Cryptography (AsiaPKC 2013), pp. 39–44. ACM Press (2013)
6. Cohen, H., Frey, G.: Handbook of Elliptic and Hyperelliptic Curve Cryptography. Discrete Mathematics and Its Applications, vol. 34. Chapmann & Hall, Boca Raton (2006)
7. Crandall, R.E.: Method and apparatus for public key exchange in a cryptographic system, U.S. Patent No. 5,159,632, October 1992
8. Crossbow Technology, Inc. MICAz Wireless Measurement System. Data sheet, January 2006. http://www.xbow.com/Products/Product_pdf_files/Wireless_pdf/MICAz_Datasheet.pdf
9. de Meulenaer, G., Standaert, F.-X.: Stealthy compromise of wireless sensor nodes with power analysis attacks. In: Chatzimisios, P., Verikoukis, C., Santamaría, I., Laddomada, M., Hoffmann, O. (eds.) MOBILIGHT 2010. LNICST, vol. 45, pp. 229–242. Springer, Heidelberg (2010)
10. Eisenbarth, T., Gong, Z., Güneysu, T., Heyse, S., Indesteege, S., Kerckhof, S., Koeune, F., Nad, T., Plos, T., Regazzoni, F., Standaert, F.-X., van Oldeneel tot Oldenzeel, L.: Compact implementation and performance evaluation of block ciphers in ATtiny devices. In: Mitrokotsa, A., Vaudenay, S. (eds.) AFRICACRYPT 2012. LNCS, vol. 7374, pp. 172–187. Springer, Heidelberg (2012)
11. Gallant, R.P., Lambert, R.J., Vanstone, S.A.: Faster point multiplication on elliptic curves with efficient endomorphisms. In: Kilian, J. (ed.) CRYPTO 2001. LNCS, vol. 2139, pp. 190–200. Springer, Heidelberg (2001)
12. Großschädl, J.: TinySA: a security architecture for wireless sensor networks. In: Diot, C., Ammar, M., Sá da Costa, C., Lopes, R.J., Leitão, A.R., Feamster, N., Teixeira, R. (eds.) Proceedings of the 2nd International Conference on Emerging Networking Experiments and Technologies (CoNEXT 2006), pp. 288–289. ACM Press (2006)

13. Großschädl, J., Hudler, M., Koschuch, M., Krüger, M., Szekely, A.: Smart elliptic curve cryptography for smart dust. In: Zhang, X., Qiao, D. (eds.) QShine 2010. LNICST, vol. 74, pp. 623–634. Springer, Heidelberg (2012)
14. Großschädl, J., Kamendje, G.-A.: Architectural enhancements for montgomery multiplication on embedded RISC processors. In: Zhou, J., Yung, M., Han, Y. (eds.) ACNS 2003. LNCS, vol. 2846, pp. 418–434. Springer, Heidelberg (2003)
15. Gura, N., Patel, A., Wander, A., Eberle, H., Shantz, S.C.: Comparing elliptic curve cryptography and RSA on 8-bit CPUs. In: Joye, M., Quisquater, J.-J. (eds.) CHES 2004. LNCS, vol. 3156, pp. 119–132. Springer, Heidelberg (2004)
16. Hankerson, D.R., Menezes, A.J., Vanstone, S.A.: Guide to Elliptic Curve Cryptography. Springer, New York (2004)
17. Heyse, S., von Maurich, I., Wild, A., Reuber, C., Rave, J., Poeppelmann, T., Paar, C.: Evaluation of SHA-3 candidates for 8-bit embedded processors. Presentation at the 2nd SHA-3 Candidate Conference, Santa Barbara, CA, USA, August 2010. http://csrc.nist.gov/groups/ST/hash/sha-3/Round2/Aug2010/
18. Hutter, M., Schwabe, P.: NaCl on 8-Bit AVR microcontrollers. In: Youssef, A., Nitaj, A., Hassanien, A.E. (eds.) AFRICACRYPT 2013. LNCS, vol. 7918, pp. 156–172. Springer, Heidelberg (2013)
19. Hutter, M., Wenger, E.: Fast multi-precision multiplication for public-key cryptography on embedded microprocessors. In: Preneel, B., Takagi, T. (eds.) CHES 2011. LNCS, vol. 6917, pp. 459–474. Springer, Heidelberg (2011)
20. Kargl, A., Pyka, S., Seuschek, H.: Fast arithmetic on ATmega128 for elliptic curve cryptography. Cryptology ePrint Archive, Report 2008/442 (2008). http://eprint.iacr.org
21. Koç, Ç.K., Acar, T., Kaliski, B.S.: Analyzing and comparing Montgomery multiplication algorithms. IEEE Micro **16**(3), 26–33 (1996)
22. Lederer, C., Mader, R., Koschuch, M., Großschädl, J., Szekely, A., Tillich, S.: Energy-efficient implementation of ECDH key exchange for wireless sensor networks. In: Markowitch, O., Bilas, A., Hoepman, J.-H., Mitchell, C.J., Quisquater, J.-J. (eds.) Information Security Theory and Practice. LNCS, vol. 5746, pp. 112–127. Springer, Heidelberg (2009)
23. Liu, A., Ning, P.: TinyECC: a configurable library for elliptic curve cryptography in wireless sensor networks. In: Proceedings of the 7th International Conference on Information Processing in Sensor Networks (IPSN 2008), pp. 245–256. IEEE Computer Society Press (2008)
24. Liu, Z., Großschädl, J.: New speed records for Montgomery modular multiplication on 8-bit AVR microcontrollers. Cryptology ePrint Archive, Report 2013/882 (2013). http://eprint.iacr.org
25. Mangard, S., Oswald, E., Popp, T.: Power Analysis Attacks: Revealing the Secrets of Smart Cards. Springer, New York (2007)
26. Montgomery, P.L.: Modular multiplication without trial division. Math. Comput. **44**(170), 519–521 (1985)
27. Montgomery, P.L.: Speeding the Pollard and elliptic curve methods of factorization. Math. Comput. **48**(177), 243–264 (1987)
28. Oswald, E.: Enhancing simple power-analysis attacks on elliptic curve cryptosystems. In: Kaliski, B.S., Koç, Ç.K., Paar, C. (eds.) CHES 2002. LNCS, vol. 2523, pp. 82–97. Springer, Heidelberg (2002)
29. Sakai, Y., Sakurai, K.: Simple power analysis on fast modular reduction with NIST recommended elliptic curves. In: Qing, S., Mao, W., López, J., Wang, G. (eds.) ICICS 2005. LNCS, vol. 3783, pp. 169–180. Springer, Heidelberg (2005)

30. Scott, M., Szczechowiak, P.: Optimizing multiprecision multiplication for public key cryptography. Cryptology ePrint Archive, Report 2007/299 (2007). http://eprint.iacr.org

31. Seo, H., Kim, H.: Multi-precision multiplication for public-key cryptography on embedded microprocessors. In: Lee, D.H., Yung, M. (eds.) WISA 2012. LNCS, vol. 7690, pp. 55–67. Springer, Heidelberg (2012)

32. Seo, S.C., Han, D.-G., Kim, H.C., Hong, S.: TinyECCK: efficient elliptic curve cryptography implementation over $GF(2^m)$ on 8-bit Micaz mote. IEICE Trans. Inf. Syst **E91–D**(5), 1338–1347 (2008)

33. Solinas, J.A.: Generalized Mersenne numbers. Technical report CORR-99-39, Centre for Applied Cryptographic Research (CACR), University of Waterloo, Waterloo, Canada (1999)

34. Stebila, D., Thériault, N.: Unified point addition formulæ and side-channel attacks. In: Goubin, L., Matsui, M. (eds.) CHES 2006. LNCS, vol. 4249, pp. 354–368. Springer, Heidelberg (2006)

35. Szczechowiak, P., Oliveira, L.B., Scott, M., Collier, M., Dahab, R.: NanoECC: testing the limits of elliptic curve cryptography in sensor networks. In: Verdone, R. (ed.) EWSN 2008. LNCS, vol. 4913, pp. 305–320. Springer, Heidelberg (2008)

36. Ugus, O., Westhoff, D., Laue, R., Shoufan, A., Huss, S.A.: Optimized implementation of elliptic curve based additive homomorphic encryption for wireless sensor networks. In: Wolf, T., Parameswaran, S. (eds.) Proceedings of the 2nd Workshop on Embedded Systems Security (WESS 2007), pp. 11–16 (2007). http://arxiv.org/abs/0903.3900

37. Uhsadel, L., Poschmann, A., Paar, C.: Enabling full-size public-key algorithms on 8-bit sensor nodes. In: Stajano, F., Meadows, C., Capkun, S., Moore, T. (eds.) ESAS 2007. LNCS, vol. 4572, pp. 73–86. Springer, Heidelberg (2007)

38. Walter, C.D.: Simple power analysis of unified code for ECC double and add. In: Joye, M., Quisquater, J.-J. (eds.) CHES 2004. LNCS, vol. 3156, pp. 191–204. Springer, Heidelberg (2004)

39. Wang, H., Li, Q.: Efficient implementation of public key cryptosystems on mote sensors (short paper). In: Ning, P., Qing, S., Li, N. (eds.) ICICS 2006. LNCS, vol. 4307, pp. 519–528. Springer, Heidelberg (2006)

40. Wenger, E., Großschädl, J.: An 8-bit AVR-based elliptic curve cryptographic RISC processor for the Internet of things. In: Proceedings of the 45th Annual IEEE/ACM International Symposium on Microarchitecture Workshops (MICROW 2012), pp. 39–46. IEEE Computer Society Press (2012)

41. Woodbury, A.D., Bailey, D.V., Paar, C.: Elliptic curve cryptography on smart cards without coprocessors. In: Domingo-Ferrer, J., Chan, D., Watson, A. (eds.) Smart Card Research and Advanced Applications. International Federation for Information Processing, vol. 180, pp. 71–92. Kluwer Academic Publishers, Amsterdam (2000)

42. Yanık, T., Savaş, E., Koç, Ç.K.: Incomplete reduction in modular arithmetic. IEE Proc. Comput. Digit. Tech. **149**(2), 46–52 (2002)

43. Zhang, Y., Großschädl, J.: Efficient prime-field arithmetic for elliptic curve cryptography on wireless sensor nodes. In: Proceedings of the 1st International Conference on Computer Science and Network Technology (ICCSNT 2011), vol. 1, pp. 459–466. IEEE (2011)

Public Key Cryptography

Secure One-to-Group Communications Escrow-Free ID-Based Asymmetric Group Key Agreement

Lei Zhang[1], Qianhong Wu[2]([⊠]), Josep Domingo-Ferrer [3], Bo Qin[4],
Sherman S.M. Chow[5], and Wenchang Shi[4]

[1] Shanghai Key Laboratory of Trustworthy Computing, Software Engineering
Institute, East China Normal University, Shanghai, China
leizhang@sei.ecnu.edu.cn
[2] School of Electronic and Information Engineering,
Beihang University, Beijing, China
qianhong.wu@buaa.edu.cn
[3] UNESCO Chair in Data Privacy,
Department of Computer Engineering and Mathematics,
Universitat Rovira i Virgili, Catalonia, Spain
josep.domingo@urv.cat
[4] School of Information, Renmin University of China, Beijing, China
{bo.qin,wenchang}@ruc.edu.cn
[5] Department of Information Engineering,
Chinese University of Hong Kong, Sha Tin, Hong Kong
sherman@ie.cuhk.edu.hk

Abstract. Group key agreement (GKA) is widely employed for secure group communications. Yet there is an increasing demand for secure one-to-group communications in distributed computing applications. Asymmetric group key agreement (AGKA) is a handy tool to answer this need. In AGKA, a group of members can establish a group public key while each member has a different secret key. Any sender can encrypt under this group key such that any of the members who hold the secret key can decrypt. This paper proposes an identity-based AGKA protocol which is secure against active attackers, with an emphasis on optimal round efficiency, sender dynamics, and escrow freeness. The last feature offers security of the previously established ciphertexts even when either all the involved participants or the key generation center of the identity-based cryptosystem are compromised. The proposed protocol is shown to be secure under the k-Bilinear Diffie-Hellman exponent assumption in the random oracle model. Regarding performance, our protocol is comparable to the state-of-the-art AGKA protocols.

Keywords: Communication security · Key management · Identity-based cryptography · Asymmetric group key agreement

© Springer International Publishing Switzerland 2014
D. Lin et al. (Eds.): Inscrypt 2013, LNCS 8567, pp. 239–254, 2014.
DOI: 10.1007/978-3-319-12087-4_15

1   Introduction

In ubiquitous computing applications such as wireless mesh networks and mobile *ad hoc* networks, there is a need to efficiently and securely broadcast to a remote cooperative group. A popular approach to secure group communications is to exploit group key agreement (GKA) [5]. Conventional GKA protocols allow a group of members to interact over an open network to establish a common secret key; thereafter, the group members can securely exchange messages using this shared key. Thus, conventional GKA protocols are *sender restricted* in the sense that, when a sender wants to send a secret message to a group of receivers, the sender has to first join the receivers to form a group and then run a GKA protocol. To see the limitations, let us consider the following scenarios.

Scenario 1. A group of users in different time zones would like to discuss on some sensitive topics over an untrusted medium, e.g., via a social network service provider.

Scenario 2. One or more soldiers may want to securely report to a group of tactical units.

Up to now, most existing efficient GKA protocols need at least two rounds [12,19]. In Scenario 1, all the users have to stay online to finish the protocol before they can wait for encrypted contents, which is a prohibitive way for users in different time zones. In Scenario 2, the same key will be derived from the GKA protocol for a soldier and the tactical units. The compromise of any one soldier will compromise the secrecy of the communication among the tactical units as well. This is also prohibitive since a soldier is conceivably under a poor communication environment.

Motivated by above scenarios, Wu *et al.* [21] introduced the notion of asymmetric group key agreement (AGKA) and proposed a concrete *one-round* AGKA protocol. Unlike regular GKA, AGKA allows the members to negotiate a common *group encryption key* while holding different *(group) decryption keys*. The group encryption key is publicly accessible and enables any sender to securely encrypt to the group members. The decryption key, which is different from the long-term private key of the user, can be used to decrypt every ciphertexts encrypted under the group encryption key.

The above AGKA protocol, and the subsequent improvements [22,23], are based on traditional public-key infrastructure (PKI). The idea of identity-based cryptosystem (IBC) proposed by Shamir [18] eliminates complicated certificate management in PKI, with the help of a trusted key generation centre (KGC) for creating the long-term identity-based secret keys for the group members. Identity-based AGKA (IBAGKA) protocols have been proposed [26,27]. Using these identity-based secret keys with AGKA, the members can securely establish a secure broadcast channel among them, without relying on PKI.

The original AGKA notion and the instantiated protocol are only secure against passive attackers who just eavesdrop the open communications. This is not sufficient against realistic attackers who may fully control the open networks and launch more powerful active attacks such as member impersonation, communication tampering, replay of early protocol transcripts, etc. To counter this kind of attackers, an additional identity-based signature scheme is used on top of the IBAGKA protocol [26, 27].

The authenticated AGKA protocol in [26, 27] achieves partial forward secrecy. That is, if only one or some specific group members' long-term keys are compromised, the secrets exchanged before the compromise stay unknown to the attacker. However, if all the group members' long-term keys are leaked, then the previously established secrets will be exposed to the attacker and the protocol will no longer be secure. Obviously, since the long-term keys for the group members are generated by the KGC, the KGC can always read the secrets. This is known as the *key escrow problem*. Further, in practice, we do not know which members might be compromised after the protocol is deployed and, in the worst case, all the members and even the KGC might be compromised. These observations motivate us to investigate authenticated AGKA protocols with stronger active security.

1.1 Our Contributions

This paper contributes to the study of authenticated AGKA in the IBC setting, in the following aspects.

We first formalize the notion of IBAAGKA without escrow. Our notion captures the typical active security properties of secrecy and known-key security [26, 27] derived from their analogs in conventional authenticated GKA protocols. The former means that only the group members can read the message exchanged after the AGKA protocol is executed. The latter means that an attacker who knows the decryption keys of previous sessions cannot compute subsequent group decryption keys. Furthermore, our notion also captures *escrow freeness* [7] (just like the standard perfect forward secrecy [1,2]) by allowing an attacker to corrupt the KGC. True, a KGC can always generate the long-term identity-based secret keys of any user. However, even such an attacker cannot read any secret messages exchanged before the corruption.

To motivate our design of authenticated AGKA protocol, we first propose and realize our new notion of strongly unforgeable stateful identity-based batch multi-signatures (IBBMS). Borrowing its design, we propose an IBAAGKA protocol without escrow. The protocol is shown to be secure against active attacks in our strengthened model. The proof relies on the k-Bilinear Diffie-Hellman Exponent assumption (which is widely used in recent cryptographic constructions) and the strong unforgeability of our stateful IBBMS. The protocol needs only one round to enable a group of members to establish a common encryption and their respective decryption keys. A detailed analysis shows that the complexity in computation and communication of our authenticated AGKA protocol is comparable to that of up-to-date AGKA protocols, but our protocol achieves the strongest active security in AGKA protocols, so far.

1.2 Related Work

As a fundamental primitive of secure group communications, GKA has attracted considerable attention in cryptography. The best-known among these are perhaps the works of Ingemarsson et al. [16], Burmester and Desmedt [5], and Steiner et al. [20]. These proposals require two or more rounds to obtain a secret key and an additional round for each member to confirm the established secret key. Boneh and Silverberg [4] showed that a one-round GKA protocol can be constructed if multilinear maps [15] exist. However, the key confirmation step cannot be eliminated. Further, these GKA protocols only allow secure intra-group communications.

Wu et al. [21] constructed a one-round AGKA protocol allowing a sender not in the group to encrypt to the members while offering short ciphertexts and efficient encryption. Unlike previous GKA protocols, an interesting property of Wu et al.'s AGKA protocol is that it allows key confirmation without extra communication. That is, a member just needs to locally encrypt a message using the encryption key and then decrypt the corresponding ciphertext using her secret decryption key. If the messages are equal, then she obtains the keys correctly. Their protocol requires $\mathcal{O}(1)$-size ciphertext and $\mathcal{O}(1)$ encryption operations after the group encryption key is negotiated. One may note that a trivial solution of one-round AGKA is to let each member publish a public key and withhold the respective secret key. A sender can then separately encrypt to each member and can generate the final ciphertext by concatenating all the underlying individual ones. However, this solution leads to $\mathcal{O}(n)$-size ciphertext and requires $\mathcal{O}(n)$ encryption operations for a group of n receivers. The challenge is to design one-round AGKA protocols with efficient encryption and short ciphertexts.

Subsequently, Wu et al. strengthened AGKA and presented contributory broadcast encryption [22] so that the sender could exclude some members from reading the transmissions. In [23], Wu et al. showed how to shorten the size of protocol transcripts in AGKA protocols.

To alleviate complicated certificate management of authenticated GKA in the PKI setting, identity-based authenticated GKA protocols (e.g., [8,17]) have been suggested. These protocols require two or more rounds and cannot cope with sender changes. The recent IBAAGKA protocol [26,27] is one-round and can handle sender changes efficiently. However, this protocol only achieves partial forward secrecy. Further, to guarantee the security of the protocol, an additional identity-based signature is used which makes the protocol less interesting. One may consider adding random secret value(s) [6] in the key agreement phase of conventional GKA protocols to achieve *escrow freeness* in identity-based AGKA protocols. However, it is unclear how to use this method without affecting the round efficiency of AGKA protocols.

Another notion close to IBAGKA is identity-based broadcast encryption [11] due to Delerablée. However, since the long-term key derived from a member's identity is directly used for decryption, identity-based broadcast encryption cannot even achieve partial forward secrecy and is weaker than our protocol with escrow freeness, which implies perfect forward secrecy.

Escrow freeness is especially important in the IBC setting since the KGC is the Achilles' heel and the most vulnerable spot for an attacker to break. Many works have considered solutions to address this problem. For example, forward secrecy in identity-based (anonymous) key agreement protocols [9], anonymous ciphertext indistinguishability against KGC attack in identity-based encryption [10,25], and resilience against continual auxiliary leakage of the master secret key in (hierarchical) identity-based encryption [24].

1.3 Paper Outline

The rest of the paper is organized as follows. Section 2 defines the security for IBAAGKA protocols. A strongly unforgeable stateful IBBMS signature is proposed in Sect. 3. Section 4 proposes our IBAAGKA protocol. Section 5 compares our AGKA protocol with other two AGKA protocols. Finally, Sect. 6 gives a conclusion.

2 System Model

In this section, we formalize our IBAAGKA model without escrow.

2.1 Notations

Let $\mathbb{P}$ be a polynomial-size set of participants. At any point of time, any subset $\mathbb{U} = \{\mathcal{U}_1, \ldots, \mathcal{U}_n\} \subseteq \mathbb{P}$ may decide to establish a confidential channel. Let $\Pi^\pi_{\mathcal{U}_i}$ represent instance π of participant $\mathcal{U}_i$. We will require the following notations:

- $\mathsf{pid}^\pi_{\mathcal{U}_i}$ is the *partner ID* of $\Pi^\pi_{\mathcal{U}_i}$, defined by a set containing the identities of the participants in the group with whom $\Pi^\pi_{\mathcal{U}_i}$ intends to establish a session key including $\mathcal{U}_i$ itself. The identities in $\mathsf{pid}^\pi_{\mathcal{U}_i}$ are lexicographically ordered.
- $\mathsf{sid}^\pi_{\mathcal{U}_i}$ is the *session ID* of instance $\Pi^\pi_{\mathcal{U}_i}$. The session IDs are unique. All members taking part in a given execution of a protocol have the same session ID. *The session ID of $\Pi^\pi_{\mathcal{U}_i}$ can be instantiated by concatenating $\mathsf{pid}^\pi_{\mathcal{U}_i}$, a time interval (e.g., date of the day) and a counter of the number of sessions executed by the participants with* partner ID $\mathsf{pid}^\pi_{\mathcal{U}_i}$ *in the time interval.*
- $\mathsf{ms}^\pi_{\mathcal{U}_i}$ is the concatenation of all messages sent and received by $\Pi^\pi_{\mathcal{U}_i}$ during its execution, where the messages are ordered by round, and within each round lexicographically by the identities of the purported senders.
- $\mathsf{ek}^\pi_{\mathcal{U}_i}$ is the group encryption key held by $\Pi^\pi_{\mathcal{U}_i}$.
- $\mathsf{dk}^\pi_{\mathcal{U}_i}$ is the group decryption key held by $\Pi^\pi_{\mathcal{U}_i}$.
- $\mathsf{state}^\pi_{\mathcal{U}_i}$ represents the current (internal) state of instance $\Pi^\pi_{\mathcal{U}_i}$. $\Pi^\pi_{\mathcal{U}_i}$ is *terminated*, if it stops sending and receiving; and it is *successfully terminated* if $\Pi^\pi_{\mathcal{U}_i}$ is *terminated* and no incorrect behavior has been detected, *i.e.*, it possesses $\mathsf{ek}^\pi_{\mathcal{U}_i}(\neq null)$, $\mathsf{dk}^\pi_{\mathcal{U}_i}(\neq null)$, $\mathsf{ms}^\pi_{\mathcal{U}_i}$, $\mathsf{pid}^\pi_{\mathcal{U}_i}$ and $\mathsf{sid}^\pi_{\mathcal{U}_i}$.

Definition 1 (Partnering). *Two instances $\Pi_{\mathcal{U}_i}^{\pi}$ and $\Pi_{\mathcal{U}_j}^{\pi'}$ (with $i \neq j$) are partnered if and only if (1) they are successfully terminated; (2) $\mathsf{pid}_{\mathcal{U}_i}^{\pi} = \mathsf{pid}_{\mathcal{U}_j}^{\pi'}$; and (3) $\mathsf{sid}_{\mathcal{U}_i}^{\pi} = \mathsf{sid}_{\mathcal{U}_j}^{\pi'}$.*

2.2 Security Model

Our security model for IBAAGKA protocols is defined by the following game, which is run between a challenger $\mathcal{C}$ and an adversary $\mathcal{A}$. The adversary has full control of the network communications. This game has the following stages:

Initialize: Taking as input a security parameter ℓ, $\mathcal{C}$ generates the *master-secret* and initializes the system parameters Υ. Υ is passed to $\mathcal{A}$.

Probing: At this stage, $\mathcal{A}$ is allowed to make the following types of queries:

- Send($\Pi_{\mathcal{U}_i}^{\pi}, \Psi$): It sends a message Ψ to instance $\Pi_{\mathcal{U}_i}^{\pi}$, and outputs the reply generated by this instance. In particular, if $\Psi = (\mathsf{sid}, \mathsf{pid})$, this query prompts $\mathcal{U}_i$ to initiate the protocol using session ID sid and partner ID pid. If Ψ is of incorrect format, the query returns *null*.
- Corrupt($\mathcal{U}_i$): It outputs the private key of participant $\mathcal{U}_i$ and can be used to model forward secrecy.
- Corrupt(KGC): It outputs the *master-secret* and can be used to model escrow freeness.
- Ek.Reveal($\Pi_{\mathcal{U}_i}^{\pi}$): It outputs the group encryption key $\mathsf{ek}_{\mathcal{U}_i}^{\pi}$.
- Dk.Reveal($\Pi_{\mathcal{U}_i}^{\pi}$): It outputs the group decryption key $\mathsf{dk}_{\mathcal{U}_i}^{\pi}$. It is used to model known-key security.
- Test($\Pi_{\mathcal{U}_i}^{\pi}$): At some point, $\mathcal{A}$ returns two messages (m_0, m_1) and a fresh instance $\Pi_{\mathcal{U}_i}^{\pi}$ (see Definition 2). $\mathcal{C}$ randomly chooses a bit $b \in \{0, 1\}$, encrypts m_b under $\mathsf{ek}_{\mathcal{U}_i}^{\pi}$ to produce a ciphertext c, and returns c to $\mathcal{A}$. This query can be queried only once and is used to model secrecy.

Following [21,26,27], we use the confidentiality of the final broadcast channel to define the secrecy of IBAAGKA protocols. That is, secrecy is defined by the indistinguishability of a message encrypted under the negotiated group encryption key from a random string in the ciphertext space.

Guess: Finally, $\mathcal{A}$ returns a bit b'. If $b' = b$, $\mathcal{A}$ wins the game. $\mathcal{A}$'s advantage is defined to be $\epsilon = |2\Pr[b = b'] - 1|$.

Definition 2 (Freshness). *An instance $\Pi_{\mathcal{U}_i}^{\pi}$ is fresh if none of the following happens:*

1. *$\Pi_{\mathcal{U}_i}^{\pi}$ has not successfully terminated.*
2. *$\mathcal{A}$ has queried Dk.Reveal($\Pi_{\mathcal{U}_i}^{\pi}$) or Dk.Reveal($\Pi_{\mathcal{U}_j}^{\pi'}$), where $\Pi_{\mathcal{U}_j}^{\pi'}$ is any partnered instance of $\Pi_{\mathcal{U}_i}^{\pi}$.*
3. *Before $\Pi_{\mathcal{U}_i}^{\pi}$ successfully terminated, the query Corrupt(KGC) has been made or the query Corrupt(participant) has been made for some participants whose identities are in $\mathsf{pid}_{\mathcal{U}_i}^{\pi}$.*

Definition 3 (Secrecy). *An IBAAGKA protocol is said to be semantically indistinguishable against chosen identity and plaintext attacks (Ind-ID-CPA) if ϵ is negligible for any probabilistic polynomial time (PPT) active adversary in the above model.*

We stress that, in our IBAAGKA secrecy definition, escrow freeness is incorporated since the attacker is allowed to corrupt the PKG. Even if such an attacker cannot understand the secret messages exchanged among the group members. The escrow freeness naturally implies perfect forward secrecy. This strong security is important in practice as IBAAGKA protocols are assumed to be deployed in ad hoc network like scenarios. In these applications, end users are usually connected by open wireless communications and exposed to attackers. Furthermore, the centralized PKG is the single point of the system and may be compromised by attackers. Our key-escrow free secrecy guarantees that IBAAGKA protocols can be securely employed in such hostile environments.

Similarly to [21,26,27], in the above model, we only consider chosen-plaintext attacks (CPA) against IBAAGKA protocols. We note our definition is readily extended to resist chosen-ciphertext (CCA) attacks. Indeed, there are some generic approaches that convert a CPA secure encryption scheme into a CCA secure one, such as the Fujisaki-Okamoto conversion [13].

3   Building Block: Strongly Unforgeable Stateful IBBMS

Here we propose a strongly unforgeable stateful IBBMS scheme as a building block of our IBAAGKA protocol.

3.1   Definition

A stateful IBBMS allows multiple signers to sign t messages under a piece of state information in an efficient way to generate a batch multi-signature. Furthermore, the batch multi-signature can be separated into t individual multi-signatures. A stateful IBBMS scheme consists of the following five algorithms:

- BM.Setup, taking as input a security parameter ℓ, outputs a *master-secret* and a list of system parameters. For brevity, we omit the inclusion of the system parameters as part of the inputs for the other algorithms.
- BM.Extract, taking as inputs an entity's identity ID_i and the *master-secret*, outputs the entity's private key.
- Sign, taking as inputs t messages, a piece of state information $info$, a signer's identity ID_i and private key, outputs a batch signature.
- Aggregate, taking as input a collection of x batch signatures on the same t messages from x signers, under the same state information $info$, outputs a batch multi-signature.
- BM.Verify, taking as input a batch multi-signature on t messages generated by x signers, under the same state information $info$, outputs either "all valid" if the batch multi-signature is valid or an index set, which means that the multi-signatures on the messages with indices in that set are valid.

As the state information, one can use the identities of all the signers and concatenate a specification of each time interval together with a counter of the number of signatures issued by these signers in the time interval.

3.2   Security Model

This section defines the strong unforgeability of stateful IBBMS schemes. Roughly speaking, a stateful IBBMS scheme is strongly unforgeable if an adversary cannot generate a different multi-signature on a message m under any state information and x signers' identities even if he can get the signature(s) on m under the same state information and identities. The formal definition of strong unforgeability of stateful IBBMS schemes is defined using the following game between a challenger $\mathcal{C}$ and an adversary $\mathcal{A}$.

Initialize: $\mathcal{C}$ runs BM.Setup to generate a *master-secret* and the system parameter list Υ. Υ is passed to $\mathcal{A}$ while *master-secret* is kept secret.

Probing: $\mathcal{A}$ can adaptively issue the following queries:

- BM.Extract: $\mathcal{A}$ can request the private key of an entity with identity ID_i. On receiving such a query, $\mathcal{C}$ outputs the private key of this entity.
- Sign: $\mathcal{A}$ can request a batch signature on messages $(m_1, \ldots, m_{t_i})$ under an identity ID_i and a piece of state information. For simplicity, we assume the messages are lexicographically ordered. On input

$$(ID_i, info_i, m_1, \ldots, m_{t_i})$$

the challenger $\mathcal{C}$ outputs a valid batch signature on those messages. If $\mathcal{A}$ asks a batch signature query with a previously used state information but different messages as input, $\mathcal{C}$ returns *null*.

Note that, to generate the IBBMS on messages $(m_1, \ldots, m_{t_i})$ under identities $(ID_1, \ldots, ID_x)$ (lexicographically ordered) and a piece of state information, $\mathcal{C}$ just needs to simulate via repeated calls to the Sign queries and then generate an IBBMS by using the Aggregate algorithm.

Forgery: Finally, $\mathcal{A}$ outputs x identities $(ID_1^*, \ldots, ID_x^*)$, a piece of state information $info^*$, a message m^* and a multi-signature σ^*. $\mathcal{A}$ wins the game if the following conditions are satisfied:

1. σ^* is a valid multi-signature on message m^* under identities $(ID_1^*, \ldots, ID_x^*)$ and $info^*$.
2. None of the identities in $\{ID_1^*, \ldots, ID_x^*\}$ has been submitted during the BM.Extract queries.
3. For $ID_i^* \in \{ID_1^*, \ldots, ID_x^*\}$, the forged signature σ^* is not generated by using the batch signatures output by calling the Sign queries with

$$(ID_i^*, info^*, m_1, \ldots, m_{\mathcal{I}}, \ldots, m_t)$$

as input, where $m_{\mathcal{I}} = m^*$ and $\mathcal{I}$ defines the index of the message.

In the **Forgery** stage, $\mathcal{A}$ is only required to output a single multi-signature, but not a batch multi-signature. This is due to the property of batch multi-signatures. A batch multi-signature can be separated into t individual multi-signatures. We only require that one of them is a forgery. As a result, we require that none of the identities in $\{ID_1^*, \ldots, ID_x^*\}$ has been submitted during the BM.Extract queries. This restriction is stronger than the restriction in the security models for normal multi-signature schemes which allow an adversary to query $x-1$ private keys corresponding to the identities in $\{ID_1^*, \ldots, ID_x^*\}$. However, this level of security suffices for our higher level applications in IBAAGKA. Indeed, we will be reducing the security of our IBAAGKA to that of our IBBMS.

Definition 4. *A stateful IBBMS scheme is strongly existentially unforgeable under adaptively chosen-message attacks if and only if the success probability ϵ' of any PPT adversary in the above game is negligible.*

3.3 Strongly Unforgeable Stateful IBBMS Scheme

Before delving into the details of our construction, we would like to remark that, although our final goal is not to propose an identity-based multi-signature scheme, we borrow some of its design principles to achieve our final goal of building IBAAGKA. Hence, we do not consider the generic approach of building identity-based signatures from the certification approach of standard signatures [14].

Our scheme is built over bilinear groups. Let $\mathbb{G}_1$ and $\mathbb{G}_2$ be two multiplicative groups of prime order q, and g be a generator of $\mathbb{G}_1$. An efficient map $\hat{e} : \mathbb{G}_1 \times \mathbb{G}_1 \to \mathbb{G}_2$ is called a bilinear map if it satisfies the following two properties.

1. **Bilinearity:** It holds that $\hat{e}(g^\alpha, g^\beta) = \hat{e}(g, g)^{\alpha\beta}$ for all $\alpha, \beta \in \mathbb{Z}_q^*$.
2. **Non-degeneracy:** There exists $u, v \in \mathbb{G}_1$ such that $\hat{e}(u, v) \neq 1$.

Now we are ready to describe our strongly unforgeable stateful IBBMS scheme.

– BM.Setup: On input a security parameter ℓ, KGC chooses two cyclic multiplicative groups $\mathbb{G}_1, \mathbb{G}_2$ with prime order q, such that there exists a bilinear map $\hat{e} : \mathbb{G}_1 \times \mathbb{G}_1 \longrightarrow \mathbb{G}_2$, where $\mathbb{G}_1$ is generated by g; KGC chooses a random $\kappa \in \mathbb{Z}_q^*$ as the *master-secret* and sets $g_{pub} = g^\kappa$; KGC chooses cryptographic hash functions

$$H_1, H_2, H_3 : \{0,1\}^* \longrightarrow \mathbb{G}_1, H_4 : \{0,1\}^* \longrightarrow \mathbb{Z}_q^*$$

Finally, KGC publishes the system parameter list

$$\Upsilon = (q, \mathbb{G}_1, \mathbb{G}_2, \hat{e}, g, g_{pub}, H_1 \sim H_4)$$

– BM.Extract: This algorithm takes κ and an entity's identity $ID_i \in \{0,1\}^*$ as inputs. It generates the private key for the entity as follows:

1. Compute
$$id_{i,0} = H_1(ID_i, 0), id_{i,1} = H_1(ID_i, 1)$$

2. Output the private key
$$(s_{i,0} = id_{i,0}^\kappa, s_{i,1} = id_{i,1}^\kappa)$$

- Sign: To sign t messages $(m_1, \ldots, m_t)$ under a piece of state information $info$, a signer with identity ID_i and private key $(s_{i,0}, s_{i,1})$ performs the following steps:

1. Choose random $\eta_i, \theta_i \in \mathbb{Z}_q^*$ and compute

$$r_i = g^{\eta_i}, u_i = g^{\theta_i}, v = H_2(info), \varpi_i = H_4(info, ID_i, r_i, u_i)$$

$$f_j = H_3(info, m_j), z_{i,j} = s_{i,0} s_{i,1}^{\varpi_i} v^{\theta_i} f_j^{\eta_i}, \text{ for } 1 \leq j \leq t.$$

2. Output batch signature $\sigma_i = (r_i, u_i, z_{i,1}, \ldots, z_{i,t})$.

- Aggregate: Anyone can aggregate a collection of signatures

$$\{\sigma_i = (r_i, u_i, z_{i,1}, \ldots, z_{i,t})\}_{1 \leq i \leq x}$$

on the messages $\{m_j\}_{1 \leq j \leq t}$ from x signers, under same $info$, into a batch multi-signature. In particular, the signatures can be aggregated into

$$(r_1, \ldots, r_x, u_1, \ldots, u_x, d_1, \ldots, d_t), \text{ where } d_j = \prod_{i=1}^{x} z_{i,j}.$$

- BM.Verify: To check the validity of the above batch multi-signature

$$(r_1, \ldots, r_x, u_1, \ldots, u_x, d_1, \ldots, d_t)$$

the verifier computes

$$w = \prod_{i=1}^{x} r_i, y = \prod_{i=1}^{x} u_i, v = H_2(info),$$

$$f_j = H_3(info, m_j), \Gamma_j = \hat{e}(f_j, w) \text{ for } 1 \leq j \leq t,$$

$$\varpi_i = H_4(info, ID_i, r_i, u_i) \text{ for } 1 \leq i \leq x,$$

$$\Omega = \hat{e}(\prod_{i=1}^{x} H_1(ID_i, 0) H_1(ID_i, 1)^{\varpi_i}, g_{pub}) \hat{e}(v, y).$$

For $1 \leq j \leq t$, the verifier checks

$$\hat{e}(d_j, g) \stackrel{?}{=} \Omega \Gamma_j.$$

If all the equations hold, the verifier outputs "all valid"; otherwise, it outputs an index set $\mathbb{I}$, which means that the multi-signatures with indices in that set are valid.

The security of our protocol is based on the following computational Diffie-Hellman (CDH) assumption.

CDH Assumption: In a finite cyclic group $\mathbb{G}$ with order q, the CDH assumption states that, given $g, g^\alpha, g^\beta \in \mathbb{G}$ for randomly chosen $\alpha, \beta \in \mathbb{Z}_q$, there exists no efficient algorithm to compute $g^{\alpha\beta}$.

The following result relates the security of the IBBMS primitive with the difficulty of breaking the CDH assumption.

Theorem 1. *Let H_1, H_2, H_3 and H_4 be random oracles. Suppose an adversary $\mathcal{A}$ makes at most q_{H_i} queries to H_i, for $1 \leq i \leq 3$, q_E Extract queries, q_σ Sign queries with maximal message size N, and wins the game in Sect. 3.2 with advantage ϵ' in time τ'; and the forged IBBMS is by at most x users. Then, there exists an algorithm to solve the CDH problem with advantage*

$$(\frac{x+2}{q_E + q_{H_3} + x + 1})^{x+2} \frac{q_{H_3}}{e^{x+2}} \epsilon'$$

in time

$$\tau' + \mathcal{O}(4q_{H_1} + q_{H_2} + q_{H_3} + 5Nq_\sigma)\tau_{\mathbb{G}_1}$$

where $\tau_{\mathbb{G}_1}$ is the time to compute a scalar exponentiation in $\mathbb{G}_1$ and e is Euler's number.

The proof will be presented in the full version of this paper.

4 Identity-Based Authenticated Asymmetric Group Key Agreement Protocol

In this section, we propose our one-round IBAAGKA protocol.

- Setup: It is the same as BM.Setup, except that an additional cryptographic hash function $H_5 : \mathbb{G}_2 \longrightarrow \{0,1\}^\iota$ is chosen, where ι defines the bit-length of plaintexts. The system parameter list is

$$\Upsilon = (q, \mathbb{G}_1, \mathbb{G}_2, \hat{e}, g, g_{pub}, H_1 \sim H_5, \iota)$$

- Extract: It is the same as BM.Extract.
- Agreement: Assume the group scale is n and the session ID is sid_λ. A protocol participant $\mathcal{U}_i$, whose identity is ID_i and private key is $(s_{i,0}, s_{i,1})$, performs the following steps:

  1. Choose $\eta_i, \theta_i \in \mathbb{Z}_q^*$ and compute

$$r_i = g^{\eta_i}, u_i = g^{\theta_i}$$

  2. Compute

$$v = H_2(\text{sid}_\lambda), \varpi_i = H_4(\text{sid}_\lambda, ID_i, r_i, u_i)$$

3. For $1 \leq j \leq n$, compute

$$f_j = H_3(\text{sid}_\lambda, j)$$

4. For $1 \leq j \leq n$, compute

$$z_{i,j} = s_{i,0} s_{i,1}^{\varpi_i} v^{\theta_i} f_j^{\eta_i}$$

5. Publish

$$\sigma_i = (r_i, u_i, \{z_{i,j}\}_{j \in \{1,\ldots,n\}, j \neq i})$$

- EncKeyGen: To get the group encryption key, for $j \in \{1, 2\}, i \in \{1, \ldots, n\}$, an entity computes

$$v = H_2(\text{sid}_\lambda), f_j = H_3(\text{sid}_\lambda, j), \varpi_i = H_4(\text{sid}_\lambda, ID_i, r_i, u_i).$$

Define $\Delta = 1$, if Eqs. (1) and (2) hold, and $\Delta = 0$ in other cases.

$$\hat{e}(z_{1,2}, g) \stackrel{?}{=} \hat{e}(H_1(ID_1, 0)H_1(ID_1, 1)^{\varpi_1}, g_{pub})\hat{e}(v, u_1)\hat{e}(f_2, r_1) \tag{1}$$

$$\hat{e}(\prod_{i=2}^{n} z_{i,1}, g) \stackrel{?}{=} \hat{e}(\prod_{i=2}^{n} H_1(ID_i, 0)H_1(ID_i, 1)^{\varpi_i}, g_{pub})\hat{e}(v, \prod_{i=2}^{n} u_i)\hat{e}(f_1, \prod_{i=2}^{n} r_i) \tag{2}$$

The Δ is used to check whether r_i and u_i are well formatted. If $\Delta = 1$, the entity outputs (w, Ω) as the group encryption key, where

$$w = \prod_{i=1}^{n} r_i, \Omega = \hat{e}(\prod_{i=1}^{n} H_1(ID_i, 0)H_1(ID_i, 1)^{\varpi_i}, g_{pub})\hat{e}(v, \prod_{i=1}^{n} u_i);$$

otherwise it aborts. We note that a protocol participant does not need to test the value of Δ, since it will do a similar check in the following DecKeyGen stage.

- DecKeyGen: Each participant $\mathcal{U}_i$ computes

$$w = \prod_{l=1}^{n} r_l, \Gamma_i = \hat{e}(f_i, w), d_i = \prod_{l=1}^{n} z_{l,i}$$

and tests

$$\hat{e}(d_i, g) \stackrel{?}{=} \Omega \cdot \Gamma_i.$$

If the equation holds, $\mathcal{U}_i$ accepts d_i as the group decryption key; otherwise, it aborts. The above test is also used by $\mathcal{U}_i$ to determine whether the encryption key is valid.

- Enc: To encrypt a plaintext m, select $\rho \in \mathbb{Z}_q^*$ and compute the ciphertext $c = (c_1, c_2, c_3)$ where

$$c_1 = g^\rho, c_2 = w^\rho, c_3 = m \oplus H_5(\Omega^\rho).$$

- Dec: To decrypt the ciphertext $c = (c_1, c_2, c_3)$, $\mathcal{U}_i$, whose group decryption key is d_i, computes

$$m = c_3 \oplus H_5(\hat{e}(d_i, c_1)\hat{e}(f_i^{-1}, c_2)).$$

The following theorem characterizes the security of our IBAAGKA protocol. The security of our protocol relies on the k-Bilinear Diffie-Hellman Exponent (BDHE) assumption [3] which states that, in the bilinear group setting, given g, h, and $g_i = g^{\alpha^i}$ in $\mathbb{G}_1$ for $i = 1, 2, \ldots, k, k + 2, \ldots, 2k$ as inputs, there exists no efficient algorithm to compute $\hat{e}(g, h)^{\alpha^{k+1}}$.

Theorem 2. *Let H_2, H_3 and H_5 be random oracles. Suppose that an adversary $\mathcal{A}$ makes at most q_{H_i} queries to H_i, $i \in \{2, 3, 5\}$, q_C Corrupt queries, q_S Send queries, q_{EK} Ek.Reveal queries and q_{DK} Dk.Reveal queries, and wins the game with advantage ϵ in time τ. Then there exists an algorithm to solve the k-BDHE problem with advantage at least*

$$\frac{1 - 2\epsilon'}{q_{H_5}(q_{DK} + 1)e}\epsilon$$

in time

$$T = \tau + \mathcal{O}(10q_{EK})\tau_{\hat{e}} + \mathcal{O}(q_{H_2} + q_{H_3} + 2q_C + 8q_S + 3q_{EK})\tau_{\mathbb{G}_1}$$

where ϵ' is the advantage for $\mathcal{A}$ to forge a valid IBBMS in time T, $\tau_{\hat{e}}$ is the time to compute a bilinear map, $\tau_{\mathbb{G}_1}$ is the time to compute a scalar exponentiation in $\mathbb{G}_1$ and e is Euler's number.

The proof will be presented in the full version of this paper.

5   Comparison

In this section, we compare our AGKA protocol with the unauthenticated AGKA protocol in [21] and the IBAAGKA in [26,27]. We only consider the costly operations and omit the operations that can be pre-computed.

Table 1 shows the computational overhead of three protocols in the last five stages, where $\tau_{\hat{e}}, \tau_{\mathbb{G}_1}, \tau_H, \tau_{\mathbb{G}_2}, \tau_{sg}$ are the times to compute a bilinear map, a scalar exponentiation in $\mathbb{G}_1$, a MapToPoint hash, a scalar exponentiation in $\mathbb{G}_2$, and the signing algorithm of an identity-based signature (IBS), respectively. Let τ_{sv} denote the verification time of an IBS. The efficiency of an AGKA protocol is mainly determined by stages Enc and Dec, since Agreement, EncKeyGen and DecKeyGen only need to be run once. Hence, for simplicity, in EncKeyGen, we only consider the computational cost for a participant to generate the group encryption key; the computational cost for a sender to generate the group encryption key is omitted. From this table, one can find that our protocol has comparable efficiency in stages Agreement, EncKeyGen and DecKeyGen as protocols in

Table 1. Computational overhead (†: it can be done in EncKeyGen or DecKeyGen)

Protocols	Agreement	EncKeyGen	DecKeyGen	Enc	Dec
AGKA in [21]	$1\tau_{\hat{e}} + n\tau_{\mathbb{G}_1}$	–	$1\tau_{\mathbb{G}_1}$	$2\tau_{\mathbb{G}_1} + 1\tau_{\mathbb{G}_2}$	$2\tau_{\hat{e}} + 1\tau_{\mathbb{G}_2}$
AGKA in [26,27]	$(n+1)\tau_{\mathbb{G}_1} + n\tau_H + 1\tau_{sg}$	$1\tau_{\hat{e}}$	$2\tau_{\hat{e}} + n\tau_{sv}^{\dagger}$	$2\tau_{\mathbb{G}_1} + 1\tau_{\mathbb{G}_2}$	$2\tau_{\hat{e}} + 1\tau_{\mathbb{G}_1}$
Our protocol	$(n+4)\tau_{\mathbb{G}_1} + (n+1)\tau_H$	$2\tau_{\hat{e}} + 1\tau_{\mathbb{G}_1}$	$2\tau_{\hat{e}}$	$2\tau_{\mathbb{G}_1} + 1\tau_{\mathbb{G}_2}$	$2\tau_{\hat{e}} + 1\tau_{\mathbb{G}_1}$

[21,26,27]. For stages Enc and Dec, our protocol is as efficient as [26,27], and it has similar efficiency as [21].

Let P_1, P_2, P_{ID}, P_m denote the binary length of an element in $\mathbb{G}_1$, $\mathbb{G}_2$, an identity, and a message, respectively. Let P_{sig} be the length of an identity-based signature. Table 2 compares our protocol with two other protocols regarding transmission cost. From this table, one may find that the transmission overhead of our protocol is slightly lower than the one in [21,26,27] for the Agreement stage, if we consider an identity of length 160 bits. Further, the length of a ciphertext in our protocol is the same as the one in [21,26,27], assuming that the plaintexts in the three protocols are of the same size.

Table 2. Transmission Overhead

Protocols	Agreement	Ciphertext Size
AGKA in [21]	$nP_1 + P_2$	$2P_1 + P_2$
AGKA in [26,27]	$nP_1 + P_{sig} + P_{ID}$	$2P_1 + P_m$
Our protocol	$(n+1)P_1 + P_{ID}$	$2P_1 + P_m$

6 Conclusion

We have extended the security model for IBAAGKA protocols, in which an attacker is allowed to learn the master secret of the KGC. A one-round IBAAGKA protocol has been proposed and proven secure in our extended model under the k-BDHE assumption. It offers secrecy and known-key security, and it does not suffer from the escrow problem. Therefore, not even the KGC can decrypt the ciphertexts sent to a group.

Acknowledgment. This work was supported in part by the Natural Science Foundation of China under Grants 61202465, 61021004, 11061130539, 61103222, 61173154, 61370190, 61003214, 61070192 and 61272501, the National Key Basic Research Program (973 program) under grants 2012CB315905, the Beijing Natural Science Foundation through project 4132056, the Fundamental Research Funds for the Central Universities, and the Research Funds of Renmin University of China and the Open Research Fund of Beijing Key Laboratory of Trusted Computing; the European

Commission under FP7 projects "DwB" and "Inter-Trust"; the Spanish Government under projects TIN2011-27076-C03-01 and CONSOLIDER INGENIO 2010 "ARES" CSD2007-0004; the Government of Catalonia under grant SGR2009-1135; the Shanghai NSF under Grant No. 12ZR1443500, 11ZR1411200; the Shanghai Chen Guang Program (12CG24); the Science and Technology Commission of Shanghai Municipality under grant 13JC1403500; the Fundamental Research Funds for the Central Universities of China; the Open Project of Shanghai Key Laboratory of Trustworthy Computing (No. 07dz22304201101).

The fifth author is supported by the Early Career Scheme and the Early Career Award of the Research Grants Council, Hong Kong SAR (CUHK 439713), and Direct Grant (4055018) of the Chinese University of Hong Kong.

The third author is with the UNESCO Chair in Data Privacy, but the views in this paper are his own and do not commit UNESCO.

References

1. Bellare, M., Canetti, R., Krawczyk, H.: A modular approach to the design and analysis of authentication and key exchange. In: STOC 1998, pp. 419–428 (1998)
2. Bellare, M., Rogaway, P.: Entity authentication and key distribution. In: Stinson, D.R. (ed.) CRYPTO 1993. LNCS, vol. 773, pp. 232–249. Springer, Heidelberg (1994)
3. Boneh, D., Boyen, X., Goh, E.-J.: Hierarchical identity based encryption with constant size ciphertext. In: Cramer, R. (ed.) EUROCRYPT 2005. LNCS, vol. 3494, pp. 440–456. Springer, Heidelberg (2005)
4. Boneh, D., Silverberg, A.: Applications of multilinear forms to cryptography. Contemp. Math. **324**, 71–90 (2003)
5. Burmester, M., Desmedt, Y.G.: A secure and efficient conference key distribution system. In: De Santis, A. (ed.) EUROCRYPT 1994. LNCS, vol. 950, pp. 275–286. Springer, Heidelberg (1995)
6. Chen, L., Cheng, Z., Smart, N.P.: Identity-based key agreement protocols from pairings. Int. J. Inf. Secur. **6**(4), 213–241 (2007)
7. Chen, L., Kudla, C.: Identity based authenticated key agreement protocols from pairings. In: IEEE CSFW 2003, pp. 219–233 (2003)
8. Choi, K.Y., Hwang, J.Y., Lee, D.-H.: Efficient ID-based group key agreement with bilinear maps. In: Bao, F., Deng, R., Zhou, J. (eds.) PKC 2004. LNCS, vol. 2947, pp. 130–144. Springer, Heidelberg (2004)
9. Chow, S.S.M., Choo, K.-K.R.: Strongly-secure identity-based key agreement and anonymous extension. In: Garay, J.A., Lenstra, A.K., Mambo, M., Peralta, R. (eds.) ISC 2007. LNCS, vol. 4779, pp. 203–220. Springer, Heidelberg (2007)
10. Chow, S.S.M.: Removing escrow from identity-based encryption. In: Jarecki, S., Tsudik, G. (eds.) PKC 2009. LNCS, vol. 5443, pp. 256–276. Springer, Heidelberg (2009)
11. Delerablée, C.: Identity-based broadcast encryption with constant size ciphertexts and private keys. In: Kurosawa, K. (ed.) ASIACRYPT 2007. LNCS, vol. 4833, pp. 200–215. Springer, Heidelberg (2007)
12. Dutta, R., Barua, R.: Provably secure constant round contributory group key agreement in dynamic setting. IEEE Trans. Inf. Theory **54**(5), 2007–2025 (2008)
13. Fujisaki, E., Okamoto, T.: Secure integration of asymmetric and symmetric encryption schemes. In: Wiener, M. (ed.) CRYPTO 1999. LNCS, vol. 1666, pp. 537–554. Springer, Heidelberg (1999)

14. Galindo, D., Herranz, J., Kiltz, E.: On the generic construction of identity-based signatures with additional properties. In: Lai, X., Chen, K. (eds.) ASIACRYPT 2006. LNCS, vol. 4284, pp. 178–193. Springer, Heidelberg (2006)
15. Garg, S., Gentry, C., Halevi, S.: Candidate multilinear maps from ideal lattices. In: Johansson, T., Nguyen, P.Q. (eds.) EUROCRYPT 2013. LNCS, vol. 7881, pp. 1–17. Springer, Heidelberg (2013)
16. Ingemarsson, I., Tang, D.T., Wong, C.K.: A conference key distribution system. IEEE Trans. Inf. Theory **28**(5), 714–720 (1982)
17. Reddy, K.C., Nalla, D.: Identity based authenticated group key agreement protocol. In: Menezes, A., Sarkar, P. (eds.) INDOCRYPT 2002. LNCS, vol. 2551, pp. 215–233. Springer, Heidelberg (2002)
18. Shamir, A.: Identity-based cryptosystems and signature schemes. In: Blakely, G.R., Chaum, D. (eds.) CRYPTO 1984. LNCS, vol. 196, pp. 47–53. Springer, Heidelberg (1985)
19. Snoeyink, J., Suri, S., Varghese, G.: A lower bound for multicast key distribution. In: IEEE INFOCOM 2001, pp. 422–431 (2001)
20. Steiner, M., Tsudik, G., Waidner, M.: Key agreement in dynamic peer groups. IEEE Trans. Parallel Distrib. Syst. **11**(8), 769–780 (2000)
21. Wu, Q., Mu, Y., Susilo, W., Qin, B., Domingo-Ferrer, J.: Asymmetric group key agreement. In: Joux, A. (ed.) EUROCRYPT 2009. LNCS, vol. 5479, pp. 153–170. Springer, Heidelberg (2009)
22. Wu, Q., Qin, B., Zhang, L., Domingo-Ferrer, J., Farràs, O.: Bridging broadcast encryption and group key agreement. In: Lee, D.H., Wang, X. (eds.) ASIACRYPT 2011. LNCS, vol. 7073, pp. 143–160. Springer, Heidelberg (2011)
23. Wu, Q., Qin, B., Zhang, L., Domingo-Ferrer, J., Manjón, J.A.: Fast transmission to remote cooperative groups: a new key management paradigm. IEEE/ACM Trans. Netw. **21**(2), 621–633 (2013)
24. Yuen, T.H., Chow, S.S.M., Zhang, Y., Yiu, S.M.: Identity-based encryption resilient to continual auxiliary leakage. In: Pointcheval, D., Johansson, T. (eds.) EURO-CRYPT 2012. LNCS, vol. 7237, pp. 117–134. Springer, Heidelberg (2012)
25. Yuen, T.H., Zhang, C., Chow, S.S.M., Liu, J.K.: Towards anonymous ciphertext indistinguishability with identity leakage. In: Susilo, W., Reyhanitabar, R. (eds.) ProvSec 2013. LNCS, vol. 8209, pp. 139–153. Springer, Heidelberg (2013)
26. Zhang, L., Wu, Q., Qin, B., Domingo-Ferrer, J.: Identity-based authenticated asymmetric group key agreement protocol. In: Thai, M.T., Sahni, S. (eds.) COCOON 2010. LNCS, vol. 6196, pp. 510–519. Springer, Heidelberg (2010)
27. Zhang, L., Wu, Q., Qin, B., Domingo-Ferrer, J.: Provably secure one-round identity-based authenticated asymmetric group key agreement protocol. Inf. Sci. **181**(19), 4318–4329 (2011)

Security Model and Analysis of FHMQV, Revisited

Shengli Liu[1,6], Kouichi Sakurai[2], Jian Weng[3,7], Fangguo Zhang[4], and Yunlei Zhao[5,6(✉)]

[1] Department of Computer Science and Engineering, Shanghai Jiao Tong University, Shanghai 200240, China
slliu@sjtu.edu.cn
[2] Department of Computer Science and Communication Engineering, Kyushu University, Fukuoka, Japan
sakurai@csce.kyushu-u.ac.jp
[3] Department of Computer Science, Emergency Technology Research Center of Risk Evaluation and Prewarning on Public Network Security, Jinan University, Guangzhou, China
cryptjweng@gmail.com
[4] School of Information Science and Technology, Sun Yat-sen University, Guangzhou 510006, China
isszhfg@mail.sysu.edu.cn
[5] Software School, Fudan University, Shanghai 201203, China
ylzhao@fudan.edu.cn
[6] State Key Laboratory of Information Security, Institute of Information Engineering, Chinese Academy of Sciences, Beijing 100093, China
[7] Shanghai Key Laboratory of Scalable Computing and Systems, Shanghai, China

Abstract. HMQV is one of the most efficient (provably secure) authenticated key-exchange protocols based on public-key cryptography, and is widely standardized. In spite of its seemingly conceptual simplicity, the HMQV protocol was actually very delicately designed. The provable security of HMQV is conducted in the Canetti-Krawczyk framework (CK-framework, in short), which is quite complicated and lengthy with

Shengli Liu—Funded by Natural Science Foundation of China (No. 61170229, 61373153), Innovation Project (No.12ZZ021) of Shanghai Municipal Education Commission.

Kouichi Sakurai—Supported by Grant-in-Aid for Scientific Research KAKENHI-No.23650008 from the Japan Society for the Promotion of Science (JSPS).

Jian Weng—Funded by the National Science Foundation of China under Grant Nos. 61272413, 61133014 and 61272415, the Fok Ying Tung Education Foundation under Grant No. 131066, the Program for New Century Excellent Talents in University under Grant No. NCET-12-0680, and the R&D Foundation of Shenzhen Basic Research Project under Grant No. JC201105170617A.

Yunlei Zhao—Contact author, funded by the National Basic Research Program of China (973 Program) No. 2014CB340600, and National Natural Science Foundation of China Grant No. 61070248, and No. 61272012, Innovation Project (No.12ZZ013) of Shanghai Municipal Education Commission, and Joint Project of SKLOLS. Work partially done during his visiting Sakura-lab of Kyushu Univ. JAPAN with support by Invitation Programs for Foreign-based Researchers provided from NICT, JAPAN.

© Springer International Publishing Switzerland 2014
D. Lin et al. (Eds.): Inscrypt 2013, LNCS 8567, pp. 255–269, 2014.
DOI: 10.1007/978-3-319-12087-4_16

many subtleties actually buried there. However, lacking a full recognition of the precise yet subtle interplay between HMQV protocol structure and provable security can cause misunderstanding of the HMQV design, and can cause potential flawed design and analysis of HMQV protocol variants. In this work, we explicitly make clear the interplay between HMQV protocol structure and provable security, showing the delicate design of HMQV. We then re-examine the security model and analysis of a recently proposed HMQV protocol variant, specifically, the FHMQV protocol proposed by Sarr et al. in [25]. We clarify the relationship between the traditional CK-framework and the CK-FHMQV security model proposed for FHMQV, and show that CK-HMQV and CK-FHMQV are incomparable. Finally, we make a careful investigation of the CDH-based analysis of FHMQV in the CK-FHMQV model, which was considered to be one of the salient advantages of FHMQV. We identify that the CDH-based security analysis of FHMQV is actually flawed. The flaws identified in the security proof of FHMQV just stem from lacking a full realization of the precise yet subtle interplay, as clarified in this work, between HMQV protocol structure and provable security.

1   Introduction

Diffie-Hellman key-exchange (DHKE) protocols [9] marked the birth of modern cryptography, and are one of the main pillars of both theory and practice of cryptography [5]. The plain DHKE protocol proposed in [9] is later observed to be insecure against active, man-in-the-middle adversaries. Much research efforts have been being made to achieve authenticated DHKE protocols secure against such active adversaries. One common approach is to add explicit authentication of the messages being exchanged by the use of signatures, encryptions and MACs, e.g., Internet Key-Exchange (IKE) [15] (that is based on SIGMA [14]), deniable IKE [29], and TLS [8]. Such protocols are referred to *explicitly authenticated* DHKE (EA-DHKE). However, the EA-DHKE approach usually incurs significant computational and communication complexity as compared with the plain DHKE.

Matsumoto et al. [18] initiated one ambitious line of investigation to design implicitly authenticated DHKE (IA-DHKE) protocols, which then triggered a list of subsequent (ad-hoc) designs of IA-DHKE protocols. By implicitly authenticated DHKE, we mean DHKE protocol whose communication is identical to the basic DH protocol, yet it is implicitly authenticated by the sole ability of the parties in computing the resultant session key [16]. This approach, i.e., the combination of authentication with the key derivation procedure, can potentially result in significant computational and communication savings. An IA-DHKE protocol is called *role-dependent* (resp., role-independent), if its session-key derivation is dependent (resp., independent) of players' roles (i.e., initiator or responder).

The MQV and HMQV protocols ((H)MQV, in short) marked the great milestones of IA-DHKE developments, and are widely standardized [1,2,10,11,21,22,26]. In particular, the first formal analysis of IA-DHKE, say the HMQV protocol, within the Canetti-Krawczyk framework (CK-framework) [5] is conducted in [16], which is particularly helpful in understanding the protocol design insights and the parameter choices.

Recently, Sarr et al. [25] proposed a variant of HMQV, named FHMQV (depicted in Fig. 1),[1] and claimed that FHMQV "preserves the efficiency and security attributes of HMQV" and provides "stronger security than HMQV". FHMQV is proved to be secure, under merely the CDH assumption, in a variant of the CK-framework for role-dependent IA-DHKE that is referred to as CK-FHMQV for presentation simplicity. The CDH-based provable security of FHMQV in the CK-FHMQV model, besides others, was considered to be one of the major advantages of FHMQV. Also, the work of [25] proposed, as a interesting future research question, to investigate the actual relationship between the CK-framework and the CK-FHMQV variant.

Despite its seemingly conceptual simplicity, designing "*sound*" and "*right*" key-exchange protocols turns out to be extremely error prone and can be notoriously subtle, particularly witnessed by the evolution history of (H)MQV [13,16, 18–20,32]. Also, the analysis of even a simple cryptographic protocol in intricate adversarial settings like the Internet can be a luxury and dauntingly complex task [4,16]. The reason for this is the high system complexity and plenty of subtleties surrounding the design, definition and analysis of key-exchange protocols.

In particular, in spite of the seemingly conceptual simplicity and similarity with MQV, the HMQV protocol was actually very delicately designed with a precise interplay between the protocol structure and provable security, in the sense that slight changes in the design structure or parameters can lose provable security or even be totally insecure. Unfortunately, the precise interplay between the protocol structure of HMQV and its provable security is quite subtle, and many subtleties were buried in the highly complicated and lengthy security proof of HMQV [16]. However, as we shall see, such a precise yet subtle interplay (between HMQV protocol structure and provable security) plays a key role in understanding and evaluating the HMQV design.

Our contribution. In this work, we explicitly make clear the interplay between HMQV protocol structure and provable security, showing the delicate design of HMQV. As (H)MQV is widely standardized and deployed in practice, and due to the high system complexity nature of KE security proof, we suggest that explicitly making clear of such an interplay is important for deep understanding of HMQV design as well as for evaluating potential HMQV variants.

Then, we re-examine the security model and analysis of FHMQV proposed in [25]. We first clarify the relationship between traditional CK-framework [5] and the CK-FHMQV variant proposed in [25], and show that CK-HMQV (for role-dependent IA-DHKE) and CK-FHMQV are incomparable. Then, we make a careful investigation of the CDH-based analysis of FHMQV in the CK-FHMQV model, and identify that the security analysis of FHMQV is actually flawed. The flaws identified in the security proof of FHMQV just stem from lacking a full

---

[1] Actually, the FHMQV can be viewed as variant of a protocol proposed in [28], where $d = h(\hat{A}, A, \hat{B}, B, X, Y)$ and $e = h(d)$.

realization of the precise yet subtle interplay, as clarified in this work, between HMQV protocol structure and provable security.

2 Preliminaries

We recall some preliminaries in this section, which is almost verbatim from [30]. If S is a finite set then $|S|$ is its cardinality, and $x \leftarrow S$ is the operation of picking an element uniformly at random from S. If α is neither an algorithm nor a set then $x \leftarrow \alpha$ is a simple assignment statement. A string or value α means a binary one, and $|\alpha|$ is its binary length. We denote by $\mathbb{N}$ the set of natural numbers. Two ensembles $X = \{X_l\}_{k \in \mathbb{N}}$ and $Y = \{Y_l\}_{k \in \mathbb{N}}$ are computationally indistinguishable, if for any probabilistic polynomial-time (PPT) algorithm $\mathcal{D}$ and for all sufficiently large k's, $|\Pr[D(1^k, X_k) = 1] - \Pr[D(1^k, Y_k) = 1]|$ is negligible in k.

Let G' be a finite Abelian group of order N, G be a subgroup of prime order q in G'. Throughout this work, we denote by $k = |q|$ the underlying security parameter. Denote by g a generator of G, by 1_G the identity element, by $G \setminus 1_G = G - \{1_G\}$ the set of elements of G except 1_G and by $t = \frac{N}{q}$ the cofactor. In this work, we use multiplicative notation for the group operation in G'. Roughly speaking, the discrete logarithm (DL) assumption over G says that given $X = g^x$, where $x \leftarrow Z_q^*$, no efficient, specifically probabilistic polynomial-time (PPT), DL-solver algorithm can output x with non-negligible probability. The computational Diffie-Hellman (CDH) assumption says that given $X = g^x, Y = g^y$, where $x, y \leftarrow Z_q^*$, no efficient CDH-solver algorithm can compute $CDH(X, Y) = g^{xy}$ with non-negligible probability.

Gap Diffie-Hellman (GDH) assumption [23]. Let G be a cyclic group generated by an element g, and a decision predicate algorithm $\mathcal{O}$ be a (*full*) Decisional Diffie-Hellman (DDH) Oracle for the group G and generator g such that on input (U, V, Z), for *arbitrary* $(U, V) \in G^2$, oracle $\mathcal{O}$ outputs 1 if and only if $Z = CDH(U, V)$. We say the GDH assumption holds in G if for any polynomial-time CDH solver for G and for any sufficiently large security parameter k, the probability that on a pair of random elements $(X, Y) \leftarrow G$ the solver computes the correct value $CDH(X, Y)$ is negligible (in k), even when the algorithm is provided with the (full) DDH-oracle $\mathcal{O}$ for G. The probability is taken over the random coins of the solver, and the choice of X, Y (each one of them is taken uniformly at random in G).

Knowledge-of-Exponent Assumption (KEA) [7]. Let G be a cyclic group of prime order q generated by an element g, and consider algorithms that on input a triple $(g, C = g^c, z)$ output a pair $(Y, Z) \in G^2$, where c is taken uniformly at random from Z_q^* and $z \in \{0, 1\}^*$ *is an arbitrary string that is generated independently of* C. Such an algorithm $\mathcal{A}$ is said to be a KEA algorithm if with non-negligible probability (over the choice of g, c and $\mathcal{A}$'s random coins) $\mathcal{A}(g, g^c, z)$ outputs $(Y, Z) \in G^2$ such that $Z = Y^c$. Here, $C = g^c$ is the random challenge to the KEA algorithm $\mathcal{A}$, and z captures the auxiliary input of $\mathcal{A}$ that is independent of the challenge C.

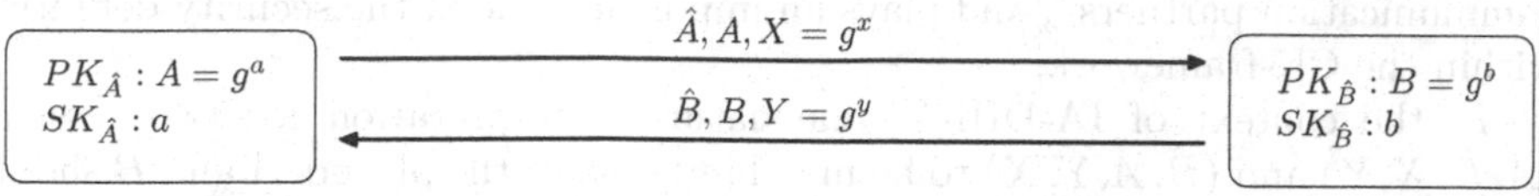

$$\hat{A}, A, X = g^x$$

$$PK_{\hat{A}} : A = g^a \qquad\qquad \hat{B}, B, Y = g^y$$
$$SK_{\hat{A}} : a \qquad\qquad\qquad\qquad\qquad\qquad PK_{\hat{B}} : B = g^b$$
$$\qquad\qquad\qquad\qquad\qquad\qquad\qquad\qquad SK_{\hat{B}} : b$$

(H)MQV Family: $K_{\hat{A}} = (YB^e)^{x+da} = (XA^d)^{y+eb} = K_{\hat{B}}, K = H_K(K_{\hat{A}}, aux) = H_K(K_{\hat{B}}, aux)$

MQV: $d = 2^l + (X \bmod 2^l), e = 2^l + (Y \bmod 2^l), aux = \varepsilon$

HMQV: $d = h(X, \hat{B}), e = h(Y, \hat{A}), aux = \varepsilon$

FHMQV: $d = h(X, Y, \hat{A}, \hat{B}), e = h(Y, X, \hat{A}, \hat{B}), aux = (\hat{A}, \hat{B}, X, Y)$

Fig. 1. Specifications of (H)MQV and FHMQV

We say that the KEA assumption holds over G, if for every probabilistic polynomial-time KEA algorithm $\mathcal{A}$ for G there exists another efficient algorithm $\mathcal{K}$, referred to as the KEA-extractor, such that for sufficiently large security parameter the following property holds except for a negligible probability: let (g, g^c, z) be an input to $\mathcal{A}$ and ρ a vector of random coins for $\mathcal{A}$ on which $\mathcal{A}$ outputs $(Y, Z = Y^c)$, then, on the same inputs and random coins, $\mathcal{K}(g, C, z, \rho)$ outputs the triple $(Y, Z = Y^c, y)$ where $Y = g^y$.

Specification of (H)MQV and FHMQV. Let $(A = g^a, a)$ (resp., $(X = g^x, x)$) be the public-key and secret-key (resp., the DH-component and DH-exponent) of player $\hat{A}$, and $(B = g^b, b)$ (resp., $(Y = g^y, y)$) be the public-key and secret-key (resp., the DH-component and DH-exponent) of player $\hat{B}$, where a, x, b, y are taken randomly and independently from Z_q^*. (H)MQV and FHMQV are presented in Fig. 1, where, on the security parameter k, H_K (resp., h) is a hash function of k-bit (resp., l-bit) output and l is set to be $|q|/2$. Notice that, (H)MQV is role-independent (i.e., session-key derivation is independent of players' roles), while FHMQV is role-dependent as players' identities are put into the input of H_K in the fixed order of $(\hat{A}, \hat{B})$.

2.1   Overview of the CK-Framework for IA-DHKE

The following brief description of the CK-framework for IA-DHKE is almost verbatim from [30,31]. For more details, the reader is referred to [16].

In the CK-framework for an IA-DHKE protocol, a session run at the side of player $\hat{A}$ with a peer player $\hat{B}$, where the outcoming (resp., incoming) DH-component is X (resp., Y), is assigned with a session identifier as $(\hat{A}, \hat{B}, X, Y)$. In each session, a party can be activated as the role of either initiator (who sends the first DH-component) or responder (who sends the second DH-component). During a normal protocol run (*without adversary interference*) between two players $\hat{A}$ and $\hat{B}$, we require that both sessions (one at $\hat{A}$ and one at $\hat{B}$) should compute the same session-key, which is referred to as the completeness property. The completeness property within the CK-framework is captured by the definition of *matching sessions*, which aims to capture when two sessions are "intended communication partners", and plays an important role in the security definition within the CK-framework.

In the context of IA-DHKE, one natural interpretation for two sessions $(\hat{A}, \hat{B}, X, Y)$ and $(\hat{B}, \hat{A}, Y, X)$ to be matching is that: the players $\hat{A}$ and $\hat{B}$ should have matching roles in the two sessions, i.e., if $\hat{A}$ is the initiator (resp., responder) then $\hat{B}$ is the responder (resp., initiator) in both of the two sessions. However, as the basic (H)MQV is role-independent, for two sessions between the same pair of players $\hat{A}$ and $\hat{B}$ but with the opposite order of DH-component exchange (which may be made by a cross-message attack [6]),[2] player $\hat{A}$ (resp., $\hat{B}$) thinks it is interacting with a responder $\hat{B}$ (resp., $\hat{A}$), while the session-key outputs in these two sessions are the same. That is, two sessions (between the same pair of players) output the *same session-key* but with *role confusion* between each other. The work [16] was (implicitly) clear of this situation, and such a problem is ruled out, by definition, by simply defining two sessions $(\hat{A}, \hat{B}, X, Y)$ and $(\hat{B}, \hat{A}, Y, X)$ to be matching, *no matter whether the two players have matching roles or not.* That is, two sessions with adversary interference under a cross-message attack [6] are defined to be matching. However, from our view, in light of the cross-message attack [6](that causes role confusion between two matching sessions for role-independent IA-DHKE), such a definition of matching sessions is "ill", as it does not well capture the intuition of "intended communication partners" *without adversary interference.* We notice that FHMQV is role-dependent as $(\hat{A}, \hat{B})$ are involved in a fixed order in session-key derivation, and the more natural definition of matching sessions, *where the two players are required to have matching roles,* is used.

A concurrent man-in-the-middle (CMIM) adversary $\mathscr{A}$ controls all the communication channels among concurrent session runs of the KE protocol. In addition, $\mathscr{A}$ is allowed access to secret information via the following three types of queries: (1) state-reveal queries for ongoing incomplete sessions; (2) session-key queries for completed sessions; (3) corruption queries upon which all information in the memory of the corrupted parties will be leaked to $\mathscr{A}$. A session $(\hat{A}, \hat{B}, X, Y)$ is called *exposed,* if itself or its matching session $(\hat{B}, \hat{A}, Y, X)$ suffers from any of these three queries. The session-key security (SK-security) within the CK-framework is captured as follows. For any complete session $(\hat{A}, \hat{B}, X, Y)$ between two *uncorrupted* players $\hat{A}$ and $\hat{B}$, which is adaptively chosen by $\mathscr{A}$ and is referred to as the *test session,* as long as it is unexposed (in particular its matching session, if it exists, was not exposed during its ongoing incomplete

---

[2] In a cross-message attack, an adversary $\mathscr{A}$ *concurrently* interacts, *as the responder,* with $\hat{A}$ (resp., $\hat{B}$) in the name of $\hat{B}$ (resp., $\hat{A}$) in two sessions. After getting X and Y respectively *as the first-round message in both of the two sessions,* it sends Y (resp., X) to $\hat{A}$ (resp., $\hat{B}$) as the second-round message in both of the two sessions. For the basic (H)MQV, both of the two players will output the same session-key in the two sessions but with role confusion.

stage before $\mathscr{A}$ stops[3]) the followings hold with overwhelming probability.
(1) Completeness: the session-key outputs of the test-session and its matching
session are identical. (2) Randomness: $\mathscr{A}$ cannot distinguish, with non-negligible
probability/advantage over $1/2$, the session-key output of the test-session from
a random value.

Here, we would like to stress that, as already explicitly clarified in [6], the SK-
security defined for role-dependent IA-DHKE (referred to as role-dependent SK-
security) and that for role-independent IA-DHKE (referred to as role-independent
SK-security), differentiated by the definition of matching sessions, are
fundamentally incomparable. On the one hand, *any* role-dependent IA-DHKE,
e.g., FHMQV, does not satisfy, by definition, the completeness property of
role-independent SK-security. On the other hand, *any* role-independent IA-DHKE,
e.g., (H)MQV, is totally broken according to role-dependent SK-security (as the
session-key of the test-session can exist in a non-matching session by the cross-
message attack [6]), which might be considered as more dangerous.

3   Overview of HMQV Analysis, and Interplay Between HMQV Protocol Structure and Provable Security

In this section, we present the overview of the HMQV analysis in the CK-
framework, and clarify the underlying interplay between the HMQV protocol
structure and its provable security, and some subtleties actually buried in the
complicated security analysis of HMQV. In particular, we clarify the key role of
the setting mechanism of $d = (X, \hat{B})$ and $e = (Y, \hat{A})$ in the CDH-based security
proof of HMQV assuming no secrecy leakage. In view of the high complexity of
HMQV proof, our clarifications may be of independent interest, and can play a
guide in designing other provably secure protocol variants of HMQV.

3.1   Overview of HMQV Analysis with Secrecy Leakage

Denote by $(\hat{A}, \hat{B}, X_0, Y_0)$ the test-session between two uncorrupted players $\hat{A}$ and
$\hat{B}$, and by $H_K(\sigma_0)$ the corresponding session-key, where $\sigma_0 = (X_0 A^{d_0})^{y_0 + e_0 b}$,
$d_0 = h(X_0, \hat{B})$ and $e_0 = h(Y_0, \hat{A})$. Note that in case the test-session does not
have a matching session, the DH-component Y_0 is actually generated by the
attacker, otherwise it is generated by the uncorrupted player $\hat{B}$ in the matching
session. The provable security of HMQV within the CK-framework, assuming the

---

[3] For IA-DHKE, this makes sense mainly when the test-session is held by a responder. Consider that the attacker first activates an initiator $\hat{A}$ to get X, and then
suspends this session held by $\hat{A}$ till finishing the test-session $(\hat{B}, \hat{A}, Y, X)$ run by $\hat{B}$.
If the session run by $\hat{A}$ is never completed, the DH-exponent x can be exposed to
adversary (while $\hat{A}$ cannot be corrupted as the test-session is required to be between
two uncorrupted players); but if later this session is completed and thus becomes
matching to the test-session, it should be unexposed for the SK-security.

leakage of DH components and exponents,[4] distinguishes two cases, according to whether $\hat{A} = \hat{B}$ or not.

Analysis for the case of $\hat{A} \neq \hat{B}$. On a pair of challenge DH-components $U \in G$ and $B \in G$, a simulator $\mathcal{C}$ runs an attacker $\mathscr{A}$ as an subroutine with the aid of a DDH solver oracle (to make its answers to queries from $\mathscr{A}$ consistent). The public key of the uncorrupted user $\hat{B}$, which is chosen uniformly at random by $\mathcal{C}$ from all players in the system, is set just to be B. The DH-component X_0 to be sent in the test-session, which is also chosen uniformly at random by $\mathcal{C}$ from all the sessions in the system, is just set to be $X_0 = U$. But the public and secret keys of all the other uncorrupted players (other than $\hat{B}$) in the system, and all the DH-components exchanged in all the sessions except the test-session, are just generated by $\mathcal{C}$ itself. Supposing the attacker $\mathscr{A}$ can break the SK-security of HMQV in this case, the goal of the simulator $\mathcal{C}$ is to compute $CDH(X_0, B)$, which then contradicts the GDH assumption.

In the random oracle (RO) model [3] assuming both h and H_K are random oracles, there are only two strategies for the adversary $\mathscr{A}$ to distinguish $H_K(\sigma_0)$ from a random value:

- Key-replication attack. $\mathscr{A}$ succeeds in forcing the establishment of a session (other than the test-session or its matching session) that has the same session-key output as the test-session. In this case, $\mathscr{A}$ can learn the test-session key by simply querying that session to get the same key. To rule out the Key-replication attack, the KEA assumption is employed in [16].
- Forging attack. At some point in its run, with non-negligible probability $\mathscr{A}$ queries the RO, H_K, with the value $\sigma_0 = (X_0 A^{d_0})^{y_0 + e_0 b}$. In this case, the simulator $\mathcal{C}$ always rewinds to the point that $\mathscr{A}$ just made the RO-query $e_0 = h(Y_0, \hat{A})$, redefines $h(Y_0, \hat{A})$ to be a new independently random value $e_0' \in Z_q^*$, and repeats the run of $\mathscr{A}$ from this point. In the repeated run, by the forking lemma [24], $\mathcal{C}$ will get $\sigma_0' = (X_0 A^{d_0'})^{y_0 + e_0' b}$ also with non-negligible probability. As $\hat{A}$ is uncorrupted and its secret-key a is generated by $\mathcal{C}$, from (a, σ_0, σ_0') $\mathcal{C}$ can compute $CDH(X_0, B)$.

Analysis for the case of $\hat{A} = \hat{B}$. The HMQV analysis the case of $\hat{A} = \hat{B}$ further considers two cases according to whether $X_0 = Y_0$ or not. The provable security of HMQV for the case of $X_0 = Y_0$ can be based on the CDH assumption. Below, we focus on the more complicated case of $X_0 \neq Y_0$. Specifically, in comparison with the analysis for the case of $\hat{A} \neq \hat{B}$, the analysis of HMQV for the case of $\hat{A} = \hat{B}$ yet $X_0 \neq Y_0$ makes the following key differences ($\mathcal{C}$ still uses the DDH oracle to ensure answer consistency and the KEA assumption to rule out the possibility of session collisions):

- The DH-component X_0 to be sent at the test-session is set to be $X_0 = U/A^{d_0}$, i.e., $U = X_0 A^{d_0}$.

---

[4] It is clarified in [31] that the provable security of HMQV, in this case, actually does not allow the leakage of all the pre-computable secrecy values; for example, the pre-computable value $y + eb$ or $x + da$ is not allowed to be exposed for the provable security of HMQV in the CK-framework.

- The simulator $\mathcal{C}$ defines the value $d_0 = h(X_0, \hat{B} = \hat{A})$ at the onset of its simulation to ensure that the RO query d_0 is always prior to $e_0 = h(Y_0, \hat{A} = \hat{B})$. Thus, redefining e_0 will not change the value of d_0 and accordingly the value $X_0 = U/A^{d_0}$. *This is allowed by the setting mechanism of $d_0 = h(X_0, \hat{B} = \hat{A})$, because X_0 is generated at the onset of the simulation and $\hat{B} = \hat{A}$ in this case.*
- By redefining the RO-query e_0 to a new random value e_0', and repeating the run of $\mathscr{A}$ from this rewinding point, by the forking lemma the simulator will get $\sigma_0' = (X_0 A^{d_0})^{y_0 + be_0'} = U^{y_0 + be_0'}$. Then, from σ_0 and σ_0', the value $CDH(U, B)$ can be computed, which contradicts the GDH assumption.

3.2   Interplay Between HMQV Protocol Structure and CDH-Based Provable Security Without Secrecy Leakage

The CDH-based security proof of HMQV, assuming no secrecy leakage, is based on the CDH-based security proof of the underlying XCR and HCR signatures defined for HMQV. Here, *the setting mechanism of $d = h(X, \hat{B})$ and $e = h(Y, \hat{A})$ in HMQV plays a key role for the CDH-based provable security of HMQV, assuming no secrecy (particularly any DH component or exponent) leakage.* However, to our knowledge, this subtlety was somewhat buried in the complicated security proof of HMQV, and was not made clear.

In the CDH-based security proof of the underlying XCR and DCR signatures for the provable security HMQV assuming no leakage of DH component or exponent (Theorem 5 and 7, [16]), as noted in Remark 4.3 there, consider the following interaction order between a forger $\mathcal{F}$ and a challenger $\mathcal{C}$ who impersonates the uncorrupted player $\hat{B}$ of public key $B = g^b$ but *without knowing the secret key b*. The forger $\mathcal{F}$ first presents a message, say the peer's identity $\hat{A}$ in the context of HMQV, to be signed by the challenger $\mathcal{C}$. Then, $\mathcal{C}$ randomly take $s \leftarrow Z_q$ and $e \leftarrow \{0,1\}^l$, sets $Y = g^s/B^e (= g^{s-be})$, $h(Y, \hat{A}) = e$ and sends Y back to $\mathcal{F}$. Notice that, from $Y = g^s/B^e = g^{s-be}$, we have that $s = y + be$. Finally, after receiving the DH-challenge X from $\mathcal{F}$, $\mathcal{C}$ sets $d = h(X, \hat{B})$, and returns back $(XA^d)^s (= (XA^d)^{y+be})$ to $\mathcal{F}$ (*though the challenger $\mathcal{C}$ does not know the secret key b*). Such an interaction order between $\mathcal{C}$ and $\mathcal{F}$ corresponds to that the signer plays the role of the initiator in the run of a session of HMQV.

Here, what buried in the above CDH-based security proof of HMQV is: if both X and Y are put into the inputs of d and e, e.g., $d = h(X, Y, \hat{A}, \hat{B})$ and $e = h(Y, X, \hat{A}, \hat{B})$ as in FHMQV, the CDH-based security proof of HMQV will fail. To be precise, in this case, the challenger $\mathcal{C}$ cannot define the value e before receiving the DH-challenge X, as now the value X is also a part of the input of e.

Specifically, consider the following attacker $\mathcal{F}$, who, after receiving Y, makes a list of queries to the RO h with the following forms: $(Y, X_1, \hat{A}, \hat{B}), \cdots, (Y, X_m, \hat{A}, \hat{B})$, where $m > 1$ and for each j, $1 \leq j \leq m$, X_j is taken uniformly at random from G. Only after these RO queries, $\mathcal{F}$ presents X_i as the DH-challenge, where i is taken uniformly at random from $\{1, \cdots, m\}$. For such an attacker, the CDH-based security proofs of XCR or DCR signatures for HMQV in [16] do not work.

On the one hand, when the DH-component $Y = g^s/B^e$ is sent (without knowing the DH-challenge X), the value e (as well as s) has already been determined. Then, for the challenger $\mathcal{C}$ to successfully answer the queries made by $\mathcal{F}$, $\mathcal{C}$ has to correctly guess, before sending Y, the value X_i that is to be used by the forger as the actual DH-challenge in that session. However, the random DH-components $(X_1, \cdots, X_m)$, appearing in the queries to the RO H_K, can only be determined after the value Y is sent and fixed. As each X_j, $1 \leq j \leq m$ is taken uniformly at random from G, $\mathcal{C}$ can correctly guess X_i only with negligible probability.

On the other hand, another way for the challenger $\mathcal{C}$ to bypass the above obstacle is to send Y with d and e being undefined, and only defines the value e after X_i is presented. However, with this approach, to correctly output the value s, the challenger $\mathcal{C}$ needs to compute the discrete logarithm of YB^e, which is infeasible under the DLP assumption.

We conclude that, in any case, the CDH-based security proof of HMQV will get stuck whenever both X and Y are put into the inputs of d and e. However, this subtlety was buried in the security proof of HMQV, and was not made clear to our knowledge.

4   Revisiting FHMQV

The work [25] proposed a variant of HMQV, named FHMQV (that is depicted in Fig. 1),[5] and claimed that FHMQV "preserves the efficiency and security attributes of HMQV" and provides "stronger security than HMQV". The security of FHMQV is analyzed in a variant of the CK-framework for role-dependent IA-DHKE, which is referred to as CK-FHMQV for presentation simplicity.[6] The authors of [25] proposed, as a interesting future research question, to investigate the actual relationship between the CK-framework and the CK-FHMQV variant.

In this section, we first review the CK-FHMQV model, and clarifies the relationship between CK-framework and CK-FHMQV. In particular, we show that CK-HMQV (for role-dependent IA-DHKE) and CK-FHMQV are incomparable. Then, we make a careful investigation of the analysis of FHMQV in the CK-FHMQV model, and identify that the security analysis of FHMQV is actually flawed. The flaws in the security proof of FHMQV just stem from lacking a full realization of the precise yet subtle interplay between HMQV protocol structure and provable security as clarified in Sect. 3.

4.1   On the Relationship Between CK-Framework and the CK-FHMQV Variant

The work of [25] considers a tree like computation of the shard DH-secret, e.g., $K_{\hat{A}} = W^{s_A}$ (referred to as the session signature), where $W = YB^e$ and $s_A =$

---

[5] Actually, the FHMQV can be viewed as variant of a protocol proposed in [28], where $d = h(\hat{A}, A, \hat{B}, B, X, Y)$ and $e = h(d)$.

[6] The work of [25] also considers a variant of the eCK model proposed in [17]. In this work, we mainly focus on the CK-FHMQV variant.

$x + da$. The CK-FHMQV model proposed in [25] follows the CK-framework for role-dependent IA-DHKE, but with the following modifications.

Firstly, in comparison with the traditional CK-framework (for role-dependent IA-DHKE), in the CK-FHMQV model the attacker is provided with a different set of secrecy reveal queries [25].

- $StaticKeyReveal(party)$ to obtain the static private key of a party.
- $SessionKeyReveal(session)$ to obtain the derived session-key in a session.
- $SecretExponentReveal(session)$ to obtain the ephemeral secret exponent, $s = x + da$ or $s = y + eb$, in a session.
- $SecretGroupElementReveal(session)$ to obtain the session signature W^{s_A}.
- $EstablishParty(party)$ to register a static public key on behalf of a party; from there, the party is supposed totally controlled by $\mathscr{A}$. A party, against which this query is not issued, is said to be *honest*.

Let sid be the identifier of a completed session at an honest party $\hat{A}$, with some honest peer $\hat{B}$, and sid^* be the matching session's identifier (in case the matching session exists). The session sid is said to be *unexposed* (*ck-fresh* in [25]), if none of the following conditions hold:

- $\mathscr{A}$ issues a $SecretExponentReveal$ query on sid or sid^* (if sid^* exist).
- $\mathscr{A}$ issues a $SecretGroupElementReveal$ query on sid or sid^*.
- $\mathscr{A}$ issues a $SessionKeyReveal$ query on sid or sid^*.
- sid^* does not exit, and $\mathscr{A}$ makes a $StaticKeyReveal$ query on $\hat{B}$.

Claim 1. *The traditional CK-framework (for role-dependent IA-DHKE) and the CK-FHMQV variant are incomparable.*

Proof. Firstly, the CK-framework allows a more general and flexible *state-reveal* query, which can be dependent upon the actual protocols and allows for various possible IA-DHKE protocol designs. In particular, the queries of $SecretExponentReveal(session)$ and $SecretGroupElementReveal(session)$ specified in the CK-FHMQV model are some specific forms of the more general *state-reveal* query defined in the traditional CK-framework.

Secondly, usually, the *state-reveal* query in the traditional CK-framework can be used to obtain some (*offline pre-computed*) DH components and exponents, as well as some pre-computed components of the session-key, etc. In comparison, the CK-FHMQV model only allows very limited access to the ephemeral DH-exponent. Specifically, through the $StaticKeyReveal(party)$ query and the $SecretExponentReveal(session)$ query, an attacker can retrieve the ephemeral DH-exponent x or y. However, this way implies that the DH-exponent x or y can only be leaked after the value $s = x + da$ or $s = y + eb$ is online generated during a session run and after the static secret-key a or b is exposed. In particular, in the CK-FHMQV model, the DH-exponent x or y is not allowed to be leaked to the attacker at the beginning or before the session run, and the pre-computed DH-components are not allowed to be leaked as well.

Thirdly, the leakage of DH-exponent x or y in the CK-FHMQV model implies the leakage of static secret key a or b. This is unrealistic, as in practice the static secret-key is better protected than the ephemeral DH-exponents.

Fourthly, it is unrealistic for the CK-FHMQV model to provide the attacker the access to the secret exponent $s = x + da$ or $s = y + eb$ and the secret group element W^s, while the DH-exponent x or y is essentially denied to get accessed as clarified above. In practice, the DH-exponents are usually offline pre-computed and stored, which are more vulnerable by adversarial leakage than the more volatile secret exponent s or group element W^s that are usually generated on the fly during a session run and will be erased once the session is finished.

Fifthly, adaptive party corruption is allowed in the CK-framework; that is, an attacker can adaptively corrupt (during its attack) some existing honest parties in the system. Adaptive party corruption is not allowed in CK-FHMQV, where a party is corrupted via the *Establisharty* query *before* it takes part in the system.

Finally, the CK-framework does not explicitly allow attacker to make the *StaticKeyReveal* query, which is, however, explicitly specified for CK-FHMQV. Specifically, the CK-framework for IA-DHKE [16] does not explicitly separate *party corruption* and *StaticKeyReveal*, and the security vulnerabilities against static secret-key leakage (e.g., KCI security and weak forward security) are considered separately in [16].   □

4.2   On the Security Proof of FHMQV in CK-FHMQV Model

The work of [25] showed that the FHMQV is provably secure in the CK-FHMQV model under *merely the CDH assumption*. However, by a careful investigation, we show that the CDH-based security proof in [25] is flawed. The identified flaws just stem from lacking full realization of the precise yet subtle interplay between HMQV protocol structure and provable security as clarified in Sect. 3.

Claim 2. *The CDH-based security proof of FHMQV in the CK-FHMQV model is flawed.*

Proof. The security proof of FHMQV in CK-FHMQV considered two cases: (1) Case E1, where the test-session has the matching session; and (2) Case E2, where the test-session has no matching session. The security proof flaw lies in the analysis of Case E.2. Specifically, in the analysis of Case E2 in [25], when the challenger/simulator $\mathcal{C}$ is activated as a session initiator $\hat{B}$ (interacting with a peer player $\hat{A}$ that may be impersonated by the attacker), $\mathcal{C}$ works as follows: it chooses $s_B \leftarrow Z_q$, $d, e \leftarrow \{0,1\}^l$, sets $Y = g^{s_B} B^{-e}$, $d = h(\star, Y, \hat{A}, \hat{B})$ and $e = h(Y, \star, \hat{A}, \hat{B})$. Then, $\mathcal{C}$ provides the attacker with $(\hat{B}, \hat{A}, Y)$, and stores $(\hat{B}, \hat{A}, Y, \star)$ as an incomplete session (waiting for the DH-challenge X from the attacker). That is, the challenger $\mathcal{C}$ pre-defines d and e with the unknown input X to be received from the attacker. It is claimed in [25] that "when the challenger is later queried with $h(Y, X, \hat{A}, \hat{B})$ (resp., $h(X, Y, \hat{A}, \hat{B})$), it responds with $h(Y, \star, \hat{A}, \hat{B})$ (resp., $h(\star, Y, \hat{A}, \hat{B}))$". This argument is flawed.

Specifically, consider an attacker $\mathscr{A}$, who activates the honest player $\hat{B}$ (simulated by the challenger $\mathcal{C}$) as the session initiator by playing the role of the session responder $\hat{A}$. After receiving Y from $\mathcal{C}$, $\mathcal{A}$ makes a list of queries to the random oracle h with the following forms: $(Y, X_1, \hat{A}, \hat{B}), \cdots, (Y, X_m, \hat{A}, \hat{B})$ and $(X_1, Y, \hat{A}, \hat{B}), \cdots, (X_m, Y, \hat{A}, \hat{B})$, where $m > 1$ and each X_i, $1 \leq i \leq m$, is taken uniformly at random from G. After these RO queries, $\mathcal{F}$ presents X_i as the DH-challenge, where i is taken uniformly at random from $\{1, \cdots, m\}$. For such an attacker, to make the simulation go through, the challenger $\mathcal{C}$ can work in the following two ways.

- For each query $(Y, X_i, \hat{A}, \hat{B})$ (resp., $(X_i, Y, \hat{A}, \hat{B})$), to the random oracle h, it always relies with the pre-defined e (resp., d). But this way clearly indicates inconsistency in simulating the random oracle h.
- $\mathcal{C}$ tries to correctly guess the DH-component X_i, $1 \leq i \leq m$, to be actually used as the DH-component for the session with which the pre-defined Y and (d, e) are involved. But, as each X_i is taken uniformly at random from G, and i is taken uniformly at random from $\{1, \cdots, m\}$, the probability that $\mathcal{C}$ correctly guesses X_i is negligible.

We remark that we do not know how to fix the above flaws in the CDH-based security proof of FHMQV.[7] We also note that such a security proof flaw just stems from lacking the full recognition of the precise yet subtle interplay between HMQV protocol structure and provable security as clarified in Sect. 3 (particularly for the CDH-based security analysis of HMQV).

Flaws in security proof of FXCR and FDCR signatures. The CDH-based security proof of FHMQV in CK-FHMQV was relied upon that of the underlying building tools, named FXCR signature and FDCR signature. We show that the CDH-based security proofs of FXCR and FDCR signatures in [25] are also flawed. The security proof of FXCR signature in [25] only considered a regular interaction order: the attacker presents (σ, X) where σ denotes the message to be signed, and the challenger $\mathcal{C}$ (simulating the signer $\hat{B}$ but without knowing the secret key b) sets $s_B \leftarrow Z_q$, $Y = g^{s_B} B^{-e}(= g^{s_B - be})$, defines $e = h(X, Y, m)$, and responds (Y, X^{s_B}) to the attacker. Notice that, from $Y = g^{s_B} B^{-e}(= g^{s_B - be})$, we have that $s_B = y + be$. Here, a key point is: the challenger $\mathcal{C}$ defines Y and e on the fly only after seeing the DH-challenge X. This situation corresponds to that the signer plays the role of the responder in a session run of FHMQV. However, suppose the signer plays the role of the session initiator, i.e., $\mathcal{C}$ first forwards $Y = g^{s_B} B^{-e}$ to the attacker, and then receives the DH-challenge X. In this case, the CDH-based security proof of FXCR signature fails in general. The reason is that, the value $e = h(X, Y, \sigma)$ is undefined when sending Y before receiving X. As X is a random value in G, it is infeasible for the challenger $\mathcal{C}$ to correctly guess this value when defining Y. Specifically, as clarified in Sect. 3.2 about the CDH-based security proof of HMQV, consider

---

[7] According to our investigation, FHMQV might be proved secure under the stronger GDH assumption, with the underlying security proof, nevertheless, being significantly changed. But our result indicates that the CDH-based security proof of FHMQV, which was claimed in [25] as one of the major security advantages of FHMQV, is indeed flawed.

an attacker who, after receiving Y, make a list of queries to the random oracle h with the forms $(X_1, Y, \sigma), \cdots, (X_m, Y, \sigma)$. The same flaw applies to the CDH-based security proof of FDCR signature as well. $\square$

Acknowledgments. We are grateful to the anonymous referees for many helpful suggestions.

References

1. American National Standard (ANSI) X9.42-2001. Public Key Cryptography for the Financial Services Industry: Agreement of Symmetric Keys Using Discrete Logarithm Cryptography
2. American National Standard (ANSI) X9.42-2001. Public Key Cryptography for the Financial Services Industry: Agreement of Symmetric Keys Using Elliptic Curve Cryptography
3. Bellare, M., Rogaway, P.: Random oracles are practical: a paradigm for designing efficient protocols. In: ACM Conference on Computer and Communications Security, pp. 62–73 (1993)
4. Canetti, R.: Security and composition of cryptographic protocols: a tutorial. SIGACT News **37**(3,4), 67–92 (2006)
5. Canetti, R., Krawczyk, H.: Analysis of key-exchange protocols and their use for building secure channels. In: Pfitzmann, B. (ed.) EUROCRYPT 2001. LNCS, vol. 2045, pp. 453–474. Springer, Heidelberg (2001). Available also from Cryptology ePrint Archive, Report No. 2001/040
6. Cremers, C.: Formally and practically relating the CK, CK-HMQV, and eCK security models for authenticated key exchange. Cryptology ePrint Archive, Report 2009/253, 2009. Extended abstract appears in AsiaCCS 2011
7. Damgård, I.B.: Towards practical public key systems secure against chosen ciphertext attacks. In: Feigenbaum, J. (ed.) CRYPTO 1991. LNCS, vol. 576, pp. 445–456. Springer, Heidelberg (1992)
8. Dierks, T., Allen, C.: The TLS Protocol, Version 1.0. Request for Comments: 2246, January 1999
9. Diffie, W., Hellman, M.: New directions in cryptography. IEEE Trans. Inf. Theory **22**(6), 644–654 (1976)
10. IEEE 1363–2000: Standard Specifications for Public Key Cryptography
11. ISO/IEC IS 15946-3. Information Technology - Security Techniques - Cryptographic Techniques Based on Elliptic Curves - Part 3: Key Establishment (2002)
12. ISO/IEC. Identification Cards Integrated Circuit Cards Programming Interface Part 6: Registration procedures for the authentication protocols for interoperability. Technical report ISO/IEC FDIS 24727-6, International Organization for Standardization, Geneva, Switzerland (2009)
13. Kaliski, B.: An unknown key-share attack on the MQV key agreement protocol. ACM Trans. Inf. Syst. Secur. (TISSEC) **4**(3), 275–288 (2001)
14. Krawczyk, H.: SIGMA: the 'SIGn-and-MAc' approach to authenticated Diffie-Hellman and its use in the IKE protocols. In: Boneh, D. (ed.) CRYPTO 2003. LNCS, vol. 2729, pp. 400–425. Springer, Heidelberg (2003)
15. Kaufman, C.: Internet Key Exchange (IKEv2) Protocol. INTERNET-DRAFT, The Internet Engineering Task Force (2002)

16. Krawczyk, H.: HMQV: a high-performance secure Diffie-Hellman protocol. In: Shoup, V. (ed.) CRYPTO 2005. LNCS, vol. 3621, pp. 546–566. Springer, Heidelberg (2005)
17. LaMacchia, B.A., Lauter, K., Mityagin, A.: Stronger security of authenticated key exchange. In: Susilo, W., Liu, J.K., Mu, Y. (eds.) ProvSec 2007. LNCS, vol. 4784, pp. 1–16. Springer, Heidelberg (2007)
18. Matsumoto, T., Takashima, Y., Imai, H.: On seeking smart public-key distribution systems. Trans. IECE Jpn. **E69**(2), 99–106 (1986)
19. Menezes, A., Qu, M., Vanstone, S.: Some new key agreement protocols providing mutual implicit authentication. In: Second Workshop on Selected Areas in Cryptography (SAC'95) (1995)
20. Menezes, A., Ustaoglu, B.: On the importance of public-key validation in the MQV and HMQV key agreement protocols. In: Barua, R., Lange, T. (eds.) INDOCRYPT 2006. LNCS, vol. 4329, pp. 133–147. Springer, Heidelberg (2006)
21. NIST Special Publication 800–56 (DRAFT): Recommendation on Key Establishment Schemes. Draft 2, January 2003
22. NSAs Elliptic Curve Licensing Agreement. Presentation by Mr. John Stasak (Cryptography Office, National Security Agency) to the IETF's Security Area Advisory Group, November 2004
23. Okamoto, T., Pointcheval, D.: The gap-problems: a new class of problems for the security of cryptographic schemes. In: Kim, K. (ed.) PKC 2001. LNCS, vol. 1992, pp. 104–118. Springer, Heidelberg (2001)
24. Pointcheval, D., Stern, J.: Security arguments for digital signatures and blind signatures. J. Cryptol. **13**, 361–396 (2000)
25. Sarr, A.P., Elbaz-Vincent, P., Bajard, J.-C.: A secure and efficient authenticated Diffie–Hellman protocol. In: Martinelli, F., Preneel, B. (eds.) EuroPKI 2009. LNCS, vol. 6391, pp. 83–98. Springer, Heidelberg (2010)
26. SP 800–56 (DRAFT), Special Publication 800–56, Recommendation for Pair-Wise Key Establishment Schemes Using Discrete Logarithm Cryptography, National Institute of Standards and Technology, July 2005
27. Yao, A.C., Zhao, Y.: On-line Efficient, Deniable and Non-Malleable Key-Exchange Methods, Domestic patent (in Chinese), No. 200710047344.8, August 2007
28. Yao, A.C., Zhao, Y.: Method and Structure for Self-Sealed Joint Proof-of-Knowledge and Diffie-Hellman Key-Exchange Protocols. PCT Patent. August 2008. This is the PCT version of [27], with [27] serving as the priority reference
29. Yao, A.C., Zhao, Y.: Deniable internet key exchange. In: Zhou, J., Yung, M. (eds.) ACNS 2010. LNCS, vol. 6123, pp. 329–348. Springer, Heidelberg (2010)
30. Yao, A.C., Zhao, Y.: A New Family of Implicitly Authenticated Diffie-Hellman Protocols. Cryptology ePrint Archive: Report 2011/035
31. Yao, A.C., Zhao, Y.: OAKE: A new family of implicitly authenticated Diffie-Hellman protocols. ACM CCS (2013, to appear)
32. Yoneyama, K., Zhao, Y.: Taxonomical security consideration of authenticated key exchange resilient to intermediate computation leakage. In: Boyen, X., Chen, X. (eds.) ProvSec 2011. LNCS, vol. 6980, pp. 348–365. Springer, Heidelberg (2011)

RSA-OAEP is RKA Secure

Dingding Jia[1,2](✉), Bao Li[1], Xianhui Lu[1], and Yamin Liu[1]

[1] Institute of Information Engineering,
Chinese Academy of Sciences, Beijing, China
[2] Data Assurance and Computation Security,
University of Chinese Academy of Sciences, Beijing, China
{ddjia,lb,xhlu,ymliu}@is.ac.cn

Abstract. In this paper we show that RSA-OAEP is secure against related key attacks (RKA) in the random oracle model under the strong RSA (sRSA) assumption. The key related functions can be affine functions. Compared to the chosen ciphertext security proof of OAEP, we overcome two major obstacles: answering the decryption queries under related keys; and preventing the adversary from promoting queries that are corresponding to the same message with the challenge ciphertext. These two obstacles also exist in the RKA security proof of RSA-OAEP+ and RSA-SAEP$^+$. By combining our technique and the chosen ciphertext security proofs, RSA-OAEP+ and RSA-SAEP$^+$ can also be proved RKA secure. In our proof, the security of the scheme relies substantially on the algebraic property of the sRSA function.

Keywords: Related key attack · RSA-OAEP · Strong RSA assumption · RSA assumption

1 Introduction

Since "cold-boot" attacks demonstrated a practical threat to cryptography systems [15], researchers have contributed much effort to constructing schemes against side channel attacks. Among these attacks there is one kind called related key attacks (RKA) [8], which means that attackers can modify keys stored in the memory and observe the outcome of the cryptographic primitive under this modified key [9,11].

In this paper we study the security of public key encryption (PKE) schemes against chosen ciphertext RKA (CC-RKA), which is formulated by Bellare et al. [3]. Following the original theory given by Bellare and Kohno [4], the definition is parameterized by a class of Φ functions that the adversary can apply to the secret key. As denoted by Bellare et al. [5], let S be the secret key space. If S

This work is Supported by the National Basic Research Program of China (973 project)(No. 2013CB338002), the National Nature Science Foundation of China (No. 61070171, No. 61272534), the Strategic Priority Research Program of Chinese Academy of Sciences under Grant XDA06010702 and IIE's Cryptography Research Project (No.Y3Z0027103, No.Y3Z0024103).

D. Lin et al. (Eds.): Inscrypt 2013, LNCS 8567, pp. 270–281, 2014.
DOI: 10.1007/978-3-319-12087-4_17

is a group, $\Phi^{\text{lin}} = \{\phi_a\}_{a \in S}$ denotes the class of linear functions; if S is a ring, $\Phi^{\text{affine}} = \{\phi_{a,b}\}_{a,b \in S}$ denotes the class of affine functions; $\Phi^{\text{poly}(d)}$ denotes the class of polynomial functions bounded by degree d.

Bellare, Cash and Miller [3] showed that CC-RKA secure PKE can be transformed from RKA secure pseudorandom functions (PRF) and RKA secure identity based encryption (IBE) separately for the same class of Φ. In [2] Bellare and Cash gave a framework of building RKA secure PRFs for $\Phi = \Phi^{\text{lin}}$. In [5] Bellare, Paterson and Thomson gave a framework of building RKA secure IBE for $\Phi = \Phi^{\text{poly}(d)}$. So by combining [2,3], a Φ-CC-RKA secure PKE for $\Phi = \Phi^{\text{lin}}$ can be achieved; and by combining [3,5], a Φ-CC-RKA secure PKE for $\Phi = \Phi^{\text{poly}(d)}$ can be achieved. In [19] Wee proposed a framework of constructing Φ-CC-RKA secure PKE from adaptive trapdoor relations for $\Phi = \Phi^{\text{lin}}$.

The OAEP scheme was introduced by Bellare and Rogaway [7] to build CCA secure PKE from one way trapdoor permutations. RSA-OAEP is the industry-wide standard for RSA encryption (PKCS#1 version 2, IEEE P1363). In 2001, Shoup [18] pointed out that the CCA security proof against OAEP under one way trapdoor permutations had some flaw and presented a modified scheme named OAEP+ that can be proved CCA secure under one-way trapdoor permutation. And Fujisaki and Okamoto et al. [13,14] showed that RSA-OAEP was secure under the RSA assumption in the same year. Later Boneh [10] gave simplified versions called SAEP and SAEP$^+$, they also proved that RSA-SAEP$^+$ was secure under the RSA assumption, with restrictions that the reduction was not tight and the "message expansion rate" was not good enough. However, as far as we know, the security of the OAEP against RKA has not been studied.

Our Result. In this paper we prove that RSA-OAEP is Φ-CC-RKA secure for $\Phi = \Phi^{\text{affine}}$ in the random oracle model under the strong RSA (sRSA) assumption [1]. In the security proof we overcome two major obstacles:

- Firstly, how the queries (ϕ, C) are answered? In the CCA security proofs of previous works such as RSA-OAEP, RSA-OAEP+, RSA-SAEP$^+$, the adversary answers the decryption queries by traversing the queries to the random oracles G, H, computing the corresponding s', t' and checking whether there is some s', t' satisfying $(s' \| t')^e = C$. Here we denote the affine function as $\phi(d) = ad + b$, and the checking equation should be $(s' \| t')^{e'} = C$ for some e'. However, we cannot computing such a e' according to the equation $s' \| t' = C^{ad+b}$. We construct a new equation by raising both sides of the previous equation to the e-th power, hence get that $(s' \| t')^e = C^{a+be}$. So we can find the message corresponding to (ϕ, C) by checking the equation above.
- Secondly, can the adversary promote a (ϕ, C) such that $C^{\phi(sk)} = C^{*sk}$ and thus corresponding to the same message with C^*? Here for any probabilistic polynomial time (PPT) adversary $\mathcal{A}$ that can produce such a query, we can build a PPT adversary $\mathcal{B}$ to break the sRSA assumption.

Using similar methodology, we can prove that RSA-OAEP+ and RSA-SAEP$^+$ are also secure in the random oracle model under the sRSA assumption. Note that our proof relies substantially on the algebraic properties of the sRSA assumption. Whether OAEP is Φ-CC-RKA secure under the partial-domain one-wayness and whether OAEP+ is Φ-CC-RKA secure under the one-wayness respectively of the underlying permutation are still open problems. Another open problem is whether Φ can be extended to the class of polynomial functions or even larger classes.

The rest of our paper is organized as follows: in Sect. 2 we give definitions and preliminaries; in Sect. 3 we review the construction of RSA-OAEP and prove its security against RKA; Sect. 4 is the conclusion of the whole paper.

2   Definitions and Preliminaries

2.1   Notation

We use PPT as the abbreviation of probabilistic polynomial time. Let $l(X)$ denote the bit length of X. Let X and Y be probability spaces on a finite set S, the statistical distance $SD(X,Y)$ between X and Y is defined as $SD(X,Y) := \frac{1}{2}\Sigma_{\alpha \in S} |\Pr_X[\alpha] - \Pr_Y[\alpha]|$. For a bitstring z, $z[k_1...k_2]$ is used to denote the k_1-th to the k_2-th bit of z. Let k be the security parameter.

2.2   Random Oracle Model

To analyze the security of certain natural constructions, Bellare and Rogaway introduced an idealized world called the random oracle model [6]. We say a construction is in the random oracle model if at least one function in the construction has the following property: before querying the function at a new point, the output is completely random distributed in the range and after querying the function, the output is fixed. Although security in the random oracle model does not imply security in the real world [12], and Kiltz and Pietrzak have proved that no instantiated OAEP can be black-box proved secure in [16], we believe that our proof still has some heuristic significance.

2.3   Public Key Encryption

A Public key encryption scheme (PKE) is a tuple of four PPT algorithms: (**Setup, Keygen, Enc, Dec.**)

$Setup(1^k)$: take as input the security parameter k and output public parameters pp.

$Keygen(pp)$: take as input the public parameters pp and output a pair of keys (pk, sk).

$Enc(pk, m)$: take as input public key pk and message m and output a ciphertext C.

$Dec(sk, C)$: take as input the ciphertext C and secret key sk and output the message m.

For correctness, we require that all properly generated ciphertexts can be decrypted correctly.

Here we give the formal definition of Φ-CC-RKA security, here Φ represents a class of functions that the adversary can apply to the secret keys. The RKAsecurity of a PKE scheme is defined using the following game between an adversary $\mathcal{A}$ and a challenger.

Setup: The challenger runs the key generation algorithm to generate the public and secret keys. $Keygen(pp) \rightarrow (pk, sk)$. Then it sends pk to the adversary $\mathcal{A}$, and keeps the secret key sk to itself.

Phase 1: $\mathcal{A}$ adaptively issues queries (ϕ, C) where $\phi \in \Phi$, the challenger responds with $Dec(\phi(sk), C)$.

Challenge: $\mathcal{A}$ gives two messages (m_0, m_1) to the challenger. The challenger picks a random bit b and responds with $Enc(pk, m_b)$.

Phase 2: $\mathcal{A}$ adaptively issues additional queries as in Phase 1, with the restriction that $(\phi(sk), C) \neq (sk, C^*)$.

Guess: $\mathcal{A}$ outputs a guess b' of b.

The advantage of $\mathcal{A}$ is defined as $Adv_{\mathcal{A},\Phi} = \left| \Pr[b' = b] - \frac{1}{2} \right|$.

Definition 1 (Φ-CC-RKA Security). *A PKE scheme is Φ-CC-RKA secure if for all PPT adversary $\mathcal{A}$, $Adv_{\mathcal{A},\Phi}$ is negligible in k.*

Here our security definition follows the definition given by Bellare et al. [3]. However, in [3] it is required that the public key is completely determined by the secret key, but in our paper part of the elements in the public key can be randomly chosen and irrelevant to the secret key.

2.4 Complexity Assumptions

Strong RSA Assumption (sRSA). The strong RSA assumption is an assumption that is firstly promoted by Barić and Pfitzmann in [1]. In this paper we state the sRSA assumption that is slightly different from that in [1]:

Let $IGen$ be a PPT algorithm that, on input a security parameter k, generates $(N = PQ, P, Q)$, where P, Q are two random primes with similar size. Choose a random $y \in \mathbb{Z}_N^*$. The advantage of $\mathcal{A}$ is defined as

$$Adv_{\mathcal{A}}^{sRSA} = \Pr[x^e = y \ (\mathrm{mod}\, N) \wedge x \in \mathbb{Z}_N^* \wedge e > 1, \text{where } (x, e) \leftarrow \mathcal{A}(N, y)].$$

Definition 2 (sRSA). *We say that $IGen$ satisfies the sRSA assumption if for all PPT algorithm $\mathcal{A}$, $Adv_{\mathcal{A}}^{sRSA}$ is negligible in k.*

RSA Assumption. Let $IGen$ be a PPT algorithm that, on input a security parameter k, generates $(N = PQ, P, Q)$, where P, Q are two random primes with similar size. Choose random $y, e \in \mathbb{Z}_N^*$ with the restriction that $(e, \varphi(N)) = 1$. The advantage of $\mathcal{A}$ is defined as

$$Adv_{\mathcal{A}}^{RSA} = \Pr[x^e = y \ (\mathrm{mod}\, N) \wedge x \in \mathbb{Z}_N^*, \text{where } x \leftarrow \mathcal{A}(N, e, y)].$$

Definition 3 (RSA). *We say that IGen satisfies the RSA assumption if for all PPT algorithm $\mathcal{A}$, $Adv_{\mathcal{A}}^{RSA}$ is negligible in k.*

It is easy to see that the RSA assumption can be implied by the sRSA assumption.

3　RSA-OAEP Is RKA Secure

In this section we first recall the RSA-OAEP scheme that is proposed by Bellare and Rogway in [7]. Then we prove that RSA-OAEP is Φ-CC-RKA secure in the random oracle model under the sRSA assumption, where Φ is a family of affine functions.

Let k_0, k_1 be parameters satisfying $k_0 + k_1 < k$ and $2^{-k_0}, 2^{-k_1}$ are negligible. The length of encrypted messages m is n, where $n = k - k_0 - k_1$. Let G, H be random oracles that will be used in the RSA-OAEP scheme.

$$G : \{0,1\}^{k_0} \rightarrow \{0,1\}^{n+k_1},$$

$$H : \{0,1\}^{n+k_1} \rightarrow \{0,1\}^{k_0}.$$

$Keygen(1^k)$: The key generation algorithm runs $IGen(k) \rightarrow (N, P, Q)$, it chooses a random $e \in \mathbb{Z}_N^*$ satisfying $(e, \varphi(N)) = 1$ and computes d such that $ed = 1(\mathrm{mod}\ \varphi(N))$. The public key is set as $pk = (N, e)$ and the secret key is set as $sk = d$.

$Enc(pk, m)$: The encryption algorithm chooses random $r \in \{0,1\}^{k_0}$ and computes the ciphertext C as:

$$s = G(r) \oplus (m\|0^{k_1}) \tag{1}$$

$$t = H(s) \oplus r \tag{2}$$

$$w = s\|t \tag{3}$$

$$C = w^e \ (\mathrm{mod}\ N) \tag{4}$$

$Dec(C, sk)$: The decryption algorithm computes $w = C^d \ (\mathrm{mod}\ N)$, it sets the fist $n + k_1$ bit of w as s and the rest k_0 bit as t, then it computes

$$r = H(s) \oplus t \tag{5}$$

$$M = G(r) \oplus s \tag{6}$$

$$z = M[n...n + k_1 - 1] \tag{7}$$

If $z = 0^{k_1}$, the algorithm outputs $m = M[0...n - 1]$ and rejects otherwise.

3.1　Security Proof

Theorem 1. *Let $\mathcal{A}$ be a Φ-CC-RKA adversary against the RSA-OAEP scheme with advantage ϵ and running time t, making q_D, q_G and q_H queries to the decryption oracle, random oracles G and H respectively, Φ being a family of affine functions, then we can construct an adversary $\mathcal{B}$ breaking the sRSA problem with advantage ϵ' and time t', where $\epsilon' \geq \frac{A(A-B)}{2Aq_D - Bq_D + 1}$ and $t' \leq t + q_G \cdot q_H \cdot \mathcal{O}(k^3)$. Here $A = 2\epsilon - \frac{2q_D}{2^{k_1}} - \frac{2q_D q_G + q_D + q_G}{2^{k_0}}$ and $B = 2^{2k_0 - k + 6}$.*

First let us reproduce two lemmas that will be used in our proof.

Lemma 1 *[13]. For any probability events E, F and G,*

$$\Pr[E \wedge F | G] \leq \begin{cases} \Pr[E | F \wedge G] \\ \Pr[F | G] \end{cases}$$

Lemma 2 *[13]. Let $\mathcal{A}$ be an algorithm that outputs a q-set containing $k - k_0$ of the most significant bits of the e-th root of its input (partial-domain RSA, for any $2^{k-1} < N < 2^k$, with $k > 2k_0$), within time bound t, with probability ϵ. Then there exists an algorithm $\mathcal{B}$ that solves the RSA problem (N, e) with success probability ϵ', within time bound t', where*

$$\epsilon' \geq \epsilon \times (\epsilon - 2^{2k_0 - k + 6}),$$

$$t' \leq 2t + q^2 \times \mathcal{O}(k^3).$$

Proof (of Theorem 1). Similar to that in [13], we prove Theorem 1 in two steps. Firstly, we present a reduction from a Φ-CC-RKA adversary $\mathcal{A}$ to an adversary $\mathcal{B}$ breaking the sRSA assumption. And then we analyze the success probability.

Suppose that the public key is (N, e) and the secret key is d. The challenge ciphertext is denoted by C^*. We denote the affine function in the decryption query (C, ϕ) as $\phi(x) = ax + b$. Let G-List, H-List be query/answer lists for the oracles G and H respectively, both are initially set to empty lists.

The Simulation Process. $\mathcal{B}$ receives (N, y) and its task is to compute $(x, \bar{e})$ such that $y = x^{\bar{e}} \pmod{N}$. $\mathcal{B}$ picks a random $e \in \mathbb{Z}_N^*$ and sends (N, e) as the public key to $\mathcal{A}$.

When $\mathcal{A}$ submits (m_0, m_1), $\mathcal{B}$ selects a random bit b, sets $C^* = y$ as the ciphertext of m_b and sends C^* to $\mathcal{A}$. $\mathcal{B}$ simulates the answers to the queries of $\mathcal{A}$ to the decryption oracle and random oracles G and H respectively. The description of the simulations are given below.

When $\mathcal{A}$ outputs an answer b', $\mathcal{B}$ checks its H-List and gets the partial pre-image s^* of y if such an s^* has been found. Then by applying Lemma 2, one can find a w^* such that $w^{*e} = y$ and thus solve the sRSA problem.

The simulation of random oracles G and H are the same with that in [13] and we put the concrete process in the appendix.

Simulation of the Decryption Oracle. Whenever $\mathcal{A}$ submits a decryption query (ϕ, C), $\mathcal{B}$ traverses all pairs $(\gamma, G_\gamma) \in$ G-List and $(\delta, H_\delta) \in$ H-List. For each pair from both lists, it defines

$$\sigma = \delta, \tau = \gamma \oplus H_\delta, \mu = G_\gamma \oplus \delta,$$

and checks whether

$$(\sigma \| \tau)^e = C^{a+be} \text{ and } \mu[n...n + k_1 - 1] = 0^{k_1}$$

If both equations hold, $\mathcal{B}$ outputs $m = \mu[0...n-1]$ and rejects the query (ϕ, C) if no such pair is found. Note that when $(\sigma\|\tau)^e = C^{a+be}$ then $C^{\phi(d)} = C^{ad+b} = (\sigma\|\tau)^{\frac{e(ad+b)}{a+be}} = \sigma\|\tau$, so the decryption process is correct.   □

Notations. We denote by w, s, t, r, m, z the values related to the decryption query C, and by $w^*, s^*, t^*, r^*, m^*, z^*$ the values related to the challenge ciphertext C^*. Since y is defined to be the encryption of m_b with random value r^*, so $r^* \leftarrow H(s^*) \oplus t^*$ and $G(r^*) \leftarrow s^* \oplus (m_b\|0^{k_1})$.

For analysis, we define the following events as that in [13].

- AskG denotes the event that r^* has been asked to G. And AskH denotes the event that s^* has been asked to H.
- GBad denotes the event that r^* has been asked to G, but the answer is something other than $s^* \oplus (m_b\|0^{k_1})$.
- DBad denotes the event of decryption failure. And let us denote Bad= DBad∨GBad.

Note that the event GBad implies AskG.

For every query (ϕ, C) to the decryption oracle:

- CBad denotes the union of the bad events, CBad = RBad ∨ SBad, where
  - SBad denotes the event that $s = s^*$;
  - RBad denotes the event that $r = r^*$, which means that $H(s) \oplus t = H(s^*) \oplus t^*$.
- AskRS denotes the intersection of both events about the oracle queries, AskRS = AskR ∧ AskS, which means both r and s has been asked to G and H respectively,
  - AskR denotes the event that $r(= H(s) \oplus t)$ has been asked to G;
  - AskS denotes the event that s has been asked to H;
- Fail denotes the event that the above decryption simulator outputs a wrong decryption answer to query (ϕ, C). Therefore, in the global reduction, the event DBad will be set to true as soon as one decryption simulation fails, so $\Pr[\text{DBad}] \leq q_D \cdot \Pr[\text{Fail}]$.

Analysis of the Decryption Simulation. From the simulation procedure, we can see that for the ciphertext with the corresponding r and s having been asked to G and H respectively, the simulation will output the correct answer. However, it will reject ciphertexts that are valid but the corresponding r and s have never been asked to the random oracles G and H, so the Fail event is limited to the situation in which the simulation rejects a ciphertext which would be accepted by the actual decryption oracle.

Let event E be that RBad ∧ ¬AskR ∧ SBad ∧ ¬AskH, it means that $r = r^*$ and $s = s^*$, neither r nor s has been asked to the random oracles. Furthermore, it means that $w = w^*$, and the adversary $\mathcal{A}$ produces a query (C, ϕ) such that $C^{\phi(d)} = y^d$, then $y = C^{\frac{ad+b}{d}} = C^{a+be}$ and $\mathcal{B}$ can solve the sRSA problem with answer $(C, a + be)$. So we have $\Pr[\text{E}] \leq \epsilon'$.

Now let us analyze the probability of the event Fail, while ¬AskH occurs.

$$\Pr[\text{Fail}|\neg\text{AskH}] = \Pr[\text{Fail} \wedge \text{E}|\neg\text{AskH}] + \Pr[\text{Fail} \wedge \neg\text{E}|\neg\text{AskH}]$$
$$\leq \Pr[\text{E}] + \Pr[\text{Fail} \wedge \neg\text{E}|\neg\text{AskH}]$$
$$\leq \epsilon' + \Pr[\text{Fail} \wedge \neg\text{E}|\neg\text{AskH}]$$
$$\leq \Pr[\text{Fail} \wedge \text{CBad} \wedge \neg\text{E}|\neg\text{AskH}] + \Pr[\text{Fail} \wedge \neg\text{CBad} \wedge \text{AskRS}|\neg\text{AskH}]$$
$$+ \Pr[\text{Fail} \wedge \neg\text{CBad} \wedge \neg\text{AskRS}|\neg\text{AskH}] + \epsilon'$$

Note that when ¬CBad ∧ AskRS happens, the simulation is perfect and cannot fail, so $\Pr[\text{Fail} \wedge \neg\text{CBad} \wedge \text{AskRS}|\neg\text{AskH}] = 0$.

The analysis of the third item is the same as that in [13], here we put the concrete process in the appendix. In a word, we can get that

$$\Pr[\text{Fail} \wedge \neg\text{CBad} \wedge \neg\text{AskRS}|\neg\text{AskH}] \leq 2^{-k_1} + q_G \cdot 2^{-k_0}.$$

Now let us focus on the first item, since

$$\text{CBad} = \text{SBad} \vee \text{RBad} = \text{SBad} \vee (\text{RBad} \wedge \neg\text{SBad}),$$

Then

$$\Pr[\text{Fail} \wedge \text{CBad} \wedge \neg\text{E}|\neg\text{AskH}] \leq \Pr[\text{Fail} \wedge \text{SBad} \wedge \neg\text{E}|\neg\text{AskH}] + \Pr[\text{Fail} \wedge \neg\text{SBad} \wedge \text{RBad}|\neg\text{AskH}]$$

$$\leq \Pr[\text{Fail} \wedge \neg\text{E}|\text{SBad} \wedge \neg\text{AskH}] + \Pr[\text{RBad}|\neg\text{SBad} \wedge \neg\text{AskH}] \tag{8}$$

$$\leq \Pr[\text{Fail} \wedge \neg\text{E}|\text{SBad} \wedge \neg\text{AskH}] + 2^{-k_0} \tag{9}$$

$$\leq \Pr[\text{Fail} \wedge \text{AskR}|\text{SBad} \wedge \neg\text{AskH}] + \Pr[\text{Fail} \wedge \neg\text{AskR} \wedge \neg\text{E}|\text{SBad} \wedge \neg\text{AskH}] + 2^{-k_0} \tag{10}$$

$$\leq \Pr[\text{AskR}|\text{SBad} \wedge \neg\text{AskH}] + \Pr[\text{Fail} \wedge \neg\text{E}|\neg\text{AskR} \wedge \text{SBad} \wedge \neg\text{AskH}] + 2^{-k_0} \tag{11}$$

$$\leq q_G \cdot 2^{-k_0} + \Pr[\text{Fail} \wedge \neg\text{E}|\neg\text{AskR} \wedge \text{SBad} \wedge \neg\text{AskH}] + 2^{-k_0} \tag{12}$$

$$\leq (q_G + 1) \cdot 2^{-k_0} + 2^{-k_1} \tag{13}$$

In Eq. 8 can be acquired according to Lemma 1. Equation 9 is split according to the event AskR. The computation of the probability inequations are the same as that in [13] and we put the formal explanation in the appendix.

To sum up, we got that

$$\Pr[\text{Fail}|\neg\text{AskH}] \leq \frac{2}{2^{k_1}} + \frac{2q_G + 1}{2^{k_0}} + \epsilon'.$$

Success Probability. First let us analyze the probability that $\mathcal{B}$ outputs the partial pre-image s^* of y, that is the probability of the event AskH occurs during the reduction.

Split event AskH according to event Bad:

$$\Pr[\text{AskH}] = \Pr[\text{AskH} \wedge \text{Bad}] + \Pr[\text{AskH} \wedge \neg\text{Bad}].$$

The analyze of the two items on the righthand side is almost the same with that in [14] and we put the formal analysis in the appendix.

$$\Pr[\text{AskH} \wedge \text{Bad}] \geq \Pr[\text{Bad}] - \frac{2q_D}{2^{k_1}} - \frac{2q_D q_G + q_D + q_G}{2^{k_0}} - q_D \epsilon'.$$

$$\Pr[\mathtt{AskH} \wedge \neg \mathtt{Bad}] \geq 2\epsilon - \Pr[\mathtt{Bad}].$$

Then

$$\Pr[\mathtt{AskH}] \geq 2\epsilon - \frac{2q_D}{2^{k_1}} - \frac{2q_D q_G + q_D + q_G}{2^{k_0}} - q_D \epsilon'.$$

From Lemma 2 one can get that

$$\epsilon' \geq (2\epsilon - \frac{2q_D}{2^{k_1}} - \frac{2q_D q_G + q_D + q_G}{2^{k_0}} - q_D \epsilon') \times (2\epsilon - \frac{2q_D}{2^{k_1}} - \frac{2q_D q_G + q_D + q_G}{2^{k_0}} - q_D \epsilon' - 2^{2k_0 - k + 6})$$

Let $A = 2\epsilon - \frac{2q_D}{2^{k_1}} - \frac{2q_D q_G + q_D + q_G}{2^{k_0}}$ and $B = 2^{2k_0 - k + 6}$, hence

$$\epsilon' \geq (A - q_D \epsilon')(A - B - q_D \epsilon')$$
$$(1 + 2Aq_D - Bq_D)\epsilon' \geq q_D^2 \epsilon'^2 + A(A - B)$$
$$(1 + 2Aq_D - Bq_D)\epsilon' > A(A - B)$$
$$\epsilon' > \frac{A(A - B)}{2Aq_D - Bq_D + 1}$$

Note that the running time of the simulator includes the modular multiplication for all possible pairs and thus bounded by $q_H \cdot q_G \cdot \mathcal{O}(k^3)$. Hence the whole running time is $t' = t + q_H \cdot q_G \cdot \mathcal{O}(k^3)$.

By combining the original proofs in [10, 18]) and our proof methodology, one can prove that RSA-OAEP+ (RSA-SAEP$^+$) is secure under the sRSA assumption as well.

4   Conclusion

In this paper we show that RSA-OAEP is Φ-CC-RKA secure in the random oracle model under the sRSA assumption, where Φ is a family of affine functions. Using similar techniques, we can also prove that RSA-OAEP+ and RSA-SAEP$^+$ are RKA secure. Note that our proof relies substantially on the algebraic properties of the sRSA assumption. Whether OAEP is Φ-CC-RKA secure under the partial-domain one-wayness or whether OAEP is Φ-CC-RKA secure under the one-wayness respectively of the underlying permutation are still open problems. Another open problem is whether Φ can be extended to the class of polynomial functions or even larger classes.

Acknowledgments. We are very grateful to anonymous reviewers for their helpful comments.

Appendix

Simulation of Random oracles G and H

- for a fresh query γ to G, $\mathcal{B}$ looks at the H-List, and enumerating all queries δ asked to H with answer H_δ, one builds $z = \gamma \oplus H_\delta$, and checks whether $y = (\delta \| z)^e$. If for some δ the equation holds, we find the partial preimage s^* of c^*, and we can still correctly simulate G by answering the query with $G_\gamma = \delta \oplus (m_b \| 0^{k_1})$. Note that G_γ is uniformly distributed since $\delta = s^*$ is uniformly distributed. Otherwise, one outputs a random value G_γ. In both cases, the pair (γ, G_γ) is added to the G-List.
- For a fresh query δ to H, one outputs a random value H_δ, and add the pair (δ, H_δ) to the H-List. Then for any $(\gamma, G_\gamma) \in$ G-List, one may build $z = \gamma \oplus H_\delta$, and checks whether $y = (\delta \| z)^e$. If for some γ the equation holds, we find the partial preimage s^* of c^*.

Probability Analysis

(1) $\Pr[\text{Fail} \wedge \neg\text{CBad} \wedge \neg\text{AskRS} | \neg\text{AskH}] \leq 2^{-k_1} + q_G \cdot 2^{-k_0}$.

$$\neg\text{AskRS} = \neg\text{AskR} \vee \neg\text{AskS} = \neg\text{AskR} \vee (\text{AskR} \wedge \neg\text{AskS})$$

$$\neg\text{CBad} = \neg\text{RBad} \wedge \neg\text{SBad}$$

$\Pr[\text{Fail} \wedge \neg\text{CBad} \wedge \neg\text{AskRS}]$
$\leq \Pr[\text{Fail} \wedge \neg\text{RBad} \wedge \neg\text{AskR}] + \Pr[\text{Fail} \wedge \neg\text{SBad} \wedge (\text{AskR} \wedge \neg\text{AskS})]$
$\leq \Pr[\text{Fail} | \neg\text{RBad} \wedge \neg\text{AskR}] + \Pr[\text{AskR} | \neg\text{SBad} \wedge \neg\text{AskS})]$

But when r is not asked to G and $r \neq r^*$, $G(r)$ is unpredictable, thus the probability that $(s \oplus G(r))[0...k_1 - 1] = 0^{k_1}$ is less than 2^{-k_1}. On the other hand, when $H(s)$ has not been asked and $s \neq s^*$, $r = H(s) \oplus t$ is unpredictable. On this condition, the probability of having asked r to G is less than $q_G \cdot 2^{-k_0}$. In addition, this event is independent of AskH, which yields

$$\Pr[\text{Fail} \wedge \neg\text{CBad} \wedge \neg\text{AskRS} | \neg\text{AskH}] \leq 2^{-k_1} + q_G \cdot 2^{-k_0}.$$

(2) $\Pr[\text{RBad} | \neg\text{SBad} \wedge \neg\text{AskH}] \leq 2^{-k_0}$.
The event means that RBad occurs provided $s \neq s^*$ and the adversary has not queried s^* from H. So $H(s^*)$ is unpredictable and independent of $H(s)$ as well as t and t^*, and the probability that $r = r^*$, which means $H(s^*) = H(s) \oplus t \oplus t^*$ is at most 2^{-k_0}.

(3) $\Pr[\text{AskR} | \text{SBad} \wedge \neg\text{AskH}] \leq q_G \cdot 2^{-k_0}$.
The event means that r has been asked to G whereas $s = s^*$ and $H(s^*)$ is unpredictable, hence $r = H(s) \oplus t$ is unpredictable and the probability of this event is at most $q_G \cdot 2^{-k_0}$.

(4) $\Pr[\text{Fail} \wedge \neg E | \neg \text{AskR} \wedge \text{SBad} \wedge \neg \text{AskH}] \leq 2^{-k_1}$.

Note that $\neg E$ means that events RBad, $\neg$AskR, SBad, $\neg$AskH cannot happen at the same time. So the whole event means that $s = s^*, r \neq r^*, r$ has not been asked to G, and $(G(r) \oplus s)[n...n + k_1 - 1] = 0^{k_1}$, which lead to that $(G(r) \oplus G(r^*))[n...n + k_1 - 1] = 0^{k_1}$. Then the equation holds with probability upper bound by 2^{-k_1}.

(5) $\Pr[\text{AskH} \wedge \text{Bad}] \geq \Pr[\text{Bad}] - \frac{2q_D}{2^{k_1}} - \frac{2q_D q_G + q_D + q_G}{2^{k_0}} - q_D \epsilon'$.

$\Pr[\text{AskH} \wedge \neg \text{Bad}] \geq 2\epsilon - \Pr[\text{Bad}]$.

$$
\begin{aligned}
\Pr[\text{AskH} \wedge \text{Bad}] &= \Pr[\text{Bad}] - \Pr[\neg \text{AskH} \wedge \text{Bad}] \\
&\geq \Pr[\text{Bad}] - \Pr[\neg \text{AskH} \wedge \text{GBad}] - \Pr[\neg \text{AskH} \wedge \text{DBad}] \\
&\geq \Pr[\text{Bad}] - \Pr[\text{GBad}|\neg \text{AskH}] - \Pr[\text{DBad}|\neg \text{AskH}] \\
&\geq \Pr[\text{Bad}] - \Pr[\text{AskG}|\neg \text{AskH}] - \Pr[\text{DBad}|\neg \text{AskH}] \\
&\geq \Pr[\text{Bad}] - \frac{q_G}{2^{k_0}} - q_D \left(\frac{2}{2^{k_1}} + \frac{2q_G + 1}{2^{k_0}} + \epsilon' \right) \\
&\geq \Pr[\text{Bad}] - \frac{2q_D}{2^{k_1}} - \frac{2q_D q_G + q_D + q_G}{2^{k_0}} - q_D \epsilon'.
\end{aligned}
$$

The above inequations can be get from Lemma 1 and previous results. Let P_A denote $\Pr[\text{AskH} \wedge \neg \text{Bad}]$, then we have:

$$
\begin{aligned}
\Pr[\text{AskH} \wedge \neg \text{Bad}] &\geq \Pr[b = b' \wedge \text{AskH} \wedge \neg \text{Bad}] \\
&= \Pr[b = b' \wedge \neg \text{Bad}] - \Pr[b' = b \wedge \text{AskH} \wedge \neg \text{Bad}] \\
&\geq \Pr[b = b'] - \Pr[\text{Bad}] - \Pr[\neg \text{AskH} \wedge \neg \text{Bad}] \cdot \Pr[b = b' | \neg \text{AskH} \wedge \neg \text{Bad}] \\
&= \frac{1}{2} + \epsilon - \Pr[\text{Bad}] - \frac{1}{2} \cdot (1 - P_A - \Pr[\text{Bad}]) \\
P_A &\geq 2\epsilon - \Pr[\text{Bad}]
\end{aligned}
$$

Note that when $\neg$AskH occurs, $H(s^*)$ is unpredictable, thus $r^* = t^* \oplus H(s^*)$ is unpredictable and b as well. This fact is independent of the event $\neg$Bad, hence $\Pr[b' = b | \neg \text{AskH} \wedge \neg \text{Bad}] = \frac{1}{2}$. In addition, $\Pr[\text{Bad}] + (\Pr[\text{AskH} \wedge \neg \text{Bad}] + \Pr[\neg \text{AskH} \wedge \neg \text{Bad}]) = 1$, so $\Pr[\neg \text{AskH} \wedge \neg \text{Bad}] = 1 - P_A - \Pr[\text{Bad}]$.

References

1. Barić, N., Pfitzmann, B.: Collision-free accumulators and fail-stop signature schemes without trees. In: Fumy, W. (ed.) EUROCRYPT 1997. LNCS, vol. 1233, pp. 480–494. Springer, Heidelberg (1997)
2. Bellare, M., Cash, D.: Pseudorandom functions and permutations provably secure against related-key attacks. In: Rabin, T. (ed.) CRYPTO 2010. LNCS, vol. 6223, pp. 666–684. Springer, Heidelberg (2010)
3. Bellare, M., Cash, D., Miller, R.: Cryptography secure against related-key attacks and tampering. In: Lee, D.H., Wang, X. (eds.) ASIACRYPT 2011. LNCS, vol. 7073, pp. 486–503. Springer, Heidelberg (2011)
4. Bellare, M., Kohno, T.: A theoretical treatment of related-key attacks: RKA-PRPs, RKA-PRFs, and applications. In: Biham, E. (ed.) EUROCRYPT 2003. LNCS, vol. 2656, pp. 491–506. Springer, Heidelberg (2003)

5. Bellare, M., Paterson, K.G., Thomson, S.: RKA security beyond the linear barrier: IBE, encryption and signatures. In: Wang, X., Sako, K. (eds.) ASIACRYPT 2012. LNCS, vol. 7658, pp. 331–348. Springer, Heidelberg (2012)
6. Bellare, M., Rogaway, P.: Random oracles are practical: a paradigm for designing efficient protocols. ACMCCS 28(4), 62–73 (1993)
7. Bellare, M., Rogaway, P.: Optimal asymmetric encryption. In: De Santis, A. (ed.) EUROCRYPT 1994. LNCS, vol. 950, pp. 92–111. Springer, Heidelberg (1995)
8. Biham, E.: New types of cryptanalytic attacks using related keys. In: Helleseth, T. (ed.) EUROCRYPT 1993. LNCS, vol. 765, pp. 398–409. Springer, Heidelberg (1994)
9. Biham, E., Shamir, A.: Differential fault analysis of secret key cryptosystems. In: Kaliski Jr., B.S. (ed.) CRYPTO 1997. LNCS, vol. 1294, pp. 513–525. Springer, Heidelberg (1997)
10. Boneh, D.: Simplified OAEP for the RSA and Rabin functions. In: Kilian, J. (ed.) CRYPTO 2001. LNCS, vol. 2139, pp. 275–291. Springer, Heidelberg (2001)
11. Boneh, D., DeMillo, R.A., Lipton, R.J.: On the importance of checking cryptographic protocols for faults. In: Fumy, W. (ed.) EUROCRYPT 1997. LNCS, vol. 1233, pp. 37–51. Springer, Heidelberg (1997)
12. Canetti, R., Goldreich, O., Halevi, S.: The random oracle methodology. JACM 51(4), 557–594 (2004). (Revisited)
13. Fujisaki, E., Okamoto, T., Pointcheval, D., Stern, J.: RSA-OAEP is secure under the RSA assumption. In: Kilian, J. (ed.) CRYPTO 2001. LNCS, vol. 2139, pp. 260–274. Springer, Heidelberg (2001)
14. Fujisaki, E., Okamoto, T., Pointcheval, D., Stern, J.: RSA-OAEP is secure under the RSA assumption. J. Cryptology 17(2), 81–104 (2004). (Springer, Heidelberg)
15. Halderman, J.A., Schoen, S.D., Heninger, N., Clarkson, W., Paul, W., Calandrino, J.A., Feldman, A.J., Appelbaum, J., Felten, E.W.: Lest we remember: cold-boot attacks on encryption keys. Commun. ACM 52(5), 91–98 (2009)
16. Kiltz, E., Pietrzak, K.: On the security of padding-based encryption schemes – or – why we cannot prove OAEP secure in the standard model. In: Joux, A. (ed.) EUROCRYPT 2009. LNCS, vol. 5479, pp. 389–406. Springer, Heidelberg (2009)
17. Naccache, D., Stern, J.: A new public key cryptosystem based on higher residues. CCS 1998, 59–66 (1998)
18. Shoup, V.: OAEP reconsidered. In: Kilian, J. (ed.) CRYPTO 2001. LNCS, vol. 2139, pp. 239–259. Springer, Heidelberg (2001)
19. Wee, H.: Public key encryption against related key attacks. In: Fischlin, M., Buchmann, J., Manulis, M. (eds.) PKC 2012. LNCS, vol. 7293, pp. 262–279. Springer, Heidelberg (2012)

A Note on a Signature Building Block
and Relevant Security Reduction
in the Green-Hohenberger OT Scheme

Zhengjun Cao[1]($\boxtimes$), Frederic Lafitte[2], and Olivier Markowitch[3]

[1] Department of Mathematics, Shanghai University, Shanghai, China
caozhj@shu.edu.cn
[2] Department of Mathematics, Royal Military Academy, Brussels, Belgium
[3] Departement d'informatique, Universite Libre de Bruxelles, Brussels, Belgium

Abstract. In Asiacrypt'08, Green and Hohenberger presented an adaptive oblivious transfer (OT) scheme which makes use of a signature built from the Boneh-Boyen Identity Based Encryption. In this note, we show that the signature scheme is vulnerable to known-message attacks and the reduction used in the proof of Lemma A.6 is flawed. We also remark that the paradigm of "encryption and proof of knowledge" adopted in the OT scheme is unnecessary because the transferred message must be "recognizable" in practice, otherwise the receiver cannot decide which message to retrieve. However, we would like to stress that this work does not break the OT scheme itself.

Keywords: Oblivious transfer · Signature · Selective security · Encryption and proof of knowledge · Recognizable message

1 Introduction

When designing new cryptographic schemes, it is not unusual to make use of some simple schemes as building blocks. Nevertheless this may lead to complicated constructions with intricate security proofs; and it is often very likely that the resulting scheme is doubtful if an underlying building block is insecure.

When investigating the security of a signature scheme, we usually consider [11] either a *total break* when an adversary is able to retrieve the private key of the signer or is able to find an efficient signing algorithm functionally equivalent to the valid signing algorithm, either a *selective forgery* when an adversary is able to create a valid signature for a particular message or class of messages chosen a priori, or an *existential forgery* when an adversary is able to create a valid signature for a random message. The effort required to mount these attacks depends on the resources that the adversary would have access to, and it is common to consider scenarios where an adversary is able to obtain signatures on messages of his choice. In this note, we consider unforgeability under the weaker *known-message attack* scenario where an adversary has signatures for a set of messages which are known to him but over which he has no control.

© Springer International Publishing Switzerland 2014
D. Lin et al. (Eds.): Inscrypt 2013, LNCS 8567, pp. 282–288, 2014.
DOI: 10.1007/978-3-319-12087-4_18

In Asiacrypt'08, Green and Hohenberger [7] presented a universally composable adaptive oblivious transfer scheme based on symmetric external Diffie-Hellman [2,4,9,13], decision linear assumption [4], and q-hidden LRSW assumption [1,10]. The scheme is complex since it results from the combination of four existing schemes: Groth-Sahai proof system [9], a weak variant of the Camenisch-Lysanskyaya signature [5], a weak signature scheme built from the Boneh-Boyen selective-ID IBE [3], and a variant of the Boneh-Boyen-Shacham encryption [4] with a double trapdoor for decryption.

It was previously believed that the signature built from the Boneh-Boyen IBE is selective-message secure. In this note, we show that the signature scheme is vulnerable to known-message attacks and the reduction used in the proof of Lemma A.6 is flawed. Besides, we remark that the paradigm of "encryption and proof of knowledge" in the OT scheme is unnecessary because the transferred message must be "recognizable" in practice, otherwise, the receiver does not know which message is to be retrieved. This note discusses the issues in a signature building block and the relevant security reduction in the Green-Hohenberger OT Scheme, but we would like to stress that this work does not break the OT scheme itself.

2   The Signature Proposed by Green and Hohenberger

In Ref. [7], the authors proposed two signature schemes as building blocks for their OT scheme. One is called Modified CL signature. The other is called Selective-message secure Boneh-Boyen signature.

Let BMsetup be an algorithm that, on input 1^κ, outputs the parameters for a bilinear mapping as

$$\gamma = (p, \mathbb{G}_1, \mathbb{G}_2, \mathbb{G}_T, e, g \in \mathbb{G}_1, \tilde{g} \in \mathbb{G}_2),$$

where g generates $\mathbb{G}_1$ and $\tilde{g}$ generates $\mathbb{G}_2$, the groups $\mathbb{G}_1, \mathbb{G}_2, \mathbb{G}_T$ each are of prime order p, and $e : \mathbb{G}_1 \times \mathbb{G}_2 \to \mathbb{G}_T$ is a bilinear map such that $e(g, \tilde{g}) \neq 1$.

The latter signature can be described as follows:

BBKeyGen. Select a generator $h \in \mathbb{G}_1$, $\alpha, z \in \mathbb{Z}_p^*$, and compute

$$g \leftarrow g_1^{1/\alpha}, \tilde{g} \leftarrow \tilde{g}_1^{1/\alpha}, g_2 \leftarrow g^z, \tilde{g}_2 \leftarrow \tilde{g}^z.$$

Output $pk = (\gamma, g, \tilde{g}, g_1, g_2, h, \tilde{g}_2)$, and $sk = g_2^\alpha$.

BBSign. In order to sign a message $m \in \mathbb{G}_1$, pick a random $r \in \mathbb{Z}_p^*$ and compute the signature

$$((mh)^r g_2^\alpha, \tilde{g}^r, g^r).$$

BBVerify. The signature $(s_1, \tilde{s}_2, s_3)$ on message m is considered valid if

$$e(s_1, \tilde{g})/e(mh, \tilde{s}_2) = e(g_1, \tilde{g}_2)$$

and

$$e(g, \tilde{s}_2) = e(s_3, \tilde{g}).$$

3   A Known Message Attack

In Sect. 3 of Ref. [7], the authors claim that the signature built from the Boneh-Boyen IBE is selective-message secure. As shown below, the signature is not immune against the following known message attack.

Given a valid signature $(s_1, \tilde{s}_2, s_3) = ((mh)^r g_2^\alpha, \tilde{g}^r, g^r)$ on message m for some $r \in \mathbb{Z}_p^*$, an adversary can pick any $\theta \in \mathbb{Z}_p^*$ and output the signature $(s_3^\theta s_1, \tilde{s}_2, s_3)$ on message $g^\theta m$. The forged message-signature pair passes the verification process since we have:

$$e(s_3^\theta s_1, \tilde{g})/e(g^\theta mh, \tilde{s}_2) = e(g^{r\theta}(mh)^r g_2^\alpha, \tilde{g})/e(g^\theta mh, \tilde{g}^r)$$
$$= e((g^\theta mh)^r g_2^\alpha, \tilde{g})/e((g^\theta mh)^r, \tilde{g})$$
$$= e(g_2^\alpha, \tilde{g}) = e(g^{z\alpha}, \tilde{g}) = e(g^\alpha, \tilde{g}^z) = e(g_1, \tilde{g}_2)$$
$$e(g, \tilde{s}_2) = e(g, \tilde{g}^r) = e(g^r, \tilde{g}) = e(s_3, \tilde{g})$$

Notice that this attack is not a total break because forging the signature of an arbitrary message m' would require an adversary to solve $m' = mg^\theta$ for θ; therefore the signature scheme is selectively forgeable.

It seems unlikely that this selective forgery can be used to attack the OT scheme built from the vulnerable signature scheme. The OT scheme actually requires to use BBSign to sign some value ab where both $a \in \mathbb{G}_1$ and $b \in \mathbb{G}_1$ are separately signed using a different signature algorithm (i.e. the Modified CL signature).

4   The Lemma A.6 Revisited

In the latest revision [7], the authors believe that their security argument is sound although they admit that the building block "signature-like" scheme may be not selective secure. We find, however, the relevant proof of Lemma A.6 (see [7], p. 22) seems difficult to revise. Now, we show the security argument of Case-1 is flawed.

4.1   Review the Original Argument of Case-1 (Lemma A.6)

Consider the case where $\mathcal{A}$ produces $(\omega, \omega_2) = (c_{i,1}, c_{j,2})$ for $i \neq j$, and show that an $\mathcal{A}$ that produces such a query can be used to solve the Computational co-Diffie-Hellman problem in $\mathbb{G}_1, \mathbb{G}_2$, i.e., given $(g, g^a, g^b, \tilde{g}, \tilde{g}^a, \tilde{g}^b)$ for $a, b \in_R \mathbb{Z}_p$, solve for g^{ab}.

Given an input $(g, g^a, g^b, \tilde{g}, \tilde{g}^a, \tilde{g}^b)$ to the co-CDH problem: select random values $u, v, \omega, y \xleftarrow{\$} \mathbb{Z}_p$. Set $(u_1, u_2) \leftarrow (g^a, g^{au}), (\tilde{u}_1, \tilde{u}_2) \leftarrow (\tilde{g}^a, \tilde{g}^{au})$ and $h' \leftarrow (g^a)^{-v} g^\omega$. Generate $(vk_1, sk_1), (vk_2, sk_2)$ as in the normal scheme, but set $vk_3 = (\gamma, g, \tilde{g}, g^a, g^a, h', \tilde{g}^b)$. Set $pk \leftarrow (u_1, u_2, \tilde{u}_1, \tilde{u}_2, vk_1, vk_2, vk_3)$. Randomly select two ciphertext indices i^*, j^* such that $i^* \neq j^*$.

Now for $i = 1$ to N, choose r_i, s_i, y_i uniformly from $\mathbb{Z}_p$ with the restriction that $(r_{i*} + us_{j*}) = v \bmod p$. Set $z_i = (r_i + us_i) \bmod p$. Generate $\text{sig}_1 \leftarrow \text{CLSign}_{sk_1}(u_1^r)$, $\text{sig}_2 \leftarrow \text{CLSign}_{sk_2}(u_2^s)$, and set

$$\text{sig}_3 \leftarrow \left((g^b)^{\frac{-\omega}{z_i - v}} ((g^a)^{z_i - v} g^\omega)^{y_i}, (\tilde{g}^b)^{\frac{-1}{z_i - v}} \tilde{g}^{y_i}, (g^b)^{\frac{-1}{z_i - v}} g^{y_i} \right).$$

Construct the ith ciphertext as:

$$C_i = (u_1^{r_i}, u_2^{s_i}, g_1^{r_i}, g_2^{s_i}, m_j h^{r_i + s_i}, \text{sig}_1, \text{sig}_2, \text{sig}_3)$$

Now set $T \leftarrow (pk, C_1, \cdots, C_N)$ and send T to $\mathcal{A}$. Whenever $\mathcal{A}$ submits a request $Q = (d_1, d_2, \pi)$ where π verifies correctly, use the extraction trapdoor to obtain the values $(\omega_1, \omega_2, \omega_3, \omega_4)$ and the values $s_1', \tilde{s}_2', s_3'$ corresponding to sig_3. Now:

1. If, for some $j \in [1, N]$, the pair $(\omega_1, \omega_2) = (u_1^{r_j}, u_2^{s_j})$: then output a valid response to $\mathcal{A}$ by selecting $s' = (h^{r_j + s_j} \omega_3 \omega_4)$, constructing the proof δ', and sending $R = (s', \delta')$ to $\mathcal{A}$. Continue the simulation.
2. If $(\omega_1, \omega_2) = (u_1^{r_{i*}}, u_2^{s_{j*}})$, then compute $s_1' / s_3'^\omega$ as the solution to the co-CDH problem.
3. In all other cases, abort the simulation.

Observe that in case (2) the soundness of the G-S proof system ensures that for some y' we can represent $(s_1', \tilde{s}_2', s_3') = ((g^a)^v h)^{y'} g^{ab}, \tilde{g}^{y'}, g^{y'})$. By substitution we obtain $((g^a)^v (g^a)^{-v} g^\omega)^{y'} g^{ab}, \tilde{g}^{y'}, g^{y'}) = (g^{\omega y'} g^{ab}, \tilde{g}^{y'}, g^{y'})$, and thus $s_1' / s_3'^\omega = g^{ab}$. In this case, we can obtain the value g^{ab} and output a correct solution to the co-CDH problem.

4.2 Remarks on the Flawed Argument

We first remind readers that the randomly chosen numbers $r, s \in \mathbb{Z}_p$ in the OT initialization are not parallelly used later. Concretely, see the generations of

$$\text{sig}_1 \leftarrow \text{CLSign}_{sk_1}(u_1^r), \text{sig}_2 \leftarrow \text{CLSign}_{sk_2}(u_2^s),$$

and

$$\text{sig}_3 \leftarrow \text{BBSign}_{sk_3}(u_1^r u_2^s).$$

In the phase of OTRespond, s is directly sent to the receiver $\mathcal{R}$, but r is not exposed (see [7], pp. 11–12). Thus, in the generation of sig_3 the signer is not forced to sign $u_1^r u_2^s$.

Based on the key observation, we remark that in the case where $\mathcal{A}$ produces $(\omega, \omega_2) = (c_{i,1}, c_{j,2})$ for $i \neq j$, $\mathcal{A}$ cannot produce a query which can be used to solve the Computational co-Diffie-Hellman problem in $\mathbb{G}_1, \mathbb{G}_2$. In fact, it only needs to transform the corresponding part of the original simulation as follows:

For $i = 1$ to N, choose r_i, s_i, y_i and θ_i uniformly from $\mathbb{Z}_p$ with the restriction that $(r_{i*} + us_{j*}) = v \bmod p$. Set $z_i = (r_i + us_i) \bmod p$. Generate $\text{sig}_1 \leftarrow \text{CLSign}_{sk_1}(u_1^r)$, $\text{sig}_2 \leftarrow \text{CLSign}_{sk_2}(u_2^s)$, and set

$$\text{sig}_3 \leftarrow \left(\underline{((g^b)^{\frac{-1}{z_i-v}} g^{y_i})^{\theta_i}} (g^b \, \underline{g^{\theta_i}})^{\frac{-\omega}{z_i-v}} ((g^a)^{z_i-v} g^\omega \, \underline{g^{\theta_i}})^{y_i}, (\tilde{g}^b)^{\frac{-1}{z_i-v}} \tilde{g}^{y_i}, (g^b)^{\frac{-1}{z_i-v}} g^{y_i} \right).$$

According to the proposed attack in Sect. 3, it is easy to find that the signature sig_3 is valid. Thus, the transformed simulation runs well. But in such case, we have

$$s_1'/s_3'^\omega = \left((g^b)^{\frac{-1}{z_i-v}} g^{2y_i} g^{\frac{-\omega}{z_i-v}} \right)^{\theta_i} \neq g^{ab}.$$

5 Further Discussion

The oblivious transfer primitive, introduced by Rabin [12], is of fundamental importance in multi-party computation [8,14]. Most OT schemes follow the paradigm of "encryption and proof of knowledge" to force the sender to keep the consistency of the committed messages, so does the Green-Hohenberger OT scheme. From the practical point of view, we should remark that the paradigm is unnecessary. In most reasonable applications of OT, *the transferred messages must be recognizable for the receiver*, or *the sender is willing to disclose some messages to the receiver*. The property has been explicitly specified in the earlier works by Rabin, Even, Goldreich and Lempel. We refer to the following descriptions.

In Ref. [12], Rabin explained that:

> Bob and Alice each have a secret, SB and SA, respectively, which they wish to exchange. For example, SB may be the password to a file that Alice wants to access (we shall refer to this file as Alice's file), and SA the password to Bob's file. To exclude the possibility of randomizing on the possible digits of the password, we assume that if an incorrect password is used then the file is erased, and that Bob and Alice want to guarantee that this will not happen to their respective files.

In Ref. [6], Even, Goldreich and Lempel stressed that:

> The notion of a "recognizable secret message" plays an important role in our definition of OT. A message is said to be a recognizable secret if, although the receiver cannot compute it, he can authenticate it once he receives it.
>
> The notion of a recognizable secret message is evidently relevant to the study of cryptographic protocols, in which the sender is reluctant to send the message while the receiver wishes to get it. In such protocols, it makes no sense to consider the transfer of messages that are either not secret (to the receiver) or not recognizable (by the receiver).

In symmetric case, such as exchanging secrets, signing contracts, both two participators can easily verify the correctness of the received messages. In unsymmetric case, for example when a database manager plays the role of the sender and a client plays the role of the receiver, it is usual that the sender is willing to disclose some messages to the receiver.

To sum up, *if the transferred messages are not recognizable then the receiver cannot decide which message to retrieve*. It is reasonable to assume that the transferred messages in an OT scheme are correctly formed. It is unnecessary for the sender to provide any proofs of knowledge. By the way, the definition of "proof of knowledge" is more strong than that of "recognizable message". The below three common examples of recognizable messages are due to the Ref. [6]:

(i) A signature of a user to some known message is a recognizable secret message for everybody else.
(ii) The key K, by which the plaintext M is transformed using cryptosystem F into ciphertext $F_K(M)$.
(iii) The factorization of a composite number, which has only large prime factors.

Many OT schemes, frankly speaking, have neglected the above warning. Thus increasingly complicated OT constructions have been presented in the past decades.

6 Conclusion

In this paper, we show that the signature in Green-Hohenberger OT Scheme is vulnerable to known-message attacks and the reduction used in the proof of Lemma A.6 is flawed. The full version of the OT scheme is available at http://eprint.iacr.org/2008/163 (last revised, 14 Sep 2013). The paper highlights the difficulty to deal with complicated (OT) schemes and with their corresponding security proof ; moreover the interpretation of such proofs should be clearly related with the precise corresponding security notions. In fact, "the theorem-proof paradigm of theoretical mathematics is often of limited relevance and frequently leads to papers that are confusing and misleading" [N. Koblitz and A. Menezes: another look at "provable security", J. Cryptology 20(1), 2007]. We hope this note will help to right the balance between academic researches of OT and its practice.

Acknowledgments. We are grateful to the referees and the shepherd for their valuable suggestions to revise the paper. We thank Green and Hohenberger for their kindly responses on this note. This work is supported by the National Natural Science Foundation of China (Project 61303200), the Shanghai Leading Academic Discipline Project (S30104), and the Scientific Research Foundation for the Returned Overseas Chinese Scholars, State Education Ministry.

References

1. Ateniese G., Camenisch J., Medeiros B.: Untraceable RFID tags via insubvertible encryption. In: 12th ACM Conference on Computer and Communications Security (CCS 2005), pp. 92–101. ACM Press (2005)
2. Ballard L., Green M., Medeiros M., Monrose F.: Correlation-resistant storage from keyword searchable encryption. Cryptology ePrint Archive, Report 2005/417 (2005)

3. Boneh, D., Boyen, X.: Efficient selective-ID secure identity-based encryption without random oracles. In: Cachin, C., Camenisch, J. (eds.) EUROCRYPT 2004. LNCS, vol. 3027, pp. 223–238. Springer, Heidelberg (2004)
4. Boneh, D., Boyen, X., Shacham, H.: Short group signatures. In: Franklin, M. (ed.) CRYPTO 2004. LNCS, vol. 3152, pp. 45–55. Springer, Heidelberg (2004)
5. Camenisch, J., Lysyanskaya, A.: Signature schemes and anonymous credentials from bilinear maps. In: Franklin, M. (ed.) CRYPTO 2004. LNCS, vol. 3152, pp. 56–72. Springer, Heidelberg (2004)
6. Even, S., Goldreich, O., Lempel, A.: A randomized protocol for signing contracts. Commun. ACM 28(6), 637–647 (1985)
7. Green, M., Hohenberger, S.: Universally composable adaptive oblivious transfer. In: Pieprzyk, J. (ed.) ASIACRYPT 2008. LNCS, vol. 5350, pp. 179–197. Springer, Heidelberg (2008). http://eprint.iacr.org/2008/163
8. Goldreich, O., Micali, S., Wigderson, A.: How to play any mental game or a completeness theorem for protocols with honest majority. In: STOC '87, pp. 218–229 (1987)
9. Groth, J., Sahai, A.: Efficient non-interactive proof systems for bilinear groups. In: Smart, N. (ed.) EUROCRYPT 2008. LNCS, vol. 4965, pp. 415–432. Springer, Heidelberg (2008)
10. Lysyanskaya, A., Rivest, R., Sahai, A., Wolf, S.: Pseudonym systems. In: Heys, H., Adams, C. (eds.) SAC 1999. LNCS, vol. 1758, pp. 184–199. Springer, Heidelberg (1999)
11. Menezes, A., Oorschot, P., Vanstone, S.: Handbook of Applied Cryptography. CRC Press, Boca Raton (1996)
12. Rabin, M.: How to exchange secrets by oblivious transfer. Technical Report TR-81, Aiken Computation Laboratory, Harvard University (1981)
13. Scott M.: Authenticated id-based key exchange and remote log-in with simple token and pin number. Cryptology ePrint Archive, Report 2002/164 (2002)
14. Yao, Y.: How to generate and exchange secrets. In: FOCS, pp. 162–167 (1986)

Hash Function

LHash: A Lightweight Hash Function

Wenling Wu[1,2(✉)], Shuang Wu[1], Lei Zhang[1], Jian Zou[1], and Le Dong[1]

[1] Trust Computing and Information Assurance Laboratory, Beijing, China
[2] State Key Laboratory of Computer Science Institute of Software,
Chinese Academy of Sciences, Beijing 100190, People's Republic of China
{wwl,zhanglei}@tca.iscas.ac.cn

Abstract. In this paper, we propose a new lightweight hash function supporting three different digest sizes: 80, 96 and 128 bits, providing preimage security from 64 to 120 bits, second preimage and collision security from 40 to 60 bits. LHash requires about 817 GE and 1028 GE with a serialized implementation. In faster implementations based on function T, LHash requires 989 GE and 1200 GE with 54 and 72 cycles per block, respectively. Furthermore, its energy consumption evaluated by energy per bit is also remarkable. LHash allows to make trade-offs among security, speed, energy consumption and implementation costs by adjusting parameters. The design of LHash employs a kind of Feistel-PG structure in the internal permutation, and this structure can utilize permutation layers on nibbles to improve the diffusion speed. The adaptability of LHash in different environments is good, since different versions of LHash share the same basic computing module. The low-area implementation comes from the hardware-friendly S-box and linear diffusion layer. We evaluate the resistance of LHash against known attacks and confirm that LHash provides a good security margin.

Keywords: Lightweight · Hash function · Sponge function · Feistel · Security · Performance

1 Introduction

RFID products have been widely implemented and deployed in many aspects in our daily life, e.g. automated production, access control, electronic toll collection, parking management, identification and cargo tracking. The need for security in RFID and sensor networks is dramatically increasing, which requires secure yet efficiently implementable cryptographic primitives including secret-key ciphers and hash functions. In such constrained environments, the area and power consumption of a primitive usually comes to the fore and standard algorithms are often prohibitively expensive to implement. Hence, lightweight cryptography has become a hot topic. A number of lightweight cryptographic algorithms are proposed, such as stream cipher Trivium [11] and Grain [16], block cipher PRESENT [5], HIGHT [18], LBlock [35], LED [15], Piccolo [31]

© Springer International Publishing Switzerland 2014
D. Lin et al. (Eds.): Inscrypt 2013, LNCS 8567, pp. 291–308, 2014.
DOI: 10.1007/978-3-319-12087-4_19

and PRINCE [7]. Recently, some significant works on lightweight hash functions have also been performed. In [6], the proposed lightweight hash function is constructed from block cipher PRESENT in Hirosei's double-block mode [17]. The ARMADILLO [2] hash function was found to be insecure after proposed at CHES 2010. Then a new version of ARMADILLO (version 3) [33] was proposed at CARDIS 2012. QUARK [1] uses sponge structure [3] and internal permutation similar to feedback shift registers used in Grain. PHOTON [14] proposed at CRYPTO 2011 and Spongent [4] proposed at CHES 2011 also used sponge structure, but different internal permutations, which are based on AES-like and PRESENT-like structures, respectively. Moreover, Kavun et al [20] presented a lightweight implementation of Keccak at RFIDSec 2010.

In this paper, we propose a new lightweight hash function LHash with digest sizes from 80 to 128 bits. LHash is based on extended sponge functions framework, which allows trade-offs among security, speed, energy consumption and implementation costs by adjusting parameters. The internal permutation is designed using a structure, named as Feistel-PG, which is an extended variant of improved generalized Feistel. Feistel-PG has faster diffusion, shorter impossible differential paths and integral distinguishers than similar structures. The S-box and MDS linear layer used in the internal permutation are designed to be hardware-friendly. Both of them have very compact hardware implementation. The MDS linear layer has an iterated implementation, which is similar to and more compact than the linear layer used in PHOTON. We present that LHash achieves remarkably compact implementation in hardware. In our smallest implementation, the area requirements are 817 and 1028 GE with 666 and 882 cycles per block, respectively. Meanwhile, its efficiency on energy consumption evaluated by the metric of energy per bit proposed in [31] is the smallest class among current lightweight hash functions in literature. Especially, for the competitors with similar preimage and collision resistance levels, it also compete well in terms of area and throughput trade-off as shown in Fig. 7. Comparative results regarding the hardware efficiency for lightweight hash functions are summarized in Table 1. Regarding security, the internal permutation of LHash provides a good security margin against all kinds of attacks, including differential attack, impossible differential attack, zero-sum distinguisher, rebound attack etc. Since LHash is built on the internal permutation using extended sponge structure, we believe that the security bounds claimed can be reached.

This paper is organized as follows. Specification of LHash is given in Sect. 2. Section 3 describes the design rationale. Sections 4 and 5 provide results on security and implementation evaluations, respectively. Finally, we conclude in Sect. 6.

2   Specification of LHash

2.1   Notations

In the specification of LHash, we use the following notations:
- M: The original message
- n: The digest size

Table 1. Comparison of LHash with existing lightweight hash functions

| Algorithm | Parameters | | | | | Bounds | | | Area [GE] | Cycle [clks] | Throughput [kbps] | | FOM [nb/clk/GE²] | | Energy/bit* |
	n	b	c	r	r'	Pre	2nd Pre	Col			long	96-bit	long	96-bit	
LHash	80	96	80	16	16	64	40	40	817	666	2.40	1.44	35.96	21.59	34008
									989	54	29.63	17.78	302.9	181.75	3338
	96	96	80	16	16	80	40	40	817	666	2.40	1.31	35.96	19.63	34008
									989	54	29.63	16.16	302.9	165.2	3338
	128	128	112	16	32	96	56	56	1028	882	1.81	1.21	17.13	11.44	56669
									1200	72	22.22	14.81	154.3	102.89	5400
	128	128	120	8	8	120	60	60	1028	882	0.91	0.40	8.61	3.81	113337
									1200	72	11.1	4.94	77.15	34.29	10800
PHOTON	80	100	80	20	16	64	40	40	865	708	2.82	1.51	37.73	20.12	30621
									1168	132	15.15	8.08	111.13	59.27	7709
	128	144	128	16	16	112	64	64	1122	996	1.61	0.69	12.78	5.48	69845
									1708	156	10.26	4.40	35.15	15.06	16653
Spongent	80	88	80	8	8	80	40	40	738	990	0.81	0.42	14.84	7.74	91328
									1127	45	17.78	9.28	139.97	73.03	6339
	128	136	128	8	8	120	64	64	1060	2380	0.34	0.14	2.99	1.28	315350
									1687	70	11.43	14.90	40.16	17.21	14761
U-Quark	128	136	128	8	8	120	64	64	1379	544	1.47	0.61	7.73	3.20	93772
									2392	68	11.76	4.87	20.56	8.51	20332
H-PRESENT-128	128	–	128	64	–	128	64	64	2330	559	11.45	5.72	21.09	10.54	20351
									4256	32	200	100	110.41	55.21	2128
Keccak-f[100]+	80	100	80	20	20	60	40	40	1250	800	2.50	1.50	16.00	9.60	50000
Keccak-f[200]	128	200	128	72	72	64	64	64	2520	900	8.00	3.56	12.6	5.60	31500
Keccak-f[400]	128	400	256	144	144	128	128	64	5090	1000	14.40	9.60	5.56	3.71	35347

*: Energy/bit = (Area[GE]×required cycles for one block process)/block size[bit]. [31]
+: Implementation data is estimated based on the same serialized architecture in [20].

- b: The block size of internal permutation
- F_{96}, F_{128}: The 96(128)-bit internal permutation
- C_i: The i-th round constant
- P_b: Nibble permutation on $b/2$ bits state
- s: 4×4 S-box
- S: Concatenation of four S-boxes
- T: Non-linear function on 16-bit word
- G_b: Concatenation of $b/32$ function T
- A: 4×4 MDS linear transformation on 16-bit word
- $\bigoplus$:   Bitwise exclusive-OR operation
- $\times 2, \times 4$:   Constant multiplications on finite field $\mathbb{F}_2[x]/x^4 + x + 1$

2.2 Domain Extender

In LHash, we choose the extended sponge function [3] as illustrated in Fig. 1. The message is padded and split into r-bit blocks, each of which is XORed to part of the state and enter the permutation. After the message blocks are all

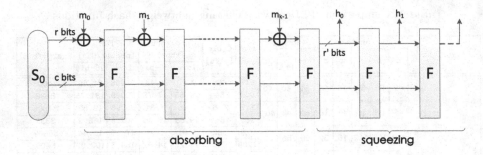

Fig. 1. Extended sponge function

Table 2. Suggested parameters and security bounds of LHash

n	b	c	r	r'	collision	2nd preimage	preimage
80	96	80	16	16	2^{40}	2^{40}	2^{64}
96	96	80	16	16	2^{40}	2^{40}	2^{80}
128	128	112	16	32	2^{56}	2^{56}	2^{96}
128	128	120	8	8	2^{60}	2^{60}	2^{120}

processed, output r' bits of the state as a digest block and continue iterating the permutation until the output digest size is reached.

In Fig. 1, m_i is the i-th message block split from the padded message, h_i is the i-th digest block and F stands for a fixed internal permutation. r is the length of input message blocks, c is the size of the capacity, $b = r+c$ is the size of the fixed permutation and r' is the output size for each output digest block. S_0 is the initial value for the iteration. For different versions, the initial values are different. We set initial values as the concatenation of 8-bit binary expressions of the four parameters n, b, r and r' and filling zeros in the higher bits if the size is not enough, *i.e.* $S_0 = 0||...||0||n||b||r||r'$.

The padding works as follows. Suppose the length of the original message is *len*, the padding rule is to append one bit of "1" and x bits of "0". The value x is the smallest non-negative integer such that $x + 1 + len \equiv 0 \ modr$.

As shown in Table 2, four versions of LHash are constructed based on two permutations F_{96} and F_{128} with sizes of 96 and 128 bits. The parameters and security bounds can be found in Table 2. We refer to its various parameterizations as LHash-$n/b/r/r'$ for different digest sizes n, block sizes b, absorbing sizes r and squeezing sizes r'.

2.3   Internal Permutation

The internal permutations F_{96} and F_{128} are constructed using 18-round Feistel structure. The round transformations are shown in Fig. 2. The permutation works as follows.

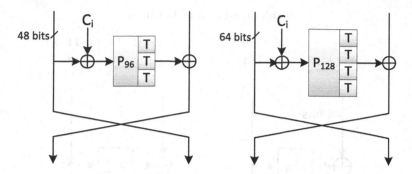

Fig. 2. Round transformations for internal permutation F_{96} and F_{128}

Table 3. Nibble permutation P_{96} and P_{128}

i	0	1	2	3	4	5	6	7	8	9	10	11
$P_{96}(i)$	6	0	9	11	1	4	10	3	5	7	2	8

i	0	1	2	3	4	5	6	7	8	9	10	11	12	13	14	15
$P_{128}(i)$	3	6	9	12	7	10	13	0	11	14	1	4	15	8	5	2

First split the b-bit input (b=96 or 128) into two halves $X_1\|X_0$. Then for $i = 2, 3, ..., 19$, calculate

$$X_i = G_b(P_b(X_{i-1} \oplus C_{i-1})) \oplus X_{i-2}$$

At last, $X_{19}\|X_{18}$ is the output of the permutation.

Here the transformation G_b is the concatenation of $b/32$ function T which is the non-linear transformation on 16-bit word. The details of function T will be introduced in the following paragraphs. P_b is a simple permutation on $b/8$ nibbles, as defined in Table 3.

The function T is defined as

$$T(x_3, x_2, x_1, x_0) = A(S(x_3, x_2, x_1, x_0))$$

where S is the concatenation of four S-boxes:

$$S(x_3, x_2, x_1, x_0) = s(x_3)\|s(x_2)\|s(x_1)\|s(x_0).$$

The definition of the 4-bit S-box is shown in Table 4.

The linear layer A is an 4×4 MDS transformation on 16-bit word, it is calculated as four iterations of the linear transformation B as shown below, *i.e.* $A = B^4$. In this figure ×2 and ×4 are constant multiplications on finite field $\mathbb{F}_2[x]/x^4 + x + 1$.

The round constants C_i is used in both F_{96} and F_{128}. In each round, C_i is XORed to the most significant 16 bits of the state. The round constants are

Table 4. S-box used in LHash

x	0	1	2	3	4	5	6	7	8	9	10	11	12	13	14	15
$s(x)$	14	9	15	0	13	4	10	11	1	2	8	3	7	6	12	5

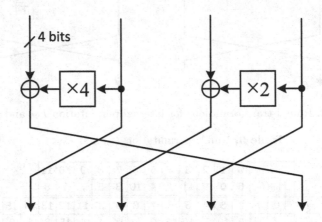

Fig. 3. Linear transformation B

Table 5. Round constants

round	0	1	2	3	4	5	6	7	8
C_i	0012	0113	1301	3725	7E6C	ECFE	C9DB	9280	2436
round	9	10	11	12	13	14	15	16	17
C_i	485A	8193	1200	2537	5A48	A5B7	5B49	B7A5	7F6D

generated by a 5-bit LFSR. The initial state is zero: $x_4 = x_3 = x_2 = x_1 = x_0 = 0$, for $i > 4$, $x_i = x_{i-3} \oplus x_{i-5} \oplus 1$. Let $a_i = x_i||x_{i+1}||x_{i+2}||x_{i+3}$, $a'_i = x_i||x_{i+1}||x_{i+2}||\overline{x_{i+3}}$, $b_i = x_{i+1}||x_{i+2}||x_{i+3}||x_{i+4}$ and $b'_i = x_{i+1}||x_{i+2}||\overline{x_{i+3}}||x_{i+4}$. Then $C_i = a_i||b_i||a'_i||b'_i$. $\overline{x_{i+3}}$ stands for the complement of the bit x_{i+3}. The values of C_i are listed in Table 5 (Fig. 3).

3   Design Rational

3.1   Extended Sponge Function and the Choice of Paramenters

In most of the known RFID protocols, a hash function is required for privacy. In such cases, only the first preimage resistance is needed. Thus the second preimage bound can be sacrificed to have a more compact hardware implementation. LHash is based on extended sponge functions framework, which allows trade-offs among security, speed, energy consumption and implementation costs by adjusting parameters. Compared to the traditional construction based on block ciphers, the advantages are:

- Sponge function is based on fixed permutation. The cost of key expansion in block ciphers can be avoided. For encryption, the same secret key are used multiple times. As a result, the key expansion is done once and the subkeys can be stored and used again and again. But for block cipher based hash, we need to do the key expansion for every new message block.
- Avoiding feeding forward operation and saving storage. The cost of storage is high in lightweight computing environment. Thus for lightweight hash, we need to use as less storage as possible. In block cipher based hash, the feeding forward mode is necessary, thus the plaintext/key needs to be stored after the encryption is finished. If we need optimal resistance of second preimage attack, the capacity in sponge function needs to be of twice the size as the digest length and the storage requirement is similar to the block cipher based hash. But for sponge function, we can sacrifice the second preimage resistance by adjusting the parameters and reduce the storage requirement to about the same as the digest size.
- The security reduction of Sponge function has been proved. Thus we only need to analyze the security of the internal permutation. If the internal permutation doesn't have any flaw, we can have confidence in the security of the hash based on it in sponge mode.

3.2   Internal Permutation

Structure. The structure of the internal permutation is as shown in Fig. 5 in Appendix B. P_n is a vector permutation whose unit size is the same as the size of sbox and G is the concatenation of several function $T's$. This structure is a kind of Feistel-type and combines the advantage of generalized Feistel structure. Its basic non-linear module T is small and parallelable, which make LHash can be implemented efficiently in both software and hardware.

Compared to traditional Feistel structure, the diffusion effect of generalized Feistel structure is slower and hence more rounds are needed to achieve the desired security level. In order to overcome the disadvantage, we propose an extended variant of improved generalized Feistel structure which represented as Feistel-PG. We utilize a permutation layer P_n on nibbles to improve the diffusion effect. The unit size of P_n is the same as the size of the S-box and requires no extra hardware area cost. However, the choice of P_n has impact on the security. After a lot of attempts and tests, we decide to choose current permutations since they are the best ones we found. Assuming the same block length and size of non-linear module T, compared to traditional generalized Feistel structure such as Type-2 GFS and improved GFS [32], Feistel-PG can achieve full diffusion [32] in less rounds which means its diffusion speed is faster, and the attackable round number of impossible differential and integral path is fewer. The comparison between different structures are listed in Table 6.

Moreover, compared to the usually utilized SP structure in the design of internal permutation of hash functions, Feistel-type structure has completely different properties. Therefore, most of the hash function attack techniques suitable for the property of SP-type structure, such as the most famous rebound

Table 6. Comparison of structures

Structure	Size	Full Diffusion	Impossible Differential	Integral Path
Type-2 generalized Feistel	96	7	13	12
Improved GFS	96	5	9	10
Feistel-PG	96	4	8	8
Type-2 generalized Feistel	128	9	17	16
Improved GFS	128	6	10	11
Feistel-PG	128	4	8	8

attack, super-sbox techniques etc., will be less effective. Therefore, we believe that Feistel-type internal permutation can achieve good immunity against known attacks, and later in Sect. 4 we will evaluate the security of LHash against known attacks in detail.

S-Box. On the pursuit of hardware efficiency, we use 4×4 S-boxes $s : F_2^4 \to F_2^4$ in LHash. Compared with the regular 8×8 S-box, small S-box has much more advantage when implemented in hardware. For example, to implement the S-box of AES in hardware more than 200 GE are needed. On the other hand, the S-box used in LHash requires two AND operations, two ORs, one NOT and six XORs. The area costs for AND, OR, NOT and XOR are 1.33 GE, 1.33 GE, 0.5 GE and 2.67 GE. Thus the S-box costs 21.84 GE in total. Furthermore, in the aspect of security, the S-box used in LHash is complete, has no fixed points, optimal differential and linear characteristics probability of 2^{-2} and algebraic degree of 3.

Linear Diffusion Layer. The diffusion of the internal permutation is achieved by both the nibble permutation P_n and the linear layer A used in function T. Their combination results in good security. The lower bound for the active S-boxes for 17 out of 18 rounds of F_{96} and F_{128} are 48 and 64, respectively. P_n is the nibble permutation with no hardware cost. A is a linear transformation on 16 bits, the branch number of A regarding 4 nibbles is 5, which is optimal.

A follows the 4-branch generalized Feistel structure, the round function uses constant multiplications $\times 2$ and $\times 4$ on $\mathbb{F}_2[x]/x^4 + x + 1$. After four iterations, the branch number of 5 can be reached. The linear transformation A has two advantages:

- Easy to invert. The reason why we consider the inversion is for compact hardware implementation, which will be explained in the following sections. Since generalized Feistel structure is used to implement A, we only need to change the permutation of the round function to invert it and the round function can be reused.
- Low area cost for hardware implementation. In the generalized Feistel structure, there are two XOR operations between 4-bit branches, which requires 8 bits of XORs. The multiplication by 2 and 4 can be implemented using 1 and

2 bits of XORs. The total area cost of A is 11 bits of XORs and is less than the iterated MDS layer used in PHOTON, which requires 15 bits of XORs.

The circuits for multiplications by 2 and 4 in $\mathbb{F}_2[x]/x^4 + x + 1$ can be found in Fig. 6.

4 Security Evaluation

Since extended sponge function is used, the desired security of the internal permutation is that the permutation is indistinguishable with a random permutation with no more than $2^{c/2}$ queries. The parameter r is small for all versions of LHash. Thus for the adversary, the controllable freedom degree is small (no more than 16 bits for each permutation). It is difficult for the adversaries to take advantage of the vulnerability of the internal permutation and turn it into an attack on the hash function. Based on the reasoning above, we only propose analysis of the internal permutation. All analyses in this section are based on the stronger assumption that the input can be completely controlled by the adversary.

4.1 Generic Security Bounds

With the assumption that the internal permutation is ideal, the security bounds for extended sponge function are as follows [14].

- Collision bound: $min\{2^{n/2}, 2^{c/2}\}$.
- Second preimage bound: $min\{2^n, 2^{c/2}\}$.
- Preimage bound: $min\{2^{min\{n,b\}}, max\{2^{min\{n,b\}-r'}, 2^{c/2}\}\}$.

According to our analysis on the internal permutations F_{96} and F_{128}, we believe the bounds shown in Table 2 can be reached.

4.2 Differential Analysis

For differential analysis of LHash, it is highly dependent on the maximum differential characteristic probability of the internal permutations F_{96} and F_{128}. Considering the internal permutations are built based on block cipher structure, we can adopt the regular method of searching least number of active sboxes to evaluate the upper bound of differential characteristic probability for F_{96} and F_{128}. This method is widely used in security evaluation of Feistel cipher against differential analysis such as Camellia and CLEFIA.

The search program is usually a truncated differential path search with Viterbi algorithm. Considering that the sbox is a bijective and deterministic nonlinear function, its input and output differences can be truncated to 1-bit. Namely if its input and output differences are not zero, then we call it an active sbox and denote it as "1" in the truncated differential path. Otherwise, if the input and output differences are both zero, then we call it a passive sbox and denote it as "0". Notice that for a passive sbox its differential probability $DP_S = 1$, and for an active sbox $DP_S = p < 1$. Therefore, by counting the minimum number of active sboxes, we can evaluate the upper bound of differential characteristic probability. In the truncated differential path search, we start from input state $\Delta D^{(0)}$, and transit toward output state $\Delta D^{(r)}$ round by round so as to minimize the number of active sboxes at every round as follows.

For every possible truncated differential path $(\Delta D^{(i)} \to \Delta D^{(i+1)})$, assign the right-hand value to left-hand if the inequation is satisfied where $z(\Delta D^{(i+1)})$ is a temporal variable of the minimum active sbox number.

$$z(\Delta D^{(i+1)}) > AS_{min}(\Delta D^{(i)}) + AS(\Delta D^{(i)} \to \Delta D^{(i+1)})$$

where $AS_{min}(\Delta D^{(i)})$ is the total minimum active sbox number of the truncated path from the first round to $\Delta D^{(i)}$, and $AS(\Delta D^{(i)} \to \Delta D^{(i+1)})$ denotes the active sbox number of truncated path $(\Delta D^{(i)} \to \Delta D^{(i+1)})$. Then the temporal variable $z(\Delta D^{(i+1)})$ after finishing the above steps becomes $AS_{min}(\Delta D^{(i+1)})$. Finally, the minimum result of $AS_{min}(\Delta D^{(r)})$ is the guaranteed minimum number of active sboxes for r-round.

After our searching of the guaranteed minimum number of active sboxes for internal permutations F_{96} and F_{128} by computer program, the results are listed in Table 7. Since the maximal probability for differential distribution of the sbox is 2^{-2}, 17 rounds of F_{96} and F_{128} cannot be distinguished from a random permutation by using differential paths. Thus we believe LHash is secure regarding differential attack.

4.3   Rebound Attack

Rebound attack is proposed in recent years [26], which is very effective against AES-like structures. Till now, lots of works have been done to improve it [19,23–25,27,28,30,34]. The original rebound attack works on AES structure itself, which cannot be directly applied to LHash. Sasaki tried to analyze the resistance of Feistel-SP structure against rebound attack [29]. Here we propose the preliminary rebound attack on LHash.

11-Round Rebound Distinguishers on the Internal Permutations. First, we can present 5-round inbound paths for both F_{96} and F_{128}. Then the full 11-round path can be obtained by extending the inbound rounds 3 rounds backward and 3 rounds forward. For F_{128}, the total complexity to find a solution to the

Table 7. The guaranteed minimum number of active sboxes for F_{96} and F_{128}

Round	2	3	4	5	6	7	8	9	10	11	12	13	14	15	16	17	18	19	20
F_{96}	1	2	6	10	14	18	22	24	26	29	32	36	40	42	46	48	51	54	58
F_{128}	1	2	6	10	16	22	27	31	35	37	41	45	51	54	61	64	67	71	75

11-round path is 2^{16}. For a random permutation, finding a solution fulfilling the input and output truncated differences is a limited birthday problem [13]. The complexity to solve this limited birthday problem for a random permutation is 2^{24}, which is higher than the complexity using our differential path. That is how this distinguisher works. For F_{96}, it takes 2^{12} complexity to find a solution, which is slower than the generic case (2^{18}).

Remarks on Super-Sbox Technique. Super-Sbox technique [13] exploits the independency between columns in 2 rounds of AES-like structure and improves the attackable rounds of rebound attack. In Feistel-PG structure, there is no independent structure like this. Therefore, we believe super-sbox technique doesn't work on LHash.

4.4   Zero-Sum Distinguisher

For a given permutation F, zero-sum distinguisher aims to find a partition of the input values X such that $\bigoplus_{x\in X} x = \bigoplus_{x\in X} F(x) = 0$ with low complexity. Here we consider another kind of distinguisher called half zero-sum distinguisher. Suppose permutation F is $2n$ bits, we aim to find set X such that $\bigoplus_{x\in X} Trunc_n^1(x) = \bigoplus_{x\in X} Trunc_n^2(F(x)) = 0$, where $Trunc_n^1$ and $Trunc_n^2$ are truncation functions with half of the state size.

We have measured the algebraic degree of F_{96} and F_{128}, using the technique proposed by Boura et al. [8–10]. For F_{96}, half of the state doesn't reach maximal algebraic degree of 95 after 7 rounds. Then we can propose a 15-round half zero-sum distinguisher for F_{96}. Choose 20 nibbles (except the first 4 nibbles of left branch) to be active, and then we can obtain 8 independent active nibbles after 3 rounds. When we choose one bit from the other part of the state and fix it, the 8 nibbles will go over all the 2^{32} values no matter which bit value we choose and fix besides the 8 nibbles. Then we can deduce that the algebraic degree of half of the state after another 5 rounds is no more than 27 and the sum of these bits will be zero. Therefore, in the forward direction, we have an 8-round half zero-sum distinguisher. Similarly, we can deduce that it is a 7-round half zero-sum distinguisher in the backward direction when we select the same active nibbles. Combining the forward and backward paths, we get a 15-round half zero-sum distinguisher for F_{96}, and the data complexity is 2^{80}. Apply the same technique on F_{128}, we can find a 15-round half zero-sum distinguisher with 2^{96}, which can be improved using the algebraic bounding techniques. In the forward direction, we choose all the nibble on the left side(64 bits) and 63 bits on the right side as active bits. In the forward direction, we can ensure that after 9 rounds, half of the state is balanced(with zero-sum). In the backward direction, we can only go back for 8 rounds. As a result, we have a 17-round half zero-sum distinguisher on F_{128} with 2^{127} data complexity.

4.5   Slide Attacks

Slide attacks are proposed for block ciphers, which take advantage of the self-similarity in the key expansion by constructing plaintext-ciphertext pairs fulfilling the slide conditions and recover the internal state or the secret key. Since hash function can be used to construct MACs, e.g. HMAC and NMAC, and sponge function itself can be used to construct MACs, we need to consider this type of attacks.

We can have two different types of slide attacks: sliding on round transformations inside the internal permutation and sliding on iterations of the internal permutations, *i.e.* sliding message blocks. First, slide inside the internal permutation is prevented by adding different round constants in each round. Second, slide attack between iterations of the internal permutations can be prevent if our padding rule ensures the last message block is always non-zero. The padding rule of LHash fulfills this property. Thus we can conclude that slide attack doesn't work on LHash.

4.6   Other Attacks

Rotational Distinguisher. Rotational distinguisher [21,22] was proposed to analyze ARX structures. Calculate the output of a rotational pair and check if the rotational condition is still fulfilled. In the design based on S-boxes and MDS linear layer, rotational distinguisher doesn't work well. The using of S-boxes ensure that if the rotational amount is not multiple of the size of the S-box, the rotational relation will be destroyed. The only possible way to apply rotational distinguisher on LHash, is to use a rotational amount as multiple of 4. Furthermore, the rotational pair will be destroyed by the nibble permutation layers. Based on this reasoning, we conclude that LHash is immune to rotational distinguisher.

Self Differential Attack. In a self differential attack, the difference between different partitions of a single value is considered, instead of the difference between a pair of values. The best collision attack on Keccak is based on this kind of attack [12]. The self similarity property can be found in AES, if there is no constants, the similarity can be preserved forever. In LHash, the nibble permutation can destroy the self similarity and ensures LHash immune to this kind of attack.

5   Implementation

5.1   Hardware Implementation

We evaluate hardware implementation of LHash using the *Virtual Silicon* (VST) standard cell library based on *UMC L180 0.18* μm *1P6M logic process* (*UMCL18G212T3*). We propose two different hardware implementations:

(1) minimal area (serialized) implementation and (2) implementation based on function T. In the second implementation, the area cost is higher while the speed is significantly increased and the energy consumption is significantly reduced.

Serialized Implementation. In hardware implementation of AES-like structures, such as PHOTON, the value before S-boxes don't need to be stored. The output values of the S-boxes can be stored in the same storage units of the inputs, *i.e.* the input values are overwritten. During the calculation of the iterated MDS layer, the intermediate values are also stored in the same place. For Feistel structure, the situation is different. Since the value of the left branch needs to be kept for the next round, we cannot just discard the original values before S-boxes. If the round function cannot be calculated in one cycle, we need extra storage to store the intermediate values for the following calculations, which is bad for compact implementations. In order to achieve compact serialized implementation, we introduce an equivalent expression of the round transformation. Figure 4 shows the equivalent round transformation with one T module. It can be expressed as follows, and the equation ensures that we don't need to store the intermediate output value of sbox during the calculation.

$$A(S(P_n(X_{i-1} \oplus C_i))) \oplus X_{i-2} = A(S(P_n(X_{i-1} \oplus C_i)) \oplus A^{-1}(X_{i-2}))$$

First, we applied the inversion of the linear layer, *i.e.* A^{-1}, to the right branch of the state. The updated value is stored at the original storage unit. Then we calculate the constant addition, nibble permutation, and sbox operation of the left branch nibble by nibble and XOR the output of the sbox into the right branch storage. After all sboxes have been processed, the linear transformation A is applied to the right branch again and we get the value of X_i. During the calculation, no extra storage is required. After finishing all the nonlinear T modules in one round, another operation is needed to swap the left and right branches.

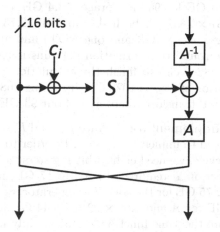

Fig. 4. Equivalent round transformation

In the serialized implementation of LHash, we use a 4-bit width datapath and only one instance of sbox, A^{-1} and A need to be implemented respectively. First of all, state storage needs 96(128) bits flip-flop cells to store the data, and each bit flip-flop requires 6 GE. Therefore, for F_{96} and F_{128} this module requires $96 \times 6 = 576$ GE and $128 \times 6 = 768$ GE respectively, which occupies the majority of the total area required. Then for the round transformation, six kinds of operations need to be done, including constant addition, nibble permutation, sbox, 4-bit XOR operation, linear transformation A^{-1} and A. Notice that in the design of LHash, the constants only apply to the first 16-bit of left branch and for the other bits the constants equal to zero. Therefore, we only need four 4-bit XOR to implement the constant addition operation which requires about 42.72 GE. Moreover, another 32.75 GE is needed for the constant generator(5-bit storage, one XNOR and one NOT). Then the nibble permutation can be implemented by simple wiring and costs no area and the choice of data is controlled by the Controller module where a Finite State Machine is used to generate the control signals. As specified in Sect. 3.2, the modules of sbox, A^{-1} and A require 21.84 GE, 29.37 GE(11 bits XOR), and 29.37 GE respectively. Finally, to XOR the output of sbox into the right branch nibble, a 4-bit XOR is needed which costs 10.68 GE. In the end of the round transformation, the swap operation can be implemented by wiring and need no additional area. Furthermore, an overall Controller module is needed to generate all the control signals and logic circuits. The Controller module is realized by a Finite State Machine and its gate varies depending on the size of internal permutation: about 74 GE for F_{96} and 93 GE for F_{128}.

In summary, for F_{96}, the round transformation contains three function T's. Each of them requires 4 cycles for A^{-1}, 4 cycles for the combination operation of constant addition, S-box and 4-bit XOR, and another 4 cycles for A. After the calculation of three function T, another 1 cycle is required to swap the left and right branches. Thus the round transformation requires $12 \times 3 + 1 = 37$ cycles and F_{96} requires $37 \times 18 = 666$ cycles in total. The area cost of F_{96} is about 817 GE, including 576 GE for 96-bit storage, 53.4 GE for five 4-bit XORs, 22 GE for the sbox, 29.37×2 GE for both A^{-1} and A, 32.75 GE for the constant generator(5-bit storage, one XNOR and one NOT) and about 74 GE for logic circuits. For F_{128}, the round transformation contains four T modules. It takes $(12 \times 4 + 1) \times 18 = 882$ cycles to finish the calculation. The area cost of the serialized implementation of F_{128} is 1028 GE, including 768 GE register storage, 166.89 GE for the round transformation, and about 93 GE for logic circuits.

Function T Based Implementation. Since F_{96} and F_{128} share the same module T, thus we only need to implement it once. In order to finish the calculation of function T in one cycle, we need eight 4-bit registers, constant generator and 16-bit XOR. The function T requires about 515.17 GE, including 192 GE for eight 4-bit storage, 32.75 GE for the constant generator, 88 GE for four S-boxes, $29.37 \times 4 = 117.84$ GE for A and $2.67 \times 32 = 85.44$ GE for 32-bit XOR. Both F_{96} and F_{128} can share the same function T and we only need extra storage for both of them. Therefore F_{96} requires $515.17 + 384 = 899.17$ GE, with additional

Table 8. Software performances in cycles per byte of the LHash variants

LHash-80/96/16/16	LHash-96/96/16/16	LHash-128/128/16/32	LHash-128/128/8/8
139c/B	139c/B	156c/B	312c/B

89.8 GE control logic circuits, and the total area cost is about 989 GE. It takes $3 \times 18 = 54$ cycles to finish the calculation of F_{96}. Similarly, F_{128} costs about $(515.17 + 576 + 108.8) \approx 1200$ GE and 72 cycles.

5.2 Software Implementation

We give in Table 8 our software implementation performances for the LHash variants. The processor used for the benchmarks is an Intel Core i7-3612QM @2.10 GHz. We have also benchmarked other lightweight hash function designs. QUARK reference code [1], which is very likely to be optimized, runs at 8k, 30k and 22k cycles per byte respectively for U-QUARK, D-QUARK and S-QUARK. The speed for PHOTON-80/20/16 and PHOTON-128/16/16 [14] are 96 and 156 cycles per byte, respectively.

6   Conclusion

We proposed a new lightweight hash function LHash, supporting digest length of 80, 96 and 128 bits, providing from 64 to 120 bits of preimage security and from 40 to 60 bits of second preimage and collision security. The internal permutation is designed based on structure Feistel-PG, using nibble permutations to improve the resistance to different attacks of the structure. The component S-box and linear layer are designed to be secure and suitable for hardware implementations. Serialized implementation of the internal permutation in LHash requires 817 and 1028 GE. LHash has the lowest energy consumption among existing lightweight hash functions. We offer the trade-offs among security, speed, energy consumption and implementation cost by adjusting the parameters. We also evaluate the security of LHash and our cryptanalytic results show that LHash achieves enough security margin against known attacks. In the end, we strongly encourage the security analysis of LHash and helpful comments.

Acknowledgement. We wish to thank Florian Mendel for his kind communication and many useful suggestions, and also the anonymous reviewers for their helpful comments. This work is partly supported by the National Basic Research Program of China (No. 2013CB338002) and the National Natural Science Foundation of China (No. 61272476, 61232009, 61202420).

A   Test Vectors

Test vectors for LHash are shown in hexadecimal notation as follows.

B   Figures

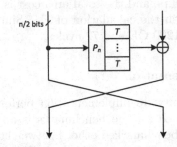

Fig. 5. Feistel-PG structure

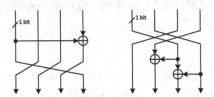

Fig. 6. Circuits for multiplications by 2 and 4 on $\mathbb{F}_2[x]/x^4 + x + 1$

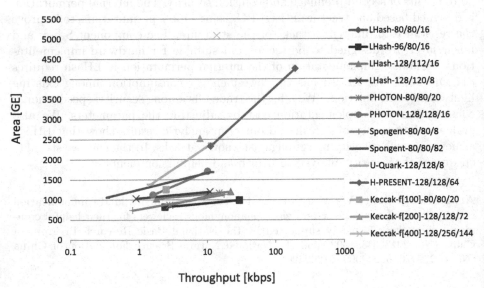

Fig. 7. Area versus throughput trade-off of lightweight hash functions

References

1. Aumasson, J.-P., Henzen, L., Meier, W., Plasencia, M.N.: Quark: a lightweight hash. J. Cryptol. **26**(2), 313–339 (2013)
2. Badel, S., Dağtekin, N., Nakahara Jr., J., Ouafi, K., Reffé, N., Sepehrdad, P., Sušil, P., Vaudenay, S.: ARMADILLO: a multi-purpose cryptographic primitive dedicated to hardware. In: Mangard, S., Standaert, F.-X. (eds.) CHES 2010. LNCS, vol. 6225, pp. 398–412. Springer, Heidelberg (2010)
3. Bertoni, G., Daemen, J., Peeters, M., Assche, G.V.: Sponge functions. In: Ecrypt Hash Worksop (2007)
4. Bogdanov, A., Knežević, M., Leander, G., Toz, D., Varıcı, K., Verbauwhede, I.: SPONGENT: a lightweight hash function. In: Preneel, B., Takagi, T. (eds.) CHES 2011. LNCS, vol. 6917, pp. 312–325. Springer, Heidelberg (2011)
5. Bogdanov, A.A., Knudsen, L.R., Leander, G., Paar, C., Poschmann, A., Robshaw, M., Seurin, Y., Vikkelsoe, C.: PRESENT: an ultra-lightweight block cipher. In: Paillier, P., Verbauwhede, I. (eds.) CHES 2007. LNCS, vol. 4727, pp. 450–466. Springer, Heidelberg (2007)
6. Bogdanov, A., Leander, G., Paar, C., Poschmann, A., Robshaw, M.J.B., Seurin, Y.: Hash functions and RFID tags: mind the gap. In: Oswald, E., Rohatgi, P. (eds.) CHES 2008. LNCS, vol. 5154, pp. 283–299. Springer, Heidelberg (2008)
7. Borghoff, J., et al.: PRINCE – a low-latency block cipher for pervasive computing applications (extended abstract). In: Wang, X., Sako, K. (eds.) ASIACRYPT 2012. LNCS, vol. 7658, pp. 208–225. Springer, Heidelberg (2012). http://eprint.iacr.org/2012/529.pdf
8. Boura, C., Canteaut, A.: Zero-sum distinguishers for iterated permutations and application to KECCAK-f and Hamsi-256. In: Biryukov, A., Gong, G., Stinson, D.R. (eds.) SAC 2010. LNCS, vol. 6544, pp. 1–17. Springer, Heidelberg (2011)
9. Boura, C., Canteaut, A.: On the influence of the algebraic degree of f^{1} on the algebraic degree of gf. IEEE Trans. Inf. Theory **59**(1), 691–702 (2013)
10. Boura, C., Canteaut, A., De Cannière, C.: Higher-order differential properties of KECCAK and *Luffa*. In: Joux, A. (ed.) FSE 2011. LNCS, vol. 6733, pp. 252–269. Springer, Heidelberg (2011)
11. De Cannière, C., Preneel, B.: TRIVIUM. In: Robshaw, M., Billet, O. (eds.) New Stream Cipher Designs. LNCS, vol. 4986, pp. 244–266. Springer, Heidelberg (2008)
12. Dinur, I., Dunkelman, O., Shamir, A.: Self-differential Cryptanalysis of Up to 5 Rounds of SHA-3 (2012). http://eprint.iacr.org/2012/672.pdf
13. Gilbert, H., Peyrin, T.: Super-Sbox cryptanalysis: improved attacks for AES-Like permutations. In: Hong, S., Iwata, T. (eds.) FSE 2010. LNCS, vol. 6147, pp. 365–383. Springer, Heidelberg (2010)
14. Guo, J., Peyrin, T., Poschmann, A.: The PHOTON family of lightweight hash functions. In: Rogaway, P. (ed.) CRYPTO 2011. LNCS, vol. 6841, pp. 222–239. Springer, Heidelberg (2011)
15. Guo, J., Peyrin, T., Poschmann, A., Robshaw, M.: The LED block cipher. In: Preneel, B., Takagi, T. (eds.) CHES 2011. LNCS, vol. 6917, pp. 326–341. Springer, Heidelberg (2011)
16. Hell, M., Johansson, T., Maximov, A., Meier, W.: The grain family of stream ciphers. In: Robshaw, M., Billet, O. (eds.) New Stream Cipher Designs. LNCS, vol. 4986, pp. 179–190. Springer, Heidelberg (2008)
17. Hirose, S.: Some plausible constructions of double-block-length hash functions. In: Robshaw, M. (ed.) FSE 2006. LNCS, vol. 4047, pp. 210–225. Springer, Heidelberg (2006)

18. Hong, D., et al.: HIGHT: a new block cipher suitable for low-resource device. In: Goubin, L., Matsui, M. (eds.) CHES 2006. LNCS, vol. 4249, pp. 46–59. Springer, Heidelberg (2006)
19. Jean, J., Naya-Plasencia, M., Peyrin, T.: Improved rebound attack on the finalist Grøst. In: Canteaut, A. (ed.) FSE 2012. LNCS, vol. 7649, pp. 110–126. Springer, Heidelberg (2012)
20. Kavun, E.B., Yalcin, T.: A lightweight implementation of keccak hash function for radio-frequency identification applications. In: Ors Yalcin, S.B. (ed.) RFIDSec 2010. LNCS, vol. 6370, pp. 258–269. Springer, Heidelberg (2010)
21. Khovratovich, D., Nikolić, I.: Rotational cryptanalysis of ARX. In: Hong, S., Iwata, T. (eds.) FSE 2010. LNCS, vol. 6147, pp. 333–346. Springer, Heidelberg (2010)
22. Khovratovich, D., Nikolić, I., Rechberger, C.: Rotational rebound attacks on reduced skein. In: Abe, M. (ed.) ASIACRYPT 2010. LNCS, vol. 6477, pp. 1–19. Springer, Heidelberg (2010)
23. Lamberger, M., Mendel, F., Rechberger, C., Rijmen, V., Schläffer, M.: Rebound distinguishers: results on the full whirlpool compression function. In: Matsui, M. (ed.) ASIACRYPT 2009. LNCS, vol. 5912, pp. 126–143. Springer, Heidelberg (2009)
24. Lamberger, M., Mendel, F., Rechberger, C., Rijmen, V., Schläffer, M.: The Rebound Attack and Subspace Distinguishers: Application to Whirlpool. http://eprint.iacr.org/2010/198.pdf. Accepted for publication in J. Cryptology
25. Matusiewicz, K., Naya-Plasencia, M., Nikolić, I., Sasaki, Y., Schläffer, M.: Rebound attack on the full LANE compression function. In: Matsui, M. (ed.) ASIACRYPT 2009. LNCS, vol. 5912, pp. 106–125. Springer, Heidelberg (2009)
26. Mendel, F., Rechberger, C., Schläffer, M., Thomsen, S.S.: The rebound attack: cryptanalysis of reduced whirlpool and Grøstl. In: Dunkelman, O. (ed.) FSE 2009. LNCS, vol. 5665, pp. 260–276. Springer, Heidelberg (2009)
27. Naya-Plasencia, M.: How to improve rebound attacks. In: Rogaway, P. (ed.) CRYPTO 2011. LNCS, vol. 6841, pp. 188–205. Springer, Heidelberg (2011)
28. Rijmen, V., Toz, D., Varıcı, K.: Rebound attack on reduced-round versions of JH. In: Hong, S., Iwata, T. (eds.) FSE 2010. LNCS, vol. 6147, pp. 286–303. Springer, Heidelberg (2010)
29. Sasaki, Y.: Double-SP is weaker than single-SP: rebound attacks on feistel ciphers with several rounds. In: Galbraith, S., Nandi, M. (eds.) INDOCRYPT 2012. LNCS, vol. 7668, pp. 265–282. Springer, Heidelberg (2012)
30. Sasaki, Y., Wang, L., Wu, S., Wu, W.: Investigating fundamental security requirements on whirlpool: improved preimage and collision attacks. In: Wang, X., Sako, K. (eds.) ASIACRYPT 2012. LNCS, vol. 7658, pp. 562–579. Springer, Heidelberg (2012)
31. Shibutani, K., Isobe, T., Hiwatari, H., Mitsuda, A., Akishita, T., Shirai, T.: *Piccolo*: an ultra-lightweight blockcipher. In: Preneel, B., Takagi, T. (eds.) CHES 2011. LNCS, vol. 6917, pp. 342–357. Springer, Heidelberg (2011)
32. Suzaki, T., Minematsu, K.: Improving the generalized feistel. In: Hong, S., Iwata, T. (eds.) FSE 2010. LNCS, vol. 6147, pp. 19–39. Springer, Heidelberg (2010)
33. Sušil, P., Vaudenay, S.: Multipurpose cryptographic primitive ARMADILLO3. In: Mangard, S. (ed.) CARDIS 2012. LNCS, vol. 7771, pp. 203–218. Springer, Heidelberg (2013)
34. Wu, S., Feng, D., Wu, W.: Practical rebound attack on 12-round cheetah-256. In: Lee, D., Hong, S. (eds.) ICISC 2009. LNCS, vol. 5984, pp. 300–314. Springer, Heidelberg (2010)
35. Wu, W., Zhang, L.: LBlock: a lightweight block cipher. In: Lopez, J., Tsudik, G. (eds.) ACNS 2011. LNCS, vol. 6715, pp. 327–344. Springer, Heidelberg (2011)

Cryptanalysis of the Round-Reduced GOST Hash Function

Jian Zou[1,2]($\boxtimes$), Wenling Wu[1], and Shuang Wu[3]

[1] TCA, Institute of Software, Chinese Academy of Sciences,
Beijing 100190, People's Republic of China
{zoujian,wwl}@is.iscas.ac.cn
[2] Graduate University of Chinese Academy of Sciences,
Beijing 100049, People's Republic of China
[3] Huawei International, Shenzhen, China
wushuang@huawei.com

Abstract. The GOST hash function, defined in GOST R 34.11-2012, was selected as the new Russian standard on August 7, 2012. It is designed to replace the old Russian standard GOST R 34.11-94. The GOST hash function is an AES-based primitive and is considered as an asymmetric reply to the SHA-3. It is an iterated hash function based on the Merkle-Damgård strengthening design. In addition to the common iterated structure, it defines a checksum computed over all input message blocks. The checksum is then needed for the final hash value computation. In this paper, we show the first cryptanalytic attacks on the round-reduced GOST hash function. Using the combination of Super-Sbox technique and multi-collision, we present collision attacks on 5-round of the GOST-256 and GOST-512 hash function, respectively. The complexity of these collision attacks are both $(2^{122}, 2^{64})$ (in time and memory). Furthermore, we combine the guess-and-determine MitM attack with multi-collision to construct a preimage attack on 6-round GOST-512 hash function. The complexity of the preimage attack is about 2^{505} and the memory requirements is about 2^{64}. As far as we know, these are the first attacks on the round-reduced GOST hash function.

Keywords: GOST · Preimage attack · Collision attack · Multi-collision · Rebound attack · Meet-in-the-middle · Guess-and-determine

1 Introduction

Cryptographic hash functions are playing important roles in the modern cryptography. They have many important applications, such as authentication and digital signatures. In general, hash function must satisfy three security requirements: preimage resistance, second preimage resistance and collision resistance. In the last few years, the cryptanalysis of hash functions has been significantly improved. After the pioneering work of Wang [21–23], there is a strong need for a secure and efficient hash function. In 2012, GOST R 34.11-2012 [17] was

© Springer International Publishing Switzerland 2014
D. Lin et al. (Eds.): Inscrypt 2013, LNCS 8567, pp. 309–322, 2014.
DOI: 10.1007/978-3-319-12087-4_20

selected as the new Russian National hash function standard. In addition, NIST announced that Keccak [3] was the winner of the SHA-3 competition [15] in 2012.

GOST R 34.11-94 [18] was theoretically broken in 2008 [12,13]. As a result, GOST R 34.11-2012 is designed to replace the old Russian standard GOST R 34.11-94 that no longer fits performance and security requirements. The new GOST hash function was approved on August 7, 2012 and deployed on January 1, 2013 by the Federal Agency on Technical Regulating and Metrology of Russian Federation (FATRMRF). It provides operation of digital signature systems using the asymmetric cryptographic algorithm in compliance with GOST R 34.10-2012. The GOST hash function is widely used in Russia and is developed by the Center for Information Protection and Special Communications of the FATRMRF with participation of the Open joint-stock company "Information Technologies and Communication Systems". Note that for the remainder of this article we refer to the new GOST hash function simply as GOST.

GOST is an iterated hash function based on the Merkle-Damgård strengthening design. In addition to the common iterated structure, GOST specifies a checksum consisting of the modular addition of all message blocks, which is the input to the final application of the compression function. The compression function of GOST employs an SPN structure following the AES design strategy. GOST has an output length of 256/512-bit. In the following, the two hash functions are called GOST-256 and GOST-512, respectively. The designers [6] claimed that GOST made many attacks harder to apply, such as multi-collision attacks, differential attacks, rebound attacks, and the meet-in-the-middle attacks. However, the design principles of GOST and Whirlpool are very similar, and hence the attacks on Whirlpool can be extended to GOST in a quite straightforward way. In addition, Gauravaram [4] showed some weaknesses on hash functions using checksums.

At Crypto 2004, Joux [7] presented a method to construct multi-collision by using the flaw of the iterated structure of the hash function. Based on the result, Joux pointed out that the concatenation of several hash function does not increase the security.

With respect to the collision attack, the rebound attack proposed by Mendel et al. [14] is very effective with the differential attack against AES based structure. From then on, many techniques are proposed to improve the original rebound attack such as start-from-the-middle technique [11], linearized match-in-the-middle technique [11], Super-Sbox analysis [5,9], and multiple-inbound technique [8–10].

In the past few years, many techniques have been proposed to improve the preimage attacks. One of them is the meet-in-the-middle (MitM) preimage attack with the splice-and-cut technique. This method is first proposed by Aoki and Sasaki to attack MD4 [1]. In CRYPTO 2009, Aoki and Sasaki [2] combined the MitM attack with the guessing of carry bits technique to improve their preimage attack on SHA-0 and SHA-1. In FSE 2012, Wu et al. [24] improved its complexity and proposed the pseudo preimage attack on Grøstl. Using the combination of the guess-and-determine and the MitM attack, Sasaki et al. [20] improved the preimage attacks on Whirlpool in AsiaCrypt 2012. In addition, Zou *et al.* [25] combined the guess-and-determine with the MitM attack to propose an improved pseudo-preimage attack on Grøstl.

Our Contributions. Since GOST adopts the Merkle-Damgård strengthening design, it seems difficult to attack the GOST hash function. In addition, the compression function of GOST employs well-studied and time-tested constructions, which makes many known attacks harder to apply. In this paper, we present a security analysis of GOST with respect to collision and preimage resistance. Our attacks are composed of some known attacks, such as multi-collision attack, rebound attack and the MitM attack. Using the combination of Super-Sbox technique and multi-collision attack, we can construct collision attacks on 5-round of the GOST-256 and GOST-512 hash function. Then we combine the guess-and-determine technique with the MitM preimage attack to propose preimage attacks on 6-round of the compression function of GOST-256 and GOST-512. Utilizing the multi-collision technique, we extend the preimage attack on the compression function to the GOST-512 hash function. As far as we know, this is yet the first published security analysis of the GOST hash function. Our cryptanalytic results of GOST are summarized in Table 1.

Table 1. Summary of attack results for GOST

Algorithm	Target	Attack type	Rounds	Time	Memory	Source
GOST-256 (12 rounds)	Compression function	Collision	5	2^{120}	2^{64}	Sect. 3.1
	Compression function	Preimage	6	2^{240}	2^{64}	Sect. 4.1
	Hash function	Collision	5	2^{122}	2^{64}	Sect. 3.2
GOST-512 (12 rounds)	Compression function	Collision	5	2^{120}	2^{64}	Sect. 3.1
	Compression function	Preimage	6	2^{496}	2^{64}	Sect. 4.1
	Hash function	Collision	5	2^{122}	2^{64}	Sect. 3.2
	Hash function	Preimage	6	2^{505}	2^{64}	Sect. 4.2

Outline of the Paper. The rest of the paper is organized as follows. We give a short description of GOST in Sect. 2. In Sect. 3, we present the collision attacks on the round-reduced GOST. Then we show our preimage attacks on the round-reduced GOST in Sect. 4. Section 5 concludes the paper.

2 Description of GOST

GOST is an iterated hash function with an SPN structure following the AES design strategy. The basic construction of GOST is shown in Fig. 1. GOST outputs a 256 or 512-bit hash value and can process up to 2^{512}-bit message. The initial value for GOST-256 is $(00000001)^{64}$, while the initial value for GOST-512 is 0^{512}. For the GOST-256 hash function, a truncation function is needed to produce the final hash value. Assume a message M is padded and divided into 512-bit message blocks $M_1, \ldots M_t$. The hash value H is generated as follows:

$$CV_0 \leftarrow IV_{256} \; (or \; IV_{512})$$

$$CV_i \leftarrow CF(CV_{i-1}, M_i) \; for \; 1 \leq i \leq t$$

$$CV_{t+1} \leftarrow CF(CV_t, |M|)$$

$$CV_{t+2} \leftarrow CF(CV_{t+1}, M_1 + M_2 + \ldots + M_t)$$

$$H = \begin{cases} Trunc_{256}(CV_{t+2}) & for \; 256 - bit \; hash \; value \\ CV_{t+2} & for \; 512 - bit \; hash \; value \end{cases}$$

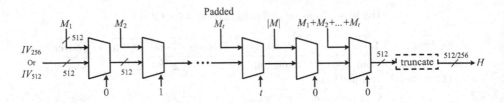

Fig. 1. Structure of the GOST hash functions

Here the IV_{256} and IV_{512} are initial values for two hash values $n = 256$ bits and $n = 512$ bits, respectively. $|M|$ represents the bit-length of the entire message prior to padding, and '+' denotes addition modulo 2^{512}. The $CF(CV_{i-1}, M_i)$ is the compression function of GOST. Before applying the compression function, the input message M is processed to be a multiple of 512 bits by the padding procedure. According to the padding procedure, a single bit '1' and len_0 '0's are put at the end of the message M. Here len_0 satisfies the following equation, $len_M + 1 + len_0 \equiv 0 \mod 512$ (len_M and len_0 are short for the length of M and the number of '0', respectively).

The compression function $CF(\cdot)$ of GOST basically consists of two parts: the key schedule and the state update transformation. As shown in Fig. 2, the underlying block cipher E operates in the Miyaguchi-Preneel mode. The state update transformation and the key schedule of E update an 8×8 state of 64 bytes in 12 rounds and 13 round separately. The round transformations of GOST are briefly described here:

- AK: The key addition AK operation XORs the round key to the state.
- S: The S transformation applies an S-box to each byte of the state independently.
- P: The P transformation rearranges each byte of the 8×8 state in the predefined order. See Fig. 3.
- L: In the L operation, each row of the state is multiplied by an MDS matrix.

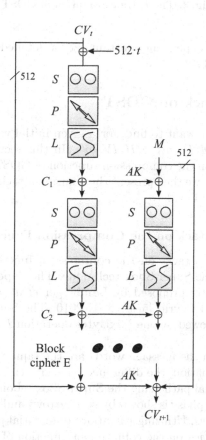

Fig. 2. The compression function of GOST

The compression function $CF(\cdot) : F_2^{512} \times F_2^{512} \mapsto F_2^{512}$, $N \in F_2^{512}$ is defined as follows:

$$CF_N(CV_{i-1}, M_i) = E(L \circ P \circ S(CV_{i-1} \oplus N), M_i) \oplus CV_{i-1} \oplus M_i, \quad CV_{i-1}, M_i \in F_2^{512},$$

where $E(K, m) = AK \circ \prod_{j=1}^{12} L \circ P \circ S \circ AK(m)$, and $N = 512 \cdot i$. The i is the block counter.

The key schedule transformation is computed as follows:

$$K_1 = L \circ P \circ S(CV_i \oplus N), \quad K_i = L \circ P \circ S(K_{j-1} \oplus C_{j-1}), j \in \{2, \ldots 13\},$$

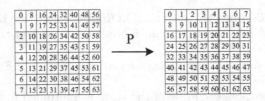

Fig. 3. The P transformation of GOST

where C_{j-1} is a round-dependent constant. For a detailed explanation, we refer to the original paper [17].

3   Collision Attack on GOST

In a collision attack, we want to find, for a given initial value IV, two messages m and m' such that $H(IV, m) = H(IV, m')$. In this section, we will first propose collision attacks on the compression function of GOST-256 and GOST-512. Based on these attacks, we then present the collision attacks on the hash function of GOST-256 and GOST-512.

3.1   A Collision Attack on the Compression Function of GOST

We show the collision attacks on the compression function of GOST-256 and GOST-512 by using the Super-Sbox technique. The Super-Sbox rebound technique was independently proposed by Lamberger *et al.* at ASIACRYPT 2009 [8] and by Gilbert and Peyrin [5] at FSE 2010. The Super-Sbox consists of 8 parallel S-boxes S, followed by one MixBytes operation L and another 8 parallel S-boxes S: S-L-S.

If the differences in the message words are the same as in the output of the state update transformation, the differences cancel each other through the feedforward. Our differential path using the Super-Sbox rebound technique is shown in Fig. 4. The inbound phase is shown by solid arrows and the outbound phase is shown by dashed arrows. Utilizing the above differential path, we can construct a 5-round collision attack on the compression function of GOST. Note that the differential path can be used in the collision attack for both the GOST-256 and GOST-512. Here we want to construct the collision attack on the compression function of GOST, so we can not make use of the freedom degree of the key schedule.

For the inbound phase, the procedure proceeds as follows:

1. Fix the input difference of the 2nd round Mix Column operation L, then compute the input difference of the 3rd round Sbox operation S. For each Super-Sbox, calculate the output differences of the Super-Sbox for all possible pairs of inputs that have the fixed input difference. Make tables of the output difference and the corresponding input pair. This step takes time and memory 2^{64}.

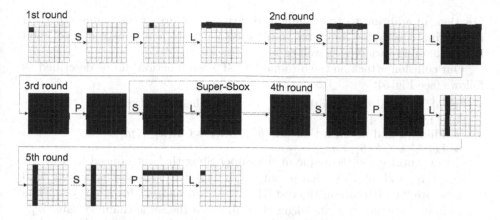

Fig. 4. Differential path for the Super-Sbox technique

2. Fix the output difference of the 4th round L and compute the output difference of the 4th round Sbox operation S.
3. For each Super-Sbox, use the difference distribution table of Step 1 to find the pairs of the inputs such that the output difference of the 4th round Sbox operation S is equal to the output difference of the Step 2. Note that this can be done for each Super-Sbox independently. If the number of the solutions of the inbound phase is not sufficient, Step 2 and 3 can be repeated until the output differences of the 4th round L are exhausted. After exhausting the differences at Step 2, the adversary can also repeat the procedure from Step 1 by changing the input difference of the 2nd round L.
4. For the whole inbound phase, we expect 2^{64} solutions with a complexity of 2^{64} in time and memory.

All in all, the average time complexity to generate an internal state pair that follows the differential path of the inbound phase is one. In the outbound phase, the state pairs of the inbound phase are propagated outwards probabilistically. The transition from 8 active bytes to one active byte through the Mix column transformation L has a probability of 2^{-56}. Since there are two $8 \rightarrow 1$ transitions (the L operation in round 1 and round 5), the probability of the outbound phase is $2^{-2 \cdot 56} = 2^{-112}$. In other word, we have to repeat the inbound phase about 2^{112} times to generate 2^{112} starting points for the outbound phase of the attack. To construct a collision at the output of this 5-round compression function, the exact value of the input and output difference has to match. Since these is only one byte is active, this can be fulfilled with a probability of 2^{-8}. As a result, the complexity to generate a collision for 5-round compression function of GOST-256 and GOST-512 are both $2^{112+8} = 2^{120}$. The memory requirement are 2^{64}.

3.2   A Collision Attack on GOST Hash Function

In this section, we show how to extend the collision attack on the compression function to the hash function. According to the definition of the GOST hash function, in addition to the common iterative structure, a checksum is needed for the final hash value computation. As a result, we have to construct a collision in the chaining variables as well as in the checksum.

Our collision attack on the 5-round GOST hash function can be described as follows (see Fig. 5):

1. Let h'_0 be equal to the initial value IV of the hash function.
   For i from 1 to 4 do:
   - Find m_i and m'_i such that $CF(h'_{i-1}, m_i) = CF(h'_{i-1}, m'_i)$
   - Let $h'_i = CF(h'_{i-1}, m_i)$.
   Here we utilize the technique of the Super-Sbox that introduced in Sect. 3.1 to find m_i and m'_i. Note that m_i and m'_i only differ in the same one byte, and these are no difference in the rest 63 bytes of m_i and m'_i, for $1 \le i \le 4$. Then we have constructed 2^4 messages that all reach the same chaining value h'_4.
2. Randomly choose m_5. Here we just require that m_5 satisfies the padding rule. As shown in Fig. 5, all the 2^4 messages reach the same chaining value h'_5. Since the length of the 2^4 messages $|m|$ are equal, the chaining value h'_6 of the 2^4 messages are still the same. Note that the 2^4 checksums of the above messages are only different in one byte. Based on the birthday paradox, the probability to find a collision among the 2^4 checksums is high. As a result, we have constructed a collision in the chaining variables as well as in the checksum. Then we construct a collision attack on the GOST hash function.

Find collision in the chaining variables h'_i as well as in the checksum

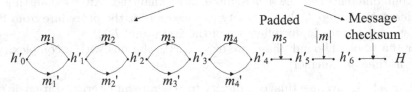

Fig. 5. Overview of the collision attack on GOST

It takes $4 \cdot 2^{120}$ computations and 2^{64} memory to construct the $2^4 - collision$ in Step 1. According to the attack process, the collision attack has a complexity of about 2^{122} evaluations of the compression function of GOST. The memory requirement is 2^{64}. Note that our collision attack can be applied to both the GOST-256 and GOST-512 hash function.

4   Preimage Attack on GOST

In this section, we present a preimage attack on the GOST-512 hash function with a complexity of about 2^{505} evaluations of the compression function. Firstly, we will show how to construct the preimage attacks for the compression function of GOST-256 and GOST-512. Secondly, we show the preimage attack for the GOST-512 hash function based on the preimage attack on the compression function of GOST-512.

4.1   Preimage Attack on 6-Round Compression Function of GOST

Here we fix the key-input (chaining value) when we perform the MitM attack, and the goal is to find the plaintext-input (message) that provides the given target. The 6-round chunk separation of the state update transformation is illustrated in Fig. 6. Using the combination of the guess-and-determine technique and the MitM attack, we can construct 6-round preimage attacks on the compression function of GOST-256 and GOST-512. By guessing some unknown bytes, all the possible values of the guessed bytes are used as extra freedom degrees in the MitM preimage attack. As a result, more matching points can be obtained. Note that the guessed bytes are extra constraints. After a partial match is found, we should check if the guessed value produces a valid preimage. We will talk about more details about the guessing technique in the following attack algorithm.

Parameters for the Guess-and-Determine MitM Attack. As shown in Fig. 6, we use the purple bytes as the guessed bytes. The red/blue color means neutral message. They are independent from each other. The white color stands for the bytes whose values are affected by red bytes and blue bytes both, and we can't determine their values until a partial match is found. The gray bytes are constants that come from the hash value or the initial structure. In order to evaluate the complexity for the attack, we should define these parameters: freedom degrees in red and blue bytes (d_r, d_b), the guessing red and blue bytes (D_{gr}, D_{gb}), the bits of the matching point b_m.

The Attack Algorithm and Complexity. The guess-and-determine MitM attack algorithm can be described as follows:

1. Set random values to constants in the initial structure.
2. For all possible values 2^{d_r} of the red bytes and $2^{D_{gr}}$ of the guessing red bytes, compute backward from the initial structure and obtain the value at the matching point. Store the values in a lookup table L_{comp}.
3. For all possible values 2^{d_b} of the blue bytes and $2^{D_{gb}}$ of the guessing blue bytes, compute forward from the initial structure and obtain the value at the matching point. Check if there exists an entry in L_{comp} that matches the result at the matching point. Expected number of the partial matches is $2^{d_r+d_b+D_{gr}+D_{gb}-b_m}$.
4. Once a partial match is found, compute and check if the guessed value is right. The probability of the validity is $2^{-D_{gr}-D_{gb}}$. There are $2^{d_r+d_b-b_m}$ valid partial matches left. Then we continue the computation and check the full match. The probability that a partial match is a full match is $2^{-(n-b_m)}$.
5. The success probability for the above steps is $2^{d_r+d_b+D_{gr}+D_{gb}-b_m} \cdot 2^{-(D_{gb}+D_{gr})} \cdot 2^{-(n-b_m)} = 2^{d_r+d_b-n}$. Then repeat the above steps for $2^{n-d_b-d_r}$ to find one full match.

The complexity for each step can be calculated as follows:

1. In Step 2, building the lookup table L_{comp} takes $2^{d_r+D_{gr}}$ computations and memory.

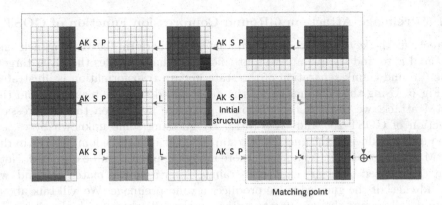

Fig. 6. Preimage attack on the compression function of GOST

2. In Step 3, it takes $2^{d_b+D_{gb}}$ computations to find the partial matches. Expected number of the partial matches is $2^{d_b+D_{gb}+d_r+D_{gr}-b_m}$.
3. In Step 4, testing all the partial matches in step 3 needs $2^{d_b+D_{gb}+d_r+D_{gr}-b_m}$ computations. The probability of the validity is $2^{-D_{gb}-D_{gr}}$, and there are $2^{d_b+d_r-b_m}$ valid partial matches left.
4. In Step 5, repeat the above four step for $2^{n-d_b-d_r}$ times.

Then the complexity of the above attack algorithm is:

$$2^{n-d_b-d_r} \cdot (2^{d_r+D_{gr}} + 2^{d_b+D_{gb}} + 2^{d_b+D_{gb}+d_r+D_{gr}-b_m})$$
$$= 2^n \cdot (2^{D_{gr}-d_b} + 2^{D_{gb}-d_r} + 2^{D_{gb}+D_{gr}-b_m}). \tag{1}$$

As shown in Fig. 6, the parameters for the attack on the 6-round compression function of GOST-512 are as follow: $d_r = 16$, $d_b = 64$, $D_{gr} = 48$, $D_{gb} = 0$, $b_m = 64$ and $n = 512$. According to equation (1), the overall complexity is $2^{512} \cdot (2^{48-64} + 2^{0-16} + 2^{48-64}) \approx 2^{496}$ compression function calls. Only Step 2 requires $2^{16+48} = 2^{64}$ memory.

Note that our attack can also be applied to the last block compression function of GOST-256. In this case, the parameters for the attack are as follows: $d_r = 16$, $d_b = 64$, $D_{gr} = 48$, $D_{gb} = 0$, $b_m = 64$ and $n = 256$. The overall complexity is $2^{256} \cdot (2^{48-64} + 2^{0-16} + 2^{48-64}) \approx 2^{240}$ compression function calls. The memory requirement is also 2^{64}.

4.2 Preimage Attack on the GOST-512 Hash Function

We show how to extend the preimage attack on the compression function to the GOST-512 hash function. Our technique combine the multi-collision attack with the guess-and-determine MitM attack.

Our preimage attack on the GOST-512 hash function can be described as follows (see Fig. 7):

1. Make use of the multi-collision technique proposed by Joux. Find w successive collisions by performing w successive birthday attacks, as follows: Let h_0 be equal to the initial value IV of the hash function.

$$CF(h_0, M_1) = CF(h_0, M_1') = h_1(say),\ where\ M_1 \neq M_1'$$
$$CF(h_1, M_2) = CF(h_1, M_2') = h_2(say),\ where\ M_2 \neq M_2'$$
$$\dots$$
$$CF(h_{w-1}, M_w) = CF(h_{w-1}, M_w') = h_w(say),\ where\ M_w \neq M_w'$$

The 2^w different messages built as above all reach the same final value h_w. Store the $2 \cdot w$ messages M_i and M_i' for $1 \leq i \leq w$ in a lookup table L_M.

2. Randomly choose 2^k M_{w+1}. For each M_{w+1}, choose a corresponding message M_{w+2} such that $M_{w+1} + M_{w+2} = 0$ (Here '+' denotes addition modulo 2^{512}). For each M_{w+1} and the corresponding M_{w+2}, calculate the corresponding chaining value h_{w+3} that is marked in Fig. 7.

3. For each h_{w+3} and the given H, compute the corresponding message M_{target} by the method introduced in Sect. 4.1. Since the number of h_{w+3} is 2^k, we can find out the corresponding 2^k message M_{target} for the given digest H. Store the 2^k message M_{target} in a lookup table L_{hash}.

4. For the 2^w collision found in Step 1, we can compute the sum modulo 2^{512} of the 2^w message blocks. Check if there exists an entry in L_{hash} that matches the result such that $M_{target} = M_0 + M_1 + \dots + M_w + M_{w+1} + M_{w+2}$. Since $M_{w+1} + M_{w+2} = 0$, M_{w+1} and M_{w+2} have no effect on the sum of all message blocks. When $w + k \geq 512$, we expect to find a match. Then we construct a preimage attack on the GOST.

The complexity for each step can be calculated as follows:

1. In Step 1, finding the 2^w-collision takes $w \cdot 2^{256}$ computations. Here we can search the collisions by the memory-less algorithms such as the Rho algorithm [16] and the distinguished points [19]. The memory requirement for building the lookup table L_M is $2 \cdot w$.

2. In Step 3, it takes 2^{496} computations to find a message M_{target} for each h_{w+3} and the given H. Then the complexity to find 2^k M_{target} is 2^{k+496}. The memory requirement for building the lookup table L_{hash} is 2^k.

3. In Step 4, checking the final match for 2^w candidates requires 2^w table look-ups.

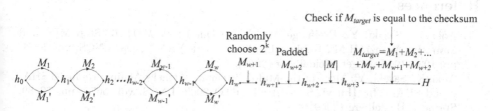

Fig. 7. Preimage attack on the GOST hash function

All in all, the overall complexity to calculate a preimage of GOST-512 hash function is $w \cdot 2^{256} + 2^{k+496} + 2^w$. Note that the condition of $w + k \geq 512$ should be satisfied in order to find one final match. The memory requirement is 2^{64} (needed to solve the M_{target} in Sect. 4.1). As a result, the minimum complexity is 2^{505}, when $k = 8$, $w = 504$. Since the complexity 2^{505} is far greater than 2^{256}, our preimage attack can not attack GOST-256 hash function.

5 Conclusion

In this article, we propose the collision attacks and the preimage attacks on the GOST hash function. As opposed to most commonly used hash functions such as SHA-1 and SHA-2, GOST adopts the Merkle-Damgård strengthening design, that defines a checksum computed over all input message blocks besides the common iterated structure. The checksum is needed for the final hash value computation. This design approach makes many known attacks harder to apply. The original MitM attack [1] can not be used to solve a preimage of the GOST hash function due to the checksum operation. In addition, we can not construct the collision attack on the GOST hash function only by the rebound attack. Our solution is the combination of some known attacks such as the multi-collision, rebound attack and the MitM preimage attack. To sum up, we present the first public security analysis of the GOST hash function. Firstly, we construct collision attacks on the compression function of GOST-256 and GOST-512 by using the Super-Sbox technique. Utilizing the Multi-collision attack, the collision attacks on the compression function can be extended to the hash function. Furthermore, we propose the preimage attacks on 6-round compression function of GOST-256 and GOST-512 by combining the guess-and-determine with the MitM attack. At last, we present the preimage attack on the 6-round of the GOST-512 hash function by using the combination of the guess-and-determine MitM attack with the multi-collision attack. However, our attacks do not threat any security claims of GOST.

Acknowledgments. We would like to thank anonymous referees for their helpful comments and suggestions. This work is supported by the National Basic Research Program of China 973 Program (2013CB338002), and the National Natural Science Foundation of China (61272476, 61232009).

References

1. Aoki, K., Sasaki, Y.: Preimage Attacks on One-Block MD4, 63-Step MD5 and More. In: Avanzi, R.M., Keliher, L., Sica, F. (eds.) SAC 2008. LNCS, vol. 5381, pp. 103–119. Springer, Heidelberg (2009)
2. Aoki, K., Sasaki, Y.: Meet-in-the-Middle Preimage Attacks Against Reduced SHA-0 and SHA-1. In: Halevi, S. (ed.) CRYPTO 2009. LNCS, vol. 5677, pp. 70–89. Springer, Heidelberg (2009)
3. Bertoni, G., Daemen, J., Peeters, M., Van Assche, G.: The keccak sha-3 submission. Submission to NIST (Round 3) (2011).

4. Gauravaram, P., Kelsey, J., Knudsen, L.R., Thomsen, S.S.: On hash functions using checksums. Int. J. Inf. Sec. **9**(2), 137–151 (2010)
5. Gilbert, H., Peyrin, T.: Super-Sbox Cryptanalysis: Improved Attacks for AES-Like Permutations. In: Hong, S., Iwata, T. (eds.) FSE 2010. LNCS, vol. 6147, pp. 365–383. Springer, Heidelberg (2010)
6. Grebnev, S, Dmukh, A, Dygin, D., Matyukhin, D., Rudskoy, V, Shishkin, V.: Asymmetric reply to sha-3: Russian hash function draft standard. http://www.tc26.ru/CTCrypt/2012/abstract/streebog_corr.pdf/
7. Joux, A.: Multicollisions in Iterated Hash Functions. Application to Cascaded Constructions. In: Franklin, M. (ed.) CRYPTO 2004. LNCS, vol. 3152, pp. 306–316. Springer, Heidelberg (2004)
8. Lamberger, M., Mendel, F., Rechberger, C., Rijmen, V., Schläffer, M.: Rebound Distinguishers: Results on the Full Whirlpool Compression Function. In: Matsui, M. (ed.) ASIACRYPT 2009. LNCS, vol. 5912, pp. 126–143. Springer, Heidelberg (2009)
9. Lamberger, M., Mendel, F., Rechberger, C., Rijmen, V., Schläffer, M.: The rebound attack and subspace distinguishers: application to whirlpool. IACR Cryptology ePrint Archive **2010**, 198 (2010)
10. Matusiewicz, K., Naya-Plasencia, M., Nikolić, I., Sasaki, Y., Schläffer, M.: Rebound Attack on the Full LANE Compression Function. In: Matsui, M. (ed.) ASIACRYPT 2009. LNCS, vol. 5912, pp. 106–125. Springer, Heidelberg (2009)
11. Mendel, F., Peyrin, T., Rechberger, C., Schläffer, M.: Improved Cryptanalysis of the Reduced Grøstl Compression Function, ECHO Permutation and AES Block Cipher. In: Jacobson Jr., M.J., Rijmen, V., Safavi-Naini, R. (eds.) SAC 2009. LNCS, vol. 5867, pp. 16–35. Springer, Heidelberg (2009)
12. Mendel, F., Pramstaller, N., Rechberger, C.: A (Second) Preimage Attack on the GOST Hash Function. In: Nyberg, K. (ed.) FSE 2008. LNCS, vol. 5086, pp. 224–234. Springer, Heidelberg (2008)
13. Mendel, F., Pramstaller, N., Rechberger, C., Kontak, M., Szmidt, J.: Cryptanalysis of the GOST Hash Function. In: Wagner, D. (ed.) CRYPTO 2008. LNCS, vol. 5157, pp. 162–178. Springer, Heidelberg (2008)
14. Mendel, F., Rechberger, C., Schläffer, M., Thomsen, S.S.: The Rebound Attack: Cryptanalysis of Reduced Whirlpool and Grøstl. In: Dunkelman, O. (ed.) FSE 2009. LNCS, vol. 5665, pp. 260–276. Springer, Heidelberg (2009)
15. National Institute of Standards and Technology. Announcing Request for Candidate Algorithm Nominations for a New Cryptographic Hash Algorithm (SHA-3) Family. Federal Register 27(212), 62212–62220, November 2007. http://csrc.nist.gov/groups/ST/hash/documents/FR_Notice_Nov07.pdf. 17 October 2008
16. Pollard, J.M.: Monte carlo methods for index computation (mod p). Math. Comput. **32**(143), 918–924 (1978)
17. Information Protection and Special Communications of the Federal Security Service of the Russian Federation. Gost r 34.11.2012 information technology cryptographic date security hash-functions (in english). http://tk26.ru/en/GOSTR3411-2012/GOST_R_34_11-2012_eng.pdf/
18. Information Protection and Special Communications of the Federal Security Service of the Russian Federation. Gost r 34.11.94 information technology cryptographic date security hash-functions (in russian)
19. Quisquater, J.-J., Delescaille, J.-P.: How Easy Is Collision Search. New Results and Applications to DES. In: Brassard, G. (ed.) CRYPTO 1989. LNCS, vol. 435, pp. 408–413. Springer, Heidelberg (1990)

322   J. Zou et al.

20. Sasaki, Y., Wang, L., Wu, S., Wu, W.: Investigating Fundamental Security Requirements on Whirlpool: Improved Preimage and Collision Attacks. In: Wang, X., Sako, K. (eds.) ASIACRYPT 2012. LNCS, vol. 7658, pp. 562–579. Springer, Heidelberg (2012)
21. Wang, X., Yin, Y.L., Yu, H.: Finding Collisions in the Full SHA-1. In: Shoup, V. (ed.) CRYPTO 2005. LNCS, vol. 3621, pp. 17–36. Springer, Heidelberg (2005)
22. Wang, X., Yu, H.: How to Break MD5 and Other Hash Functions. In: Cramer, R. (ed.) EUROCRYPT 2005. LNCS, vol. 3494, pp. 19–35. Springer, Heidelberg (2005)
23. Wang, X., Yu, H., Yin, Y.L.: Efficient Collision Search Attacks on SHA-0. In: Shoup, V. (ed.) CRYPTO 2005. LNCS, vol. 3621, pp. 1–16. Springer, Heidelberg (2005)
24. Wu, S., Feng, D., Wu, W., Guo, J., Dong, L., Zou, J.: (Pseudo) Preimage attack on round-reduced Grøstl hash function and others. In: Canteaut, A. (ed.) FSE 2012. LNCS, vol. 7549, pp. 127–145. Springer, Heidelberg (2012)
25. Zou, J., Wu, W., Wu, S., Dong, L.: Improved (pseudo) preimage attack and second preimage attack on round-reduced grostl. IACR Cryptology ePrint Archive 686 (2012).

Side-Channel and Leakage

Multivariate Leakage Model for Improving Non-profiling DPA on Noisy Power Traces

Suvadeep Hajra$^{(\boxtimes)}$ and Debdeep Mukhopadhyay

Department of Computer Science and Engineering,
Indian Institute of Technology Kharagpur, Kharagpur, India
{suvadeep.hajra,debdeep.mukhopadhyay}@gmail.com

Abstract. Profiling power attacks like Template attack and Stochastic attack optimize their performance by jointly evaluating the leakages of multiple sample points. However, such multivariate approaches are rare among non-profiling Differential Power Analysis (DPA) attacks, since integration of the leakage of a higher SNR sample point with the leakage of lower SNR sample point might result in a decrease in the overall performance. One of the few successful multivariate approaches is the application of Principal Component Analysis (PCA) for non-profiling DPA. However, PCA also performs sub-optimally in the presence of high noise. In this paper, a multivariate model for an FPGA platform is introduced for improving the performances of non-profiling DPA attacks. The introduction of the proposed model greatly increases the success rate of DPA attacks in the presence of high noise. The experimental results on both simulated power traces and real power traces are also provided as an evidence.

Keywords: Differential Power Attack (DPA) · Correlation Power Attack (CPA) · Leakage model · Multivariate leakage model · Non-profiling attack · Multivariate distinguisher · Multivariate DPA

1 Introduction

The success rate of the Differential Power Analysis (DPA) [12,13] attacks is largely influenced by the Signal-to-Noise Ratio (SNR) [13] of the power traces. As a consequence, in many applications, Power Analysis attacks are either preceded by various pre-processing techniques like integration (Chap. 4.5.2 of [13]), PCA [4], filtering [15] for the reduction of noise in the power traces or followed by some post-processing techniques like averaging [2,4,7] for the reduction of the effect of noise on the outputs of the distinguisher. These techniques attempt to improve the performance of the DPA attacks directly or indirectly by extracting information from multiple sample points. However, those techniques are mainly based on some heuristic approaches and do not exhibit performance improvement in many scenarios.

Various profiling attacks like Template attack [6] and Stochastic attack [16] provide optimal performance by jointly evaluating the leakages at multiple sample points. However, they use a separate profiling step for approximating the

© Springer International Publishing Switzerland 2014
D. Lin et al. (Eds.): Inscrypt 2013, LNCS 8567, pp. 325–342, 2014.
DOI: 10.1007/978-3-319-12087-4_21

multivariate leakage distribution [18] of the power traces. The profiling step requires a large number of power traces to estimate the multivariate leakage distribution with sufficient accuracy. Moreover, in most of the cases, it needs the knowledge of the secret key. Thus, optimising the performance of non-profiling DPA by considering the joint distribution of the leakages of multiple sample points is an open issue. This work attempts to do so using a model based approach.

In this work, our goal is to gain partial information of the multivariate leakage distribution of the power traces from the overall trace statistics like mean, variance etc. which can be easily computed without knowing the secret key. It should be noted that such attempt already exists in the form of using Principal Component Analysis (PCA) [1,4,17] in side-channel analysis. PCA projects the data-dependent variations from all the sample points of the power traces into the first principal component by analysing its covariance matrix. However, it performs sub-optimally on noisy power traces (see Sect. 6.2). In this paper, we extend the conventional leakage model for multiple sample points which, in turn, leads us to a multivariate leakage model. The proposed multivariate leakage model, once verified for a device, can be used to predict the (relative) SNR of each sample point of the power traces. Hence, it can strengthen the existing non-profiling DPA attacks by introducing new multivariate distinguishers which can combine the results from multiple sample points according to their relative SNR. Additionally, it can be applied to improve the sub-optimal behavior of PCA (described in [4]) for low SNR power traces. The model is experimentally verified for iterative hardware architectures on the Xilinx Virtex-5 FPGA embedded in a side-channel evaluation SASEBO-GII board (see Appendix A). A multivariate distinguisher based on the multivariate leakage model has been introduced. We also experimentally verified the effectiveness of the new distinguisher using both simulated traces with varying SNR and real traces. The results show a significant improvement in the performance of the new distinguisher for low SNR traces as compared to other existing distinguishers.

Rest of the paper is organized as follows. In Sect. 2, preliminaries of Differential Power Analysis are described. Section 3 describes some profiling results on AES power traces. In Sect. 4, the multivariate model has been introduced. Section 5 provides a way to compute the relative SNR's of sample points using the multivariate leakage model. In Sect. 6, a new multivariate distinguisher has been introduced along with its application to principal component decomposition of the traces. Sections 7 and 8 describe the attack results on simulated traces and real traces respectively. Finally conclusions have been drawn in Sect. 9.

2   Preliminaries

2.1   Notations

For the rest of the paper, we will use a calligraphic letter like $\mathcal{X}$ to denote a finite set and the corresponding capital letter X to denote a random variable over the set. Corresponding small letter x is used to denote a particular realisation of X.

$P(.)$ is used to denote the probability of the event. $E[X]$, σ_X and $Var(X)$ are used to denote mean, standard deviation and variance of the random variable X respectively. We also denote by $Cov(X, Y)$ and $Corr(X, Y)$, the covariance and the Pearson's correlation coefficient between random variables X and Y respectively. We denote a vector $\{x_0, x_2, \cdots, x_k\}$ by $\{x_i\}_{0 \leq i \leq k}$. Gaussian distribution with mean m and standard deviation σ is represented by $N(m, \sigma)$.

2.2   Differential Power Analysis

We will mainly follow the formalisation of Differential Power Analysis by Standaert et al. in [18]. It is briefly described below.

Let E be an iterative block cipher with block size b and number of rounds r. Let S be a key dependent intermediate variable of E. S is called *target* and satisfies $S = F_{k^*}(X)$, where X be a random variable representing a part of the known plaintext or ciphertext and $F_{k^*} : \mathcal{X} \rightarrow \mathcal{S}$ be a function determined by both the algorithm and the subkey $k^* \in \mathcal{K}$ (note that subkey is a small part of the secret key such that it is efficiently enumerable). We denote by L_t the random variable that represents the side channel leakage of an implementation of E at time instant t, $0 \leq t < rT$ where T is the number of samples collected per round.

In DPA, the attacker collects a set of traces $O = \{o_0, \cdots, o_{q-1}\}$ resulted from the encryption (or decryption) of a sequence of q plaintexts (or ciphertexts) $\{p_0, \cdots, p_{q-1}\}$ (or $\{c_0, \cdots, c_{q-1}\}$) using the fixed but unknown key with subkey $k^* \in \mathcal{K}$ in a physical implementation of E. It should be noted that each o_i is a vector of size rT i.e. $o_i = \{o_{i,j}\}_{j=0}^{rT-1}$ where $o_{i,j}$ be the leakages of the jth time instant during the ith encryption (or decryption). Then, a distinguisher D is used which by taking the leakage vector $\{o_0, \cdots, o_{q-1}\}$ and the corresponding input vector $\{x_0, \cdots, x_{q-1}\}$ as inputs, outputs a distinguishing vector $D = \{d_k\}_{k \in \mathcal{K}}$. For a successful attack, $k^* = argmax_{k \in \mathcal{K}} d_k$ holds with a non-negligible probability.

2.3   Leakage Model and Univariate Distinguisher

In DPA, it is assumed that the power consumption of a CMOS device at a time instant is dependent on the intermediate value manipulated at that point. Suppose the *target* S is manipulated at time instant t^* (call it *interesting* time instant). According to the conventional leakage model [5]:

$$L_{t^*} = \tilde{\Psi}(S) + N \tag{1}$$

$$= \tilde{\Psi}(F_{k^*}(X)) + N \tag{2}$$

where the function $\tilde{\Psi} : \mathcal{S} \rightarrow \mathbb{R}$ maps the target S to the deterministic part of the leakage and $N \sim N(m, \sigma)$ accounts for the independent noise.

At the time of attack, the attacker chooses a suitable prediction model $\Psi : \mathcal{S} \rightarrow \mathbb{R}$ and computes the hypothetical leakage vector denoted by random variable $P_k = \Psi(S_k) = \Psi(F_k(X))$ for each key hypothesis $k \in \mathcal{K}$. In *univariate* DPA, the attacker is provided with the leakage of the interesting time instant t^*, $L_{t^*} = \tilde{\Psi}(F_{k^*}(X)) + N$. On receiving the leakage, she computes the distinguishing vector $D = \{d_k\}_{k \in \mathcal{K}}$ such that $d_k = D(L_{t^*}, P_k) = D(\tilde{\Psi}(F_{k^*}(X)) + N, \Psi(F_k(X)))$ using a distinguisher D.

When the hardware leakage behavior follows a well known leakage model like Hamming weight model or Hamming distance model, some known prediction model Ψ closely approximates $\tilde{\Psi}$ i.e. $\tilde{\Psi}(s) \approx a \cdot \Psi(s)$ holds for some real constant a and for all $s \in \mathcal{S}$. Then, Eq. (1) can be approximated as

$$L_{t^*} = a \cdot \Psi(S) + N \tag{3}$$

Thus, the actual leakage vector L_{t^*} is linearly related to the hypothetical leakage vector for the correct key $P_{k^*} = \Psi(F_{k^*}(X))$. On the other hand, there is no such relation between L_{t^*} and the hypothetical leakage vector for a wrong key $P_k = \Psi(F_k(X))$ since $F_{k^*}(X)$ and $F_k(X)$ are almost independent for $k \neq k^*$. In Correlation Power Analysis (CPA) [5], Pearson's correlation is used to detect the linearity between L_{t^*} and P_k by computing $d_k = Corr(a \cdot \Psi(F_{k^*}(X)) + N, \Psi(F_k(X)))$ for all $k \in \mathcal{K}$. Since, Pearson's correlation detects the linear relation between two variables, it performs better than other attacks like Mutual Information Analysis (MIA) [8], Difference of Mean (DoM) [12]. When the hardware leakage model is not sufficiently known, 'generic' attacks like MIA perform better than CPA. In the rest of the paper, we will consider only the scenarios where the hardware follows a well known leakage behavior.

2.4 Multivariate DPA

In most of the practical scenarios, the point of interest t^* is not known before hand. Thus in practice, DPA attacks are multivariate in nature i.e. they take the leakages of multiple sample points as the inputs and generate the output. Most common form of multivariate DPA attacks applies a univariate distinguisher on each of the sample points independently and then, simply chooses the best result among those. However, in a different strategy, the attacker sometimes uses multivariate distinguishers which produce results based on the joint evaluation of the leakages at multiple sample points. Such multivariate distinguishers are common in profiling attacks like Template attack [6] and Stochastic attack [16].

Though multivariate distinguishers on unprotected implementations are rare in non-profiling context (example exists in [19]), there have been several attempts to improve the success rates of non-profiling DPA attacks by *integrating* the outputs of a univariate distinguisher at multiple sample points [2,4,15]. However, unlike profiling attacks where the multivariate leakage distribution of the power traces is approximated in an explicit profiling step, non-profiling attacks are vulnerable to decrease in success rate resulting from the integration of the output of a high SNR sample point to that of low SNR sample point. Thus, a successful integration of the leakages of multiple sample points requires the successful determination of the relative SNR of each sample point. We take a step in this direction in the next section.

3 Profiling the Power Traces of AES

In this section, we investigate the behaviour of the leakages of an AES implementation over a wide range of sample points due to the computation of an intermediate variable. We start with an unprotected implementation of AES on the setup described in Appendix A using parallel iterative hardware architecture. We choose the target S to be the 128-bit input to the last round which is computed from the ciphertext using the secret key. Consequently, predicted leakage $P = P_{k^*}$ is calculated using Hamming distant model i.e. by computing the Hamming distance of the target S and the ciphertext. To examine how the dependency between the actual leakage L_t and the correct predicted leakage P varies over a range of sample points, we estimate the following metrics over 300 sample points around the register update of the last round of AES using 20,000 power traces.

1. *Squared Pearson's Correlation between Data Dependent Leakage and Predicted Leakage (SCDP)*: It is defined as follows:

$$SCDP_t = Corr^2(E[L_t|P], P)$$

It reveals the linear dependency between the deterministic leakage $E[L_t|P]$ at sample point t and the predicted leakage P. It should be noted that if the leakage of a sample point t follows Eq. (3), then the empirical estimation of $SCDP_t$ using a finite number of traces will be close to one. On the other hand, if no such relation holds for a sample point t, $SCDP_t$ will be almost zero.

2. *Variation of Data Dependent Leakage (VDL)*:

$$VDL_t = Var(E[L_t|P])$$

It reveals the variations in leakage due to the predicted leakage P at sample point t. Sometimes, it is used to quantify the signal in the leakage. On the other hand, noise is quantified by $Var(L_t - E[L_t|P])$.

3. *Squared Mean Leakage (SML)*:

$$SML_t = E^2[L_t]$$

It has been included to study the behavior of the other metrics in relation with the mean leakage.

Figure 1(a) shows that as the cycle begins, with the mean leakage (SML), SCDP also rises rapidly, remains almost constant for about 150 sample points and then it decreases slowly. The slight fluctuations in the curve are due to the presence of small amount of noise after averaging a limited number of power traces. This leads us to the following observation:

Observation 1. *The deterministic part of the leakages at a large number of sample points show high linear dependencies with the correct predicted leakage P.*

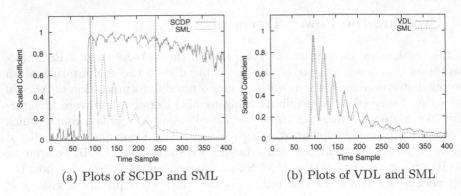

(a) Plots of SCDP and SML   (b) Plots of VDL and SML

Fig. 1. Plots of the chosen metrics in the last round of unprotected implementation of AES

Various profiling attacks also take advantage of the data dependency of multiple leakage points. However, they are more generic since they can consider different prediction model for different sample points at the cost of expensive profiling step.

From Fig. 1(b), we see that VDL almost superimposes on SML i.e. VDL is highly correlated to SML. This leads us to the following observation:

Observation 2. *The variation in the deterministic part of the leakages is correlated to the square of the mean leakages.*

In other words, the second observation states that the magnitude of the variation at a sample point due to target S is proportional to the mean value (strength) of the leakage at that sample point. It should be noted that a similar kind of observation can be found in Chap. 4.3.2 of [13] for the leakages of a microcontroller. The authors have also suggested several trace compression techniques based on the observation and have shown their usefulness to attack software implementation of AES. However, to the best of the authors' knowledge, no attempt has been made to incorporate these observations into the conventional leakage model. In the next section, we extend the conventional leakage model by using these two observations.

4 Introducing Multivariate Leakage Model

In [12], Kocher et al. mentioned the possibility of using the leakages of multiple sample points by the attacker in higher-order DPA. Later in [14], Messerges formalized the notion of *nth-order DPA* as an attack mechanism which exploits the leakages of n different sample points corresponding to n *different* intermediate values calculated during the execution of the algorithm. In this paper, we are interested in *n-variate* DPA which can exploit the leakages of n different sample points related to a *single* intermediate value calculated during the execution of the algorithm. Motivated by the observations of Sect. 3, we define *n-variate* leakage model as follows.

Definition 1. *In* **n-variate leakage** model, *leakages of n distinct sample points are assumed to be dependent upon a single intermediate value calculated during the execution of an algorithm.*

Note that since $Corr(E[L_t|P], P) \approx 1$ for $t_0 \leq t < t_0 + \tau$, in a noise-free environment, all the leakage samples in the window contain almost same information about the target S (as far as the linear part of the leakage is considered). Thus, combining those would not provide any advantage. But, in practical scenarios i.e. in the presence of noise, combining the information from multiple leakage samples would actually help to reduce the noise.

4.1   A Multivariate Leakage Model for Iterative Hardware Architecture on FPGA Platform

Observations 1 and 2 immediately extend the conventional leakage model given by Eq. (3), into the following multivariate leakage model:

$$L_t = a_t \cdot \Psi(S) + N_t$$
$$= a_t \cdot P + N_t, \quad t_0 \leq t < t_0 + \tau \tag{4}$$

where $a_t \in \mathbb{R}$ and the random vector $\{N_{t_0}, \cdots, N_{t_0+\tau-1}\}$ follows a multivariate Gaussian distribution with zero mean vector. It should be noted that the linear relation in Eq. (4) is a consequence of Observation 1 while Observation 2 enforces mean vector of the multivariate Gaussian distribution to be a zero vector. In a parallel iterative hardware architecture, a single round consists of several parallel S-boxes and the attacker targets only a part of it (usually a single S-box). Thus, in addition to the predicted leakage P due to the computation of the target $S = F_{k^*}(X)$, leakage due to the computation of the other parallel bits adds to it. This is known as algorithmic noise and we denote it by U. It should be noted that for a fully serialized architecture, U takes the value zero. Leakages due to the key bits and the control bits is denoted by c. Since key scheduling and the controlling operations are fixed for a fixed round in all the encryptions, c is constant for all the inputs.

Thus, we can adopt Eq. (4) to incorporate these new variables as follows:

$$L_t = a_t \cdot (P + U + c) + N_t, \quad t_0 \leq t < t_0 + \tau \tag{5}$$
$$= a_t \cdot (I + c) + N_t \tag{6}$$

where $I = P + U$. We are interested in the leakages of the above window namely $\{t_0, t_0 + 1, \cdots, t_0 + \tau - 1\}$ that can be roughly determined by the clock cycle in which the target operation is being performed (see Sect. 6.3). We denote this time span by $\{0, 1, \cdots, \tau - 1\}$ and in the rest of the paper, power trace is referred by the sample points of this time span only.

Next section demonstrates how this model can be useful for predicting the relative SNR of each sample point of a power trace in low SNR scenarios.

5   Application of the Multivariate Leakage Model to Estimate the SNR of the Sample Points

Mangard et al. quantifies the information leakage for each sample point of a trace using signal-to-noise ratio (SNR) [13]. In our context, it can be defined as

$$SNR_t = \frac{Var(E[L_t|I])}{Var(L_t - E[L_t|I])} \tag{7}$$

Here, $Var(E[L_t|I])$ quantifies the signal part of the leakage and $Var(L_t - E[L_t|I])$ quantifies the electronic noise.

There are several existing techniques to compute the SNR of the sample points. They are mostly used to compress the traces in profiling attacks. But, most of them such as *sosd, sost* [9] assume the key to be known. Other techniques like PCA perform sub-optimally in the presence of high noise [4]. However, the multivariate leakage model provides a way to estimate the relative SNR (i.e. SNR of a sample point with respect to the SNR of the other sample points instead of the absolute value of the SNR) of each sample point without the knowledge of the secret key, hence, makes it applicable to non-profiling setup also. Let $\alpha(t)$, $\mu_L^2(t)$ and $\sigma_L^2(t)$ be the functions over time such that $\alpha(t) = SNR_t$, $\mu_L^2(t) = SML_t = E^2[L_t]$ and $\sigma_L^2(t) = Var(L_t)$. Then, the multivariate leakage model given in Eq. (6) leads us to Proposition 1.

Proposition 1. *Suppose that the power traces are following the* multivariate leakage model *described in Eq. (6). If the variance of the electronic noise at each sample point is significantly higher than the signal variance i.e. $Var(E[L_t|I]) \ll Var(L_t - E[L_t|I])$ for $0 \le t < \tau$, then the SNR of a sample point t, $\alpha(t)$ is proportional to Squared Mean to Variance Ratio (SMVR) $\frac{\mu_L^2(t)}{\sigma_L^2(t)}$.*

Proof. By taking the expectation of both sides of Eq. (6), we get

$$E[L_t] = a_t \cdot (E[I] + c)$$
$$\text{or,} \quad a_t = \frac{E[L_t]}{E[I] + c} \tag{8}$$

From the definition of SNR in Eq. (7), we get

$$\alpha(t) \quad = \frac{Var(E[L_t|I])}{Var(L_t - E[L_t|I])},$$

$$= \frac{Var(a_t \cdot (I + E[U] + c))}{Var(L_t) - Var(E[L_t|I])}, \quad \text{from Eq. (5) and independent noise assumption}$$

$$\approx \frac{Var(a_t I)}{Var(L_t)}, \quad \text{since} \quad Var(E[L_t|I]) \ll Var(L_t - E[L_t|I]) < Var(L_t)$$

$$= \frac{a_t^2 Var(I)}{Var(L_t)},$$

$$= \frac{E^2[L_t]Var(I)}{(E[I]+c)^2Var(L_t)}, \qquad \text{from Eq. (8)}$$

$$= \frac{\mu_L^2(t)}{\sigma_L^2(t)} \times \frac{Var(I)}{(E[I]+c)^2} \qquad \text{from the definition of } \mu_L^2(t)$$
$$\text{and } \sigma_L^2(t)$$

$\square$

It should be noted that both $\mu_L(t)$ and $\sigma_L(t)$ can be computed without knowing the correct key. Thus, Proposition 1 can be used to determine the relative SNR of a sample point in the presence of high noise. Next, we will see how it can be useful for designing multivariate distinguishers in non-profiling DPA attacks.

6 Designing New Multivariate Distinguishers

The performances of many univariate distinguishers including CPA and classical DPA are susceptible to the level of SNR. Their performances get better at a sample point with higher SNR and become worse at a sample point with lower SNR [13]. We can adopt a univariate distinguisher for multivariate DPA by applying the univariate distinguisher on each sample point of the power traces separately and combining the result of each sample point using a second level distinguisher according to their relative SNR.

To elaborate the above approach, let us consider D to be a univariate distinguisher and we apply it to each sample point t, $0 \le t < \tau$, of the power traces independently. At the end, D outputs τ distinguishing vectors $\{D(t)\}_{t=0}^{\tau-1}$ where each $D(t)$ is a vector of $|\mathcal{K}|$ elements i.e. $D(t) = \{d_k(t)\}_{k\in\mathcal{K}}$. Thus, the vector $\{d_k(0), \cdots, d_k(\tau-1)\}$ represents the distinguishing values for the key hypothesis k at all the τ sample points. Since the correct key hypothesis k^* can compute the target S correctly, the distinguishing values for the correct key at time t, $d_{k^*}(t)$ depends on the SNR at t, and thus on SMVR $\mu_L^2(t)/\sigma_L^2(t)$ (thanks to Proposition 1). In other words, the vector $\{d_{k^*}(0), \cdots, d_{k^*}(\tau-1)\}$ will be strongly 'correlated' to the SMVR vector $\{\frac{\mu_L^2(0)}{\sigma_L^2(0)}, \cdots, \frac{\mu_L^2(\tau-1)}{\sigma_L^2(\tau-1)}\}$. On the other hand, since a wrong key hypothesis $k \ne k^*$ wrongly guesses the value of S i.e. $S \ne F_k(X)$, there is almost no correlation between $\{d_k(0), \cdots, d_k(\tau-1)\}$ and the SMVR vector. Thus, we can deploy a second level distinguisher $\tilde{D}$ to detect the correlation between the vectors $\{\frac{\mu_L^2(t)}{\sigma_L^2(t)}\}_{t=0}^{\tau-1}$ and $\{d_k(t)\}_{t=0}^{\tau-1}$ for all key hypothesis $k \in \mathcal{K}$ and return k as the correct key for which the correlation is maximum.

To summarise, a univariate distinguisher D can be extended for multivariate DPA as follows:

1. Apply the distinguisher D for each sample point t, $0 \le t < \tau$, of the power traces independently. At the end, D outputs τ distinguishing vectors $\{D(t)\}_{t=0}^{\tau-1}$ where each $D(t)$ is a vector of $|\mathcal{K}|$ elements i.e. $D(t) = \{d_k(t)\}_{k\in\mathcal{K}}$.
2. Construct $|\mathcal{K}|$ vectors $\{d_k(t)\}_{t=0}^{\tau-1}$ for each key hypothesis $k \in \mathcal{K}$. And also construct the SMVR vector $\{\frac{\mu_L^2(t)}{\sigma_L^2(t)}\}_{t=0}^{\tau-1}$.

3. Employ a second univariate distinguisher $\tilde{D}$ which outputs a distinguishing vector $\tilde{D} = \{\tilde{d}_k\}_{k \in \mathcal{K}}$ where $\tilde{d}_k = \tilde{D}(\{d_k(t)\}_{t=0}^{\tau-1}, \{\frac{\mu_L^2(t)}{\sigma_L^2(t)}\}_{t=0}^{\tau-1})$.

4. Return k as the correct key for which $\tilde{d}_k$ is maximum.

We will now explore this approach in several contexts in the following sections.

6.1   Extending CPA for Multivariate Leakage Model

In order to construct an effective multivariate distinguisher, we choose CPA as the first level univariate distinguisher since it is well accepted as one of the best performer when the hardware leakage follows a standard leakage model [3, 20]. To choose a proper second level distinguisher, we compute the Pearson correlation $\rho_{k^*}(t)$ between the leakage at sample point t and the predicted leakage for the correct key hypothesis $P = \Psi(S) = \Psi(F_{k^*}(X))$ using Eq. (5).

$$
\begin{aligned}
\rho_{k^*}(t) &= \frac{Cov(L_t, P)}{\sqrt{Var(L_t)Var(P)}} \\
&= \frac{Cov(a_t(P + U + c) + N_t, P)}{\sqrt{Var(L_t)Var(P)}} \\
&= \frac{a_t Cov(P, P)}{\sqrt{Var(L_t)Var(P)}} \\
&= \frac{a_t Var(P)}{\sqrt{Var(L_t)Var(P)}} \\
&= \frac{\mu_L(t)}{\sigma_L(t)} \times \frac{\sigma_P}{E[I] + c}, \quad \text{from Eq. (8)}
\end{aligned}
\tag{9}
$$

According to Eq. (9), not only the magnitude of $\rho_{k^*}(t)$ is proportional to $\frac{\mu_L(t)}{\sigma_L(t)}$ but the sign of $\rho_{k^*}(t)$ is also determined by the sign of $\mu_L(t)$. Moreover, the relation no more depends on the high noise condition as in Proposition 1, thus, is applicable to power traces with all SNR levels.

Figure 2 plots the mean leakage $\frac{\mu_L(t)}{\sigma_L(t)}$ and the correlation $\rho_{k^*}(t)$ between leakage L_t and the correct key guess for the first S-box at 600 sample points during the last round of the encryptions. To generate it, we have used 32,000 traces collected from parallel iterative implementation of AES on SASEBO-GII (please refer to Appendix A). The figure clearly indicates that the correlation curve has high positive correlation with the mean leakage curve.

To exploit the above knowledge of the relation between $\rho_{k^*}(t)$ and $\frac{\mu_L(t)}{\sigma_L(t)}$, we propose the following distinguisher.

Scalar Product. It takes the scalar product of the vectors $\{\rho_k(t)\}_{t=0}^{\tau-1}$ and $\{m(t)\}_{t=0}^{\tau-1}$ i.e. $\tilde{d}_k = \sum_{t=0}^{\tau-1} \rho_k(t)m(t)$ where $m(t) = sgn(\mu_L(t))\mu_L^2(t)/\sigma_L^2(t)$. Here function $sgn(\mu_L(t))$ takes the value 1 if $\mu_L(t) \geq 0$ and -1 otherwise.

In other words, the distinguisher takes the sum of the outputs of CPA at all the sample points weighted by the 'signed' SMVR of each sample point.

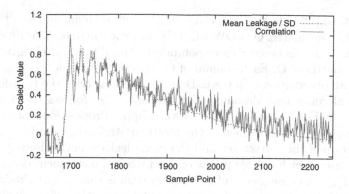

Fig. 2. Plots of the mean leakage normalised by the standard deviation and correlation of the correct key during the last round register update during AES encryption.

6.2 Improving the Performance of PCA for Low SNR Traces

PCA is a well known statistical technique for dimensionality reduction based on variations of data. It converts a set of interrelated observations (variables) into a set of new variables called principle components (PCs) such that the PCs are uncorrelated to each other and they are ordered decreasingly by their variance. Thus, first few PCs contain most of the variations in data while the later components capture a small amount of variations which are assumed to be caused by noise. Thus, the removal of the later components (which have lower variance) while preserving the first few components is a common noise reduction technique.

PCA was first introduced in the context of SCA by Archambeau et al. [1] where they used it to reduce the dimensions of the traces for Template attack. Later, in [17], Souissi et al. introduced it as a non-profiling distinguisher and in [4], Batina et al. introduced it as a pre-processing technique. For low noise traces, the PCA on the power traces (represented as matrix with rows containing different traces and columns containing different sample points) projects the variations caused by the target S into the first PC (since it is the largest component). Thus, univariate DPA on the first PC yields better result.

However in [4], Batina et al. also mentioned the limitation of PCA in high noise scenarios. Since, in high noise scenarios, the larger part of the variations is caused by the noise rather than the signal, the SNR's of the first few PCs are in fact quite low. Thus, univariate distinguishers on the first PC perform badly. Moreover, it is difficult to identify the sample points with higher SNR. However, based on some empirical observations, [4] has suggested a new distinguisher, namely *CPA Abs-Avg* distinguisher, which takes the average of the absolute value of the correlations of each sample points to compute the final output.

We suggest to use the multivariate model to find the principal components (PCs) having more information. Since PCA is a linear transformation, the principal component decomposition of the power trace matrix $O = \{o_{i,j}\}_{(i,j)=(0,0)}^{(q-1,\tau-1)}$

(recall that, $o_{i,j}$ stands for the leakage of jth sample point of the ith trace) is given by the $q \times \tau$ matrix $\tilde{O} = OW$ where W is a $\tau \times \tau$ matrix. The jth column of W represents the eigenvector corresponding to the jth largest eigenvalue of the covariance matrix of O. Each column of $\tilde{O}$ represents a single PC and each row represents an observation or a trace. Due to the linearity of the transformation, the principal component decomposition traces $\tilde{O}$ also follows the multivariate model given by Eqs. (5) and (6). Thus, we can apply Proposition 1 on $\tilde{O}$. Figure 3 validates Eq. (9) (a consequence of the multivariate leakage model) by plotting the correlation of the correct key and the mean leakage normalised by the standard deviation at each sample points of the principal component decomposition of the set T_{sim}^8. A consequence of this observation is that *Scalar Product* can be directly applied to the principal component decomposition of the power traces.

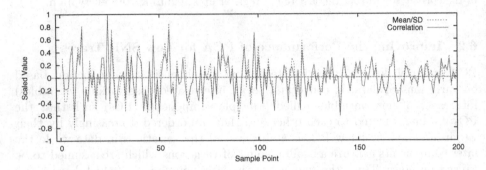

Fig. 3. Plots of the mean leakage normalised by the standard deviation and the correlation of the correct key at the first 200 PCs of the principal component decomposition of the set T_{sim}^8.

It should be noted that most of the tools like MATLAB® removes the mean of each sample point of the original traces as the first step of the transformation. Thus, we computed the mean vector $\mu_L = \{\mu_L(t)\}_{t=0}^{\tau-1}$ of the observation matrix O before applying the transformation. And after the transformation, we multiplied μ_L by the eigenvector matrix W obtained from the MATLAB® function 'princomp' to get $\mu_{\tilde{L}} = \mu_L W$, the mean vector of the principal component decomposition traces.

6.3   Determination of Window

For an iterative hardware architecture, the window can be set to the whole period of the clock cycle in which the target operation is being performed. However, to reduce the computational complexity resulting from performing computations on all points in the clock period, other measures can be taken based on SMVR. For our experiments, we have roughly chosen the window from the beginning of the target clock cycle up to a sample point for which the SMVR is slightly greater than zero.

7   Attacks on Simulated Traces with Different SNR Levels

To test the effectiveness of the new approaches, we collected a set of 20,000 power traces: T_{org} of the encryptions of AES implemented on the setup described in Appendix A using parallel iterative hardware architecture. We then removed the noises of all the traces (using the correct key) and created a set of noise-less traces: T_{nl}. Next, we created 4 sets of simulated traces each having 20,000 traces: T_{sim}^1, T_{sim}^2, T_{sim}^4 and T_{sim}^8 by adding a Gaussian noise to each sample point of T_{nl} having standard deviation 1, 2, 4 and 8 times the standard deviation of the noise at the same sample point of T_{org} respectively. It should be noted that the average noise variance of T_{sim}^2, T_{sim}^4 and T_{sim}^8 are respectively 2^2, 4^2 and 8^2 times the average noise variance of T_{sim}^1 while all the four sets are having same signal variances. Thus, average SNR of T_{sim}^2, T_{sim}^4 and T_{sim}^8 are $1/2^2$, $1/4^2$ and $1/8^2$ times the SNR of T_{sim}^1 respectively.

We applied *Scalar Product*, classical CPA [5] and *CPA Abs-Avg* [4] to attack the above 4 sets of simulated traces. We also applied the above three distinguishers on the principal component decomposition of the four sets by transforming them using MATLAB® function 'princomp' (refer to Sect. 6.2). For CPA on PCs, we tested both *CPA on first PC* and standard multivariate CPA on all the PCs. However, *CPA on first PC* yields better results. Profiling phase of Stochastic attack also determines the correct key as a byproduct of estimating the deterministic leakages. We also implemented that as a distinguisher. In the rest of the paper, we refer to this distinguisher as *Stochastic* distinguisher.

To compare the performances of the distinguishers, we have used *average guessing entropy* as a metric. The guessing entropy [18] of a distinguisher is given by the average rank of the correct key. Thus, it decreases as the attack becomes better and reaches one if it can find the correct key in all the trials. Average guessing entropy is computed by taking the average of the guessing entropy's of all the 16 S-boxes. To compute the guessing entropy of the above distinguishers, we divided each set of 20,000 simulated traces among four groups of 5,000 traces and applied the distinguishers on each group separately and took the average of their results.

Average guessing entropy of the attacks on the four sets of simulated traces are shown in Fig. 4. From this figure, we can summarise the following observations:

1. *Scalar Product* performs far better than the other distinguishers on both the original traces and the principal component decomposition of the traces. Moreover, the differences of the performances are more if the average noise level of the trace-set is more.
2. When the average noise level is comparatively low i.e. for the trace-sets T_{sim}^1 and T_{sim}^2, *CPA on first PC* performs almost equally well to *Scalar Product*. This is due to the fact that most of the data dependent variations (signal part of the leakage) have been projected to the first PC by PCA. Thus *Scalar Product* does not get any extra advantage over *CPA on first PC* by extracting information from multiple sample points.

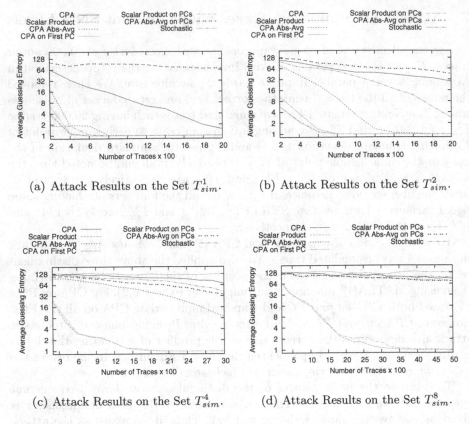

(a) Attack Results on the Set T_{sim}^1.   (b) Attack Results on the Set T_{sim}^2.

(c) Attack Results on the Set T_{sim}^4.   (d) Attack Results on the Set T_{sim}^8.

Fig. 4. Plots of the average guessing entropy of various distinguishers with the increase in the number of power traces on the four trace-sets having different average SNR.

3. The average noise levels of the trace-sets T_{sim}^4 and T_{sim}^8 are high enough to make PCA unable to project all the data dependent variations into the first PC. Rather, in Fig. 3, we can see that data gets correlated to multiple sample points of the principal component decomposition traces of T_{sim}^8. As a result, *Scalar Product on PCs* performs far better than *CPA on first PC*.

4. *Scalar Product* on the original traces and *Scalar Product on PCs* perform similarly though the later requires PCA as a pre-processing step which is computationally intensive.

5. The performance of *CPA Abs-Avg* on the principal component decomposition degrades for high SNR traces also. This is due to the fact that for high SNR traces most of the data variations are captured by the first few PCs only. Thus, *CPA Abs-Avg* reduces the effective SNR of the first few PCs by averaging them with rest of the low SNR sample points.

6. Though the non-profiling *Stochastic* attack performs quite well for T_{sim}^1, it performs badly for other sets of traces.

8   Attacks on Real Traces

To verify the effectiveness of the proposed distinguisher on real traces, we collected 20 sets of 2,000 traces of an AES implementation on SASEBO-GII (please refer to Appendix A). The implementation is based on parallel iterative architecture. The S-boxes are implemented using Xilinx device primitive: distributed ROM. Using our setup, the maximum SNR of the obtained power traces is close to 0.42 which is quite high.

Average Guessing entropy's of *Scalar Product* along with classical CPA, *CPA Abs-Avg* and non-profiling *Stochastic* attacks are shown in Fig. 5. It should be noted that the obtained power traces contain some correlated noise (noises in multiple sample points are correlated among themselves). As a result, the third PC instead of the first PC shows the maximum SNR in the principal component decomposition of the traces. Thus, *CPA on PCs* performs better than *CPA on first PC* and is included in the figure. Due to the computational limitation, *Stochastic* attack is performed on 160 sample points while other attacks are performed on 300 sample points.

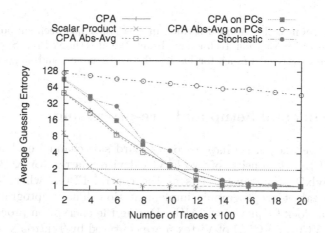

Fig. 5. Average Guessing Entropy of various attacks on the real traces of a parallel iterative implementation of AES on Xilinx FPGA device Virtex-5.

It is clear from Fig. 5 that *Scalar Product* is performing better than all the other attacks. It takes about 400 traces to bring down the average guessing entropy below two, while all other attacks take more than 1,000 traces for the same.

9   Conclusion

In this paper, we have introduced a *multivariate leakage model* for iterative hardware architecture on FPGA device Virtex-5. The introduced model allows an attacker to predict the relative SNR of each sample point of the power traces without even knowing the correct key. We have further discussed how existing univariate distinguishers can be strengthened by extending it to *multivariate* distinguishers with the help of the relative SNR of the sample points. We have also introduced and empirically verified one multivariate distinguisher namely *Scalar Product* using both simulated power traces and real power traces. The results show that *Scalar Product* performs far better than the classical CPA as well as the recently introduced *CPA Abs-Avg Distinguisher* on low SNR scenarios which are more likely in future devices.

Several advanced DSP techniques like Wavelet transforms have been recently introduced in side-channel literature. However, optimal application of such techniques either requires the knowledge of the correct key or depends on some heuristically chosen parameters such as 'scale level'. It can be an interesting study to see the applicability of the proposed multivariate leakage model in those situations.

The multivariate leakage model is validated on FPGA device Virtex-V. However, similar kinds of observations have been noticed in the literature on other platforms like micro-controllers. Hence, in future, exploring approaches based on multivariate leakage model on such other platforms could be worthy.

Acknowledgements. The work described in this paper has been supported in part by Department of Information Technology, India. We also thank Prof. Sylvain Guilley of TELECOM-ParisTech, France for his insightful discussion and suggestion on the work.

A   Experimental Setup and Pre-processing

For all the experiments, we have used standard side-channel evaluation board SASEBO-GII [11]. It consists of two FPGA device Spartan-3A XC3S400A and Virtex-5 xc5vlx50. Spartan-3A acts as the control FPGA where as Virtex-5 contains the target cryptographic implementation. The cryptographic FPGA is driven by a clock frequency of 2 MHz. During the encryption process, voltage drops across VCC and GND of Virtex-5 are captured by Tektronix MSO 4034B Oscilloscope at the rate of 2.5 GS/s i.e. 1, 250 samples per clock period.

The traces acquired using the above setup are already horizontally aligned. However, they are not vertically aligned. The vertical alignment of the traces are performed by subtracting the DC bias from each sample point of the trace. The DC bias of each trace is computed by averaging the leakages of a window taken from a region when no computation is going on. This step is also necessary since the distinguisher *Scalar Product* is sensitive to the absolute value of mean leakages.

References

1. Archambeau, C., Peeters, E., Standaert, F.-X., Quisquater, J.-J.: Template attacks in principal subspaces. In: Goubin and Matsui [10], pp. 1–14
2. Batina, L., Gierlichs, B., Lemke-Rust, K.: Differential cluster analysis. In: Clavier, C., Gaj, K. (eds.) CHES 2009. LNCS, vol. 5747, pp. 112–127. Springer, Heidelberg (2009)
3. Batina, L., Gierlichs, B., Prouff, E., Rivain, M., Standaert, F.-X., Veyrat-Charvillon, N.: Mutual information analysis: a comprehensive study. J. Cryptol. 24(2), 269–291 (2011)
4. Batina, L., Hogenboom, J., van Woudenberg, J.G.J.: Getting more from PCA: first results of using principal component analysis for extensive power analysis. In: Dunkelman, O. (ed.) CT-RSA 2012. LNCS, vol. 7178, pp. 383–397. Springer, Heidelberg (2012)
5. Brier, E., Clavier, C., Olivier, F.: Correlation power analysis with a leakage model. In: Joye, M., Quisquater, J.-J. (eds.) CHES 2004. LNCS, vol. 3156, pp. 16–29. Springer, Heidelberg (2004)
6. Chari, S., Rao, J.R., Rohatgi, P.: Template attacks. In: Kaliski Jr., B.S., Koç, Ç.K., Paar, C. (eds.) CHES 2002. LNCS, vol. 2523, pp. 13–28. Springer, Heidelberg (2003)
7. Clavier, C., Coron, J.-S., Dabbous, N.: Differential power analysis in the presence of hardware countermeasures. In: Koç, Ç.K., Paar, C., et al. (eds.) CHES 2000. LNCS, vol. 1965, pp. 252–263. Springer, Heidelberg (2000)
8. Gierlichs, B., Batina, L., Tuyls, P., Preneel, B.: Mutual information analysis. In: Oswald, E., Rohatgi, P. (eds.) CHES 2008. LNCS, vol. 5154, pp. 426–442. Springer, Heidelberg (2008)
9. Gierlichs, B., Lemke-Rust, K., Paar, C.: Templates vs. stochastic methods. In: Goubin and Matsui [10], pp. 15–29
10. Goubin, L., Matsui, M. (eds.): CHES 2006. LNCS, vol. 4249. Springer, Heidelberg (2006)
11. Katashita, T., Satoh, A., Sugawara, T., Homma, N., Aoki, T.: Development of side-channel attack standard evaluation environment. In: European Conference on Circuit Theory and Design, 2009. ECCTD 2009, pp. 403–408 (2009)
12. Kocher, P.C., Jaffe, J., Jun, B.: Differential power analysis. In: Wiener, M. (ed.) CRYPTO 1999. LNCS, vol. 1666, pp. 388–397. Springer, Heidelberg (1999)
13. Mangard, S., Oswald, E., Popp, T.: Power Analysis Attacks - Revealing the Secrets of Smart Cards. Springer, New York (2007)
14. Messerges, T.S.: Using second-order power analysis to attack DPA resistant software. In: Koç, Ç.K., Paar, C., et al. (eds.) CHES 2000. LNCS, vol. 1965, pp. 238–251. Springer, Heidelberg (2000)
15. Messerges, T.S., Dabbish, E.A., Sloan, R.H.: Investigations of power analysis attacks on smartcards. In: Proceedings of the USENIX Workshop on Smartcard Technology on USENIX Workshop on Smartcard Technology. WOST'99, p. 17. USENIX Association, Berkeley, CA, USA (1999)
16. Schindler, W., Lemke, K., Paar, C.: A stochastic model for differential side channel cryptanalysis. In: Rao, J.R., Sunar, B. (eds.) CHES 2005. LNCS, vol. 3659, pp. 30–46. Springer, Heidelberg (2005)
17. Souissi, Y., Nassar, M., Guilley, S., Danger, J.-L., Flament, F.: First principal components analysis: a new side channel distinguisher. In: Rhee, K.-H., Nyang, D.H. (eds.) ICISC 2010. LNCS, vol. 6829, pp. 407–419. Springer, Heidelberg (2011)

18. Standaert, F.-X., Malkin, T.G., Yung, M.: A unified framework for the analysis of side-channel key recovery attacks. In: Joux, A. (ed.) EUROCRYPT 2009. LNCS, vol. 5479, pp. 443–461. Springer, Heidelberg (2009)
19. Whitnall, C., Oswald, E.: A comprehensive evaluation of mutual information analysis using a fair evaluation framework. In: Rogaway, P. (ed.) CRYPTO 2011. LNCS, vol. 6841, pp. 316–334. Springer, Heidelberg (2011)
20. Whitnall, C., Oswald, E., Standaert, F.-X.: The myth of generic DPA...and the magic of learning. IACR Cryptology ePrint Archive 2012, 256 (2012)

Partially Known Nonces and Fault Injection Attacks on SM2 Signature Algorithm

Mingjie Liu[1]([✉]), Jiazhe Chen[2], and Hexin Li[2]

[1] Beijing International Center for Mathematical Research,
Peking University, Beijing 100871, China
liumj9705@pku.edu.cn
[2] China Information Technology Security Evaluation Center,
Beijing 100085, China

Abstract. SM2 digital signature scheme, which is part of the Chinese public key cryptosystem standard SM2 issued by Chinese State Cryptography Administration, is based on the elliptic curve discrete logarithm problem. Since SM2 was made public, very few cryptanalytic results have been found in the literatures. In this paper, we discuss the partially known nonces attack against SM2. In our experiments, the private key can be recovered, given 100 signatures with 3 bits of nonces known for 256-bit SM2. We also provide a byte-fault attack on SM2 when a byte of random fault is injected on the secret key during the signing process.

Keywords: Digital signature · SM2 · Cryptanalysis · Nonces leakage · Fault injection attack

1 Introduction

SM2 is the public-key cryptosystem based on elliptic curve published by Chinese State Cryptography Administration as a standard for commercial applications in 2010 [31]. It consists digital signature algorithm, key exchange protocol and public key encryption algorithm. Since SM2 was recently made public and the document is in Chinese[1], very few cryptanalytic results [38] on it could be found in the public literatures. However, being a national standard, it should be analyzed into more details.

In this paper, we focus on the SM2 digital signature algorithm[2]. Digital signature is first proposed by Diffie and Hellman [12], which is used to demonstrate the authenticity and integrity of the message. A valid digital signature of a message that only a single entity is able to generate, can be verified by anybody.

The first official digital signature standard is the DSA signature scheme [27] that was proposed in 1991 by U.S. National Institute of Standards and Technology (NIST). Its security relies on the discrete logarithm problem (DLP) over

---

[1] An informal English translation can be found in [36].
[2] In the rest of the paper, when we say SM2, we refer to SM2 digital signature algorithm.

© Springer International Publishing Switzerland 2014
D. Lin et al. (Eds.): Inscrypt 2013, LNCS 8567, pp. 343–358, 2014.
DOI: 10.1007/978-3-319-12087-4_22

finite fields. The elliptic curve version of DSA is ECDSA. Elliptic curves were first employed in cryptography by Miller [24] and Koblitz [21] independently. Compared with the widely used public-key schemes that based on integer factoring or computing discrete logarithms over finite fields, the elliptic curve cryptosystems achieve the same security level with significantly smaller system parameters. Similar to ECDSA, the security of SM2 relies on the elliptic curve discrete logarithm problem (ECDLP); however, the signature of SM2 employs a different signing procedure and different parameters.

Although the DLP and ECDLP are hard, the adversary in practice may bypass the mathematical hard problems by using the physical obtained information, i.e., he may mount side-channel attacks (SCA) and/or fault injection attacks (FIA) on the signing process. For example, during the signing procedure of DSA (ECDSA), one can observe the power/EM leakage of the nonce k. If the device running the cryptographic algorithms is not well protected, k can be recovered bit by bit using simple power analysis (SPA) [22]. Once k is disclosed, the private key can be recovered. Actually, the adversary only needs several bits of k: Howgrave-Graham and Smart [18] gave several heuristic lattice attacks on DSA to recover the secret key provided that for a reasonable number of signatures, a small fraction of the corresponding nonce is revealed. Later, Nguyen and Shparlinski improved the analysis in [28] and showed that there is a provable polynomial-time attack against DSA when the nonces are partially known. In their experiments, they can recover the 160-bit DSA private key by 3 known bits of each nonce from 100 signatures. In [23], this result is improved to 2-bit nonce leakage. These attacks can be generalized to the ECDSA case [29]. Bleichenbacher [4,5] and Mukder etc. [25] gave different attacks against nonces leaking which need many more signatures. However, they expected that their attacks can succeed with fewer bits' nonce leakage.

FIA is also used to evaluate the security of DSA and ECDSA. In this model, faults occur when the device performs the cryptographic operations, e.g., the attacker can use clock glitch, laser, etc. to inject the faults, then he tries to obtain the information about the secret key from these faults. The first fault attack on DLP-based signature schemes including DSA was given in 1997 [1]. In this attack, bit-flip errors were induced on random bits of the private key. In 2000, Dottax extended this attack to ECDSA and other signature schemes [13]. In 2004, Giraud and Kundsen [16] considered the more practical model — byte errors instead of bit errors. The improved analysis of Giraud and Kundsen's attack was presented in [17]. In [30], Nikodem discussed the immunity of DSA to such type of fault attack. By inducing faults on the nonces k [26], the public parameter g [33] and the size of the field p of DSA [2], the attacker can obtain part of the nonces k; then by invoking Nguyen and Sparlinski's technique [28] of constructing the HNP problem, the secret key can be recovered.

Our contributions. As mentioned, SM2 is the elliptic curve digital signature algorithm, thus probably the attacks on ECDSA can also be applied to SM2. However, no public literatures about the security of SM2 against partially-known nonces attack or FIA are found. In this paper, we deal with these issues.

Our discussion shows that the leak of nonces is very dangerous for SM2 as well. For a 256-bit SM2, given 100 signatures with 3 least significant bits of nonces known, we can recover the private key in a personal laptop within several hours. We also provide a byte-fault attack on SM2 when a byte of random fault is induced on the secret key during the signing procedure.

The reminder of this paper is organized as follows: Sect. 2 introduces SM2 signature scheme and some background about lattices. In Sect. 3, we describe the attack on SM2 with partially known nonces. Section 4 discusses the fault attack on SM2. Conclusions are given in Sect. 5.

2 Background

2.1 SM2 Digital Signature

Elliptic curve cryptography is defined over finite fields. In this paper, we focus on prime fields $\mathbb{F}_p$ with characteristic $p > 3$. Such a curve is the set of points (x, y) satisfying an equation of the following form:

$$y^2 = x^3 + ax + b \mod p,$$

where $a, b \in \mathbb{F}_p$ satisfy $4a^3 + 27b^2 \neq 0 \mod p$. To form a group, an extra infinity point $\mathcal{O}$ is included in this set. So, the elliptic curve $\mathbb{E}(\mathbb{F}_p)$ is defined as

$$\mathbb{E}(\mathbb{F}_p) = \{P = (x, y) | y^2 = x^3 + ax + b \mod p. \ x, y \in \mathbb{F}_p\} \cup \{\mathcal{O}\}.$$

This set of points form a group under a group operation which is denoted as "+". The detailed definition of this "+" operation and some basic results of the elliptic curves are provided in appendix.

SM2 digital signature is the elliptic curve digital signature algorithm. Its security is based on the intractability of the elliptic curve discrete logarithm problem. The SM2 digital signature algorithm is as follows:

Key Generation: Choose an elliptic curve $\mathbb{E} : y^2 = x^3 + ax + b$ over $\mathbb{F}_p$ where p is a prime. Select a $G \in \mathbb{E}(\mathbb{F}_p) = (x_G, y_G)$ to be a fixed point of order n, where n is a prime. That is $nG = \mathcal{O}$. For a user A, the private key is d_A. The corresponding public key is $P_A = d_A G$.

Signature Generation

1. Compute $w = h(M)$, here $M = Z_A \parallel m$, m is the message, Z_A is the hash value about the user, h is the hash algorithm SM3.
2. Randomly choose an integer $k \in [1, n-1]$. k is called a nonce.
3. Calculate $(x_1, y_1) = kG$.
4. Compute $r = w + x_1 \mod n$. If $r = 0$ or $r + k = n$, go to step 2.
5. Compute $s = ((1 + d_A)^{-1}(k - rd_A)) \mod n$. If $s = 0$, go to step 2.
6. Return (r, s) as the signature.

Signature Verification: A verifier receives $(m', (r', s'))$.

1. If $r' \notin [1, n-1]$ or $s' \notin [1, n-1]$, return FALSE.
2. Compute $M' = Z_A \parallel m'$, $w' = h(M')$.
3. Compute $t = r' + s' \mod n$. If $t = 0$, return FALSE.
4. Compute $(x_1', y_1') = s'G + tP_A$.
5. Compute $R = w' + x_1' \mod n$. If $R = r'$, return TRUE; else return FALSE.

2.2 Lattices

Our attack against SM2 digital signature algorithm with partially known nonces is a lattice-based attack. Hence, we introduce some related results on lattice in this subsection.

A lattice is a discrete subgroup of $\mathbb{R}^m$ whose elements are integer linear combinations of n ($n \leq m$) linearly independent vectors. Shortest vector problem (SVP) and closest vector problem (CVP) are two classical hard problems in computer science.

- **Shortest Vector Problem (SVP):** Given a basis of a lattice $\mathcal{L}$, find a shortest nonzero vector in $\mathcal{L}$.
- **Closest Vector Problem (CVP):** Given a basis of a lattice $\mathcal{L}$ and a target vector $\mathbf{t} \in \mathbb{R}^m$, find the lattice vector closest to $\mathbf{t}$. When the distance is small, the problem is called Bounded Distance Decoding (BDD) problem.

In cryptanalysis, attacks against many non-lattice based schemes have been reduced to solving SVP or CVP by constructing proper lattice since 1980s. In theory, for an n-dimensional lattice, there exist polynomial-time algorithms for both SVP and CVP with approximation factor $2^{\gamma n \log \log n / \log n}$ [14,35] where γ is any constant. When the approximation factor decreases to n^c, the best algorithm needs $2^{O(n)}$ [14] operations. There are many deterministic enumeration algorithms [19,32,34], with computational time ranging from $2^{O(n^2)}$ to $2^{O(n \log n)}$ and with polynomial space for exact SVP and CVP. Usually, in practice, these algorithms behave better than their proved worst-case theoretical bounds. Hence, researchers can obtain the shortest (closest) vector of lattices with dimensions not too large or with special structures. The best algorithm known in practice is the improved version of Schnorr-Euchner's BKZ [34] algorithm proposed by Chen and Nguyen [10] in 2011.

In practice, embedding technique [20] is widely used to reduce CVP to SVP. Given a lattice $\mathcal{L}$ with basis $\mathbf{B} = [\mathbf{b}_1, \mathbf{b}_2, \cdots, \mathbf{b}_m]$, and a target vector $\mathbf{t} \in span(B)$, the embedding method is to construct a new lattice $\mathcal{L}'$ with basis $\mathbf{B}' = [\mathbf{b}_1', \mathbf{b}_2', \cdots, \mathbf{b}_{m+1}']$:

$$
\begin{aligned}
\mathbf{b}_1' &= (b_{11}, b_{12}, \ldots, b_{1m}, 0) \\
&\vdots \\
\mathbf{b}_m' &= (b_{m1}, b_{m2}, \ldots, b_{mm}, 0) \\
\mathbf{b}_{m+1}' &= (t_1, t_2, \ldots, t_m, \beta),
\end{aligned}
\tag{1}
$$

where β is a parameter to be determined. If the distance between the target vector and the lattice is small enough, finding the shortest vector in this embedding lattice implies solving the CVP instance. In fact, we expect that the vector $(\mathbf{u} - \mathbf{t}, -\beta)$ to be the shortest vector in the embedding lattice, where $\mathbf{u}$ is the lattice vector closest to $\mathbf{t}$.

3   Attacking SM2 with Partially Known Nonces

Either the device is not well protected or the SPA countermeasure is not correctly implemented, the scalar multiplication leaks information about the nonce k. In this section, we will discuss the attack on SM2 digital signature scheme, suppose that for a reasonable number of signatures, a small fraction of the corresponding nonce is revealed.

Each SM2 signature generation requires the use of a nonce k modulo n, where n is usually a 256-bit prime number. We will first show that disclosing the full nonce k of a single (message, signature) pair allows to recover the SM2 secret key in polynomial time.

In fact, since $s = ((1 + d_A)^{-1}(k - rd_A)) \mod n$, we deduce that $d_A = (k - s)(s + r)^{-1} \mod n$. Note that $s + r \neq 0 \mod n$, otherwise the signature is not valid because the verification process will return FALSE in step 3.

This section shows that it is also very dangerous when only several bits of the nonces are known. A polynomial time attack will be given. As will be shown in Sect. 3.2, the attack on SM2 with partially known nonces can be reduced to a hidden number problem. Consequently, we first recall the hidden number problem and related results in Sect. 3.1. Then, we give our attack and experimental results in Sects. 3.2 and 3.3.

3.1   Hidden Number Problem (HNP)

The hidden number problem is first introduced by Boneh and Venkatesan [8,9]. For integer s and $m \geq 1$, $\lfloor s \rfloor_m$ denotes the remainder of s on division by m. For any real number z, let the symbol $|\cdot|_n$ be $|z|_n = \min_{b \in \mathbb{Z}} |z - bn|$. $APP_{\ell,n}(m)$ denotes any rational number r satisfying $|m - r|_n \leq \frac{n}{2^{\ell+1}}$. The HNP asks to recover $\alpha \in \mathbb{Z}_q$, given many approximations $u_i = APP_{\ell,n}(\alpha t_i)$ where each t_i is known and chosen uniformly at random in $[1, n-1]$, for $1 \leq i \leq d$.

This HNP problem can be reduced to a BDD problem which is a special case of closest vector problem. When we obtain d such t_i, u_i, the reduction to BDD can be done as follows. One constructs the $(d + 1)$-dimensional lattice spanned by the following row matrix:

$$
\begin{pmatrix}
n & 0 & \cdots & 0 & 0 \\
0 & n & \ddots & \vdots & \vdots \\
\vdots & \ddots & \ddots & 0 & \vdots \\
0 & \cdots & 0 & n & 0 \\
t_1 & \cdots & \cdots & t_d & \frac{1}{2^{\ell+1}}
\end{pmatrix}
\tag{2}
$$

The target vector is $\mathbf{u} = (u_1, u_2, \ldots, u_d, 0)$. There exists a lattice vector $\mathbf{h} = (\alpha t_1 + nh_1, \ldots, \alpha t_d + nh_d, \frac{\alpha}{2^{\ell+1}})$, such that $\| \mathbf{h} - \mathbf{u} \| \leq \sqrt{d+1} \frac{n}{2^{\ell+1}}$. Hence, finding $\mathbf{h}$ discloses α.

To assess the hardness of solving BDD in this lattice, we need to consider the distribution of the sequences t_i.

The work of Nguyen and Shparlinski on DSA [28] shows that the distribution of multiplier $t(k, M)$ is not necessarily perfectly uniform. They use the definition of $\triangle$-homogeneously distributed modulo n to measure the distance between the distribution of the sequences $t(k, M)$ and the uniform distribution. The larger $\triangle$ implies the distribution is farther from the uniform distribution. For the perfect uniform distribution, $\triangle$ is zero. Combine the behaviour of lattice-based attacks, the following lemma is proved.

Lemma 1 *[28]. Let $w > 0$ be an arbitrary absolute constant. For a prime q, define $l = \lceil w \left(\frac{\log q \log \log \log q}{\log \log q} \right)^{1/2} \rceil$ (resp. $l = \lfloor \log \log q \rfloor$) and $d = \lceil 3 \log q / l \rceil$ (resp. $\lceil 4 \frac{\log q}{\log \log q} \rceil$). Let Γ be a $\triangle$-homogeneously distributed modulo q sequence of integer numbers. When $\triangle \leq 2^{-l}$, there exists a probabilistic polynomial-time algorithm (resp. a probabilistic algorithm which runs in time $q^{O(1/\log \log q)}$) such that for any fixed integer α in the interval $[0, q-1]$, given as input a prime q, d integers $t_1, t_2, \ldots, t_d$ and d rationals $u_i = APP_{l,q}(\alpha t_i)$, $i = 1, 2, \ldots, d$, for sufficiently large q, with probability higher than $1 - 1/q$, it outputs α, where the probability is taken over all $t_1, t_2, \ldots, t_d$ chosen uniformly and independently at random from the elements of Γ and all coin tosses of the algorithm.*

If there is a CVP_∞ oracle (the algorithm can output an exact CVP solution in l_∞ norm), they obtain a better result.

Lemma 2 *[28]. Let $\eta > 0$ be fixed. For a prime q, define $l = 1 + \eta$ and $d = \lceil \frac{8}{3} \eta^{-1} \log q \rceil$. Let Γ be a $f(q)$-homogeneously distributed modulo q sequence of integer numbers where $f(q)$ is any function with $f(q) \to 0$ as $q \to \infty$. There exists a polynomial-time algorithm using a CVP_∞ oracle such that for any fixed integer α in the interval $[0, q-1]$, given as input a prime q, d integers $t_1, t_2, \ldots, t_d$ and d rationals $u_i = APP_{l,q}(\alpha t_i)$, $i = 1, 2, \ldots, d$, for sufficiently large q, with probability higher than $1 - 1/q$, it outputs α, where the probability is taken over all $t_1, t_2, \ldots, t_d$ chosen uniformly and independently at random from the elements of Γ.*

3.2   Insecurity of SM2 with Partially Known Nonces

Based on the discussion of HNP, in this subsection, we consider how to reduce the case of SM2 to an HNP problem.

If we know the l least significant bits of k, we have $k = 2^l b + a$. Here a is known and $b \in [0, n/2^l]$. Now we connect the attack with partially known nonces against SM2 and an HNP problem by the following formulas.

Given the user A and the message m signed with the nonce k, then $M = Z_A \parallel m$. We have:

$$(1 + d_A)s(k, M) = k - r(k, M)d_A \mod n.$$

This equation can be written as

$$2^{-l}(s(k, M) + r(k, M))d_A - 2^{-l}(a - s(k, M)) = b \mod n.$$

Here let $t(k, M) = \lfloor 2^{-l}(s(k, M) + r(k, M)) \rfloor_n$, $u(k, M) = \lfloor 2^{-l}(a - s(k, M)) \rfloor_n$. Both $t(k, M)$ and $u(k, M)$ can be obtained easily by the known information. Since $b \in [0, n/2^l]$, we get

$$0 \leq \lfloor d_A t(k, M) - u(k, M) \rfloor_n \leq n/2^l, \tag{3}$$

Furthermore,

$$0 \leq |d_A t(k, M) - u(k, M) - \frac{n}{2^{l+1}}|_n \leq \frac{n}{2^{l+1}}. \tag{4}$$

By collecting d signatures with l least significant bits of the corresponding nonces k, we can obtain d relations of (4). In this way, the problem of recovering d_A is reduced to an HNP problem.

Next, we consider the distribution of sequences $t(k, M)$:

$$\begin{aligned}
t(k, M) &= 2^{-l}(s(k, M) + r(k, M)) \mod n \\
&= 2^{-l}(1 + d_A)^{-1}(k + r(k, M)) \mod n \\
&= 2^{-l}(1 + d_A)^{-1}(k + x(kG) + h(M)) \mod n
\end{aligned}$$

Here, $x(kG)$ is the x-coordinate of kG and $h(M)$ is a hash value in $[0, n-1]$. In the well-known random oracle model, it is assumed that hash functions behave as random oracles, that is, the values of $h(M)$ are independent and uniformly distributed. $\{k + x(kG) \mod n\}$ can be seen as a random variable in $[0, n-1]$ and is independent of $h(M)$.

Now, let's consider the following probabilistic model: ξ and η are two independent random variables in $[0, n-1]$, ξ is uniformly distributed. Let $\varsigma = c(\xi + \eta) \mod n$, here c is an invertible constant modulo n. We discuss the distribution of ς: in fact, for any $u \in [0, n-1]$, we have,

$$\begin{aligned}
Pr(\varsigma = u) &= Pr(c(\xi + \eta) = u \mod n) = Pr(\xi + \eta = c^{-1}u \mod n) \\
&= \sum_{i=0}^{n-1} Pr(\xi = i \mod n)Pr(\eta = c^{-1}u - i \mod n) \\
&= \frac{1}{n}\sum_{i=0}^{n-1} Pr(\eta = c^{-1}u - i \mod n) \\
&= \frac{1}{n}
\end{aligned}$$

We remark that $t(k, M) \neq 0 \mod n$. Because in step 4 of the signing process, when $k + r = 0 \mod n$, we choose a new nonce k and recompute the signature. Therefore, the sequences $t(k, M)$ is uniformly distributed in $[1, n-1]$ under the above assumption about the hash function. Note that the conditions $r \neq 0$ and $s \neq 0$ will not affect the uniformity of $t(k, M)$. As a result, both Lemma 1 and Lemma 2 can be applied to SM2 with l least significant bits of nonces k known.

Lemma 1 invokes Schnorr's algorithm [35] and Kannan's algorithm [20] to solve this BDD problem. More precisely, when about $(\log n)^{1/2}$ signatures with about $(\log n)^{1/2}$ least significant bits of k known, the secret can be recovered in polynomial time. When the number of disclosed bits of k decreases to $\log \log q$, given about $\log q / \log \log q$ signatures, a subexponential time algorithm is needed. If there is an ideal oracle for CVP_∞, the secret key can be revealed with only 2-bit leakage. We note that in Lemma 2, the assumption on the distribution of Γ is very weak.

In practice, it has been widely reported that lattice algorithms behave better than their proved worst-case theoretical bounds. So experiments are very crucial to evaluate the efficiency of this attack. In next subsection, we will report our experiments about the attack.

3.3   Experimental Results and Remarks

In this subsection, we summarize our experimental results on the attack in Sect. 3.2. In practice, the embedding strategy [20] are widely used to solve BDD problem. Recently, Liu and Nguyen [23] showed that any security estimate of BDD-based cryptosystems must take the enumeration with extreme pruning technique [15] into account. Therefore, we do experiments by these two methods. Our experiments are implemented in a computer with Intel Xeon E7330 at 2.40 GHz using one of the cores for one instance.

Our results show that, for 256-bit p and n, given the $l = 3$ least significant bits of each one-time key for about 100 signatures, the enumeration with linear pruning can recover the secret key with success probability about 0.22 within several hours.

To verify our discussion in the previous subsection, we implement the SM2 signature algorithm to construct the corresponding HNP-lattice. According to the SM2 document [31], we choose both p and n to be 256 bits. The test vector (a, b, p, n, P_A, d_A) in [31] has been tested as well.

In fact, to avoid the fraction in computation and balance the values in coordinates, one needs to modify the coefficients of the row matrix (2) by some scaling factor.

$$\begin{pmatrix} 1732 \cdot 2^{l+1} n & 0 & \cdots & 0 & 0 \\ 0 & 1732 \cdot 2^{l+1} n & \ddots & \vdots & \vdots \\ \vdots & & \ddots & 0 & \vdots \\ 0 & \cdots & 0 & 1732 \cdot 2^{l+1} n & 0 \\ 1732 \cdot 2^{l+1} t_1 & \cdots & & \cdots 1732 \cdot 2^{l+1} t_d & 1000 \end{pmatrix} \quad (5)$$

We invoke the BKZ algorithm in NTL library [37]. First, we try embedding method with the last basis vector $\mathbf{b}_{d+2} = (1732 \cdot (u_1 2^{l+1} + n), 1732 \cdot (u_2 2^{l+1} + n), \ldots, 1732 \cdot (u_d 2^{l+1} + n), 0, 1000n)$ in matrix (1) with $m = d+1$. For BKZ with blocksize 20, $l = 4$, $d = 100$ case can be solved within several minutes. But it fails for $l = 3$ even with BKZ30 reduction.

Then, we use enumeration algorithm with linear pruning in BKZ 20 basis. The choice of radius determines the number of nodes in the enumeration tree and the success probability. Take the set of parameters in SM2 document [31] as an example. We list the data for different radius, corresponding estimations of numbers of nodes and success probabilities in Table 1.

Table 1. Enumeration complexity

Radius	11.5×10^{80}	10×10^{80}	8×10^{80}	7×10^{80}	6.5×10^{80}
No.of nodes	1.22×10^{25}	1.3×10^{22}	3.33×10^{15}	3.95×10^{13}	1.22×10^{11}
Success Pro	0.925	0.853	0.628	0.389	0.22

The rate of enumeration is very close to 6.5×10^6 nodes per second. We do enumeration for radius 6.5×10^{80}. The average actual running time is about 18104.8 s per enumeration. Our experiments solved 21 out of 100 instances.

We do not claim this kind of pruning is optimal for this attack. Our experiments only show that 100 signatures with 3 least significant bits of nonces known is insecure. The implementation of BKZ developed by Chen and Nguyen [10] achieves several exponential speedups compared to NTL's implementation. Therefore, if we invoke this stronger basis reduction algorithm, it may be possible to solve $l = 2$ case.

Remark 1. As discussed in [28], this attack can be generalized to the case of consecutive bits at other known position. If the known bits of nonces are the most significant bits, similar attack exists. We note that there are two definitions of most significant bits in [28]: the most significant usual bits and the most significant modular bits. All the above analysis holds for both cases. The only difference is that, we have to add one more bit in the case of the most significant usual bits. For l consecutive bits in the middle position, twice as many bits are required (See [28]).

In CHES 2013, Mukder etc. described a method to solve HNP using an FFT based attack [25]. Their method is an improved version of Bleichenbacher's solution [4,5]. BKZ is invoked to collect data for FFT. They did experiments on 384-bit ECDSA and could recover the private key using a 5-bit nonce leak from 4000 signatures. Their attack can also be applied to the SM2-HNP instance. They believed, although, this attack performs worse than standard lattice-based attacks now, their technique will continue to scale with fewer bits, because it can utilize many more signatures than that of the standard lattice attacks.

4 Fault Injection Attack on SM2

Fault injection attack was first introduced in 1996 by Boneh, Demillo and Lipton [7]. This type of attack is a serious threat for implementing cryptographic algorithms in practice. Therefore, it is important to look into the security of SM2 against fault injection attacks. In this section, we provide a byte-fault attack on SM2 when a byte of random fault is induced on the secret key during the signature generation.

4.1 The Model of the Attack

Our fault attack induces a byte error on the private key before the step 5 of the signature generation. Both the position and the value of this error are unknown. Let d_A be the secret key and $\widetilde{d}_A$ be the corresponding faulty secret key. $d_A^i, \widetilde{d}_A^i$ denote the i-th byte of d_A and $\widetilde{d}_A$, respectively. We assume a one-byte fault induced on d_A, which means the bytes of $\widetilde{d}_A$ satisfying

$$\widetilde{d}_A^{i_0} = e + d_A^{i_0} \tag{6}$$

$$\widetilde{d}_A^i = d_A^i \quad i \neq i_0 \tag{7}$$

Here $d_A^i, \widetilde{d}_A^i \in \{0, ..., 255\}$ ($i \in \{0, 1, ..., 31\}$) and $e \in \{-255, ..., 255\}$ is the random byte induced on the secret key d_A during the signing process of SM2. In fact, from Eq. (6), we have $-d_A^{i_0} \leq e \leq 255 - d_A^{i_0}$.

The faulty signature is $(r, \widetilde{s})$ where $\widetilde{s} = ((1 + \widetilde{d}_A)^{-1}(k - r\widetilde{d}_A)) \mod n$.

Now, we show how to detect the value of e and its position i_0. First, one computes

$$H = \widetilde{s}G + (\widetilde{s} + r)P_A = \widetilde{s}G + (\widetilde{s} + r)d_A G$$

and

$$J_{i,j} = (\widetilde{s} + r)e_{i,j}G$$

where $e_{i,j} = 2^{8i} + j$ with $i \in \{0, ..., 31\}$ and $j \in \{0, ..., 255\}$.

Then we obtain

$$H + J_{i,j} = (\widetilde{s} + (\widetilde{s} + r)(d_A + e_{i,j}))G = (x_{i,j}^+, y_{i,j}^+),$$

$$H - J_{i,j} = (\widetilde{s} + (\widetilde{s} + r)(d_A - e_{i,j}))G = (x_{i,j}^-, y_{i,j}^-).$$

It is clear that if $\widetilde{d}_A > d_A$, there exists an e_{i_0,j_0} satisfying $\widetilde{d}_A = d_A + e_{i_0,j_0}$. Otherwise, an e_{i_0,j_0} makes $\widetilde{d}_A = d_A - e_{i_0,j_0}$ hold. Therefore, by computing all $H \pm J_{i,j}$ with $i \in \{0, ..., 31\}$ and $j \in \{0, ..., 255\}$, we can find the correct e by finding the J_{i_0,j_0} such that either $x_{i_0,j_0}^+ = r - h(M) \mod n$ or $x_{i_0,j_0}^- = r - h(M) \mod n$ holds.

Remark 2. In fact, the correct e_{i_0,j_0} satisfies one of the following equations:

$$\tilde{s} + (\tilde{s} + r)(d_A + e_{i_0,j_0}) = k \mod n \tag{8}$$
$$\tilde{s} + (\tilde{s} + r)(d_A - e_{i_0,j_0}) = k \mod n \tag{9}$$

We remark that, in very rare cases, there exists another e_{i_1,j_1} that makes either $x_{i_1,j_1}^+ = r - h(M) \mod n$ or $x_{i_1,j_1}^- = r - h(M) \mod n$ hold as well, which happens when

$$\tilde{s} + (\tilde{s} + r)(d_A + e_{i_1,j_1}) = -k \mod n, \tag{10}$$
$$or \quad \tilde{s} + (\tilde{s} + r)(d_A - e_{i_1,j_1}) = -k \mod n. \tag{11}$$

If this e_{i_1,j_1} exists, we can obtain d_A directly from Eq. (8)–(11).

As long as the value of the error e is known, we can get information on the i_0-th byte of d_A. More precisely, if there exist two error bytes e_1, e_2 with a large enough difference, we can reduce the value of $d_A^{i_0}$ to very few choices. Once we find a pair (e_1, e_2) s.t.

$$e_2 - e_1 \geq 256 - x, \tag{12}$$

from Eq. (6), we get

$$-e_i \leq d_A^{i_0} \leq 255 - e_i, \quad i = 1, 2. \tag{13}$$

Combine equations (12) and (13), we deduce that $-e_1 \leq d_A^{i_0} \leq x - e_1 - 1$.

In this way, we restrict $d_A^{i_0}$ to x values. By exhaustive search, a byte of d_A is recovered.

Since the error is induced randomly, by repeating this procedure, the other bytes can be recovered similarly.

4.2   Analysis of the Attack

To estimate the complexity of this fault attack, we need to consider the number of errors induced before we can restrict the byte of the private key in x values.

In [16], the authors prove the following lemma.

Lemma 3. *For any $1 \leq x \leq 255$ and any $t \geq 2$, the probability of having $e_2 - e_1 \geq 256 - x$ after t faulty signatures, is $P(T_x \leq t) = 1 - (x+1)(\frac{256-x}{256})^t + x(\frac{255-x}{256})^t$. Here for series $(e_i)_{i \geq 1}$, $0 \leq e_i \leq 255$, $T_x = min\{t \geq 2 | \exists 1 \leq i, j \leq t : e_i - e_j \geq 256 - x\}$. The expected waiting time is given by $E[T_x] = \frac{2x+1}{x(x+1)} 256$.*

Applying this lemma to our 256-bit SM2 case, for $x = 1, ..., 4$, the expected number of faulty signatures required are 12288, 6816, 4768 and 3680, respectively. The corresponding maximum number of candidate private keys are 1, $2^{32}, 3^{32} \approx 2^{50.7}$ and $4^{32} = 2^{64}$, respectively.

A more practical analysis of this value has been presented in [17]. They discussed the expected number of guesses an attacker would have to conduct and obtain that the expected size of an exhaustive search is $\sum_{s=1}^{N}(\frac{s}{N})^t$, where t is the number of faulty signatures. Applying this formula to SM2, we have $N = 256$. Therefore, the expected number of guesses for private keys are $2^{32}, 2^{50.7}$ and 2^{64}, the corresponding number of faulty signatures needed are 5648, 3290 and 2327, respectively.

4.3   Countermeasure

A trivial countermeasure to the previous attack is verifying the signature, i.e., one executes the signature verification procedure. If the result of the verification is true, then one concludes that the signature is correct and outputs it; otherwise, nothing will be output. However, this countermeasure is vulnerable to a second order fault injection: The adversary can inject another fault to bypass the conditional operation; thus the faulty signature will still be output. Therefore, a countermeasure without conditional operations is a better choice.

This subsection proposes a modified version of SM2 as a countermeasure. Compared with the original version, any induced error on the private key is spread during the signing process. If no error is induced, the signature of the modified version is the same as the standard SM2. Otherwise, the diffusion of the error makes it difficult to find the useful information about the private key.

The modified SM2 signature generation is as follows:

1. Compute $w = h(M)$, here $M = Z_A \parallel m$, m is the message, Z_A is the hash value about the user, h is the hash algorithm SM3.
2. Randomly choose a nonce $k \in [1, n-1]$.
3. Calculate $(x_1, y_1) = kG$.
4. Compute $r = w + x_1 \mod n$. If $r = 0$ or $r + k = n$, go to step 2.
5. Compute $v = k + d_A r \mod n$.
6. Compute $T = x(vG - rP_A) - (r - h(M)) \mod n$.
7. Compute $k' = k \oplus T$.
8. Compute $s = ((1 + r^{-1}v - r^{-1}k)^{-1}(k' - v + k)) \mod n$. If $s = 0$, go to step 2.

The signature is (r, s).

If an attacker tries to do the fault attack by inducing a byte-fault on d_A in the signature generation, he obtains $\tilde{v} = k + \tilde{d}_A r \mod n$ and $\tilde{s} = ((1 + r^{-1}\tilde{v} - r^{-1}k)^{-1}(k' - \tilde{v} + k) \mod n$. To collect information about the error, he needs to find an x satisfying $(r + \tilde{s})P_A + \tilde{s}G + xG = kG = (x_1', y_1')$ where $x_1' = x_1 = r - h(M) \mod n$. It is equivalent to solving

$$(r + \tilde{s})d_A + \tilde{s} + x = k \mod n$$
$$(1 + d_A)\tilde{s} + rd_A + x = k \mod n$$
$$(1 + \tilde{d}_A)\tilde{s} + (d_A - \tilde{d}_A)\tilde{s} + rd_A + x = k \mod n$$

$$k' - (r + \widetilde{s})e - k = -x \quad \bmod n$$
$$-k \oplus T + (r + \widetilde{s})e + k = x \quad \bmod n$$

The value of x is related to both k and e, and hence x can not be obtained easier than exhaustive search.

Compared with the original SM2, the major extra operations required by our modified algorithm are two more scalar multiplications and one more point addition. Note that these extra computations are also needed by the trivial countermeasure.

There exist fault attacks on elliptic curve cryptosystems which induce faults into the computation of public key P_A by a scalar multiplication (e.g., [3,6,11]). These attacks are potential threats to all the elliptic curve based cryptosysems that are not specially protected. As a result, we are not going to discuss this type of attacks. Note that when implementing SM2, countermeasures against these attacks should be considered as well.

5   Conclusion

In this paper, we show that SM2 is vulnerable to the partially known nonces and fault injection attacks that are applicable to ECDSA. However, we would like to claim that there are some inherent differences between SM2 and ECDSA, as well as the attacks on them. For the partially known nonces attack, our discussion in Sect. 3.2 implies that the uniformity of the multiplier $t(k, M)$ of SM2 is much easier to analyze than that of ECDSA. In fact, in SM2, we have $s = ((1 + d_A)^{-1}(k - rd_A)) \bmod n$, while in ECDSA, the formula is $s = k^{-1}(h(m) + rd_A) \bmod n$. In the process of computing $(1 + d_A)^{-1}$, the information of d_A is more vulnerable to side channel attacks; injecting errors to d_A when computing $(1 + d_A)^{-1}$ can lead to a fault attack similar to that in Sect. 4.1. On the other hand, the part of $k - rd_A$ may be more secure than $h(m) + rd_A$ because of the unknown k.

Acknowledgement. We thank the anonymous referees for their careful reading and constructive comments.

This work is supported by China Postdoctoral Science Foundation (No. 2013M-540786), China's 973 Program (No. 2013CB834201) and National Natural Science Foundation of China (No. 61202493).

A   Background About Elliptic Curves

The elliptic curve is defined as $\mathbb{E}(\mathbb{F}_p) = \{P = (x, y) | y^2 = x^3 + ax + b \bmod p. \, x, y \in \mathbb{F}_p\} \cup \{\mathcal{O}\}$, where an $\mathcal{O}$ is an extra infinity point.

This set of points form a group under a group operation which is denoted as "+". This addition is defined as follows:

- $\mathcal{O} + \mathcal{O} = \mathcal{O}$
- $\forall P = (x, y) \in \mathbb{E}(\mathbb{F}_p) \backslash \mathcal{O}, \ P + \mathcal{O} = \mathcal{O} + P = P$
- $\forall P = (x, y) \in \mathbb{E}(\mathbb{F}_p) \backslash \mathcal{O}$, the inverse of P is $-P = (x, -y), P + (-P) = \mathcal{O}$
- $\forall P_1 = (x_1, y_1) \in \mathbb{E}(\mathbb{F}_p) \backslash \mathcal{O}, \ \forall P_2 = (x_2, y_2) \in \mathbb{E}(\mathbb{F}_p) \backslash \mathcal{O}, \ x_1 \neq x_2$, let $P_3 = P_1 + P_2 = (x_3, y_3)$, then

$$\begin{cases} x_3 = \lambda^2 - x_1 - x_2 \\ y_3 = \lambda(x_1 - x_3) - y_1, \end{cases}$$

where $\lambda = \frac{y_2 - y_1}{x_2 - x_1}$
- $\forall P_1 = (x_1, y_1) \in \mathbb{E}(\mathbb{F}_p) \backslash \mathcal{O}, \ y_1 \neq 0, \ P_3 = P_1 + P_1 = (x_3, y_3)$, then

$$\begin{cases} x_3 = \lambda^2 - 2x_1 \\ y_3 = \lambda(x_1 - x_3) - y_1, \end{cases}$$

where $\lambda = \frac{3x_1^2 + a}{2y_1}$

Elliptic curve discrete logarithm problem. Given $P \in \mathbb{E}(\mathbb{F}_p)$ and an integer m, there are many efficient scalar multiplication algorithms to compute mP. However, it is widely believed that given P and mP, computing m is hard when the point P has a large prime order. This problem is called elliptic curve discrete logarithm problem (ECDLP).

It is well known that the number of rational points in $\mathbb{E}(\mathbb{F}_p)$ is in the interval $[p + 1 - 2\sqrt{p}, p + 1 + 2\sqrt{p}]$. Therefore, for a curve over $\mathbb{F}_p$, it is easy to find a subgroup with order n which is a large prime and slightly smaller than p. Solving ECDLP in this subgroup is expensive.

References

1. Bao, F., Deng, R.H., Han, Y., Jeng, A.B., Narasimhalu, A.D., Ngair, T.H.: Breaking public key cryptosystems on tamper resistant devices in the presence of transient faults. In: Christianson, B., Lomas, M., Crispo, B., Roe, M. (eds.) Security Protocols 1997. LNCS, vol. 1361, pp. 115–124. Springer, Heidelberg (1998)
2. Berzati, A., Canovas-Dumas, C., Goubin, L.: Secret key leakage from public key perturbation of DLP-based cryptosystems. In: Naccache, D. (ed.) Cryphtography and Security: From Theory to Applications. LNCS, vol. 6805, pp. 233–247. Springer, Heidelberg (2012)
3. Biehl, I., Meyer, B., Müller, V.: Differential fault attacks on elliptic curve cryptosystems. In: Bellare, M. (ed.) CRYPTO 2000. LNCS, vol. 1880, pp. 131–146. Springer, Heidelberg (2000)
4. Bleichenbacher, D.: On the generation of one-time keys in DL signature schemes. Presentation at IEEE P1363 Working Group meeting (2000)
5. Bleichenbacher, D.: On the generation of DSA one-time keys. Presentation at Cryptography Research Inc. (2007)
6. Blömer, J., Otto, M., Seifert, J.-P.: Sign change fault attacks on elliptic curve cryptosystems. In: Breveglieri, L., Koren, I., Naccache, D., Seifert, J.-P. (eds.) FDTC 2006. LNCS, vol. 4236, pp. 36–52. Springer, Heidelberg (2006)

7. Boneh, D., DeMillo, R.A., Lipton, R.J.: On the importance of checking cryptographic protocols for faults. In: Fumy, W. (ed.) EUROCRYPT 1997. LNCS, vol. 1233, pp. 37–51. Springer, Heidelberg (1997)
8. Boneh, D., Venkatesan, R.: Hardness of computing the most significant bits of secret keys in Diffie-Hellman and related schemes. In: Koblitz, N. (ed.) CRYPTO 1996. LNCS, vol. 1109, pp. 129–142. Springer, Heidelberg (1996)
9. Boneh, D., Venkatesan, R.: Rounding in lattices and its cryptographic applications. In: Saks, M.E. (ed.) SODA 1997, pp. 675–681. ACM/SIAM (1997)
10. Chen, Y., Nguyen, P.Q.: BKZ 2.0: better lattice security estimates. In: Lee, D.H., Wang, X. (eds.) ASIACRYPT 2011. LNCS, vol. 7073, pp. 1–20. Springer, Heidelberg (2011)
11. Ciet, M., Joye, M.: Elliptic curve cryptosystems in the presence of permanent and transient faults. Des. Codes Crypt. **36**(1), 33–43 (2005)
12. Diffie, W., Hellman, M.E.: New directions in cryptography. IEEE Trans. Inf. Theor. **22**(6), 644–654 (1976)
13. Dottax, E.: Fault attacks on NESSIE signature and identification schemes. Technical report, NESSIE (2002)
14. Gama, N., Nguyen, P.Q.: Finding short lattice vectors within Mordell's inequality. In: Dwork, C. (ed.) STOC 2008, pp. 207–216. ACM (2008)
15. Gama, N., Nguyen, P.Q., Regev, O.: Lattice enumeration using extreme pruning. In: Gilbert, H. (ed.) EUROCRYPT 2010. LNCS, vol. 6110, pp. 257–278. Springer, Heidelberg (2010)
16. Giraud, C., Knudsen, E.W.: Fault attacks on signature schemes. In: Wang, H., Pieprzyk, J., Varadharajan, V. (eds.) ACISP 2004. LNCS, vol. 3108, pp. 478–491. Springer, Heidelberg (2004)
17. Giraud, C., Knudsen, E.W., Tunstall, M.: Improved fault analysis of signature schemes. In: Gollmann, D., Lanet, J.-L., Iguchi-Cartigny, J. (eds.) CARDIS 2010. LNCS, vol. 6035, pp. 164–181. Springer, Heidelberg (2010)
18. Howgrave-Graham, N., Smart, N.P.: Lattice attacks on digital signature schemes. Des. Codes Crypt. **23**(3), 283–290 (2001)
19. Kannan, R.: Improved algorithms for integer programming and related lattice problems. In: Johnson, D.S., Fagin, R., Fredman, M.L., Harel, D., Karp, R.M., Lynch, N.A., Papadimitriou, C.H., Rivest, R.L., Ruzzo, W.L., Seiferas, J.I. (eds.) STOC 1983, pp. 193–206. ACM (1983)
20. Kannan, R.: Minkowski's convex body theorem and integer programming. Math. Oper. Res. **12**(3), 415–440 (1987)
21. Koblitz, N.: Elliptic curve cryptosystems. Math. Comput. **48**(177), 203–209 (1987)
22. Kocher, P.C., Jaffe, J., Jun, B.: Differential power analysis. In: Wiener, M. (ed.) CRYPTO 1999. LNCS, vol. 1666, pp. 388–397. Springer, Heidelberg (1999)
23. Liu, M., Nguyen, P.Q.: Solving BDD by enumeration: an update. In: Dawson, E. (ed.) CT-RSA 2013. LNCS, vol. 7779, pp. 293–309. Springer, Heidelberg (2013)
24. Miller, V.S.: Use of elliptic curves in cryptography. In: Williams, H.C. (ed.) CRYPTO 1985. LNCS, vol. 218, pp. 417–426. Springer, Heidelberg (1986)
25. De Mulder, E., Hutter, M., Marson, M.E., Pearson, P.: Using Bleichenbacher's solution to the hidden number problem to attack nonce leaks in 384-bit ECDSA. In: Bertoni, G., Coron, J.-S. (eds.) CHES 2013. LNCS, vol. 8086, pp. 435–452. Springer, Heidelberg (2013)
26. Naccache, D., Nguyên, P.Q., Tunstall, M., Whelan, C.: Experimenting with faults, lattices and the DSA. In: Vaudenay, S. (ed.) PKC 2005. LNCS, vol. 3386, pp. 16–28. Springer, Heidelberg (2005)

27. National Institute of Standards and Technology (NIST): Fips publication 186–3:digital signature standard (2009)
28. Nguyen, P.Q., Shparlinski, I.: The insecurity of the digital signature algorithm with partially known nonces. J. Cryptology **15**(3), 151–176 (2002)
29. Nguyen, P.Q., Shparlinski, I.: The insecurity of the elliptic curve digital signature algorithm with partially known nonces. Des. Codes Crypt. **30**(2), 201–217 (2003)
30. Nikodem, M.: DSA signature scheme immune to the fault cryptanalysis. In: Grimaud, G., Standaert, F.-X. (eds.) CARDIS 2008. LNCS, vol. 5189, pp. 61–73. Springer, Heidelberg (2008)
31. Office of State Commercial Cryptography Administration: Public Key Cryptographic Algorithm SM2 Based on Elliptic Curves (in Chinese). http://www.oscca.gov.cn/UpFile/2010122214822692.pdf
32. Pohst, M.: On the computation of lattice vectors of minimal length, successive minima and reduced bases with applications. SIGSAM Bull **15**, 37–44 (1981)
33. Rosa, T.: Lattice-based fault attacks on DSA - another possible strategy. In: Proceedings of the Conference Security and Protection of Information, vol. 2005, pp. 91–96 (2005)
34. Schnorr, C.P., Euchner, M.: Lattice basis reduction: improved practical algorithms and solving subset sum problems. Math. Program. **66**, 181–191 (1994)
35. Schnorr, C.P.: A hierarchy of polynomial time lattice basis reduction algorithms. Theor. Comput. Sci. **53**, 201–224 (1987)
36. Shen, S., Lee, X.: SM2 Digital Signature Algorithm draft-shen-sm2-ecdsa-01. http://tools.ietf.org/pdf/draft-shen-sm2-ecdsa-01.pdf
37. Shoup, V.: Number Theory C++ Library (NTL) version 5.5.2. http://www.shoup.net/ntl/
38. Xu, J., Feng, D.: Comments on the SM2 key exchange protocol. In: Lin, D., Tsudik, G., Wang, X. (eds.) CANS 2011. LNCS, vol. 7092, pp. 160–171. Springer, Heidelberg (2011)

Application and System Security

Environment-Bound SAML Assertions: A Fresh Approach to Enhance the Security of SAML Assertions

Kai Chen[1]([✉]), Dongdai Lin[1], Li Yan[2], and Xin Sun[2]

[1] State Key Laboratory of Information Security, Institute of Information Engineering, Chinese Academy of Sciences, Beijing 100093, People's Republic of China
chenk@iie.ac.cn, ddlin@iie.ac.cn
[2] State Grid Zhejiang Electric Power Company, Hangzhou, China

Abstract. SAML plays an import role in authentication and authorization scenarios. People have paid much attention to its security, and find that major SAML applications have critical vulnerabilities, including XML signature wrapping (XSW) vulnerabilities and SAML assertion eavesdropping vulnerabilities. The countermeasures now available cannot address these two types of problems simultaneously, and always require a large change of the server modules.

In this paper, we propose to break this stalemate by presenting a fresh approach to SAML. A key cause of XSW and SAML assertion eavesdropping is that SAML assertions can be verified independently of the environment related to them. So we present an improved version of SAML (environment-bound SAML) that provides SAML assertions with the ability to defeat XSW and SAML assertion eavesdropping by binding SAML assertions to environment, and keeps tiny deployment overhead. To ensure the integrity of the binding relationship, we present the Master-Slave signature (MSS) scheme to replace the original signature scheme. We implement our scheme in OpenSAML, and provide a performance evaluation of this implementation.

Keywords: Master-Slave signature · Environment information bound SAML · XML signature wrapping · SAML assertion eavesdropping

1 Introduction

The **Security Assertion Markup Language** (SAML) [1] is an XML-based framework for exchanging user authentication, authorization and attribute information. SAML allows business entities to make assertions about the identity, entitlements and attributes of a subject. SAML is widely deployed. SAML assertions are usually used as the identity token in web Single Sign-On (SSO) scenario, or as the authorization grant in OAuth 2.0 scenario.

The security of SAML has a major impact on these web services. Based on previous analysis, major SAML applications have critical vulnerabilities. The

© Springer International Publishing Switzerland 2014
D. Lin et al. (Eds.): Inscrypt 2013, LNCS 8567, pp. 361–376, 2014.
DOI: 10.1007/978-3-319-12087-4_23

most harmful vulnerabilities are XML signature wrapping (XSW) and SAML assertion eavesdropping. An SAML signature is looked as a node of an XML tree, which is presented by the *Signature element*. A new class of vulnerabilities named XSW utilizes the features of the SAML signature to break the security of SAML. By using XSW, an attacker can inject forged elements without invalidating the SAML signature. The XSW details are described in Sect. 2.1. In SAML application scenarios, it is inevitable that SAML assertions are transferred between different roles. So the security of SAML assertions is subject to the application environment. SAML applications are always built upon the existing web infrastructures, including principal agents (typically browsers), networks, and servers. Many prevalent vulnerabilities of these infrastructures can be exploited to weaken the security of SAML assertions. The details about SAML assertion eavesdropping vulnerabilities are described in Sect. 2.2.

Some countermeasures have been presented to mitigate the effects of XSW and SAML assertion eavesdropping. J. Somorovsky et al. [2] presented two countermeasures against XSW. S. Sun et al. [3] suggested seven recommendations that can mitigate the effects of OAuth 2.0 eavesdropping vulnerabilities. SAML assertions can be used as token in OAuth 2.0. So their recommendations are suited to SAML. But these countermeasures have their own drawbacks, which limit their practical use. We summarize the drawbacks as following:

- **Limited Capacity:** None of countermeasures described above can address XSW and SAML assertion eavesdropping simultaneously. And it is hard to combine the existing countermeasures to resolve the two issues altogether. Because each countermeasure requires a big change for the logic process, the result of combining several countermeasure simply is usually that the original business logic in the service is affected.
- **Poor Universality:** None of countermeasures described above is a universal measure. Any one of the countermeasures described above is only designed for a specific application scenario. So a countermeasure suited to a server maybe not suit others.
- **Heavy Deployment Overhead for Servers:** Each countermeasure described above requires SAML servers to modify more than one module. It means wide-scale code changes. These changes introduce unwanted complications to SAML servers, and increase the overhead of deploying the countermeasures.

1.1   Contribution

We present a improved version of SAML, which provides SAML assertions efficient immunity against XSW and SAML assertion eavesdropping simultaneously. A key cause of XSW and SAML assertion eavesdropping is that SAML assertions can be verified independently of the environment related to them. So, in our scheme, SAML assertions are bound to environment (including the generation environment and the application environment). Unlike the existing countermeasures, the modifications of our scheme are limited to the SAML module. So all

SAML servers can deploy our scheme with tiny overhead. In our scheme, when SAML assertions are generated, the SAML assertion issuer server binds SAML assertions to the generation environment (SAML assertions - generation environment binding) to prevent SAML assertions from tampering via XSW. When SAML assertions are used, the principal binds SAML assertions to the application environment (SAML assertions - application environment binding), to prevent SAML assertions from eavesdropping. Our scheme ensures that SAML assertions are only valid in the environment with which the SAML assertions are bound. So we name our new scheme as environment-bound SAML assertion scheme. To ensure the integrity of binding relationship, we propose a new sequential aggregate signature scheme to replace the original SAML signing scheme. By using the new sequential aggregate signature scheme, we modify the SAML signature process from only SAML assertion issuer server signing to SAML assertion issuer server co-signing with principal. The SAML assertion issuer server signs SAML assertion firstly to ensure the integrity of "SAML assertions - generation environment" binding relationship. Subsequently, the principal adds his signature onto issuer's signature to ensure the integrity of "SAML assertions - application environment" binding relationship. Because there are only two signers in the new signature scheme, and the sequence of signing is fixed, we name this new sequential aggregate signature as Master-Slave signature (the first signer is the master user, and the second signer is the slave user). The Master-Slave signature is a restricted version of sequential aggregate signature.

We also give the implementation procedure of environment-bound SAML assertion scheme in detail, and analyse its security. At last, to demonstrate the feasibility of the environment-bound SAML assertion scheme, we evaluate the performance of a demo program which is based on OpenSAML. Comparing with existing countermeasures, the environment-bound SAML assertion scheme can provide SAML assertions effective immunity against XSW and SAML assertion eavesdropping simultaneously, keeping a tiny deployment overhead. And it is suitable to all application scenarios.

2   Related Work

XSW and SAML assertion eavesdropping pose a direct threat to SAML. In this section, we introduce some related works about these vulnerabilities and the corresponding countermeasures.

2.1   XML Signature Wrapping (XSW)

M. Mcintosh and P. Austel [4] and M. Jensen et al. [5] presented the XML signature wrapping (XSW) attacks. The cause of XSW attack is that different module of a application has different view on the same XML document. The security module of the application only performs security check on the signature part of the XML message. But the logic processing module of the application focuses on different parts of the same message. If an attacker modifies the XML message structure by injecting some forged elements keeping the XML signature valid, the security module may verify the signature successfully while the logic processing module processes the forged elements. Hence, by using XSW, an attacker can circumvent the security check and inject arbitrary content.

XSW on SAML. J. Somorovsky et al. [2] described the XSW attack on SAML. The simplest attack is the XML signature exclusion attack. Some servers' security modules have poor implementation. If these security modules do not find the *signature* element, they skip the verification step directly. The attacker can simply insert arbitrary elements and remove the *signature* element. The other attack is the refined XSW attack. Figure 1 are two refined XSW attack examples. As shown in Fig. 1(a), the attacker injects a different *ID* element into the original assertion. Because the SAML 2.0 schema allows to have multiple assertions in a SAML document, the modification doesn't invalidate the SAML assertions. But the logic processing module reads the forged <*assertion*> element. What Fig. 1(b) describes is similar with Fig. 1(a) but inserting the forged element into different place.

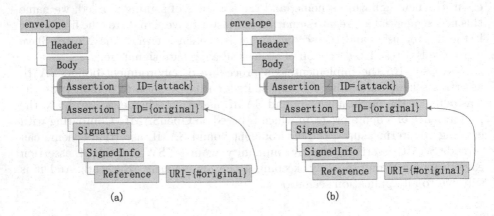

Fig. 1. Refined XSW attack example

Countermeasures for XSW. J. Somorovsky et al. [2] presented two countermeasures against XSW. The SAML consumer server is regarded as an aggregation of a security module and a logic processing module. The first countermeasure is "Only process what is hashed". The security module acts as a filter and only forwards the hashed parts of a SAML assertion to the logic processing module. The second countermeasure is "Mark signed elements". The security module marks the signed parts of a SAML assertion. And then the security module forwards the marked SAML assertion to the logic processing module. The logic module only processes the trusted parts of a SAML assertion. But these countermeasures only address the XSW problems. They do not consider the eavesdropping issues. Both "Only process what is hashed" countermeasure and

"Mark signed elements" countermeasure require the SAML application servers to modify the logic processing module. They all involve a large deployment overhead for SAML application servers.

2.2 SAML Assertion Eavesdropping

S. Sun et al. [3] analysed eavesdropping vulnerabilities of OAuth 2.0, and suggested some recommendations that can mitigate the effects of these vulnerabilities. SAML assertions can be used as token in OAuth 2.0 [6]. So their analyses and recommendations are suited to SAML.

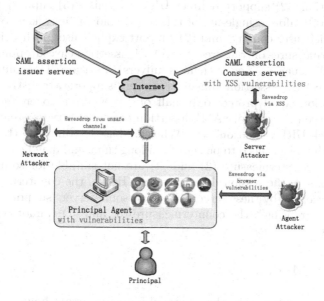

Fig. 2. SAML assertions eavesdropping

SAML Assertion Eavesdropping in OAuth 2.0. OAuth 2.0 protocol [7] is an open and standardized web resource authorization protocol. Due to poor implementation, some OAuth 2.0 web applications are not indeed secure in practice. S. Sun et al. [3] uncovered several critical vulnerabilities that allowed an attacker to gain access to the victim's resource or impersonate a victim. As described in Fig. 2, an attacker can eavesdrop on SAML assertions by sniffing on the unencrypted communication. According to the OAuth 2.0 specification, SSL/TLS should be used to provide end-to-end protection between any two parties. However, SSL/TLS imposes management and performance overhead and introduces undesired side-effects. So many service providers only use SSL/TLS for a few pages, such as login pages. An attacker can eavesdrop on SAML assertions via the communications without SSL/TLS protection. Due to poor implementation, some pages of SAML assertion consumer server have XSS vulnerability. An attacker can inject a malicious script into any page with XSS vulnerability to enforce the principal log again and send SAML assertions to him. Moreover, any vulnerabilities found in the principal agents (typically the browsers) also lead to security breaches. The security of browsers faces the challenge of the browser extension mechanism [8,9]. If an attacker controlled the principal agent, he would obtain any data through the principal agent, including SAML assertions.

Countermeasures for SAML Assertion Eavesdropping. S. Sun et al. [3] suggested recommendations that allow to mitigate discovered vulnerabilities. The SAML assertion consumer server should (1) provide explicit authorization flow registration, (2) support redirect URIs whitelist, (3) support token fresh mechanism, (4) enforce single-use of token, (5) void saving token to cookie, (6) support explicit user consent, and (7) support explicit user authentication. But these countermeasures only address the SAML assertion eavesdropping problems in OAuth 2.0 scenario. None of them is universal measure. The countermeasure (1) requires SAML assertion consumer servers support a registration option. And this option could protect only half of servers from token theft. For the countermeasure (2), most of SAML assertion consumer servers prefer "Domain-based redirect URI validation" to "Whitelist-based redirect URI validation". Sometimes, the tokens need to be kept for a long time, and may be used for many times. So the countermeasure (3) and (4) are not suitable for some scenarios. Many servers save the session data to cookie. Hence, the countermeasure (5) is hard to be accepted by these servers. Because some servers support "Automatic authorization granting", the countermeasure (6) and (7) cannot be applied in these servers.

3   Threat Model

In this section, we define the threat model for environment-bound SAML assertion scheme, including the attacker type and the attacker capability. There are three types of attackers in our threat model. Their capabilities describes as following:

Server attacker: The server attacker can exploit the vulnerabilities of server web pages, such as XSS, to setup malicious web pages. As Fig. 2 described, the malicious pages enforce the principal agent to execute the scripts implanted by the attacker. The scripts usually send the SAML assertions of the victim principal to the attacker. The attacker injects forged elements into the original assertions by using XSW, and then he submits the modified assertions to the SAML assertion consumer server. Or he replays the stolen assertions directly.

Agent attacker: The principal agent attacker can exploit the vulnerabilities of principal agents (such as browsers) to eavesdrop, such as man-in-the-browser malware [10]. As Fig. 2 described, SAML assertions are often forwarded by the principal agents. They *must* be cached in the memory of the principal agents. If the attacker controlled the principal agents, he would analyse agent caches to obtain SAML assertions. Similar to the server attacker, the agent attacker can submit the modified assertions or replay the stolen assertions.

Network attacker: The network attacker can sniff network traffic between different parties to steal SAML assertions. As Fig. 2 described, the attacker can sniff SAML assertions from the unencrypted channels. Moreover, we also assume that the attacker is able to "pry open" SSL/TLS sessions and extract the sensitive data by exploiting the bugs of SSL/TLS [11]. After obtaining SAML assertions, the attacker can handle them just like what the server attacker and the agent attacker does.

In short, our threat model gives attackers the ability to exploit XSW vulnerability and SAML assertion eavesdropping vulnerability. By combining these two vulnerabilities, a attacker can gain unauthorized access to the victim's resource or impersonate victim principal.

4   Environment-Bound SAML Assertions

In this section, we describe the environment-bound SAML assertion scheme in detail. To provide SAML assertions efficient immunity against XSW and SAML assertion eavesdropping simultaneously, SAML assertions are bound to environment by using the Master-Slave signature scheme. Figure 3 describes the environment-bound SAML assertion scheme. Firstly, we present the Master-Slave signature in detail. And then we demonstrate how to bind SAML assertions to environment by using Master-Slave signature scheme.

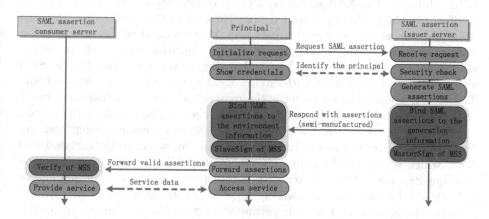

Fig. 3. Environment-bound SAML assertions flow chart

4.1   Master-Slave Signature

The key point for the environment-bound SAML assertion scheme is that SAML assertions are bound with a specified environment. So the security of binding relationship is the prerequisite and the foundation of the environment-bound SAML assertion scheme. To ensure the integrity of binding relationship, we present the Master-Slave signature (MSS) scheme. By using MSS, we modify the SAML signature process [1,12,13] from only SAML assertion issuer server signing to SAML assertion issuer server co-signing with principal. The signature of the SAML assertion issuer server ensures the integrity of "SAML assertions - generation environment" binding relationship. And the signature of the principal ensures "SAML assertions - application environment" binding relationship.

Definition of MSS. G. Neven [14] proposed a sequential aggregate signed data (SASD) scheme. The SASD scheme is based on families of trapdoor permutations except that it doesn't require the permutations to be certified. But this scheme is not a strong sequential aggregate signature scheme. The signing sequence can be changed without invalidating the signature. The MSS scheme is derived from SASD. We give the definition of MSS as following:

Definition 1. The Master-Slave signature (MSS) is a restricted version of sequential aggregate signature. There are only two signer in the MSS scheme: the master signer and the slave signer. It allows these two signers to sign different messages while aggregating into a single signature. And the sequence of signing is fixed. The master signer creates the initial signature, and the slave signer generates the aggregate signature subsequently. Any change to signing sequence would invalidate the signature.

MSS Details. The MSS scheme is a tuple of four algorithms (KeyGen, MasterSign, SlaveSign, Verify). And it defines three roles: the master user, the slave user, and the verifier. The master user uses MasterSign algorithm to create the initial signature. The slave user uses SlaveSign algorithm to generate the aggregate signature. The verifier uses Verify algorithm to verify the final Master-Slave signature. This is consistent with environment-bound SAML assertion scheme. The SAML assertion issuer server is the master user. The principal corresponds to the slave user. The SAML assertion consumer server plays a role as the verifier.

We present our Master-Slave aggregate signature scheme arising from any family of claw-free trapdoor permutations. So it can be easily instantiated with RSA, which is the default signing algorithm of SAML. We first introduce some prerequisites. Let $k, l \in \mathbb{N}$ be security parameters. l is system-wide parameter. k is chosen by each user as long as $k > l$. Let Π be a family of claw-free trapdoor permutations. For each permutation π in Π, there exists an abelian group $\mathbb{G}_\pi \subseteq D_\pi$. Let $enc_\pi : \{0,1\}^* \to \{0,1\}^* \times \mathbb{G}_\pi$ be a encoding algorithm which divides a message M into a shorter message m and an element $\mu \in \mathbb{G}_\pi$. Let $dec_\pi : \{0,1\}^* \times \mathbb{G}_\pi \to \{0,1\}^*$ be the corresponding decoding algorithm. The decoding algorithm must be injective: $dec_\pi(m, \mu) = dec_\pi(m', \mu') \Rightarrow (m, \mu) = (m', \mu')$. Let $H_\pi : \{0,1\}^* \to D_\pi$, $H' : \{0,1\}^* \to \{0,1\}^l$, $H'' : \{0,1\}^* \times \{0,1\}^* \to \{0,1\}^l$ and $G_\pi : \{0,1\}^l \to \mathbb{G}_\pi$ be public hash functions modeled as random oracle.

KeyGen. For a particular user, the KeyGen algorithm uniformly selects a pair of claw-free trapdoor permutation $(\pi, \rho, \pi') \leftarrow \Pi$. Here π is the permutation

Evaluate$(pk, \cdot)$, and π' is the inverse permutation *Invert*$(sk, \cdot)$. The KeyGen algorithm return pk as the public key and sk as the private key.

MasterSign. For the master user, given the private key sk_m of the master user and a message $M_m \in \{0,1\}^*$, the MasterSign algorithm computes

$$h_m \leftarrow H_\pi(M_m), \ \sigma_m \leftarrow Invert(sk_m, h_m)$$

where $h_m \in D_\pi$. The MasterSign algorithm returns σ_m as the master signature.

SlaveSign. The slave signing algorithm is given a tuple of *six* parameters $(sk_s, pk_m, pk_s, M_m, M_s, \sigma_m)$: the private key sk_s of the slave user; the public key pk_m of the master user; the public key pk_s of the slave user; the message M_m signed by the master user; the message M_s to be signed by the slave user; the master signature σ_m. Firstly, the slave signing algorithm checks the validity of the master signature. The slave signing algorithm computes

$$h_m \leftarrow H_\pi(M_m).$$

If $h_m \neq Evaluate(pk_m, \sigma_m)$, the algorithm return $\bot$. Secondly, the slave signing algorithm computes

$$M' \leftarrow H''(M_m, M_s).$$

Thirdly, the algorithm encodes the string $(M' \parallel \sigma_m)$ by running

$$(m, \mu) \leftarrow enc_\pi(M' \parallel \sigma_m).$$

m is a shorter string than $(M' \parallel \sigma_m)$. μ is an element of $\mathbb{G}_\pi$. Fourthly, the algorithm computes

$$h_s \leftarrow H'((pk_m, pk_s) \parallel M' \parallel \sigma_m), \ g_s \leftarrow G_\pi(h_s), \ \chi \leftarrow Invert(sk_s, g_s + \mu).$$

Lastly, the SlaveSign algorithm returns a slave signature $\sigma_s \leftarrow (m, \chi, h_s)$.

Verify. The verification algorithm is given a tuple of *five* parameters $(pk_m, pk_s, M_m, M_s, \sigma_s)$: the public key pk_m of the master user; the public key pk_s of the slave user; the message M_m signed by the master user; the message M_s signed by the slave user; the slave signature σ_s. Firstly, the verification algorithm parses σ_s as (m, χ, h_s) and checks the validity of parameters. If $|\mathbb{G}_\pi| < 2^l$, the algorithm returns 0 to indicate rejection. Secondly, the verification algorithm computes

$$g_s \leftarrow G_\pi(h_s), \ \mu \leftarrow Evaluate(pk_s, \chi) - g_s.$$

Thirdly, the master signature is reconstructed from (m, μ) by running

$$(M' \parallel \sigma_m) \leftarrow dec_\pi(m, \mu).$$

Lastly, the verification algorithm computes $h_m \leftarrow H_\pi(M_m)$. If M' is equal with $H''(M_m, M_s)$, h_s is equal with $H'((pk_m, pk_s) \parallel M' \parallel \sigma_m)$, and h_m is equal with $Evaluate(pk_m, \sigma_m)$, then the algorithm return 1 to indicate that the slave signature σ_s is valid. Otherwise it returns 0.

4.2   Binding SAML Assertions to Environment

The environment-bound SAML assertion scheme ensures that SAML assertions are only valid in special environment. In this section, we present how the SAML assertion issuer server binds SAML assertions to the generation environment, how the principal binds SAML assertions to the application environment, and how the SAML assertion consumer server verifies the SAML assertions.

Binding SAML Assertions to Generation Environment. The SAML assertion issuer server is responsible to generate SAML assertions and bind SAML assertions to generation environment by using the MSS scheme. The generation environment information includes: (1) the issuer information – who initializes SAML assertions, and (2) the objective principal information – who can use SAML assertions. The issuer information has been included in SAML assertions [1]. To prevent SAML assertions from a attacker tampering via XSW, the SAML assertion issuer server must indicates which principal can use SAML assertions. The SAML assertion issuer server adds the public key of the objective principal into each SAML assertion. The public key information is placed in the <*Advice*> element. The <*Advice*> element is a sub-element of the <*Assertion*> element. The integrity of <*Advice*> element is protected by the <*Signature*> element that envelops a master signature (by using MasterSign algorithm of MSS). Figure 4(a) is an example of a HTTP response message with a environment-bound SAML assertion. An X.509 certification, which includes the public key of the principal, is placed in <*Advice*> element.

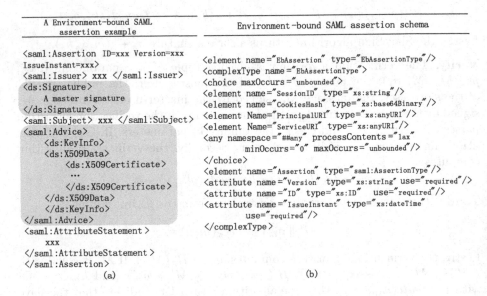

Fig. 4. Binding SAML assertions to environment

Binding SAML Assertions to Application Environment. The principal is responsible to bind SAML assertions to the application environment before forwarding them to the SAML assertion consumer server. To resist SAML assertion eavesdropping, the principal creates a new XML element, called *<EbAssertion>* element, which envelops the application environment information and the original SAML assertion. Figure 4(b) defines the *<EbAssertion>* element and its complex type (**EbAssertionType**). The **EbAssertionType** type specifies the basic information of the application environment, including the following elements and attributes:

- <SessionID> The identifier for session between the principal and the SAML assertion consumer server.
- <CookiesHash> The hash value of cookies. The default case is that hash value comes from total cookies by using SHA1 [15] algorithm. But the SAML assertion consumer server can negotiate with the principal to decide how to get hash value. The hash value is encoded by Base64 [16].
- <PrincipalURI> The unique URI for the principal.
- <ServiceURI> The unique URI for the SAML assertion consumer server.
- <Assertion> The original SAML assertion received from the SAML assertion issuer.
- <Version> The version of the enveloped assertion.
- <ID> The identifier for this environment-bound SAML assertion.
- <IssueInstant> The time instant of issue in UTC.

And then the principal signs the *<EbAssertion>* element by using SlaveSign algorithm of MSS. Only the principal indicated by the SAML assertion issuer server can generate a valid MSS signature, because the other principals including attackers do not have the private key which can match the public key in the *<Advice>* element of SAML assertions. The principal removes the original signature and places his final signature in the *<ds:Signature>* element of *<Assertion>*. Lastly, he forwards the valid environment-bound SAML assertions to the SAML assertion consumer server.

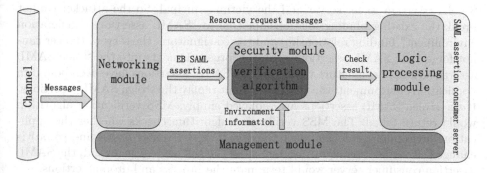

Fig. 5. The SAML assertion consumer server model

Verifying SAML Assertions. The SAML assertion consumer server is responsible to verify environment-bound SAML assertions. The environment-bound SAML assertion scheme only substitutes the Verify algorithm of MSS for the original verification algorithm. The verification process describes in Fig. 5. Firstly, the verification algorithm uses the SAML assertion issuer's public key together with the public key in the <*Advice*> element (namely, the principal's public key is extracted from "SAML assertions - generation environment" binding relationship), to verify the slave signature. Secondly, the verification algorithm checks the validity of "SAML assertions - application environment" binding relationship. The current application environment information is input to the verification algorithm. And then the verification algorithm compares the current application environment information with the application environment information bound to SAML assertions. It returns the check result to the logic processing module of the SAML assertion consumer server. The check result is reliable enough. The logic processing module need to do nothing more.

5   Security Analysis

In this section, we demonstrate how the environment-bound SAML assertion scheme can be used to improve the security of SAML applications.

The security of MSS has a direct impact on the environment-bound SAML assertions scheme. It can be proved in the random oracle model. If a MSS adversary $\mathcal{A}$ broke our MSS scheme with $AdvMSS_{\mathcal{A}}$, we could construct an algorithm $\mathcal{B}$ to break the SASD scheme [14] with the same probability. As space is limited, the detailed proof is not described here.

The major adversary types have been described in Sect. 3. We explain how the environment-bound SAML assertion scheme can be used to harden SAML applications against adversaries.

Against server attacker. The server attacker exploits the vulnerabilities of server's web pages to steal victim's SAML assertions. The stolen SAML assertions have been bound to the generation environment and the application environment. We assume that the attacker does not know the private key of the SAML assertion issuer server and the victim principal. So the attacker cannot break the existing binding relationship. Due to "SAML assertions - generation environment" binding relationship and the co-signature, the server attacker cannot forge valid SAML assertions or inject forged elements into the stolen SAML assertions keeping signature valid. Because SAML assertions have been bound to application environment, the attacker cannot replay the stolen SAML assertions. If the stolen SAML assertions are replayed simply, MSS verification algorithm would return failed. The MSS verification algorithm checks whether the application environment information (<*SessionID*>, <*CookiesHash*> and so on) is changed. If verification algorithm indicated the signature was invalid, the SAML assertion consumer server would terminate the process and drop assertions.

Against agent attacker. The agent attacker exploits the vulnerabilities of principal agent to steal SAML assertions. In environment-bound SAML assertion scheme, the principal is required to bind SAML assertions to the application environment. Once the application environment is changed, the corresponding SAML assertions become invalid. The agent attacker can steal *three* kinds of SAML assertions: the semi-manufactured SAML assertions (the assertions are only bound to the generation environment), the valid SAML assertions (the assertions are bound not only to the generation environment but also to the application environment, and the corresponding application environment is unchanged), and invalid SAML assertions (the assertions are invalid due to the changes in the corresponding application environment – for example, the session was close). Because the agent attacker does not know the private key of the victim principal, he is not able to bind the semi-manufactured SAML assertions to the application environment just as what the legal principal does. It means that the agent attacker cannot validate the semi-manufactured SAML assertions, no matter whether the semi-manufactured SAML assertions are tampered by using XSW or not. Similar to the server attacker, even if the agent attacker stole a valid SAML assertion or a invalid SAML assertion, he would not circumvent the environment information check of the MSS verification algorithm.

Against network attacker. The network attacker sniffs network traffic between different parties. The network attacker can steal *two* kinds of SAML assertions: the semi-manufactured SAML assertions (when the attacker sniffs network traffic between the SAML assertion issuer server and the principal), and the valid SAML assertions (when the attacker sniffs network traffic between the principal and the SAML assertion consumer server). Due to missing the victim principal's private key, the network attacker is not able to validate a semi-manufactured SAML assertion. Due to "SAML assertion - application environment" binding relationship and the co-signature, both tampering attack via XSW and replay attack have no impact on the environment-bound SAML assertions. The network attacker cannot use the stolen SAML assertions to gain access to unauthorized resource or to impersonate victim principal.

6 Implementation and Performance Evaluation

In order to demonstrate the feasibility of the environment-bound SAML assertion scheme, we implemented our scheme and evaluated its performance.

6.1 Implementation

We re-developed the OpenSAML. OpenSAML is a set of open source libraries. The OpenSAML libraries support developers working with SAML. The current version, OpenSAML 2, supports SAML 1.0, 1.1, and 2.0 specification. Open-SAML has been applied widely by many projects, such as: Shibboleth, Globus Toolkit, gLite, JBoss, Apache WSS4J, and so on.

We modified the original signing and verification algorithm into the Master-Slave signature algorithm. We instantiate the Master-Slave signature algorithm by using the default algorithm of XML signature as following:

1. using RSA private key encryption as *Invert*();
2. using RSA public key decryption as *Evaluate*();
3. using SHA1 as $H_\pi()$, $H'()$, H'', and $G_\pi()$ (SHA2 or SHA3 could be used to replace SHA1. But we suggested using SHA1 to be compatible with existing systems).

And then, we added support for environment-bound functions to OpenSAML. We implemented "generation environment bound" functions during the generation phase of SAML assertions. And we implemented "application environment bound" functions during the use phase of SAML assertions.

We chose Linux (version 3.2.0) as our development platform. We used OpenSAML version 2.5.2 as the development base line. It was the prerequisite to OpenSAML that we compiled and installed XMLTooling (version 1.5.2) library and XML-Security-C (version 1.6.1-5+deb7u2) library into the development platform. All modifications for the environment-bound SAML assertions scheme required an additional 2,878 lines added (across 27 files) to the OpenSAML source code.

6.2 Performance Evaluation

In order to demonstrate the performance impact of using environment-bound SAML assertions in SAML servers, we evaluated the performance of our scheme in SAMLSign program which was released together with OpenSAML. All experiments ran on Debian (version 7.0) Linux system with a 3.4 GHz Core i7-2600 CPU and 4 GB of RAM.

We analysed the slowdown in processing speed. The test results were gathered with Linux "time" command, which was able to show the total run time and the CPU time of a specified progress. Because there was no principal signing process in the original OpenSAML, we defined that the run time of the principal signing process in original OpenSAML was equal to 0. These tests considered two cases: (1) both the SAML assertion issuer and the principal signing assertions by using 1024 bit RSA keys; (2) both the SAML assertion issuer and the principal signing assertions by using 2048 bit RSA keys.

We analysed time performance with 1024 bits RSA keys firstly. The results of the run time tests were shown in Fig. 6(a). The run time of the issuer signing process was up 8.4 % from the original. The run time of the signature verification process was up 9.0 %. But the test environment has a significant impact on the test results (The impact came from the concurrent processes in the system). The CPU time was more accurate than the total run time to reflect the slowdown in processing speed. The data described in Fig. 6(b) showed the CPU time comparison, when the 1024 bits RSA keys were used. The CPU time of the issuer signing process was up 3.5 % from the original. The run time of the signature verification process was up 3.6 %.

We repeated time tests with 2048 bits RSA keys subsequently. Figure 6(c) showed the total run time comparison. The run time of the issuer signing process was up 7.6 % from the original. The run time of the signature verification process

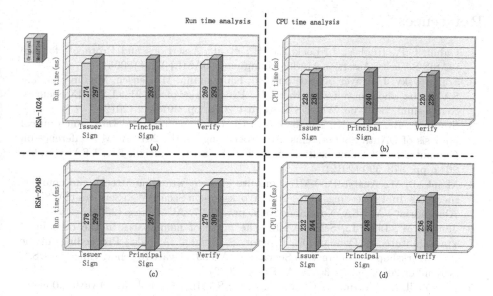

Fig. 6. Time performance analysis

was up 10.8 %. Figure 6(d) showed the CPU time comparison. The CPU time of the issuer signing process was up 5.2 % from the original. The run time of the signature verification process was up 6.8 %.

7   Conclusion

In this paper we presented the environment-bound SAML assertion scheme as a new approach to enhance the security of SAML assertions. We described how to bind SAML assertions to the environment, and explained why it was able to protect SAML assertions against XSW and SAML assertion eavesdropping. To finish binding task, we introduced the Master-Slave signature, which was well suited for environment-bound SAML assertion scheme. At the end of this page, we demonstrated the feasibility of the environment-bound SAML assertion scheme by the experiment data and result.

We see the environment-bound SAML assertion scheme as a first step to enhance the security of SAML-based protocols and applications.

Acknowledgements. This work was partially supported by a National Key Basic Research Project of China (2011CB302400), the "Strategic Priority Research Program" of the Chinese Academy of Sciences, Grant No. XDA06010701, and No. XX17201200048 of State Grid Corporation of China. We would like to thank all anonymous reviewers for helping us make this paper better.

References

1. Cahill, C.P., Hughes, J., Lockhart, H., et al.: Assertions and Protocols for the OASIS Security Assertion Markup Language (SAML) V2.0 (2005)
2. Somorovsky, J., Mayer, A., Schwenk, J., Kampmann, M., Jensen, M.: On breaking SAML: be whoever you want to be. In: Proceedings of the 21st USENIX Security Symposium, Bellevue, WA, USA, August 2012, pp. 397–412 (2012)
3. Sun, S.T., Beznosov, K.: The devil is in the (implementation) details: an empirical analysis of OAuth SSO systems. In: Proceedings of the 2012 ACM Conference on Computer and Communications Security (CCS'12), Raleigh, NC, USA, October 2012, pp. 378–390 (2012)
4. Mcintosh, M., Austel, P.: XML signature element wrapping attacks and counter-measures. In: Proceedings of the 2005 Workshop on Secure Web Services (SWS'05), Alexandria, VA, USA, November 2005, pp. 20–27. ACM press (2005)
5. Jensen, M., Liao, L., Schwenk, J.: The curse of namespaces in the domain of xml signature. In: Damiani, E., Proctor, S., Singhal, A. (eds.) Proceedings of the 2009 Workshop on Secure Web Services (SWS'09), Hyatt Regency, Chicago, USA, November 2009, pp. 29–36. ACM Press (2009)
6. Campbell, B., Mortimore, C., Jones, M.B.: SAML 2.0 profile for OAuth 2.0 client authentication and authorization grants (draft-ietf-oauth-saml2-bearer-16), March 2013
7. Hardt, D.: The OAuth 2.0 authorization framework, October 2012
8. Chia, P.H., Yamamoto, Y., Asokan, N.: Is this app safe? a large scale study on application permissions and risk signals. In: Proceedings of the 21st International Conference on World Wide Web (WWW'12), Lyon, France, April 2012, pp. 311–320 (2012)
9. Bandhakavi, S., King, S.T., Madhusudan, P., Winslett, M.: VEX: vetting browser extensions for security vulnerabilities. In: Proceedings of the 19th USENIX Security Symposium, Washington, DC, USA, August 2010, pp. 339–354 (2010)
10. Mushtag, A.: Man in the Browser: Inside the Zeus Trojan, February 2010
11. Duong, T., Rizzo, J.: Beast, September 2011
12. Cahill, C.P., Hughes, J., Metz, R., et al.: Profile for the OASIS Security Assertion Markup Language (SAML) V2.0 (2005)
13. Cahill, C.P., Hughes, J., Beach, M., et al.: Bindings for the OASIS Security Assertion Markup Language (SAML) V2.0 (2005)
14. Neven, G.: Efficient sequential aggregate signed data. IEEE Trans. Inf. Theor. **57**(3), 1803–1815 (2011)
15. Reagle: Schema for XML signatures (2001)
16. Josefsson, S.: The Base16, Base32, and Base64 Data Encodings, October 2006

One-Time Programs with Limited Memory

Konrad Durnoga[1], Stefan Dziembowski[1,2], Tomasz Kazana[1],
and Michal Zając[1(✉)]

[1] University of Warsaw, Warsaw, Poland
m.zajac@mimuw.edu.pl
[2] Sapienza University of Rome, Rome, Italy

Abstract. We reinvestigate a notion of *one-time programs* introduced
in the CRYPTO 2008 paper by Goldwasser *et al.* A one-time program
is a device containing a program C, with the property that the program
C can be executed on at most one input. Goldwasser *et al.* show how
to implement one-time programs on devices equipped with special hardware gadgets called *one-time memory* tokens.

We provide an alternative construction that does not rely on the
hardware gadgets. Instead, it is based on the following assumptions: (1)
the total amount of data that can leak from the device is bounded, and
(2) the total memory on the device (available both to the honest user
and to the attacker) is also restricted, which is essentially the model
used recently by Dziembowski *et al.* (TCC 2011, CRYPTO 2011) to construct one-time computable *pseudorandom* functions and key-evolution
schemes.

Keywords: Pseudorandom functions · One-time device · One-time program · Circuit garbling

1 Introduction

A notion of *one-time programs* was introduced by Goldwasser *et al.* [13]. Informally speaking, a one-time program is a device D containing a program C, that
comes with the following property: the program C can be executed on at most
one input. In other words, any user, even a malicious one, that gets access to
D, should be able to learn the value of $C(x)$ for exactly one x at his choice. As
argued by Goldwasser *et al.*, one-time programs have vast potential applications
in software protection, electronic tokens and electronic cash.

It is a simple observation that one-time programs cannot be solely software-
based, or, in other words, one always needs to make some assumptions about
the physical properties of the device D. Indeed, if we assume that the entire

This work was partly supported by the WELCOME/2010-4/2 grant founded within
the framework of the EU Innovative Economy (National Cohesion Strategy) Operational Programme. The European Research Council has provided financial support
for this work under the European Community's Seventh Framework Programme
(FP7/2007-2013)/ERC grant agreement no CNTM-207908.

D. Lin et al. (Eds.): Inscrypt 2013, LNCS 8567, pp. 377–394, 2014.
DOI: 10.1007/978-3-319-12087-4_24

contents $\mathcal{P}$ of D can be read freely, then an adversary can create his own copies of D and compute C on as many inputs as he wishes. Hence, it is natural to ask what kind of "physical assumptions" are needed to construct the one-time programs. Of course, a trivial way is to go to the extreme and assume that D is fully-trusted, i.e. the adversary cannot read or modify its contents. Obviously, then one can simply put any program C on D, adding an extra instruction to allow only one execution of C. Unfortunately, it turns out that such assumption is often unrealistic. Indeed, a number of recent works on side-channel leakage and tampering [11] attacks have demonstrated that in real-life constructing leakage- and tamper-proof devices is hard, if not impossible.

Therefore it is desirable to base the one-time programs on weaker physical assumptions. The construction of Goldwasser *et al.* [13] is based on the following physical assumption: they assume that D is equipped with special gadgets that they call *one-time memory (OTM)* devices. At the deployment of D an OTM can be initialized with a pair of values (K_0, K_1). The program $\mathcal{P}$ that is stored on D can later ask the OTM for the value of exactly one K_i. The main security feature of the OTMs is that the OTM under no circumstances releases both K_0 and K_1. Technically, it can be implemented by (a) storing on each OTM a flag f initially set to 0, that changes its value to 1 after the first query to this OTM, and (b) adding a requirement that if $f = 1$ then an OTM answers $\perp$ to every query. Under this assumption one can construct a general complier that transforms any program C (given as a boolean circuit) into a one-time program that uses the OTMs. Hence, in some sense, Goldwasser *et al.* [13] replace the unrealistic assumption that the whole device D is fully secure, with a much weaker one that the OTM gadgets on D are secure. Here, by "secure" we mean that they are leakage-proof (in particular: they never leak both K_0 and K_1) and tamper-proof (and hence the adversary should not be allowed to tamper with f).

Our Contribution. One can, of course, still ask how reasonable it is to assume that all the OTMs placed on D are secure, and it is natural to look for other, perhaps more realistic, models where the transformation similar to the one of [13] would be possible. In this paper we propose such an alternative model, inspired by recent work of Dziembowski *et al.* [8] on one-time computable self-erasing functions. In contrast to the assumption used by Goldwasser *et al.*, in our model we do not assume security of individual gadgets on D, but rather impose "global" restrictions on what kind of attacks are possible.

To explain and motivate the use of the model of [8] in our context, let us come back to the observation that a "physical assumption" that is obviously needed is that the adversary cannot copy the entire contents $\mathcal{P}$ of D, or more precisely, that the amount of information $f(\mathcal{P})$ about $\mathcal{P}$ that *leaked* to the adversary is bounded. There has been lot of work recently on modeling such bounded leakage. A common approach, that we follow in this paper, is to model it as an *input shrinking function*, i.e. a function f whose output is much shorter than its input (the length c of the output of f is a parameter called the *amount of leakage*). Such functions were first proposed in cryptography in the so-called bounded-storage model of Maurer [17]. Later, they were used to define the memory leakage occurring during the virus attacks in the bounded-retrieval model [2,5,6]. In the context of the side-channel leakages they were first used by Dziembowski and Pietrzak [9] with an additional restriction that the memory is divided into two separate parts that do not leak information simultaneously, and in the full generality in the paper of Akavia *et al.* [1].

Obviously, if we want to incorporate the tampering attacks into our model then we also need some kind of a formal way to define the class of admissible tampering attacks. To see that some kind of limitations on tampering attacks are always needed let us first consider the broadest possible class of such attacks, i.e. let us assume that we allow the adversary to transform the contents $\mathcal{P}$ of the device in an arbitrary way. More precisely, suppose the adversary is allowed to substitute $\mathcal{P}$ with some $g(\mathcal{P})$, where g is an arbitrary function chosen by him. Obviously in this case there is no hope for any security, as the adversary can design a function g that simply calculates "internally" (i.e.: on the device) the values of the encoded program on two different inputs, and leaks them to the adversary (if these values are short then this can be done even if the amount of leakage is small). Hence, some limitations on g are always needed. Unfortunately, it is not so obvious what kind of restrictions to use here, as currently, unlike in the case of leakage attacks, there does not seem to be any widely-adopted model for tampering attacks. In fact, most of the anti-tampering models either assume that some part of the device is tamper-proof [12], or they are so strong that they permit only very limited constructions [10].

As mentioned before, in this paper we follow the approach of [8], where the authors model the tampering attacks by restricting the size of memory available to the tampering function g. More precisely, we assume that there is a general bound s on the space available on D, that can be used by anybody who performs computations on D, including the honest program $\mathcal{P}$ and the adversary. This assumption can be justified by the following observations: (1) it is reasonable to assume that in practice the bound on the memory size of the device is known, and no adversary can "produce" additional space on it by tampering with it, and (2) in general it is also reasonable to assume that the tampering function is "simple", and hence it cannot have a large space-complexity.

What remains is describing the way in which the restrictions c on leakage and s on communication are combined into a single model. The way it is done by [8] is as follows: they model the adversary as two entities: a *big* adversary $\mathcal{A}_{big}$ and a *small* adversary $\mathcal{A}_{small}$. The small adversary represents the tampering function, and hence it has a full access to the contents $\mathcal{P}$ of the device[1]. It can perform any computation on D subject to the constraint that it cannot use more memory than s. The fact that it can leak information to the outside is modeled by allowing

---

[1] In the work of Dziembowski *et al.* [8] the adversary $\mathcal{A}_{small}$ is used to model the malicious code executed on the device (e.g. a computer virus), while in our case it models the tampering function. While in real life mallware is usually much more powerful than hardware tampering functions, we adopt the model of [8] since we do not see any other natural restriction on the tampering function that would lead to better parameters or the simpler proofs.

him to communicate up to c bits outside of the device. This leakage information can later be processed by the big adversary $\mathcal{A}_{big}$ that has no restrictions on his space complexity. In order to make the model as strong as possible we actually allow $\mathcal{A}_{big}$ to communicate with $\mathcal{A}_{small}$ in several rounds (and we do not impose any restriction on the amount of information communicated by $\mathcal{A}_{big}$ back to $\mathcal{A}_{small}$). We apply exactly the same approach in our paper. Our main result (see Theorem 1) is a generic compiler that takes any circuits C and transforms it into a one-time program $\mathcal{P}$ secure in the model described above. As in the case of Dziembowski et al. [8], our construction works in the Random Oracle Model, where we model as random oracles hash functions of fixed input lengths. For a complete statement of our result see Theorem 1. Let us only remark here that for a fixed circuit we get that the security holds as long as $s - 2nc \geq \gamma k$, where γ is some constant and n is the number of input bits of the circuit. Hence, the leakage size c has to be inversely-proportional to n, which may be sufficient for practical applications where n is small, e.g., if the input is a human-memorized PIN. In any case, for any realistic values of other parameters it is super-logarithmic, and hence covers all attacks where the leaking value is a scalar (e.g. the Hamming weight of the bits on the wires).

Related Work. Some related work was already described above. The feasibility of implementing the scheme of Goldwasser et al. [13] was analyzed by Jarvinen et al. [14]. The model of Dziembowski et al. [8] and related techniques were also used in a subsequent paper [7] to construct leakage-resilient key-evolution schemes. Finally, let us note that the main difference between [8] and our work is that in [8] the authors construct a one-time scheme for a concrete cryptographic functionality (i.e., a pseudorandom function), while here we show a generic way to implement *any* functionality as a one-time program.

It has been recently pointed out by Bellare et al. [4] that the original security proof of [13] had a gap. Informally speaking, this was due to the fact that the scheme of [13] was based on a statically-secure Yao garbled circuit, and hence did not provide security against the adversaries that can modify the input during the computation. We note that this problem does not affect the security of our construction. We elaborate more on this in Sect. 5.2.

Organization of the Paper. Some basic definitions we refer to later on are listed in Sect. 2. In Sect. 3, we give a formal statement of what we mean by a one-time device. Also, we announce the main theorem of the paper asserting that our construction produces programs compliant with this definition. Several tools we extensively use throughout the paper are synopsized in Sect. 4. These include: circuit garbling [16,19], universal circuits [15,18], and one-time computable pseudorandom functions [8]. In Sect. 5, we describe a compiler that converts a boolean circuit to a one-time device. A proof-sketch of the main theorem from Sect. 3 follows in Sect. 6.

2 Preliminaries

Across the paper, we often make use of boolean circuits. We use a capital C to label such a circuit. If C has n inputs and m outputs then we identify C with a function $C\colon \{0,1\}^n \to \{0,1\}^m$. For simplicity, we confine the analysis to the case where every gate of C has a fan-in of 2. Each wire, including the input and output ones, and every gate is assigned a unique label. A size of C, defined as a number of gates in C, is denoted by $|C|$.

We write $C(x)$ for a result of evaluating C on a given input x, and, more generally, $\mathcal{A}(x)$ for an outcome of running an algorithm $\mathcal{A}$ (modeled as a Turing machine, possibly a non-deterministic one) on x. Occasionally, we add a super-script $\mathcal{H}$ to $\mathcal{A}$ and write $\mathcal{A}^{\mathcal{H}}$ to signify that $\mathcal{A}$ is given access to an oracle that computes some function $\mathcal{H}$. Everywhere below it is assumed that there exists a (programmable) random oracle $\mathcal{H}\colon \{0,1\}^* \to \{0,1\}^k$ for a parameter k to be specified later. Phrases: the random oracle $\mathcal{H}$ and the function $\mathcal{H}$ are then used interchangeably. Although the declaration of $\mathcal{H}$ assumes that $\mathcal{H}$ accepts argu-ments of an arbitrary length, we only apply $\mathcal{H}$ to inputs not longer that a fixed multiple of k except for one case. In this particular case, however, the long input can be split into smaller chunks which allows cascading of $\mathcal{H}$. Overall, we can invoke the oracle only for short inputs.

When typesetting algorithms, we write $R \xleftarrow{\$} S$ for sampling a uniformly ran-dom value from some set S and assigning it to a variable R. We assume that every such a sample is independent of other choices. We conform to the common bracket notation $T[i]$ for accessing the ith element of an array T.

We say that a function is *negligible* in k if it vanishes faster than the inverse of any polynomial of k. In particularly, we use this expression to indicate that certain event can only occur with a small, i.e. negligible, probability in some security parameter k. Also, we often write just: a *negligible probability* and omit k when this parameter is clear from context.

As announced in Sect. 1, the model we adopt in the paper assumes splitting an adversary $\mathcal{A}$ into two components: $\mathcal{A}_{small}$ and $\mathcal{A}_{big}$. Both parts are interactive algorithms with access to $\mathcal{H}$, where a total number of oracle calls made is limited. Additionally, $\mathcal{A}_{small}$, which can see the internals of an attacked device, has:

- s-bounded space – a total amount of memory used by $\mathcal{A}_{small}$ does not exceed s bits, i.e., an entire configuration of $\mathcal{A}_{small}$ (contents of all tapes, a current state, and positions of all the tape heads), at any point of execution, can be described using s bits;
- c-bounded communication – a total number of outgoing bits sent by $\mathcal{A}_{small}$ does not exceed c, assuming that $\mathcal{A}_{small}$ cannot convey any extra information when communicating with $\mathcal{A}_{big}$ (e.g. by abstaining from sending anything during some period of time).

Note that $\mathcal{A} = (\mathcal{A}_{small}, \mathcal{A}_{big})$ can have an unbounded computational power. Also, the amount of bits uploaded by $\mathcal{A}_{big}$ to $\mathcal{A}_{small}$ is not restricted. We write $\mathcal{A}^{\mathcal{H}}(R) = (\mathcal{A}_{big}^{\mathcal{H}}() \leftrightarrows \mathcal{A}_{small}^{\mathcal{H}}(R))$ to denote the interactive execution of $\mathcal{A}_{big}$ and

$\mathcal{A}_{small}$, where $\mathcal{A}_{small}$ gets R as an input. We settle on a simplifying arrangement that the contents of memory (e.g. the data on all the tapes) of $\mathcal{A}_{big}$ after it finishes its run form a result of this execution. In particular, any information computed by $\mathcal{A}_{small}$ needs to be transmitted to $\mathcal{A}_{big}$ (contributing to the communication quota) in order to be included as a part of the result. Such an approach is justified by the real-world interpretation of $\mathcal{A}_{small}$ and $\mathcal{A}_{big}$ as a virus and a remote adversary controlling the virus. Here, only the data that the external adversary can receive is considered valuable.

3   One-Time Programs

In this section, we give a strict definition of one-time programs/devices. Intuitively, an ideal one-time program should mimic a black-box that internally calculates a value of some boolean circuit C. It should allow only one execution on an arbitrary input after which it self-destructs. Additionally, the black-box should not leak any information about C whatsoever. As explained in Sect. 4.2, there are theoretical obstacles that make this goal impossible to achieve in its full generality. So instead, we show that any adversary that operates a one-time device can evaluate it on a single argument x and can hardly learn anything more about the underlying circuit C but n, m, and $|C|$. It therefore gains some additional knowledge that goes beyond $C(x)$, namely the size of the circuit. Admittedly, that information is not considered substantial in practice. Definition 1 makes this property formal in terms of a simulator that is permitted to call an oracle evaluating C only once.

Definition 1. *Let c, s, δ, q, and ϵ be parameters. Let $C \colon \{0,1\}^n \to \{0,1\}^m$ be a boolean circuit with positive integers n and m. Write $\mathcal{O}$ for an oracle that computes $C(x)$ given $x \in \{0,1\}^n$. Consider an algorithm $\mathcal{A} = (\mathcal{A}_{big}, \mathcal{A}_{small})$ which is $(s + \delta)$-bounded in space, c-bounded in communication, and is allowed at most q calls to the random oracle $\mathcal{H}$. A string $\mathcal{P}$ is called a $(c, s, \delta, q, \epsilon)$–one-time program for C if both of the following conditions hold:*

- *there exists a probabilistic polynomial-time decoder $\mathcal{D}ec$ that given $x \in \{0,1\}^n$ executes $\mathcal{P}$ using at most s bits of memory, so that $\mathcal{D}ec(x, \mathcal{P}) = C(x)$, except for probability ϵ (where the probability is taken over all possible choices of x and $\mathcal{P}$);*
- *there exists a simulator $\mathcal{S}$ with one-time oracle access to $\mathcal{O}$, such that, for any adversary $\mathcal{A}$, no algorithm restricted to at most q oracle calls to $\mathcal{H}$ can distinguish $\mathcal{S}(1^n, 1^m, 1^{|C|}, \mathcal{A})$ and $\mathcal{A}(\mathcal{P})$ with a probability greater than ϵ.*

Basically, the definition states that a user can honestly execute a device containing a one-time program on a single input of his choice. Yet, even for a computationally unbounded adversary $\mathcal{A} = (\mathcal{A}_{big}, \mathcal{A}_{small})$, with $\mathcal{A}_{small}$ having extra δ bits of memory, it is infeasible to break the device. We note that the one-time property formulated above is slightly stronger than what one may need for the applications. For instance, it could be safe to give the adversary some partial information about the circuit (e.g. information about a single boolean gate). In our definition, we disallow adversary to find out anything more than n, m, $|C|$, and $C(x)$ for a single x. We also remark that the definition provides adaptive security, i.e., the adversary can freely choose x depending on the contents of $\mathcal{P}$.

Shortly, in Sect. 5.3, we construct a compiler $\text{Compile}_{k,s}(C)$ that, for some parameter k, converts any boolean circuit C to a one-time program $\mathcal{P}$ that can be organized into a device with s bits of memory. The main result of this paper is stated in the below Theorem 1 about $\text{Compile}_{k,s}(C)$. The theorem contains a reference to circuits of uniform topology. A uniform version of C, denoted $\widetilde{C}$, is produced by the algorithm of Kolesnikov and Schneider [15], which is discussed in Sect. 4.2. Transforming C to such a form introduces a small blow-up factor (see (4) below) so that $\widetilde{C}$ is slightly larger than C.

Theorem 1. *Let k be a security parameter and let $\mathcal{H}\colon \{0,1\}^* \to \{0,1\}^k$ be modeled as a random oracle. Then, for any boolean circuit $C\colon \{0,1\}^n \to \{0,1\}^m$ and $\mathcal{P} \leftarrow \text{Compile}_{k,s}(C)$, the string $\mathcal{P}$ is a (c,s,δ,q,ϵ)-one-time program for C with $\epsilon = O(q|\widetilde{C}|2^{-k})$, provided that $k \geq \max(m, 4n^2 \log q)$ and*

$$s - 2nc \geq 2n\delta + 6k(2|\widetilde{C}| \log |\widetilde{C}| + 5n^2 + 4nm), \qquad (1)$$

where $|\widetilde{C}|$ denotes the number of gates in $\widetilde{C}$ – a version of C with uniform topology.

Remark 1. We note that the above theorem holds even if a potential distinguisher is given C. Also, we impose no limits on its running time as well as on time-complexity of the adversary. $\mathcal{A}$ can be computationally unbounded but he merely subjects to restriction on the number of oracle calls made. The construction of $\mathcal{S}$ is universal, i.e., it is independent of C and $\mathcal{P}$ so no information about C is hardwired in $\mathcal{S}$. We also mention that with a minor modification of our construction we can replace the factor $2n$ on the left-hand side of (1) with $2n/\log n$. We do not present this modification here as it would make the proofs considerably more complicated.

4 Tools

For completeness of the exposition, we outline several existing constructions the architecture of one-time devices builds upon – circuit obfuscation techniques and one-time computable pseudorandom functions.

4.1 Circuit Garbling

An important landmark in the theory of multi-party computations was set up by Yao in mid '80s. His seminal work [19] provided the first general protocol that enabled two honest-but-curious users to jointly evaluate a function f without disclosing their respective private inputs x. A so called *circuit garbling* process accounted for an essential part of this method. Its role was to conceal all intermediate values that occur on internal wires (in particular: on certain input wires) of a boolean circuit representing f during computation. Since the circuit garbling seems to be well-known, we skip its description here and only give the minimal relevant excerpt just to fix the notation.

Let k be a security parameter. For a boolean circuit C the garbling procedure $\text{Garble}_k(C)$ associates two random strings K_0^w and K_1^w of length k with each wire w of C. These two keys correspond to bits 0 and 1, respectively, that could appear on the wire w when evaluating C in its plain form. The mapping between input and output keys for each gate is masked using an auxiliary encryption scheme (E, D). We call it *a garbling encryption* scheme. It enjoys some extra properties, given by Pinkas and Lindell [16], going a little beyond the standard semantic security. In what follows, $E_K(\cdot)$ denotes the encryption under a key K (similarly, $D_K(\cdot)$ stands for the decryption using K). We instantiate E_K using the following setting, compliant with the requirements listed by Pinkas and Lindell, based on the oracle $\mathcal{H}$:

$$E_K(M) := (\mathcal{H}(K), r, \mathcal{H}(K, r) \oplus M) \quad \text{where } r \xleftarrow{\$} \{0, 1\}^k. \tag{2}$$

A double-encryption under two keys, say K_1 and K_2, each of length k, which is written as $E_{K_1; K_2}(\cdot)$ with $D_{K_1; K_2}(\cdot)$ being the complementary double-decryption, is a paramount ingredient of the garbling process. Departing from the original solution by Pinkas and Lindell for technical reasons, we specify $E_{K_1; K_2}(\cdot)$ separately extending (2) with:

$$E_{K_1; K_2}(M) := (\mathcal{H}(K_1, K_2), r, \mathcal{H}(K_1, K_2, r) \oplus M) \quad \text{for } r \xleftarrow{\$} \{0, 1\}^k. \tag{3}$$

In the remainder of this paper we assume that ciphertexts in a garbling encryption scheme are all of length $3k$ as implied by (2) and (3).

Below, we assume that the garbling procedure outputs a triple $(I, \mathfrak{C}, O)$, where $\mathfrak{C}$ is the actual garbled circuit, while I and O are arrays mapping plain bits to keys for input and output wires. $\mathfrak{C}$ is just a list of encrypted keys and each ciphertext on that list was produced using the double-encryption (3). Closely related to $\text{Garble}_k(C)$ is the procedure for evaluating the garbled circuit $\mathfrak{C}$ on a given input x. We write $\text{Eval}(\mathfrak{C}, O, K_x)$ to name this procedure.

4.2   Uniform Circuit Topology

One of the requirements a one-time program has to stand up to is ensuring that no eavesdropping into program's internals is possible. It is also a common problem in practical computer science to create software invulnerable to reverse engineering. Usually, satisfactory results can be achieved by ad-hoc techniques that decrease readability of a program (e.g. by obscuring a source code syntactically or inserting NOOPs). From a theoretical point of view, however, an ideal obfuscator cannot exist. Barak *et al.* [3] provide an artificial example of a family of functions that are inherently unobfuscatable. That is, there always exists a predicate which leaks when we are given a function in its plain form but cannot be reliably guessed if the function is implemented as a black-box. Fortunately, some *partial* obfuscation is attainable. There are several works describing methods for hiding circuit topology [15,18,20]. The most recognized one, which is asymptotically optimal in terms of additional overhead it incurs, comes from Valiant [18]. Recently, Vladimir Kolesnikov has pointed out to us that his construction [15], while being slightly worse asymptotically than Valiant's, achieves a smaller implied constant and thus performs better for circuits of up to 5000 gates. We recall his joint result on topology erasing algorithm UniformCircuit(C) below.

Theorem 2 (Kolesnikov and Schneider [15]**).** *Let* $C \colon \{0,1\}^n \to \{0,1\}^m$ *be a boolean circuit. Then, the topology erasing algorithm UniformCircuit(C) constructs a circuit* $\widetilde{C}$ *with*

$$|\widetilde{C}| = \left(\tfrac{3}{2} + o(1)\right) \cdot |C| \log^2 |C|. \tag{4}$$

such that $\widetilde{C}(x) = C(x)$ *for all* $x \in \{0,1\}^n$ *and the topology of* C *(i.e., the connectivity graph of* C *where each gate is stripped of information about what functionality it actually implements) discloses (in the information-theoretic sense) nothing more than* n, m, *and* $|C|$.

The below Proposition 1 follows from the analysis given by Kolesnikov and Schneider.

Proposition 1. *The algorithm UniformCircuit(C) uses at most* $4|\widetilde{C}| \log |\widetilde{C}|$ *bits of memory. Put differently, given* n, m, *and* $|C|$ *it is possible to generate a uniform topology that is common for all circuits with n-bit input, m-bit output, and* $|C|$ *gates, within space of* $4|\widetilde{C}| \log |\widetilde{C}|$ *bits.*

4.3   One-Time Computable Pseudorandom Functions (PRFs)

A notion of the one-time computable pseudorandom functions was introduced by Dziembowski *et al.* [8]. A salient development of this work is a construction of a pseudorandom function, or, more generally, a set of n such functions, where each function can be calculated for a single argument in the computation model with $\mathcal{A}_{big}$ and $\mathcal{A}_{small}$ having limited space and communication. Dziembowski *et al.* assume the existence of the random oracle $\mathcal{H}$. The underlying idea is to store a long random key, say R, on a device that $\mathcal{A}_{small}$ operates on. Now, R and $\mathcal{H}$ determine n distinct pseudorandom functions $(F_{1,R}^{\mathcal{H}}, \ldots, F_{n,R}^{\mathcal{H}})$. It is possible to evaluate each one on any input but the computation forces an erasure of R so that no one can viably compute both $F_{i,R}^{\mathcal{H}}(x)$ and $F_{i,R}^{\mathcal{H}}(x')$ for any two points $x \neq x'$ and the same index i. Below, we borrow some basic definitions from the original paper to formalize the mentioned properties.

Consider an algorithm $\mathcal{W}^{\mathcal{H}}$ that takes a key $R \in \{0,1\}^{\mu}$ as an input and has access to the oracle $\mathcal{H}$. Let $(F_{1,R}^{\mathcal{H}}, \ldots, F_{n,R}^{\mathcal{H}})$ be a sequence of functions depending on $\mathcal{H}$ and R. Assume that $\mathcal{W}^{\mathcal{H}}$ is interactive, i.e., it may receive queries, say

$x_1, \ldots, x_n$, from the outside. The algorithm $\mathcal{W}^{\mathcal{H}}$ replies to such a query by issuing a special *output query* to $\mathcal{H}$. We assume that after receiving each $x_i \in \{0,1\}^*$ the algorithm $\mathcal{W}^{\mathcal{H}}$ always issues an output query of a form $((F_{i,R}^{\mathcal{H}}(x_i), (i, x_i)), \mathsf{out})$. We say that an adversary *breaks PRFs* if a transcript of oracle calls made during its entire execution contains two queries $((F_{i,R}^{\mathcal{H}}(x), (i, x)), \mathsf{out})$ and $((F_{i,R}^{\mathcal{H}}(x'), (i, x')), \mathsf{out})$, appearing at any point, for some index i and $x \neq x'$.

Definition 2 (Dziembowski *et al.* [8]). *An algorithm $\mathcal{W}^{\mathcal{H}}$ with at most q queries to the oracle $\mathcal{H}$ defines $(c, \mu, \sigma, q, \epsilon, n)$–one-time computable PRFs if:*

- *$\mathcal{W}^{\mathcal{H}}$ has μ-bounded storage and 0-bounded communication;*
- *for any $\mathcal{A}^{\mathcal{H}}(R)$ that makes at most q queries to $\mathcal{H}$ and has σ-bounded storage and c-bounded communication, the probability that $\mathcal{A}^{\mathcal{H}}(R)$ (for a randomly chosen $R \xleftarrow{\$} \{0,1\}^\mu$) breaks PRFs, is at most ϵ.*

Basically, what this definition states is that no adversary with σ-bounded storage and c-bounded communication can viably compute a value of any $F_{i,R}^{\mathcal{H}}$ on two distinct inputs. Dziembowski *et al.* [8] prove the existence of the one-time computable PRFs in the Random Oracle model under some plausible assumption on parameters c, μ, σ, q, ϵ, and n.

The use case we investigate in the paper requires a slightly stronger primitive than the PRFs of Definition 2. In this work, we introduce *extended one-time computable PRFs*. An observation we come out with is that the limits on memory available to an adversary can be relaxed moderately. Namely, once all $F_{i,R}^{\mathcal{H}}$ are computed on some arguments, an adversary might be given unrestricted space, yet it still gains no advantage in breaking PRFs in the remainder of its execution. Now, the *computing phase* is a time interval between the beginning of an execution and the moment when all output queries of the form $((F_{i,R}^{\mathcal{H}}(x_i), (i, x_i)), \mathsf{out})$ were made (for some x_i and every $i = 1, \ldots, n$), provided that no i appears twice in that part of transcript. The below Definition 3 strengthens the notion of one-time computable PRFs.

Definition 3. *An algorithm $\mathcal{W}^{\mathcal{H}}$ defines extended $(c, \mu, \sigma, q, \epsilon, n)$–one-time computable PRFs if:*

- *$\mathcal{W}^{\mathcal{H}}$ defines $(c, \mu, \sigma, q, \epsilon, n)$–one-time computable PRFs;*
- *for any adversary $\mathcal{A}^{\mathcal{H}}(R)$ that makes at most q queries to $\mathcal{H}$, has σ-bounded storage and c-bounded communication during the computing phase, but is not bounded on space afterwards, the probability that $\mathcal{A}^{\mathcal{H}}(R)$ breaks PRFs, is at most ϵ.*

In full version of the paper, we verify that the theorem about the extended one-time computable PRFs holds with essentially the same parameters as in the base theorem by Dziembowski *et al.* [8]. Here, we present one more result about the existence of the extended PRFs that stems from the one proven in the full version and provides a condition which is more convenient to use in our particular application.

Theorem 3. *Let c, μ, δ, q, and n be positive integers. Then, for any $\epsilon \leq q2^{-4n^2}$, there exist extended $(c, \mu, \mu+\tau, q, \epsilon, n)$-one-time computable PRFs, provided that*

$$\mu \geq 2n \cdot (\tau + c + 4 \log q + 6 \log \epsilon^{-1} + 6). \tag{5}$$

A proof of Theorem 3 appears in full version of the paper.

5   The Construction

In this section, we give a high-level description of what a one-time device is made up of. Our solution, in principle, combines the hardware-based construction [13] and the primitive developed by Dziembowski *et al.* [8]. We replace the OTM units present in the former work with the extended one-time computable PRFs to achieve a purely software-based construction. There are, however, certain subtleties that occur when attempting to compose these both worlds together. Before proceeding to the correct construction we ultimately propose, we detail why a security proof for the most straightforward solution simply does not work out of the box.

5.1   Naïve Approach

A simple composition of techniques outlined in Sect. 4 one might conceive of could be the following. Garble a circuit as per Yao's method in the same way as it is done by Goldwasser *et al.* [13], and conceal its input keys using one-time computable PRFs. That is, let $K_0^{\mathrm{in}_i}$ and $K_1^{\mathrm{in}_i}$ be two keys corresponding to the ith input wire of the garbled circuit. Pick a long random string R and calculate both $F_{i,R}^{\mathcal{H}}(0)$ and $F_{i,R}^{\mathcal{H}}(1)$ for each member function $F_{i,R}^{\mathcal{H}}$ of the one-time computable PRFs. Then, a one-time device can store just the garbled circuit, the key R together with both $K_0^{\mathrm{in}_i} \oplus F_{i,R}^{\mathcal{H}}(0)$ and $K_1^{\mathrm{in}_i} \oplus F_{i,R}^{\mathcal{H}}(1)$ for each i. Intuitively, since the one-time PRFs only allow any space restricted algorithm to discover each $F_{i,R}^{\mathcal{H}}(b_i)$ for a single bit $b_i = 0$ or 1, keeping its counterpart $F_{i,R}^{\mathcal{H}}(\bar{b_i})$ entirely random, we can guarantee that such an algorithm can learn at most one input key $K_0^{\mathrm{in}_i}$ or $K_1^{\mathrm{in}_i}$. In that way we simulate the OTM gadgets and the original reasoning [13] should apply from this point. This would seemingly satisfy the requirements of Definition 1.

However, there are several problems arising in the above construction. Firstly, there is more space available on a device than just space needed to store the key R for the one-time computable PRFs. For instance, the garbled circuit resides in this additional memory. The extra space could be possibly used by an adversary to break PRFs, i.e., to compute both $F_{i,R}^{\mathcal{H}}(0)$ and $F_{i,R}^{\mathcal{H}}(1)$ for some i. There are several ways to fix this issue. Perhaps the most basic and the cleanest one is asserting that the garbled circuit is read-only. This is not a viable option for us as long as we aim at a solution that does not assume any tamper- nor even leakage-resistant components. Another way to circumvent the problem would be increasing the amount of free memory (cf. the parameter δ in Definition 1) available to an adversary, which would, however, worsen the parameters in Theorem 1 substantially. We take a different path and, in fact, ensure that an adversary may not erase the garbled circuit partially, reuse the claimed memory to break PRFs, and then still be able to evaluate the circuit. What makes establishing this property a bit tricky is an observation that a limited erasure is always possible, e.g., a constant number of bits from the circuit can be safely dropped and then guessed back correctly with large enough probability. A new element we introduce in the construction secures that an adversary cannot reliably do more than that. This is made formal in full version of the paper.

An important consequence of putting the garbled circuit into writable memory is that the basic one-time computable PRFs, as given by Definition 2, fall short of providing suitable security. The reason is that once an adversary computes each member function of the PRFs honestly for a single input and evaluates the circuit, then it can erase the circuit and, again, break the PRFs soon after using the increased amount of memory. This justifies turning to the extended one-time computable PRFs of Definition 3. Studying the details of the construction by Dziembowski *et al.* it is not hard to notice that their PRFs effectively self-destruct themselves when evaluating and thus prevent any further evaluations even by space unrestricted algorithms. This makes a transition to the extended PRFs rather straightforward.

Finally, it is not evident whether such a vague construction provides adaptive security or suffers from the same issue Bellare *et al.* [4] identified in the work of Goldwasser *et al.* [13].

5.2   One-Time Device

Our concluding construction of one-time programs does not differ significantly from the basic idea sketched above. Therefore, it involves garbling a circuit and masking its input keys with the extended one-time computable PRFs. However, it features an additional layer between these two components which is needed to address the issues we have mentioned. This auxiliary element can be viewed as a simple all-or-nothing transform. The main purpose it serves is splitting each execution of a one-time program into two phases. In the first stage any user, an honest or a malicious one, has to commit himself to the entire input he intends to compute the program on. The garbled circuit can be evaluated in the second phase, yet this process cannot begin before input bits for *all* the input wires are decided.

The exact way how such a separation can be accomplished is not very complex. Each input wire of the circuit is associated with an additional random key. We refer to a set of these keys as to *latchkeys*. Then, every latchkey gets encrypted using the outputs of the extended PRFs. We ensure that the ith latchkey can be recovered given $F_{i,R}^{\mathcal{H}}(0)$ or $F_{i,R}^{\mathcal{H}}(1)$. Lastly, we apply n-out-of-n secret sharing, where each latchkey forms a share, and combine the resulting secret with the garbled circuit using the random oracle $\mathcal{H}$. This produces a new string which we call the *master key*. Intuitively, by the property of $\mathcal{H}$, this value cannot be determined without all the latchkeys and the circuit. We now require the master key to be known to anyone attempting to discover the actual input keys of the garbled circuit. Technically, we adjust the naïve approach and replace the one-time pad encryption keys $F_{i,R}^{\mathcal{H}}(0)$ and $F_{i,R}^{\mathcal{H}}(1)$ present there with the keys that also depend on the master key.

There are two goals we achieve with this transform. First, the garbled circuit cannot be partially erased during the first phase as this would make computing the master key impossible, block opening all its input keys and render the circuit unusable. Second, it makes our construction immune to the attack devised by Bellare *et al.* [4]. The fact that the one-time programs of Goldwasser *et al.* permit what Bellare *et al.* call *partial evaluations* is the fundamental reason that makes these programs susceptible to the attack. In our construction a user cannot attempt to evaluate the circuit if he has learnt keys corresponding only to a proper subset of input wires. In other words, partial evaluations are not feasible. Also, we note that Bellare *et al.* consider a family garbling schemes and construct an artificial scheme for which the proof of Goldwasser *et al.* fails. We, in turn, use only a single, explicitly defined garbling scheme (3). It leaves no room for attaching any security-exploiting superfluous data as Bellare *et al.* do. Finally, our garbled circuits look entirely random to any adversary who does not know the input keys. Seeing this random string does not help the adversary in choosing his input.

Overall, one-time devices we propose contain the following data:

- a garbled circuit $\mathfrak{C}$ together with a table O mapping output keys of the circuit back to plain bits;
- a random key R that determines the extended one-time computable PRFs;
- an array L of encrypted latchkeys;
- an array K consisting of one-time pad encrypted input keys for the garbled circuit $\mathfrak{C}$ – the encryption keys depend on all the latchkeys and $\mathfrak{C}$;
- the number m of output wires of the original circuit.

5.3   One-Time Compiler

The purpose of a one-time compiler is to transform an arbitrary boolean circuit $C\colon \{0,1\}^n \to \{0,1\}^m$ into a deliberately obscured form accompanied with some additional logic (a procedure) that enables evaluations of the circuit on every single n-bit input.

The compiler routine $\text{Compile}_{k,s}$ constructs a one-time program deployable on a device with a grand total of s bits of writable memory (including registers, RAM, flash memory, and any other persistent storage). We, however, introduce no extra assumptions on the amount of read-only memory available. $\text{Compile}_{k,s}$ is allowed unrestricted use of a source of random bits, as well as access to the aforementioned random oracle $\mathcal{H}\colon \{0,1\}^* \to \{0,1\}^k$ with k being a security parameter. Algorithm 1 presents a listing of the one-time compiler procedure.

Firstly, the compiler prepares (Lines 2 and 3 of Algorithm 1) a set of random latchkeys L^{in_i}. A value L^{in_i} corresponds to the ith input wire in_i of C. A string $\text{Latch} := L^{\text{in}_1} \oplus \ldots \oplus L^{\text{in}_n}$ combines all the latchkeys into a single key. From Latch we derive (Line 5), by means of the oracle, one more random value, denoted

---

Algorithm 1. One-time compiler $\text{Compile}_{k,s}(C)$

INPUT: a boolean circuit $C \colon \{0,1\}^n \to \{0,1\}^m$, a security parameter $k \geq m$, a total amount of memory on the device s

OUTPUT: a one-time program $\mathcal{P} = (m, R, L, K, \mathfrak{C}, O)$

1: **procedure** $\text{Compile}_{k,s}(C)$
2:     **for** $i \leftarrow 1$ **to** n **do**
3:         $L^{\text{in}_i} \overset{\$}{\leftarrow} \{0,1\}^k$
4:     $\text{Latch} \leftarrow L^{\text{in}_1} \oplus \cdots \oplus L^{\text{in}_n}$
5:     $\text{Mask} \leftarrow \mathcal{H}(\text{Latch})_{|m}$
6:     $\widetilde{C} \leftarrow \text{UniformCircuit}(C \oplus \text{Mask})$
7:     $(I, \mathfrak{C}, O) \leftarrow \text{Garble}_k(\widetilde{C})$
8:     $\text{Master} \leftarrow \mathcal{H}(\text{Latch}, \mathfrak{C})$
9:     $\mu \leftarrow s - (12|\widetilde{C}| + 8n + 2m)k - \log m$
10:     round μ down to the largest multiple of k
11:     $R \overset{\$}{\leftarrow} \{0,1\}^\mu$
12:     **for each** input wire in_i of C **do**   ▷ in_i is the ith input wire of C
13:         $(K_0^{\text{in}_i}, K_1^{\text{in}_i}) \leftarrow I[i]$
14:         compute $F_{i,R}^{\mathcal{H}}(0)$ and $F_{i,R}^{\mathcal{H}}(1)$
15:         $L[i] \leftarrow \left(E_{F_{i,R}^{\mathcal{H}}(0)}(L^{\text{in}_i}), E_{F_{i,R}^{\mathcal{H}}(1)}(L^{\text{in}_i}) \right)$
16:         $K[i] \leftarrow \left(K_0^{\text{in}_i} \oplus \mathcal{H}(F_{i,R}^{\mathcal{H}}(0), \text{Master}), K_1^{\text{in}_i} \oplus \mathcal{H}(F_{i,R}^{\mathcal{H}}(1), \text{Master}) \right)$
17:     **end for each**
18:     **return** $(m, R, L, K, \mathfrak{C}, O)$
19: **end procedure**

Mask, trimming the output of $\mathcal{H}$ to the leading $m \leq k$ bits. The exact role that all these auxiliary components play should become clear later, in Sect. 6. Having calculated these values, the compiler enters its main phase in Line 6. There, the obfuscation algorithm is run, yet on a biased version of C, say C^*, defined as $C^*(x) := C(x) \oplus \text{Mask}$. At this point Mask is merely a constant that does not depend on x. Obviously, C^* can be viewed as a boolean circuit and implemented in such a way that $|C^*| = |C|$ (it suffices to flip, if needed, a functionality of each gate an output wire of C is attached to, depending on the corresponding bit of Mask). The reason behind switching to C^* instead of working with C directly is that the simulator from Theorem 1 needs to alter an output of a circuit when interacting with an adversary. This trick can be exercised by changing the value of Mask in a transparent way, which is done by $\mathcal{S}$ in Sect. 6.

The obfuscated circuit is garbled (Line 7) using Yao's method. Next, extended one-time computable PRFs (in the sense of Definition 3) are set up (Line 10). Actually, this step boils down to picking a random string R that determines (together with $\mathcal{H}$) said pseudorandom functions $F_{i,R}^{\mathcal{H}}$. The embedded extended one-time computable PRFs are a primitive that protects input keys of the garbled circuit. Namely, in order to evaluate a one-time program on some input $x = b_1 b_2 \ldots b_n$, one has to compute each $F_{i,R}^{\mathcal{H}}(b_i)$ for $i = 1, \ldots, n$. By virtue of the property of extended PRFs, this computation erases an essential portion of memory available on the device and makes evaluations of $F_{i,R}^{\mathcal{H}}(\bar{b}_i)$ infeasible.

The compiler, however, needs to find both: $F_{i,R}^{\mathcal{H}}(0)$ and $F_{i,R}^{\mathcal{H}}(1)$ for all i's (this requires a larger amount of memory than just s bits but still Compile$_{k,s}$ is clearly polynomial in space and time).

Stored on the device are two encryptions of each latchkey L^{in_i} under $F_{i,R}^{\mathcal{H}}(0)$ and $F_{i,R}^{\mathcal{H}}(1)$ as encryption keys. For this purpose, in Line 15 where these cipher-texts are accumulated in array L, we use the garbling encryption scheme as given by (2). The input keys for $\mathfrak{C}$ generated by the garbling procedure get encoded too before being placed on the device. That is: the ith entry of K contains, for $b = 0$ and 1, simple one-time pad encryptions of $K_b^{\text{in}_i}$ under a key $\mathcal{H}(F_{i,R}^{\mathcal{H}}(b), \text{Master})$. Here, Master $:= \mathcal{H}(\text{Latch}, \mathfrak{C})$ is a value that depends on all the latchkeys and the garbled circuit $\mathfrak{C}$. This all-or-nothing construction ensures that a user can no sooner determine $K_b^{\text{in}_i}$ than he has computed all $F_{i,R}^{\mathcal{H}}(b_i)$. Also, this allows us to hold off the moment when an adversary can reclaim a part of memory occupied by $\mathfrak{C}$ and reuse it to enlarge space available for computing (or breaking) the extended PRFs. In this way we control the amount of free memory during the computing phase specified in Definition 3.

Now that we have described the one-time compiler, we present a decoder $\mathcal{D}ec = \mathcal{D}ec_k$ which is capable of evaluating a program produced by Compile$_{k,s}$ on an arbitrary input $x = b_1b_2\ldots b_n$. As the first step, $\mathcal{D}ec_k$ determines $F_{i,R}^{\mathcal{H}}(b_i)$ for each $i = 1,\ldots,n$. This is accomplished by computing labels of output vertices under a *random oracle labeling* of a certain on-line constructed graph (the exact method follows from the work of Dziembowski et $al.$ [8]). The key R that settles a labeling of input vertices of this graph gets erased during the process, and the region of memory that contained R can be reused by $\mathcal{D}ec$. Next, the decoder decrypts a matching entry of each $L[i]$ to find L^{in_i}. Based on these latchkeys, $\mathcal{D}ec$ computes Latch, Mask $= \mathcal{H}(\text{Latch})_{|m}$, Master $= \mathcal{H}(\text{Latch}, \mathfrak{C})$, and reveals, using $K[i]$, input garbled keys $K_{b_i}^{\text{in}_i}$ that correspond to each bit b_i. Let K_x be a vector consisting of all $K_{b_i}^{\text{in}_i}$. The decoder then executes Eval$(\mathfrak{C}, O, K_x)$ subroutine and calculates a bitwise exclusive or of the result with Mask to obtain the final value, i.e., $C(x)$. As for evaluating $\mathfrak{C}$, the garbled circuit kept on the device only includes a list of garbled tables without its actual topology. Prior to running Eval, the decoder needs to generate the unique uniform topology distinctive for all circuits of n inputs, m outputs, and $|C|$ gates. That is, $\mathcal{D}ec$ simulates the topology erasing algorithm on such an arbitrarily chosen circuit. A memory that has to be supplied by $\mathcal{D}ec$ for this step is located exactly in the same region the key R was previously stored in. By Proposition 1, this space, which is considered free after computing the extended PRFs, has a sufficient size if $\mu = |R| \geq 4|\widetilde{C}|\log|\widetilde{C}|$. The sizes of the remaining components of $\mathcal{P}$ can be easily counted: $|L| = 6nk$, $|K| = 2nk$, $|\mathfrak{C}| = 12|\widetilde{C}|k$, and $|O| = 2mk$. In total, the space that $\mathcal{P}$ occupies is

$$|\mathcal{P}| = \mu + (12|\widetilde{C}| + 8n + 2m) \cdot k + \log m. \tag{6}$$

6   Universal Simulator for One-Time Programs

In this section, we focus on the more intricate part of Definition 1 and describe an explicit simulator $\mathcal{S}$. We employ a similar approach to the one that appears in the work of Goldwasser *et al.* [13]. A notable difference, however, is that our construction includes a component, i.e., the extended one-time computable PRFs, which does not offer a black-box security, in opposition to the aforementioned OTMs. The condition (1) of Theorem 1 ensures that our replacement of the OTMs performs nearly equally well. Namely, it is possible to achieve $\epsilon = (q+1)2^{-k}$ in Theorem 3 so that the corresponding extended one-time computable PRFs can only be broken with a small probability. By the analysis given in full version of the paper, the extra memory the adversary can retain in the computing phase (see Definition 3) can be bounded above by $\tau = \delta + (8n + 2m + 3)k$. Now, combining (5) and (6) we get the following constraint

$$s - 2nc \geq 2n(\delta + \tau + 6k + 6) + (12|\widetilde{C}| + 8n + 2m)k + \log m \qquad (7)$$

But (1) guarantees this condition is met.

Now, we give an outline of how the simulator $\mathcal{S}$ of Definition 1 works given 1^n, 1^m, $1^{|C|}$, and an $(s+\delta)$-space bounded, c-communication bounded adversary $\mathcal{A}^{\mathcal{H}}$. Plus, $\mathcal{S}$ has access to $\mathcal{H}$. The simulator begins with assembling a uniformly random circuit $C' : \{0,1\}^n \rightarrow \{0,1\}^m$ of size $|C'| = |C|$. Then, it runs the one-time compiler $\text{Compile}_{k,s}$ on C' obtaining a protocol $\mathcal{P}' = (m, R, L, K, \mathfrak{C}, O)$. The simulator maintains two exact copies of $\mathcal{P}'$. In the next step $\mathcal{S}$ starts executing $\mathcal{A}^{\mathcal{H}}$ on a copy of $\mathcal{P}'$, recording each oracle call to $\mathcal{H}$. Depending on what the resulting transcript contains, the simulator picks one of the following paths:

1. There exists at least one index i such that none of the associated values $F_{i,R}^{\mathcal{H}}(0)$ nor $F_{i,R}^{\mathcal{H}}(1)$ has been computed. Then, $\mathcal{S}$ simply outputs a result $\mathcal{A}^{\mathcal{H}}$ has returned.
2. $\mathcal{A}^{\mathcal{H}}$ has broken the PRFs (in the sense given in Sect. 4.3). In this case an outcome of the simulation is again the same as the result $\mathcal{A}^{\mathcal{H}}$ has produced.
3. For each $i = 1, \ldots, n$, the adversary $\mathcal{A}^{\mathcal{H}}$ has issued an output query to $\mathcal{H}$ computing $F_{i,R}^{\mathcal{H}}(b_i)$ either for $b_i = 0$ or $b_i = 1$ (but not both – therefore $\mathcal{A}^{\mathcal{H}}$ has not broken PRFs). As $\mathcal{S}$ has learnt all these values in the process, it can decrypt each of the latchkeys L^{in_i} just to pinpoint for which b_i the function $F_{i,R}^{\mathcal{H}}$ has been computed. All the $F_{i,R}^{\mathcal{H}}(b_i)$'s correspond to a single value $x_A := b_1 b_2 \ldots b_n$ that $\mathcal{A}^{\mathcal{H}}$ has committed to by evaluating the extended one-time computable PRFs. Thus, $\mathcal{S}$ is also able to find out x_A, compute $C'(x_A)$ on its own, and query O on argument x_A. Let $\Delta_x := C'(x_A) \oplus C(x_A)$. If Δ_x happens to be 0^m then $\mathcal{S}$ continues by returning the value $\mathcal{A}^{\mathcal{H}}$ has outputted. Otherwise, the simulator discards this result. Using the latchkeys and querying the oracle $\mathcal{H}$ on $\text{Latch} = L^{\text{in}_1} \oplus \ldots \oplus L^{\text{in}_n}$, the simulator determines the genuine value of $\text{Mask} = \mathcal{H}(\text{Latch})_{|m}$. Then, it reprograms $\mathcal{H}$ so that $\mathcal{H}(\text{Latch})_{|m} := \text{Mask} \oplus \Delta_x$. Next, $\mathcal{S}$ rewinds $\mathcal{A}^{\mathcal{H}}$ and runs it again on a leftover copy of $\mathcal{P}'$ with substituted $\mathcal{H}$. No matter which of the above

conditions 1–3 this second execution matches, an output of $\mathcal{A}^{\mathcal{H}}$ becomes the final result of the simulation.

In full version of the paper we prove that the output of $\mathcal{S}$ is indistinguishable from a result of $\mathcal{A}^{\mathcal{H}}$ running on $\mathcal{P}$, except for $O(q|\widetilde{C}|2^{-k})$ probability.

References

1. Akavia, A., Goldwasser, S., Vaikuntanathan, V.: Simultaneous hardcore bits and cryptography against memory attacks. In: Reingold, O. (ed.) TCC 2009. LNCS, vol. 5444, pp. 474–495. Springer, Heidelberg (2009)
2. Alwen, J., Dodis, Y., Wichs, D.: Leakage-resilient public-key cryptography in the bounded-retrieval model. In: Halevi, S. (ed.) CRYPTO 2009. LNCS, vol. 5677, pp. 36–54. Springer, Heidelberg (2009)
3. Barak, B., Goldreich, O., Impagliazzo, R., Rudich, S., Sahai, A., Vadhan, S.P., Yang, K.: On the (Im)possibility of obfuscating programs. In: Kilian, J. (ed.) CRYPTO 2001. LNCS, vol. 2139, pp. 1–18. Springer, Heidelberg (2001)
4. Bellare, M., Hoang, V.T., Rogaway, P.: Adaptively secure garbling with applications to one-time programs and secure outsourcing. In: Wang, X., Sako, K. (eds.) ASIACRYPT 2012. LNCS, vol. 7658, pp. 134–153. Springer, Heidelberg (2012)
5. Di Crescenzo, G., Lipton, R.J., Walfish, S.: Perfectly secure password protocols in the bounded retrieval model. In: Halevi, S., Rabin, T. (eds.) TCC 2006. LNCS, vol. 3876, pp. 225–244. Springer, Heidelberg (2006)
6. Dziembowski, S.: Intrusion-resilience via the bounded-storage model. In: Halevi, S., Rabin, T. (eds.) TCC 2006. LNCS, vol. 3876, pp. 207–224. Springer, Heidelberg (2006)
7. Dziembowski, S., Kazana, T., Wichs, D.: Key-evolution schemes resilient to space-bounded leakage. In: Rogaway, P. (ed.) CRYPTO 2011. LNCS, vol. 6841, pp. 335–353. Springer, Heidelberg (2011)
8. Dziembowski, S., Kazana, T., Wichs, D.: One-time computable self-erasing functions. In: Ishai, Y. (ed.) TCC 2011. LNCS, vol. 6597, pp. 125–143. Springer, Heidelberg (2011)
9. Dziembowski, S., Pietrzak, K.: Leakage-resilient cryptography. In: 49th Annual IEEE Symposium on Foundations of Computer Science, FOCS 2008, pp. 293–302 (2008)
10. Dziembowski, S., Pietrzak, K., Wichs, D.: Non-malleable codes. In: Yao, A.C.-C. (ed.) Innovations in Computer Science - ICS 2010, Proceedings, pp. 434–452. Tsinghua University Press (2010)
11. ECRYPT. Side channel cryptoanalysis lounge. http://www.emsec.rub.de/research/projects/sclounge/
12. Gennaro, R., Lysyanskaya, A., Malkin, T., Micali, S., Rabin, T.: Algorithmic tamper-proof (ATP) security: theoretical foundations for security against hardware tampering. In: Naor, M. (ed.) TCC 2004. LNCS, vol. 2951, pp. 258–277. Springer, Heidelberg (2004)
13. Goldwasser, S., Kalai, Y.T., Rothblum, G.N.: One-time programs. In: Wagner, D. (ed.) CRYPTO 2008. LNCS, vol. 5157, pp. 39–56. Springer, Heidelberg (2008)
14. Järvinen, K., Kolesnikov, V., Sadeghi, A.-R., Schneider, T.: Garbled circuits for leakage-resilience: hardware implementation and evaluation of one-time programs. In: Mangard, S., Standaert, F.-X. (eds.) CHES 2010. LNCS, vol. 6225, pp. 383–397. Springer, Heidelberg (2010)

15. Kolesnikov, V., Schneider, T.: A practical universal circuit construction and secure evaluation of private functions. In: Tsudik, G. (ed.) FC 2008. LNCS, vol. 5143, pp. 83–97. Springer, Heidelberg (2008)
16. Lindell, Y., Pinkas, B.: A proof of security of Yao's protocol for two-party computation. J. Cryptol. **22**(2), 161–188 (2009)
17. Maurer, U.M.: Conditionally-perfect secrecy and a provably-secure randomized cipher. J. Cryptol. **5**(1), 53–66 (1992)
18. Valiant, L.G.: Universal circuits (preliminary report). In: Chandra, A.K., Wotschke, D., Friedman, E.P., Harrison, M.A. (eds.) STOC '76, pp. 196–203. ACM (1976)
19. Yao, A.C.-C.: How to generate and exchange secrets. In: Proceedings of the 27th Annual Symposium on Foundations of Computer Science, SFCS '86, pp. 162–167 (1986)
20. Yu, Y., Leiwo, J., Premkumar, B.: Hiding circuit topology from unbounded reverse engineers. In: Batten, L.M., Safavi-Naini, R. (eds.) ACISP 2006. LNCS, vol. 4058, pp. 171–182. Springer, Heidelberg (2006)

Cryptanalysis of Three Authenticated Encryption Schemes for Wireless Sensor Networks

Xiaoqian Li[1,2](✉), Peng Wang[1,2], Bao Li[1,2], and Zhelei Sun[1,2]

[1] State Key Laboratory of Information Security,
Institute of Information Engineering, Chinese Academy of Sciences, Beijing, China
[2] University of Chinese Academy of Sciences, Beijing, China
{xqli,wp,lb,zhlsun}@is.ac.cn

Abstract. In this paper we analyse three authenticated encryption schemes, CMBC-MAC, SCMA and CBC-X, which were proposed for wireless sensor networks (WSN). Our research shows that these three schemes all have serious security problems either in authenticity or in privacy. More specifically, we only need one query to break the authenticity of CMBC-MAC and SCMA with success probability of 1. Meanwhile, we only need one query of block length of at least three to break the authenticity of CBC-X with success probability of 0.63, and we need two queries to break the privacy of CBC-X with success probability of $1 - 2^{-64}$.

Keywords: Authenticated encryption · Cryptanalysis · CMBC-MAC · SCMA · CBC-X

1 Introduction

The application of wireless sensor networks (WSN) ranges widely from battlefield surveillance, environmental monitoring, medical application, to industrial process monitoring and control. For most WSN applications, security and efficiency are often significant or even rigorous requirements. When several security provisions are required, authenticated encryption with associated data (AEAD) [1] schemes are able to cover the need. AEAD schemes can have the payload portion encrypted and authenticated while the associated header portion unencrypted, so that packet can be routed expeditiously.

This work was supported by the National Basic Research Program of China (973 Project, No.2013CB338002), the National High Technology Research and Development Program of China (863 Program, No.2013AA014002), the National Natural Science Foundation Of China (No. 61272477, 61202422), the IIE's Cryptography Research Project (No.Y3Z0027103, Y3Z0025103), and the Strategic Priority Research Program of Chinese Academy of Sciences under Grant XDA06010702.

© Springer International Publishing Switzerland 2014
D. Lin et al. (Eds.): Inscrypt 2013, LNCS 8567, pp. 395–406, 2014.
DOI: 10.1007/978-3-319-12087-4_25

Generally speaking, AEAD schemes can be classified as two-pass and single-pass modes. In a two-pass mode, such as CCM [2], EAX [3], CWC [4] and GCM [5], every block is processed twice, one for authenticity, the other for privacy. In a single-pass mode, such as IAPM [6] and OCB [7], the single pass can provide privacy and authenticity simultaneously. Characteristically, single-pass mode generally exhibits a lower computational cost.

The security provisions of WSN have given rise to a number of proposals for well-defined AEAD schemes, including CCM [2], which is IEEE 802.11i security standard, TinySec [8], which is the de facto standard for WSN data communication security, and CCFB+H [9]. Compared to CCM and TinySec which are both two-pass modes, three single-pass modes CMBC-MAC [10], SCMA [11] and CBC-X [12] are more resource saving and energy efficient and thus perform better in WSN environment. However, as not expected, these three schemes all suffer from serious security problems either in authenticity or in privacy.

In this paper we examine these three single-pass AEAD modes, CMBC-MAC, SCMA and CBC-X. Our first target CMBC-MAC is designed for improving CCM. Our second target is Simultaneous Combined Mode Algorithm (SCMA), whose encrypting portion is a variant of Counter Output Feedback mode (CTR-OFB) [13] and the authentication portion is a variant of QBC-MAC [14]. Both CMBC-MAC and SCMA can be viewed as encrypt-then-MAC scheme, but with tinny authentication portions, and the tags of schemes are only determined by the sum of ciphertext blocks. Our attacks on CMBC-MAC and SCMA is simple, but not negligible from an industrial view point. Our third target is CBC-X, which adopts a novel padding technique. It is important to note that the description of CBC-X in the original paper has some errors which may cause contradiction and confusion, which are corrected in this paper. Our main results are exhibited in Table 1 where the computation complexity in the forgery attack against CBC-X is trivial.

Table 1. Main results of this paper

	CMBC-MAC	SCMA	CBC-X	
Attack	Forgery	Forgery	Forgery	Chosen Plaintext
Query	1	1	1	2
Probability	1	1	0.63	$1 - 2^{-64}$
Complexity	$\mathcal{O}(1)$	$\mathcal{O}(1)$	-	$\mathcal{O}(1)$

The paper is organized as follows: Sect. 2 describes the notations used and the security mode we adopt in this paper. Section 3 describes the mechanism of CMBC-MAC and the forgery attack on it. Section 4 describes the mechanism of SCMA and the forgery attack on it. Section 5 describes the mechanism of CBC-X, the forgery attack and chosen plaintext attack on it. In Sect. 6 we make some remarks on our attacks. And we conclude in Sect. 7.

2   Notations and Security Models

2.1   Notations

- A *block cipher* is a function $E : \{0,1\}^k \times \{0,1\}^m \to \{0,1\}^m$, where m and k are the block-length and key-length respectively. $E_K(\cdot) = E(K, \cdot)$ is a permutation for all $K \in \{0,1\}^k$.
- $X \oplus Y$ denotes the *exclusive or* (XOR) of two strings X and Y.
- $X \boxplus Y / X \boxminus Y$ denotes the add/minus modulo 2^m in which $m = |X| = |Y|$.
- $X \gg f$ denotes the bitwise right-shift by f bits on the string X.

These notations are suitable for all the three AE schemes.

2.2   Security Models

We adopt the standard security models as those mentioned in [15].

Authenticity Model. The adversary $\mathcal{A}$ queries the Enc with messages, observing the outputs. After some queries, he tries to return a new ciphertext which does not appear before. Formally, the advantage of $\mathcal{A}$ is defined by

$$\mathbf{Adv}^{auth}(\mathcal{A}) = \Pr[\mathcal{A}^{\text{Enc}} \text{ forges}].$$

In this authenticity model we break the authenticity of CMBC-MAC, SCMA and CBC-X.

Privacy Model. The adversary $\mathcal{B}$ also queries the Enc with messages, observing the outputs, and tries to distinguish it from random bits. Formally, the advantage of $\mathcal{B}$ is defined by

$$\mathbf{Adv}^{priv}(\mathcal{B}) = |\Pr[\mathcal{B}^{\text{Enc}} \Rightarrow 1] - \Pr[\mathcal{B}^{\$} \Rightarrow 1]|.$$

where $\$$ returns a random string with the same length of real ciphertext. Just like in the security analysis of the GCM or OCB mode, we assume that the adversary can choose but can not repeat the initial vector (IV) or nonce used in the scheme, in this model which is also known as nonce-respecting model [15], we break the privacy of CBC-X.

3   Forgery Attack on CMBC-MAC

3.1   Description of CMBC-MAC

CMBC-MAC [10] is a hybrid CCM design with merged Counter Mode Encryption and CBC-MAC variant. It is designed for enhancing the efficiency of CCM, which is IEEE 802.11i standard for wireless local area network (WLAN). CMBC-MAC scheme uses 128-AES as the underlying cryptographic primitive. The CMBC-MAC

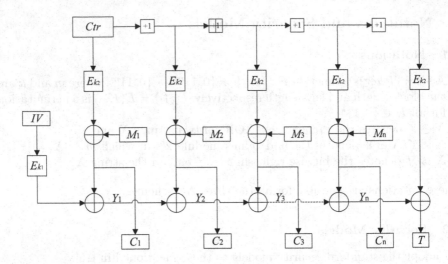

Fig. 1. CMBC-MAC

scheme is illustrated in Fig. 1. Suppose the input message M (having been padded if necessary) is divided into a sequence of 128-bit plaintext blocks, $M = M_1 M_2 M_3 \cdots M_n$. A nonce N is chosen to derive the initial value (IV) and the counter value (Ctr). Using Y_i as intermediate results, the encryption of the plaintexts $M_1, M_2, M_3, \cdots, M_n$ is defined as $C_1 = M_1 \oplus E_{k_2}(Ctr), C_i = M_i \oplus E_{k_2}(Ctr \boxplus i \boxminus 1)$ $(2 \le i \le n)$, where $Y_1 = E_{k_1}(IV) \oplus C_1, Y_i = Y_{i-1} \oplus C_i$ $(2 \le i \le n)$. The tag is computed as $T = Y_n \oplus E_{k_2}(Ctr \boxplus n)$.

CMBC-MAC is a single-pass mode that requires two keys k_1, k_2 for encryption and authentication. The generation of IV and Ctr is not explicitly stated in the original paper [10], we assume that IV and Ctr can not be chosen by the adversary in the forgery attack on CMBC-MAC.

3.2 Breaking Authenticity of CMBC-MAC

In the following we exhibit a simple forgery attack on CMBC-MAC. This attack only makes one special query to the encryption oracle, then returns a valid triple of initial value, ciphertext and tag which do not appear before.

1. Query $(M_1 M_2 \cdots M_l)$ to the encryption oracle, where M_i $(1 \le i \le l)$ are arbitrary blocks, and get $(IV, C_1 C_2 \cdots C_l, T)$, where C_i $(1 \le i \le l)$ are ciphertext blocks, T is the tag.
2. Return $(IV, C_1^* C_2^* \cdots C_l^*, T)$ such that $\bigoplus_{i=1}^{l} C_i = \bigoplus_{i=1}^{l} C_i^*$.

The corresponding plaintext blocks M_i^* of C_i^* under the same initial value IV are $M_i \oplus C_i \oplus C_i^*$ $(i = 1, 2, \cdots, l)$. The proof for the validation of $(N, C_1^* C_2^* \cdots C_l^*, T)$ is trivial, and we can get $Adv_{CMBC}^{auth}(\mathcal{A}) = 1$.

4   Forgery Attack on SCMA

4.1   Description of SCMA

The encrypting portion of SCMA [11] is a variant of Counter Output Feedback mode (CTR-OFB) [13] and the authentication portion is a variant of QBC-MAC [14]. SCMA scheme uses a 64-bit block cipher as the underlying cryptographic primitive. The graphical implementation of SCMA is in Fig. 2. Let message $M = M_1M_2M_3\cdots M_n$ be a sequence of 64-bit plaintext block. Using X_i, Y_i as intermediate results, we suppose $Y_0 = E_{k_1}(N), X_1 = E_{k_2}(Y_0 \oplus 1 \boxplus Twk)$ and $X_i = E_{k_2}(Y_0 \oplus i \boxplus X_{i-1})$ $(2 \le i \le n)$, $Y_i = Y_{i-1} \boxplus C_i$ $(1 \le i \le n)$. Then the encryption of the plaintexts is defined as $C_i = X_i \oplus M_i$ $(1 \le i \le n)$. The tag is computed as $T = Y_n \boxplus E_{k_1}(Y_n)$.

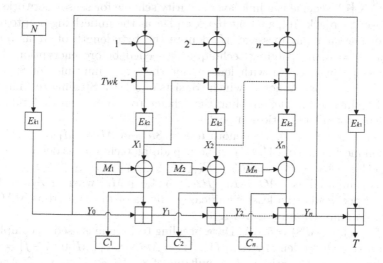

Fig. 2. SCMA

Like CMBC-MAC, SCMA is also a single-pass mode that requires two keys for encryption and authentication. The adversary is allowed to manipulate both the nonce and the associated-data while no nonce is repeated. Twk is a tweak value chosen by the application designer to be a security parameter.

4.2   Breaking Authenticity of SCMA

Now we exhibit a simple forgery attack to the authenticity of SCMA which is similar to the attack we give against the authenticity of CMBC-MAC.

1. Query $(M_1M_2\cdots M_l)$ to the encryption oracle, where M_i $(1 \le i \le l)$ are arbitrary blocks, and get $(N, C_1C_2\cdots C_l, T)$, where C_i $(1 \le i \le l)$ are ciphertext blocks, T is the tag.
2. Return $(N, C_1^*C_2^*\cdots C_l^*, T)$ such that $\boxplus_{i=1}^{l} C_i = \boxplus_{i=1}^{l} C_i^*$.

The corresponding plaintext blocks M_i^* of C_i^* under the same Nonce N are $M_i \oplus C_i \oplus C_i^*$ ($1 \leq i \leq l$). The verification of the legacy of the forgery is omitted here, since it is the same as of CMBC-MAC.

SCMA and CMBC-MAC have something in common: the authentication portion of both schemes is a sum of ciphertexts. The method of linear combining of ciphertexts for authentication is the key for our forgery attack. For future design principle, this construction method should not be directly used for data integrity.

5   Forgery Attack on CBC-X

5.1   Description of CBC-X

The CBC-X [12] scheme is a link layer security scheme for sensor networks. This scheme uses Skipjack [16], a 64-bit block cipher as the underlying cryptographic primitive. For an input message M, denote the byte-length of M as len. For $len \; (mod \; 8) = 0$, no padding technique is needed before encryption. For an input message byte-length with length not the exact multiples of 8, a novel padding technique is promoted, which consists of a Data Stealing technique and a MAC Stealing technique, enabling the scheme to achieve zero-redundancy on sending encrypted/authenticated packets.

For $len \; (mod \; 8) = 0$, we denote $len = 8n$ and $M = M_1 M_2 \cdots M_n$. The encryption mechanism of (M, IV) without padding technique is denoted as $C_1 = E_{k_1}(E_{k_1}(IV) \oplus M_1) \oplus IV$, and $C_i = E_{k_1}(M_i \oplus C_{i-1}) \oplus M_{i-1}$ ($2 \leq i \leq n$). Then the tag is computed as $TAG = E_{k_2}(PAD \oplus C_n) \oplus M_n$, where $PAD = $ "0^8" is constant. Specifically, the least significant 4 bytes of tag is used as MAC, and the diagram representation is in Fig. 3.

For $f = len \; (mod \; 8) = 5, 6, 7$, Data Stealing technique is used to complement the plaintext with "stolen" bytes in IV. $M' = M \gg 8 - f$, $M'[0 : 7 - f] = IV[f : 7]$, enabling the byte length of M' a multiple of 8. $IV' = IV \gg 8 - f$. And then the encryption of (M', IV') without MAC stealing can proceed.

For $len \; (mod \; 8) = 4$, we denote $len = 8(n-1)+4$ and $M = M_1, M_2, \cdots, M_{n-1},$ $M[8n - 8 : 8n - 5]$. Only the MAC Stealing technique is used, $M_n = M[8n - 8 : 8n - 5]||PAD$, where $PAD = ABCD$ is constant. This technique enables the byte length of plaintext concatenated MAC a multiple of 8. Then the encryption of the plaintexts is defined as $C_1 = E_{k_1}(E_{k_1}(IV) \oplus M_1) \oplus IV$, and $C_i = E_{k_1}(M_i \oplus C_{i-1}) \oplus M_{i-1}$ ($2 \leq i \leq n - 1$). The tag is computed as $TAG = E_{k_2}(E_{k_1}(M_n \oplus C_{n-1}) \oplus M_{n-1})$, which is used as MAC without truncation. The diagram representation is in Fig. 4.

For $f = len \; (mod \; 8) = 1, 2, 3$, first the Data Stealing technique is used to complement the plaintext with "stolen" bytes in IV, $M' = M \gg 4 - f$, $M'[0 : 3 - f] = IV[f + 4 : 7]$, enabling the byte length of M' to be 4 modular 8. $IV' = IV \gg 4 - f$. Then a MAC Stealing technique is used for (M', IV').

Like the previous two schemes, CBC-X is a single-pass mode that requires two keys for encryption and authentication. In the original designing paper,

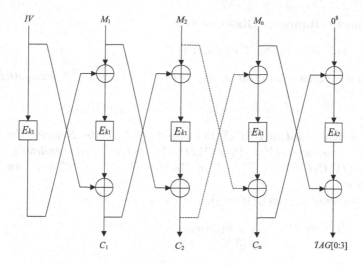

Fig. 3. CBC-X mechanism without MAC Stealing

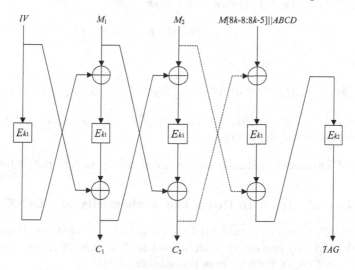

Fig. 4. CBC-X mechanism with MAC Stealing

IV has a pattern, so that only three bytes in IV is randomly chosen, and IV cannot be reused. Any error alteration during message transmission can be detected by re-computing the MAC before decryption.

In 2005, Chris J. Mitchell adopted a Birthday Paradox search to make a forgery attack on a PCBC+ [17]. A similar Birthday Paradox search is applied in this paper to break the integrity of CBC-X. In the rest of this section we exhibit a known plaintext attack on CBC-X in the case that the byte-length of plaintext is a multiple of 8, while other analogous attacks in other cases are omitted here.

5.2   Some Preliminary Observations

Our main result is based on Theorem 1 [17].

Theorem 1. *Suppose an attacker knows* r ($r \geq 2$) *pairs of blocks satisfying:*

$$\{(u_i, w_i) \mid 1 \leq i \leq r, w_i = E_{k_1}(u_i)\},$$

where k_1 *is a key used in CBC-X to compute ciphertexts. Suppose the attacker also knows a message* $(IV, P_1 P_2 \cdots P_s, PAD)$ *and its corresponding ciphertexts and MAC* $(IV, C_1 C_2 \cdots C_s, T)$, *where* $PAD = 0^8, T = TAG[0:3]$ *in the case that* $len \pmod 8 = 0$.
*   If the sequence* $(u_1, w_1), (u_2, w_2), \cdots, (u_r, w_r)$ *satisfies*

(i) $B_1 = M_s \oplus w_1, B_2 = C_s \oplus u_1 \oplus w_2,$
(ii) $B_j = B_{j-2} \oplus u_{j-1} \oplus w_j$ $(3 \leq j \leq r),$
(iii) $B_r = C_s,$

then the CBC-X decrypted version of the ciphertext

$$IV, C_1, \cdots, C_s, B_1, B_2, B_3, \cdots, B_r, T'$$

is equal to

$$IV, M_1, \cdots, M_s, C_s \oplus u_1, B_1 \oplus u_2, B_2 \oplus u_3, \cdots, B_{r-1} \oplus u_r, PAD,$$

where $T' = TAG[0:3] \oplus M_s[0:3] \oplus B_{r-1}[0:3] \oplus u_r[0:3]$. *That is, the modified message is an existential forgery.*

The proof of Theorem 1 is similar to the proof in [17], so we omit it here.

5.3   A General Attack to Break the Authenticity of CBC-X

We now exhibit a forgery attack on CBC-X in the case that $len \pmod 8 = 0$. This attack need only one query with block length of at least three, to break the authenticity of CBC-X with success probability of 0.63.

1. Query $(IV, M_1 \cdots M_l M_{l+1})(l \geq 2)$ to the encryption oracle, where M_i $(1 \leq i \leq l+1)$ are arbitrary blocks, and get $(IV, C_1 \cdots C_l C_{l+1}, T)$. We then compute $u_i = C_i \oplus M_{i+1}, w_i = M_i \oplus C_{i+1}$ $(1 \leq i \leq l)$ and gain l pairs $(u_1, w_1), (u_2, w_2), \cdots, (u_l, w_l)$ which satisfy $w_i = E_{k_1}(u_i)$ $(1 \leq i \leq l)$.
2. Let $v = min\{v \text{ is even} \mid l^v \geq 2^{m/2}, l \geq 2\}$. Then generate l^v possible sequences $(u_{i_1}, w_{i_1}), (u_{i_2}, w_{i_2}), \cdots, (u_{i_v}, w_{i_v})$ $(1 \leq i_1, i_2, \cdots, i_v \leq l)$, and for each such sequence compute B_v using the equations:
   (i) $B_1 = M_{l+1} \oplus w_{i_1}, B_2 = C_{l+1} \oplus u_{i_1} \oplus w_{i_2},$
   (ii) $B_j = B_{j-2} \oplus u_{i_{j-1}} \oplus w_{i_j}$ $(3 \leq j \leq v).$
   Sort and store all the B_v values. This step will take $\mathcal{O}(2^{m/2})$ XOR operations and $\mathcal{O}(2^{m/2})$ memory space.

3. Now repeat the same process as step 2, working backwards from $B'_v = C_{l+1}$. Generate l^v possible sequences $(u'_{i'_1}, w'_{i'_1}), (u'_{i'_2}, w'_{i'_2}), \cdots, (u'_{i'_v}, w'_{i'_v})$ $(1 \leq i'_1, i'_2, \cdots, i'_v \leq l)$, and for each such sequence compute B'_0 using the equations:
   (i) $B'_v = C_{l+1}$,
   (ii) $B'_j = B'_{j+2} \oplus u'_{i'_{j+1}} \oplus w'_{i'_{j+2}}$ (j is even, $v - 2 \geq j \geq 0$).
   If any of the values B'_0 equal any of the B_v values stored before, then set $(u_{i_v+j}, w_{i_v+j}) = (u'_{i'_j}, w'_{i'_j})$ $(1 \leq j \leq v)$ and concatenate the corresponding two sequences to yield a new sequence $(u_1, w_1), (u_2, w_2), \cdots, (u_{2v}, w_{2v})$. It is easy to testify that this new sequence has the desired properties as required in Theorem 1.
4. Let $B_j = B_{j-2} \oplus u_{i_{j-1}} \oplus w_{i_j}$ $(v + 1 \leq j \leq 2v)$, and we can easily get $B_{2v} = B'_v = C_{l+1}$. Return

$$IV, C_1, \cdots, C_{l+1}, B_1, B_2, \cdots, B_{2v}, T'$$

where $T' = T \oplus M_{l+1}[0:3] \oplus B_{2v-1}[0:3] \oplus u_{2v}[0:3]$.

Note that $l \geq 2$ so that there exists v satisfying $l^v \geq 2^{m/2}$, hence our attack needs one query with block length of at least three. Because of the choice of the parameter v, the probability of such a match occurring is 0.63. The total number of operations is clearly $\mathcal{O}(2^{m/2})$, where m is the block-length of underlying block cipher. It is worth emphasizing that $\mathcal{O}(2^{m/2})$ does not imply a complexity of birthday bound. In birthday bound, it implies a query of $\mathcal{O}(2^{m/2})$ plaintext blocks, while in our attack, only one query with block length of at least three is needed and it impies $\mathcal{O}(2^{m/2})$ off-line XOR operations. In CBC-X where the underlying block cipher has block length of $m = 64$, it means we need $\mathcal{O}(2^{32})$ XOR operations and $\mathcal{O}(2^{32})$ memory space to break its authenticity. The computation complexity is trivial.

5.4   Remarks on the General Attack

We can derive another attack directly from Theorem 1:

1. Query $(IV, 0^8)$ to the encryption oracle, and get (IV, C, T).
2. Return $(IV, C, IV + C, C, T + C[0:3])$.

The corresponding plaintext blocks is $(0^8, E_{k_1}(IV) + C, C)$. So it is easy to verify that $(IV, C, IV + C, C, T + C[0:3])$ is valid.

To compare with this attack, the general attack is of more practical values. This attack requires adversary the ability to choose a special plaintext, which is not realistic in most cases. In the general attack, a new ciphertext can be forged from any pair of plaintext and ciphertext.

5.5   Breaking Privacy of CBC-X

We exhibit an chosen plaintext attack to the encryption mechanism of CBC-X using the weakness in Data Stealing technique. This attack is in the case that $f = len \ (mod \ 8) = 6$, where len denotes the byte-length of M. Analogous attacks in other cases are omitted here.

1. Query (IV, M) to the encryption oracle and get (IV', C, T), in which M is with byte-length of 6 modular 8.
2. Query (IV^*, M^*) to the encryption oracle, where M^* is with byte-length of multiple of 8. The input satisfies $IV^*[0,1] = 0^2, IV^*[2,7] = IV[0,5]$, $M^*[0,1] = IV[6,7], M^*[2,7] = M[0,5]$. We can get (IV'^*, C^*, T^*). If $(C^*, T^*) = (C, T)$, then return 1, otherwise return 0.

In the first step of this attack, by definition we get $M'[0,1] = IV[6,7]$, $M'[2,7] = M[0,5], IV'[0,1] = 0^2, IV^*[2,7] = IV[0,5]$, such that $M^* = M'$, $IV'^* = IV^* = IV$. Therefore, we can get CBC-X.$Enc(IV, M) =$ CBC-X. $Enc(IV^*, M^*)$, i.e., $(C^*, T^*) = (C, T)$ with probability of $1 - 2^{-64}$.

According to the original designing paper of CBC-X, the generation of IV is random in three bytes. Consequently, by birthday paradox, we only need to encrypt 2^{12} messages to get a repeat IV with non-negligible probability.

In nonce-respecting privacy model, we restrain the adversary from repeating IV, but we allow the adversary to chose it. This chosen plaintext attack proves that, on the contrary to OCB [7] and GCM [5], CBC-X is insecure under the nonce-respecting privacy model.

6   Remarks on Attacks of Three Schemes

None of these three AE scheme has used reduction technique to prove security in the original paper. The analysis of integrity security of three AE schemes is built on the assumption that the values of tags will be randomly distributed due to the avalanche effect. However, respectively for each scheme, once the IV is fixed, specific structure of ciphertexts will lead to a corresponding structure in tags. For example, in the first two schemes we attack, the equality of sum of ciphertexts will lead to equality of tags, which results in a forgery attack. For schemes which don't have obvious structures, this attack cannot work, such as OCB [7] and GCM [5]. Though the reuse of IV under the same key is not allowed when an adversary gets access to the encryption oracle, the retain of IV in the forgery of triple (IV, C, T) is feasible when the adversary questions the verification oracle. In reality, it is also possible for the unauthorized party to intercept a data (IV, C, T), substitute it with another forgery triple (IV, C^*, T), in which $C^* \neq C$.

In the forgery attack on CMBC-MAC and SCMA, a structure of ciphertexts (C, C^*) satisfying $\sum_i C_i = \sum_i C_i^*$, will lead to a structure of a pair of equal tags. The data complexity of this attack is only one known ciphertext message with arbitrary blocks, and the computation complexity is negligible.

Whilst in the forgery attack on CBC-X, as is stated in Theorem 1, a structure of ciphertexts satisfying all the three conditions, will lead to a structure of a pair of well-related tags (T, T^*). The data complexity of this attack is only one known plaintext message with at least three known plaintext blocks, and the computation complexity is trivial.

The attack of integrity on these three schemes suggests that when designing an AE, the security should not be excessively weakened, though it has to be compromised with simplicity and efficiency.

7 Conclusion

In this paper we have demonstrated forgery attacks against three authenticated encryption schemes for WSN: CMBC-MAC, SCMA and CBC-X. These are all practical, easy-to-perform, known plaintext attacks, which imply that all these three modes are unacceptably weak when used to provide ciphertext integrity. We can therefore conclude that these three authenticated encryption modes are not as secure as described in their designing papers, and should not be used in the environment of Wireless Sensor Networks. The attacks of integrity on these three schemes also suggest that security should not being excessively weakened though it has to be compromised with simplicity and efficiency.

Acknowledgments. To the anonymous reviewer for useful comments and suggestions which improved the clarity and content of the manuscript.

References

1. Phillip, R.: Authenticated-encryption with associated-data. In: ACM Conference on Computer and Communications Security CCS 2002, pp. 98–107. ACM Press (2002)
2. Whiting, D., Housley, R., Ferguson, N.: IEEE 802.11-02/001r2: AES Encryption and Authentication Using CTR Mode and CBC-MAC (March 2002)
3. Bellare, M., Rogaway, P., Wagner, D.: The EAX mode of operation. In: Roy, B., Meier, W. (eds.) FSE 2004. LNCS, vol. 3017, pp. 389–407. Springer, Heidelberg (2004)
4. Kohno, T., Viega, J., Whiting, D.: CWC: A high-performance conventional authenticated encryption mode. In: Roy, B., Meier, W. (eds.) FSE 2004. LNCS, vol. 3017, pp. 408–426. Springer, Heidelberg (2004)
5. McGrew, D.A., Viega, J.: The galois/counter mode of operation (GCM) (2004). http://csrc.nist.gov/groups/ST/toolkit/BCM/
6. Jutla, C.S.: Encryption modes with almost free message integrity. In: Pfitzmann, B. (ed.) EUROCRYPT 2001. LNCS, vol. 2045, pp. 529–544. Springer, Heidelberg (2001)
7. Rogaway, P., Bellare, M., Black, J., Krovetz, T.: OCB: a block-cipher mode of operation for efficient authenticated encryption. In: Reiter, M.K., Samarati, P. (eds.) ACM Conference on Computer and Communications Security, pp. 196–205. ACM (2001)

8. Karlof, C., Sastry, N., Wagner, D.: TinySec: A link security architecture for wireless sensor networks. In: SenSys '04 (2004)

9. Lucks, S.: Two-pass authenticated encryption faster than generic composition. In: Gilbert, H., Handschuh, H. (eds.) FSE 2005. LNCS, vol. 3557, pp. 284–298. Springer, Heidelberg (2005)

10. Razvi Doomun, M., Sunjiv Soyjaudah, K.M.: Resource saving AES-CCMP design with hybrid counter mode block chaining - MAC. IJCSNS Int. J. Comput. Sci. Netw. Secur. 8(10), 1–13 (2008)

11. Adekunle, A.A., Woodhead, S.R.: An efficient authenticated-encryption with associated-data block cipher mode for wireless sensor networks. In: Osipov, E., Kassler, A., Bohnert, T.M., Masip-Bruin, X. (eds.) WWIC 2010. LNCS, vol. 6074, pp. 375–385. Springer, Heidelberg (2010)

12. Li, S., Li, T., Wang, X., Zhou, J., Chen, K.: Efficient link layer security scheme for wireless sensor networks. In: Proceedings of Journal on Information and Computational Science. Binary Information Press (2007)

13. Sung, J., Lee, S.-J., Lim, J.-I., Lee, W.I., Yi, O.: Concrete security analysis of CTR-OFB and CTR-CFB modes of operation. In: Kim, K. (ed.) ICISC 2001. LNCS, vol. 2288, pp. 103–113. Springer, Heidelberg (2002)

14. Adekunle, A., Woodhead, S.: On efficient data integrity and data origin authentication for wireless sensor networks utilising block cipher design techniques. In: Al-Begain, K. (ed.) NGMAST09, pp. 419–424. IEEE Computer Society, Los Alamitos (September 2009)

15. Bellare, M., Namprempre, C.: Authenticated encryption: relations among notions and analysis of the generic composition paradigm. In: Okamoto, T. (ed.) ASIACRYPT 2000. LNCS, vol. 1976, pp. 531–545. Springer, Heidelberg (2000)

16. Skipjack and KEA Algorithm Specifications, Version 2.0, 29 May 1998. Available at the National Institute of Standards and Technology's web page. http://csrc.nist.gov/encryption/skipjack-kea.htm

17. Mitchell, C.J.: Cryptanalysis of two variants of PCBC mode when used for message integrity. In: Boyd, C., González Nieto, J.M. (eds.) ACISP 2005. LNCS, vol. 3574, pp. 560–571. Springer, Heidelberg (2005)

Author Index

Printed in the United States
By Bookmasters